The French Polity

The French Polity

SIXTH EDITION

William Safran
University of Colorado–Boulder

New York   San Francisco   Boston
London   Toronto   Sydney   Tokyo   Singapore   Madrid
Mexico City   Munich   Paris   Cape Town   Hong Kong   Montreal

Vice President and Publisher: Priscilla McGeehon
Executive Editor: Eric Stano
Senior Marketing Manager: Megan Galvin-Fak
Production Manager: Douglas Bell
Project Coordination, Text Design, and Electronic Page Makeup: Nesbitt Graphics, Inc.
Senior Cover Designer/Manager: Nancy Danahy
Cover Photo: Copyright © Getty Images/PhotoDisc, Inc.
Manufacturing Buyer: Roy L. Pickering Jr.
Printer and Binder: The Maple-Vail Book Manufacturing Group
Cover Printer: Phoenix Color Corporation

Library of Congress Cataloging-in-Publication Data
Safran, William.
    The French polity / William Safran. — 6th ed.
        p. cm.
    Includes bibliographical references and index.
    ISBN 0-321-07774-1
        1. France—Politics and government—1958- I. Title.
JN2594.2.S23 2003
320.944—dc21   2002016227

Please visit our website at
http://www.ablongman.com

ISBN 0-321-07774-1

1 2 3 4 5 6 7 8 9 10—MA—05 04 03 02

For Eva and Frieda

CONTENTS

Tables and Figures   xi

Preface   xiii

Abbreviations and Acronyms   xv

CHAPTER 1
France: The Historical and Constitutional Background   1
    The Legacy of the Revolution   3
    The Rise and Fall of the Fourth Republic   7
    The Sources and Nature of the Fifth Republic Constitution   9
    Constitutional Interpretation and Adaptation   14
    Notes   21

CHAPTER 2
The Economic and Social Context   23
    Economic Development   23
    Social Classes and Mobility   28
    Religion and Culture   32
    The Educational System   38
    The Position of Women   41
    Notes   44

CHAPTER 3
Patterns and Perspectives of Political Culture   51
    Approaches to French Political Culture   51
      Civic and Uncivic Attitudes   51
      Verbal and Practical Behavior   55
    Conceptions of the State   59
    National Identity   63
    Notes   66

CHAPTER 4

Political Parties and Elections   73

The Socialist Party   79

The Communists   80

The Origins and Evolution of Gaullism: From the RPR to the *Union pour la Majorité*   82

The Political "Center": From Classic Provincialism to the *Union pour la Démocratie Française*   83

Radicalism   84

Catholicism   84

Centrist Coalition Games   84

The Elections of 1974 and the Emergence of Giscardo-Centrism   85

The Left in Power: 1981 and After   88

The Right and Center in Opposition   91

The Rise of the National Front   92

The Parliamentary Election of 1986: Introduction to Power Sharing   93

The Presidential and Parliamentary Elections of 1988   94

The Greens   96

The Parliamentary Elections of 1993   97

The Collapse of the Left   97

The Victory of the Right   100

The Marginalization of the Environmentalists and the Containment of the Extreme Right   102

The Presidential Elections of 1995   103

The Parliamentary Elections of 1997   105

The Elections of 2002   108

The Functional Relevance of Political Parties   116

Unnatural Alliances   116

Political Wanderings   117

The Place of Ideology   119

Voters' Choices, Programs, and Personalities   122

The Electoral System: Its Impact on Parties and Voting Behavior   126

Political Fringe Groups, Clubs, and Movements   133

Summary and Conclusion   136

Notes   137

CHAPTER 5

Interest Groups   147

Trade Unions   147

Business Associations   152

Agriculture   154

Students and Teachers   155
Miscellaneous Interest Groups   157
The Access and Input of Interest Groups   157
Pluralist, Corporatist, and Other Models of Interest-Group Politics   159
Notes   171

CHAPTER 6
Instruments and Patterns of Decision Making: The Executive   177
The Position of the President   177
The Premiers   181
Cohabitation I: Precedent-Setting Pattern or Political Parenthesis?   185
Cohabitation II: A "Civilized" Waiting Game   187
Cohabitation III: Co–Decision Making or a Neo-Parliamentary Regime?   188
The Government   190
The Construction and Reshuffling of Cabinets   199
The Executive and Parliament   204
Article 16   206
The President and Charisma   208
Summary   213
Notes   214

CHAPTER 7
Instruments and Patterns of Decision Making: The Parliament   221
Parliament in the Fifth Republic   222
The Committee System   224
The Senate   231
Limits on Parliamentary Decision Making   234
The Constitutional Council   238
Questions and Censure Motions   241
The Incompatibility Rule   243
The Role of the Deputy   245
Notes   253

CHAPTER 8
The Administrative System   259
Background, Structure, and Recruitment   259
The Political Complexion of Civil Servants   262
Controls over the Civil Service   266
Subnational Administration   271
The Commune   272

Administrative Reform and Decentralization   274

The Reforms of 1981–1983   277

Functional Decentralization   283

The Administration of Paris   284

Corsica and Overseas Territories   285

Bureaucracy, Technocracy, and Economic Administration   287

Notes   289

CHAPTER 9
Law, Justice, and Civil Liberties   297

The Judicial System   297

Justice and the Democratic State   300

The Legal Protection of Aliens and Minorities   305

The Police   306

Freedom of Expression   308

Notes   312

CHAPTER 10
Political Changes and Public Policies   319

Economic Policy from the Liberation to the Giscard Presidency   320

Capitalist Planning   320

Economic Policy Under the Mitterrand Presidency   324

The Politics of Austerity   324

The Chirac Cohabitation Government and the Politics of Neoliberalism   326

The Governments of Rocard, Cresson, and Bérégovoy: Prospects and Growing Constraints   326

The Balladur Government: Redressement *and* Rigueur   327

Economic Policy Under the Chirac Presidency   328

The Juppé Plan   328

The Jospin Government: Squaring the Circle   330

Raffarin's Policies: Pressures and Prospects   331

Education, Research, and Culture   332

Aspects of Foreign Policy   335

France and Europe   341

Constitutional and Institutional Issues: Conclusions   346

Notes   349

Appendix: The French Constitution of 1958   355

Selected Bibliography   373

Index   381

TABLES AND FIGURES

Tables

1.1 Fifth Republic Features and Their Precedents   10

1.2 Political Cycles and Regimes   13

1.3 Constitutional Amendments: Successes and Failed Attempts   15

1.4 Constitutional Principles and Adaptations   18

2.1 France: Selected Demographic Changes, 1946–2000   25

2.2 The Largest Conurbations in France, 1999 Census   26

2.3 Structure of the Active Population, 1968–2002   27

2.4 Incomes, Taxes, and Social Deductions: Six Countries, 1999   31

3.1 Responsibilities of the State   62

3.2 State Intervention in the Economy: Views of Young People
(Ages 18–25), 1996   63

4.1 Parliamentary Elections: Distribution of Votes, 1958–2002   74

4.2 Presidential Elections: Distribution of Votes, 1965–2002   78

4.3 Presidential Elections: Popular Vote, 2002   109

4.4 Parliamentary Elections: Popular Vote, 2002   111

4.5 European Parliament and French Subnational Elections: Votes by Party,
1998–2001   114

4.6 Issue Salience and Candidate Preference, Presidential Elections of 2002   123

4.7 Electoral Systems in France   129

4.8 Abstentions in Elections, 1978–2002   131

4.9 National Referenda   132

5.1 Membership in the Economic and Social Council, by Sector, 1979, 1984,
and 1998   163

5.2 Trade Unions and Elections to Labor Relations Tribunals
(Conseils de Prud'hommes) 165

6.1 Fifth Republic Premiers 183

6.2 Party Composition of Fifth Republic Governments 190

6.3 The French Government in June 2002 193

7.1 Composition of the National Assembly, 1956–2002 227

7.2 Assembly Committees of Inquiry, Investigation, and Control,
1989–2002 229

7.3 Activities of the National Assembly, 1997–2002 230

7.4 Composition of the Senate, 1959–2001 232

7.5 Use of Conference Committees, 1994–2001 234

7.6 Professions of Members of the Twelfth Assembly, 2002 246

8.1 Subnational Authorities and Jurisdictions 279

8.2 Public and Other Employees on Subnational Levels 280

8.3 Sources of Revenue and Expenses of Subnational Units 281

9.1 Important Parisian Newspapers, 1999 310

10.1 Public Opinion Survey on Needed Institutional Reforms 347

Figures

4.1 Fragmentation and Consolidation of Political Parties 76

7.1 Steps in the Legislative Process 225

8.1 The Council of State 268

8.2 The 22 Regions of France 276

9.1 The French Court Structure 299

Since the appearance of the last edition five years ago, significant changes have taken place in France. These include the following: further institutional democratization; an amplification of pluralism; an increasing pace of privatization; and a shift of power from the state to civil society. There has also been a growth of European supranationalism and a corresponding weakening of national sovereignty—a development signaled, inter alia, by the adoption of the euro. The economy has held steady and there have been signs of improvement: a stable currency, low inflation, sustained though modest growth, and the introduction of a 35-hour workweek. At the same time, unemployment has persisted, and despite efforts to reduce the gap between the well-to-do and the poor, there are still too many economically marginalized inhabitants. There have been ongoing problems in the relationship between subnational and national government, in particular with respect to Corsica. The balancing of power within the dual executive assumed new forms during the third period of cohabitation, revealing, on the one hand, a weakened president and, on the other, a seemingly strong prime minister beset with tensions within his own coalition. The party system has continued to evolve, with most parties becoming even weaker than they had been. There has been a modification of relations between the Right and the Left in the face of fissions and recombinations within both camps. At the same time, a selective depolitization has taken place, as reflected in an increasing dealignment from political parties and the growth of electoral abstention. Normal interest-group politics is alive and well, supplemented, as usual, by strikes, mass demonstrations, and other forms of extrainstitutional articulation.

These developments are taken into account in the present edition. The chapter arrangements have been retained; the approach of the book remains unambiguously institutional but is marked by attention to the evolution of institutions and the behavior of the people associated with them. The focus on the Constitution has been expanded in order to deal with recent amendments and with the never-ending debate about the need to adjust interinstitutional relationships. The treatment of political culture (Chapter 3) has been considerably enlarged. The chapter on political parties and elections (Chapter 4) has been revised: The historical discussion has been shortened in order to make room for recent developments. While this edition was in preparation, the elections of 2002 took place; their unexpected outcome dictated a rethinking about the nature of political parties and their role in the political process. All the chapters have been updated, especially those dealing with the social and economic system (Chapter 2), law and justice (Chapter 9), and public policies (Chapter 10).

For descriptive material and analysis I have relied as much as possible on recent documentation and periodical literature as well as discussions I have had with French scholars during several visits to France. As in the case of earlier editions, I have tried to obtain new material from a variety of sources: official publications, economic and electoral statistics, public opinion polls, recent books, and the daily and periodical press. The voluminous notes at the end of each chapter are indicative of my sources. These notes contain supplementary information, selective (and sometimes contradictory) statistical and survey data, illustrations, references to quoted material, and variable interpretations that may prompt the reader to further study.

I am indebted to a large number of colleagues and friends. Many of those who helped me in the preparation of the fifth edition have helped me again, either directly (by reviewing parts of preliminary drafts or by discussing selected issues with me orally, often at length) or by means of their writings. I want to record my gratitude to Pierre Bréchon, Jacques Coeuillet, Paul Godt, Dominique Labbé, Michael Lewis-Beck, Pierre Martin, Vincent Hoffmann-Martinot, Nonna Mayer, Jean-Luc Parodi, Pascal Perrineau, Françoise Praderie, Jean-Louis Quermonne, Philippe Roqueplo, Daniel-Louis Seiler, and Jean Tournon. I would like to thank Frieda Sanidas, Honorary French Consul in Denver, who has been helpful in obtaining important documentation, and Maduratna Black, Julie Chernov, and Michelle Williams for tracking down essential sources. In addition, I want to express my appreciation to Maria McColligan for steering the book through the production stages, and to Executive Editor Eric Stano for his infinite patience. Last but not least, I thank my wife, Marian, who has shared my experiences in France, acted as a sounding board for my interpretations, and scrutinized every line of the manuscript. For all errors of commission, omission, or interpretation I remain, of course, alone responsible.

WILLIAM SAFRAN

ABBREVIATIONS AND ACRONYMS

ATTAC   *Association pour une taxation des transactions financiers pour l'aide aux citoyens* (Association in Favor of Taxing Financial Transactions to Help Citizens)

CAP   Common Agricultural Policy

CDS   *Centre des démocrates sociaux* (Center of Social Democrats)

CERES   *Centre d'études, de recherches, et d'éducation socialistes* (Center for Socialist Study, Research, and Education)

CES   *Conseil Economique et Social* (Economic and Social Council)

CFDT   *Confédération française démocratique du travail* (French Democratic Confederation of Labor)

CFE   *Confédération française de l'encadrement* (French Confederation of Managerial Staff)

CFTC   *Confédération française des travailleurs chrétien* (French Confederation of Christian Workers)

CGC   *Confédération générale des cadres* (General Confederation of Managerial Personnel)

CGP   *Commissariat général du plan* (General Commission on Planning)

CGPME   *Confédération générale des petites et moyennes entreprises* (General Confederation of Small and Medium-Sized Enterprises)

CGT   *Confédération générale du travail* (General Confederation of Labor)

CGT-FO   See FO

CID-UNATI   *Confédération intersyndicale de défense–Union nationale des artisans et travailleurs indépendants* (Interunion Protective Confederation–National Union of Artisans and Independent Workers)

CIR   *Convention des institutions républicaines* (Convention of Republican Institutions)

CNIP   *Centre national des indépendants et paysans* (National Center of Independents and Peasants)

CNJA   *Centre national des jeunes agriculteurs* (National Center of Young Farmers)

CNPF   *Conseil national du patronat français* (National Council of French Employers)

CODER   *Commission de développement économique régional* (Regional Economic Development Commission)

CPNT   *Chasse, pêche, nature et traditions* (Hunting, Fishing, Nature, and Traditions—Hunters' party)

CSA   *Conseil supérieur de l'audiovisuel* (Supreme Council for Audiovisual Policy)

CSMF   *Confédération des syndicats médicaux français* (Confederation of French Medical Associations)

DATAR   *Délégation à l'aménagement du territoire et à l'action régionale* (Delegation for Space Planning and Regional Action)

DL   *Démocratie libérale* (Liberal Democrats)

ENA   *École Nationale d'Administration* (National School of Administration)

ENM   *École Nationale de la Magistrature* (National School for the Judiciary)

EU   European Union

FD   *Force démocrate* (Democratic Force—formerly, CDS)

FEN   *Fédération d'éducation nationale* (National Education Association)

FGDS   *Fédération de la gauche démocratique et socialiste* (Federation of the Democratic and Socialist Left)

FN   *Front national* (National Front)

FNSEA   *Fédération nationale des syndicats des exploitants agricoles* (National Federation of Farmers' Unions)

FO   *Force ouvrière* (Workers' Force), commonly used for CGT-FO

FSU   *Fédération syndicale unitaire de l'enseignement, de l'éducation, de la recherché et de la culture* (Interunion Federation of Education, Research, and Culture)

GE   *Génération écologie* (Ecological Generation)

INSEE   *Institut national de la statistique et des études économiques* (National Statistical Office)

MDC   *Mouvement des citoyens* (Citizens' Movement)

MEDEF   *Mouvement des entrepreneurs de France* (Association of French Entrepreneurs—formerly, CNPF)

MNR   *Mouvement national républicain* (National Republican Movement)

MPF   *Mouvement pour la France* (Movement for France)

MRG   *Mouvement des radicaux de gauche* (Movement of the Radical Left—Left Radicals)

MRP   *Mouvement républicain populaire* (Popular Republican Movement)

ORTF	*Office pour la télévision et la radiodiffusion françaises* (Office of French Television and Radio Broadcasting)
PACS	*Pacte civil de solidarité* (Civil Solidarity Pact)
PCF	*Parti communiste français* (Communist Party of France)
PDM	*Progrès et démocratie moderne* (Progress and Modern Democracy)
PPDF	*Parti populaire pour la démocratie française* (People's Party for French Democracy)
PR	*Parti républicain* (Republican party)
PRG	*Parti des radicaux de gauche* (Party of the Radical Left—Left Radicals)
PS	*Parti socialiste* (Socialist party)
PSU	*Parti socialiste unifié* (Unified Socialist party)
PT	*Parti des travailleurs* (Workers' party)
RI	*Républicains indépendants* (Independent Republicans)
RMI	*Revenu minimum d'insertion* (minimum income for integrating into the economy)
RPF	*Rassemblement du peuple français* (Rally of the French People [Fourth Republic])
RPF	*Rassemblement pour la France* (Rally for France [Pasqua's party])
RPR	*Rassemblement pour la République* (Rally for the Republic)
SFIO	*Section française de l'internationale ouvrière* (French Section of the Workers' International—Socialist party)
SMIC	*Salaire minimum interprofessionnel de croissance* (minimum wage dependent on productivity growth)
SMIG	*Salaire minimum industriel garanti* (guaranteed minimum wage)
SNESup	*Syndicat national d'enseignement supérieur* (National Union of Higher Education)
TVA	*Taxe à valeur ajoutée* (value-added tax)
UDC	*Union du centre* (Center Union)
UDF	*Union pour la démocratie française* (Union for French Democracy)
UDR	*Union des démocrates pour la République* (Democratic Union for the Republic); formerly: *Union pour la défense de la République* (Union for the Defense of the Republic)
UEM	*Union en mouvement* (Union in Motion)
UER	*Unité d'enseignement et de recherche* (instructional and research unit)
UMP	*Union pour la majorité présidentielle* (Union for the Presidential Majority)
UNR	*Union pour la nouvelle République* (Union for the New Republic)
UNSA	*Union nationale des syndicats autonomes* (National Federation of Independent Unions)
UPF	*Union pour la France du progrès* (Union for a Progressive France)
WTO	World Trade Organization

CHAPTER 1

France: The Historical and Constitutional Background

The study of France has long been a matter of interest to students of comparative politics. It is one of the major democracies in the world, and its institutional system has served as a model for a number of European countries. Like the United States, France has a written constitution that commits it to basic liberties, separation of state and religion, and competitive elections based on universal suffrage; it has not, however, adopted the American idea of separation of powers. Like Germany, France has had an uneven political development, facing challenges by antidemocratic forces. Like Great Britain, it is a unitary country, but with increasing cognizance of regional and local variations; and like most continental democracies, it has a multiparty system. Finally, as a host to many immigrants, it is, like other Western democracies, beset by collective self-doubts about its national identity.

At the same time, French politics has been a source of fascination for its own sake. The long history of France as a unified state, its high culture, and, above all, its aspirations toward a progressive republican system that would serve as a model for the rest of the world—all these have led many citizens of other countries to regard France as a "second homeland." Some political scientists have viewed the French polity as an ideal type by which other republics might be judged, whereas others have considered it as an exceptional or "deviant" case because of its periodic instability and because of its citizens' unusual excitement over political issues. The analysis of the politics of France is confounded by contradictory images: a high standard of living alongside massive unemployment; rapid urbanization and the persistence of tradition-bound villages; a commitment to civic equality and the continued existence of socioeconomic privilege; the active involvement of citizens in political life at various levels and the durability of administrative elitism; and vocal disagreements among parties and politicians despite a decline of programmatic differences.

Since the Revolution of 1789 there have been many changes of regime, accompanied by changes in social structure, public attitudes, and political style. These changes have been interpreted in various ways. To some, they are steps in a continual upward climb toward freedom, equality, reason, and prosperity; to others, they are deplored as signifying the abandonment of order and authority; to still others, change has occurred at too slow a pace, so that France has lagged behind some of its neighbors. Disagreements about the political system and anxieties about the country's future have in the past been reflected in polarized political parties, arguments about the constitution, and, often enough, street fights, general strikes, and rebellions. Yet the majority of French men and women have shared a highly developed sense of national identity and an immense pride in their country, the beauty of its landscape, the glory of its monarchs, its global diplomatic role, its intellectual and artistic achievements, the variety of its cuisine, the spread of its language, and the influence of its political ideas.

At the same time, the French have been increasingly concerned about the loss of their uniqueness, which has been challenged by the internationalization and popularization of their national culture, increasing American influence on their language and mores, and the growing irrelevance of many of their ideologies. Nothing has been more unsettling to the French than the question of how France can maintain its national character and its independence while at the same time becoming part of an increasingly integrated European Union (EU).

France is the third largest country in Europe (after Russia and Ukraine), its boundaries having been more or less fixed some two centuries ago. It achieved national unity earlier than did Germany or Italy; it was the first important European country to produce a revolution, to commit itself to republican rule, and to export its democratic ideals to foreign countries. Its great natural wealth, once measured in agricultural terms, led to relative economic self-sufficiency and inward-looking tendencies, whereas its universalist principles and its military entanglements contributed to its international outlook. It is a country in which revolutionary mythologies persisted alongside social and economic traditionalism and in which the apparent disorder in politics contrasted with orderly and relatively rigid patterns of culture in general: the geometric layout of Paris and other cities, its neoclassical architecture, its formal gardens, a strictly codified etiquette, uniform school curricula, and continuing attempts by the authorities to exert formal control over the purity of the French language.[1]

France owes much to Julius Caesar. Survivals of the Roman conquest are obvious: the Romance language, Roman law, the mixed racial stock (Latin grafted onto the indigenous Celtic and Germanic), and the French toleration (at least in principle) of different races. The movement toward centralization of the various autonomous provinces was gradual and occurred essentially from about the eleventh to the sixteenth century.

Geographically, France is far from a uniform country. There are mountainous areas, such as the Alps, the Jura, and the Vosges in the east, the Pyrenees in the south, and the Auvergne (Massif Central) in the south center. In the south, there is the subtropical vegetation typical of the Mediterranean; in the Paris area and its surrounding regions, there are forested areas and extensive wheat fields; in the west, the flat coastal Vendée fronts on the Atlantic Ocean; and the flatlands of the northwest spill over into Belgian Flanders. The French like to point to these diverse features, in addition to the moderate climate and the fertile soil, and to relate them to the development of national pride, the hexagonal symmetry of the country's map, and the peculiar mix of national and local orientations.

France is at least as complex as the United States, and as geographically and culturally diverse. It is noteworthy that the two countries share many features, regardless of differences in historical development. To name just a few common traits: (1) the belief that a constitution does not "evolve" organically but is the result of deliberate choice—a belief reflected in the United States in the founders' conviction that a political experiment could be started from scratch and that previous political formulas could be summarily rejected; and in France, in the politics, culture, and religion of reason, which after the Revolution of 1789 led to the temporary "abolition" of God, of the Christian calendar, and of traditional social institutions; (2) the principle of popular sovereignty, that is, the axiom that governmental powers are derived from the people; (3) a commitment to the principle of equal rights for all; (4) a persistent localism in politics; and (5) a commitment to equal representation and to a public and secular educational system for the masses.

THE LEGACY OF THE REVOLUTION

Five of France's 11 political systems since 1789 have been republics. The remainder comprised three monarchies, two empires, and one fascist puppet state. Each republic has given France new institutions and patterns, which were at least partly incorporated into succeeding regimes. The First Republic (1792–1799) proclaimed the notion of popular sovereignty, produced the Declaration of the Rights of Man and the Citizen, reduced the power of the Catholic church, and inaugurated the secular age in politics. During the Second Republic (1848–1852), universal male suffrage was introduced, and a plebiscitary element—the election of the president by popular vote—was injected into French political life. During the Third Republic (1875–1940), the church was formally disestablished, the executive branch was weakened and made responsible to a Parliament that asserted its supremacy, and the French nation, it seemed, was decisively converted to republicanism.

Still, many innovations introduced during the old monarchical system (the *ancien régime*) and many prerepublican social patterns persisted well into the twentieth century. The centralization of administration, introduced by Cardinal de Richelieu, Mazarin, and Colbert during the seventeenth century, continued to the present republic with only minor modifications, and the preeminence of Paris, secured by the Bourbon rulers, still informs French political, economic, and cultural life. The old social and legal distinctions between the nobility and the middle class that had marked the *ancien régime* gave way, but they were replaced by almost equally pronounced distinctions between the bourgeoisie and the working class. The French republic, whatever its latest constitutional expression, continued to be adorned with several monarchist glosses: the glorification of French kings and of the royal and martial tradition in the history books, châteaux, and museums; the refurbishing of old buildings and neighborhoods in the name of cultural continuity; and the nostalgia for a national hero.

Just as popular dissatisfactions with existing monarchies expressed themselves in periodic uprisings that culminated in republican experiments, republics were inevitably overlaid with reactionary institutions and ideologies. The attempt in 1789 to moderate the absolute rule of the Bourbon dynasty ended with its abolition. The revolutionary republic that replaced it was in turn replaced by a Reign of Terror, a Directory, and, finally, a Consulate. This last gave way to the First Empire of Napoleon Bonaparte (who had been first consul) in 1804. When that empire collapsed, largely from external causes, the French regime returned to Bourbon rule with the accession of Louis XVIII to the throne in 1814. That regime retained, at least in theory, some of Napoleon's accomplishments: the establishment of a merit-based civil service, the abolition of feudal tax obligations, and a system of codified laws. The Charter of 1814 provided a framework for a constitutional monarchy based on the English model. The Charter called for religious freedom, the sanctity of property, procedural safeguards against arrest, equality before the law, and some participation in the legislative process by a bicameral Parliament.

But when Charles X ascended to the throne in 1824, monarchical rule became increasingly arbitrary. The subsequent replacement of the Bourbon king by Louis-Philippe (of the House of Orléans) after the Revolution of July 1830 was intended to provide a better opportunity for the development of constitutional rule. As if to underline its republican spirit, the "July Monarchy" used as its symbol, not the fleur-de-lis of the Bourbons, but the tricolor flag of the Revolution of 1789. Censorship was abolished; equality before the law was guaranteed; extraordinary courts were forbidden; trial by jury was instituted; and the Parliament was granted more significant lawmaking responsibilities. But that regime too was a disappointment, for Parliament continued to be disregarded, opposition leaders were arrested, and political liberty failed to flourish.

In 1848, the French rebelled again and instituted the Second Republic. The Constitution of (November) 1848 was a remarkably democratic and modern document, its social provisions foreshadowing the constitutions of twentieth-century welfare states. The one plebiscitary feature of the Constitution—the provision for the direct election of the president—was soon used injudiciously by the French people when they voted for Louis Napoleon, the nephew of the great emperor, as president and elected an Assembly with a monarchist majority, and when, three years later, they acquiesced in the establishment of a Second Empire, under Napoleon III.

The Second Empire was, in theory, a "popular" empire in the sense that it was inaugurated by a plebiscite. The Constitution of January 1852, on which it was based, confirmed "the great principles proclaimed in 1789." The chief executive was "responsible to the French people" (rather than to God), and legislative power was to be exercised collectively by the president,[2] the Senate, and the Chamber of Deputies. The Senate was appointed by Napoleon III, but the Chamber was elected on the basis of universal male suffrage. However, legislative initiative rested with the president (later emperor) and ministers were responsible to him rather than to Parliament. The republican features of the Constitution were progressively subverted by imperial interference in legislative elections, the persecution of opposition candidates, and the requirement of an oath of imperial support and allegiance for all deputies. To counteract growing popular disenchantment—perhaps boredom—with the regime after 1860, Napoleon III made half-hearted attempts to liberalize it by increasing the power of the Parliament, which even obtained the right of legislative initiative. But it was too late. France's defeat at the hands of the Prussians in 1870 discredited and disorganized the Second Empire, and a rebellion in Paris hastened its demise.

The regime that followed the Second Empire was a republic by default. The National Assembly that was hurriedly elected in 1871 to provide a government capable of negotiating peace with Bismarck's Germany did not want a republic at all: More than 400 of its

650 deputies were monarchists. But since the Assembly could not agree on which of the three dynasties (Bourbon, Orléans, Bonaparte) should be called on to provide a king, the precise nature of the regime was left unsettled. The Assembly adopted a skeleton constitution that dealt merely with "the organization of public powers"—the executive and legislature—and the relationship between them. This constitution contained neither a preamble nor a bill of rights. The first provisional president, Adolphe Thiers, who had served as a minister in several preceding monarchical regimes, had become convinced that "a republic divides us least." His successor, Marshall Mac-Mahon, was a conservative, a clericalist, and a monarchist. The question of the regime was tentatively and surreptitiously settled in 1875 when the Parliament adopted (by a one-vote majority) an amendment providing that "the president of the *Republic* shall be elected by a plurality of votes of the Senate and the Chamber of Deputies meeting in joint session."[3]

The "provisional" Third Republic was to last 65 years, and the political patterns established in it were to influence succeeding republican regimes. There was a popularly elected Chamber of Deputies, juxtaposed with a Senate dominated by indirectly elected, relatively aged, and conservative representatives of rural communes. The cabinet, though appointed by the president, was collectively responsible to Parliament, which could oust it by a vote of censure. The president, elected for seven years, was not "responsible," in that his acts had to be countersigned by a minister. But he did have the power to dissolve the Chamber (after consulting the Senate).

The conflict between the legislature and the executive was never fully resolved, at least in formal constitutional terms, and was to lead to several crises. The first and most important of these was the episode of 16 May 1877, when President Mac-Mahon ousted a republican prime minister with whom he did not get along (in spite of the latter's solid support in the Chamber of Deputies), appointed a monarchist in his stead, and dissolved Parliament. The newly elected Chamber was even more solidly republican (or "leftist," in the context of that period) than its predecessor; and when, early in 1879, the Senate, too, was brought under the control of the republicans, Mac-Mahon saw himself as effectively repudiated and he resigned. Thereafter, nearly all Third Republic presidents were deliberately selected on the basis of their lack of ambition. The presidential dissolution power atrophied, and the chief of state became a figurehead, like an English monarch, rather than an active decision maker. In fact, of the 14 presidents of the Third Republic, only six served full seven-year terms.[4] The Third Republic became a parliamentary regime that proved durable but unstable, with the legislature recklessly overturning cabinets at an average rate of once every eight months.

While in Britain a gradually evolving democracy and parliamentary supremacy could easily accommodate the retention of traditional institutions and patterns, such as the Crown, the House of Lords, the established church, and a deferential and hierarchical social order, the French, with their Cartesian intellectualism,[5] were unable to compromise among clashing political norms. "Republicanism" was grudgingly accepted, but its precise meaning was subject to disagreement. Its dominant expression was Jacobinism, which could be traced to a belief (espoused by Rousseau as well as the men of the Reign of Terror) in a direct democracy that excluded all intermediaries or mediating structures such as political parties, interest groups, and local governments; in egalitarianism and anticlericalism (opposition to the [Catholic] church, particularly its political role); and in the supremacy of the state as the embodiment of the "general will" (or the public interest). Yet the Paris Commune of 1871,[6] the first French egalitarian (or "social-ist") uprising, was mercilessly crushed by the bourgeoisie that led the new republic. Despite the distrust of institutions that would interpose themselves between people and government, the role of the Senate, an indirectly elected body, became very important. A commitment to the republic did not necessarily mean acceptance of a particular manifestation of it: The government was hated, even though the state was depended on for protection and subvention.

Nor did the commitment to the republic resolve a deep-seated disagreement about political values. This dissent stemmed from the confusion of three strains coexisting in French political culture: rationalism, historicism, and hero worship. The rationalistic spirit has been reflected in recurring attempts to elevate a particular set of abstract principles and to construct a "logical" political system on their basis.[7] This attitude was personified by Abbé Sieyès, who, after the Revolution of 1789, wrote several draft constitutions based on his principles of an "indivisible popular sovereignty" and a "just representation"—principles first embodied in the Constitution of 1791. Historicism implies the belief that a political system cannot be constructed from logical blueprints; it is a reaction to, and an evolution from, a nation's collective experiences, which do not always follow rational patterns. In order to "explain" their political positions, many French citizens used to refer, without more specific identification, to "18 Brumaire" (1799, when Napoleon instituted his coup d'état); the "July Monarchy" (1830); the "Affair of 16 May" (1877); the "Episode of 13 May" (the revolt of the French officers in Algeria in 1958); and the "May events" (1968) as if the references were clearly understood by all French schoolchildren. Moreover, all French political attitudes are said to be shaped by the Revolution of 1789. The republicans have considered themselves the true heirs of the revolution because they trace their own faith in a secular and parliamentary government to the years following that great event. The moderates believed that the revolution established, once and for all, the political ascendancy of the bourgeoisie. Leftists considered it their task to "complete" the revolution by adding economic rights to the political rights already gained, thereby achieving "liberty, equality, and fraternity"; and the Right saw the revolution as a mistake to be rectified. The hero-worshipping French are essentially anti-rationalist and historicist. The belief that institutions are run by people and are therefore corruptible is coupled with the belief that there are individuals who are untainted by corruption and who must be called on to rectify the evils of the "system" and to advance national unity. The French have had numerous historical models for such heroes.

The remembrance of these heroes and the revolt against reason explain why the Third Republic was confronted with repeated eruptions of traditionalism, Bonapartism, monarchism, and fascism. In 1886, General Boulanger, a "man on horseback," was encouraged by antirepublican and clericalist forces to institute a coup d'état, and he might have succeeded had he not lost his nerve. The Dreyfus Affair, in which militarism, monarchism, clericalism, and anti-Semitism, abetted by a corrupt judiciary, colluded in trumped-up espionage charges against a Jewish military officer, occurred in the 1890s; it divided France into two hostile camps and almost destroyed the republic. A century has passed since that affair began, but it is still evoked as a reminder of how hatred and injustice can undermine democracy.[8] In the 1920s and 1930s, the *Action française*, the *Croix de feu*, and other extreme nationalist and antidemocratic movements challenged the legitimacy of the regime. Yet the Third Republic survived these challenges. In the first decade of the twentieth century, the church was separated from the state. The regime was on solid enough foundations to emerge intact from the experience of World War I. Parliament had asserted its supremacy, at least in theory, and much progress was achieved despite chronic cabinet instability and legislative immobility; and when the Popular Front, a left-wing coalition under Léon Blum, attempted to institute far-reaching social reforms in 1936, it seemed that the egalitarian aspect of republicanism would finally be taken into account.

The Third Republic—so far, the longest-lasting regime since 1789—ended with the fall of Paris to the invading German armies in the summer of 1940. Whether the Vichy regime that followed was constituted legally; whether the republic could have survived if France had not been defeated; whether the political institutions had been so subverted from within by apathy, defeatism, or antidemocratic sentiment that France's ability to fight Germany was destroyed—all these are questions that have no clear answers, even after a half century.[9] France has only gradually been freeing itself from a Vichy guilt complex stemming from the fact that many of its citizens collaborated with the Nazi regime, and has been reexamining the Occupation period objectively in fiction, nonfiction, and films.[10] In July 1995, two months after his inauguration as president, Jacques Chirac revived the controversy about "a past that will not pass" by doing what his predecessors had refused to do: He publicly acknowledged France's responsibility for deporting thousands of Jews to Nazi extermination camps.[11]

THE RISE AND FALL OF THE FOURTH REPUBLIC

When France was liberated in 1944, monarchism was dead. A new spirit of unity had been forged during the Resistance, and there was general agreement that the republic should be continued or renewed. Most Catholics had become republican, and their party, the Popular Republican Movement (*Mouvement républicain populaire*—MRP), had emerged from the Resistance as the largest party; the Communist party, too, was considered respectable and patriotic. An unprecedented leftist majority, composed of the MRP, the Socialists, and the Communists, participated in the first postwar government coalition and agreed on the need to establish a progressive, welfare-oriented republic.

Nevertheless, there was disagreement about the *form* of that republic. The Communists and Socialists favored a strong unicameral legislature and a weak executive. The first draft constitution that embodied these ideas was, however, rejected in a popular referendum held in May 1946. A second draft constitution provided for bicameralism. This Constitution, which inaugurated the Fourth Republic, was ratified by a bare plurality of the French people: Only 60 percent of the electorate participated in the referendum, and of those, only two-thirds voted yes. The Communists remained unenthusiastic about the Constitution, for they opposed a second parliamentary chamber. The most vocal opposition came from General Charles de Gaulle, the wartime leader of the Free French and the head of the provisional government that had been formed after the Liberation. The general and his supporters were convinced that the Constitution was doomed to failure because of its imperfections (chief among them being the absence of a strong executive).

They started a vigorous campaign against the document, a campaign that gave rise to the Rally of the French People (*Rassemblement du peuple français*—RPF), the first Gaullist mass movement.

The Fourth Republic Constitution had many structural weaknesses. The Assembly was given too much power, whereas the role of the Council of the Republic, a pale copy of the Third Republic Senate, was ill defined and ambiguous. The dual executive was reminiscent of the Third Republic: The president, elected by Parliament, was a mere figurehead; the prime minister, the real decision maker, was chosen by and responsible to the legislature. The prime minister theoretically possessed dissolution power, but he exercised that power only once.

The Assembly remained sensitive about its constitutionally defined legislative supremacy, but in the absence of coherent and stable majorities, that chamber could not fully play its role. Unable or unwilling to make unpleasant decisions, the Assembly delegated legislative or decree powers to cabinets (in violation of the Constitution) only to oust them once decisions had been made. Cabinet instability was aggravated by the ambitions of politicians who considered themselves of ministerial caliber *(ministrables)* and were eager for cabinet posts.

Any postmortem of the Fourth Republic is of course incomplete if it disregards the accomplishments of that regime. It instituted the first national modernization plan for the economy and thereby helped bring prosperity to France. It initiated extensive social legislation, including paid vacations for all workers,[12] comprehensive medical insurance, and subsidies to families with children. It started France on the road to decolonization and committed the nation to participation in the European Coal and Steel Community and, subsequently, the Common Market.[13]

To be sure, there were policy failures, foremost among them the failure to reform the tax system, to provide adequate wages to industrial workers, and to reduce significantly the gap between the rich and the poor. These problems might have been resolved and the imperfections of the Constitution might have been transcended by political practice had it not been for the colonial question, the military's frustration, and the scarcity of strong leaders capable of dealing with these issues.

Members of the military, in particular, brought up with the historical memories (or myths) of a glorious national army, had in their lifetimes experienced mainly defeats: the fall of France in 1940, the defeat at Dien Bien Phu in Indochina in 1954, the Suez misadventure of 1956, and a continuing inability to pacify the rebels in North Africa. Just as German officers had blamed the "politicians" for the defeat of Germany in 1918, so French generals had tried to assign the blame for their lack of military victories to the politicians and the republic that had brought these men forward.

The final years and months of the Fourth Republic saw a rapid succession of "prosystem" (i.e., essentially centrist) governments that were unable to deal with the problem of Algeria (whose indigenous population was fighting to free itself from French colonial rule) and, as it turned out, to save the regime. The Parliament had made a few last-ditch attempts to remove certain constitutional difficulties. In 1954, the Constitution had been amended to make the investiture of prime ministers easier—and thus to make deadlocks less likely—by requiring a relative rather than an absolute majority. In March 1958, in order to reduce the scope of irresponsible behavior on the part of deputies, a reform was instituted that forbade backbenchers to introduce bills resulting in an increase of public expenditure. In addition, the Assembly sharply limited its own power to oust a cabinet by a vote of censure.[14] But these reforms came too late. General de Gaulle, who had "saved" France's honor in the past, waited in his country home at Colombey-les-deux-Églises for the opportunity to act as the savior of his nation once more.

In April 1958, the resident military in Algeria set up—in a manner reminiscent of 1793—a Committee of Public Safety. Its demand for the return of de Gaulle to power was echoed by the general's political supporters on the mainland of France. In May, the president of the Republic, René Coty, sent a letter to de Gaulle exploring the possibility of the general's return. De Gaulle promptly held a press conference in which he announced his "availability" and began to take steps to form a government. The coup de grâce of the Fourth Republic was finally delivered by President Coty when he somewhat belatedly informed Parliament that he had asked the general to form a government and that he would resign if the formation of such a government were prevented.[15]

THE SOURCES AND NATURE OF THE FIFTH REPUBLIC CONSTITUTION

On June 1, 1958, de Gaulle was formally invested as prime minister by the Assembly and empowered by the latter to undertake a revision of the Constitution. The Fifth Republic Constitution, which was written in record time, is an eclectic document that incorporates monarchical, plebiscitary, and traditional republican features (see Table 1.1), in addition to specifically Gaullist innovations.[16]

In modern French political history, there have been two conflicting constitutional theories: Rousseau's theory of complete popular sovereignty, as enunciated in the *Social Contract*,[17] and the doctrine of a "mixed government." According to Rousseau's theory, a truly democratic constitution is based on the principle that all political sovereignty rests inalienably with the people, who can delegate decision-making power only imperfectly, if at all, to a legislature. The second constitutional principle envisages a balanced mixture of executive, legislative, and judicial institutions, all of which derive equally from the people and are therefore "coordinate" (but not as separate from each other as Montesquieu had envisaged them in his *Spirit of the Laws*).[18] The Rousseau doctrine was reflected in the "Jacobin" Constitution of 1792, which gave unlimited power to a constituent assembly as the best possible articulator of the "general will," and in the Fourth Republic's grant of legislative supremacy to the National Assembly. The doctrine of a mixed government was generally embodied in monarchist regimes (e.g., the Constitutions of 1791, 1814, and 1830). In these, the principle of popular sovereignty was reaffirmed but was institutionally reflected only in an elected lower house. That chamber, rather than being the sole decision maker, had to act in "concert" with a nonelective king and a chamber of the nobility.[19] To some extent, the idea of a mixed government was embodied in the scanty constitutional articles of the Third Republic, which granted legislative power to the Assembly but gave the executive the power to appoint ministers and to dissolve Parliament.

TABLE 1.1
Fifth Republic Features and Their Precedents

Feature of the Fifth Republic Constitution	Precedent or Model
Popular election of president (amendment: 1962; first election: 1965)	Constitution of 1848 (Second Republic)
Seven-year term of president (until 2000)	Fourth Republic
Power to appoint prime minister without prior parliamentary consultation	Second Republic
Presidential dissolution power	Third Republic (until 1879)
Presidential lawmaking (by decree)	Second Republic
Economic and Social Council	Third and Fourth Republics
Referenda or plebiscites for constitutional amendments	1802 (Napoleon Bonaparte made consul for life) 1852 (Napoleon III vested with imperial powers)
Limit of Parliament's budget-making powers	End of Fourth Republic
President as "co-initiator" of legislation	Second and Third Republics
President as negotiator of treaties	Second and Third Republics
Plebiscitary appeal to the people	Constitution of 1852 (Napoleon III)
Constitution adopted by referendum	Year I (1792)
	Year III (1795)
	Year VIII (1799)
	Fourth Republic (1946)
Incompatibility of cabinet office with parliamentary mandate	Constitution of 1791 (constitutional monarchy)

The Fifth Republic Constitution, on the face of it, adheres neither to Jacobin principles nor to the idea of a mixed system. The very order of the constitutional provisions—sovereignty, the president, the government, Parliament—implies an enhanced position for the executive, and the provisions detailing the power of the legislature seem to render that branch neither supreme nor coordinate.

The president's powers—to preside over the cabinet, to appoint the prime minister, and to dissolve the legislature—are basically Third Republic features, though after the "Affair of 16 May," these powers had eroded. The provision for the independent (and later direct) election of the president is reminiscent of the Second Republic, whereas the incompatibility of cabinet office and parliamentary mandate is a feature found in both the Constitution of 1791 and the Constitution of 1852 (Second Empire). The extralegislative election of the president, his power to introduce measures through his ministers, and his power to appoint the prime minister (and, in effect, the cabinet) without prior parliamentary consultation were based on provisions found in the Constitution of 1848 (Second Republic). The president's appeal to the people was based on the Constitution of 1852. The president's power to negotiate treaties and to dissolve Parliament, the makeup of the Senate and its relatively equal position vis-à-vis the Assembly, and the omission of a clearly stipulated set of provisions regarding civil liberties are all features reminiscent of the Third Republic's Constitutional Laws of 1875. The Fourth Republic

Constitution, too, is heavily reflected in the provisions of the Fifth, notably with respect to the following: the seven-year term of the president; the president's power to send messages to Parliament and to ask that body to reconsider bills it has passed; the election of senators by an electoral college of local politicians; provisions concerning martial law and the establishment of an Economic and Social Council; and, of course, an Assembly chosen by universal suffrage. The specifically "Gaullist" aspects of the Constitution are not easy to determine, because the sources of Gaullism are diverse and its nature is intertwined with Bonapartism. In his Bayeux speech of 16 June 1946, de Gaulle, while publicly opposing the first draft of a constitution for the Fourth Republic, had proposed a system of separation of powers, an indirectly elected Senate in which, in conformity with corporatist tradition, socioeconomic and professional sectors would be represented, and a chief executive who would be above parties[20] and would select his prime minister and preside over the cabinet. Some of the Gaullist notions of government had been espoused by Michel Debré and René Capitant (a "left-wing" Gaullist), who suggested the shortening of the sessions of a parliament that would operate within the framework of enumerated powers.

The central feature of the Fifth Republic Constitution, a strong, quasimonarchical executive, is considered to be the most Gaullist of the innovations, because the general, in his memoirs and public utterances, had consistently advocated it. However, it is important to keep in mind that de Gaulle merely embraced a constitutional preference that was a recurrent theme in France. The restoration of a genuine monarchy became unthinkable in that country long ago, but the glorification of kings and the association of national greatness with monarchical regimes are still emphasized in its public schools. Moreover, most of the French regimes after 1789, including republics, have been adorned (or encumbered) with certain monarchist elements. The Constitution of the Year III (1795) empowered the executive to appoint and dismiss ministers; the Charter of 1814 gave the king extensive legislative powers; the laws of 1830 reaffirmed the royal veto power; the Constitution of 1848 (Second Republic) provided for a relatively weak president who was still entitled to convoke the Assembly for special sessions, introduce bills, and negotiate treaties; the Constitution of 1852 (put into effect after the coup d'état by Napoleon III) granted most legislative and other powers to the executive; and the Constitutional Laws of 1875 (Third Republic) gave legislative initiative both to the president and to the chambers, and granted the president the power to appoint ministers.

In the course of the Third Republic, the Parliament had asserted its supremacy at the expense of the president, whose legislative, appointive, and dissolution powers had gradually atrophied. Parliamentary supremacy and presidential weakness had become republican constitutional norms, which were embodied in the Fourth Republic Constitution of 1946. But throughout the Third and Fourth Republics, the myth of an authoritarian president had persisted and had been propagated by various movements and individuals who (like General Boulanger in the 1880s) had viewed Parliament as ill suited to express the general will. Reflecting a growing hostility toward deputies for their alleged selfishness and incompetence, numerous proposals to strengthen the presidency were made in the early part of the twentieth century.[21]

Immediately after World War II, the overreaction to Marshal Pétain's authoritarianism was so widespread that few Frenchmen seriously thought that a strong executive was feasible in a republican regime or accepted the idea of either the people or an electoral college replacing Parliament as the instrument for selecting the executive. Between 1941 and 1943 even Michel Debré, who was later to become the orthodox Gaullist par excellence, had written essays and letters expressing opposition to a popularly elected president and opposing a presidential regime altogether because he feared that France would be governed by a general on the basis of proclamations.[22] Nonetheless, at various times throughout the postwar period, especially during the last few years of the Fourth Republic, notions of presidentialism were disseminated not only by de Gaulle himself, but also by Socialists, Christian Democrats, and others.[23] The president came to be viewed as an ideal person to hold the overseas territories and France together—perhaps following the example of Britain, where the queen was the focal point of cohesion for the Commonwealth. After 1956, many elements of the intellectual Left and Right favored the direct election of the president (following the U.S. model).[24] Others proposed the direct election of the prime minister, but this alternative was not held out as a serious possibility for France because of its chronic multiparty tendencies and imperfect party discipline. As noted, some reforms had been instituted between 1954 and 1958 to strengthen the executive vis-à-vis Parliament, but these reforms had not been effective or credible, because they had not been endorsed by the people.

The plebiscitary features of the Fifth Republic Constitution, introduced by the Gaullists in order to weaken Parliament and other intermediaries and to strengthen the president, were not Gaullist innovations. One aspect of plebiscitarism, popular ratification of the Constitution, has had a particularly hallowed place in French constitutional history: The Constitutions of 1792, 1795, 1799, and 1946 had all been submitted to the people. But the same is true of the *invalidation of republican rule* and its replacement by authoritarian and Bonapartist regimes: The naming of Napoleon I as consul for life in 1802, the establishment of the Bonapartist hereditary line in 1804, and the investiture of Napoleon III as emperor in 1852 had all been approved by plebiscite.[25] Even where clear French precedents do not exist, certain Fifth Republic features are not entirely novel: They probably drew on foreign examples. Thus, the authors of Article 16 (emergency powers) may have based their work partly on Article 48 of the Weimar Constitution, and the use of referenda for ordinary legislation may have been based on the examples of Switzerland and contemporary Italy.

The Fifth Republic does, however, represent a sharp break with the Fourth Republic because its Constitution tilts power decisively on the side of the executive and because it mirrors the political doctrines and institutional preferences of one man. Furthermore, the circumstances surrounding its establishment are in many ways different from those of earlier French republics, which were attempts to reconstitute republican regimes after authoritarian experiences. The First Republic was the consequence of a rebellion against the monarchs of the *ancien régime*; the Second Republic followed the Revolution of 1848 and the deposition of the July Monarchy; the Third Republic was a reaction to the military failures of Napoleon III, as well as to the bloody suppression of the Paris Commune; the Fourth Republic was both a reaction to the Vichy regime and an attempt to restore the democratic *status quo ante bellum*.

The Fifth Republic, in contrast, was not a reaction to the authoritarianism of an earlier regime. Therefore, to many observers *at that time* it did not represent a step forward in republican terms: Insofar as republicanism was equated with the elevation of Parliament at the expense of a powerful executive, the Fifth Republic was considered institutionally retrogressive. Yet much of the Fifth Republic Constitution—in particular its executive-administrative character—can be explained by the fact that the new regime was historically opportune (i.e., fitted into a cyclical pattern of French constitutional development). According to Dorothy Pickles, modern French political history has been divided into three-part cycles, each beginning with a moderate monarch, followed by a liberalized ("republican") regime, and ending in a conservative reaction (see Table 1.2).[26] But whereas the conservative reactions to the Republic of 1792, the July Monarchy, and the Third Republic since the 1880s had been institutionally reflected in empires or dictatorships, the response to the parliamentary excesses of the Fourth Republic was a regime in which many republican features were retained. These features (as we shall see later) lent themselves easily enough to democratic interpretation.

Nonetheless, the Fifth Republic Constitution contains more innovations than its immediate predecessor. First, there is the notion of presidential *arbitrage:* The president is responsible for both observing and interpreting the Constitution. Second, the Fifth Republic Constitution limits the length of parliamentary sessions, reduces the number and the power of legislative committees, and streamlines the budgetary process in a way that leaves it essentially an executive matter. Third, it contains a specific mention of political parties, including a stipulation (also found in the constitutions of Italy and the German Federal Republic) that political parties "must respect the principles of national sovereignty and democracy."[27] Fourth, it provides a sharing of legislative power among the executive, the legislature, and the people and for that reason differentiates among organic laws, ordinary laws, regulations and decrees, and referenda (see Chapter 7). A fifth feature is the double responsibility of the prime minister to the president and to Parliament. Finally, Article 16 (discussed more fully in Chapter 6) gives the president discretionary power to act in case the constitutionally established institutions do not function normally.

One might even argue that the Fifth Republic is unique because, unlike other republics, it was inaugurated in a somewhat unconstitutional manner. After investing de Gaulle as prime minister of a provisional government, the Fourth Republic Parliament

TABLE 1.2
Political Cycles and Regimes

Modern Monarchy	Liberalization	Conservative Reaction
Constitutional monarchy of 1791	Republic of 1792	Dictatorial government of 1795
		First Empire, 1804
Restoration of 1815	July Monarchy (1830)	Second Empire
Early Third Republic (1870–1879)	Third Republic from presidency of Jules Grévy	Vichy regime
	Fourth Republic	Fifth Republic (1958–1981)
	Fifth Republic (1981–)	

SOURCE: Adapted from Dorothy Pickles, *The Fifth French Republic*, 3d ed. (New York: Praeger, 1965), pp. 3–5.

granted that government the power to change the constitution, in violation of Article 90 of the Fourth Republic Constitution (then still in effect), which provided that constitutional changes could be initiated only in Parliament. Hence one prominent anti-Gaullist argued that the installation of the Fifth Republic was a coup d'état that had only a thin veneer of legality.[28] Indeed, the law of 3 June 1958, which empowered the government to draw up a new constitution, could be considered almost as "unconstitutional"—and the result as "illegal"—as the law of 10 July 1940, by which the Chamber of Deputies of the Third Republic ceded all power (including the power to set aside the constitution) "to the Government of the Republic, under the authority and signature of Marshal Pétain."[29] This does not mean that the Gaullist regime should be compared to the Vichy regime, because the Fifth Republic Constitution, unlike Pétain's "French State," was endorsed in a popular referendum and therefore legitimated. Indeed, if one attaches a quantitative element to the criterion of popular endorsement, one may even argue that the Fifth Republic Constitution (which was approved by 80 percent of the electorate) was more "legitimate" than its immediate predecessor (which had been endorsed by only about 40 percent of registered voters). It remains true that in France, popular sovereignty is the source of a republican constitution, just as it is in Britain, where parliamentary enactments or cabinet actions that have the consequence of "amending" the constitution are based on general or "mandate" elections.

The Fifth Republic Constitution was also legitimated by its internal character, that is, by virtue of the fact that it included certain traditional republican principles. First, the principle of universal suffrage applies as before to the election of the Assembly. Second, the government, although selected by the president, continues to be subject to criticism and revocation by the Parliament. Third, there is an independent judiciary. The inclusion of these features had been demanded by the multipartite Consultative Committee, the Council of State, and other agencies and individuals whose advice had been sought at the constitution-drafting stage.[30] Without these provisions, the Fifth Republic Constitution would very likely have been rejected in the popular referendum. Finally, the Constitution continues to be legitimated by its growing (and now overwhelming) acceptance by the French people.

CONSTITUTIONAL INTERPRETATION AND ADAPTATION

Most observers agree that the Fifth Republic today is not the same as it was when it was established. Yet there is a considerable difference of opinion about the extent to which the Constitution has been stretched beyond the intentions of the founders by means of formal amendment, interpretation, and practice.[31] Thus far, the Constitution has worked well enough to make frequent resort to formal amendment (as is the case in the Federal Republic of Germany) unnecessary. The amendment process is not particularly cumbersome; it involves two alternative methods: After an amendment bill has been passed in each house of Parliament, it is ratified either by a "congress," that is, a joint session of both houses, by a three-fifths vote; or by popular referendum (see Table 1.3).[32]

TABLE 1.3
Constitutional Amendments: Successes and Failed Attempts

Subject	Date	Ratification
Membership of former colonies in French Community	4 June 1960	Special method[a]
Self-determination of Algeria	8 January 1961	By referendum
Evian Accords (end of Algerian war)	8 August 1992	By referendum
Election of president by universal suffrage	26 October 1962	By referendum
Dates of parliamentary sessions	20 December 1963	By a congress
Reform of Senate	27 April 1969	Rejected by referendum
Reduction of presidential term to five years	20 October 1973	Passed by both chambers but not submitted to ratification process
Right of parliamentarians to appeal to Constitutional Council	21 October 1974	By a congress
Death, incapacity, or withdrawal of candidates during presidential election campaign	14 June 1976	By a congress
Extension of use of referendum to matters regarding civil liberties	July–September 1984	Approved by Assembly, rejected by Senate
Right of citizens to appeal to Constitutional Council	April–June 1989	Approved by Assembly, rejected by Senate
Acceptance of selected rules and norms of European Community[b]	26 June 1992	By a congress
Reform of judicial authority	19 July 1993	By a congress
Reform of right of asylum	19 November 1993	By a congress
Expansion of referenda, restriction on parliamentary immunity, single parliamentary session, and control over parliamentary agenda	4 August 1995	By a congress
Financing social security	19 February 1996	By a congress
Future of New Caledonia	20 July 1998	By referendum
Dispositions relating to the ratification of Treaty of Amsterdam	25 January 1999	By a congress
Dispositions permitting the recognition of International Court of Criminal Justice	8 July 1999	By a congress
Dispositions relating to equality between women and men	8 July 1999	By a congress
Amsterdam Treaty, empowering European Union to set common immigration and asylum rules	25 January 1999	By a congress
Reduction of presidential term to five years	2 October 2000	By referendum

NOTE: Congresses, or joint sessions of the two parliamentary chambers, take place in the Château of Versailles.

[a]Use of Article 85 of the Constitution, which provided for ratification by Parliament and a special legislative body composed of members of Parliament and of the legislatures of the newly independent states. Since the creation of that Community was aborted, this article and certain others became irrelevant.

[b]This prepared the groundwork for the popular referendum on the Treaty of European Union itself, which took place the following September.

Not all the constitutional changes to date have moved the Fifth Republic in the classic parliamentary direction, possibly because the French today, as in earlier regimes, have not been able to make up their minds between direct (plebiscitary) and representative democracy. Whereas the amendment of 1962 that provided for the popular election of the president was a shift in the plebiscitary direction, the failure of the constitutional amendment of 1969, which would have "reformed" the Senate out of existence, demonstrated that institutions traditionally associated with republican regimes (or with parliamentary supremacy) cannot be abolished so easily.[33] In 1992, in conformity with the Treaty of European Union (which reflected the parliamentary norms of most of France's neighbors), the Constitution was amended (Art. 88, sec. 4) to require parliamentary approval of all legislative proposals submitted to the European Council of Ministers. The amendments of 1995 appear to expand direct as well as representative democracy. The amendment to Article 12 not only makes it possible to have a referendum on economic and social policy, but also requires that the government justify its referendum proposal before each chamber of Parliament and permit a debate on the proposal there. The amendments to Articles 28 and 48 grant Parliament expanded powers over the agenda, the legislative process, and the surveillance of the executive (see Chapter 7).[34]

Regardless of the formal balance of power between the executive and the legislature, constitutional *practice* has tended to reinforce patterns that are reminiscent of earlier regimes. The Fifth Republic has had to operate at least partially within the parameters of traditional republican expectations because, apart from General de Gaulle himself, a large number of cabinet members and one president (Mitterrand) had been prominent politicians in the Fourth Republic, and many more deputies, especially in the early years of the new regime, were holdovers from the Fourth Republic's National Assembly. It was natural for such politicians to operate according to their traditional styles and to help perpetuate old practices. Among these have been the occasional practice of parliamentary "investiture" of prime ministers, the custom of proxy voting, the enforcement of party discipline, and the simultaneous service of deputies as regional or local councillors or as mayors.

Nevertheless, certain practices have not conformed with the traditions of parliamentary democracy—indeed, they have been situated in the twilight zone between constitutional and unconstitutional behavior. Thus, it is not clear that de Gaulle acted constitutionally when, in October 1962, he dissolved Parliament after it had adopted a censure motion against Premier Pompidou. According to Article 50, the premier, when censured, must submit the resignation of his government (therefore ceasing to be premier). According to Article 8, the president names the premier; and according to Article 11, the president can dissolve the Assembly, but before doing so must consult the speakers of the two chambers *and* the premier. The question is whether an ousted premier is still premier, or whether there is any premier left to "consult"! Even if one admits that these provisions are vague enough to lend themselves to presidential interpretation for political purposes—in this case, the purpose of taking revenge on, and thereby cowing, the Assembly—could one not say that the spirit of the Constitution was violated? Note that the exercise of the dissolution power is not always motivated by vengefulness. After his election to the presidency in 1981, and again after his reelection in 1988, Mitterrand called for new legislative elections in the hope that the new Assembly would be ideologically better aligned with the Socialist-oriented executive, and therefore easier to work with, than the old Assembly.

De Gaulle and at least two of his successors interpreted presidential power in such a way as to undercut the premier's independent position even more than envisaged by the constitutional wording. They did so by retaining responsibility for foreign and defense affairs; interfering, on a selective basis, in domestic policy matters; and "helping" their premiers in the selection of cabinet ministers. But they got away with that because the majority of deputies had been too submissive. During the three "cohabitation" interludes (1986–1988, 1993–1995, and 1997–2002), the Assembly was more independent vis-à-vis the president; as a result, the premier, whom the Assembly had in effect selected, became a more important decision maker than the president. Most Fifth Republic premiers have interpreted *their* powers in such a way as to deprive the Parliament of meaningful legislative initiative by giving legislators little time to debate policies and by enacting measures by decree. But one must remember that in the Fourth Republic, a regime characterized by parliamentary supremacy, the prohibition against "delegated legislation" (i.e., lawmaking by the executive) was disregarded when Parliament in fact granted decree powers to cabinets (see Table 1.4, page 18).

Having noted the digressions from the explicit text of the Fifth Republic Constitution, one should not assume that France is unique in this respect. In Britain, too, adaptations of the constitution have become necessary in order for government to function effectively. One of these adaptations is the "complementing" of the principle of parliamentary supremacy by the practice of cabinet government. In France, constitutional provisions have been sidetracked or adapted not only in the Fifth Republic but also in preceding republics; however, this process has not necessarily been antidemocratic or dysfunctional for the system. In the Third Republic, the constitutional provisions regarding strong presidential powers had to be ignored and certain executive powers had to be permitted to wither in order to facilitate democratic political development. In the Fourth Republic, provisions against the delegation of rule-making power had to be ignored in order to allow decisions to be made by *someone* (usually the prime minister). In the Fifth Republic, not all failures to adhere strictly to constitutional provisions and not all extraconstitutional practices have merely enhanced presidential power. For example, the interpretation of Article 23 that permits cabinet members to seek formal election to parliamentary seats (which they do not occupy) provides a grassroots legitimation of ministers. The constitutional reference (Art. 2) to France as a secular state has not interfered with legislation that provides for governmental support of parochial schools—nor should it, given the historic and present importance of Catholicism in France. In interpreting the constitutional requirement (Art. 4) that political parties adhere to a democratic order, France could have followed the example of the Federal Republic of Germany by declaring extremist groups such as the Communist party or the National Front to be illegal. But such a "strict construction" might well create disorder, given the vehemence of supporters of such groups.

Most of the adaptations found in Western constitutions have been legitimated by their popular acceptance and democratic intent. This is also true of the Fifth Republic Constitution; and even the president's interpretations of it that have tended to favor executive power to the detriment of parliamentary power are democratic because he himself is (since 1965 at any rate) a product of majority rule.

TABLE 1.4
Constitutional Principles and Adaptations

	Principle	Practice
Third Republic	Presidential dissolution and appointive powers	Parliamentary arrogation of these powers
	President to serve seven years	Premature abdication of several presidents forced by Parliament
Fourth Republic	Prohibition against delegated legislation	Decree powers in fact given to the cabinet
	Investiture of prime minister	"Double investiture" of premier and cabinet
Fifth Republic	Selection of cabinet by premier	Presidential involvement in selection process
	Incompatibility of cabinet office with parliamentary mandate (Art. 23)	Ministers permitted to seek parliamentary mandate, and senators and deputies serving as "temporary" ministers
	Prohibition against undemocratic parties (Art. 4)	Certain extremist parties allowed to exist
	No precise enumeration of civil liberties	Continuation of traditional rights due to their "incorporation" by the Constitutional Council
	Separation of church and state (Art. 2)	Governmental support of parochial schools: public salary of clerics in Alsace; church holidays as legal holidays
	Equality of all before the law (Art. 2)	Legal disabilities of women, abolished in the past few decades
	Vote of censure by Parliament leading to dismissal of cabinet	Vote of censure by Parliament leading to its dissolution by the president
	Prohibition against binding instructions upon members of Parliament (Art. 27)	Enforcement of party discipline in most parliamentary parties
	Government determines policy (Art. 20)	President (normally) tells premier what policies to pursue

Neither the "rules of the game" nor notions of legitimacy in France—and, indeed, in other European countries—have been based exclusively on the text of the Constitution currently in effect. Certain constitutional adaptations have been legitimate because they have been based on laws or declarations that antedated, or existed alongside, a particular constitution. Thus, although the preamble of the Fifth Republic Constitution alludes to a tradition of civil liberties in France, there are still-valid statutes providing for the punishment of speech that is seditious or *lèse majesté*; and although the Constitution provides for equality of all citizens before the law (Art. 2), there were until recently laws that placed women in a legally inferior position. This is similar to the situation in the Federal

Republic of Germany, where statutes providing for punishment of seditious statements and laws giving the police extensive power to make preventive arrests coexisted for many years with constitutional provisions regarding freedom of speech and due-process protections. French constitutions have been revised too frequently for the legal norms contained therein to be easily absorbed in the French citizen's political consciousness. In the face of this apparent constitutional impermanence, it has been natural for intellectuals, lawyers, and others to base many of their notions of legality on the old statute laws and their ideas of legitimacy on popular sovereignty. Constitutional practice must therefore be viewed in this light. Some of the advances in constitutional democracy have been accomplished through formal constitutional change, such as the amendment ratified in 1999 providing for gender parity in the nominations of candidates for elective office. Others have been achieved by the imposition of supranational (European Union) norms regarding substantive rights and procedural protections of French citizens.

The Fifth Republic Constitution contains its share of imprecisions and internal contradictions, of which the following may be cited as examples: Article 23 provides for the incompatibility of a parliamentary mandate with incumbency in the national executive branch, but Article 25 permits Parliament to provide legislation that may moderate this incompatibility. Article 16 provides for purely presidential action in cases of emergency, but Article 36 provides for the declaration of martial law by the cabinet and the prorogation of that law by Parliament. Article 21 provides that the premier is in charge of national defense, but Article 15 makes the president commander of the armed forces. Article 20 says that the government "determines the policy of the nation," but Article 5 stipulates that the president is the "guarantor of national independence [and] the integrity of its territory."[35] The ambiguity of the president's position in the Fifth Republic is seen by some as an attempt to find a middle way between two extremes: the Caesaristic chief of state embodied, on the one hand, by Napoleon I under the Consulate and by Napoleon III during the short-lived Second Republic and, on the other hand, the impotent presidents of the Third and Fourth Republic.[36]

During the first decade, most of these ambiguities were resolved by a kind of "preferred position" doctrine under which—when the situation was in doubt—presidential power would prevail. This was the case because most French citizens knew that the Constitution was tailor-made for General de Gaulle and accepted the fact that he was the main institutional bulwark of the system. The "institutional" (if not regal) qualities of de Gaulle, based largely on charisma, did not carry over to his successors; consequently, they were bound more closely to the letter of constitutional provisions, and they had to contend more seriously with parliamentarians (especially from other political parties). Thus the Gaullists after 1974—and the right-wing parties in general after 1981—began to complain about the "ostentation of power" made possible by a "bastard" constitution and called for the strengthening of countervailing powers.[37]

For many years, the president was the main interpreter of the Constitution because judicial review in the American sense had not yet sufficiently evolved, that is, before the Constitutional Council developed into a guardian of constitutional propriety (see Chapter 7). Practices and laws that violated the Constitution were considered valid if these violations (such as the procedural violation by de Gaulle in 1962 in connection with a referendum to amend the Constitution) were "vindicated" by popular vote, the ultimate expression of popular sovereignty, and other adaptations were legitimated by the fact that they were anchored in French tradition.

The Fifth Republic Constitution is unusual for a twentieth-century "law of the land" in that, like its U.S., British, and Third Republic counterparts, it is essentially "mechanistic" (i.e., confines itself largely to institutional features and relationships); unlike the Italian, German Federal, Spanish, and French Fourth Republic constitutions, it contains virtually no "programmatic" (i.e., policy-oriented) features and no bill of rights. Whereas the Fourth Republic Constitution spelled out in its preamble the right to work, to organize trade unions, to strike, to bargain collectively, and to receive social benefits, free and secular education, and so on, the Fifth Republic Constitution shies away from such clear specifications.[38] However, a plethora of customary rights and freedoms exists alongside the Constitution, and these have been periodically extended by means of legislation, especially since the presidency of Valéry Giscard d'Estaing. Furthermore, the preamble of the Fifth Republic Constitution contains an affirmation of "attachment" to the Declaration of the Rights of Man of 1789 and of the civil rights mentioned in the Fourth Republic Constitution; these rights have been gradually incorporated into the operative body of constitutional law by interpretation of the Constitutional Council.[39]

Every constitution is said to be based on a particularly dominant principle and to be instituted for an overriding political purpose. The major principle of the U.S. Constitution is the separation of powers; of the British Constitution, a gradual development of freedoms and the progressive adjustment of relations among certain dominant institutions (e.g., the queen, Parliament, and cabinet); and of the Fourth Republic Constitution, parliamentary supremacy. The guiding principle of the Fifth Republic Constitution has been the maintenance of traditional republican institutions, but with relations between them adjusted in such a way that effective decision making would be possible. For the first two (Gaullist) chiefs of state, this meant that the executive, especially the president, would be strengthened at the expense of the legislature. While in the opposition, the Socialists, and many centrists, had reservations about the Fifth Republic Constitution because they had always equated republicanism with a powerful legislature, and because the first president had been an overly Olympian and conservative figure. But as the years passed, and especially after the Socialists themselves had captured the presidency, they came to share a growing national consensus about the Constitution, which they found quite usable and which could be adapted to a variety of institutional relationships. As we will see (Chapter 6), Mitterrand had little difficulty in adopting certain Gaullist interpretations of the presidency; at the same time, he never abandoned the idea of leaving behind him a Constitution that would be adjusted in favor of the rights of Parliament and the citizen. In 1992, he appointed an ad hoc commission (the *Commission Vedel*) to suggest revisions of the Constitution that would embody his own preferences as well as those of parliamentary leaders. Among the recommendations contained in its final report to the president (early in 1993) were the following: the obligation of newly appointed prime ministers to obtain formal parliamentary investiture; an increase in the number of legislative standing committees; abolition of Article 16; and granting to citizens the right to bring cases before the Constitutional Council (see Chapter 7) and to initiate popular referenda.[40] One of the recommendations, the lengthening of ordinary parliamentary sessions, was achieved by amendment (Art. 28) in 1995; the adoption of most of the other recommendations would go a long way toward returning France to a more traditional parliamentary republic.

NOTES

1. See Raymond Rudorff, *The Myth of France* (New York: Coward, McCann, 1970), pp. 183–87; and William Safran, "Politics and Language in Contemporary France: Facing Supranational and Infranational Challenges," *International Journal of the Sociology of Language*, no. 137 (1999), 39–66.
2. According to the Constitution of January 1852, Napoleon was to be president for a ten-year period. He was proclaimed emperor in December of that year.
3. Emphasis added. The joint sessions were usually held at the royal palace in Versailles.
4. Of the remaining chiefs of state, one died in office, two were assassinated, one resigned after six months in office because of alleged involvement in scandals, one relinquished his position because of insanity, and four were prematurely forced out by the Chamber of Deputies.
5. "Cartesian" refers to the intellectual tradition inspired by René Descartes through his best-known work, *Discours de la méthode* (1637). According to the popular conception of this method, particulars are deduced from general principles (based on reason) in an orderly, logical, and clear fashion. See Ernst Robert Curtius, *The Civilization of France* (New York: Vintage Books, 1962), pp. 93–96.
6. The *Communards*, a motley force of many thousands ranging from pure revolutionaries to anarchists and "federalists," were motivated in their three-month rebellion variously by lack of food, the desire for a moratorium on the repayment of debts, and the quest for local self-government.
7. Charles Morazé, *The French and the Republic* (Ithaca, NY: Cornell University Press, 1958), pp. 20–31.
8. According to a poll conducted in 1994 by the Institut CSA, 64 percent of those questioned thought that the Dreyfus Affair continued to be of current significance. See *Le Point*, 26 February 1994, p. 10. See also William Safran, "The Dreyfus Affair, Political Consciousness, and the Jews: A Centennial Retrospective," *Contemporary French Civilization* 19:1 (1995), 1–32.
9. For a massive study of these questions, see William Shirer, *The Collapse of the Third Republic: An Inquiry into the Fall of France in 1940* (New York: Simon and Schuster, 1969).
10. For a recent crop of studies, see Michèle Cointet, *Vichy Capitale (1940–1944)* (Paris: Perrin, 1993); Asher Cohen, *Persécutions et Sauvetages: Juifs et Français sous l'Occupation et sous Vichy* (Paris: Cerf, 1993); and "Présence du passé, lenteur de l'histoire: Vichy, l'Occupation, les juifs," *Revue des Annales*, May–June 1993 (Paris: Armand Colin); Robert Soucy, *French Fascism: The Second Wave, 1933–1939* (New Haven: Yale University Press, 1995); Philippe Burrin, *La France à l'heure allemande, 1940–1944* (Paris: Seuil, 1995).
11. Jean-Baptiste de Monvallon, "M. Chirac reconnaît la 'faute collective' commise envers les juifs," *Le Monde*, 18 July 1995, p. 6. See also Renée Poznanski, *Être juif en France pendant la Seconde Guerre mondiale* (Paris: Hachette, 1994).
12. The groundwork for this measure had been laid during the Popular Front government of 1936.
13. For a recent study of the achievements and failures of the Fourth Republic, see Frank Giles, *The Locust Years: The Story of the Fourth French Republic, 1946–1958* (New York: Carroll & Graf, 1994).
14. Specifically, it was provided that if the prime minister made a bill a matter of confidence, the text of the bill was automatically considered adopted unless the Assembly actually produced a censure (or "no-confidence") vote; that such a vote could be introduced only if there were a government program before Parliament; and that the president could dissolve the legislature if, after having sat for a minimum of 18 months, it censured a prime minister who had been in office less than two years. Some of these features found their way into the Fifth Republic Constitution.
15. A succinct and useful account of the end of the Fourth Republic is found in Nicholas Wahl, *The Fifth Republic: France's New Political System* (New York: Random House, 1959), pp. 18–24.
16. Regarding the haste and confusion amid which the Constitution was drafted, see Nicholas Wahl, "The French Constitution of 1958: The Initial Draft and Its Origins," *American Political Science Review* 53 (June 1959), 358–82.

17. Jean-Jacques Rousseau, *Le Contrat social* (original French edition published in Amsterdam: Rey, 1762), Bk. 3, sect. 4.

18. Charles Secondat, Baron de Montesquieu, *L'Esprit des lois* (first of numerous French editions published in Paris in 1748), Bk. 11, sect. 6.

19. M. C. J. Vile, *Constitutionalism and the Separation of Powers* (New York: Oxford University Press, 1967), pp. 202–03. For a discussion of eighteenth-century constitutional doctrines, see Jean Bart, ed., *1789–1799: Les Premières Expériences constitutionnelles en France*, Documents d'études, droit constitutionnel et institutions politiques (Paris: Documentation Française, 1989); and Yves Guchet, *Histoire constitutionnelle française, 1789–1958* (Paris: Erasme, 1990), esp. pp. 18–28 and 57–105.

20. Léo Hamon, *De Gaulle dans la République* (Paris: Plon, 1958), p. 70.

21. Hughes Tay, *Le Régime présidentiel et la France* (Paris: Librairie Générale de Droit et de Jurisprudence [hereafter cited as LGDJ], 1967), pp. 69ff.

22. Jacquier-Bruère (pseud.), *Refaire la France* (Paris: Plon, 1945), p. 120.

23. Tay, *Le Régime présidentiel*, pp. 185–94.

24. See Club Moulin, *L'État et le citoyen* (Paris: Seuil, 1961).

25. Hervé Duval et al., *Référendum et plébiscite* (Paris: Armand Colin, 1970), pp. 15–16.

26. For a detailed breakdown of the succession of regimes from 1789 to the present, see Olivier Duhamel, *Le Pouvoir politique en France* (Paris: Seuil, 1993), pp. 15–17.

27. The Fourth Republic Constitution (Art. 2) had merely referred to "political associations," the aim of which was "the preservation of the natural . . . rights of man," specifically, "liberty, property, security, and resistance to oppression."

28. Pierre Mendès-France, "De Gaulle's Betrayal of de Gaulle," *Le Monde Weekly*, 18 November 1970. This view was once also shared by François Mitterrand. See his *Le Coup d'État permanent* (Paris: Plon, 1964).

29. Michel-Henri Fabre, *Principes républicains de droit constitutionnel*, 2d ed. (Paris: LGDJ, 1970), pp. 339f.

30. For a brilliant analysis of Fifth Republic constitution-making (in comparison with the U.S.A.), see John A. Rohr, *Founding Republics in France and America: A Study in Constitutional Governance* (Lawrence: University Press of Kansas, 1995).

31. See the discussion by Olivier Duhamel, "Les Logiques cachées de la Constitution de la Cinquième République," in O. Duhamel and Jean-Luc Parodi, eds., *La Constitution de la Cinquième République* (Paris: Presses de la Fondation Nationale des Sciences Politiques [hereafter, PFNSP], 1985), pp. 11–23.

32. For a recent textual analysis of constitutional amendments, see Christian Bigaut, *Les Revisions de la Constitution de 1958*, Documents d'études, no. 1.2 (Paris: La Documentation Française, 2000).

33. On formal amendments as "surgical operations" to correct the weaknesses of the Constitution, see François Luchaire, "La Constitution à l'épreuve du temps," *Revue politique et parlementaire*, September–October 1980, pp. 19–31.

34. For a discussion of these amendments, see Guy Carcassonne, *La Constitution* (Paris: Seuil, 1996), pp. 145–50, 202–05.

35. For a more detailed treatment of textual ambiguities, see Stanley Hoffmann, "The French Constitution of 1958: The Final Text and Its Prospects," *American Political Science Review* 53 (June 1959), 332–57.

36. Jean-Michel Gaillard, "Les Nouveaux Impératifs de la fonction présidentielle," interview in *Revue politique et parlementaire*, September–October 2000, pp. 2–8.

37. See the roundtable discussion, "Un Bilan constitutionnel du septennat," *Revue politique et parlementaire*, March–April 1981, pp. 3–95.

38. For a more general discussion of the differences between mechanistic and programmatic constitutions, see Karl Loewenstein, *Political Power and the Governmental Process*, 2d ed. (Chicago: University of Chicago Press, 1963), pp. 136–43.

39. On the preamble and other sources of "constitutional values," see John Bell, *French Constitutional Law* (Oxford: Clarendon Press, 1992), esp. pp. 57–77.

40. See Charles Zorgbibe, "Le Rapport Vedel: Un Retour aux sources de la Ve République?" *Revue politique et parlementaire*, 95 année, no. 963 (January–February 1993), 3–12. See also "Les Institutions de la Ve République en question," *Le Monde, Dossiers et Documents*, no. 207 (February 1993), 1–5; and *La Révision de la Constitution* (Paris: Fondation Jean Jaurès), no. 1 (January 1994).

CHAPTER 2

The Economic and Social Context

ECONOMIC DEVELOPMENT

By all measures, France is one of the most advanced industrialized nations today. Spurred by the French experiment in economic planning inaugurated in 1946, the country's rate of growth averaged close to 5 percent annually in the 1950s and 1960s. Some of France's industries, notably mass transportation, aeronautics, and communications, are among the most modern in the world. Its railroad system, renovated in the late 1940s, is one of the best in Europe. In the past three decades, other signs of economic modernization have been apparent. The mass ownership of durable goods, the proliferation of supermarkets throughout the country, a high per capita ownership of automobiles, and a tendency among increasing numbers of middle-class families to acquire second homes attest to France's economic dynamism.

This dynamism, however, is uneven and is of relatively recent date. Only about two generations ago, the French economy was still marked by a predominance of small, family-owned firms, an agricultural sector accounting for a third of the labor force and heavily dependent on government protection, and relatively slow urbanization. Since the end of World War II, however, economic growth has been impressive. Heir to a long tradition of state intervention in industrial development and economic transactions *(dirigisme)*—reflected in the fact that more than 20 percent of France's enterprises were once under government ownership—France has faced increasing competition within the European Union and the global market by resorting to a policy of consolidation and privatization. It has become the fourth-largest exporting country in the world. In 2001, France had an estimated trade surplus of 23.7 billion euros.[1]

France's economic progress is attested by statistics showing that in the mid-1970s the per capita income of the French was already among the highest in Western Europe. The hourly wage rates of industrial workers in France have kept up with inflation better than wages in the United States, largely as a result of periodic adjustments of the minimum wage (SMIG and subsequently SMIC).[2] The situation began to deteriorate in the 1980s and early 1990s, as the consumer price index rose more rapidly than hourly wages. Whereas there was a modest growth of net incomes in the 1970s, there was a virtual standstill in that growth in the 1990s. This was compensated to some extent by a decline in the rate of inflation.[3] The lot of the lowest income earners improved somewhat after 1988, when the government instituted a guaranteed minimum monthly family income, the *revenu minimum d'insertion* (RMI). In 1995, about 946,000 households received the RMI.[4]

French governments have striven earnestly to remedy the situation of the poorest segment of the population—by raising the SMIC and the RMI, and by providing free medical coverage to the 6 million inhabitants with the lowest incomes, a measure that in effect made medical coverage universal in 2000.[5] Between 1994 and 1999 the number of *SMICards* (those receiving the minimum wage) rose by about 40 percent.[6] The number of RMI recipients, too, increased; the cost of paying them rose from 5 billion francs in 1989 (when RMI came into effect) to 25 billion francs in 1998, and has continued to go up. This explains why the special wealth tax introduced in 1982 was retained. But this source, which affected nearly 180,000 households, yielded only 12 billion francs in 1999; to cover these outlays, an additional tax of 1.8 percent was imposed on the 800 households whose wealth was more than 100 million francs.[7]

In any case, wages and social benefits had been increased so much that comparative labor costs were too high for many industries to compete in the global market. Many firms complained that excessive wage rates and ever-increasing social security contributions forced them to close down.[8] These developments added to the growth of unemployment, which in 1996 reached 12.6 percent of the labor force. By 2000, the figure had gone down to 9.5 percent, largely as a result of the creation of about a million jobs; many of them (especially those of young people), however, were temporary, and others filled openings made available as a result of the reduction of the workweek to 35 hours—a measure for which the participating employers were rewarded with a reduction of social security charges.[9] Despite the various redistributive measures, inequality has persisted.[10] In 2000, the poor made up 8.4 percent of the population in France (compared to 6.0 percent in Germany, 10.6 percent in Britain, and 17.3 percent in the United States).[11]

The population of the country has grown at a relatively slow rate. The demographic stagnation was caused in part by the many wars in which France had been embroiled. As a consequence, the country had lost much of its productive manpower. In 1789, France, with 26 million inhabitants, was the most populous country in Europe apart from Russia; in the late 1960s, when the French population reached 50 million, it had long been surpassed by the populations of Germany, Britain, and Italy (see Table 2.1). In order to counteract this deficit, de Gaulle's postwar appeal to French families to produce "12 millions de beaux bébés" in the name of patriotism was not enough; it had to be supplemented by a system of income support to families with two or more children *(allocations familiales)* and by liberal immigration policies.

Between 1946 and 1975, more than 3 million immigrants entered France, in addition to about 1 million repatriates, French citizens from the former colonies in North Africa. These figures were augmented by a large number of workers from Spain, Portugal, and the Third World, now forming a significant percentage of the workforce in French factories. The presence of foreign workers was welcomed for a number of rea-

TABLE 2.1
France: Selected Demographic Changes, 1946–2000

	1946	1975	1985	1990	1995	2000
Total population (in millions)	40.5	52.6	55.0	56.6	58.3	59.8
Birthrate (per 1,000)	20.9	14.1	14.0	13.8	12.3	12.6[a]
Infant mortality (per 1,000 live births)	84.4	13.8	10.1	7.5[b]	4.9	4.4
Longevity of males (in years)	61.9	69.1	71.0[c]	73.3	73.8	75.2
Longevity of females (in years)	67.4	77.0	79.0[c]	80.6	81.9	82.7
Average annual duration of full-time work (hours)	2,100	1,875	1,763[d]	na	1,500	1,355
Number of adolescents over 14 enrolled in school (in 1,000s)	650	4,000	4,200	5,400	5,600	5,649[e]
Number of private cars in circulation (in 1,000s)	1,000	15,300	20,800	22,750[b]	na	27,500

SOURCES: Based on Jean Fourastié, *Les Trente glorieuses ou la révolution invisible* (Paris: Fayard, 1979), p. 36; *Quid 1988, 1992, 1996, 2001* (Paris: Robert Laffont); Dominique Borne, *Histoire de la société française depuis 1945* (Paris: Armand Colin, 1988), p. 95; Gérard Mermet, *Francoscopie 2001* (Paris: Larousse, 2000), pp. 195, 301–302; and *L'État de la France 2001–2002* (Paris: La Découverte, 2001), p. 140.
[a]1998.
[b]1989.
[c]1982.
[d]1986.
[e]1999.

sons: They contributed to the growth of the internal market; because they were, for the most part, unskilled, they formed a cheap labor force, and because they were largely not unionized and easily subject to deportation, their ability to press for higher wages was limited. They did not require an unreasonable outlay for housing or social benefits, for (at the outset) they tended to be young people without dependents. They brought more money into the social security funds than they took out and cost the government less for education than the natives. Yet because of these low labor costs, employer incentives to make "postindustrial" innovations (e.g., automation) were reduced. Today there is a widespread belief that the presence of large numbers of immigrants has a negative impact in the long run. There is, however, a powerful counterargument: Although the birthrate increased somewhat in the late 1990s and the population reached nearly 60 million in 2000, population growth is still too low. The population is expected to be between 61 and 66 million in 2020 and will probably rise only slightly thereafter. It is estimated that within three decades there will be only 2.5 active members of the workforce (as opposed to the current 4.5) for each retired person, so that the only way to keep the social security funds solvent will be to import more workers.[12]

Meanwhile, the growth of immigrant communities has created resentment among the indigenous workers; in addition, the rootlessness and cultural maladjustments from which many immigrants suffer have caused social disorganization that has, on occasion, erupted into violence. Finally, the dependents they bring into the country have special problems and impose a burden on local welfare and educational facilities.[13]

For many years, France's economic growth was impeded by a geographic imbalance of its population (due to a variety of factors such as soil conditions, topography, transport facilities, and distances to markets). The Paris region and parts of the northwest bordering on Belgium are heavily populated, whereas the Massif Central and parts of southwestern France are sparsely settled and show little growth. With only four conurbations of over a million inhabitants (Paris, Lyons, Marseilles, and Lille [see Table 2.2]), France is still a country of small towns and rural communes.

The agricultural sector, which in 1945 accounted for one-third of the labor force, had been reduced to less than 4 percent by 2000,[14] but it is still larger than in Britain, Germany, and the United States. The majority of French people are recently urbanized, and their cultural and emotional roots are in the provinces. The French succeeded for a long time in keeping the economy dominated by small farms and family firms producing for a limited market. Since the end of the nineteenth century, when high tariffs on imported wheat were imposed, the French farmer has been accustomed to governmental protection against foreign competition. Indeed, many of the great political parties of the Third and Fourth Republics, aware of their dependence on the votes of the provincial farmer and shopkeeper, embraced a protectionist policy and thereby helped to perpetuate in France what has been called a "peasant republic."[15]

TABLE 2.2
The Largest Conurbations in France, 1999 Census
(population in 1,000s, rounded)

	Metropolitan Area	Town
Paris	9,645	2,148
Marseilles/Aix-en-Provence	1,350	807
Lyons	1,349	453
Lille	1,001	191
Nice	889	346
Toulouse	761	398
Bordeaux	754	219
Nantes	545	278
Toulon	520	166
Doui-Lens[a]	519	na
Strasbourg	427	267
Grenoble	419	156
Rouen	390	109
Valenciennes	357	108
Nancy	331	106

SOURCE: Barry Turner, ed., *The Statesman's Yearbook, 2002* (New York: Palgrave, 2002), pp. 631–32.
[a]This highly urbanized area comprises Douai and Lens as well as other small- and medium-sized towns.

However, in the past 50 years, there has been a transformation of agriculture, marked by the abandonment of more than a million farms, the consolidation of farmland, the modernization of agricultural production, and the reduction of farm subsidies. At the same time, the government made credit more easily available for the purchase of farm machinery, so that the number of tractors increased more than twentyfold. Many farmers who left the land sought employment in industry and added to the growth of urban agglomerations. Yet some vestiges of rural domination in politics still exist. In the Third and Fourth Republics, the rural element, largely because of the electoral system, had controlling power in the Senate, and that element (together with the electorate of small, provincial towns) dominates the Senate today via right-of-center parties.

The pressure for agricultural efficiency was reduced somewhat when the European Community's Common Agricultural Policy (CAP), put in place in the late 1960s, created a captive market for French farm products in Europe. Furthermore, growing unemployment in the cities slowed down the rural exodus. Nonetheless, the postwar modernization of the French economy contributed both to a consolidation of industries and to the rise of the tertiary sector (see Table 2.3). Immediately after World War II, when France faced the challenge of rebuilding a war-torn economy, it tried (under pressure from bourgeois and province-based parties that reflected the nonmarket orientations of the peasant, the artisan, and the small shopkeeper) to protect the small entrepreneur through favorable tax and tariff policies. Later, with the competitive pressures of the Common Market and, still later, the energy crisis, French governments changed their policies abruptly. By means of cheap, long-term credit, tax exemptions for capital gains, outright subsidies, and the gradual abolition of price controls, the government encouraged industrial mergers. This policy had been inaugurated with some hesitation in the early 1960s but was advanced with particular dogmatism by President Giscard d'Estaing and his prime minister Raymond Barre (1976–1981) and was taken up again during the "cohabitation" government of Jacques Chirac (1986–1988), and, selectively, by Socialist governments as well.

TABLE 2.3
Structure of the Active Population, 1968–2002
(selected sectors and years, in 1,000s, rounded)

	1968	1975	1980	1994	2000
Agriculture/fishing	3,123	2,104	1,841	1,048	292
Mining and quarrying	251	177	144	66	44
Manufacturing	5,317	5,780	5,445	4,162	3,833
Commerce	2,628	3,215	3,386	3,715	3,320
Transport	1,388	1,250	1,334	1,397	1,425
Services	4,802	4,812	5,436	7,733	10,403

SOURCES: International Labor Office, *Yearbook of Labor Statistics* (Geneva: ILO, 1983, 1995); *Annuaire statistique de la France* (Paris: INSEE, 1990); *Labour Force Statistics, 1980–2000* (Paris: OECD, 2001), 144–45.

As a result of this policy, more than 400,000 independent firms went out of business during the past 35 years. Yet several hundred thousand small shopkeepers (including more than 30,000 bakers) remain. These continue to fight unsympathetic governments by means of lobbying, the ballot, and spontaneous acts of violence. Several organizations representing small and medium-sized businesses have intermittently pressed for legislation to impede the growth of "hypermarkets" and curb their ability to resort to selective price-cutting. One of the reasons for the growth of the Socialist party (and for its victories in 1981 and thereafter) was that it was supported by many small entrepreneurs who were disgruntled over the apparent favoritism of Giscard and his government to big business.

In recent years, both the remainder of the agricultural sector and the industrial sector have been challenged—the former by the agreements between the European Union and the United States in the context of the World Trade Organization—under which France is obliged to lower its farm price support levels and reduce agricultural production; and the latter by the relocation of industries from France to countries with lower labor costs.

France's farmers have accounted for 25 percent of the European Union's total agricultural production, a fact that explains why, in 2000, they received about 60 billion francs (compared to Germany's 36 billion) out of the 150 billion francs of the total agricultural subsidies disbursed by the EU under the Common Agricultural Policy. For many farmers the payments (15,000 francs [or about $2,500] annually per farmer) fell far short of their needs, especially with the spread of BSE ("mad cow" disease), which forced the government to slaughter tens of thousands of infected cattle and threatened to bankrupt numerous cattle farmers. The emergency aid promised by the government in 2001 was far from enough, and the farmers reacted by continued mass demonstrations.

SOCIAL CLASSES AND MOBILITY

Historically, the social system of France was much like that of any other Western European country that experienced feudalism and inherited a society divided into classes of nobles, clergy, townspeople (bourgeoisie), and peasants. This division was reflected toward the end of the *ancien régime* in the "estate" representation of the old Parliament. Since that time, the bourgeoisie has gained in political and economic power; much of the landed aristocracy has disappeared or lost its importance because of revolutions, expulsions, and the impact of the guillotine. The number of independent farmers increased because of the parceling of land among all the sons of the landowner. In the nineteenth century, with the rise of the factory system, the industrial working class (the proletariat) made its appearance. Today French society is still divided into the following groups: (1) the upper class, including graduates of the prestigious national universities, the upper echelons of the civil service, the directors of large and successful enterprises, bankers, and what remains of the old aristocracy; (2) the bourgeoisie, including members of the liberal professions (e.g., physicians, lawyers, architects), university and lycée professors, engineers and *cadres* (upper-echelon technical and administrative personnel), and owners of medium-sized shops and family firms; (3) the middle and lower-middle class *(classe moyenne)*, including white-collar employees, petty shopkeepers, lower-echelon civil servants, elementary school teachers, and, possibly, artisans; and finally (4) the lower classes *(classes populaires)*, comprising in the main industrial workers and small farmers. There is a correlation between class and ideology: Membership in the working class is often associated with membership in the socialist "ideological family," whereas peasant status usually implies sociopolitical conservatism and, in many cases, a continuing commitment to Catholicism.

But such correlations are simplistic and unreliable. It is important to keep in mind the following: (1) In France, a person's social origins may be just as important as actual class membership. A middle-class technician or engineer whose father was a worker would be almost twice as likely to vote for the Left as one whose father had himself belonged to the middle class. (2) Ideological and class divisions have tended to overlap in complex industrial societies; in France (as in Italy) there are workers who are revolutionary, reformist, Catholic, or apathetic,[16] although in recent years both revolutionary inclinations and Catholic commitment have greatly diminished. The self-worth of a unionized factory worker may be enhanced by the presence of foreign workers; the economic insecurity of a bourgeois may be compensated by his becoming a knight in the Legion of Honor; and the diminishing purchasing power of a lycée professor may be made up in part by the "psychic income" of her academic prestige (which itself has suffered as a result of the democratization of education). (3) There is a growing postindustrial sector, whose members (e.g., computer technologists and marketing specialists) are difficult to place in terms of the traditional class system. Indeed, a person's social status according to customary "objective" criteria (such as type of employment and wages) does not clearly correlate with his or her self-classification. In 1966, 69 percent of the workers referred to themselves as members of the working class and only 13 percent as belonging to the middle class; in 1994, 47 percent of the workers regarded themselves as working class and 30 percent middle class.[17] This change in self-classification may be attributed to an improved lifestyle, a reduced class consciousness, or an enhancement of the workers' status in relation to immigrants, the homeless, and the unemployed.

Furthermore, geographic variables may compensate for objective class membership: There is still a status difference between living in Paris and living in the provinces. Thus, entry into the National School of Administration (ENA), which has been training most higher civil servants since the end of World War II, has been rare for provincials, especially children of workers and farmers (see Chapter 8). Social mobility has tended to be lateral rather than upward; statistics indicate that the majority of the various elites have fathers who were in elite positions and that higher civil servants have little difficulty in moving to responsible positions in the private sectors of industry, commerce, and banking.[18]

During the past four decades, an increasing number of French men and women passed from agriculture or salaried-worker status to positions of self-employment. Still, most of the adults who left the farm entered the low-paid urban labor force, and the majority of workers' children remained workers. This lack of upward mobility in France, fortified by a continuing inequality of educational opportunity and housing conditions, and a pronounced lower-class lifestyle, sharpened the workers' perception of themselves as a deprived segment of society.[19]

In a discussion of the evolution of the class system, two observers argue that "the peasantry and the working class are disappearing in favor of a spreading middle class composed of cadres and white-collar employees. At the fringes of this new class of wage earners certain young people without education as well as older people whose jobs have brutally disappeared survive somehow."[20] (Many of these used to vote on the left, but now increasingly support the extreme Right: During the legislative elections of 2002, one out of five workers voted for the National Front). These observers also see a growth of jobs in the service sector (e.g., hotels, supermarkets, banking, and information technology). They note that while many of the larger enterprises have "delocalized," that is, moved their operations to countries with lower labor costs, some small business firms (employing fewer than 50 people) have resisted globalization.

Class cleavages and working-class consciousness have been moderated by the gradual democratization of primary and secondary education and the somewhat enhanced possibilities of the recruitment of children of working-class and lower-middle-class parents to the lower echelons of the national civil service. Class divisions have also been reduced by the expansion of the welfare state, the introduction of paid vacations, and the statutory medical care system. However, the worker has had to finance social security protection with ever-increasing payroll deductions. Although an annual paid vacation of five weeks is guaranteed by law to virtually all employed categories, a sizable number of industrial and agricultural workers do not take full advantage of it. Family allowances are less effective than they might be as a means of encouraging the growth of the birthrate; many of the French delay marrying and having children because of the persistent difficulty of finding adequate housing. Although individual home ownership has become increasingly common (with more than half of the population owning their homes in 2000), a large number of families (and the majority of the immigrants and the indigenous working class) live in substandard apartments.

About four decades ago, the government began to build housing for low- and middle-income families (*habitations à loyer modéré*—HLMs) in the center of Paris and other cities. These were later supplemented by massive high-rise projects along the periphery of towns (*zones d'urbanisation à priorité*—ZUPs), where many immigrants and indigenous poor live, and where crime and juvenile delinquency are rampant. About two-thirds of the HLM inhabitants are blue- or white-collar workers; however, an increasing number of such housing units are inhabited by petit-bourgeois French families. The ZUPs often became instant slums—a situation that has not contributed to an easing of interclass resentments.

After the accession of de Gaulle, co-management boards and profit-sharing plans were introduced in order to "associate" the working class with industrial entrepreneurs and reduce proletarian resentments. In addition, interclass resentments were channeled into nationalistic (and often anti-American) sentiments, which were widespread and were counted on to unite various socioeconomic sectors. With the partial eclipse of Gaullism, beginning with the election of Giscard d'Estaing in 1974, the resentment of the less privileged had to be addressed in a more concrete fashion. Despite the decline in economic output induced by the petroleum crisis,[21] Giscard allocated generous amounts of money for increases in unemployment and pension payments, and even initiated measures aimed at the democratization of the tax system. Despite the relatively generous social expenditures by the government, the tax bite on families in France with modest incomes does not seem particularly harsh compared with other consolidated western democracies, including those (like the United States), whose social expenditures

TABLE 2.4
Incomes, Taxes, and Social Deductions: Six Countries, 1999
(married couples with two children, average annual income,[a] in percent)

	Total Tax	Income Tax	Social Deductions	Family Income Supplement
Great Britain	17.8	14.3	7.7	−4.2
France	19.8	10.0	13.4	3.6
United States	21.3	13.6	7.6	0.0
Germany	33.3	12.6	20.7	0.0
Italy	25.5	17.3	9.2	−1.0
Sweden	28.3	26.2	6.9	−4.8

SOURCE: Philippe Chatenay, "Paie-t-on vraiment plus d'impôts en France qu'ailleurs?" *Marianne*, 25 June–1 July 2001, p. 60.
[a] Gross income, including salary of spouse, of 227,167 francs in 1999 = ca. $35,000 (U.S.).

are lower (see Table 2.4); moreover, taxes are compensated by family income supplements and other welfare measures.

However, these measures could not immediately reverse the fiscally conservative policies introduced earlier in the Fifth Republic. Among these policies were the reduction of social security benefits and the introduction of the regressive value-added tax system (*taxe à valeur ajoutée*—TVA). Spurts of inflation and devaluations of the franc were rarely counterbalanced by sufficient wage increases, because the fragmented trade union movement was in a poor position to bargain collectively; and the officially fixed minimum wage seldom made up for increases in the cost of living. Finally, the decline of the role of Parliament—in which the working class, through Socialist and Communist parties, had reasonably effective representation—and the corresponding enhancement of the position of the higher civil service since 1958 had greatly weakened working-class access to decision-making organs.

For many years, the gap between the white-collar worker (*salariat*) and the blue-collar worker (*prolétariat*) in France remained one of the largest in Western Europe. The radical trade unions, including the Communist-dominated *Confédération générale du travail* (CGT), despite their verbal commitment to social equality, hesitated to close this gap because they hoped to recruit and retain as members the very status-conscious white-collar and *cadre* elements. Moreover, some leaders of political parties most given to egalitarian rhetoric, particularly the Socialist party, were of bourgeois descent and status, and they did not wish to lose their social and economic privileges as a result of a precipitate policy of social leveling.

The salary and status gaps between blue- and white-collar employees have narrowed during the past half century. In fact, in 1999, skilled workers were earning slightly more than white-collar employees.[22] This salary convergence can be interpreted as a sign that France has entered the postindustrial phase and as proof of the corollary proposition regarding the embourgeoisement of the masses, the weakening of the class struggle, and the "end of ideology." It is true that the proportion of blue-collar workers in the labor force has decreased dramatically. However, many of these, particularly the unskilled, are immigrant or temporary workers, and they often tend to be ignored because they are "by definition, hardly members of French society."[23] Conversely, although there has been an increase in the number of white-collar employees as a consequence of the explosion of the service sector, there has been a corresponding socioeconomic decline among members of the sector.

During the second half of the twentieth century, in which the white-collar segment more than doubled, its female component increased markedly (see further on), but women's salaries continued to lag behind those of men. Furthermore, white-collar workers of both sexes have routinized jobs and low pay, experience unemployment, and resent the inequities of the tax system. Occasionally, blue- and white-collar workers discover that they have interests in common with intellectuals and students—for example, during the "Events of May 1968," these social groups attempted (or pretended) to support one another in public demonstrations against the Gaullist system. But such camaraderie is tenuous at best, largely because of the history of mutual distrust, the different backgrounds, and the divergent concerns of these groups. More than three decades after the "May events," the "mandarins" (the Sorbonne professors), no matter how far to the Left, still live in their spacious apartments in the bourgeois neighborhoods of Paris, while the poor continue to live in the suburban slums, the "Red Belt," around Paris.

RELIGION AND CULTURE

Constitutionally, France is a secular country. The Catholic church was disestablished three generations ago; public education, even in the provinces, is consciously and officially nonreligious; and many political parties, in addition to a large percentage of the parliamentary deputies (from the Third Republic to the present), have had a decidedly anticlerical outlook. Until well into the Fourth Republic, it was the view of Radical-Socialists that Catholicism was incompatible with republicanism, and it was the view of many Socialists that religion was incompatible with socioeconomic progress and equality. As if to advertise its commitment to laicism in public life, after the 1880s, the Third Republic accorded few chances for practicing Catholics to serve as cabinet ministers. With the outbreak of World War II, Catholicism reestablished itself as a positive political force when a number of priests joined the Resistance; after the war, a new Catholic party, the *Mouvement républicain populaire* (MRP), emerged with the fullest republican credentials.

The traditional attacks on religion by left-wing political parties have abated considerably, especially during the past three decades, and both religious and antireligious influences on politics have been greatly moderated due to two major factors: the "republicanization" of devout Christians and the decline of religious observance. Although the majority of the population is nominally Catholic, the appeal of the Church to the French people has continued to weaken, in particular among the working class, about 80 percent of which was more or less detached from Catholicism.

According to a poll on religious practice conducted at the beginning of 2000, 21 percent of the population declared no religion. Of those having religious sentiments, 62 percent were close to Catholicism; 19 percent, to Protestantism; 11 percent, to Buddhism; 6 percent, to Islam; and 2 percent, to Judaism.[24] According to an earlier poll, the proportion of baptized individuals declined from 85 percent in 1970 to 58 percent in 1995; marriages performed by priests plummeted from 95 percent to 50 percent; the number of priests, from 45,259 to 28,694; and the number of ordinations, from 264 to 122 (in 1997).

To be sure, religious practice varies according to region and gender. About two-thirds of devout Catholics are women. To the extent that France is urbanized, it is largely de-Christianized. Religious practice is relatively insignificant in selected regions around Paris and more noticeable in the rural areas of Brittany, Alsace, and Auvergne. But throughout the provinces there are many small communities from which the priest has departed and where churches are in a state of disrepair.

Although the principle of *laïcité* is widely accepted, there are certain policies that depart from it. These include not only religious programming on public television and courses on comparative religion in public secondary schools but also the subsidy of clergy in Alsace and part of Lorraine (Moselle)[25] and the public subsidies of parochial schools. The parochial (mainly Catholic) schools are maintaining their enrollments, which in 1996 embraced about 20 percent of all French schoolchildren from kindergarten through secondary school. There are several explanations for the survival of this aspect of religious culture. Undoubtedly the Debré law of 1959, under which teachers in Catholic (as well as other private) schools receive their salaries from public funds when these schools "contract" with the national Ministry of Education to include state-approved subject matter in their curricula, have helped to sustain the Catholic school system financially.

In some less-developed provinces—for example, Brittany, where Catholic school enrollment is high (nearly 40 percent)—parochial education may be viewed as a way of asserting the region's cultural uniqueness. And in the cities, parents may see parochial schools as a means of preserving many traditional moral values that are threatened by industrialization and other social changes or of preserving discipline and ensuring more personalized instruction (and higher standards than those believed to exist in public schools with large proportions of poor immigrant children). It is a reflection of both the persistence of Catholic values and of pluralism that, in the past two decades, the Catholic-secular issue has been muted and that many secular French citizens failed to support the Socialist government's attempt in 1983–1984 to bring the parochial schools under closer government control. The issue was revived in 1993 with the introduction of a bill to augment government support of parochial schools (see Chapter 10).

In many respects, France, once considered "the eldest daughter of the Church," manages to be a thoroughly Catholic country. The town cathedral remains in subtle ways a focal point of French culture. Most public holidays (except for May 1, the international Labor Day, and July 14, Bastille Day) are Catholic holidays, and public institutions are shut down. There is still little commerce on Sundays, and the major newspapers do not appear on that day. Until the mid-1960s, the list of officially approved first names for children born in France was based largely on the calendar of saints. Many Catholic charitable, educational, professional, and social-action groups exist; one of them, the Association of Christian Working Youth *(Jeunesse ouvrière chrétienne)*, claimed nearly 100,000 members in 1999.

The statistics cited above are only a partial reflection of Catholic identity. Catholic celebrations tend to be more cultural-familial than theological, and religion in general more personal than institutional. Only a minority of Catholics identify with the stand of the Church on certain issues (e.g., contraception, abortion, or homosexuality).[26] According to a 1996 poll, while 59 percent of respondents had a favorable opinion of the Catholic church, 67 percent (and 49 percent of practicing Catholics) thought that Pope John Paul II's orientations were retrograde, and a majority of both the general population and of practicing Catholics were in disagreement with his attitude toward important social and family problems, notably his opposition to the use of contraception.[27]

The controversy about Catholicism and, more generally, about the place of religion in politics was reignited with the public Catholic burial ceremonies of former president Mitterrand following his death in January 1996 and the official visit to the Vatican by his successor, Jacques Chirac, during which the latter stressed France's historical role as a Christian country. During the Pope's visit in September 1996, Chirac tried to rectify the situation by reiterating the "republican and secular" character of the French republic.

Non-Catholics enjoy full religious, civil, and political liberties. Until the Revolution of 1789, Protestants (mainly Huguenots) were subjected to forcible conversion, expulsion, and occasional massacres, punctuated by periods of toleration. Today, many Protestants—they are said to number about 2 million—are prominent in commerce, banking, the professions, and (since the end of World War II) in the higher civil service and politics, especially in the upper echelons of the Socialist party.[28]

There are about 700,000 to 800,000 Jews in France today. The Nazi Holocaust nearly decimated the Jewish community, whose roots in France go back to Roman times, but its remnants were augmented by refugees from Eastern Europe during the immediate postwar years. Jewish religious life was revitalized in the early 1960s with the influx of repatriates from North Africa, who, together with their descendants, now account for more than half of the total Jewish population. Like their Protestant compatriots, Jews have consistently supported republicans (rather than monarchists, who were traditionally identified with Catholicism) and have shown a preference for Radical-Socialist and (since the beginning of the postwar period) Socialist politicians. Jews are fully assimilated and participate prominently in the country's cultural life.

It has been suggested that anti-Semitism is one of the constant, though latent, factors of French sociopolitical thinking common to the bourgeoisie and working class.[29] Sometimes this anti-Semitism was theologically inspired. But there seemed to have been a decline in popular anti-Semitism during the past half century, perhaps attributable to the guilty conscience of many French citizens about their behavior vis-à-vis Jews during the Vichy regime. Moreover, it is widely believed that since the Muslim Arabs, who are much more numerous than the Jews, constitute the major target of xenophobia, anti-Semitism in France has decreased.

Despite a relaxation of prejudice toward Jews, anti-Semitism is never far below the surface. After the Arab-Israeli war of 1967, the phenomenon received a new respectability as a result of pronouncements and actions by de Gaulle, Pompidou, and Giscard that were widely construed as anti-Jewish. The government's pro-Arab and anti-Israel policies arose from economic considerations rather than anti-Semitism, yet these policies had the effect of sparking attacks on Jewish targets, including the desecration of cemeteries and the bombing of synagogues and Jewish-owned stores—which in turn led to greater

Jewish community solidarity and, subsequently, massive hostility on the part of that community to Giscard's leadership.[30] After the election of Mitterrand, the discomfort of Jews was greatly reduced, although Jean-Marie Le Pen, the leader of the National Front, continued to make them uneasy with his anti-Jewish innuendos. However, since the latter part of 2000, the Arab-Israeli conflict, in particular the growing violence in the Middle East, has again inspired attacks on Jewish targets in France. The overt identification of the French foreign-policy establishment with the Arab side has culminated in a demonization of Israel and its government, of Zionism, and of Jews who are believed to support it, a process that has revived anti-Semitism. The major difference between this and the more traditional anti-Semitism is that the former is identified with much of the elite, especially of the Left.

It is possible, however, to exaggerate the extent to which anti-Semitism exists in France. The phenomenon cannot always be clearly separated from negative attitudes toward "outgroups" in general. During the height of the Dreyfus Affair, most anti-Semites were also anti-Protestant, anti-Masonic, and anti-foreigner.[31] Many French people then viewed—and still view today—French culture as thoroughly bound up with Catholicism (albeit in increasingly secularized form) and with the idea of an organic evolution of Gallic tribes rooted in the soil of France. Like most European countries, France traditionally based citizenship on *jus sanguinis* as opposed to *jus soli*—that is, on French parentage rather than birth in France. However, during the French Revolution, ideological and "voluntary" criteria, such as the adherence to republican principles and a willingness to share the fate of the nation became more important in the determination of citizenship. The acceptance of these criteria, as well as the need to increase the population of the country, explains why France encouraged immigration and enacted relatively liberal naturalization laws.[32] In response to growing unemployment and racism, there have been pressures on the government to limit the number of immigrants and to make naturalization more difficult. Nevertheless, in 2000 there were well over 4 million immigrants, about 1.6 million of them already naturalized citizens, apart from the North African repatriates and tens of thousands of seasonal workers.

France's ambivalent attitude as both a welcoming host country and a hotbed of xenophobia is illustrated today most sharply in the case of the Muslim immigrants from North Africa, most of them Arabs. The presence of a large community of Muslims—estimates of their number in France range from 2.5 million to more than 4 million (compared to 90,000 in 1967)—has made many French people uncomfortable, because that presence is often equated with the unemployment problem and with the rising incidence of delinquency and crime.[33] The National Front, the *Club de l'Horloge*, and, to a lesser extent, other right-wing organizations have exploited that discomfort for their own ends, arguing that Islam, unlike Christianity (or what is increasingly referred to as the "Judeo-Christian" tradition), is not only a religion but also an "oriental" and foreign way of life, and that the cultural background of these "Arabs" makes it difficult to assimilate them into French society.[34] Some fear that Islam's "fundamentalism" will undermine French secular and republican values, while others hope that Muslims and their religion will become "westernized" (as has Judaism) and accept the dominance of French civil law over Islamic *(sharia)* law.[35]

French citizens, however, are no more racist than Americans, Britons, or Germans. They continue to consider France as a welcoming country for immigrants and have not lost their faith in the role of the public school in the integration of foreigners and non-Christians.[36] That faith has not been misplaced; for Muslim immigrants (and especially their children) are gradually becoming integrated into French society and acculturated to its way of life.[37]

Islam has been grudgingly acknowledged as a major religion in France. In 2001 there were 1,500 mosques and prayer halls, and their number is growing, in response to the fact that Muslims are more religiously observant than they were a decade earlier. In a recent poll, 36 percent of Muslims declared themselves to be "believing and practicing"; still, only 20 percent said they went regularly to Friday mosque, and for many, religion was essentially a private affair.[38] The opinion of non-Muslims regarding their Islamic fellow citizens has been steadily improving. Nevertheless, only about 30 percent favor the construction of additional mosques (but 51 percent of practicing Catholics favor it). Curiously, 41 percent of those who are politically on the left favor the building of mosques (compared to 25 percent of those on the right), which is probably a reflection of overall tolerance rather than religiosity.[39]

At the same time, the French are worried that certain elements associated with normative Islam—among them a weak commitment to pluralism, rejection of the separation of state and religion, and discrimination against women—may have a harmful effect on principles associated with French republicanism, among them gender equality and laïcité. The public debate on this matter was sharpened in the wake of an incident involving two Muslim schoolgirls who came to their public-school classes with their hair covered by a scarf. The incident, which was seen as challenging the ability of the public school to shape the secular national identity of children in France, divided the government and the Socialist party and provided extra ammunition for the National Front.[40]

Another disquieting factor was the discovery in the mid-1990s of fundamentalist Islamic cells in France that are closely associated with Algerian Muslim terrorists. Such cells have appealed primarily to the socioeconomically disprivileged Muslims found in certain towns and suburbs.[41] Worries about the political impact of a constantly growing Islamic presence and Islamic fundamentalism in France were heightened in the wake of the September 2001 terrorist attack on American targets, as, according to estimates, 10 percent of French Muslims were said to support the Taliban Islamic fundamentalists.

Religion is not the only challenge to the cohesion of French society. There has also been the fear that the survival of the cultures and languages of regional subcommunities would fragment the nation. For many generations, the suppression of ethnic minority cultures reflected the thinking of much of the French elite. Most intellectuals and politicians, especially of the Left, were committed to the Jacobin tradition, according to which all provincialisms and particularisms were equated with feudal backwardness and anti-republicanism. To nationalists, the ethnolinguistic minorities were "internal exiles" who "compromised national ideology";[42] to Marxists, they impeded the development of class consciousness, without which there could be no class struggle.[43] This explains why for many years children in Basque areas were punished for speaking their native tongue in public schools; the same was true in the case of children using Breton, spoken in several variants by several hundred thousand people in Brittany.

In the past three decades, however, France has been confronted with a new cultural assertiveness on the part of Bretons, Corsicans, and, to a lesser extent, Alsatians. This assertiveness has many sources: the independence movements of the Third World; the influence of foreign workers; the transnational regionalism and open borders of the European Union; and the examples of culturally focused "regionalization" policies of Belgium, Italy, and other European countries.

France could not accept regional aspirations for outright independence. Corsican, Breton, and Basque separatist movements (or "liberation fronts") were suppressed, and their leaders were tried for subversion in the State Security Court, which existed from 1963 to 1981. The government responded to the *cultural* aspirations of its ethnic minorities more positively—by providing radio broadcasts in Breton and Alsatian, legalizing Celtic first names, and permitting localities to post bilingual street signs.

About two decades ago, a further change began to take place. Postwar immigration was so massive that France—with its hundreds of thousands of Portuguese, black Africans, Southeast Asians, and North African Muslims—had become a complex multiracial and multiethnic mosaic. Shortly before President Giscard d'Estaing was ousted by the voters, he admitted publicly that France was a "pluralistic society." The Socialists, too, adjusted their principles and advocated the teaching of regional languages; after gaining control of the government in 1981, they promoted policies accordingly.[44] Nevertheless, while refusing to ratify European conventions legitimating the use of minority languages, France has selectively subsidized the teaching of regional languages and in 2001 sponsored the enactment of a law on Corsican autonomy that accorded special status to the island's language.

Cultural chauvinism has been directed not only at indigenous minorities or immigrants but also at foreign influences. A major target is the English language and American culture, whose impact has been so great that—so it is feared—they threaten to undermine the dominance of the French language and of the intellectual elite that are its guardians.[45] Several associations exist specifically for the "defense of the French language," and the government of France spends a great deal of money promoting the use of French abroad. The French elite's sensitivity to the position of the French language is reflected in attempts to limit the import of American films and in the enactment in June 1992 of an amendment to Article 2 of the Constitution stipulating that "the language of the Republic is French." It was reflected even more strongly in the Toubon law of 1994 (named after Jacques Toubon, its sponsor, who was then minister of culture). The law made the use of French obligatory in product labeling, advertising (both in print and in the audiovisual media), public announcements, public transport, and contracts, and it forbade the use of foreign terms by public authorities if equivalent French terms approved by the public authorities existed.[46]

This law has not been fully implemented, thereby demonstrating that the power of the state is not absolute, despite the heavy hand of the Napoleonic centralizing tradition. The latter had brought about the unquestioned preeminence of Paris, which still has the largest number of industries and controls the financial, cultural, and political life of the country. Despite some halfhearted efforts to bring "culture" to the provinces, music, theater, and dance do not have an impressive existence outside the capital.[47] The continued dominance of Paris explains why ambitious politicians and businesspeople, even though they might pride themselves on their rural roots, endeavor to maintain a foothold in the capital and why many provincial university professors try to obtain supplementary lecture assignments in Paris. In order to breathe some economic life into the provinces and, incidentally, to limit the urban sprawl around Paris, the government took several measures in the 1960s and 1970s, such as the siting of selected nationalized enterprises in provincial cities and the granting of subsidies or tax exemptions to private firms willing to build industrial plants in the hinterlands, but these measures have not met with much success.

In recent years, provincials have felt less isolated than before because they have been tied more effectively to the national (i.e., Parisian) scene by the constant modernization of telecommunications and the rail transport system, including high-speed train service between the Paris region and many provincial cities. As a result of these developments, the differences in attitudes between provincial small town residents and Parisians have narrowed.

To the extent that provincialism has been maintained or revived, it has been emotional rather than functional: Despite the increasing fiscal powers granted to local and regional authorities (see Chapter 8), typical French citizens are still clearly oriented toward the national government in a *policy* sense; they expect the national government to do more for them than the local government, and their participation in national elections is normally higher than in local ones (see Chapter 4). Still, Paris is farther away from the village than is the principal city *(chef-lieu)* of the department, and citizens can relate much better to their national parliamentary deputy if, as is often the case, the latter is also their mayor.

THE EDUCATIONAL SYSTEM

The educational system, like so many other aspects of French life and culture, may be viewed as traditional or innovative, depending on the observer's criteria. Since the nineteenth century, the school system in France has been largely public, compulsory, uniform, and centralized, with the Ministry of Education determining the educational policy and curricula at all levels and standards of virtually all examinations for diplomas. The primary schools in particular have served as relatively efficacious agencies of republican, secular, and nationally oriented political socialization and have prepared most pupils to find productive places in the economy.

Until the end of the 1950s, the French school system was highly stratified, with the children of working-class or peasant families rarely going beyond primary school (and entering the labor market at 15 and, later, 16 years of age) and bourgeois children advancing to the lycée in early adolescence, and thence to the university. In fact, the educational content of the lycée, which stressed classics, literature, and theory rather than technical or "modern" subjects, was little related to the labor market and was mainly designed for those who belonged to educated or otherwise privileged families.

Although in principle most French lycées are equal, certain Parisian lycées have been more highly regarded than the less pretentious secondary schools in the provinces. In higher education, too, a distinction has been made between the ordinary universities and the specialized *grandes écoles*, such as the *École Polytechnique* and the *École Normale Supérieure*. The *grandes écoles*, which have catered largely to the upper-middle and upper classes, have provided France with its intellectual and political leadership.[48] The status distinctions among the university faculty ranks *(professeur titulaire, maître de conférences, chargé de cours,* and *assistant)* and between these and the student have traditionally been precise and rigid, a microcosm of the hierarchy of society at large.

Nevertheless, there has been an impulse toward the democratization of education, particularly since the beginning of the Fifth Republic. In 1959, the government decided to raise the school-leaving age to 16 (a decision fully implemented only in 1971), and soon there was widespread agreement that secondary schooling was the right of all French children. The traditional screening of pupils for entry into the lycée at the ages of 10 to 11 was replaced by a system *(cycle d'observation)* in which a uniform curriculum was provided for all students up to the age of 14 or 15; this system evolved into a kind of comprehensive middle school (the *collège,* which comprises the lower four years of the lycée). Thereafter (i.e., during the final three years—the lycée properly speaking), students are guided into one of several "streams" *(filières):* letters, social sciences, physical science, mathematics, the life sciences, and (since 1983) agriculture, music and art, physical education, and other tracks. As a consequence of the baby boom in the immediate postwar period, growing social pressures, and easier access, the number of students in secondary schools rose from 1 million in 1950–1951 to 3 million in 1964–1965 and more than 6 million in 2000.

The demand for admission to universities created by this growth caused serious problems for the higher education system, which in 2000 encompassed more than 1.6 million students in 90 universities (in addition to about half a million in other postsecondary institutions, including the *grandes écoles)* and enrolled about 30 percent of the 20- to 24-year-old-age group. The overcrowding of lecture halls, the inadequacy of physical facilities and libraries, and, above all, the persistence of a university curriculum that, notwithstanding its overall excellence, bore an ever-diminishing relationship to the labor market—these were problems that demanded solutions.

In the 1960s, the government began to build additional universities, often with American-style campuses, and introduced more "technical" courses. But these measures were inadequate and came too late, and the clamor for a thorough overhauling of the French higher education system figured heavily in the rebellion of May 1968. After this event, the Ministry of Education initiated several significant reforms, including granting some autonomy to universities in determining curricula, creating new technical institutes, forming American-style academic departments (UERs),[49] and instituting a system of "participatory democracy" under which a university's governing personnel would in part be elected by professors, staff, and students.

These reforms were continued, particularly in regard to greater decentralization of academic decision making, the shaping of interdisciplinary curricula, and the founding of new university centers in the Paris region to relieve the congestion of the old Sorbonne. In the mid-1970s, the focus was on making higher education more relevant to the modern economy by giving a larger place in the curriculum to economics, mathematics, and a variety of technical subjects. In the 1990s, there were attempts to make the curriculum more flexible and to pay greater attention to students' different abilities and interests.

Most of the academic establishment welcomed certain aspects of educational reform because they were in consonance with egalitarian principles. These reforms included the virtual universalization of the public nursery school *(école maternelle);* the mixing of the sexes in elementary schools (at first in Paris, and later in the provinces);

and the program of literacy and basic education for adults inaugurated in the early 1970s. At the same time, the academic elite has been concerned about the decline in overall standards of culture and in levels of literacy resulting from the *massification* of education. There have been complaints that many students taking the examinations for the *baccalauréat* (the lycée diploma) are insufficiently prepared in grammar and writing. Many of these complaints were substantiated by reports issuing from special committees of inquiry set up shortly after the Socialist government was installed in 1981.[50] Despite such complaints, the government has been committed to a continuing democratization of education: It announced that the proportion of secondary-school students who received the *baccalauréat* would rise from 60 percent in 1983 to 80 percent in 2000—a goal that was actually reached in 1995—by means of an enlarged budget, better counseling, and further modernization of the curriculum.

Some professors objected to the increased attention to modern subjects because they did not conform to an idealized conception of culture; they saw their own elite status threatened by a cheapening of the commodity they produced. This attitude was brought into sharp focus in 1976 in reaction to a government proposal to reform the university curriculum in order to channel a large number of students from humanistic to more practical subjects. This aim was to be accomplished with the participation of the business community. Many professors opposed the reform on the ground that it would destroy the function of the universities "as places where culture is dispensed to those worthy to receive it."[51] Despite the good intentions of politicians, the rate of expansion of university admissions was reduced, and at the end of the 1970s the Ministry of Education abruptly dismantled selected graduate programs at various universities and reduced the financial support of institutions that had taken their autonomy too seriously. Since the early 1980s, a number of reforms have been undertaken that seem to move France in an "American" direction: downgrading the prestige of the professor; ending automatic admission of holders of lycée diplomas to selected faculties; pressuring universities to seek grants from the private sector; and suggesting that universities take account of the market in paying higher salaries to professors of business administration, engineering, and other "practical" fields than to professors of the more traditional subjects.[52] In the meantime, the number of entrants into universities continued to grow so rapidly that individual faculties began to limit the number of students admitted to graduate ("third cycle") studies. One of the proposals to accomplish this goal (made by the Balladur government early in 1995) was to ban graduates of technical secondary schools from entry into anything other than technical postsecondary schools, but after vehement student protest the proposal was withdrawn.[53]

The commitment to democratization was an article of faith under governments run by Socialists, because they were wedded to the Napoleonic principle of admission to universities on the basis of objective academic achievement rather than ascribed status; because of the close ties between the National Education Association (FEN) and the Socialist party; and because of the dominance of educators in the higher echelons of the party and in the government. For these reasons, the scholarship aid to university students *(bourses)*, especially those from low-income families, was increased and the salaries of teachers were raised. Irrespective of the changing commitments to structural reforms in education, the democratization of education at all levels is a fact and is unlikely to be reversed under more conservative governments.

THE POSITION OF WOMEN

Nowhere is the ambiguous relationship between modernism and traditionalism illustrated better than in the position of women in France. As a Latin and predominantly Roman Catholic country, France tended to assign the customary family and household roles to women. The Napoleonic code of 1804, under which women were legally incompetent, remained in force until 1938. Since that time, the legal and political disabilities of women have gradually been removed. In 1945, women obtained the right to vote; in 1965, married women were granted the right to open bank accounts without their husbands' express permission, to dispose of property in their own name, and, subsequently, to be legal heirs. Further progress was made, in part as a result of the general liberalization of social relations since the rebellions of 1968.

Women have made even greater strides economically. Between the mid-1950s and mid-1960s, the number of women in the professions, particularly in teaching, rose by nearly 70 percent. In 1992, women accounted for 56 percent of graduates of secondary schools and nearly 54 percent of university students, over 75 percent of elementary-school teachers and about 60 percent of secondary-school teachers, but only 20 percent of university professors.[54] The proportion of women in medical and related professions has grown considerably. The entry of women into the labor market has been facilitated by a generous system of paid maternity leave, which was raised to 16 weeks in 1980, and by the availability (especially in the Paris region) of free nursery schools for children from the age of three up. The proportion of women in France's working population as a whole changed very little during most of the twentieth century: It was 39 percent in 1906, 38 percent in 1979, and 47 percent in 1994, but by 2000 it had jumped to 74.4 percent.[55]

Nevertheless, the unemployment rate of women is still much higher than that of men, as is the proportion of women holding part-time or temporary jobs. Moreover, they are paid less than men.[56] Although the pay differential has narrowed somewhat in the past two decades (partly in response to a law passed in 1983 forbidding wage discrimination based on gender), the average salary of women in the private sector is still about 25 percent lower than that of men.

Women have made great strides in public service employment, but they are underrepresented in the higher administrative positions. The situation has greatly improved since the enactment of a law in 1982 that provided for equality of access to public employment. The proportion of women among the entrants to the National School of Administration (ENA) grew from 20 percent in 1980 to nearly 30 percent in 1990. Nevertheless, in the mid-1990s, fewer than 10 percent of the incumbents in the *grand corps* were women.[57] Moreover, the average salaries of women in all echelons of the civil service were 17 percent lower than those of men.[58] In 1999, 60 percent of civil servants were women; but they accounted for less than 20 percent of central administration and 13 percent of the highest administrative class.[59] About half of the judges have been women; but it was not until 1992 that a breakthrough occurred with the National

Assembly's appointment of the first woman to the Constitutional Council. In 2000, a woman was chosen as president of that institution.

The political role of women is more difficult to assess. Most observers agree that women have traditionally been more conservative ideologically than men. Thus, in the parliamentary elections of 1967, 65 percent of the women voted for right-wing candidates, compared to 48 percent of the men; by 1978, this 17-point differential had been reduced to 6 points, and by 1986, when the Right got 55 percent of the vote of both sexes, the differential had virtually disappeared. The one remaining difference had to do with support for extremist parties.[60] In the past several elections, women have voted less heavily than men for the Communist party and the National Front. In the first round of the presidential elections of 1988, only 10 percent of women voters (as compared to 17 percent of male voters) supported Jean-Marie Le Pen. In the elections of 1993 and 1997, the right- and left-wing preferences of women approximated those of men, except that women were somewhat more attracted to candidates of environmentalist parties.[61] Women in national executive posts have tended to be on the Left rather than on the conservative side.[62]

Some women have attained high positions within political parties and interest groups. In the 1980s, Nicole Notat became the president of the CFDT, one of the three major trade unions, and held that position until 2002. In the 1990s, Dominique Voynet assumed the leadership of the Green party and Michèle Alliot-Marie was chosen to head the Gaullist party; and at the end of 2001, Marie-George Buffet was chosen to be Robert Hue's successor as the national secretary of the Communist party.

Women have, however, done less well in elective offices; compared to most other European countries, the number of women in the French national legislature has been low. In the parliamentary elections of 1945—a year after gaining the right to vote—only 33 women were elected as deputies, that is, less than 6 percent of the total, a figure that put the parliamentary representation of women in France in seventieth rank globally. This proportion (which was even lower in the Senate) remained more or less constant until the elections of 1997, when the representation of women almost doubled.[63]

The presence of women in cabinets also grew at a slow pace. Only 3 women cabinet members during the Third Republic served as junior ministers in the Popular Front government of Léon Blum in 1936; and between 1946 and mid-1997 only about two dozen women held ministerial posts: 5 during the Giscard presidency and the remainder under Mitterrand. Women were particularly important in the Socialist government headed by Edith Cresson (1991), the first and as yet only woman prime minister in French history: 8 of her 46 ministers were women; 5 of them full members of the cabinet. In the Balladur government set up in March 1993, only 3 of the 30 ministers were women; one of them, Simone Veil, held three portfolios successively (social affairs, health, and urban affairs) and was the highest-ranking cabinet officer after the prime minister. In the first Juppé government, set up in May 1995, 12 out of 42 ministers were women; but when the government was reshuffled and tightened six months later, only 4 women remained among the 32 ministers. The Socialist government of Jospin, which came to power in June 1997, had quite a different appearance: Of its 27 members, 8 were women, 5 of them full cabinet members. In the reshuffled Jospin government of 2000, 11 of the 33 ministers were women. Women were a respectable presence during the presidential elections of 2002, with 4 of the 16 first-round candidates. But in the Raffarin government appointed after these elections, women did not do as well as their electoral weight would have presupposed: They accounted for only 9 of the 39 ministers, and 3 of the 15 members of the cabinet (other than the prime minister).

Women have not fared well in subnational elective offices either. Although since the end of the 1970s, women have constituted about 53 percent of the electorate, in 1996 they provided only 3.9 percent of the senators,[64] 21 percent of the municipal councillors, 5 percent of the general councillors, and 7 percent of the mayors. Before the 2001 municipal elections, only 10 percent of communes had women mayors. Although the number of women mayors has been growing, only two large cities have been governed by women.[65]

Some observers speak of a continued hostility toward women on the part of the "political class." They argue that such hostility has been particularly pronounced among the Socialists, who are accused of having done little to promote greater parliamentary representation of women.[66] However, after gaining power in 1981, the Socialist government introduced a bill to institute a minimum quota of 30 percent for women on all electoral candidate lists, but it was rejected by the Constitutional Council.[67] Nevertheless, the Socialist party adhered to that quota for the parliamentary elections of 1997; as a result, 63 women—10.9 percent of the total: 42 of them Socialists and 9 belonging to other left-wing parties—were elected to the Assembly.

In order to rectify the imbalance between men and women in elective office, a constitutional amendment was ratified in 1999 stating that "the law favors the equal access of women and men to elective mandates and functions." This was followed by specific legislation in June 2000 mandating that every effort would be made to achieve parity, that is, to create electoral lists on which there were as many women as men.[68] There had been some progress, however, in anticipation of the amendment's taking effect. The number of women in the Senate rose from 20 in 1997 to 35 in September 2001.[69]

The gender parity law was applied for the first time in the municipal elections of March 2001, resulting in the election of 39,373 women to municipal councils, that is, 47.43 percent of the total (compared to 21.7 percent in the 1995 municipal elections).[70] However, women did not do well in the parliamentary elections of 2002, the first time the law was applied at that level. As barely 40 percent of the candidates were women (compared to 20 percent in the 1997 elections), the gender parity of the lists was not achieved, and none of the major parties distinguished itself. The final result was equally disappointing. The overall number of women elected was 71 out of 577 (12.71 percent), only a slight improvement over the 1997 result (62, or 12.2 percent).[71]

The formal approaches to parity are not necessarily approved by all citizens. Some have argued that they constitute a quota system that amounts to a form of "affirmative action" and might open the door to quotas for ethnic and/or religious minorities.[72] Moreover, they argue, a formal provision of gender parity is unnecessary in view of Article 6 of the Declaration of the Rights of Man and the Citizen of 1789, which provides that "all citizens are equal and are entitled to all privileges, positions, and public employment on the basis of their abilities and without distinction other than their virtues and their talents"; and of Article 1 of the Constitution, which provides for equality of all citizens regardless of origin, race and religion—and presumably also of gender.[73]

One indication of the changing societal position of women has to do with birth control. The Gaullist party had disapproved of contraception and abortion because of the leadership's social conservatism and its desire to encourage population growth. But in the past four decades, family planning has become more acceptable, and since 1969, contraceptive devices for women could be purchased legally. In 1972, children born out of wedlock obtained the same rights as other children.

After the accession of Giscard, the policy of liberalization in regard to women's rights advanced considerably. Abortions were decriminalized, and their cost covered by social security funds. By 1980, women had achieved equality with men with respect to choice of domicile, authority over children, and initiative in divorce proceedings. As a sign of his commitment to women's rights, Giscard created a Ministry for the Condition of Women, and Mitterrand retained such an office during the first few years of his presidency.[74] In 1985, women were given equal rights in the administration of family property. In 1986, French citizens obtained the right to bear the maiden name of their mothers; and in 1992, a law was passed to criminalize sexual harassment at work.[75]

The independent existence of the women's movement is fairly recent.[76] Among the most important women's organizations have been the *Union des femmes françaises*, which was formed in 1945 out of Resistance committees; the *Mouvement de la libération des femmes*, established in 1968 as a federation of several associations of different leftist tendencies; and the *Mouvement pour la liberté de l'avortement et de la contraception*.[77] In 1989 a new women's organization, the *Alliance des femmes pour la démocratisation*, was founded; it included representatives of virtually all political parties and age groups and concerned itself with general political issues, particularly on local levels. Much of the credit for the social, legal, and political changes in the status of women is owed to the women's movement.

NOTES

1. Compared to 33.2 billion in 1999 and 20.2 billion in 2000. See Éric Heyer, "Le Commerce extérieur," in Françoise Milewski, ed., *L'Économie française 2002* (Paris: La Découverte, 2002), p. 38.
2. SMIG—*salaire minimum industriel garanti*, the ordinary minimum wage; SMIC—*salaire minimum interprofessionel de croissance*, a minimum wage dependent on productivity growth. In 1982, the SMIC was 2.77 € (18.15 francs, or ca. $2.50) per hour; in 2001, 6.67 € (ca. $6.50). This brought the minimum monthly wage (at 39 hours per week) to 7,388 francs, or about $1,200. Between 1982 and 2001, the SMIC rose by an annual average of 3.2%, or by 2.4% in real terms (i.e., ahead of cost-of-living increases). The SMIC benefits 2.2 million wage earners, or 11 percent of the workforce. Cf. www.insee.fr/fr/indicateur/smic.htm, and Gérard Mermet, *Francoscopie 2001* (Paris: Larousse, 2001), p. 324.
3. The rate of inflation was 7.2% in 1973; 9.6% in 1983, 0.8% in 1995, and 1.0% in 2001.
4. At the beginning of 2002, individuals entitled to the RMI received 405.62 € euros per month and couples, 608.43 € per month, plus more than 120 € per child.
5. The cost of this measure (9 billion francs or $1.3 billion) was to come from the state, various departments, and the health insurance funds. See *News from France*, 7 February 2001.
6. Alexandre Garcia, "Des SMICards plus nombreux," *Le Monde*, 25 August 1999.
7. Laurent Mauduit, "L'Impôt sur la fortune ne fait plus recette," *Le Monde*, 26 July 1999.

8. The proportion of social security deductions furnished by the employer went up from 30% in 1970 to 42% in 1990; that of the employee rose from 6% to 24% during the same period. See Gérard Mermet, *Francoscopie 1995: Les Français: Qui sont-ils? Où vont-ils?* (Paris: Larousse, 1994), p. 327.

9. See Xavier Timbeau, "L'Emploi et le chômage," in *L'Économie française 2001* (Paris: La Découverte, 2001), pp. 54–55.

10. In 1998, 10% of the richest decile owned 53% of the wealth; the next decile, 16%; and the lowest three deciles, 1%. Figures from Laurent Mauduit, "10% des ménages détiennent la moitié des fortunes," *Le Monde, Dossiers et Documents,* 16 June 1998.

11. Jean Gadrey, "La 'Nouvelle Économie' entre réalité et mythe," in *L'État de la France 2001/2002.* (Paris: La Découverte, 2001), p. 29. According to another source, 1.6 million households (7.3 percent of the total), were below the poverty threshold. See Virginie Malengre, "Le Taux de pauvreté est resté stable malgré la croissance," *Le Monde,* 23 March 2001.

12. Pascale Bessy-Pietri, Mohamed Hilal, and Bertrand Schmidt, "Bilan démographique de recensement de 1999," in *Ruralités,* ed. Pierre Alphanderi et al., Problèmes Politiques et Sociaux, no. 84 (Paris: Documentation Française, 2000), pp. 10–11.

13. See "Immigrés: Le Dossier explosif," a series of articles in *L'Express,* 4 February 1983, pp. 46–66, for statistics and public opinion data.

14. See Régis Guyotat, "En douze ans, un tiers des paysans français ont disparu," *Le Monde,* 22 February 2002.

15. Gordon Wright, *Rural Revolution in France: The Peasantry in the Twentieth Century* (Stanford, CA: Stanford University Press, 1964), p. 1.

16. This was true even during the first two decades after the end of World War II, when ideological and class divisions were much sharper than today. Mattei Dogan, "Political Cleavage and Social Stratification in France and Italy," in S. M. Lipset and S. Rokkan, eds., *Party Systems and Voter Alignments* (New York: Free Press, 1967), pp. 175–77.

17. Guy Michelat and Michel Simon, "1981–1995: Changements de société, changements d'opinion," SOFRES, *L'État de l'opinion 1996,* p. 176.

18. See Dominique Goux and Éric Maurin, "La Mobilité sociale en France," *Données sociales, 1996* (Paris: INSEE, 1996).

19. See Serge Cordellier, "L'Ascenseur social est en panne," in *L'État de la France, 95–96* (Paris: La Découverte, 1995), pp. 199–202. For earlier studies, see Pierre Birnbaum, *La Classe dirigeante française* (Paris: Presses Universitaires de France [hereafter PUF], 1978), pp. 68–70. This study notes (p. 104) that in 1974, 15% of the "ruling class" was composed of sons of members of the middle and lower classes, and 4 percent were sons of farmers—at a time when sons of members of the lower classes constituted 40% of the population and sons of farmers 26%. See also Pierre Birnbaum, ed., *Les Élites socialistes au pouvoir, 1981–1985* (Paris: PUF, 1985).

20. Dominique Goux and Éric Maurin, "Une Société sans classes?" in Daniel Cohen, ed., *France: Les révolutions invisibles* (Paris: Calmann-Lévy, 1998), p. 127.

21. This crisis resulted from a quadrupling of oil prices by the Organization of Petroleum-Exporting Countries (OPEC) following the Arab-Israeli war of October 1973.

22. See the (sometimes conflicting) statistics of the *Centre d'études des revenus et des coûts* (CERC) and INSEE for various years.

23. Jacques Lautman, "Où sont les classes d'antan?" in Henri Mendras, ed., *La Sagesse et le désordre* (Paris: Gallimard, 1980), p. 81.

24. Seven percent of the population were regularly practicing Catholics; 24%, occasionally practicing; 41%, nonpracticing Catholics; 2%, practicing Muslims; 2%, Protestants; 2%, other religions. See Mermet, *Francoscopie 2001,* pp. 253–58.

25. These provinces had been annexed by Germany as a result of the Franco-Prussian War of 1870; when they reverted to France in 1918, the government decided to continue the system of official support of "established" religions that been instituted there by the Germans.

26. A few years ago, about 60% of the population (outside the Paris region) favored the maintenance of Sunday "blue laws," but only 15% gave religious reasons. For an overall statistical analysis of religious attitudes and practices, see Guy Michelat, Julien Potel, Jacques Sutter, and Jacques Maître, *Les Français sont-ils encore catholiques?* (Paris: Le Cerf, 1991).

27. IPSOS poll of August 1996. See Christian Makarian, "Ce que pèsent Catholiques de France," *Le Point*, 14 September 1996, p. 73.
28. Half of the French Protestants are members of the Reformed church, and most of the remainder belong to the Lutheran or the Evangelical sect. They are led by about 1,200 clergy (100 of whom are women). Former prime minister Jospin is a Protestant, as well as former prime minister Rocard and at least six of the cabinet ministers who served under him. About 25% of regional prefects and more than 20% of the members of the diplomatic corps are Protestants. See "La Grande Revanche des protestants," *Le Point*, 27 January 1996, pp. 71–79.
29. See Pierre Birnbaum, *Un Mythe politique: La "République juive"* (Paris: Fayard, 1988).
30. See Alain de Sédouy and André Harris, *Juifs et Français* (Paris: Seuil, 1979). See also William Safran, "France and Her Jews: From 'Culte Israélite' to 'Lobby Juif,'" *Tocqueville Review* 5:1 (Spring–Summer 1983), 101–35; and Maurice Szafran, *Les Juifs dans la Politique Française* (Paris: Flammarion, 1990).
31. Anti-Semitism was a component of the "integral nationalism" of ultraconservative thinkers such as Charles Maurras, who disliked Jews because they were not Catholics; and Maurice Barrès, who disliked Jews because they were "different." J. S. McClelland, ed., *The French Right* (London: Jonathan Cape, 1970), pp. 25–32. For instances of survival of small-town, petit-bourgeois anti-Semitism, see Edgar Morin, *Rumor in Orléans* (New York: Random House, 1971), esp. pp. 11–79.
32. Until a decade ago, a child born in France of foreign parents acquired citizenship automatically upon reaching majority (i.e., the age of 18) if he or she had lived in France for the preceding five years. Immigrants could be naturalized on demand after a minimum of five years' residence and proof of acculturation (including fluency in French). In 1993, legislation was enacted providing for tighter controls over immigration and immigrants and removing the automatic grant of citizenship. After that, local authorities were able to exercise discretion in responding to requests for naturalization. See Philippe Bernard, "Nationalité française, nouveau mode d'emploi," *Le Monde*, 1 January 1994. See also Catherine Wihtol de Wenden, *Citoyenneté, nationalité et immigration* (Paris: Arcantère Éditions, 1987); and Rogers Brubaker, "Citizenship and Naturalization: Policies and Politics," in W. R. Brubaker, ed., *Immigration and the Politics of Citizenship in Europe and North America* (Lanham, MD: University Press of America, 1989), pp. 99–127.
33. For the past century France has gathered no official statistics on religion. Moreover, Muslim organizational life is highly fragmented, and there is as yet no central Islamic authority in the country.
34. See Jocelyn Cesari, *Être musulman en France: Associations militants et mosquées* (Paris: Éditions Karthala and IREMAM, 1994), pp. 10f et passim. According to this scholar, the widespread fear of Islam is based on fantasies—associated with conquest, violence, fanaticism, terrorism, fundamentalism, and intolerance for democracy and for other religions.
35. William Safran, "Religion and *Laïcité* in a Jacobin Republic: The Case of France," in W. Safran, ed., *The Secular and the Sacred: Nation, Religion, and Politics* (London: Frank Cass, 2002), Chapter 2.
36. For a particularly strong argument, see Dominique Schnapper, *La France de l'intégration: Sociologie de la nation en 1990* (Paris: Gallimard, 1991).
37. See Rémy Leveau, Catherine Wihtol de Wenden, and Gilles Kepel, "Les Musulmans dans la société française," *Revue française de science politique* [hereafter *RFSP*] 37:6 (December 1987), 765–81. See also Gilles Kepel, *Les Banlieues de l'islam, naissance d'une religion en France* (Paris: Seuil, 1987). It is interesting to observe that in 1995, only 14% of the children whose parents were born in Algeria engaged in regular religious practice (compared to 7% of the French population as a whole). Conversely, 30% of the offspring of Algerian-born parents had no religion at all. INSEE study of March 1995, cited in *Le Monde*, 31 March 1995, p. 8.
38. IFOP poll, September 2001. For a variety of attitudes, see Xavier Ternisien, "Plus pratiquants, les musulmans de France sont aussi mieux intégrés," *Le Monde*, 5 October 2001.
39. Xavier Ternisien, "Une Meilleure Acceptation par l'opinion," *Le Monde*, 5 October 2001.
40. See "Faut-il laisser entrer l'Islam à l'école?" *Le Point*, 22 October 1989, pp. 52–57. See also David Beriss, "Scarves, Schools, and Segregation: The Foulard Affair," *French Politics and Society* 8:1 (Winter 1990), 1–13. A similar incident occurred in 1993.
41. Henri Tinq, "L'Islam de France se radicalise," *Le Monde*, 12 August 1994, p. 1. See also the case study by Philippe Aziz, *Le Paradoxe de Roubaix* (Paris: Plon, 1995).

42. Jacques Chevallier, "L'État-nation," *Revue du droit public* 96 (September–October 1980), 1271–1302; and William Safran, "The French Left and Ethnic Pluralism," *Ethnic and Racial Studies* 7:4 (October 1984), 447–61.

43. See Roger Martelli, *Comprendre la nation* (Paris: Éditions Sociales, 1979), p. 71. According to Martelli, there is no such thing as a Corsican or Breton nation. In a 1990 decision, the Constitutional Council echoed that view.

44. Parti Socialiste, *Projet Socialiste pour la France des années 80* (Paris: Club Socialiste du Livre, 1980), pp. 253–58; William Safran, "Minorities, Ethnics, and Aliens: Pluralist Policies in the Fifth Republic," in Paul Godt, ed., *Policy-Making in France* (London and New York: Pinter, 1989), pp. 176–90; and W. Safran, "The French State and Minority Cultures: Policy Dimensions and Problems," in J. R. Rudolph and R. J. Thompson, eds., *Ethnoterritorial Politics, Policy, and the Western World* (Boulder & London: Lynne Rienner, 1989), 115–57. In 2001, about 150,000 French pupils were studying regional languages.

45. Even Jack Lang, the Socialist minister of culture, 1981–1986 and 1988–1993, briefly railed against American "cultural imperialism." See also Michel Wieviorka, "La Nouvelle Question urbaine en France," in Gabriel Gosselin and Henri Ossebi, eds., *Les Sociétés Pluriculturelles* (Paris: L'Harmattan, 1994), pp. 108–10, who argues that Jacobin universalism is occasionally marked by cultural condescension.

46. See William Safran, "Politics and Language in Contemporary France: Facing Supranational and Infra-national Challenges," *International Journal of the Sociology of Language*, 137 (1999), 39–66.

47. In the 1960s, under the direction of Minister of Culture André Malraux, centers for the arts *(maisons de la culture)* began to be established in selected cities, with mixed success.

48. There are now about 300 *grandes écoles*, about half of them schools of engineering and commerce. Many of these are private, and their prestige is far below that of the *École Polytechnique*, the *École Normale Supérieure*, or the *École Nationale d'Administration*.

49. UER—*unité d'enseignement et de recherche* (instruction and research unit).

50. The *Commission Laurent Schwartz* reported at the end of 1981 that one-third of the graduates of primary schools had not mastered spelling, and that France had some 400,000 illiterate adults. Another *commission* (Louis Legrand) reported that a large proportion of upper-grade secondary-school students performed poorly in mathematics and foreign languages. See "École, pourquoi tant d'échecs," *Le Point*, 31 January 1983, pp. 50–53.

51. Alfred Kastler, "La Réforme de l'université," *Le Monde*, 23 April 1976. See also Jacques Charpentreau, "Le Snobisme de la culture," *Revue politique et parlementaire* 78 (March–April 1976), 70–79.

52. Frédéric Gaussen, "Les Enseignants et la loi du marché," *Le Monde*, 14 February 1989.

53. In order to make technical school more attractive to students, François Bayrou, the minister of education, argued in 1995 that a technical diploma had the same prestige as an academic one, but the argument was little more than rhetoric.

54. The proportion of women varies according to field of specialization. In 1991, women accounted for a clear majority of students in literature and law, slightly more than 51% in the social sciences, but only 40% in the hard sciences, medicine, and engineering. Catherine Leroy, "Les Sciences délaissées," *Le Monde*, 17 February 1993.

55. *Le Monde*, 10 November 2000, p. 18. The statistics for younger women (ages 25–49), however, are different. Their proportion in the labor force rose from 58.6% in 1975 to 79.3% in 2000.

56. For a discussion of women's employment patterns, see Mariette Sineau, "D'un perspective à l'autre: La Politique Socialiste en direction des femmes (10 mai 1981–10 mai 1991)," *French Politics and Society* 9:3–4 (Summer–Fall 1991), 63–81. In 1999, women made up 77.1% of the two deciles of people with the lowest wages and 33.3% of the two highest-paid deciles. See Martine Laronche, "Les Femmes loin de la parité," *Le Monde*, 10 March 1999.

57. According to more specific statistics for 1994, women accounted for fewer than 7% of the deputy or assistant directors of ministries; and only 5.2% of the members of the Council of State, 6.5% of the Court of Accounts, and 3.3% of the Inspectors of Finance.

58. For comparable (and sometimes variable) statistics, see Valérie Devillechabrolle, "L'Administration, un nouveau vivier," *Le Monde*, 17 February 1993; Michèle Riot-Sarcey, "Les Femmes et le pouvoir,"

in Jean-Yves Potel, ed., *L'État de la France* (Paris: La Découverte, 1985), pp. 454–56; Patricia Latour, Monique Houssin, and Madia Tovar, *Femmes et citoyennes* (Paris: Éditions de l'Atelier, 1995); and Odile Krakovitch, "Les Femmes dans l'administration," *Après-Demain*, no. 380–81 (January–February 1996), 16–19.

59. See Nathalie Raulin, "Femmes d'exception à la haute fonction publique," *Libération*, 17 February 1999.

60. *L'Élection présidentielle de 1988, Le Monde, Dossiers et Documents*, p. 43. According to *Jours de France* (7–12 November 1987), in 1977, 35% of wives had voted the same as their husbands; in 1987, only 23% did.

61. Janine Mossuz-Lavau and Mariette Sineau, "Le Revirement des femmes," *Le Monde*, 18 August 1993. For a more detailed discussion of voting trends, see Janine Mossuz-Lavau, "Le Vote des femmes en France (1945–1993), *RFSP* 43:4 (August 1993), 673–89.

62. For example, of the 10 first-round presidential candidates in 1981, 3 were women, and 2 of these ran on leftist tickets; and of the 26 women elected to the Assembly that year (compared to 18 elected in 1978), 19 were Socialists and 3 Communists. In the parliamentary elections of 1988, the situation was more balanced: Of the 32 women elected to the Assembly that year, 16 were Socialists or close to that party; 1 was Communist; 14 belonged to the Gaullist-Giscardist alliance, and 1 was elected on the ticket of the National Front. In the parliamentary elections of 1993, 35 women were victorious. In the Mauroy government, 6 of the 43 ministers were women; in the Chirac government of 1986, 4 of the 43; in the (second) Rocard government, 6 of the 49.

63. For these and other statistics, see *La Parité dans la vie politique*, Rapport de la Commission pour la parité entre les femmes et les hommes dans la vie politique, Gisèle Halimi, rapporteur (Paris: Documentation Française, 1999).

64. In 1980, 7 of the 305 senators were women, and in 1986, 9 of the 319 senators.

65. Catherine Trautmann, who was mayor of Strasbourg until 2001, when she was succeeded by another woman (Fabienne Keller); and Martine Aubry, a former cabinet member who became mayor of Lille after the municipal elections of 2001.

66. Jane Jenson and Mariette Sineau, *Mitterrand et les Françaises: Un rendez-vous manqué* (Paris: PFNSP, 1995), pp. 140f. This somewhat polemical book argues that the feminist aspects of Socialist platforms, notably the "110 Propositions pour la France" (1981), remained largely slogans, and that the Left in general, and Mitterrand in particular, had difficulty relating to women.

67. See Gisèle Halimi, *Femmes: Moitié de la terre, moitié du pouvoir* (Paris: Gallimard, 1994). A year later, Halimi, a prominent feminist and Socialist deputy, introduced a bill stipulating that "no more than 75% of the lists of candidates for elections could be of the same sex," but (although approved by both chambers of Parliament) the Constitutional Council nullified it on the grounds that it "introduced a division of citizens by categories." A similar fate met a bill passed in 1982 providing that at least 25% of candidates in municipal elections (in communes of more than 3,500 inhabitants) be women. Nonetheless, the idea of "affirmative action" quotas for women found its way into Socialist party statutes. See Latour et al., *Femmes et Citoyennes*, p. 6.

68. See *La Parité dans la vie politique*, pp. 17–29, for a historical review, and annexe 1, pp. 59–62, for statistics on women in elective office.

69. Accompanying this change there was also a degree of rejuvenation, as the average age of senators dropped from 63 to 52, and the Left made some gains at the expense of the Right (which, however, held on to its majority).

70. See Didier Hassoux, "La Parité en manque de voix," *Libération*, 23 March 2001. Note that the "parity" law does not apply to communes with fewer than 3,500 inhabitants or to cantonal elections (for general councils). Yet it had a certain impact on those elections: In 1998, 15.1% of candidates were women; in 2001, 20.1%. In 1998, 8.4% of those elected to general councils were women; in 2001, 9.9%.

71. Women accounted for 40% of the candidates in the PS but only 20% in the UMP. The National Assembly representation of women in terms of the two major parties was as follows: 38 out of 369 (10.29%) for the UMP, the Chirac alliance (see Chapter 4); and 23 out of 141 (16.42%) for the Socialists. See *Le Monde*, 18 December 2001, p. 12; and 2 May 2002, p. 8.

72. Affirmative action is already spreading. For example, in 2001 the *Institut d'Etudes Politiques* in Paris decided to admit a certain number of students from disprivileged families. These students, graduates of seven lycées in working-class suburbs, were to receive special guidance and financial support.

73. Zaïr Kedadouche, "Les Quotas sont un racisme à l'envers," *Libération*, 15 November 1999.

74. Under Mitterrand, it was called the Ministry for Women's Rights. Chirac abolished that ministry in 1986, and Rocard (in 1988) did not restore it. However, in 1991, Cresson reestablished the position, naming a junior minister for women's rights.

75. On the evolution of women's rights and their role in politics and the labor force, see *Les Femmes dans la société française au 20e siècle* (Paris: Armand Colin, 2001). See also Michelle Perrot ed., *An 2000: Quel bilan pour les femmes?* Problèmes politiques et sociaux, no. 835 (Paris: Documentation Française, 2000).

76. The women's organizations that had existed during the Fourth Republic had been connected with other movements (e.g., Communist-oriented Resistance forces and Catholic Action Groups).

77. In the parliamentary elections of 1978, a women's organization *(Choisir)* fielded 43 candidates, but it won only 1.4 percent of the first-round votes.

CHAPTER 3

Patterns and Perspectives of Political Culture

APPROACHES TO FRENCH POLITICAL CULTURE

For many years it has been acknowledged that France had long experience with democratic institutions, that it possessed the requisite socioeconomic infrastructure necessary for a stable democracy,[1] and that it was a "modern" country.[2] Yet there was a feeling, shared by American and some French political scientists, that French democracy was not fully "consolidated," that is, that for a sizable number of citizens it was not "the only game in town."[3] This state of affairs was attributed not only to faults in institutional arrangements but also to flaws in the French "national character." Until recently, discussions of the problems faced by France emphasized a number of political culture traits blamed for recurrent revolutions, legitimacy crises, and decision-making blockages. Social scientists, for example, pointed to the prevalence of class distrust, the absence of civic-mindedness *(incivisme)*, and an underdeveloped ethos of participation.[4] Some scholars even spoke of a "delinquent society" that made incessant demands on the state for benefits but refused to accept the necessary social and political obligations.[5] These characterizations have almost always proceeded from the vantage point of an ideal type of political culture. Such a culture is noted for its pragmatism, prosystem orientation, social trust, ethos of participation in political life, and high degree of civic responsibility.

Civic and Uncivic Attitudes

Several years ago there appeared a list of traits of French culture that are regarded as major causes for the policy deadlocks that have existed in French society: (1) a taste for comfort; (2) an instinct for private property; (3) a collective laziness; (4) a hexagonal vision of reality; (5) a penchant for abstraction; (6) an admiration of the intellectual and a contempt for the businessperson; (7) an "untouchable" past, that is, a sanctification of traditional views of national history and a resistance to change; (8) an orientation to the small world—the locality, the family, and the individual; and (9) an immobility based on fear of contact with outsiders.[6]

There are problems with such catalogues: (1) They are often based on survey questions that are highly selective and not placed in context. (2) The presumably negative (or dysfunctional) traits may be compensated by positive traits that are not adequately studied. (3) The characterizations have not always correlated with actual political behavior. (4) The list of traits has not fully reflected the dynamic nature of political culture—the fact that the political attitudes of the French have been in a process of constant change since the end of World War II and especially since the watershed events of 1968.

For example, the lack of civic-mindedness in France was said to be illustrated by widespread tax evasion, draft dodging, contempt for law, and alcoholism. In 1987 a public opinion survey revealed relatively high levels of indulgence toward those who behave in an uncivic manner: 52 percent were tolerant of draft dodgers; 58 percent, of those who had illegal ("moonlighting") jobs; 44 percent, of tax cheats.[7] Similar polls show that paying taxes was considered increasingly less important as an indicator of good citizenship. Conversely, the item that figured highest on civic-mindedness was "seeking to be well informed,"[8] which suggests the importance of the cognitive element of French political culture.[9] A public opinion poll conducted in 1998 on the question of what kinds of liars were unacceptable elicited the following responses: merchants lying to their customers about the quality of their products, 79 percent; corporate executives lying to their stockholders, 78 percent; persons lying to their spouses about an extramarital affair, 52 percent; physicians lying to their patients about their state of health, 49 percent; children lying to their parents about their school performance, 39 percent; persons lying to the state about their income, 33 percent; job candidates lying about their curricula vitae, 28 percent.[10]

Tax evasion—a phenomenon about which the French speak constantly (and not without a certain bluster)—is definitely related to an "evaluative" political culture, and to the extent that such evasion exists, it is at least partly indicative of a low regime-support level. But tax fraud or tax negotiations were inevitable in a society that was incompletely industrialized; moreover, tax fraud had certain "eufunctional" aspects: In permitting artisans and small shopkeepers to practice selective fiscal evasion, governments cushioned them against the vicissitudes of too-rapid economic modernization, kept their antisystem proclivities in check, and limited the growth of popular fascism, such as Poujadism (see Chapter 4). Today, tax fraud is to some extent compensated by the value-added tax, which is based on itemized production processes, but it is still facilitated by the fact that income taxes are not deducted automatically from payrolls. Finally, in France, tax advantages for the wealthy (although on the increase in recent years, especially under right-of-center governments) are not so obviously sanctioned by law as they are in the United States and are partly balanced by the extensive system of family income subsidies, university scholarships, and social security payments.

In any case, tax evasion is still unacceptably high. The majority of French people consider most forms of taxation—on inheritance, added value, real estate, income, alcohol and tobacco, and local taxes and social security deductions—to be excessive, which explains why only a small minority of the French are willing to have any of the existing taxes raised in order to help reduce their country's fiscal deficits.[11] However, barely half of the French population would want to see a tax reduction if that meant a contraction of what they consider the mission of the state.[12]

Occasional violations of the laws, or the circumvention of laws by means of personal arrangements or even bribery, have not been demonstrably more pronounced in France than in the United States, and less so than in Italy. For several generations of republican experience, the French have accepted the *principle* of government of laws and tended to be law-abiding in *practice* if they were convinced that the laws were just and fair. Today, the growing acceptance of judicial review, as practiced by the Constitutional Council, suggests that government of laws is replacing government legitimation by popular sovereignty as a norm.

Draft dodging was bound to be a problem in a country engaged in wars for a longer continuous period than any other democratic regime in the twentieth century—from the outbreak of World War II in 1939 to the settlement of the Algerian war in the early 1960s. But draft dodging has been no more significant in France than it was in the United States during the Vietnam war; and since the abolition of the draft, it can no longer be a measure of uncivic behavior. Moreover, the French are also known for their patriotism and for the readiness with which many of them sacrificed their lives during World Wars I and II.

The alcoholism that one still encounters in France might be attributed to widespread alienation. But excessive wine drinking, apart from its association with conviviality and "Latin" patterns of social intercourse, is also related to the fact that viticulture is a very important element of the French agricultural economy. In any case, the rapidly growing number of road accidents due to drinking has resulted in stricter punishment of drunk drivers since 2000–2001.

For many years, the educational elitism described in Chapter 2 impeded upward mobility, fortified inequality, and contributed to the alienation of those social sectors whose chances of advancement were blocked, while the "unrealistic" humanistic content of higher education contributed to frustration, as university graduates found their diplomas not well suited to the market. But selectivity in school admissions, which continues despite the educational reforms, has also been a means of maintaining standards and providing continuity in a cultural tradition that, today more than ever, is threatened both by popular culture and by foreign influences. The gap between elite and mass attitudes is occasionally expressed in a concern by the former with the purity of the French language, but periodic attempts to enforce such purity by legislation, as in the case of the Toubon law of 1994 (see Chapter 2), have not been successful.

Many French observers have shared a widespread assumption that a modern, democratic political culture depends heavily on an ethic of individual achievement, that the development of such a culture has been promoted best in Protestant countries,[13] and that economic and political advancement in France has been inhibited by the prevalence of Catholicism.[14] One must, however, keep in mind that (1) there is an authoritarian as well as a democratic Protestantism, and France has been subjected to the influences of both;[15] (2) France began the process of intermittent "de-Christianization" with the Revolution of 1789; (3) Napoleonic France, which was still in the grip of Catholicism, was one of the first countries to introduce nonascriptive recruitment to the civil service; and (4) postwar France, like Italy, another Catholic country, has had a more dynamic economy than Britain (where much innovation is promoted by non-Anglo-Saxons). Moreover, there has been a progressive "Protestantization" of France, as Protestants have become more prominent than ever in business, banking, and politics. (This development has been occurring at a time when the United States is becoming less "Anglo-Saxon" and more "Latino.")

About thirty years ago a scholar remarked that "in the United States, which has gone further than any other Western society in institutionalizing the ethic of achievement, acute social tensions occur at the lower levels of the reward hierarchy. These are manifested in the exceptionally high incidence of various social phenomena, including homicide, mental illness, drug addiction, alcoholism, juvenile delinquency, and organized crime."[16] All these problems can be found in France in increasing measure as that country becomes more modernized and urbanized. That their dimensions are not so great as in the United States might be attributed to the survival of forms of social orientations one tends to regard as premodern or parochial, such as the stress on family membership and on local patriotism. Despite the growing number of divorces and the increasing proportion of unmarried couples and single-parent families,[17] traditional family ties are still important, and despite a growing accent on youth, there is still a respect for, and a concern with, the older generation. In each department there are information centers for the elderly to inform them of their rights, which include generous pension payments, housing allowances, and rebates on public transport. Irrespective of this concern (which contrasts sharply with the institutionalized bias against the aged in the United States, a bias that exists despite the growth of entitlements), many French people still think that the family has a primary responsibility to take care of the aged.[18] This attitude, however, has been changing in response to the lengthening life span of the aged; although intergenerational relations remain close, there is a growing discomfort among the younger generation, based on its perception that the aged consume an ever-larger portion of welfare benefits.

The persistence of local orientations, which might be regarded as a line of defense against an overcentralized state, has been attested not only by a highly developed municipal pride but also by the fact that the mayor of a town is more favorably regarded than a deputy or senator. This has been particularly true since the decentralization measures of the 1980s, under which communes were given greater responsibility. A study of the "cognitive" dimension of French political culture shows that 92 percent of respondents to a poll knew the name of their mayor, compared with 44 percent who could identify their deputy.[19]

The localism and familism of French orientations were to some extent symptoms of a fear of outsiders. For many years, this fear was reflected in an avoidance of close relationships outside the family circle,[20] excessively formalized *politesse*, an inability to make friends easily, a reluctance to invite outsiders home, an unwillingness to join voluntary associations, and an underdeveloped tradition of philanthropy. According to some surveys, the French still exhibit a relatively low level of trust (a characteristic they are said to share with Italians and Greeks).[21] But according to other surveys, the vast majority of the French believe that people *can* be trusted.[22] In any case, some of these behavior patterns have been less a matter of political culture than a reflection of physical constraints or public policy; as these have changed, the aforementioned patterns of behavior have changed with them. For instance, more French people invite outsiders to their homes as these become more spacious. Philanthropy, too, is developing, as French families have more money and as governments use tax incentives to encourage private giving. According to one poll, 38 percent of respondents belonged to a voluntary philanthropic association in 1990, and 23 percent participated in its activities (a percentage lower than that found in the United States, Britain, and Germany, but higher than in other "Latin" countries in Western Europe).[23] In 1996–1997, about 20 million French people gave a total of more than 11 billion francs to charity, but the total amount given by the typical family was very small.[24] Nevertheless, in the past few years, French voluntary giving has been reflected in "telethons" to fund medical research, in collections for "soup kitchens" (*Restos du coeur*) and Catholic charities, and in significant contributions to the victims of famine in the Third World.[25] In response to the increase in the number of homeless and destitute people, both secular and religious private giving has grown, some of the latter inspired by the efforts of Abbé Pierre, an aged left-wing cleric. Conversely, the collection of funds for medical research has been negatively affected by revelations in the mid-1990s of corruption within the Association of Cancer Research. Government efforts, especially during the cohabitation period of 1986–1988, to encourage wealthy private individuals and corporations to help support museums, theaters, and libraries have not been so successful as in the United States, in part because the tax incentives have been too low, and in part because the promotion of culture has been considered the proper province of the government.[26] In recent years, the French have increasingly endorsed the "postmaterialist" measures of central and subnational governments and supported movements promoting such measures. These developments are manifested by the growth of local cultural associations, the growing influence of environmental movements, and the enactment of laws providing for enhanced civil liberties and gender and racial equality.

The above suggests that political culture is not static. One observer has noted three major changes in French political culture: (1) a move toward greater individualism and away from collective allegiances; (2) the weakening of loyalty toward traditional political families; (3) deepening fractures between traditional Right and extreme Right and between "liberal" Left and "radical" Left; (4) a growing gulf between an open, educated, and pro-European position and an uneducated, closed, and xenophobic one.[27]

Verbal and Practical Behavior

The local and familial orientations of the French have frequently been cited as evidence of both a faulty socialization process and a widespread disaffection for the national political system. That disaffection was said to be shown by the prevalence of an ideological approach to politics, revolutionary rhetoric, electoral abstention, and frequent outbursts of political violence. There is no doubt that a generation ago, French politics was informed by a high degree of ideological thinking, by "absolute-value rationalities," and by "apocalyptic visions."[28] This mind-set, conditioned by history and by the educational curriculum's stress on rationalistic, Cartesian, and systematic approaches to social phenomena, has influenced French interest in philosophical nuances among competing political formulas. Such approaches were said to be particularly remarkable among "Radicals, Socialist and Catholic intellectuals, and Communists,"[29] who had their own diverse views about the imperfections of the existing regime.

Are these divisions significant in terms of practical politics? The French have experienced numerous revolutions, or have at least participated in many attempts to replace inadequate regimes by experiments informed by millennial strivings. But none of the revolutions has succeeded completely, and the French have learned not to expect too much from them; as a well-known saying has it, "Plus ça change, plus c'est la même chose" (The more things change, the more they remain the same). Therefore, "apocalyptic visions" have often been pursued as if they had a life of their own, a situation that has been reflected in the behavior of political parties as well as voters.

The functional autonomy of ideological rhetoric (to the extent that such rhetoric still exists), party orientations, and programmatic preferences is illustrated by the fact that although the majority of the French adhere to an anticlerical party, an even greater majority oppose the end of subsidies to Catholic schools.[30] It is also illustrated by the fact that although there are Left "collectivist" and redistributive and Right "anticollectivist" *biases*, there is no clear correlation between general leftist orientations and approval of nationalization policies or between conservative orientations and privatization policies.[31] Although supporters of left-wing candidates in the 1995 presidential elections were most concerned with the fight against socioeconomic exclusion, and voters for the National Front candidate with immigration, supporters of all the major candidates were interested in safeguarding existing welfare state entitlements, reducing unemployment, and maintaining purchasing power and minimum incomes, and all were reluctant to accept personal sacrifices.[32] There is no indication that these attitudes changed before the 2002 elections.

The disjunction between verbal and real political behavior is illustrated in a number of ways. Many French people who embraced revolutionary rhetoric had a penchant for order in their personal lives; many who exhibited verbal antimilitarism admired the warriors of the past; and many who in the past held antiregime views had respect for civil servants and hoped that their children would enter a career in the service of the state.[33] This remains true despite the fact that in recent years the image of civil servants has declined—possibly because in the Fifth Republic the distinction between them and politicians has become increasingly obscured.

Many observers have spoken of a gradual "depoliticization" of the French, including a lagging interest in politics. Such a tendency would seem to be suggested by public opinion surveys conducted between 1993 and 2000, according to which only a small minority regarded politics as an important interest in their lives.[34] Nevertheless, it is argued that the thesis about the French having become "depoliticized," which was already questioned more than 40 years ago, continues to have little substance.[35] The measures normally used to indicate politicization—intensity of political involvement, concern with the outcome of political fights, and *specific political orientations*—suggest that the French are as interested in politics as ever. There has been a decline in trade union membership, one measure of depoliticization; but that decline is related to the evolution of society and the economy, especially the decline of low-technology industries and the displacement of many indigenous low-skilled workers by foreigners. The number of strikes has gone down; however, the massive strikes in the transport sector at the end of 1995, the frequent strikes by nurses, physicians, and teachers, and the solid support of the strikers by the population at large, including many who were inconvenienced by the strikes, indicate that anomic politics continues to be important. The number of dues-paying members in mainstream political parties and the support of left-wing parties have decreased dramatically. Yet many French citizens still describe themselves as leftist, and even more continue to be committed to the welfare state, including those who are self-identified as "centrist" and "right-wing."

Voter turnout has declined; but electoral abstentions are not significantly higher than they were a generation ago in important national elections, and they are lower in France than in certain other countries, such as the United States. The highest rates of abstention have been in elections whose outcome has made the least difference in terms of policy: selected national referenda, local elections, and elections to the European Parliament. In some cases, voter turnout has been unexpectedly high, as in the cantonal elections of 1992 and the referendum on the Maastricht Treaty in the same year. Moreover, there are other forms of electoral participation, such as voting for factory and university councils and social security boards.

Political involvement is not uniform across French society; there are variations according to class, age, gender, education, and ideology. Political involvement tends to be somewhat lower among 18- to 24-year-olds than among 45- to 74-year-olds. It is highest among the well-educated and members of the liberal professions, and lowest among workers; higher among men than women; higher among urban than rural residents; and, curiously, higher among practicing Catholics, as well as among confirmed atheists! It is also higher among those who situate themselves to the left on the political spectrum.[36] The Left seems to be more interested in "postmaterialist" concerns, such as human rights, ecology, nuclear disarmament, feminism, and the fight against racism and exclusion, whereas the Right has shown greater concern for traditional family structure.[37]

Herbert Luethy, an astute observer of France, once wrote about "the lack of consequences of political controversy" in that country.[38] The continued existence of feelings that political arguments have little impact on policy decisions is often said to be "proved" by a decline in party membership and a growing indifference to traditional political parties (especially among the young), and the increasing incidence of electoral abstention. However, the relative indifference to political parties may be due not so much to opposition to parties as such as to the belief that the old ideologies are no longer very important and that there has been a convergence on issues. The "dealignment" from the mainstream parties is, to some extent, compensated by the growth of social movements (such as antiracist ones) and single-issue parties (such as environmental ones), a development that might be seen as evidence of interest in fostering democratic expression by a more autonomous civil society. Similarly, electoral abstention may be less a testimony to disillusionment with the political system as such than a sign of protest against too many elections at short intervals (as in 1988), or an indicator of the belief that the victory of one party rather than another would neither redound to the clear material benefit of the voters nor cause them irreparable harm (see Chapter 4). The presidential elections of 2002 are a case in point. The abstention rate in the first round was the highest on record in any Fifth Republic presidential contest because voters were dissatisfied with the nominees of both major mainstream parties; but in the second round, abstentions remained high because it was clear that both right-wing and left-wing voters would support the incumbent president overwhelmingly in the interest of preserving the democratic system.

It has been pointed out that many French voters, especially the young, are relatively ignorant of political parties and politicians.[39] A study conducted a decade ago confirmed this phenomenon, but it also showed that the cognitive dimension of French political culture is strongly tied to the instrumental dimension—that the knowledge of political subject matter is related not only to a person's level of education and place in the social hierarchy but also to the concrete policy benefits derived from such knowledge. Thus, many more farmers know the name of the minister of agriculture than know the names of other ministers.[40] Young people do not inform themselves as much as do adults about politics, in part because they are not yet actively involved in the economic system and in part because they concentrate their efforts on obtaining a lycée diploma.[41]

Until a few years ago, it was customary to refer to incidents of anomic behavior such as street demonstrations and mass strikes as indicators of a negative dimension in French political culture. But anomic behavior should not automatically be equated with revolution or construed as evidence of a persistent alienation of the masses. Spontaneous events may, in fact, provide useful outlets or social catharses that obviate or sidetrack real system changes or revolutions. In the view of typical French citizens, one goes into the street, not in order to be aggressive, but "in order to feel better and in order to restore one's taste for politics."[42] Most mass protests—by farmers, workers, and students—are issue-specific and designed to supplement and energize (and sometimes "unblock") institutional processes; moreover, to the extent that these protests are encouraged by leaders of political parties and interest groups, they are not anomic. However, the issue may be one of public concern rather than narrow self-interest, as in the case of mass demonstrations early in 1997 to protest against a government bill on immigrants that was regarded as unfair.

The most interesting (and voluminously discussed) rebellion, the Events of May 1968, could be viewed as a case in point. That month, mass demonstrations organized by students and workers in the Paris area broke out, quickly spread to other segments of the population, and culminated in a series of general strikes in several cities that involved more than one-third of the nation's labor force, paralyzed France for several days, and threatened to bring down the government. The "May events" had several causes: the explosion of the number of students in universities and the government's inadequate response to it; the antiquated physical plants and overcrowded conditions, which could not be resolved with jerry-built new structures; an outdated and rigid curriculum that was as ill adapted to the changing labor market as it was to the scientific needs of an advanced industrial society; and a system of relationships (or rather, lack of relationships) between students and faculty that did not respond to the students' demands for greater say in their courses of study. For the workers, there was a growing resentment, in part fanned by the students, over low pay, a long workweek, poor housing, and a perception of general neglect by the government. Both students and workers were impatient with the authoritarian patterns of government initiated by de Gaulle and, finally, bored with the general himself.

Some radicals may have seen the "May events" as a prelude to a social and political revolution. For the majority of the rebels, however, the events were little more than a "happening" and a public festival. The events shook up part of France—and provided some momentum for the loosening of social relations. They also broke the spell of de Gaulle and led to increased demands for "participatory democracy" on the part of students and for significant wage increases on the part of workers.

Yet one should keep in mind that for several years, many of the university reforms that were initiated remained innovations on paper only; that such novel manifestations of social solidarity as the collaboration between workers and students hardly outlasted the events; and that the rise in consumer demands is not by itself revolutionary. Moreover, the leftward turn of certain social sectors (for example, the quasi-Catholic trade union, the *Confédération française démocratique du travail*—CFDT) also coincided, on the one hand, with an impressive victory of Gaullist candidates in the legislative elections of 1968 and, on the other, with the beginning of the "domestication" of the French Communist party (that is, its public disavowal of revolutionary methods for achieving power or social change, and a commitment to bourgeois political values); and that the disengagement of the French from Gaullist charisma itself signified a gradual return to institutional normalcy.[43]

To the extent that the "May events" were a spontaneous uprising rather than an ideologically motivated "proletarian" one, their duration was, by definition, limited.[44] But the events, as an affair of French young people, reflected their tendency to be critical of the regime and to situate themselves further to the left on the political spectrum than their elders (which did not necessarily imply voting for specific leftist parties) as well as their tendency to challenge traditional assumptions about the political and social order.[45]

Some political observers have regarded the massive strikes of December 1995 as a replay of the events of 1968. In both cases, the strikers and their supporters were motivated by economic considerations: in the former case, the feeling that the modernization and growing prosperity of the country had left the workers behind; in the latter case, a general pessimism about economic prospects and, more specifically, the fear that the growing transfer of economic transactions from the state to the market would endanger the socioeconomic security not only of certain public service employees (such as railroad workers, who enjoyed highly privileged retirement benefits) but also of wage earners in general.[46] There was another motivation that explains both the action of the strikers and the sympathy of much of the population at large: the defense of traditional French "civic" values such as social solidarity against the cost-benefit calculations of technocratic decision makers.[47]

CONCEPTIONS OF THE STATE

In a recent book, a well-known French author, discussing the French "religion of the state," wrote as follows: "The protective state *à la française* has not ceased increasing its responsibilities and its missions, while it is losing more and more of its economic role, including the monetary one, and [while] successive governments have not stopped transferring ever more economic and monetary power to European authorities."[48]

During the past three decades the state has been subjected to increasing scrutiny. It has been criticized for being overcentralized, inefficient, and not sufficiently cognizant of the economic, social, and cultural needs of society below the national level. It is possible to trace the onset of a process of reexamination of state-society relations—in short, of changes in the French political culture—to the Events of May 1968. One of the changes relates to the definition of society itself. Until the early postwar years, the collective consciousness of the French had revolved around an image of society that was based, if not on small-town and village life, on a nostalgia about such a life and the social system and institutions that informed it: the Catholic church, the public school, the head of the family, and the small commercial establishments. Questioning the authority of the university professor and the waning influence of the paterfamilias, of organized religion, of the schoolteacher, and of the central bureaucracy have contributed to a lowering of the image of political leaders—as attested, for instance, by the lampooning of politicians in the public media—and this has led inevitably to questioning the role of the state and the foundations on which it was built. The gradual demystification of the state has been associated with the rediscovery of "civil society"—that is, the various sectors not associated with political parties, elected politicians, or officialdom—a rediscovery that, in turn, has been reflected in another development: the spread of the idea that many decisions now made by the national government should be made by local governments or by the private sector. Although most of the French view socialism more positively than capitalism, they have an increasingly favorable appreciation of liberalism; and people attach greater value to protecting the right to engage in private enterprise than to protecting the right to strike.[49]

The growing skepticism about the omnipotent state has been accompanied by an orientation more favorable than before toward the market and its managers; increasingly, French citizens find engineers and directors of business firms more useful to society than higher civil servants or deputies.[50] This skepticism did not clearly affect their confidence in democracy, for 62 percent thought that it functioned well in France; and the figures for the younger ones (71 percent) were even more positive.[51] At the same time, there was a noticeable mistrust of "politics" and of politicians. According to a poll of August 2000, 58 percent thought that politics was an honorable profession, but 64 percent thought that their politicians were corrupt, and only 28 percent, that they were honest. According to a poll of 1999, 61 percent (against 25 percent)—two out of three—of the respondents believed that in general the elected and other leaders of the country were corrupt.[52]

The deteriorated image of the political elite has made it easier for public prosecutors to indict party leaders, parliamentarians, mayors, and high officials for money laundering and other acts of corruption. There would be many more such indictments, however, were it not for the fact that impatience with the political elite has coexisted with a relatively facile acceptance of the privileges accorded to its members, such as publicly subsidized luxury apartments and (as was revealed in 2001) secret "slush" funds for a variety of national politicians.

The distrust and suspicion of decision makers appear to be deeply embedded in the thinking of French citizens despite the relatively generous welfare state. These attitudes are reflected in the fact that many citizens do not believe the promises of candidates for elective office, so that "negative" voting has become the norm. There is a contradiction: Although the majority of citizens are convinced that the *state* (in the abstract) is powerful, they share a growing conviction about the "intrinsic powerlessness of *politics.*"[53] In any case, the electorate increasingly votes to "punish" elected officeholders for nonperformance. The public's negative attitudes toward decision makers explain several other phenomena: the sympathy of the masses for strikes by public service workers, including the national gendarmerie. Furthermore, these attitudes explain two other fairly recent developments: the growth of voluntary organizations,[54] and the more frequent alternance between the parties in and out of power.

Regardless of their dissatisfaction with political-decision makers, however, the French do not necessarily accept the retreat of the *state* as a liberating development;[55] they continue to have greater expectations of the state than do Americans, in part, perhaps, because they remember the lack of social responsibility of the traditional entrepreneurial class, and in part because one out of every five members of the workforce is paid directly by the state (although this proportion decreased somewhat with the privatization measures of recent Gaullist governments). The continuing relevance of the state as a symbol (a fact that can hardly be explained in terms of the "state-centered" paradigm currently popular among American political scientists) does not imply that the French citizen functions as an authoritarian personality (although one may find individuals— mostly members of the political Right—who would welcome a strong leader). Many French citizens continue to think about the possibility of rebellion, because such an act may help to rivet the attention of the agents of the state to their problems.[56] However, the citizen's attachment to the state is not clearly related to the popularity of the *individual incumbent* of a state position or even to the policy successes and failures of that state. Thus, while President Mitterrand was losing popularity in the early 1990s, the French continued to place the president first among the political *institutions* of the country. At that time, they continued to acknowledge the various policy achievements of Socialist governments, such as the expansion of civil liberties, the reduction of the workweek, improvements of the welfare state, and decentralization. To be sure, the electorate "punished" the Socialist party for its failure to solve the unemployment problem. However, the defeat of the Socialists in 1993 and 2002 was not simply a reflection of electoral behavior based on economic rationality; it was also related to the party's internal disunity, to widespread corruption among its politicians, and to a growing disenchantment with the "political class" as a whole. Many, especially the young, considered that class more interested in macropolitics, in Europe, and in ostentatious public works than in the quotidian concerns of ordinary citizens.[57] In 1997, punishment was meted out to the right-of-center government coalition for many of the same reasons. However, the government was disavowed, not merely because of the content of its policies and a general pessimism about economic prospects, but also because of what was widely regarded as Premier Juppé's arrogant and patronizing attitude toward the public. Conversely, the "statesmanlike" public image of President Chirac as a national political leader rose dramatically after the terrorist attacks in September 2001, and had little do with his domestic political performance. The electoral defeat of Jospin in 2002 must be attributed less to his government's failures in economic policy than to those in the area of law and order; conversely, the victory of Chirac was not a reward for his policy performance as much as the result of a choice of the lesser evil (see Chapter 4).

The French still expect much from the state, and the growth of the market economy has not transformed most citizens into classic liberals.[58] They make a distinction between the state, which they rely on, and the government, which often disappoints them, as well as the "political class"—both its elected and appointed members—which they tend to distrust. What is wrong with the state in practice is that it is often captured by special interests, excessively corporatized, or broken up and for these reasons does not perform some of its tasks well, such as securing justice. A poll conducted in 1999 revealed a high degree of cross-partisan consensus about the areas the state should deal with. They are shown in Table 3.1 in order of importance.

During the past generation there has been little change in the "etatist" consensus (except in the area of employment); conversely, since that time there has developed an increasingly "liberal" consensus relating to television and telephone. According to the same poll, the state is criticized for not doing enough to ensure personal security (81%), employment (80%), environmental protection (68%), and education (65%). Of course there are differences within the population with respect to the extent of etatism. The Left is more etatist than the Right; urban residents more than rural ones, and wage earners more than the self-employed.[59] According to a poll conducted in 2001, the majority of respondents felt that food consumption, the rights of workers, international commerce, the financial markets, the Internet, and the environment were insufficiently regulated.[60]

Similar ambiguities exist with respect to attitudes toward the state and society. There is no doubt that over the years, the concern of the French with extending individual liberties—and with establishing a certain distance between themselves and the state—has grown. But such a concern is not unqualified and has not converted the French to the laissez-faire ideologies of Ronald Reagan or Margaret Thatcher. Although the French seem to consider the state in its abstract sense somewhat removed from their concerns, they tend to have a favorable view of its *concrete* manifestations, that is, of selected governmental services.[61] This favorable view, which extends to economic activities, reaches across the ideological spectrum. According to an exit poll during the 1997 elections, 58 percent of voters for the Socialists or Left Radicals and 50 percent of Com-

TABLE 3.1
Responsibilities of the State (in percent)

"Etatist" Consensus	
Defense	98
Public order	94
Education	89
Employment	84
Pensions	81
Medical care	66
"Liberal" Consensus	
Television	23
Telephone	21

SOURCE: SOFRES poll of 20–21 September 1999, based on Olivier Duhamel, "Les Français et l'État," in SOFRES, *L'État de l'opinion 2000* (Paris: Seuil, 2000), p. 141.

munist voters held a favorable view of (classic economic) liberalism; more specifically, 39 percent of Socialist party and Party of the Left Radicals (PS-PRG) voters and 23 percent of Communist party of France (PCF) voters had a positive view of privatization, and 77 percent of PS-PRG voters and 57 percent of PCF voters favored a reduction of social charges imposed on business; conversely, 66 percent of voters for the Gaullists or the Union for French Democracy (UDF) favored an increase in the monthly minimum wage and 53 percent of Rally for the Republic (RPR) and UDF voters favored the creation of 350,000 jobs in the public sector.[62]

Despite the growing fashion of neoliberalism, and despite a disenchantment with the "political class" and a low level of confidence in the ability of politicians to solve the country's economic problems,[63] most French citizens continue to prize economic security and rely on the state to guarantee it. In 1999, the majority of the French accepted the economics of the market (the Left, 62%; the moderate Right, 69%) and thought that globalization was a good thing (the Left, 57%; the moderate Right, 54%). In fact, support for nationalization had receded among the Left—from 57% in 1995 to 44% in 1998. These responses indicate that the traditional left-right ideological distinctions regarding economic policy have been considerably attenuated.[64] The continued support of interventionism has been particularly marked among young people (see Table 3.2). The concern with concrete socioeconomic payoffs granted by the government has had important behavioral consequences. It has moderated the hero-worshipping tendencies or monarchist instincts of French people and has caused them, after a number of years, to be dissatisfied with merely symbolic gestures of presidents and governments.

NATIONAL IDENTITY

Paradoxically, the desacralization of the state has been occurring at the same time as the growth of a consensus about the constitutional system and even about public policies, which may suggest that the state is no longer desperately needed as a conceptual glue for holding the French nation together. Whereas the nation was once defined in terms of a unifying state, it has increasingly come to be defined in terms of a pluralistic society.

TABLE 3.2
State Intervention in the Economy:
Views of Young People (Ages 18–25), 1996

	Total	Sympathizers of the Left	Environmentalist Sympathizers	Sympathizers of the Right	No Party Preferences
Too much intervention	20	22	19	18	14
Just right	20	19	12	33	9
Not enough intervention	58	57	69	48	73

Source: Adapted from SOFRES poll, 19–23 March 1996, conducted for *Figaro-Magazine*, cited in SOFRES, *L'État de l'opinion 1997* (Paris: Seuil, 1997), pp. 177, 189.

That society, however, is so ethnically diverse that it has become a plurality of subcultures in which ethnic consciousness, to some extent filling the void left by a declining religious orientation, is more important than it was in the past. Thus, whereas there is no longer a question about the legitimacy of the political system, there are now constant discussions about the foundations of French society and the nature of French "identity."[65] This development, it is argued, has been associated with the decline of the prestige of the French public school, as that institution has become increasingly less effective in fulfilling its role as a disseminator of a clear cultural model and an unambiguous sense of Frenchness.[66]

In the past, membership in the French nation was defined in terms of descent. However, the ethnic origins and the provincial cultures of the Hexagon have been so diverse that France had to be "invented":[67] A French national identity had to be fabricated by means of a common language, a centralized republic, an educational system, and the evocation of a common history and common unifying myths. These have included the Revolution of 1789, the Resistance, the "May events," republican values, the universal appeal of the French language and culture, and the idea of France as a great power.[68] For most French people, symbols such as the flag are probably less necessary than for Americans to remind them of their national identity, because the French encounter material evidences of their country's history (e.g., châteaux, cathedrals, and museums) almost daily, and because several of the specific values, memories, and myths of the French Revolution are now thoroughly internalized by the majority of French citizens, among them equality before the law and universal suffrage.[69]

However, in recent years, these myths have been subjected to critical reexamination. The Revolution of 1789 has been partly demythologized as historians have evoked the unnecessary massacres of antirevolutionaries in the Vendée; the uncritical acceptance of the France of the Resistance is being modified by a more sober acknowledgment of the crimes of the Vichy regime and the collaboration of the French and, more recently, of the misbehavior of the French army in Algeria;[70] and the "May events" are often labeled as a collective fiesta that ended as quickly as it began.[71] Claims regarding the uniqueness of French culture have lost much credibility in the face of a mass culture that seems to be the same in various countries; republican ideas that the French did so much to disseminate are now accepted by most nations; and the global political importance of France, already deflated by the overwhelming presence of the United States, is being further deflated by the growing international power of Germany. Moreover, there is a feeling that the political myths and values are only incompletely shared by recent immigrants and their immediate descendants.

It is perhaps for these reasons that the French have taken to defining national identity in practical terms. A poll taken several years ago revealed that for 63 percent of the respondents, French national identity was symbolized by French cuisine; for 62 percent, by human rights; for 42 percent, by the French woman; for 34 percent, by church steeples; for 30 percent, by chauvinism; and for 22 percent, by betting on horse races.[72] These images may not reflect objective reality: Cuisine in France is becoming more international; church steeples have more to do with local color than with religion; and although many of the citizens of the Hexagon are proud to be French—and about half assert that they are ready to die for their country[73]—they are far less chauvinistic today than in earlier times. According to a cross-national poll taken in 1996, the impression the French have of the quality of life in their own country is far more negative in comparison to that of other members of the European Union than is warranted by "objective" criteria.[74]

The more sober, if not pessimistic, judgments by the French are signaled by numerous writings about what is wrong with their country.[75] At the same time, there remains a collective narcissism, which is visible in the continued insistence that "France is an idea" rather than an ordinary country defined by its geography and society—an idea that incorporates universal values.[76]

The various images of national identity of the French do not correspond clearly with their complicated attitudes toward outgroups. On the one hand, most French people no longer believe that they are descended from "[their] ancestors the Gauls," and many of them (in principle) accept the idea that membership in French society is open to all who are born on French soil, who speak French, and are ready to share the fate of France.[77] This attitude was reconfirmed in Premier Jospin's policy declaration (June 1997), in which he asserted: "France, an old country of republican integration, has been built by layers, a melting pot giving birth to an alloy as strong as the number and diversity of its components. That is why the law of the soil is consubstantial with the French nation. . . . Nothing is more alien to France than a racist and xenophobic discourse." On the other hand, there are still those who are ill at ease with a purely functional and voluntaristic definition of nationhood,[78] and for reasons already alluded to (see Chapter 2), they are reluctant to accept North African Muslims as fully qualified to be French. A major reason for that reluctance is the fear that the number of non-European immigrants might become so great that French cuisine, the commitment of republican values (e.g., laïcité and pluralism), the French language, and even the physical landscape would be denatured beyond recognition.

The concern with national identity is reflected in an impatience with the particularisms of immigrants, especially Muslims from North Africa; a growing number of racist incidents; and increasing support of the ideas of the National Front (see Chapter 4).[79] In a poll conducted in 1995 for the National Commission on Human Rights, 40 percent of the respondents admitted to having racist attitudes, in particular vis-à-vis Maghrebis and Gypsies.[80] Moreover, anti-Semitism, although having progressively diminished during the past half-century, still persists, and has revived since the renewal of Palestinian violence against Israel in 2000.[81]

Nevertheless, the xenophobia of the French is not unqualified. On the one hand, tolerance of foreigners seems to be proportional to their presence.[82] A further complication is that many French citizens who welcome immigrants in their midst do not necessarily welcome the immigrants' families or immigrant communities, a phenomenon that may suggest that economic considerations (e.g., obtaining social benefits) compete with matters of principle, that is, with the Jacobin notion of an ethnoculturally undifferentiated structure of society. Yet since the mid-1990s, thousands of people have participated in mass demonstrations in favor of granting asylum to illegal immigrants from Africa.

The nature of the French people's expectations of their government, their assessment of their leaders' capabilities, and their political culture as a whole are likely to be affected by the progressive integration of France into a supranational European Union and a transatlantic network of relationships. This process began several years ago; as a result of it, many of the distinctive attitudes of the French have already been transformed. There is now less concern with ideology and more with technology, and there has been a gradual displacement of the traditional historical and national orientation by a utilitarian, regional, and global one. An important illustration of this change is the positive reception of, and quick adjustment to, the euro in the beginning of 2002. Although many French intellectuals are still in the grip of cultural insecurity and a somewhat narcissistic concern with the French language, an increasing proportion of the French are learning other languages.[83] Although some members of the French elite still profess contempt for material values, many other French citizens are oriented toward production, efficiency, and prosperity and point with pride to the fact that the country has become the world's fourth-largest exporter. At the same time, they are looking outward for models of economic management.[84] In short, the political attitudes and behavior of the French have increasingly come to resemble those of people in other Western democracies, a development that has spelled the end of French exceptionalism.[85]

NOTES

1. Conditions such as wealth, literacy, industrialization, urbanization, the number of physicians, and so on. See S. M. Lipset, *Political Man: The Social Bases of Politics,* expanded ed. (Baltimore: Johns Hopkins University Press, 1981), pp. 27ff.
2. A "modern" political system is one in which traditional authority has been replaced by "a single national authority," decision-making patterns have become rationalized, political functions have become differentiated, political life in general has become secularized, elite recruitment is by merit rather than ascription, and meaningful institutions of (popular) political participation have developed. Samuel Huntington, "Political Modernization," *World Politics* 18 (April 1966), 378–414.
3. For the major features of democratic systems, see Robert A. Dahl, *Dilemmas of Pluralist Democracy* (New Haven: Yale University Press, 1982), pp. 10–11.
4. Gabriel Almond and Sidney Verba, *The Civic Culture* (Boston: Little, Brown, 1965), esp. pp. 7, 35–36, and 86–97; and Gabriel Almond and G. Bingham Powell, Jr., *Comparative Politics: A Developmental Approach* (Boston: Little, Brown, 1966), pp. 62, 260–66, 321ff, et passim.
5. Jesse R. Pitts, "Les Français et l'autorité," in Jean-Daniel Reynaud and Yves Grafmeyer, eds., *Français, qui êtes-vous?* (Paris: Documentation Française, 1981), pp. 285–99.
6. Gérard Mermet, *Francoscopie 1989: Les Français: Qui sont-ils? Où vont-ils?* (Paris: Larousse, 1988), pp. 200–02.
7. *Nouvel Observateur*–Europe No. 1/SOFRES poll, May 1987.
8. SOFRES, *L'État de l'opinion 1990,* p. 170.
9. On the development of notions of good citizenship, including the growth of cognitive political culture, see Sophie Duchesne, *Citoyenneté à la française* (Paris: PFNSP, 1997). This study is based on interviews with a cross-section of French women and men.
10. SOFRES, *L'État de l'opinion 2000,* p. 277. Cf. the results of earlier polls (SOFRES 1976, 1983, and 1989), which suggest that between 1976 and 1989, the equation of good citizenship with "paying one's taxes without seeking to defraud the state" went from 35 percent to 28 percent of the respondents. See Duchesne, *Citoyenneté à la française,* p. 295. A public opinion poll conducted in 1995 on the question of what acts constitute unacceptable behavior elicited the following responses: using a "doping" drug in a sports competition or smoking hashish, 54 percent; accepting bribes in connection with one's work, 50 percent; shoplifting, 47 percent; greatly exceeding the speed limit on highways, 44 percent; being unfaithful to one's spouse, 39 percent; and cheating on examinations, 35 percent. Poll conducted 21–24 February 1995 for *La Croix,* cited in SOFRES, *L'État de l'opinion 1996,* p. 318. Note that abstaining from voting in elections got a negative response of only 12 percent by the population at large and 6 percent by the 18–24 age group.
11. Poll conducted on 6–7 October 1995 for *L'Expansion.* Cited in SOFRES, *L'État de l'opinion 1996,* p. 30.
12. On this issue there is a right-left distinction, with 60 percent of the former and 41 percent of the latter favoring fewer taxes. Poll of September 1999, in SOFRES, *L'État de l'opinion 2000,* p. 143.

13. See *From Max Weber*, H. H. Gerth and C. Wright Mills, eds. (New York: Oxford University Press, 1958), esp. pp. 302–57.
14. Alain Peyrefitte, *The Trouble with France* (New York: Knopf, 1981), pp. 99–100, 121–31, 155–59, et passim.
15. Cf. Emmanuel Todd, *La Nouvelle France* (Paris: Seuil, 1988), pp. 106–20.
16. Frank Parkin, *Class Inequality and Political Order* (New York: Praeger, 1971), p. 68.
17. The number of divorces rose from 37,447 in 1970 to 116,800 in 1998. See Mermet, *Francoscopie 2001*, p. 142. Currently about one in four marriages ends in divorce.
18. According to a *Figaro*-SOFRES poll of January 1988, 71 percent of the French thought that it was primarily the responsibility of the family (versus 22 percent who believed that it should be largely the concern of the state).
19. IFOP poll, 1976, and SOFRES poll, 1983. Cited by Pascal Perrineau in "La Dimension cognitive de la culture politique," *RFSP* 35:1 (February 1985), 72–89. However, a more recent (1992) poll reveals considerable confusion or lack of knowledge about the role of subnational assemblies and the operation of regional elections. See SOFRES, *L'État de l'opinion 1993*, pp. 217–18. According to another poll (SOFRES, October 2000), 70 percent of respondents had confidence in their mayor. See Philippe Méchet and Michael Schifres, "Le Laboratoire des municipales," *L'État de l'opinion 2001*, pp. 80–81.
20. See Henry W. Ehrmann, *Politics in France*, 2nd ed. (Boston: Little, Brown, 1971), pp. 151ff; and Michel Crozier, *The Stalled Society* (New York: Viking Press, 1973), pp. 65–70, 93–99, 112–19.
21. See Ronald Inglehart, *Culture Shift in Advanced Industrial Societies* (Princeton: Princeton University Press, 1989). According to a composite of World Values surveys for 1981–1984 (p. 30), only about 25 percent of French respondents felt that "most people can be trusted."
22. According to a composite of Eurobarometer surveys for 1976–1986, more than 80 percent of the French respondents considered people of their own nationality trustworthy. Ibid., p. 17.
23. Jean-François Tchernia, "Les Français et leur société," in Hélène Riffault, ed., *Les Valeurs des Français* (Paris: PUF, 1994), pp. 202–25.
24. About 600 francs, or $75, per family. *Quid 2001* (Paris: Robert Laffont, 2000), p. 1609.
25. This has taken place despite the fact that only 40 percent of gifts are tax deductible and that no more than 5 percent of individual income and 3 percent of business income may be deducted. See Danielle Rouard, "Les Aventuriers de la générosité," *Le Monde*, 4, 5, and 6 August 1993. According to a poll conducted at the same time, the beneficiaries of French citizens' philanthropy were health agencies, 37 percent; the Church, 21 percent; international social agencies, 17 percent; education, 16 percent; miscellaneous social services, 16 percent. See Gérard Mermet, *Francoscopie 1995* (Paris: Larousse, 1994), p. 243.
26. According to some estimates, the total contribution of enterprises to culture and the arts in 1987 was 400 million francs (or about $65 million). See "Le Grand Air du mécénat," *Le Point*, 30 March 1987, pp. 136–37; and Jean-Yves Kaced, "Le Mécénat culturel d'entreprise," *Regards sur l'actualité*, no. 145 (November 1988), pp. 43–53.
27. Pierre Bréchon, Introduction, p. 13, and Grégory Derville, "Les Français entre répressivité et permissivité," pp. 71–90, in Bréchon et al., eds., *Les Cultures politiques français* (Paris: Presses de Sciences-Po, 2000).
28. Gabriel Almond and James S. Coleman, eds., *The Politics of Developing Areas* (Princeton: Princeton University Press, 1960), p. 37. See also Charles Morazé, *The French and the Republic* (Ithaca, NY: Cornell University Press, 1958), pp. 20ff, which discusses the "passion for theory" prevalent among the French.
29. Almond and Coleman, *The Politics of Developing Areas*, p. 37.
30. In a public opinion poll (*Expansion*-SOFRES) in 1983, 77 percent of the respondents would consider the abolition of "the free choice of school where children are sent" a very serious matter, 19 percent as a serious matter, and only 2 percent as not serious. SOFRES, *Opinion publique: Enquêtes et commentaires 1984* (Paris: Gallimard, 1984), p. 154.
31. According to a public opinion poll in mid-1987, while only 25 percent of Socialist voters (compared to 41 percent of the total sample of respondents) approved of the Gaullists' privatization policies, 34 percent of the new owners of privatized industries were Socialists! SOFRES, *L'État de l'opinion 1988*, pp. 33, 36.

32. According to a poll conducted in October 1995, 32 percent of the respondents were unwilling to accept any sacrifice to reduce the national deficit. The most reluctant were individuals identified with the Communist party (55 percent), followed by Socialists (38 percent), National Front (33 percent), UDF (30 percent), environmentalists (29 percent), and Gaullists (17 percent). *Expansion* poll, cited in SOFRES, *L'État de l'opinion 1996*, p. 30.

33. See François Nourissier, *The French* (New York: Knopf, 1968), pp. 117–22.

34. According to a poll of October 1999, 57% of respondents considered politics an honorable activity in principle, but when asked for their own attitudes regarding politics in reality, they responded as follows: distrust, 57%; boredom, 27%; hope, 26%; disgust, 20%; interest, 20%; fear, 11%; respect, 7%; enthusiasm, 2%. SOFRES, *L'Etat de l'opinion 2000*, p. 278. The results of a poll of August 2000 regarding more specific partisan political engagements are even more pessimistic, with only 23% attending meetings organized by a political party; 21% discussing a political party platform; 5% participating at a mass demonstration by a political party; 9% belonging to a political party; 4% giving money; 4% distributing party literature; 53% doing none of the above. SOFRES, *L'État de l'opinion 2001*, p. 219.

35. Pierre Bréchon, "Le Rapport à la politique," in Helene Riffault, ed., *Les Valeurs des Français* (Paris: PUF, 1994), pp. 163–200. The reference is to Georges Vedel, *La Dépolitisation: Mythe ou réalité?* (Paris: A. Colin, 1962). A more recent appraisal is that of Alain Duhamel, *La Politique imaginaire* (Paris: Gallimard, 1995), pp. 17–51, who argues that the French continue to be as deeply interested in politics as before.

36. Bréchon, "Le Rapport à la politique," pp. 168–70.

37. Ibid., pp. 191–97. With regard to abortion and sexual freedom, there has been no difference between Right and Left.

38. Herbert Luethy, *France Against Herself* (New York: Meridian, 1957), p. 39.

39. For older studies, see P. E. Converse and G. Dupeux, "Politicization of the Electorate in France and the United States," *Public Opinion Quarterly* 25:1 (1962), 11; Frank A. Pinner, "Parental Overprotection and Political Distrust," *Annals of the American Academy of Political and Social Science*, no. 361 (September 1965), 58–70; and Yves Agnès, "Les Jeunes et la politique," *Le Monde*, 17 February 1973.

40. Perrineau, "La Dimension cognitive," pp. 75ff. According to a poll, only 48 percent could describe the role of the Conseil Général, and only 23 percent had current information about regional elections. Poll of February 1992, cited in SOFRES, *L'État de l'opinion 1993*, p. 27.

41. For detailed statistics on voting patterns of the young compared to the electorate as a whole, see Annick Percheron, "Peut-on parler d'un incivisme des jeunes? Le Cas de la France," *International Political Science Review* 8:3 (July 1987), 273–82.

42. Ariane Chemin, "Le Temps des manifestations," *Le Monde*, 30–31 March 1997, p. 11.

43. Of the numerous works on the 1968 rebellion, the following may be mentioned: Patrick Seale and Maureen McConville, *Red Flag, Black Flag* (New York: Hill & Wang, 1970); Alain Touraine, *The May Movement* (New York: Random House, 1971); Bernard E. Brown, *Protest in Paris: Anatomy of a Revolt* (Morristown, NJ: General Learning Press, 1974). For an interesting (though somewhat premature) discussion of the subject, see Philippe Bénéton and Jean Touchard, "Les Interprétations de la crise de mai-juin 1968," *RFSP* 10 (June 1970), 503–44. The 25th anniversary of the revolt in 1993 was the occasion of many additional studies on the subject. According to one of these, the May events introduced the idea of *fraternity* for the first time, however briefly. They were also "the first anticommunist mass movement," for they took the monopoly of revolution away from the Communist party and, in so doing, laid the groundwork for the end of Marxism in France. See Michel Le Bris, "Trois ou Quatre Choses que je crois savoir de mai 1968," *Revue des deux mondes*, May 1993, pp. 17–35.

44. On this point, see Edgar Morin, Claude Lefort, and Cornelius Castoriadis, *Mai 68: La Brèche—suivi de vingts ans après* (Paris: Éditions Complexe, 1988), esp. pp. 26, 74, 129, 151, 181. The book represents an effort to see the May events from a less romantic and more detached perspective, made possible by the lapse of 20 years.

45. According to a SOFRES poll (March 1978) of 13- to 17-year-olds, 32 percent felt close to (extreme to moderate) leftist parties, 17 percent to Giscardist or Gaullists, 32 percent to no party, and 17 percent did not know. According to Harris and SOFRES polls of 1977, less than 30 percent of those aged 18

to 24 (and only 17 percent of the population as a whole) wanted radical social changes, while about half of the young wanted the status quo more or less maintained. Cited by Annick Percheron, "Se faire entendre: Morale quotidienne et attitudes politiques des jeunes," in Henri Mendras, ed., *La Sagesse et le désordre* (Paris: Gallimard, 1980), pp. 136–43, 160–63.

46. Alain Touraine et al., *Le Grand Refus: Réflexions sur la grève de décembre 1995* (Paris: Fayard, 1996). See especially Farhard Khosrokhavar, "Les Nouvelles Formes de mobilisation sociale," pp. 195–246.

47. See Alain Caillé and Jean-Pierre Le Goff, eds., *Le Tournant de décembre* (Paris: La Découverte, 1996).

48. Pierre Lellouche, *La République immobile* (Paris: Grasset, 1998), p. 19.

49. According to a SOFRES poll of December 1994, 44 percent evaluated socialism positively (versus 42 percent negatively); the evaluations of capitalism were 32 percent positive, 54 percent negative. However, the evaluations of liberalism were 60 percent positive, 29 percent negative; and of enterprise, 69 percent positive, 23 percent negative. SOFRES, *L'État de l'opinion 1996*, pp. 178, 182.

50. A survey conducted by SOFRES in September 1990 on a ranking of the societal utility of various professions, on a 0–10 scale, produced the following results: nurses, 9.3; workers, 9.2; general medical practitioners, 9.1; elementary and secondary-school teachers, 9.0; farmers, 8.8; engineers, 8.6; small businessmen, 8.2; directors of business firms, 8.2; clergy, 6.7; higher civil servants, 6.3; parliamentary deputies, 6.1; prostitutes, 4.1. Selected from results cited in SOFRES, *L'État de l'opinion 1992*, p. 32.

51. Olivier Duhamel, "Confiance institutionnelle et defiance politique: L'A-démocratie française, SOFRES, *L'État de l'opinion 2001*, p. 68.

52. Ibid. and SOFRES poll conducted 27–28 October 1999, cited in *Libération*, 19 November 1999. These results confirm earlier surveys. In 1977, 38% thought politicians were corrupt; in May 1990, 46%; in November of the same year, 55%; and in 1995, 62%. In 1991, only 49 percent considered politics an honorable activity, compared to 65 percent in 1985. Cf. SOFRES, *L'État de l'opinion, 1993*, pp. 234–35.

53. Alain Duhamel, "Une Crise à froid," *Libération*, 19 November 1999.

54. This would be the opposite of the phenomenon that some observe in the United States. See Robert D. Putnam, *Bowling Alone* (New York: Simon and Schuster, 2000).

55. Alain Touraine, "Existe-t-il encore une société française?" *Contemporary French Civilization* 15:2 (Summer–Fall 1991), 335–38.

56. See H. S. Jones, *The French State in Question* (Cambridge, UK: Cambridge University Press, 1993), pp. 6–12. See also Peyrefitte, *The Trouble with France*, pp. 260–61 et passim.

57. See Janine Mossuz-Lavau, *Les Français et la politique* (Paris: Odile Jacob, 1994), pp. 39f, 49f, 78–79.

58. Olivier Duhamel, "Les Français et l'État," SOFRES, *L'État de l'opinion 2000*, pp. 137–44.

59. Ibid., pp. 138–49. There is a significant proportion of the political Right that is concerned about the problem of unemployment and that wishes to reduce social inequalities and improve social protections. SOFRES polls of September and October 2000, in *L'État de l'opinion 2002*, p. 239.

60. Bernard Spitz, "Une Mondialisation, deux France," SOFRES, *L'État de l'opinion 2002*, p. 120. SOFRES/*Le Monde* poll July 2001.

61. In a poll conducted in 1995, 92 percent had a positive opinion of the functioning of the public telephone system *(France-Télécom)*; 80 percent, of the postal system; 65 percent, of the railroads; 63 percent, of the hospitals; 57 percent, of the schools; and 49 percent, of the social security system. SOFRES, *L'État de l'opinion 1997*, p. 151.

62. See Bréchon et al., *Les Cultures politiques des Français*, pp. 99–101.

63. According to a Harris poll of December 1988, 88 percent were disenchanted with politics; 68 percent believed that governments had failed to solve urgent problems; 61 percent that politicians had been indecisive; only 20 percent had confidence in politicians, while 40 percent indicated that they had more confidence in leaders of business. See "Les Français et la politique: C'est le divorce," *L'Express*, 16 December 1988, pp. 6–8.

64. SOFRES poll January 1999, reported in Jérôme Jaffré, "La Gauche accepte le marché, la droite admet la différence," *Le Monde*, 15–16 August 1999.

65. See, for example, Espaces 89, *L'Identité française* (Paris: Éditions Tiercé, 1985), for a social-democratic and "pluralistic" view; and Club de l'Horloge, *L'Identité de la France* (Paris: Albin Michel, 1985), for a conservative and "monistic" one.

66. Pierre Milza, speaking at a symposium at New York University in 1987, cited by Frederick L. Brown, "Crisis, Decentralization, Cohabitation: Aspects of Change in France," *Tocqueville Review* 9 (1987–1988), 371–72.

67. Hervé Le Bras and Emmanuel Todd, *L'Invention de la France* (Paris: Pluriel, 1981). For a sweeping historical approach to the subject, see Fernand Braudel, *L'Identité de la France* (Paris: Arthaud, 1986). See also William Safran, "State, Nation, National Identity, and Citizenship: France as a Test Case," *International Political Science Review* 12:3 (1991), 219–38.

68. See Suzanne Citron, *Le Mythe national: L'Histoire de France en question* (Paris: Éditions Ouvrières, 1989).

69. See polls in SOFRES, *L'Opinion publique 1986*, p. 90; and SOFRES, *L'État de l'opinion 1988*, pp. 195–96, 198.

70. A majority of young people now know that the French authorities participated in the deportation of Jews during World War II, but they are more likely to have learned of this event from the media than from their schoolteachers. However, most of the young retain a patriotic view of Marshall Pétain: 31 percent think of him primarily as the victor in the battle of Verdun during World War I; 23 percent as the person who did his best to protect French lives during World War II; 31 percent as a collaborator of the Nazis; and only 4 percent as a fascist dictator. SOFRES, *L'État de l'opinion 1993*, pp. 241–42.

71. See Alan Riding, "The '68 Uprising: Heaven in Its Way," *New York Times*, 28 May 1993; and "Que reste-t-il de 'la pensée 68'?" Interview with Luc Ferry, *Le Point*, 7 May 1993, pp. 60–61.

72. Passages/CSA, October 1987. Cited in Mermet, *Francoscopie 1989*, p. 82. Interviewees were permitted to give several responses.

73. According to a poll (SOFRES, *L'État de l'opinion 1988*, pp. 181–82), 49 percent were ready to die for France.

74. In terms of such criteria as standard of living, environment, gastronomy, social benefits, health, and the overall strength of the economy, France was placed fourth in a group of 15 countries, but the French placed their country thirteenth in that group. Eurobarometer survey, as reported in Michel Richard, "La France malade d'elle-même," *Le Point*, 19 October 1996, pp. 69–72.

75. A typical example is Alain-Gérard Slama, *La Régression démocratique* (Paris: Fayard, 1995), who complains about excessive individualism, tribalism, and lawlessness.

76. See Michael Winock, *Parlez-moi de la France* (Paris: Plon, 1994). See also Alain-Gérard Slama, "La République sous la loupe," *Le Point*, 21 January 1995, pp. 60–65.

77. In a poll on the question "What does it mean to be French," the answers were as follows: to be born in France, 52 percent; to defend freedom, 51 percent; to defend the country, 42 percent; to have the right to vote, 35 percent; to be attached to a common tradition and a common history, 33 percent; to speak French, 24 percent; to have French parents, 21 percent. See Jean Pierre Rioux, "Les Français et leur histoire," *Histoire*, no. 100 (May 1987), 72.

78. In the opinion of some observers, France has entered the "postnational" period, when many of its people feel that "[they] are the children of nobody and of everybody." See Steven Englund, "De l'usage du mot 'nation' par les historiens," *Le Monde Diplomatique*, March 1988, pp. 28–29. See also Pierre Nora, *Les Lieux de la mémoire*, 2 vols. (Paris: Gallimard, 1984–1986), which discusses at length the changes in the French national consciousness.

79. A public opinion poll conducted 18–22 June 1994 for *Figaro* revealed that 86 percent were opposed to the wearing of the Islamic scarf by schoolgirls; 61 percent to the right of immigrants to vote in local elections; and 60 percent to the construction of mosques in the large cities. SOFRES, *L'État de l'opinion 1995*, p. 52.

80. See Commission Nationale des Droits de l'Homme, *La Lutte contre le racisme* (Paris: Documentation Française, 1995).

81. According to a poll conducted in May 2000, more than 40 percent of the respondents believed that Jews had too much political and economic power. Anti-Semitic stereotypes were more strongly marked among older people than younger, and among adherents of the Right rather than the Left. SOFRES, *L'Etat de l'opinion 2001*, p. 281.

82. It was found that 76 percent of respondents living in communes where fewer than 1 percent of the inhabitants were foreigners thought that there were "too many Arabs" in France, whereas only 45

percent living in cities where that proportion was more than 10 percent shared that opinion. "Plus il y a d'étrangers, moins il y a de racistes," *Le Monde*, 21 March 1996, p. 12.

83. According to an official report, nearly 60 percent of the French, and 89 percent of those 15 to 19 years old, have an understanding of one or more foreign languages (compared to only 40 percent of those over 65). The vast majority of these know some English. See *News from France*, 7 February 1992.

84. See Michel Albert, *Capitalisme contre capitalisme* (Paris: Seuil, 1991). The author argues that the "Rhenish" (i.e., German) approach to economic policy might serve as a model for France.

85. See François Furet, Jacques Julliard, and Pierre Rosanvallon, *La République du centre: La Fin de l'exception française* (Paris: Calmann-Lévy, 1988). See also Robert Boyer, "Vers l'érosion du particularisme français?" *French Politics and Society* 10:1 (Winter 1992), 8–24.

CHAPTER 4

Political Parties and Elections

Toward the end of the Fourth Republic, a well-known commentator on French politics remarked that in France "there are two fundamental principles: that of the Right and that of the Left; three main tendencies, if one adds the center; six political families; ten parties, small and large, each opposed by multiple currents; fourteen parliamentary groups, highly undisciplined; and forty million opinions."[1] From the Third Republic to the present, dozens of political formations have existed, each holding somewhat different views about economic and social policy, the relationship between the executive and the legislature and between the national and local governments, and the place of religion in politics. Some of these formations have represented distinct social classes; others have attempted to transcend classes and appeal to a broadly based national electorate. Some parties can trace their origins to the Revolution of 1789; others to the Third or Fourth Republic; and still others have been formed recently, either to deal with specific, short-term challenges or to respond to appeals from charismatic leaders. Some have mass memberships and complex national organizations; others are little more than coalitions of local notables. Some have had fully developed ideologies and programs; others are little more than clubs, created by politicians for a variety of purposes, such as expressing their ideas in small-circulation journals, enhancing their visibility, or improving their maneuverability.

Since the end of World War II, a gradual simplification of the party system has taken place. In the mid-1930s, there were 19 recognized parties in the Chamber of Deputies; in the early 1970s, there were only 6 in the National Assembly: the Gaullists and Republicans; the (Catholic) Centrists and the (anticlerical) Radical-Socialists; and the Socialists and Communists. In terms of ideology, these pairs could be grouped into Right, Center, and Left; alternatively, they might be combined into four broad electoral and parliamentary groups or into a Right and a Left alliance system. After the elections of 2002, the Assembly had only 4 formally constituted Assembly groups: on the right, the Gaullists and *Démocratie libérale*, their republican-liberal ally, grouped into the *Union pour la majorité presidentielle* (UMP), and the UDF; and on the left, the Socialists and the Communists (see Tables 4.1 and 4.2; Figure 4.1).

TABLE 4.1
Parliamentary Elections: Distribution of Votes, 1958–2002 (in percentages)*

	Left			Center				Right		
	Communists	Socialists	Other Left	Radicals	MRP	Democratic Center	Moderates/ Independents	Right-Center Alliance	Gaullists	National Front
1958										
First round	18.9	15.5		11.5	11.6		19.9		17.6	
Second round	20.7	13.7		7.7	7.5		23.6		26.4	
1962										
First round	21.7	12.6		7.5	8.9	9.6[a]	4.4[b]		31.9	
Second round	21.3	15.2		7.0	5.3	7.8[a]	1.6[b]		40.5	
1967										
First round	22.5	18.8[c]				17.9[d]		37.8[e]		
Second round	21.4	24.1[c]				10.8[d]		42.6[e]		
1968										
First round	20.0	16.5				10.3[f]		43.7[e]		
Second round	21.0	21.4				7.8[f]		46.4[e]		
1973										
First round	21.5	21.2[g]			13.1[h]			36.4[e]		
Second round	20.6	25.1[g]			6.1[h]			46.2[e]		
1978										
First round	20.5	24.8[i]					23.9[j]		22.6	
Second round	18.6	30.6[i]					24.8[j]		26.1	
1981										
First round	16.2	37.5[i]					19.2[j]		20.8	
Second round	6.9	49.3[i]					18.6[j]		22.4	
1986										
Single round†	9.8	31.4[i]					8.3[j]	21.5[k]	11.2	9.7
1988										
First round	11.3	37.5[i]					18.5[j]	(40.4[l])	19.2	9.7
Second round	3.4	48.7[i]					21.2[j]	(46.8[l])	23.1	1.1

74

1993							
First round	9.2	20.3[m]		19.1[l]		20.4	12.4
Second round	4.6	31.6[n]		25.1[l]		27.8	5.7
1997							
First round	9.8	25.7[i]	6.7[p]	14.9	(39.7°)	16.5	15.2
Second round	3.6	39.1[i]	5.6[p]	21.2	(55.0°)	23.6	5.7
2002							
First round	4.8	24.1	8.3[p]	4.8[q]	0.4[r]	33.3[s]	11.3
Second round	3.3	35.3	6.7[p]	3.9[q]		47.3[s]	1.9

SOURCES: *Le Monde* dailies and *Dossiers et Documents*, 1958–2002, and *L'Année politique*, 1958–2002. There are slight variations among the sources.

NOTES: Extreme and minor Left and Right parties (other than the National Front) have been omitted. Figures in parentheses represent alliance totals.

* Metropolitan France.
[†] Proportional representation.
[a] Anti-Gaullist centrists.
[b] Independent Republicans (RI).
[c] FGDS.
[d] *Centre démocrate.*
[e] UDR and allies.
[f] *Progrès et démocratie moderne.*
[g] Union de la gauche démocrate et socialiste.
[h] Reformers (Radicals and anti-Gaullist centrists).
[i] Including Left Radicals (MRG).
[j] UDF and other Giscard supporters, including CDS, Radicals, and Republicans.

[k] RPR-UDF combined list.
[l] *Union de rassemblement et du centre* (URC): electoral alliance of RPR, UDF, and others.
[m] Includes PS: 17.6%; MRG: 0.9%; "presidential majority": 1.8%.
[n] Includes PS: 28.3%; MRG: 1.1%; "presidential majority": 2.2%.
[o] *Union pour la France du progrès,* (UPF): electoral alliance of RPR, UDF, and others.
[p] Includes Greens, *Mouvement pour la France,* and other democratic Left parties.
[q] UDF.
[r] *Démocratie libérale.*
[s] *Union pour la majorité présidentielle* (UMP).

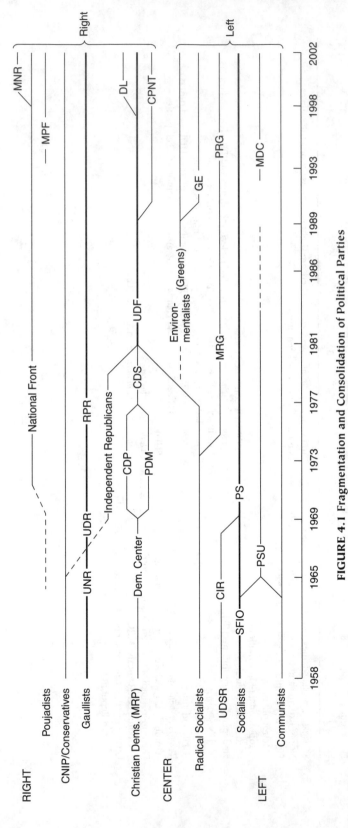

FIGURE 4.1 Fragmentation and Consolidation of Political Parties

NOTE: Heavy lines refer to major-presidential/parliamentary formations; broken lines refer to dormant state (e.g. Poujadists), preparty condition (e.g., environmentalists), or disintegration (PSU).

Abbreviations in Figure 4.1

CDP	*Centre de la démocratie et du progrès* (Center for Democracy and Progress): pro-Gaullist centrist party established in 1969
CDS	*Centre des démocrates sociaux* (Center of Social Democrats): Catholic centrist party (1976) resulting from the unification of the CDP and the anti-Gaullist centrists (PDM). In 1988, the CDS constituted itself into a separate parliamentary group, the *Union des démocrates et du center* (UDC), renamed *Force démocrate* in 1995
CIR	*Convention des institutions républicaines* (Convention of Republican Institutions): center-left formation of various political clubs
CNIP	*Centre national des indépendents et paysans* (National Center of Independents and Peasants): an amalgam of various economic conservative supporters of business and agricultural elements (often referred to as CNI)
CPNT	*Chasse, peche, nature et traditions* (Hunting, Fishing, Nature and Traditions): formed as a pressure group, became political party in 1992
DL	*Démocratie libérale* (Liberal Democracy): successor to the Republican party (PR), which left the UDF in 1997
FN	*Front national* (National Front): an extreme-right party fourced in 1972
GE	*Génération écologie*: a left-oriented splinter of the Greens
MDC	*Mouvement des citoyens* (Citizens' Movement): dissident leftist party formed in 1992
MNR	*Mouvement national républicain* (National Republican Movement): an extreme-right party that split off from the FN in 1998
MPF	*Mouvement pour la France* (Movement for France): right-wing party created in 1992 in opposition to the Maastricht Treaty
MRG	*Mouvement des radicaux de gauche* (Left Radicals): split off (1972–1973) from the main body of the Radical-Socialist party. Renamed PRG *(Parti des radicaux de gauche)* in 1996
MRP	*Mouvement républicain populaire* (Popular Republican Movement): major Christian Democratic party of the Fourth Republic. Ceased to exist in 1966
PDM	*Progrès et démocratie moderne* (Progress and Modern Democracy): anti-Gaullist centrists
PRG	See MRG
PS	*Parti socialiste* (Socialist party): successor (since 1969–1970) of the SFIO
PSU	*Parti socialiste unifié* (Unified Socialist party): established in 1960 by dissidents from the SFIO, the Communist party, and other left-wing groups
RPR	*Rassemblement pour la République* (Rally for the Republic): the "neo-Gaullist" party establishec in 1976
SFIO	*Section française de l'Internationale ouvrière* (French Section of the Workers' International): name of Socialist party from 1905 to 1969
UDF	*Union pour la démocratie française* (Union for French Democracy): a quasi-party, the Giscardist electoral alliance (1978) of the Republican party, the CDS, the Radical-Socialist party, and smaller groups, each of which retains its identity
UDR	*Union pour la défense de la République* (Union for the Defense of the Republic, later renamed the Democratic Union for the Republic): Gaullist party successor (1968) of the UNR
UDSR	*Union démocratique et socialiste de la Résistance* (Democratic and Socialist Union of the Resistance): party of former Résistance members
UNR	*Union pour la nouvelle République* (Union for the New Republic): Gaullist party, 1958

Electoral Alliances, 1958–2002

Fédération de la gauche démocratique et socialiste (FGDS—Federaticn of the Democratic and Socialist Left): alliance, between 1965 and 1968, of the SFIO, CIR, and Radical-Socialists

Réformateurs (Reformers): alliance, 1972–1974, of Radical-Socialists and (anti-Gaullist) Democratic Centrists

Union de la gauche démocrate et socialiste (UGDS—Union of the Democratic and Socialist Left): alliance, 1973, of the PS and MRG

Union du rassemblement et du centre (URC): alliance of the RPR and UDF for the parliamentary elections of 1988

Union pour la France du progrès (UPF): alliance, 1990, of the RPR and UDF for the parliamentary elections of 1993

La Droite indépendante (LDI): alliance of the CNIP and MPF for the parliamentary elections of 1997

Union pour la majorité présidentielle (UMP): alliance of the RPR, DL, and parts of the UDF for the presidential elections of 2002

TABLE 4.2
Presidential Elections: Distribution of Votes, 1965–2002 (in percentages)

	Left			Center	Right		National Front
	Communists	Socialists	Radicals	Democratic Center	Moderates/ Independents	Gaullists	National Front
1965							
First round		32.2[a]		15.8[b]		43.7[c]	
Second round		45.5[a]				54.5[c]	
1969							
First round	21.5[d]	5.1[e]		23.4[f]		43.8[g]	
Second round				42.4[f]		57.6[g]	
1974							
First round		43.2[a]			32.6[h]	15.1[i]	
Second round		49.2[a]			50.8[h]		
1981							
First round	15.3[j]	25.8[a]	2.2[k]		28.3[h]	17.9[n]	
Second round		51.8[a]			48.2[h]		
1988							
First round	6.7[l]	34.1[a]			16.6[m]	19.9[n]	14.4[o]
Second round		54.0[a]				45.9[n]	
1995							
First round	8.6[p]	23.3[q]			18.6[r]	20.8[n]	15.0[o]
Second round		47.4[q]				52.6[n]	
2002							
First round	3.4[p]	16.2[q]	2.3[k]	6.8[s]	3.9[t]	19.9[n]	16.9[o]
Second round						82.2[n]	17.8[o]

SOURCES: *Le Monde* and *L'Année politique*, 1965–2002.

NOTE: Jean-Louis Tixier-Vignancour, a candidate of the extreme Right, who received 5.3 percent in the first round of 1965, and Arlette Laguiller, the candidate of an extreme Left party *(Lutte ouvrière)*, who received 5.3 percent in the first round of 1995, have been omitted from this table. All first-round candidates who received less than 5 percent of the total have also been omitted.

[a]François Mitterrand.
[b]Jean Lecanuet.
[c]Charles de Gaulle.
[d]Jacques Duclos.
[e]Gaston Defferre.
[f]Alain Poher.
[g]Georges Pompidou.
[h]Valéry Giscard d'Estaing.
[i]Jacques Chaban-Delmas.
[j]Georges Marchais.
[k]Michel Crépeau (left-wing Radical).

[l]André Lajoinie (candidate put up by a splinter Communist party).
[m]Raymond Barre.
[n]Jacques Chirac.
[o]Jean-Marie Le Pen.
[p]Robert Hue.
[q]Lionel Jospin.
[r]Edouard Balladur (rival Gaullist candidate supported by many Giscardists).
[s]UDF.
[t]*Démocratie libérale.*

This simplification of the party system resulted from a number of developments: changes in the electoral system; the modernization of the economy; the weakening of class consciousness; reduced religious-anticlerical antagonisms; the blurring or discrediting of the image of a number of parties (because their programs were too vague or irrelevant or their leaders were distrusted); the polarizing impact of de Gaulle; and the personal ambitions of politicians who strove to mobilize a "national" electorate and appeal for support beyond traditional parties and classes. To these factors one must add a growing consensus about the legitimacy of the Fifth Republic, which reduced the number of antisystem parties, and an impatience with ideological nuances. Yet the six political families have persisted in sufficient measure—in terms of organization as well as historical points of reference—to be treated separately.

THE SOCIALIST PARTY

The Socialist party, which governed France for most of the 1980s, is the oldest existing mass party in the country. Although democratic in orientation, much like the German SPD and the British Labour Party, it was for many years more Marxist than other socialist parties in Western Europe. Although appealing to the working class with promises of radical economic change, the party has been led by bourgeois intellectuals. With the onset of the Fifth Republic, the party was greatly weakened as a national political force, but in the early 1970s it began its recovery, becoming the largest party in terms of popular support and achieving a solid victory in 1981.

The Socialist party was founded in 1905 in an attempt to unite four varieties of socialism: utopian, syndicalist, revolutionary, and reformist. Officially known as the French Section of the Workers' International (*Section française de l'internationale ouvrière*—SFIO), it was a federation of regional units whose parliamentary politicians were subject to party discipline. Although in principle committed to the class struggle and the transformation of society, the party entered into a number of coalitions with bourgeois parties, especially when the republic seemed to be in danger. Thus, the SFIO joined the government in 1914 in a "sacred union" for the defense of France against Germany; in 1936, party leader Léon Blum headed an antifascist "Popular Front" government that included the bourgeois Radical-Socialists; and during World War II, a number of Socialist politicians made common cause with non-Socialists in the Resistance against Nazi Germany.

After Liberation, the SFIO participated in a government coalition with the Communists and Christian Democrats. It contributed ministers to various cabinets until 1951 and led a government in 1956–1957. Although the SFIO was a defender of the Fourth Republic, many of the party's leaders supported the investiture of de Gaulle and the establishment of the Fifth Republic, fearing that failure to do so might lead to civil war. But the SFIO soon became disillusioned with de Gaulle's conservative domestic policies.

Having been consigned to opposition status and weakened by a massive defection of members, the SFIO experimented with a variety of alliance strategies. In 1963, some SFIO politicians promoted the presidential candidacy of Gaston Defferre, the anticommunist mayor of Marseilles, in order to encourage a rapprochement with anti-Gaullist Center parties. When this effort collapsed, the party embraced a "united Left" tactic. In

1965, in order to strengthen their position vis-à-vis the Communists, the Socialists formed the Federation of the Democratic and Socialist Left (*Fédération de la gauche démocratique et socialiste*—FGDS), a coalition of the SFIO, the Radical-Socialists, and a few democratic-leftist clubs. François Mitterrand, the leader of one of these clubs (the *Convention des institutions républicaines*—CIR), was chosen to be president of this federation and soon thereafter became the joint candidate of the democratic *and* the communist Left in the presidential elections.

The Communist-FGDS alliance continued for the parliamentary elections of 1967 and 1968, but broke down as a result of growing ideological conflict between the SFIO and the Communist party (PCF). The FGDS had collapsed, and the SFIO had become so weak that in the presidential elections of 1969 its candidate received only 5 percent of the first-round votes (compared to over 21 percent for the Communist candidate).

After those elections, the SFIO ceased to exist. It was succeeded by the *Parti socialiste* (PS), a fusion of the SFIO, the CIR, and other democratic-leftist clubs. The process of revitalization included the replacement of Guy Mollet, who had led the SFIO since 1946, by Mitterrand, and a successful effort to retain—by means of a new, progressive platform[2]—the support of the working class and to attract young people, white-collar employees, shopkeepers, farmers, and even Catholics.[3] Between 1968 and 1975, the party membership doubled, reaching 150,000. It was from this position of strength that the PS rebuilt its alliance with the PCF. In 1972, the two parties agreed on a "Common Program of the Left" and to mutual support in future elections. The Common Program called for an increased minimum wage, a reduction of the workweek, the extension of social benefits, the strengthening of union rights, and the nationalization of some industries.

The Common Program alliance began to disintegrate just before the legislative elections of 1978. A bitter quarrel arose over the meaning of the common platform, specifically, the extent of nationalization, the leveling of salaries, and the allocation of cabinet posts in the event of a victory of the Left. While the Communists questioned the good faith and the leftism of the PS, the Socialists doubted that the PCF had "de-Stalinized" itself sufficiently to be trusted with a share of power. A principal cause of the Communists' resentment was the fact that the PS had become the major party of the Left, reducing the PCF to the status of junior partner. The inability of the Left to win control of the Assembly during the 1978 elections was widely attributed to the Communists' failure to support Socialist candidates in the second round in many constituencies. At the same time, the PCF's weakened position within the Left alliance increased the voters' perception of the Socialists' moderation and improved the latter's future electoral prospects.

THE COMMUNISTS

The Communist party of France (*Parti communiste français*—PCF) was for many years the second-largest communist party in Western Europe (after Italy) and the most disciplined. It was founded in 1920 at the SFIO Congress of Tours, when about three-quarters of the delegates decided to join the Third International, which had been set up by the Russians after the Bolshevik Revolution.

Since its founding, the PCF's development has paralleled that of the SFIO. The PCF shared many of the SFIO's characteristics, notably its adherence to Marxism, its appeal to the working class, and its espousal of higher minimum wages, the nationalization of crucial industries, and the expansion of the welfare state. The PCF had a reliable electoral appeal in the Fourth Republic, obtaining more votes than any other party. From the beginning of that republic until the installation of a leftist Fifth Republic president in 1981, the PCF share of the total vote ranged from a high of 28.2 percent in 1946 to a low of 18.6 percent in 1978. It was an important party in the industrial north and in the working-class suburbs of Paris. Only about 60 percent of its members and less than 50 percent of its voters have been working class, yet the PCF has been the workers' party par excellence. It capitalized on the fact that the French working class felt a strong sense of alienation, which was not significantly diminished by improvements in its living standard.

For all its revolutionary rhetoric, the PCF made de facto concessions to bourgeois politics. In the early 1930s, the party collaborated with other left-wing parties in order to stem the tide of fascism in Europe, and in 1936, it supported the Popular Front government. As a result of the Nazi-Soviet Pact of 1939 and the PCF's defense of Stalin, many party members resigned. Dissolved by Pétain, the PCF continued in a clandestine fashion and, following the German invasion of the Soviet Union in 1941, fought seriously against fascism, compiling such an impressive record in the Resistance that it emerged from World War II with an enhanced image. The party entered the government for the first time as a component of the postwar tripartite coalition.

From 1947 to the end of the Fourth Republic, the PCF was in the opposition. In that role, the party was not only an advocate of "collectivist" domestic legislation but also an apologist for Soviet foreign policies. In 1958, the PCF opposed both de Gaulle's investiture as premier and the ratification of the Fifth Republic Constitution. Yet, although the party criticized both the institutions of the new republic and the policies pursued by President de Gaulle, it passed up several chances to promote a revolution against the regime. During the Events of May 1968, the PCF tried to contain the rebellion and favored a peaceful approach to change. In the presidential elections of 1965, it supported the Socialist candidate, but in the presidential elections of 1969, after its own candidate was eliminated in the first round, the PCF sat out the second round, preferring not to exercise a choice between "the cholera and the plague," that is, between Gaullist Pompidou and Catholic Centrist Poher, although the latter was clearly anti-Gaullist.

Throughout the 1960s and 1970s, the PCF continued to adhere to Marxist-Leninist slogans about revolution, the class struggle, and the dictatorship of the proletariat and questioned the utility of engaging in bourgeois politics. Yet the party took part in all national and local elections and embraced such bourgeois ideas as freedom of speech and competitive elections. To some observers, these developments signaled a "domestication" of the PCF; to others, they were a tactic aimed at facilitating alliances with the noncommunist Left. In any case, by the late 1970s, the image of the party had improved. A majority of French citizens no longer believed that the PCF wanted to make a revolution, and many appeared to be open to Communist participation in future governments.

The PCF had reason for optimism about its prospects for obtaining or sharing power. It had a core of disciplined activists, a tight organization, a centralized leadership, numerous affiliated organizations (of workers, professionals, students, women, and youth), many journals, a large budget, and a claimed membership of nearly 700,000. Furthermore, it provided more than 700 mayors. Yet in the 1978 legislative elections, the PCF, although still receiving nearly 6 million first-round votes, was eclipsed by the PS. While the image of the PS was improving, that of the PCF was being tarnished by a number of factors. It was blamed for the collapse of the Left alliance and accused of having fomented public disputes with the PS over the interpretation of the Common Program. Before and after the parliamentary elections, there were internal fights regarding the future orientation of the PCF: One faction called for a "de-Staliniza-tion" of the party, freer internal discussion, and less organizational rigidity; another pre-ferred a return to revolutionary Leninism and the abandonment of all "reformist" ten-dencies. Moreover, Georges Marchais, the party's secretary-general, had an increasingly negative image. His personal integrity was being questioned,[4] and his public appear-ances were marked by stridently Stalinist pronouncements.

THE ORIGINS AND EVOLUTION OF GAULLISM: FROM THE RPR TO THE *UNION POUR LA MAJORITÉ*

Gaullism is an unusual phenomenon. From its beginnings in 1947 to the end of the Fourth Republic, the Gaullist party claimed to be a national *movement,* an alternative to parties. Whereas other parties were national federations of strong local and regional po-litical machines, often run by notables, the Gaullist party, then called Rally of the French People (*Rassemblement du peuple français*—RPF), was the expression of the political be-liefs and ambitions of one man. The original Gaullists, the leaders of "Free France" in London, were a disparate group, including devout Catholics, anticlerical intellectuals, and Resistance figures of various political persuasions. After the war, those who agreed with de Gaulle's criticism of the Fourth Republic and shared his desire to replace it with a regime that would be better equipped to provide strong leadership and assert France's global role joined the Gaullist ranks.

By the end of the Fourth Republic, support for the Gaullists had declined, but in 1958, when de Gaulle reentered the political arena, the party's fortunes revived dramati-cally. Under the new republic, the Gaullist party, relabeled *Union pour la nouvelle République* (UNR), set up numerous local machines, attracted many activists, and ac-quired a mass electoral base. At the onset of the Fifth Republic, the UNR enjoyed the goodwill of a number of democratic leftists and enticed a segment of the working-class electorate.[5] Yet from the early 1960s to 1981, the party increasingly advocated conserva-tive policies and was heavily supported by entrepreneurs, higher civil servants, and other well-to-do voters. However, because of its grassroots aspects and its transformation into a "catchall" party—it received more than 45 percent of the vote in the parliamentary elections of 1968—the Gaullist party (renamed the *Union pour la défense de la République*—UDR)[6] rejected the label of "right-wing." From the very outset, the Gaullist party did not behave like a traditional party of the Right. It embraced macroeconomic planning, looked for technocratic solutions to problems, accepted the welfare state, and sought periodic popular endorsement.

Nonetheless, Gaullism must be considered right-wing because much of the social doctrine (or perhaps mood or style)[7] on which the party based its self-image related to nationalism and the enhancement of national power. Thus, the Gaullists' support of in-come subsidies for children stemmed, not from a belief in large families for their own sake, as is the case with Catholic parties, but from an interest in increasing France's population and thus enabling the country to play an enlarged global role.[8] The Gaullists for many years promoted the defense of national sovereignty by resisting European integration efforts, strengthening the country's military capacity, spreading the French language around the world, building nuclear power stations to reduce France's energy dependence, instituting worker "participation" schemes in factories to eliminate the class struggle, and curbing attempts at administrative decentralization to protect the unity of the state.

Not all Gaullists adhered to this "classical" Gaullism. Pompidou was a neoliberal who stressed industrial modernization and wished to enhance the role of the market and reduce that of the state. Léo Hamon, once the official spokesman of the government, and René Capitant, a law professor, were self-described left-wing Gaullists who wanted to see the power of the state used to expand the welfare state; Olivier Guichard, once chief economic planner, was a technocrat; and the views of Prime Minister Jacques Chaban-Delmas on socioeconomic policy had a social-democratic flavor. The factionalism and personalism within the Gaullist movement were illustrated by the fact that there were three Gaullist presidential candidates in 1981 and two in 1995.[9]

The "personalized" aspect of Gaullism is seen in the case of Jacques Chirac, whose political orientation was marked more by ambition than by ideological clarity. Serving briefly as a minister under Pompidou, he decided, upon the latter's death in 1974, to support Giscard for the presidency, rather than Chaban-Delmas, the Gaullist nominee. After his election, Giscard rewarded Chirac by appointing him as premier. Chirac's new position did not prevent him from becoming the secretary-general of the Gaullist party *and*, early in 1976, coordinator of Giscard's presidential majority. The "neo-Gaullist" successor party, the Rally for the Republic (*Rassemblement pour la République*—RPR), which Chirac founded in late 1976, a few months after his resignation as premier, and which he continued to lead, evolved both as an instrument of his presidential aspirations and as a repository of Gaullism.[10] In addition to constantly evoking de Gaulle's memory, the RPR shared with the supporters of Giscard a commitment to fighting the "socialo-communists."

THE POLITICAL "CENTER": FROM CLASSIC PROVINCIALISM TO THE *UNION POUR LA DÉMOCRATIE FRANÇAISE*

The fourth political group formally represented in the current National Assembly is the Union for French Democracy (*Union pour la démocratie française*—UDF). It was founded in 1978 to support President Valéry Giscard d'Estaing and ensure his reelection. "Giscardism" represents a confluence of political forces that have rejected both the collectivism of the Left and the nationalism and charismatic populism of the Gaullists, and whose adherents have therefore chosen to describe themselves as centrist.[11]

"Center" parties have represented the petite bourgeoisie rather than the working class, big business, or landowners. Their position in the center of the semicircular seating arrangement of the Assembly attested to their ability to turn right or left, as the occasion demanded, and act as balancers in coalition cabinets. The main components of the Giscardist electoral alliance system—traditional conservatives, Radical-Socialists, and Catholics—are sufficiently disparate to be dealt with separately.

Radicalism

The Radical-Socialist (or simply "Radical") party was officially founded in 1901, but its roots go back to the beginning of the Third Republic, if not earlier. It favored a centralized republic but derived its strength (or weakness) from the fact that it was run by local notables, mayors of towns of various sizes who used their control over political machines to be elected to Parliament. The party's "radicalism" was embodied in its anticlericalism, its support of a secular school system, and its advocacy of the separation of church and state. It favored a strong bill of rights, universal suffrage, a progressive tax system, and the protection of the small-business proprietor against the vicissitudes of economic modernization. The party's consistent antimonarchism at the turn of the century made it appear decidedly "leftist." Its center position often made it a crucial partner in multiparty governments, so that during the Third and Fourth Republics it supplied many prime ministers. Its radicalism weakened because of its ideological ambiguities; and when de Gaulle reappeared on the political scene in 1958, much of the Radical electorate voted for the General, and many of the party's leaders deserted to the UNR.

Catholicism

Another "centrist" orientation is that of Christian democracy. The Catholic church was originally monarchist and conservative, but toward the end of the Third Republic hesitantly moved toward an acceptance of republicanism. Christian democracy became an important force in French politics after the Liberation with the founding of the *Mouvement républicain populaire* (MRP). That party, led by men who had been prominent in the Resistance, was committed to the idea that Catholicism could be successfully combined with democracy and the welfare state. The party's appeal to the masses was such that in the mid-1940s it garnered more than one-fourth of the popular vote in Assembly elections and participated in a left-oriented government with the PS and the PCF. In the early 1950s, the MRP weakened, as many of its working-class supporters switched to the Socialists, and as it was forced to compete with the Radicals, and later the Gaullists, for the votes of the petite bourgeoisie. In 1958, much of the MRP leadership, already more conservative than a decade earlier, joined the Gaullist bandwagon, while the anti-Gaullist rump faced the Fifth Republic with uncertainty.

Centrist Coalition Games

Given the loss of much of their traditional electorate to the Gaullists, both the Radicals and the MRP realized that without allies neither could resist the bipolarizing impact of the electoral system—the second-round runoffs that forced voters to abandon candidates of weak parties and to turn to either a right-wing or a left-wing candidate. Consequently, each of these parties experimented with coalitions involving more powerful partners. In the mid-1960s, the Radical-Socialists entered into an electoral coalition with the Socialists—the FGDS—but that coalition had broken up by 1969. The reasons were several: (1) Many Radicals felt that the SFIO was using them to shore up its own strength. (2) The FGDS was too small to overcome de Gaulle's charismatic leadership.

(3) An expansion of the noncommunist Left by the inclusion of the MRP—a step then favored by some Radicals—was unacceptable to most Socialists, given their anticlericalism, whereas a broadening of the Left alliance to include the Communists was unacceptable to the Radicals.

After the elections of 1967, the MRP ceased to exist. Those Catholic deputies who remained and had not gone over to the Gaullists had meanwhile reorganized as the Democratic Center. Its leader, Jean Lecanuet, had run for the presidency in 1965 on a program of opposition to both Gaullism and Socialism; in the elections of 1969, the Democratic Center (organized in the Assembly under the label of *Progrès et démocratie moderne*—PDM) made a last attempt at gaining national office when it fielded Alain Poher, the speaker of the Senate and a staunch anti-Gaullist, as its presidential candidate. But when Pompidou was elected, some centrists were so starved for power that they joined the new government.

Those centrists who remained in the opposition tried an electoral alliance with the Radical-Socialists. This alliance, known as the Reformers' Movement *(Réformateurs)*, was established in 1971. The movement was not the solution to the centrist parties' dilemma, for their electoral base remained too narrow; moreover, it was torn by personal rivalries between the leaders of the two major components and beset by conflicts within the Radical party between the "liberal" probusiness faction and the protectionist faction supported by small shopkeepers.[12] Those left-wing Radicals who were offended by any collaboration with "clericalists" broke away and formed their own party, the Movement of the Left Radicals (*Mouvement des radicaux de gauche*—MRG), which promptly allied itself with the Socialists.

The Elections of 1974 and the Emergence of Giscardo-Centrism

President Pompidou's sudden death in April 1974 and Valéry Giscard d'Estaing's emergence as a presidential candidate provided an opportunity for the center parties. Positioning himself as an alternative between the Gaullists and the Left, Giscard got both the Radicals and the Democratic Centrists to support him by promising each a part of what they wanted: to the Radicals, an enlargement of civil liberties and a strengthening of local communities; to the Democratic Centrists, an expansion of the welfare state and the pursuit of less-nationalistic foreign policies. Both groups were promised an extension of the role of Parliament and a possible change of the electoral system toward proportional representation. At the same time, Giscard appealed to Gaullist voters by promising to safeguard the institutions of the Fifth Republic, a tactic that helped to ensure his election in the second round.

Giscard's background was far from ideal for a politician around whom "centrists" would cluster. A graduate of two prestigious schools, the *École Polytechnique* and the *École Nationale d'Administration* (ENA), he was also the scion of a well-to-do family with close ties to the pre-Gaullist political Right, which had defended the status quo and favored the monarchy against the republicans. Defining society in organic rather than functional terms, it favored a hierarchical social structure and had contempt for the masses. Originally, the Right was the expression of the "established" pillars of society: the Church, the army, the nobility, and the landed gentry. Later, it derived electoral support from big

business and those elements of the peasantry that were committed to religious and social conservatism. The traditional Right had tried to bring down the Third Republic, but
the Dreyfus Affair tarnished its image; moreover, the industrial revolution, the growth of
the working class, the extension of the franchise, and the rise of socialist parties weakened its position.

After Liberation, elements of the Right that had collaborated with the Germans
during World War II had been discredited; most of the remainder had accepted republicanism, and deputies identified with that remainder labeled themselves "moderates,"
"independents," or members of "peasant" parties. The main umbrella party was the
Party of Independents and Peasants (*Centre national des indépendants et paysans*—CNIP).
Founded in 1948, the CNIP was divided, on the one hand, between representatives of
business and representatives of peasants from backward regions and, on the other, between Catholic and secular elements. Because of its fragmentation, the position of the
CNIP (and of the Right as a whole) in the Fourth Republic was weak. A further source of
weakness of the CNIP was the fact that it had to compete for votes with several centrist
parties and, later, with Gaullism. One right-wing organization that had considerable appeal was the Union for the Defense of Shopkeepers and Artisans (*Union pour la défense
des commerçants et des artisans*—UDCA). Founded by Pierre Poujade after World War II as
an interest group and combining its hostility to the wealthy with anti-industrialism,
antiparliamentarism, and anti-Semitism, the "Poujadists" ran as a political party, the
Union et fraternité française, in the parliamentary elections of 1956. Convinced that
de Gaulle would end the hated Fourth Republic and keep Algeria French, most Poujadist
deputies favored his return to power, and the majority of their electoral supporters were
absorbed into the Gaullist party (with a remnant drifting into the political wilderness).
More than a decade later, Poujadism reemerged as an element in the National Front.

Giscard had entered Parliament just before the Fourth Republic collapsed. In 1958
he supported de Gaulle and his new constitution and was soon rewarded with a ministerial appointment, without, however, having joined the Gaullist party.[13] But the CNIP,
under whose label he had been reelected, was too conservative for Giscard's ambitions,
for that party had once been lukewarm about republicanism—many of its leaders had
supported the Vichy regime—and continued to represent the values of social elitism,
family, and religion. Most important, the CNIP had no mass following and no great
electoral prospects. In 1962, Giscard, together with a number of deputies, broke away
from the CNIP to found his own political organization, the *Républicains indépendants*
(RI). This group supported de Gaulle on most issues, but it diverged from the Gaullists
in favoring an enlarged role for the market; advocating greater political roles for Parliament, the parties, and interest groups; and stressing civil liberties. In 1969, Giscard
spoke out against the referendum that would have reformed the Senate, and in so doing
he helped to bring about de Gaulle's resignation. Giscard's positions were a mixture of
Gaullism, conservatism, economic liberalism, and classic parliamentarism, but they
were interpreted as sufficiently different from orthodox Gaullism to allow the Radicals
and Democratic Centrists to be co-opted by him. This co-optation enabled Giscard's
supporters, especially those who were on his side in the first round in 1974, to occupy
the parliamentary terrain situated between the Gaullists and the Socialists, and thereby
to claim the label of "centrist."

However, many observers have suggested that the term *centrist* was misappropriated and that it rested on wishful thinking—the wish for a depolarization of French political life. For the Left, both the Giscardists and the Gaullists were right-wing and indistinguishable in terms of their electoral clientele: shopkeepers, farmers, free professionals, and middle and upper-echelon white-collar employees. The Gaullists claimed that whereas *they* were populist, the Giscardists were more genuinely on the right. This claim was based on (1) the conservative and upper-class origins of Giscard and his "barons";[14] (2) the fact that, unlike the Gaullists in the late 1950s and early 1960s, the Giscardists had never received meaningful working-class support; (3) the laissez-faire liberalism embraced by most Giscardists; and (4) the fact that the Giscardists' largest component, the RI, renamed in 1977 the Republican party (*Parti républicain*—PR), was solidly conservative.[15]

An electoral alliance that included the RI, the Radical-Socialists, and the Democratic Center (which had been operating under the label of *Centre des démocrates sociaux* [CDS] since 1976, when the pro-Gaullist and anti-Gaullist factions reunited), and smaller groups,[16] the UDF was "centrist" in a tactical sense—it hoped to attract moderate supporters of the PS *and* to push the RPR further to the Right while at the same time reducing the presidential chances of Chirac. Some of the Giscardist politicians hoped that the various components of the UDF would merge and become a truly centrist political party; others wanted the UDF to remain a loose alliance in which the separate identities of the Radicals, Catholics, and Republicans would be maintained. A compromise between the two positions was soon achieved: Individuals could join the UDF directly or they could adhere to a component group, in which case they would automatically be members of the UDF. The alliance decided to put up single first-round candidates under the UDF label in many constituencies and to support Gaullist candidates only in the second round. In the parliamentary elections of 1978, the UDF received nearly one-quarter of the popular votes, gained a significant number of Assembly seats (largely at the expense of the Gaullists), and formed a single, if not very disciplined, parliamentary group.

As the presidential elections of 1981 approached, the disunity within the UDF was de-emphasized so as not to defeat the purpose for which it had been created: the reelection of Giscard. The requisite unity was provided by a common dislike for Giscard's main rival, Mayor Chirac of Paris, the leader of the Gaullists. During the campaign, Giscard and Chirac were friendly enemies: Both attacked the candidates of the Left while questioning each other's competence; both ran as presidential candidates, and both pledged to support each other in the second round if need be. When Giscard emerged as the highest vote-getter and was forced into a runoff against Mitterrand, the Gaullists officially closed ranks behind Giscard. But Chirac's failure to issue an unambiguous call to his Gaullist supporters to vote for Giscard helped to sabotage the incumbent's reelection.

There were other reasons for Giscard's defeat. During the first years of his term, the economy grew, the development of high-technology industries was encouraged, and the rate of inflation was kept low; subsequently, however, a recession occurred, unemployment increased, the gap between the rich and the poor widened, and Giscard's reformist momentum slowed down. His image had deteriorated amid charges of scandals involving himself and his ministers; his behavior had become increasingly "imperial"; and he lost the trust of small but crucial parts of the electorate on whose support he had counted.[17] The Giscardists tried desperately to salvage their position during the legislative elections that followed. In those elections, they formed an alliance with the Gaullists that was labeled, with a certain degree of optimism, the *Union pour la nouvelle majorité*, under which joint first-round candidates were put up in more than 300 constituencies, and the two groups supported each other in the second round. The results of these elections reduced the power of both the Giscardists and the Gaullists.

THE LEFT IN POWER: 1981 AND AFTER

The victories of the Socialists in 1981 were the culmination of two combined strategies: opening their party to a broad spectrum of the electorate and forming collaborative relationships with other parties of the Left. Two small democratic-left formations, the *Parti socialiste unifié* (PSU) and the *Mouvement des radicaux de gauche* (MRG), deserve mention: the former, because of its programmatic influence; the latter, because of its tactical significance.

The PSU was by turns a rival and a collaborator of the PS. Founded in 1960 by a combination of ex-Socialists, ex-Communists, left-wing Radical-Socialists, and others who opposed the Fifth Republic, the PSU placed itself to the left of the PS (although in *programmatic* terms it was not always clearly "socialist"). During the first few years of its existence, it claimed more than 15,000 members, but in 1981 it had at most 7,000; its popular vote never rose above 4 percent, and it never got more than a handful of deputies into Parliament. In the mid-1970s, a faction of the PSU, including the party's leader, Michel Rocard, accepted the Common Program of the Left and joined the PS.

The PSU is of interest because, as a party composed heavily of intellectuals, it was a source of ideas for the PS, especially via the Rocard faction (which represented about 20 percent of the PS membership). The Socialists' evolving positions regarding factory self-management *(autogestion)*, economic planning, decentralization, and the support of ethnic minority cultures owe a great deal to the PSU.[18] A consistent supporter of Mitterrand's presidential candidacies, the PSU was part of the Left's presidential majority, and in 1983 its leader, Huguette Bouchardeau, was given a ministerial post. At the end of 1988, the PSU disbanded.

The MRG consisted of those Radical-Socialists who objected to the rapprochement between the moderate politicians of their party and the Democratic Centrists. Founded in 1973, the MRG endorsed the Common Program and supported the presidential ambitions of Mitterrand. Although fielding its own first-round candidates in parliamentary elections (and sometimes its own presidential candidates), the MRG usually cast its lot with the PS in the second round. The MRG differed from the PS mainly in the following respects: It was less interested in collaboration with the Communists; it opposed the nationalization of industries; and its attitudes toward incomes and social policies attested to its petit-bourgeois electorate (as contrasted with the working-class electorate of the PS). Despite these differences, the MRG continued to be closely associated with the PS, especially in the Assembly.

A more problematic aspect of the Left alliance was the relationship between the PS and the PCF. Although the Common Program partnership remained officially intact after the 1978 elections, dealings between the two parties were embittered by the public trading of accusations. The PCF accused the PS of being more bourgeois than socialist, of not being committed to genuine reform. The PS, in turn, charged the PCF with a continuing desire to destroy democratic institutions.

In 1981, the PCF ran its own candidate for president. The party did poorly in the first round and supported the PS candidate in the second round. In the legislative elections that followed, the PCF did even worse. With its Assembly representation halved, gaining less than 10 percent of the seats, the party was reduced to relative powerlessness. The PCF put the best face on this situation, choosing to interpret Mitterrand's victory as its own and claiming credit for having helped him get elected. Having been given 4 ministerial posts (out of more than 40) in the Mauroy government, the PCF could be seen as part of the ruling coalition; but it could also be said to have been co-opted by it. The ministries allocated to the party were minor ones; in return for them, it had to accept a number of policy positions laid out by Mitterrand, including a respect for civil liberties and a nonconfiscatory approach to the nationalization of industries. Confronted with the choice between programmatic independence and a share of political power, the PCF had become somewhat schizophrenic: Its cabinet ministers counseled solidarity with the government, but the leaders of the party executive sharpened their critiques of it. One of the major reasons for the impressive victories of the PS in 1981 was the fact that the fear of Communists' having excessive (and destructive) influence on a Socialist-led government—a fear exploited in the past by Gaullists and Giscardists—was increasingly perceived as being without substance.

In 1982, Marchais was easily reelected as secretary-general of the PCF; his party, however, had been weakened by defections and the formation of dissident groups. Faced with these difficulties, the PCF was more interested in intra-Left cooperation than the PS. The leaders of the two parties agreed to have common first-ballot lists for the municipal elections of 1983, but in many constituencies the accord was not observed.

Some Socialists hoped that their capture of the presidency and the control of the Assembly would give their party the opportunity to embrace "social democracy" along the lines followed by analogous parties in the German Federal Republic and Scandinavia. That hope was based on the belief that the PS—with the help of votes from shopkeepers, farmers, teachers, and other petit-bourgeois elements—had already come to occupy part of the political *center* and that the PCF had become too weak to pressure the PS to stray from the path of moderate reform. Other Socialists insisted that the overwhelming victories of the PS would enable the party to promote a program of *socialisme à la française* that would go far beyond the reforms undertaken by social-democratic governments elsewhere in Europe.

After 1981, there were still Socialists, notably among younger party activists and, paradoxically, some of the bourgeois members of the party's top echelons, who were inspired by Marxism and expected the PS to strive for the abolition of capitalism. But it is doubtful that many of the rank-and-file members wanted radical changes. At that time, less than 50 percent of the PS electorate consisted of members of the working class; many of the industrial workers who voted Socialist belonged to the middle-income and skilled-worker categories, with the least skilled and poorest workers generally remaining loyal to the Communist party. A growing proportion of the Socialist voters between 1978 and 1981 were businesspeople, middle- and upper-middle-class managerial personnel, and practicing Catholics.[19] The embourgeoisement of the PS was also reflected in the professional backgrounds of Socialist deputies elected in 1981: Among 268, only 2 were workers, as compared to 21 physicians, 36 university professors, 84 high-school teachers, and 43 higher civil servants. The makeup of the PS leadership has not changed substantially in recent years.

It is unclear to what extent the social composition of the parliamentary contingent of the PS has reflected that of the rank and file of the party. The basic unit of the PS is the department federation, which sends delegates to the biennial national party congress. The congress elects a directorate; the latter elects an executive committee, which meets at least once every two months and is assisted by a secretariat. The federations (some of which, like those of Paris and Marseilles, carry great weight) prepare resolutions for the congresses, promote active rank-and-file involvement, and try to recruit new members. The federations are assisted in these tasks by more than a thousand party sections based in factories.

The Socialists had come to power surrounded by an aura of idealism, and many of the party's supporters expected it to "govern differently" from its predecessors.[20] During the first two years of Mitterrand's presidency, many government policies reflected traditional Socialist ideology: selective nationalizations, increased minimum wages, a reduction of the workweek, the lengthening of paid vacations, and the expansion of public employment. Other projects could not be attributed specifically to socialism (e.g., decentralization and the abolition of capital punishment), and still others were continuations of Giscard's liberal policies—for example, the infusion of capital into globally competitive industries, the promotion of gender equality, and revisions of the penal code. Finally, the austerity policies inaugurated in 1983, including a slowdown in salary raises and a limit on public sector jobs, might be attributed to the pressing needs of the day or the influence of "moderate" Socialists in the government.

The government's policy ambiguities also reflected the diversity that had marked the party since its revitalization in the early 1970s. Its various factions (courants) included a social-democratic and vociferously anticommunist group; a pro–working class segment clustered around Pierre Mauroy; the supporters of Michel Rocard; and the members of the Centre d'études, de recherches, et d'éducation socialistes (CERES), which called itself "revolutionary" and Marxist and was committed to an alliance of all left-wing parties as a matter of principle (despite the fact that about one-third of its members came from the Catholic Left).[21] There were those who were indifferent to ideology, stressed a technocratic approach to problems, and tried to cultivate good relations with the business community. Furthermore, there were the "Mitterrandists," who were concerned less with dogma than with electoral strategies and the exercise of power. This diversity was mirrored in the composition of the cabinet and the distribution of legislative committee chairs. For these reasons, the PS steadily paid less attention to the leftist demands of the PCF.

In 1984, the gulf between the two parties widened when a new government was formed under Laurent Fabius. The Communist ministers had been invited to stay on, but the PCF executive decided to withdraw them because it was unwilling to accept the austerity program begun a year earlier. The PCF still considered itself a part of the left-wing Assembly majority; it warned, however, that its support of government policies would be selective.

The conflicts within the camp of the Left were paralleled by disagreements within the PS itself. For the first several months following the 1981 electoral victories, there was a "honeymoon" atmosphere that fortified a sentiment of unity. The new government seemed prepared to respond to the claims of the varied elements that had brought it to power: trade unionists, teachers, and disgruntled white collar employees, farmers, and shopkeepers. But in 1982, discord resurfaced within the party over a number of issues: the role of Marxism in Socialist ideology and the extent to which the PS was evolving (or should evolve) toward social democracy; economic policy and the role of the unions; the degree to which private schools should be supported; and the question whether the PS should cooperate fully with, or maintain its distance from, the government. These disagreements, in addition to the jockeying for positions among party personalities, surfaced at the party congresses of the 1980s, with government supporters insisting that public policies faithfully represented socialist values and the feelings of party loyalists, and more-critical Socialist deputies demanding a better clearing of signals with the government.

THE RIGHT AND CENTER IN OPPOSITION

As a result of their loss of power, the Giscardists and Gaullists were confronted with a number of problems, apart from having to get used to opposition status. The major loser was the UDF, which, with the ouster of Giscard from the presidency, lost the focal point of its unity, if not its raison d'être. Between 1981 and 1983, many adherents of the UDF were demoralized and confused about what strategy to adopt. Some UDF politicians switched to the RPR; others suggested that the organization strengthen its position by fusing its parts into a genuine party; and still others felt that the divergences within the UDF were irreconcilable. With the restraining force of a "progressive" president gone, the Republican party and its ally, the club *Perspectives et réalités*, wanted to use their dominant positions to assert themselves and their probusiness ideas more strongly than before. Whereas the PR and the conservative elements of the CDS and Radicals favored a policy of close collaboration with the Gaullists and firm opposition to the government, the more leftist factions of those parties wished to mark themselves off more clearly from the Gaullists and toyed with the idea of leaving the UDF, forming a new center-left coalition, or even making overtures to the Socialists.

But these alternatives were straws in the wind. The system of elections impeded the construction of powerful centrist parties; a rapprochement with the new majority was out of the question as long as the Communist party was part of the government coalition. At the same time, the argument made by some Giscardists that the UDF represented the only alternative for those who rejected collectivism on the one hand and charismatic Gaullism on the other had become unconvincing, since the Socialists' policies turned out to be far from collectivist and the RPR was now much less Bonapartist-authoritarian than the old Gaullist party had been. In fact, the new RPR was not so much Gaullist as "Chiraquist"; it had become the political vehicle of the mayor of Paris, who was proving to be ideologically flexible and successful in attracting middle-of-the-road voters.

The relatively stronger position of the RPR spurred this party to greater efforts at collaboration with the UDF. In 1981, a liaison committee for the two groups was set up in the Assembly, followed in due course by a "reconciliation" meeting between Giscard and Chirac. In the municipal elections of 1983 there was a degree of second-round collaboration between the two groups, which paved the way for subsequent discussions about common platforms for future elections.

Although the UDF was ahead of the RPR in the number of municipal council seats and was holding its own in the Senate, the latter had become the dominant element within the opposition. Yet the RPR was not without problems. Its leader, Chirac, had proven to be a dynamic politician and had helped boost the party's registered membership to over 700,000 by the mid-1980s; yet he was distrusted by many. Some viewed him as too power hungry, and others doubted his commitment to genuine Gaullism. The party's programs had become noteworthy for their imprecision, and their Gaullist features were no longer distinct. The RPR was abandoning the traditional Gaullist statism in domestic policy in favor of a "neoliberal" approach (marked by deregulation, tax concessions to business, cuts in public spending, and the privatization of industries) and replacing an extreme nationalist outlook by a more pro-European one. These changes occurred for several reasons: The mystique of de Gaulle was fading; in order to capture the Giscardist electorate, it was considered necessary to absorb the liberalism of the UDF as well as the policy proposals of Raymond Barre, the former premier, whose popularity was reviving; and, finally, the opinion of the public at large seemed to be moving away from rigid statism.

THE RISE OF THE NATIONAL FRONT

While the Socialists were benefiting from the steady decline of the Communist party, the positions of the RPR and UDF, the "republican opposition," began to be threatened by the rise of the National Front (*Front national*—FN). Founded in 1972 by Jean-Marie Le Pen as a conglomerate of fascists, Pétainists, former Poujadists, right-wing Catholics, erstwhile proponents of *Algérie française*, ultranationalists, anti-Semites, and racists, the party was thrust onto the political scene during the municipal elections of 1983 when it received 17 percent of the vote in Dreux, a medium-sized industrial town near Paris, and in the elections to the European Parliament in 1984, when it got over 10 percent of the vote. After World War II, Le Pen had served as a paratrooper in Indochina; in 1956, he had been elected to the Assembly on the ticket of the Poujadist movement; later, he had fought in Algeria; and in 1965, he had managed the election campaign of Jean-Louis Tixier-Vignancour, who ran for the presidency under the aegis of an extreme-right party.

The FN appealed to various components of the electorate: the unemployed and workers afraid of losing their jobs; people who worried about the rising tide of crime in the cities and the decline of old-fashioned values concerning God, country, and family; and those who resented the presence of millions of foreigners on French soil. Given the relatively small number of Jews and their thorough assimilation, Le Pen's personal anti-Semitism (often expressed with not very subtle innuendo) has had only limited electoral utility. Although anti-Semitism is prevalent among its active membership, the FN has concentrated on stirring up hatred against the more numerous North African Muslims (Maghrebis), who are blamed for the above-mentioned problems and accused of taking advantage of France's welfare services and public housing; their presence will, it is argued, ultimately "Islamize" and "orientalize" French society.[22] For these reasons, the FN has called for the restoration of capital punishment (abolished in 1981), an end to the immigration of non-Europeans, a stricter control of the movements of foreigners, and a change in the citizenship laws to make naturalization difficult. As the appeal of the FN has appeared to increase, some of these policy positions have been gradually adopted by the RPR and UDF.

Because of its extreme-right origins, its nationalism and anticommunism, its appeal to racism, and the rabble-rousing behavior of Le Pen, the FN has often been compared to fascist parties. Yet it differs from them in several respects. It has officially embraced democratic institutions; it does not wish to replace the Fifth Republic; and unlike classic fascism, it has asserted that it does not want to strengthen the state but to curb its influence, particularly with regard to economic activity. It insists that it is not on the extreme right but rather the "liberal" right; it has frequently expressed its admiration of the United States and of the U.S. Republican party, and the FN's socioeconomic program—with its call for greater freedom of enterprise, tax concessions to business, the curbing of the trade unions, and a pruning of the welfare state—echoes the policies of Ronald Reagan and Margaret Thatcher. The FN has appealed not merely to the alienated petite bourgeoisie but to a cross-section of the electorate: middle-class suburbanites, farmers, businesspeople, professionals, and industrial workers.

Le Pen has argued that rather than speaking for the "lunatic fringe," he has merely said out loud what others, especially the politicians in the Gaullist and other conservative parties, have thought.[23] He has attempted to raid the traditional electorate of the RPR and the UDF and, for that reason, embraced a double tactic vis-à-vis these two mainstream parties. On the one hand, he has criticized RPR and UDF for being part of the "gang of four," that is, for not being very different from the PS and PCF. On the other hand, he has tried to portray his party as a republican and legitimate alternative. Although Gaullist and Giscardist politicians have made a number of second-round deals with the FN in subnational elections, the RPR and UDF have refused (officially) to make such deals. Despite the threat posed by the FN to the RPR and UDF, public opinion polls indicated that the Socialists would lose control of the Assembly as a result of the elections scheduled for 1986. In order to contain the damage, the government in 1985 rushed through Parliament a bill that replaced the two-round single-member-district method of election with a one-round system based on proportional representation. It was anticipated that although under the new system, the FN and the PCF would gain entry into the Assembly, the RPR-UDF majority would be considerably reduced.

THE PARLIAMENTARY ELECTION OF 1986: INTRODUCTION TO POWER SHARING

The results of the election of 1986 were a mixed blessing for all the political parties. The PS, although losing its majority in the Assembly, maintained its position as the most popular party in France, but remained confused about its identity. Some Socialists felt that the party should cut away the "dead wood" of ideology and turn to a German or Scandinavian type of social democracy; others yearned for a vaguely defined "ethical" socialism; and still others suggested that now that the PS was in the opposition, the time had come for a return to the sources of socialism and to its traditional working-class clientele. Still others believed that the continued leftist vocation of the PS required that the party mend fences with the PCF. These disagreements could not be resolved, since the PS had to speak for a diverse electorate in which blue-collar workers had become a minority. Moreover, the PS was hardly in a position to translate its orientations into policies.

The RPR and the UDF together, with 291 of the 577 seats, had obtained a bare majority. Although it was sufficient to enable them to produce a government and pursue a number of policy objectives, they were constrained by several factors: periodic interference by a president who still retained a number of constitutionally guaranteed powers, conflicts between the RPR and the UDF, and divisions *within* the ranks of each of these formations.

The smaller parties had their problems too. The PCF had been "saved" by the new electoral system; but with less than 10 percent of the popular vote and its Assembly representation pared to 35, it could not pretend to much influence. Some leaders of the PCF suggested that the party could save its soul and regain the support of the disadvantaged classes by returning to an uncompromising leftist orientation and equipping itself with more-appealing candidates for elective offices. In 1987, the party took a step in that direction by nominating André Lajoinie (the chairman of the Communist group in the Assembly) rather than Georges Marchais as its candidate in the forthcoming presidential elections. At the same time, however, a number of Communists, led by Pierre Juquin, split from the PCF and formed a rival party of "Reform Communists" *(Rénovateurs)*, which chose Juquin as its presidential candidate.[24]

In gaining entry to the Assembly for 35 deputies, the National Front had acquired a degree of legitimacy, but it was unsure about how it should behave. In order to achieve greater respectability, to be considered for some sort of partnership by the RPR and UDF in policy making or power sharing, and to attract uncommitted voters in the next presidential elections, the FN deputies had to eschew extremist rhetoric. However, there was a danger that in so doing, the FN would be perceived as resembling the other right-wing parties too much and risk the loss of its mystique and hence its appeal to what remained of the alienated and antisystem electorate.

THE PRESIDENTIAL AND PARLIAMENTARY ELECTIONS OF 1988

The National Front's appeal was sufficient to cause confusion in the ranks of the RPR and UDF. That confusion was compounded when Le Pen, the FN candidate in the presidential elections of 1988, got 14.5 percent of the vote in the first round. Some Gaullist leaders attempted to retrieve as many of these votes as possible for their own party in the second round by asserting that the RPR had the same concerns as the FN; other Gaullists argued that the RPR should have nothing to do with the FN; and several UDF politicians came out for Mitterrand as the person best able to maintain national unity against the threat posed by Le Pen. In this situation, Chirac temporized; on the one hand, he did not want to alienate those who felt strongly about immigration and other issues stressed by Le Pen. On the other hand, he did not want to risk losing his moderate supporters either to Mitterrand or to Raymond Barre, the UDF candidate. Chirac's fence-sitting was apparent during a television debate. Mitterrand accused Chirac of pandering to the FN electorate, and Barre, by appealing for a tolerant and inclusive society, implicitly invited his own first-round supporters to transfer their support to Mitterrand.

During the campaign for the Assembly elections following Mitterrand's election to a second presidential term, a modicum of unity between the RPR and UDF was restored, as these parties put up joint candidates in most constituencies. Having restored the single-member-district system of elections, they hoped that the smaller parties, among them the FN, would be weakened and Gaullist-Giscardist control of the Assembly would be maintained.

The Socialists expected their candidates to win the parliamentary elections in the wake of Mitterrand's victory. That hope was based in part on the fact that Michel Rocard, who had been appointed prime minister immediately after the presidential elections, projected an image of intelligence and pragmatism and enjoyed wide popularity among Socialists as well as non-Socialists. Indeed, until the eve of the parliamentary elections, public opinion polls predicted that the PS would have a comfortable majority in the Assembly. The result, however, fell short of these predictions: The PS gained merely a plurality of the Assembly seats. There were a number of reasons for that outcome. Mitterrand had been so confident about a Socialist parliamentary election victory that he had declared that "it was not a good thing for France to be governed by a single party" and had called for an "opening up" toward the political center. Therefore, many Socialists thought that their votes would not be needed. Other Socialists felt that their support of Socialist candidates would be a wasted effort, since the programmatic differences between them and those of the Right were not significant enough. Still others were angry at Rocard for having picked too many centrist ministers and therefore having ignored the election results, and others complained that Rocard had appointed too many old-guard Socialists and had thus raised doubts about the Socialist party's interest in an opening toward the political center. Furthermore, there were people who had voted for Mitterrand as a *national leader* but were not necessarily thinking of a Socialist *government*. In addition, some French citizens were tired of having to spend yet another Sunday voting. As a result, the abstention rate was the highest since 1962.

The election outcome, although not a complete victory for the PS, represented a serious enough defeat for the Right to leave it in a state of disorientation. The RPR continued to be torn between its right-wingers, who did not wish to be outflanked by the FN and favored a rapprochement with that party, and its moderates, who preferred closer collaboration with the UDF. In addition, there were politicians in the middle who dreamed of a large right-of-center confederation comprising the RPR, UDF, and CNIP. Faced with possible defections of supporters to more-moderate parties, the RPR leaders announced that their party would make no alliances with the FN in future elections.

The UDF was in a worse position. Almost immediately after the Assembly elections, several leaders of that formation insisted that although it remained an ally of the Gaullists, it was situated in the political center and therefore expected to benefit from Mitterrand's and Rocard's announced efforts at an opening toward the "centrist" mainstream of the electorate. But the UDF leaders disagreed on tactics. Giscard d'Estaing, who had become the official head of the UDF, favored a "constructive opposition"; François Léotard, who led the Republican party, the largest component of the UDF, agreed as long as the principles of his relatively conservative party were maintained; and Barre went even as far as to envisage a future cohabitation with a Rocard government. When the new Assembly met, the CDS—the most "centrist" of the Center—having increased its representation in that chamber from about 35 to 50, constituted itself into a separate parliamentary party under the label of the *Union du centre* (UDC). One result welcomed by all the major parties was the virtual elimination of the National Front's representation in the Assembly.[25]

Early in 1989, as the French were preparing for the elections to the European Parliament, the RPR and the UDF were faced with an incipient rebellion of "young Turks"—Gaullist and Giscardist politicians in their forties—who wished to rejuvenate both formations by wresting the leadership from the "old guard." To abort this rebellion, Chirac and Giscard closed ranks and decided that the latter would lead a joint RPR-UDF slate of candidates for the European elections.[26] The results were encouraging: With 28.9 percent of the vote (compared to 23.6 percent for the Socialist ticket, led by Laurent Fabius), Giscard was considered to have been politically resurrected. The CDS put up its own list, the "Center for Europe," but because of its disappointing performance (8.4 percent of the vote), its political clout was diminished. In mid-1989, a group of "rejuvenators" from both the RPR and the UDF met to discuss the possibility of merging the two formations in order to create a more potent center-right party.

THE GREENS

At the end of the 1980s, both the Right and the Left were faced with a new challenge: the rise of the "Greens." Although environmentalist groups had been in existence for several years in France, their political impact was minimal because the electoral system has not favored small parties and problems of ecology were not in the forefront. Attempts were made periodically to sponsor environmentalist candidates on regional levels, but without much success. In the presidential elections of 1981, Brice Lalonde, the environmentalist candidate, received 3.9 percent of the first-round votes. In the parliamentary election of 1986, the "Green party" *(les Verts)* made a worse showing and (with 1.2 percent of the votes) failed to secure any seats in the Assembly. In the presidential elections of 1988, the Greens (under Antoine Waechter, a young Alsatian politician) did surprisingly well, gaining 3.8 percent of the first-round votes, but his party did poorly in the Assembly elections and in the subsequent municipal elections of March 1989. There are several explanations for those poor showings. The Greens have appealed to a fairly narrow electorate—the younger and better educated. Until two decades ago, the French public was more concerned with economic issues than with environmental or other "postmaterialist" ones; before the Chernobyl disaster and the oil glut of the 1980s, there was little public worry about the safety of nuclear power stations. Furthermore, many of the platform planks of the Greens were not particularly related to environmental issues and were also found in other (especially left-center) parties,[27] and it was therefore more "rational" to vote for those parties; and, finally, environmental issues were gradually taken up by the other parties, notably the PS. In the elections for the European Parliament, the Greens received more than 10 percent of the vote, but these elections had more "expressive" than "instrumental" significance, and the abstention rate was higher than 50 percent.

The position of the Greens as the most credible articulator of environmental concerns was further complicated when Brice Lalonde created a rival party, the Ecological Generation (*Génération écologie*—GE), in 1990. Lalonde came to believe that the environmentalist agenda could best be promoted in alliance with other parties. In the regional elections of 1992, the various environmentalist parties achieved a breakthrough with over 14 percent of the vote (and 212 seats on regional councils).[28] However, the relationship between the Greens and the GE, the two main environmentalist parties, was marked by the personal rivalry between Waechter and Lalonde. The two parties agreed later that year to field a common candidate in every constituency for the next Assembly elections. But the divisions continued to be deep; Waechter envisaged the *Verts* as being neither Right nor Left, but as an alternative to both, and shunned any alliances with either. He opposed "productivism" and raised doubts about the limits of technological progress; and he favored job sharing (a theme Rocard would take up in 1993), local initiatives and referenda, the restoration of proportional representation, the reduction of the workweek, a lower consumption of energy, and support of Third World countries.[29] Lalonde, in contrast, was clearly on the left. Once a member of the PSU, he became minister for the environment in the governments of Rocard and Cresson, and he wanted to use GE as a base for promoting his own political career. While Waechter was considered too dogmatic, Lalonde was viewed as too opportunistic.[30]

THE PARLIAMENTARY ELECTIONS OF 1993

The Collapse of the Left

The 1990s began with clear signals that the Socialist party was in trouble. Many of its former supporters were disenchanted with it because the government with which it was identified seemed to have lost its reformist zeal and had proved unable to solve the problems of immigration, unemployment, and student unrest. The credibility of the PS and the government was seriously affected by evidence of incompetence and by a number of scandals involving ministers: shady business deals, bribes, the transfusion of AIDS-contaminated blood, and improprieties in party financing. An additional factor was impatience with Mitterrand, who had been in office longer than any preceding republican president, and who seemed to be losing his touch, particularly in the conduct of foreign affairs.[31] His popularity had sunk to below 30 percent, and Premier Cresson's ratings were no better. Mitterrand's attempts to freshen the image of his government by a turnover of prime ministers did not help; in the regional and cantonal elections of 1992, the PS experienced heavy losses. Public opinion polls predicted that these losses would be repeated in the forthcoming parliamentary elections.

Nevertheless, the election results came as a shock. They produced the weakest Assembly representation of the PS and its allies since 1968 and plunged the entire Left into disarray. In contrast, conservative parties gained their greatest parliamentary majority since 1815. In terms of the popular vote, the PS, with nearly 30 percent of the total, remained the largest *single* party, but given the existing electoral system, this was of little comfort. The lessons the Socialists drew from this defeat were ambiguous. Several years before the election, the leaders of the PS had been aware of the ideological and programmatic confusions within the party. There was a conflict between the two "cultures" within French socialism: (1) Jacobin, centralist, etatist, nationalist, and protectionist; and (2) decentralist, pluralist, regionalist, and European.[32] The former was dominant, but the latter won out on the level of practical politics, as the PS successfully harnessed its two conflicting impulses: the urge to reform and the need to govern. The conflict persisted in the realm of ideas and was aggravated by personal rivalries and antipathies, notably between Rocard and Fabius. At a congress in 1990, the party was nearly destroyed by its inability to agree on a program. Subsequent party meetings did not resolve these problems, which were shelved in the interest of holding on to power. The cohesion of the PS was threatened anew early in 1991 with the outbreak of the Gulf War. Many Socialist deputies were against the war but adhered to party discipline in supporting it. The exception was *Socialisme et République*, the faction led by Jean-Pierre Chevènement, whose open opposition to France's participation in the war brought about his resignation as minister of defense.

At a congress in 1992—after the defeat of the Socialists in the regional elections, and in anticipation of a legislative election defeat in 1993—Rocard was proclaimed the party's "natural" candidate for the presidency in the next elections; however, the debate about the future programmatic direction of the PS remained unresolved. Rocard called for a "big bang," an implosion of the PS and its outdated ideologies, so that the party could be reconstituted on a different basis. He suggested creating a "vast open and modern movement" embracing Socialists, reform Communists, environmentalists, Centrists, and other reform-minded citizens.[33] Mitterrand reacted by saying that there was nothing wrong with the party's trying to enlarge itself as long as it did not forget its origins and its basic values and did not abandon socialism itself.

Fabius, who had become secretary-general of the PS in 1991, denounced Rocard's proposal as a move to destroy one of the great traditions of French politics. Chevènement denounced it, too; he deplored the absence of clear principles and feared that the new party would be plunged into an ideological "primeval ooze."[34] Rocard's idea was the latest of a series of attempts to "reassemble" the democratic Left, and it rivaled Chevènement's own efforts. Chevènement, who had earlier declared his regional federation independent of the PS, quit that party altogether in mid-1993 and formed a new party, Citizens' Movement (*Mouvement des citoyens*—MDC), which was to serve as an instrument for the recomposition of the entire Left, including former Socialists, ex-Communists, left-wing Gaullists, and Christian Democrats. A prototype of such an umbrella group, the *Réfondations* movement, had in fact been created in 1991. Given its composition—it contained dissident Communists and disaffected Socialists in addition to Chevènement and his allies—the MDC resembled the old PSU in its disorganization.

At the end of 1993, the MDC claimed only 3 deputies and 7,500 members, because Chevènement's leftism was not convincing to many (except for his continued preference for *dirigisme* and his reservations about decentralization, which were shared by some old-time socialists). Chevènement's opposition to French participation in the Gulf War had been inspired by ultranationalism, anti-Americanism, and pro-Iraq connections, not by any specifically "socialist" visions; in fact, after the outbreak of the Gulf War, while still formally a member of the PS, he had proposed to gain supporters by assembling around the "republican idea."[35]

At a meeting of the executive committee in 1993, Rocard, who had been named provisional leader of the PS and charged with rebuilding it, called for a statement of "concrete utopias";[36] instead, he heard speeches affirming the "values of the Left, [among them] laïcité, humanism, and social justice" but no agreement on specific policies. Ironically, the only Socialist leader who still articulated concrete leftist positions—on incomes, immigrants, social security, and human rights—was Mitterrand himself, but he could afford to do so because he had ceased to function as an active policy maker. Since the parliamentary elections, he had distanced himself as much as possible from the PS, so that he could continue to act as a transpartisan chief of state. Resentment of Rocard's leadership was expressed both by the more dogmatic leftists and by Mitterrand's friends (among them Fabius)—all of whom undermined Rocard's chances of obtaining the party's nomination for presidential candidacy. While the committee produced a resolution entitled *"Refonder,"* which called for "a break with the Marxist dogma of the nationalized enterprises . . . and [recognized] the dynamism and efficiency of the market economy,"[37] it failed to propose a positive socialist program of action. Rocard was still regarded as the "virtual" (Socialist) candidate for the presidency, but since he had lost his election bid for Parliament in 1993, some questioned this choice. At a party congress that year, the new orientations were reconfirmed; however, the congress failed to produce a clear program of action on unemployment and other socioeconomic issues or to defend the record of the outgoing government. Despite the weakening of the party's social activism, that record was quite respectable, by and large embodying many of the traditional concerns associated with democratic leftism. But the record was marred by the corruption associated with power, with several ministers having been implicated.[38]

The job of rebuilding the PS promised to be difficult because its internal divisions persisted—between the "old guard" and the young, the intellectuals and what remained of the working-class activists, and the ideologues and the pragmatists. There was also the problem of lack of support from Mitterrand, although some PS politicians thought that in view of the president's own loss of standing nationally, such support was neither necessary nor useful. In fact, some Socialists argued that the party's electoral disaster was largely the consequence of Mitterrand's failing leadership and his indifference, as a lame-duck president, to the fate of the party he had helped to create. As a popular writer put it, "Monsieur Mitterrand is so honest that he intends to give back the Socialist party in the same condition in which he received it."[39]

Efforts at widening the party's support base were impeded by problems in its relationship with other left-wing parties. The Left-Radical group (MRG) was still formally allied to the PS, but this alliance was strained by the failure of the PS leadership to defend Bernard Tapie, a prominent MRG politician, against accusations of questionable business practices. It would be even more difficult to recruit the centrist CDS as an ally, for despite the occasional policy disagreements of its leaders with the positions of the new right-of-center government, the party leaders saw no reason to abandon the UDF, since they had been paid off with ministerial posts by Edouard Balladur, the Gaullist prime minister.

There remained the possibility of a future PS alliance with the Communists. For the time being, however, such a prospect was not favorable, given the mutual hostility between the PCF and Rocard. In 1991, the PCF had joined the Right in voting for censure of Prime Minister Rocard; it had done the same in a vote against Prime Minister Bérégovoy in 1992. The PCF had also shown little leftist solidarity in its voting on Socialist-sponsored legislation. The party remained too Stalinist for a rapprochement with the PS, even after the collapse of the Soviet Union, as long as Marchais retained the leadership, and attempts by certain Communist politicians to reform the party had been unsuccessful. The PCF had saved its Assembly seats, but with a membership of under 200,000 (compared to 630,000, 15 years earlier), it was a shadow of its former self. Its further decline was seen as unavoidable unless it became more moderate. Perhaps in recognition of this, Marchais, secretary-general since 1972, announced that he would resign his position in January 1994. He was succeeded by Robert Hue, a relatively young and moderate Communist who was supported by reformers and appeared to be more amenable to intraparty pluralism.

The Victory of the Right

The *Union pour la France du progrès* (UPF), with 85 percent of the Assembly seats, was the great victor in the 1993 elections or, rather, the beneficiary of the repudiation of the Socialist government. The UPF, an alliance of the RPR and UDF, had been created in 1990 in response to the double defeat of the Right in 1988. Some envisaged this new alliance as a step toward fusion; that, however, was out of the question because of the different traditions of the two major components and, above all, the continuing rivalry of their leaders. Although the RPR and UDF had cooperated during the campaign for the regional elections of 1992, the losses of the PS had not redounded meaningfully to the benefit of the UPF, for the biggest gains went to the FN and the environmentalist parties.

The coherence of the UPF was impaired by disagreements on the question of European unity. In 1992, during the public debate preceding the referendum on the Treaty of Maastricht, the majority of UDF politicians and their supporters favored that treaty, whereas the RPR was divided. Ultimately, most Gaullists came to support the treaty, although they denounced Giscard and other UDF politicians for appearing jointly with Socialists to argue for it. After its ratification by referendum, the two components of the UPF concentrated on a joint electoral strategy for the 1993 elections: a common platform, a common position against the Left as well as against the National Front, agreements for mutual support in the second round, and work toward a common presidential candidate. The UPF won by default, despite continued competition between the RPR and UDF in the second round in most constituencies.

The fact that the UPF had captured 80 percent of the Assembly seats and was able to constitute a cohesive government did not resolve the problem of disunity. Disagreements on political strategy persisted, specifically regarding the question of the standard-bearer in the forthcoming (1995) presidential race. Many Gaullists continued to regard Chirac as the "logical" candidate of the RPR-UDF; but some Gaullists preferred a U.S.-

style "primary" to select a common presidential nominee. The choice would be made by a national convention composed of elected officeholders at national and subnational levels and of delegates elected in local primaries by registered party members. Some UDF politicians continued to support Giscard; others, identified with the UDF as well, preferred to wait and see.

The new Assembly met amid uncertainty whether the CDS would organize as a separate parliamentary group. As we have seen, such a group had been constituted after the 1988 elections, and in 1989, the CDS had asserted its identity by running an independent slate of candidates for the European Parliament. Now the CDS demanded, as its condition for remaining in the UDF parliamentary group, that one of its members be supported for the post of Assembly speaker. The UDF agreed to that condition; but when a Gaullist was selected instead, the CDS remained in the fold because Giscard and most of the other leaders of the UDF promised to accept the pro-European orientations of the CDS. Nevertheless, many CDS deputies remained uneasy; they argued that the ministers belonging to their group were ignoring its policy orientations in the interest of government solidarity.

The uneasy relationship between the UDF and the RPR was paralleled by disagreements between the government and Parliament (especially the Senate) and within Parliament itself. There were also tensions between the government and Assembly Speaker Philippe Séguin, who differed publicly with Balladur in being both more nationalist (on Europe) and more "social" (on domestic policy). The deputies belonging to the UDF (with some exceptions, mainly in the ranks of the Republican party) were more welfare-state oriented, more tolerant toward immigrants, and more "European" than were Gaullist deputies. The UDF also remained more positive toward European unity. In constructing his government and choosing his policies, Balladur took these divergences into account; he was open to the development of the European Union, but tough in protecting the interests of the French farmer in WTO negotiations, and his policies on civil rights, employment, and constitutional reform represented compromises between conservative and progressive positions, as well as between his own preferences and those of Mitterrand.

A major source of conflict was the question of cohabitation, where positions were based less on principle than on tactical considerations. Chirac was hoping that cohabitation would be conflict-ridden, so that Mitterrand would be driven to resign prematurely, thereby provoking an early presidential election in which the mayor of Paris would be better placed than any of his rivals. Most UDF politicians preferred a "soft" cohabitation because of their "centrist" attitudes and because they wanted the government that had given them considerable power to last as long as possible. The longer it lasted and governed effectively, the less certain would be Chirac's presidential chances. Giscard had been skeptical about a renewed cohabitation several weeks before the election but afterward softened his position.[40]

Cohabitation with a Socialist president proved to be less delicate for Balladur than "cohabitation" with Chirac, who pretended to support government policy fully but did not want it to be too successful, lest Balladur become so popular that he would be preferred as the conservative presidential candidate over Chirac. Conversely, Chirac did not want to see that policy so *unsuccessful* that the French electorate, known for its quick changes of mood, would turn away from the Gaullists. At the end of 1993, Simone Veil and François Léotard, the two top non-Gaullist ministers, came out bluntly in favor of Balladur's candidacy, not only because he would provide the best way out of the endless Chirac-Giscard rivalry, but also because he was already the preferred candidate of the public at large as well as of the Gaullist electorate. Balladur himself continued to insist that his political interests were limited to his governmental tasks and kept Chirac fully informed, while the latter reaffirmed his support for Balladur's conduct as prime minister.

The Marginalization of the Environmentalists and the Containment of the Extreme Right

One of the consequences of the 1993 elections that was regarded as positive by both the UPF and the PS was the uncertain future faced by their rivals and potential spoilers, the National Front and the environmentalist parties, respectively. Full support by the environmentalists could not have saved the PS, but it could have reduced the extent of its defeat. The PS, having little to lose, offered to back environmentalist candidates unilaterally in the second round if they came out ahead in the first round, but both Waechter and Lalonde refused to reciprocate. The environmentalists' cockiness could be attributed to their respectable performance (at the expense of the PS) in the European Parliament elections of 1989 and in the regional elections of 1992. However, the environmentalists ended up with no Assembly seats at all. Some months after Balladur's appointment as premier, Lalonde said that he would not rule out future "cooperation" with a "liberal and social" government, a statement for which the Greens denounced him.[41] The "war of the chiefs" was put on hold when Waechter was replaced as secretary-general by Dominique Voynet, who was more open to collaboration with the PS.

In terms of its membership, its well-established local machines, and the clarity of its program, the National Front appeared to be in a more solid position than the environmentalist parties. Its performance in recent presidential, local, and European elections had been so respectable that some Gaullists and Giscardists were ready to make common cause with it. However, most of the UPF politicians were opposed, and in the end, the National Front was not needed. It was not a viable alternative to the right-of-center parties, because a large majority of the electorate considered it a threat to democracy.

Nevertheless, the FN had influenced the dialogue and the policies of the mainstream parties. This was reflected in expressions of intolerance vis-à-vis immigrants by Gaullists and Giscardists—for example, Chirac's statement about the "overdose" of immigrants, with their "noises and odors," and a Giscard article about the "invasion" of the country by foreigners.[42] Even the Socialists were not immune to such rhetoric. Thus, Rocard suggested that France could not receive the poor of the whole world, and Cresson spoke about chartering airplanes to fly some immigrants back to their countries of origin. Soon after assuming office, the Balladur government introduced bills to tighten controls over immigrants and limit rights of asylum, measures that potential supporters of the FN would be expected to approve.

Such expressions and measures have served to keep many French voters in the "republican" Right. Although the FN won 14 percent in regional elections in 1992, it ended up with no deputies in the Assembly. The electorate was apprehensive about the party's platform of 1991, some of whose 50 "propositions" were plainly unconstitutional. This was particularly true of provisions dealing with immigrants, such as expulsion, separate social security provisions, and detention by the police.

THE PRESIDENTIAL ELECTIONS OF 1995

The conflicts between and within the various political formations were unresolved as they prepared for the presidential elections of 1995. Each formation had its difficulties, but none more so than the Socialist party. Rocard, its most prominent personality, was no longer considered a viable candidate for the presidency, since his leadership of the PS in the European Parliament elections of 1994 had netted the party only 12 percent of the vote. Rocard had to compete for the democratic-leftist vote against a separate list of the MRG led by Bernard Tapie, which Mitterrand had apparently tacitly supported in an effort to undermine Rocard's position. After this poor performance, Rocard was eliminated from serious consideration as the standard-bearer of the PS, and he relinquished his leadership of the party. The ensuing quest for the best Socialist presidential candidate took place in an atmosphere of pessimism. The rival ambitions of the leaders of the various PS factions and the fact that the party as a whole had been increasingly discredited forced it to look for someone who was considered immune from that discredit. There were indications that the PS might still win the presidency if it chose as its candidate Jacques Delors, a former minister of finance, a political moderate, and the outgoing president of the European Commission. However, he declined to be nominated, and the PS chose Lionel Jospin as the alternative candidate at a special convention of more than 1,000 party activists. Jospin, who had been a minister of education, was not enthusiastically supported by all Socialist politicians. Mitterrand gave him only a perfunctory endorsement and refused to campaign for him.[43] That refusal was not necessarily a bad thing for Jospin; it was, in fact, the obverse of his own ambivalent relationship to the outgoing president. On the one hand, Jospin could not openly disavow Mitterrand, whom he had succeeded as secretary-general of the PS; on the other hand, he tried to distance himself from the scandals and policy failures during Mitterrand's second term by preaching a new kind of socialism and by suggesting that he represented a "new Left."[44]

The electoral victories of the Gaullists and their political allies in 1993 had augured well for them as they prepared for the presidential race. It was assumed that Chirac would be the Gaullist candidate and that Balladur would "hold the fort" for the party as prime minister. However, after several months in office, Balladur was encouraged to become a presidential candidate himself. As late as January 1995, polls showed Balladur ahead of Chirac, and it was widely believed that the former would easily be elected. Although a Gaullist of long standing, Balladur was embraced as the favored candidate of the UDF, which had declined to field a candidate of its own. He became the official choice of the Republican party (PR) and the CDS, the two major components of the UDF. Suddenly, however, the enthusiasm for Balladur began to wane; he was faulted for his patrician demeanor, the scandals involving members of his government, and a number of policy fiascos.

Voters had reservations about the three major candidates as well as the parties they represented. This situation was reflected in the fact that two weeks before the first round, 20 percent of the electorate was still undecided. This indecision, which persisted into the second round, was due to the difficulty of discerning programmatic differences between the Gaullist and Socialist candidates, specifically, between Chirac and Jospin. There were minor differences regarding domestic socioeconomic policy; while Jospin campaigned for "a more fair-minded France" *(une France plus juste)*, Chirac, like a born-again progressive, adopted a "social" (if not socialist) position with his slogan, "France for everyone" *(une France pour tous)*.[45]

In the end, nearly 40 percent of the electorate voted for minor or marginal parties. The National Front, with 15 percent of the popular vote, obtained its best score ever in presidential elections, and might have done even better had it not been for the candidacy of Philippe de Villiers and his *Mouvement pour la France*. That party was located ideologically midway between the RPR and the FN; in its nationalist and anti-European stand, its criticism of immigrant policy, and its emphasis on traditional authority and "family values," it articulated many of the positions of the FN, but did so in more measured tones.[46] The Communists managed to improve on their performance of seven years earlier, because after the collapse of the Soviet Union, the PCF was no longer regarded as a threat to the republican system and because of the reasonable and moderate rhetoric of Robert Hue, the party's new secretary-general.[47] The Greens' candidate, Dominique Voynet, won a most disappointing vote of less than 4 percent, in part because of continuing divisions within the ecologist movement and in part because the environment was not an issue during the campaign.[48] Arlette Laguiller, the candidate of the Trotskyist Workers' Struggle *(Lutte ouvrière—LO)*, received a better score than de Villiers and Voynet; but that was due less to the credibility of her party's radical program than to her personality and her dynamic campaigning style, which reflected a degree of ideological purity.[49]

The runoff between Chirac, who had edged out Balladur, and Jospin, who, surprisingly, had come in first, was a traditional bipolar contest. Those who had voted for the PCF and the other left-wing parties in the first round (including most of the Greens) now voted for Jospin, while the UDF and the first-round electorate of the *Mouvement pour la France* rallied behind Chirac. Although Le Pen refused to endorse Chirac, the latter had turned sufficiently to the right between the two rounds so that most of the FN electorate opted for him.

The contest between a Gaullist and a Socialist candidate suggested that the Right-Left division of the electorate still held. Yet it was unclear whether this presidential election—or preceding Fifth Republic contests—should be seen as a plebiscite between two persons, and hence an electors' choice between two candidates independent of political parties, or whether the process was driven by parties. Some observers have argued that the mainstream parties have remained the major driving forces behind presidential elections;[50] others have insisted that presidential elections in the Fifth Republic have personalized electoral choices and "presidentialized" the mainstream parties.[51] On the one hand, most successful aspirants to the presidency have become candidates by virtue of their status in a preexistent party, which adopted them as its standard-bearer. On the other hand, party endorsement has not always been enough, as evidenced by the poor performance of

Chaban-Delmas, the official Gaullist candidate in 1974. A presidential candidate, once chosen by his party, cannot win unless he expands his traditional electoral base by reaching out to supporters of other parties—by creating an ad hoc "presidential majority," as Giscard had done in 1974 and as Chirac was to do in 2002. The victory of a presidential candidate depends also on his ability to take advantage of shifts occurring *within* his (Right or Left) electoral camp, and to encourage movement from one camp to another.

Most observers agreed that the presidential contest in 1995 took place in the context of widespread pessimism about the future of the French economy. The voters' uncertainty about whether any of the mainstream parties could deal effectively with problems of unemployment, an overloaded social security system, and a deficit-ridden treasury was reflected in the increased vote for marginal parties in the first round and the relatively high (20 percent) abstention rate in the second round (again, much as in 2002).

THE PARLIAMENTARY ELECTIONS OF 1997

In April 1997, Chirac decided to dissolve the Assembly and call for early elections. The existing Assembly had an overwhelming RPR-UDF majority; it would have given Chirac and Alain Juppé, the prime minister, ample power to push through the legislation necessary to qualify France for participation in the European common currency (the euro), which was originally scheduled to be inaugurated in January 1999. Such participation would require reducing the government deficit to below 3 percent of the GDP, which would in turn require cutting expenditures for social security coverage and miscellaneous subsidies.

There were stumbling blocks ahead for the majority party if it waited until March 1998, the end of the five-year term of the Assembly, for new elections. All the reforms could not be enacted before that date; to expect Juppé to make the necessary decisions with elections looming was unrealistic, especially given his unpopularity; suggestions to replace him with a more popular figure were equally unrealistic, given Chirac's personal friendship with Juppé. If the election were held in 1998, the voters would rebel and punish the Juppé government and the RPR and UDF for reducing the welfare-state benefits that the people considered their due. In order to avoid such an outcome, Chirac wanted an Assembly that would support his policies for the full five years remaining of his presidential term. He calculated that if the elections took place in 1997, the right-of-center parties would maintain their control of the new Assembly, albeit in a somewhat reduced form.

The hope that the RPR-UDF would win the elections was not without merit. In contrast to the left-wing parties, which continued to be divided, the RPR and UDF appeared to be in a cohesive alliance. They were part of a "presidential majority"; they had a common electoral platform and agreed on joint candidates in more than 500 constituencies. There continued to be disagreements within both the RPR and the UDF between the neoliberals, who argued for a wider role of the market, and those who favored the retention of an important responsibility of the state in the area of social protection. In the end, however, the two factions seemed to converge.

Chirac's calculations proved wrong; the Socialists, with the help of other left-wing parties, regained control of the Assembly, thus forcing Chirac to share power with them.

The recovery of the Left from its humbling defeat only two years earlier attested to the fickleness of the French electorate. To some extent the result reflected the issue orientation of the voters, who punished the right-wing incumbents for their policy failures, notably the failure to solve the unemployment problem.[52] The result was also a disavowal of Juppé, not only for the ambiguities of his policies, but also for his failure to achieve the impossible: reduce the deficit, maintain economic growth, and at the same time keep the existing levels of wages and social benefits. Juppé was punished additionally for his style of government and for what was widely regarded as his arrogant and patronizing behavior, which had made him the most disliked premier of the Fifth Republic. Conversely, many voters opted for a leftist candidate because they preferred a government headed by Socialist Jospin, who had acquired considerable stature as the Left's major presidential candidate in 1995.

The defeat of the right-wing parties and the voters' disavowal of Juppé amounted to a defeat of Chirac as well. Because of his unfortunate call for early Assembly elections, not only was he forced into power sharing, but he also saw his decision-making authority weakened.

The contest of 1997 was remarkable in several other respects. The rallying to the support of the PS by all the left-wing parties in the second round and the minor right-wing parties' coming to the support of the RPR-UDF in that round might have suggested that France had returned to a traditional Right-Left equilibrium; but that was not quite the case. The growing importance of the FN was an important electoral factor. With nearly 15 percent of the popular vote in the first round and enough support to maintain second-round candidates in 133 out of the 577 districts, the National Front demonstrated its power, not to win elections for itself, but—as a participant in 76 "triangular" races in the second round (compared to 14 in 1993)—to influence the outcome of the elections. There is little doubt that the decision by many (perhaps one-third) of the first-round FN voters to sit out the second round or to support Socialist candidates contributed to the victory of the Left.

The PS also benefited from successful preelectoral accords with other leftist parties. An alliance with the Greens had been facilitated by the evolution of that party toward the left; an understanding with the PCF had become possible because of the attitude of its leader, Robert Hue. Under him, the PCF had achieved a new image as a relatively moderate party inclined to constructive collaboration with the PS. The PCF had acknowledged the failings of Soviet communism, embraced internal party pluralism, and accepted the market economy (albeit with modifications). Moreover, given the collapse of the Soviet Union and the end of the Cold War, the epithet "socialo-communism" had lost its relevance for the majority of the voters, who regarded the participation of the PCF in government as a positive development. Most of the parties of the Left ran separate candidates in the first round but agreed to back the best-placed candidate in the runoff. In addition, there was a special agreement between the PS and the Greens under which a number of candidates of each of these parties were supported by the other in the first round, and an agreement between the PS and the MDC on the first-round support of incumbent deputies of either party.

The election results left the RPR and the UDF in a state of turmoil, as most of their leaders distanced themselves from Juppé and began to fight for control of their party and the restoration of unity of the two formations. A number of options to achieve these aims were being discussed. One of them was the fusion of the RPR and UDF or, more ambitiously, the dissolution of both and their replacement (possibly under a new name) by an enlarged right-of-center party. This reincarnation would require ending the personal rivalries and the blurring of differences between and within the two formations, notably between the neoliberals and etatists on the one hand and the Europeanists and nationalists on the other. Chirac had tried to harmonize these conflicting positions, but after the Assembly elections he was no longer in a position to do so. This was particularly the case after a rival of Chirac's, Séguin, who was interested in running for the presidency in the future, was elected president of the RPR. In the face of the RPR's internal problems, the suggestion that the UDF merge with the Gaullists was not compelling; in contrast, some people argued that the UDF should maintain its identity and run its own candidate in the presidential elections of 2002. Precisely what that identity amounted to was, however, open to question, given the ideological gap between two components of the UDF: the increasingly laissez-faire-oriented PR and the more "social" orientation of the *Force démocrate* (FD, the former CDS), which, with about 35 deputies, had become strong enough to constitute a separate parliamentary group if it had been so inclined. In 1997, under the leadership of Alain Madelin, the PR renamed itself *Démocratie libérale* (DL)[53] and soon thereafter left the embrace of the UDF.

After the departure of the DL, little was left of the UDF except the Radical-Socialist party and the CDS. The former maintained a tenuous existence in the affiliation of a number of local and provincial notables; and the latter, having given up its status as a separate parliamentary party in 1993, was organizationally weaker than before. In order to compensate for that weakness (and to further the presidential ambitions of its leader, François Bayrou), the CDS attempted to enlarge itself in 1995 by incorporating the *Parti social-démocrate*, a smaller UDF component, and transforming itself into a new party, *Force démocrate* (FD), consisting mostly of aging Catholics.[54] The FD hoped to become a great centrist party, open to all "from Balladur to Delors," thereby contributing to the internal restructuring of the UDF. The creation of the FD was a response to a parallel move by the club *Perspectives et réalités*, which had transformed itself a few months earlier into a political party under the pretentious label *Parti populaire pour la démocratie française* (PPDF).[55] What still unites both of these parties is a mild progressivism and a strongly pro-European orientation, plus a distaste for both right-wing and left-wing extremism. The electoral prospects of each of these components, and of the UDF as a whole, are dim. Between 1998 and 2001 attempts were made to fuse these components into a single party, but arguments persisted about the division of funds between them.

The Left, meanwhile, basked in the glow of its victory. In sum, that victory was the result of a number of factors: (1) the incumbent government's unpopularity; (2) the strong leadership of Jospin, who had managed to mute the factionalism within the PS and overshadow his rivals; and (3) the fading memory of Mitterrand, whose leadership had been associated with broken promises and corruption scandals. The Left's electoral program reflected a considerable convergence of views on the following: a minimum wage increase; a reduction of the workweek from 39 to 35 hours; the end of privatization; and the creation of more than 300,000 public sector jobs.

The harmony of the Left had its limits. The PS continued to be divided between Europeanists and Euroskeptics, and the MDC and PCF persisted in their doubts about the common currency and about the extent to which the new government could be relied on to pursue its "social" goals. There was also a conflict between the old, who wished to guard their retirement benefits, and the young, who were either in the active labor force and had to pay for these entitlements or were hoping to enter the job market. However, as the Jospin government began, goodwill prevailed: PCF leader Hue reacted with understanding to Jospin's policy proposals, not all of which corresponded with the priorities of traditional Communists.

Chirac's collaboration with more conservative elements within the Gaullist party was to some extent paralleled by Jospin's collaboration with a variety of leftist deputies. The fact that the Left had a significant majority did not mean that Jospin could count on automatic parliamentary support for his policies. In order to minimize Socialist discontents and make up for having omitted prominent PS leaders—the old party "elephants"—from his cabinet, he had several of them appointed to chairs of Assembly standing committees. This move did not take sufficient account of the Left's "pluralism," for when the new Assembly met, the noncommunist allies of the PS constituted themselves into a common parliamentary group labeled Radical, Citizen, Green (*Radical, citoyen, vert*—RCV) in order to make their weight felt more strongly—and they registered their disappointment at not having been assigned committee chairs. Furthermore, almost immediately after his policy declaration to Parliament, Jospin was criticized for his insufficiently redistributive economic policies, not only by Communist deputies, but also by several Socialist ones. To be sure, there was a limit to such criticism: All leftist deputies (including the Communists) committed themselves to sufficient discipline to keep the Jospin government in power.

THE ELECTIONS OF 2002

Most observers predicted that the presidential elections of 2002 would be a replay of the 1995 elections, except that the field would be more crowded than before. There were 16 candidates (more than in any previous election) in the first round, ranging from Le Pen of the radical-Right FN to the extreme ("Trotskyist") Left; but it was widely assumed that Jospin and Chirac would emerge as the two top vote getters and face each other in the second round.

The result was so unexpected that it was characterized as a "political earthquake." Chirac came in first and Le Pen second, having edged out Jospin by less than 1 percent (see Table 4.3). Only three months before the first round, Jospin was well ahead of the other candidates in most public opinion polls, while Chirac's popularity was declining. He had been accused of corruption (while he was mayor of Paris), but was saved from indictment because of his presidential immunity. He was seen as an opportunist who had few principles and no clearly defined program.

In contrast, Jospin was regarded as a good prime minister, appreciated for his policy achievements and his personal honesty. However, unlike Chirac, who was a seasoned campaigner, Jospin was regarded as a boring speaker. He committed a number of tactical

TABLE 4.3
Presidential Elections: Popular Vote, 2002

	First Round, 21 April		Second Round, 5 May	
	Number	Percent	Number	Percent
Jacques Chirac (RPR)	5,666,440	19.88	25,537,956	82.21
Jean-Marie Le Pen (FN)	4,805,307	16.86	5,525,032	17.79
Lionel Jospin (PS)	4,610,749	16.18		
François Bayrou (UDF)	1,949,436	6.84		
Arlette Laguiller (LO)	1,630,244	5.72		
Jean-Pierre Chevènement (MDC)	1,518,901	5.33		
Noel Mamère (*Verts*)	1,495,901	5.25		
Olivier Besancenot (LCR)	1,210,694	4.25		
Jean Saint-Josse (CPNT)	1,204,863	4.23		
Alain Madelin (DL)	1,113,709	3.91		
Robert Hue (PCF)	960,757	3.37		
Bruno Mégret (MNR)	667,123	2.34		
Christiane Taubira (PRG)	660,576	2.32		
Corinne Lepage (CAP)	535,911	1.88		
Christine Boutin (FRS)	339,142	1.19		
Daniel Gluckstein (PT)	132,702	0.47		
Registered Voters	41,191,169			
Number Voting	29,498,009	71.60		

SOURCE: Ministry of the Interior.

CAP	*Citoyenneté, action, participation*	MNR	*Mouvement national républicain*
CPNT	Hunters' party	PCF	Communist party of France
DL	Liberal Democrats (*Démocratie libérale*)	PRG	Party of the Left Radicals
FN	National Front	PS	*Parti socialiste*
FRS	*Forum des Républicains sociaux*	PT	*Parti des travailleurs*
LCR	*Ligue communiste révolutionnaire*	RPR	Rally for the Republic
LO	Workers' Struggle (*Lutte ouvrière*)	UDF	Union for French Democracy
MDC	Citizens' Movement	*Verts*	Greens

errors, among them boasting too much about his record and attacking Chirac for being "old, worn-out, and tired." More important, he alienated a number of politicians who had been part of his "pluralist Left" coalition and raised doubts among working-class voters about the leftism of the Socialist party and about his own orientation. The PS platform contained the usual socialist points about employment, housing, solidarity, and equality.[56] In mid-campaign, however, Jospin leaned too far (and prematurely) to the center by insisting his program was not "socialist," thereby contributing to the demobilization of the leftist electorate: Part of it abstained or opted for one of the rival left-wing candidates, while believing that Jospin would make it to the second round anyway. Equally important was the "spoiler" candidacy of Chevènement, who took crucial votes away from Jospin by using his leftist credentials, as well as the fact that Le Pen siphoned off a number of traditionally leftist votes of those who were upset with Jospin's lack of concern about rising crime.

The second-round runoff between Chirac and Le Pen was anticlimactic; Chirac won easily, with over 80 percent of the popular vote. This impressive score should not be interpreted as a clear-cut popular endorsement, for Chirac had received only 20 percent of the first-round vote, a record low for a front-runner, or 700,000 votes less than he had received in the first round in 1995. His victory was possible only as a result of support from the Left, who opted for him in the name of "republican defense," giving him more votes than he got from the mainstream Right. The Left rejected Le Pen overwhelmingly because he was believed to endanger democracy. Symptomatic of this belief was the slogan "Vote for the crook, not the fascist!"

The 2002 presidential election was a temporary disruption of the "normal" bipolar contest, for in the first round, the electorate was split into *three* parts: One-third voted for the mainstream parties; one-third, for Right and Left extremist parties; and one-third abstained.[57] In sum, Chirac was preferred by a third of the French electorate, those well integrated into the political system. This pattern was not completely changed in the second round, in which the abstention rate remained high.

The parliamentary elections that followed revolved around two conflicting arguments. The republican Right argued for a "coherent" majority to enable Chirac to promote urgent legislative action and called for a solid vote for his supporters. The Left was reluctant to give too much power to Chirac; it wanted to preserve an executive-legislative equilibrium and asked the public to vote for the Socialists and their allies, so that cohabitation could continue.[58]

The political Right gained an unprecedented victory, capturing three-fourths of the Assembly seats (see Table 4.4). This result was no surprise. Several months before the first round of the presidential elections, Chirac had formed the *Union en mouvement* (UEM), an alliance of various right-wing formations led by Gaullist politicians, which would support his bid for reelection. The UEM was reminiscent of another presidential election alliance, the UDF of the mid-1970s. Michèle Alliot-Marie, the head of the RPR (which had been created by Chirac 25 years earlier) was not happy with the appearance of the UEM, fearing—correctly, as it turned out—that it would swallow up the RPR to the benefit of Chirac.

Many Gaullists shared Alliot-Marie's fears about the danger to the RPR. Among the proposals to avert its disappearance was a change of name (again), but that was criticized immediately as "putting a coat of paint on a dilapidated party"—a reference to the fact that the RPR membership had declined in 1999 to fewer than 80,000 members. However, Gaullism had been banalized; the invocation of the mystique of a leader no longer worked, and some intellectuals considered Gaullism a "museum piece."[59] In recognition of this reality, several proposals were made to merge the right-of-center republican parties (already cooperating in an *"intergroupe"* in Parliament) into one major electoral force. The UEM was one such proposal; it corresponded to a proposal made earlier by Balladur for a *Union pour la réforme*, which was to unite all right-of-center formations in preparation for the 2002 elections.

Just before the presidential runoff, the UEM was transformed into the *Union pour la majorité présidentielle* (UMP), composed of the RPR in addition to *Démocratie libérale,*

TABLE 4.4
Parliamentary Elections: Popular Vote, 2002

	First Round, 9 June		Second Round, 16 June	
	Number	Percent	Number	Percent
Lutte ouvrière (LO)	301,984	1.20		
Ligue communiste révolutionnaire (LCR)	320,467	1.27		
Other extreme Left	81,558	0.32		
Communist party (PCF)	1,216,178	4.82	690,807	3.26
Socialist party (PS)	6,086,599	24.11	7,482,169	35.26
Left Radicals (PRG)	388,891	1.54	455,360	2.15
Miscellaneous Left	275,553	1.09	268,715	1.27
Greens (Verts)	1,138,222	4.51	677,933	3.19
Pôle républicain	299,897	1.19	12,679	0.06
Other environmentalists	295,899	1.17		
Regionalists	66,240	0.26	28,689	0.14
Hunters (CPNT)	422,448	1.67		
Miscellaneous	194,946	0.77	13,036	0.06
Union for the Presidential Majority (UMP)	8,408,023	33.30	10,029,669	47.26
Union for French Democracy (UDF)	1,226,462	4.85	832,785	3.92
Liberal Democrats (DL)	104,767	0.41		
Rassemblement pour la France (RPF)	94,222	0.37	61,605	0.29
Mouvement pour la France (MPF)	202,831	0.80		
Miscellaneous Right	921,973	3.65	274,374	1.29
National Front (FN)	2,862,960	11.34	393,205	1.85
Mouvement national républicain (MNR)	276,376	1.09		
Extreme Right	59,549	0.24		

SOURCES: National Assembly: <www.assemblee-nat.fr/elections/resultats.asp>; EPF-Election Politique France: <www.epf.fr.fm>; and <www.2002.sofres.com/default.asp?k=1>.

part of the UDF, and smaller parties of the republican Right. Unlike the UDF, it was regarded as a full-fledged political party rather than a federation of parties. Nevertheless, it considered itself "pluralistic" and promised to respect the sensitivities of its varied components (i.e., nationalist, liberal, progressive, Catholic, etc.). In order to protect their existence, these components would be assured of a part of the party's financial resources. The effectiveness of the Chirac bandwagon was such that the legislative election results could be seen as a reconfirmation of the presidential elections. One indication of the power of presidential coattails is the fact that of the 17 members of the Raffarin government who were candidates for Assembly mandates, 16 were elected, 7 of them in the first round.[60]

The Left was unable to stop the Chirac avalanche. The Socialist party was demoralized, and—after Jospin retired from politics—leaderless. The traditional divisions within the Left continued, with each of the formations—MDC, PCF, Greens, and Trot-skyists—presenting its own slate of candidates. In order to preserve a modicum of Left unity, preelection accords were made between the PS and the smaller parties, but these brought only limited results. Yet without such accords (under which the PS gave up a number of constituencies to endorse Communist candidates in the first round), the PCF would probably not have obtained enough votes to constitute a parliamentary party. The PCF had lost the support of many members of the working class who believed that under the leadership of Hue, the party had sold out to the PS for the sake of power, and they voted for the National Front.[61] Most of the remaining members were aging.

At a national postelection conference, the PCF debated ways of retrieving its traditional electorate. Neither Marie-George Buffet, the new secretary-general, nor Hue wanted the party to be dissolved into a greater formation of the Left; but whereas the former called for a "frankly anticapitalist" orientation, the latter opposed a return to the previous (Stalinist) radicalism, as demanded by a few remaining hard-line ideologues.[62]

Other parties fared much worse. The MDC was practically dead; and the *Pôle répub-licain*, under whose label Chevènement had run for the presidency, had ceased to have meaning. The MDC's slate of candidates did very poorly in the legislative elections; Chevènement's spoiler behavior had alienated the Socialists, and he lost the Assembly seat he had held for 29 years. Now his own political future was in doubt. During the campaign, Chevènement had tried to appeal to both the Right (especially the nationalist supporters of Philippe de Villiers, a former right-wing and anti-European candidate for the presidency), arguing that the Right-Left cleavage had been transcended and the use of the two labels had become irrelevant.[63] After the elections and the collapse of his own party, Chevènement, arguing that he had always been a leftist, sought ways of "reinte-grating" into the camp of the Left.

The Greens barely managed to get a handful of seats in the Assembly, and Do-minique Voynet, the party's leader, failed to regain her own Assembly seat. The Party of the Left Radicals (*Parti des radicaux de gauche*—PRG), formerly the MRG, whose presidential candidate got less than 2.5 percent of the vote, was likely to continue its political life as an appendage of the PS, and the Trotskyists were expected to retreat to their habitual obscurity. Meanwhile the leaders of the PS were engaged in a replay of the debates of the past as it discussed its future: what leadership to choose, and whether to return to a more authentic "socialism" or evolve to a more modern "social democracy." Yet, following the rules of bipolarization, the PS remained the only realistic representative of the opposition.

The prospects of the smaller parties of the mainstream Right outside the UMP were no more auspicious than those of the non-Socialist Left. *Démocatie libérale* had too few deputies to constitute a parliamentary party, and its leader, Madelin, had no choice but to rally to the side of Chirac. The UDF was not in much better shape: After a number of its political leaders had shifted their support to the UMP, a mere rump survived under the leadership of François Bayrou, who refused to give up its independence. Although the UDF was able to constitute itself into a separate parliamentary group, it had no power, for the UMP did not need it and owed it nothing.

The National Front remained an identifiable political presence, but its future was in doubt. In a 1998 by-election, the party had lost its only Assembly seat. In the same year, Bruno Mégret, the FN's second in command, had a fight with Le Pen and seceded, forming a rival party, the *Mouvement national républicain* (MNR), which took away some of the FN's 40,000 dues-paying members. The FN and the MNR have a common ideology, including hostility to immigrants, xenophobia, a concern with national identity, opposition to abortion, a return to traditional authority structures and values (especially Christian ones), the fight against insecurity, and, in the interest of law and order, the enlargement of the police, the building of additional prisons, and the restoration of the death penalty. The two parties appeal to much the same audience. But there are differences: The FN has a larger proportion of the popular electorate, whereas the MNR, appealing to former members of the FN bureaucracy, is more bourgeois, masculine, and educated, ideologically committed, and racist. Both fight against the enlargement of the authority and membership of the European Union, are antiglobalization, and oppose multiculturalism. Both oppose NATO and American "imperialism" (and Le Pen has openly supported Saddam Hussein, the Iraqi dictator). Although originally inspired by etatism, the FN came to be a defender of market liberalism. The MNR shares this outlook, although it calls upon the state to do more to fight unemployment and protect the rights of pensioners (without being specific regarding the way to do it). Each of the two parties is supported by a number of clubs or circles.[64]

Despite Le Pen's performance in the first round of the presidential elections, his party was weak. His 16.86 percent was an antiestablishment protest vote rather than a clear endorsement of his party, for in the legislative elections, its candidates got 11.34 percent in the first round, and—owing to abstentions and switches to the UMP—only 1.85 percent in the second. Mégret's performance was even worse. Although Le Pen is aging, the FN may survive, but not the MNR. According to a specialist on the extreme Right, France has room for populist nationalism, but not technocratic nationalism.[65]

There have been other right-wing parties that were regarded as "bridges" between the RPR and the FN, and their future hangs in the balance. These included the *Mouvement pour la France* (MPF), created earlier by Philippe de Villiers, who, having questioned the Gaullism of Chirac and his dedication to national sovereignty, had left the PR (and the UDF) to become a presidential candidate in 1995. In 1999, Charles Pasqua, a former Gaullist, formed another right-wing party, the *Rassemblement pour la France* (RPF), which fused with the MPF and contained elements from the RPR as well as the FN and *Démocratie libérale*. Pasqua tried to persuade a regional right-wing politician, Charles Millon, to join it, but the RPF folded after only nine months due to personal conflicts between Pasqua and de Villiers.[66] Millon, meanwhile, after widely criticized attempts to make a deal with the FN to keep his presidency of a regional council and after leaving the UDF, had founded his own party, *La Droite*, rebaptized in 1999 *Droite libérale chrétienne* (DLC), which he hoped would be a "great pluralistic gathering of the French Right," a euphemism for an umbrella under which the FN could find a place, too.

The situation of the Hunters' party—actually "Hunting, Fishing, Nature, and Traditions" (*Chasse, Pêche, Nature et Traditions*—CPNT) is more hopeful. It was founded in the early 1990s to fight against European Union rules to limit the hunting of migratory birds. Although a small party, it has succeeded in politically mobilizing French citizens who are hunters.[67] The CPNT has exerted influence on mainstream Right and Left parties, and it has clashed in particular with the Greens, especially over the question of limiting the hunting season. During the parliamentary debate on this issue, the government-sponsored bill, which adhered to the EU position, was dramatically altered in the Senate due to CPNT pressure on the right-wing majority.[68] The appeal of that party is attested by the fact that it received 1.2 million votes (6.77 percent of the total) in the European Parliament elections of 1999 (see Table 4.5) and that its leader, Jean Saint-Josse, without waging a serious campaign, received more votes in the 2002 presidential elections than the Communist candidate.[69]

The most recent national contests illustrate several important points about parties, elections, and politicians in France. They suggest that the goal of gaining and retaining

TABLE 4.5
**European Parliament and French Subnational Elections:
Votes by Party, 1998–2001, (in percentages)**

	European Parliament 1999	Regional 1998	Cantonal 2000	Municipal 2001
LO and LCR	5.18			
Other extreme Left		4.4	0.6	0.06
PCF	6.78		9.8	
PS-PRG	21.95		22.4	23.80
Miscellaneous Left		1.1	6.2	6.20
Pluralist Left		35.4	45.8	
Greens	9.72		6.0	6.00
Other environmentalists		2.8	0.6	0.60
Miscellaneous		2.4	1.1	1.10
UDF	9.28		12.5	12.30
RPR	13.05		12.3	17.00
UDF-RPR		1.3[a]		
Miscellaneous Right		4.7	17.0	
Hunters	6.77	2.7		
National Front	5.69	15.3	7.1	7.10
MNR	3.28		3.0	3.00

Sources: European Parliament: *L'Année politique 1999*, p. 37; regional: Pierre Martin, "Les Elections régionales et cantonales des 15 et 22 mars 1998," *Regards sur l'actualité*, no. 240 (April 1998), 43; cantonal: *Le Monde*, 17 March 2001; municipal: <www.cevipof.msh-paris.fr/dossiers/municip2001>.
[a]In the 1998 regional elections, the UDF and RPR combined.

LO	*Lutte ouvrière*
LCR	*Ligue communiste révolutionnaire*
MNR	*Mouvement national républicain*
PCF	*Parti communiste français*

PRG	*Parti des radicaux de gauche*
PS	*Parti socialiste*
RPR	*Rassemblement pour la République*
UDF	*Union pour la démocratie française*

power is more important than loyalty to a program or a party and that this goal is pursued in terms of traditional Right and Left divisions. The coherence of individual parties within these divisions has weakened, in part because they no longer have clear programs. This condition applies especially to the mainstream parties, which can no longer be easily distinguished from their smaller allies or from one another. Therefore, it is not surprising that there have been shifts both within and across these divisions; that many voters did not make up their minds about their choices until the last moment before each round; that only 12 constituencies produced a victor in the first round in 1997 (compared to 80 in 1993); and that about a third of the electorate in 1997 expected little more from the new government than they received from the old.[70]

Regardless of such shifts, there continues to be a "core" party within each camp. On the Left, the PS has functioned as the nucleus for the leftist revivals since 1981. It got the largest number of popular votes in the Assembly elections of 1993 and 1997 and more than 47 percent of the popular vote in the presidential runoff in 1995. Its organizational apparatus remains in place, and despite losses in membership, it still counts about 120,000 card-carrying adherents,[71] a large proportion of whom are activists. Some of its younger leaders have been among the most popular politicians in the country.[72] Because of the strengths of the PS and the weaknesses of other leftist parties—the Left Radicals,[73] the Greens, and the PCF—those parties, although structurally independent, are likely to orient toward and collaborate with the PS.

On the right, the "core" position of the RPR could not be matched by the UDF, an umbrella organization that was unable to transcend its internal divisions. Its failure to differentiate itself convincingly from the Gaullists made it difficult to find credible presidential candidates, so that in 1995 it had to look outside its own ranks. Before the 1997 parliamentary elections, the UDF managed to preserve its identity by capitalizing on the discontent with Chirac and by selectively criticizing government policies, but these actions constituted an insufficient basis for the continued existence of that formation, neither of whose mainstays, the PR and the FD, counted more than 15,000 members. Since the PR (rebaptized DL) left the UDF in 1998 and much of the remainder of the latter was co-opted by the UMP in 2002, the future of the UDF was in doubt.

Both de Villiers's *Movement pour la France* and the CNIP are likely to remain marginal. The former, if it continues to exist at all, will remain a "flash" party dependent on its leader, but only to the extent that it is able to articulate a position sufficiently distinct from that of the FN and the right-wing Gaullists.[74] The CNIP has a longer history and, with several thousand municipal councillors, a more institutionalized presence in local elected offices. But its national electoral base is too small to figure as an effective political force, and it has been widely regarded as little more than a "passageway" between the RPR and the National Front. The FN seems to have succeeded in demarginalizing itself; its membership has grown; it is organizationally solid; it is increasingly implanted in local constituencies; and it did well enough in municipal elections in 2001 to gain about 1,000 municipal councillors and capture control of the government in four cities. Yet despite its growing electorate, its national power remains limited and it is unlikely to become strong enough to gain a significant place in the Assembly, let alone capture the presidency, as was shown clearly in 2002. The FN inspires fear in the majority of the voters; it is regarded as posing a danger to democracy because of both its overidentification with France's authoritarian interlude and its racism. The leaders of the RPR and UDF shun an alliance with the FN, at least on a national level. Finally, like the mainstream right-wing parties, the FN can no longer invoke the fear of communism.[75]

THE FUNCTIONAL RELEVANCE OF POLITICAL PARTIES

The preceding discussion has given the reader some idea of the diversity of French political forces and ideologies. Although such a discussion is meaningful from a historical point of view, the question of how ideological distinctions among parties relate to the political process and political behavior remains. Many scholars have pointed out that in the past, the multiplicity of parties rendered the maintenance of stable governments difficult, since these governments were based on tenuous coalitions. Each party's insistence on its uniqueness—an insistence that signaled the importance that French politicians (many of whom have been intellectuals) have attached to ideas—impeded the aggregation process. But it did not make the process impossible. In the Fourth Republic, there was an area of agreement among most parties about certain essentials, such as the preservation of the republican system, the pursuit of minimal welfare-state policies, and the need for economic planning.

Among members of Parliament there has been, from the Third Republic to the present, the same kind of esprit de corps that is found in other democratic legislatures. Robert de Jouvenel may have exaggerated when he asserted that "there is less difference between two deputies, one of whom is a revolutionary and the other is not, than between two revolutionaries, one of whom is a deputy and the other is not."[76] Nevertheless, it is true that often enough members of political parties have not acted in a manner conforming to the party's ideology when they entered alliances or voted on issues. There has always been a certain degree of opportunism (or pragmatism) among party leaders, particularly deputies—a phenomenon that has accounted for the widespread notion among the French, since Rousseau's time, that parliamentary parties are mainly power seeking and guilty of betraying by coalition deals the ideologies to which they are ostensibly committed.

Unnatural Alliances

This cynical view of parties can be substantiated by reference to a number of political practices. There have been "unnatural" preelectoral and parliamentary alliances involving political parties representing mutually hostile ideologies. Alliances have been determined by accidents of geography and personality, the institution of the single-member-constituency system of elections, and the fear of being left behind by political developments and of having to forgo a share of power. As noted earlier, in 1944–1945, the clerical MRP and the anticlerical Socialists and Communists collaborated in a tripartite coalition; in 1971–1972, the anticlerical Radicals and the Catholic Democratic Centrists constructed an electoral alliance and later joined the Giscardist alignment. This experiment was subsequently repeated: The *Force démocrate*, established under the leadership of a Christian

Democrat and embracing the clericalist CDS, stressed the principle of *laïcité* in order to make room for the Radicals.

In 1958, most of the SFIO supported the return of de Gaulle and the ratification of the new Constitution, despite its reservations about the man and the regime. In 1968 and 1969, the Communists tacitly supported the Gaullist regime despite their criticism of the reactionary nature of Gaullism. In the early 1960s, the Democratic Centrists were in the opposition because of their anti-Gaullism, but they were gradually co-opted into a pro-Gaullist stance in 1969 and into a new "presidential majority" in 1974. Chirac and other Gaullist leaders have at times suggested that the National Front is located within acceptable political parameters and at other times asserted that it is a danger to democracy. Le Pen himself has, on the one hand, attacked the RPR and UDF for being in collusion with the Socialists and, on the other, deplored the refusal of those parties to collaborate with him. In 1984, Raymond Barre asserted that he could identify with several of Le Pen's themes, but in a debate with Chirac four years later, Barre distanced himself from Le Pen. In 1986, Barre considered a "cohabitation" between a right-of-center Assembly majority and a Socialist president unthinkable and called for the resignation of the latter, but in 1988, he held open the possibility of participating in a Socialist government. After the Assembly elections in the same year, the CDS constituted itself as a separate parliamentary party while remaining a component of the UDF. In 1995, Giscard supported the candidacy of Chirac rather than that of Balladur, to whom he was ideologically closer. In 1996, when Giscard was factored out of the leadership of the UDF (an event presumably engineered by party leader François Léotard), Giscard, rather than supporting Léotard, (vainly) opted for Alain Madelin, a "classic" liberal, with whom he disagreed on economic policy, to succeed him. Before the first round of the presidential elections, Charles Pasqua, an anti-European Gaullist, supported the pro-European Balladur rather than Chirac, whose position on Europe was at that time more nuanced. Before and after the presidential elections of 1988, Mitterrand simultaneously played the roles of coordinator of Socialist strategies and of transpartisan father figure. The relationships between the Socialists and the Communists from 1965 on, and between the Gaullists and the Giscardists from 1962 on, have been, by turns, those of allies, rivals, and antagonists. In 1995, Robert Vigouroux, a Left-Radical senator from Marseilles, endorsed the presidential candidacy of the Gaullist Balladur, and in 1997, Le Pen, although detesting socialism, called upon his electorate not to support Chirac and Juppé and made favorable remarks about Jospin despite the latter's alliance with the Communists. As soon as their candidate was eliminated in the first round of the presidential elections of 2002, the majority of the Socialist and extreme-Left electorate decided to shelve its partisan interests and to vote for Chirac in order to prevent the election of Le Pen and preserve the republic.

Political Wanderings

France has been notorious for the political wanderings of deputies from one parliamentary party to another.[77] Examples of party switches, political fence-sitting, pragmatic adaptations, and even political "bigamy" are numerous. Practitioners have included Michel Debré and Jacques Chaban-Delmas, who switched from the Radical to the

Gaullist party during the Fourth Republic; Mendès-France, who left the Radical party to become a cofounder of a Left-Socialist party (the *Parti socialiste autonome,* the precursor of the PSU, a party that Jospin also joined in 1960 before returning to the PS in 1971); and Max Lejeune, a Socialist who started his own party, the *Mouvement démocrate-socialiste de France;* convinced that the Socialist program had already been achieved, he made his party part of the conservative majority in 1974. Other examples are Chirac, a Gaullist who in 1974 opposed the official candidate of his party and supported Giscard, only to become his bitter rival from 1976 to 1995, a rivalry moderated by intermittent "reconciliations" and appearances of collaboration; Michel Jobert, a Gaullist, who was Pompidou's foreign minister in the early 1970s but, when Giscard became president, formed his own party, the *Mouvement des démocrates,* and later, in 1981, supported Mitterrand and was rewarded with a cabinet position; Edgar Faure, who shifted uneasily between Radical party leadership and Gaullism, attempting to *combine* the two in his person. Still other examples are Alain Peyrefitte, who had been a minister of justice under Giscard and who, although himself a Gaullist, was so pro-Giscard that he tried to help the president in efforts at co-opting the rest of the Gaullist politicians; Françoise Giroud, a leftist journalist who voted for Mitterrand in 1974 but subsequently became a minister in the government headed by Gaullist Chirac; and Michel Durafour, Jean-Pierre Soisson, and Lionel Stoléru, all prominent Giscardists who became ministers in the second government of Socialist Rocard under the label of *France unie.*[78] More recent examples are Charles Fiterman, who was a prominent member of the *Refondations* movement in 1993 while continuing to be a leading figure in the PCF; Chevènement, who was a member of the same organization while simultaneously building up his *Mouvement des citoyens;* Bernard Kouchner, who moved from the PS to the Left Radicals in 1996; Yvon Blot, whose political wanderlust has taken him from the CNIP to the RPR and to the National Front; Noëlle Lenoir, a prominent Socialist who supported Chirac in his presidential campaign in 2002 and was rewarded with a cabinet post; and Brice Lalonde, who has moved toward whatever political constellation was in power.[79] A particularly interesting case is that of Olivier Stirn, a "centrist" politician, who served as a minister under Presidents Pompidou, Giscard d'Estaing, and Mitterrand. He began his political career as a left-wing Gaullist; subsequently joined the Radical-Socialist party; was elected to Parliament in 1989 on a Socialist ticket; supported Gaullist Chirac in the presidential elections of 1995; and in 1999 joined Madelin's *Démocratie libérale* in order to provide the latter with a left wing and promote an "authentic radicalism."[80] Finally, there is the case of Mitterrand himself who belonged to, and even led, four or five political organizations.[81]

Sometimes the partisan positioning of politicians is a tactical response to an electoral outcome or the consequence of strategic calculations. Thus, after the legislative elections of 1988, the CDS had enough seats in the Assembly to form a parliamentary group; but after the legislative elections of 1993, it gave up its separate identity and again became a part of the UDF Assembly contingent. The group *République et liberté* was formed in the Assembly after the parliamentary elections of 1993 to provide an organizational home for deputies who belonged to a variety of leftist parties and wished to identify neither with the Socialists nor with the Communists.

After the regional elections of 1998, Jacques Blanc and Charles Millon, right-wing members of the UDF, made deals with the National Front in order to retain the presidencies of their regional councils (Languedoc-Roussilon and Rhône-Alpes, respectively). In 2002, after Chirac's reelection, they made up with the UMP. Blanc proclaimed that he would vote in the first round of the parliamentary elections for the UMP candidate rather than for the candidate of his own party, *Démocratie libérale*. Millon withdrew the parliamentary candidates of his party, *Droite libérale chrétienne*.

The Place of Ideology

In terms of their outlooks, programs, and behavior, the political parties have evolved beyond the ideologies that originally inspired them, either because these ideologies became irrelevant or because they ceased to have adequate electoral appeal. Thus, the anti-clerical stand is now less meaningful because the rapid urbanization of France has led to a significant weakening of clericalism. The class-struggle notions of the PCF have become less compelling, partly as a result of the growing embourgeoisement of a segment of the French working class. The poorest of that class, the foreign-born workers, might still be attracted to radical-leftist ideology, but they have not voted in significant numbers, because they are not yet naturalized or politically socialized.

The split between parties advocating liberalism and those favoring interventionism is a false dichotomy today; most parties on the right were long ago converted to some measure of *dirigisme*, and leading politicians of the mainstream parties on both sides of the political divide have more recently embraced a variable number of "neoliberal" theses that stress the importance of market forces. The argument that divides the parties is not whether there should be economic guidance by the state, but what kind of incomes policy, social production, or sectoral roles a particular economic policy should entail. Colonialism and anticolonialism ceased to be relevant issues in the early 1960s, after France had completed its decolonization process. Jean-François Revel, a commentator on French politics, has listed the following as points of convergence between Right and Left: the veneration of the state; the glorification of public service; a distrust of free enterprise; a tendency to raise taxes; and the cultivation of anti-Americanism.[82]

To be sure, to the extent that is electorally feasible, the right-of-center parties continue to cater to the more privileged sectors of society; and within the Socialist party, there is still a large faction (once heavily influenced by Mitterrand himself) informed by a redistributive impulse. Despite the conversion of several PS politicians to a centrist orientation, most of the Socialist party factions are still committed to traditional socialist goals: the expansion of the welfare state, a progressive tax system, decent wages, more-democratic access to education, and the promotion of human rights. There is no longer a clear line of division between the PS and the RPR-UDF over important foreign-policy questions, such as participation in NATO, the nuclear strike force, and the Arab-Israeli conflict, but (except for the institutional development of the European Union, which most minor parties oppose for a variety of reasons) these are not matters that interest the majority of French citizens. It is true that in 1996, disagreements broke out within the RPR-UDF about policies of employment, social security, the national deficit, and a common European currency, but these conflicts reflected tactical positions rather than deeply held programmatic preferences.[83] One issue on which the Left and the Right have continued to differ is that of the (largely Muslim) immigrants, the former being committed to liberal naturalization laws and the latter to more-restrictive policies. However, in expressing its hostility to these immigrants, the Right has selectively embraced the *laïciste* positions formerly associated with the Left![84]

Emmanuel Todd, a French sociologist, remarked that "it took centuries to establish [the] ideological structures [of France]" and only five years to liquidate them.[85] This remark may be an overstatement, but it is widely agreed that all the mainstream political parties have been emptied of their traditional ideological content in much the same way as churches have been emptied of worshippers. French voters find it difficult to adhere to a major political party, because they can no longer clearly distinguish its orientation from that of a rival party. The parties have become increasingly nondescript ideologically and have "converged" because of two developments that have taken place in the past two decades in France (as elsewhere in Western Europe): (1) the decline of the appeal of the Catholic church, which "has drained the Right of its sociological substance"; and (2) the decline of the "smokestack" industries, which has ended "the proletarian dream of the Left."[86] The partisan "wars of religion," as a well-known commentator on the political scene has called them,[87] have ended because of *alternance* (the successful changing of the guard beginning in 1981) and the three "cohabitation" experiences, which have moderated the distinctions between the majority and the opposition; because of a growing consensus about the political system; and, with the celebration of the bicentennial of the French Revolution in 1989, because of the gradual ending of arguments about the heritage of that great event. To be sure, in 1995 and 2002, each presidential candidate had a "program";[88] but it is not clear whether programmatic details were decisive for the behavior of the electorate. Similarly, political values and voter preferences are not always clearly correlated with political party. It is true that those who identify with the Left (PCF, PS) tend to demarcate themselves from the Right (RPR and UDF) in terms of general values: The Left stresses liberty, equality, human rights, solidarity, and tolerance; and the Right stresses morality, authority, the nation, and individual responsibility. According to a public opinion survey, however, while on certain issues there was significant consensus between the two camps—for example, on the importance of the family, progress, the Republic, national identity, and citizenship, there were positions that both the mainstream Right and the FN had in common.[89] Such commonality, in addition to tactical opportunism, helps to explain why in the regional elections of 1998 the FN supported a number of UDF politicians in their quest for the presidencies of regional councils.[90]

In these cases, the "issue" division was so sharply drawn that some commentators have suggested that there are several orientations that have supplanted the traditional Right-Left divisions and that overlap them: (1) Europeanism versus nationalism; (2) decentralization versus centralism; (3) accommodation to the masses versus protection of the elite; (4) a pluralist versus a monistic vision of the state; and (5) the predominance of an interventionist state versus the autonomy of socioeconomic subsystems.[91] To some French political scientists, the various positions expressed during the debate over the referendum on the Maastricht Treaty overlapped the traditional party cleavages to such an extent that they posited 10 views, images, or "visions" of France instead of the simple Left-Right distinctions: a positive and optimistic vs. a negative and pessimistic outlook; a convergent vs. a centrifugal view of society; a tolerant vs. a repressive attitude; an urban vs. a rural orientation; and a national-secular vs. a social-Christian ideology. Alternatively, the division has been seen in the following cleavage lines: pro-Europeanism vs. anti-Europeanism; elitism vs. egalitarianism; pluralism vs. monism; and centralism vs. localism.[92]

These new divisions are reflected in the behavior of decision makers. Several examples of transpartisan episodes provide illustrations of the growing irrelevance of party labels for decision makers.

1. The decentralization controversy from 1982 to the present: In most cases, politicians were pitted against one another not so much on the basis of Right or Left ideology as on the basis of their individual power positions and ambitions. A similar mixture of Right-Left attitudes can be found on related issues, such as the support of multiculturalism and the question of expanded autonomy for Corsica.

2. The Gulf war in 1991: French participation was supported by most Socialist politicians (after Mitterrand had decided on that policy for reasons, not of principle, but of global opportunism), as well as by the leaders of the RPR and UDF, and opposed by the PCF, the FN, and selected ultranationalistically oriented (and anti-American) Socialist and Gaullist politicians.

3. The controversy in 1992 over the ratification of the Treaty of Maastricht that created the European Union: It was favored by Mitterrand and the majority of PS politicians, by Giscard and most of his followers, and by Chirac (in an ambiguous fashion) and half of the RPR politicians; it was opposed by the PCF, the FN, the *Mouvement pour la France*, and selected nationalists from the Socialist, Gaullist, and Giscardist camps.

4. The question of the electoral calendar: When Jospin introduced a government bill to switch the dates of the parliamentary and presidential elections scheduled for 2002, so that the latter would precede the former, he was supported not only by the Socialist deputies (who were assuming—falsely as it turned out—that he would win the presidential race, which would lead to a Socialist parliamentary victory on his coattails) but also by several UDF deputies.[93]

5. Globalization, which has been supported by *Démocratie libérale* and, with qualifications, by the RPR and a segment of the PS; and opposed by the PCF, the extreme-Left parties, the National Front, and the Greens.

6. The assessment of the Vichy regime and its connection with preceding and succeeding republics.[94]

7. The anti-terrorism bills: When these were introduced in Parliament in 2002, the Socialists, the MDC, and some UDF deputies supported them; the Greens, Gaullists, and *Démocratie libérale* opposed them; and the PCF abstained.

The programmatic eclecticism of parties does not mean that the citizens' identification with parties has come to an end, nor does it suggest that old expectations have totally disappeared. There is still a Right-Left cleavage; in the legislative elections of 1997, 88 percent of voters who labeled themselves on the left voted for candidates of the "pluralist Left", 94 percent of those labeling themselves on the right voted for right-wing parties—as did 64 percent of artisans, shopkeepers, and corporate executives—while only 51 percent of workers voted for the pluralist Left; and 75 percent of practicing Catholics voted for the Right.[95] Yet Left-Right orientations are no longer equated with specific leftist or rightist parties, because these have been constantly evolving. Since the PS became a party of government, it lost much of its oppositionist mystique and many of its left-wing supporters.

There is no doubt that the Left has been "tamed" in France (as elsewhere) and has become *embourgeoisé*. It has even been argued that since it has become the party of government, it has been "Americanized," so that it has less to do with Marxism and has come to resemble the American Democratic party.[96] This may be an exaggeration; yet in terms of public policy there is some doubt whether the general sentiments of the Left have played a decisive role. In the early 1980s the Left deregulated financial markets; during Mitterrand's 14-year presidency, the gap in incomes and wealth increased; under the Jospin government there were more privatizations than under Juppé; and it was a Socialist finance minister who restored the favorable treatments of stock options, which had been suppressed under right-wing governments. In view of the above, it is not a surprise that an increasing number of the well-to-do in France have been voting on the left.[97]

During the municipal elections of 2001, for example, dissatisfaction with the Socialist government was reflected in the formation of *"Motiv-é-s,"* a left-oriented "social movement," which generated a high degree of youthful enthusiasm on the local level. It had considerable impact in Toulouse (where it received 13 percent of the first-round vote) and a number of Parisian suburbs, and it cut into the traditional Socialist support base.

The fact that, statistically, the majority of the French electorate has been on the right side of the dividing line ideologically in most national elections does not clearly correlate with "conservative" programmatic expectations, for the majority of right-wing voters have accepted policies once associated with the Left but that have become so institutionalized that they are no longer an electoral issue, such as statutory medical coverage, minimum wages, paid vacations, and family income subsidies. According to an exit poll conducted after the first round of the presidential elections of 2002, voters indicating a preference for a specific candidate based their choice on what they believed to be his or her programmatic strong points; still, candidates of several parties shared these points (see Table 4.6). The lack of clear meaning of Right and Left may account for the steady decline of dues-paying members in most of the political parties. It may also explain why party identification is no longer as reliable as it used to be. Today, such identification tends to be based not so much on shared beliefs as on narrow instrumental considerations, disappointments in the conduct of rival parties, peer group imitation, feelings of comradeship (as in the case of many members of the PCF), cultural resentments (as in the case of many FN supporters), and the personal appeal of party politicians. It is often said that in the first round of parliamentary and presidential elections, voters exercise their true preferences, whereas in the second round they vote "intelligently," by choosing the lesser evil. There is considerable disagreement, however, about what motivates voters in either round.

Voters' Choices, Programs, and Personalities

Political scientists in France continue to argue about the meaning that voters attach to the parties' programs and the influence of the citizens' social condition on their electoral behavior. Low income and working-class status correlate significantly with voting for a

TABLE 4.6

Issue Salience and Candidate Preference, Presidential Elections of 2002 (in percentages)

	Mean	Laguiller	Besancenot	Hue	Jospin	Chevènement	Mamère	Bayrou	Madelin	Chirac	Le Pen
Law and order	48	39	29	29	36	50	26	49	54	56	68
Employment	36	56	44	41	44	30	33	30	43	32	27
Social inequities	33	51	53	56	55	32	55	20	20	18	18
Retirement pensions	27	34	24	40	29	30	16	23	36	25	29
Education and training	22	18	27	24	27	22	25	33	29	15	19
Immigration	21	9	10	7	10	19	9	11	21	17	57
Environment	20	19	26	16	19	15	73	14	12	12	13
Maintaining state authority	19	7	9	15	12	25	10	18	21	24	28
Preserving health system	16	16	20	22	21	19	17	18	18	13	16
Tax system	16	14	7	12	13	11	11	15	40	17	20
Corruption	16	17	17	18	21	26	20	14	13	6	19
Place of France in the world	16	5	6	8	13	20	11	22	26	23	17
Purchasing power	15	21	18	21	14	12	11	10	18	16	14
Length of workweek	12	19	17	15	14	6	13	7	16	11	11
Globalization	9	11	16	15	8	11	25	9	12	5	8
European integration	9	4	7	8	13	9	13	18	12	8	4

SOURCE: CSA exit poll, 21 April 2002, of 5,352 persons. Pierre Martin, personal communication.

NOTE: Responses to the question: "At the time you cast your vote, what issue counted most for you?" Each person could give three responses, indicated in percentage by column. Italic figures refer to the maximum percentage for each voting group and those higher than the mean (first column) by 10 points or more.

left-wing party, especially in parliamentary elections. There is an equally impressive correlation between middle-class status, Catholic observance, small-town background, and a conservative orientation.

But such correlations are not perfect. Catholics have been voting increasingly for left-wing parties; conversely, there are workers who vote for right-wing politicians. In public opinion surveys of 1980,[98] 35 percent of workers interviewed had confidence in Premier Barre's leadership, as had 52 percent of artisans and 62 percent of small shopkeepers (as compared with 85 percent of industrialists), indicating either that Barre's "neoliberal" economic policies were interpreted as essentially progressive or that many of Barre's supporters had a noninstrumental view of his leadership. Exit polls taken in the 1988 presidential election revealed that 38 percent of industrial workers voted for a right-wing candidate on the first ballot (about half of them casting their votes for Le Pen); and that, conversely, more than one-third of the farmers and about 30 percent of the artisans and shopkeepers voted for Mitterrand.[99] In 1995, according to another exit poll, 56 percent of industrial workers voted for a right-wing presidential candidate, with half that number (27 percent) voting for Le Pen.[100] Polls conducted in the past several years reveal that some of the traditional political labels still have positive connotations, but these polls also show that a growing number of respondents no longer consider the notions of "Right" and "Left" to be useful for understanding the positions of political parties.[101]

Furthermore, polls have shown that ideological affinities or self-classifications are not congruent with support of presidential candidates representing political parties usually labeled as right-wing and left-wing—except, perhaps, for supporters of the PCF and the National Front. It has also been noted that the votes for major presidential candidates have often been greater than those received by candidates of their parties in parliamentary and subnational elections, as has been true of de Gaulle and Chirac in relation to the Gaullist party, Le Pen and the FN, and Mitterrand and the PS. An illustration of the lack of clear relationship between the voters' electoral preferences and their views of political leaders on the one hand, and their appreciation of the political system and their policy expectations on the other hand, is a series of public opinion polls conducted in the fall of 1993, according to which a majority were dissatisfied with the way France was governed and were pessimistic about the prognosis for employment, prosperity, and social peace, yet had confidence (ranging from 57 percent to 68 percent) in Balladur's leadership and were prepared to vote for him in a presidential contest.[102]

The voters' subsequent abandonment of Balladur in favor of Chirac can be explained in part by the fact that at the time of the presidential election, the latter was not in power on a national level and was therefore not punished for the government's policy shortcomings. This may suggest that there were good "instrumental" reasons for the voters' behavior. However, it has been argued that electoral campaigns have their own logic, which does not clearly correspond to explanations in terms of rational (i.e., socioeconomic) choice.[103] In the first round of the 1995 presidential elections, 26 percent of the working-class electorate voted for Chirac; and 19 percent still rallied to him in the second round, after he had returned from a "social" orientation to a more conservative one.[104] One observer has attributed Chirac's electoral success, not to his program, which lacked precision and coherence, but to his dynamism, his flexibility, his populist campaign style, and his appeal to women and youth.[105]

The lack of a clear correlation between ideology, party identification, and policy expectations can be seen from the results of an earlier poll (1978), which revealed that 29 percent of the PS electorate declared itself to be unfavorably inclined toward the Common Program's nationalization plank (and 14 percent of Communist supporters were equally unfavorably inclined).[106] The extent of support of the Socialists in 1981 roughly corresponded with the degree of popular belief in government intervention in economic and educational matters; but, as noted earlier, it is equally true that the French have come to attach a greater value to economic security than to liberty.[107] At the same time, it is doubtful whether most of the French would accept unlimited nationalization of industry or even a radical leveling of income differentials.[108]

All the major parties or political camps have at times been forced by popular pressure or economic realities to depart from their ideological positions. The Gaullists were obliged to moderate their nationalism and, in the face of perceptions of Soviet threats during the Cold War, their anti-Americanism; the Giscardists embraced the welfare state more enthusiastically than their nucleus, the Republican party, had been willing to do in the past; many Communist politicians realized that a retrieval of the party's lost support depended on a greater effort at distancing themselves from the Soviet Union; and fiscal pressures forced the Socialists to moderate their redistributive orientations.[109]

Given these compromises, French voters have increasingly made choices on the basis of personality and other nonprogrammatic (or noninstrumental) criteria—a development that has been accentuated by the growing importance of television during election campaigns. For several years, many French people supported Giscard d'Estaing, not because they endorsed, or even understood, his "advanced liberalism" (which turned out to be a mixture of government intervention in the economy, a reliance on the market, and welfare-statism),[110] but because of the leadership qualities he was thought to possess. Many French voters on the left initially preferred Michel Rocard to Mitterrand as the Socialist party's presidential candidate—not so much because they preferred his ideas, but because Rocard was not overly identified with the Fourth Republic, he was considered to be a highly intelligent technocrat, and he was seen as a "winner."[111] In the late 1970s, many French voters were unenthusiastic about Mitterrand because of the tiredness and staleness he was thought to embody, just as they were impressed by the image of intelligence and reasonableness he projected in early 1981. Mitterrand won the presidential election in 1988, not because he was classified as a Socialist, but because he was judged to possess "presidential" qualities in greater measure than Chirac.[112] As noted, Chirac had come off equally unfavorably in comparison with Balladur, who at the end of 1993 was viewed as more *présidentiable* because of his moderate views and his calm and conciliatory behavior; but a few months later, the tables were turned: His demeanor was held against him and he was judged less qualified than Chirac.

According to a poll conducted a few days before the first round of the presidential elections of 2002, the personalities of the two candidates who were expected to be in the runoff—Chirac and Jospin—played a greater role than their programs.[113] As the elections drew near, it was increasingly clear that although Jospin was widely considered to have been one of the best prime ministers of the Fifth Republic, Chirac would win, simply because people liked him better as a person.[114]

Similarly, the decline of electoral support for the Communist party in 1981 and thereafter should not be attributed entirely to the voters' rejection of the party's domestic and foreign policy orientations; many voters were "turned off" by the buffoonery displayed by that party's leader, Marchais, during television appearances; others refused to vote for the party, because they wished to enhance the electoral prospects of Mitterrand, and still others, because the party was seen as having become too strong![115] Finally, the electoral failures of the MNR must be attributed in large part to the lack of charisma of its leader, Mégret, especially in comparison with Le Pen.

THE ELECTORAL SYSTEM: ITS IMPACT ON PARTIES AND VOTING BEHAVIOR

The electoral successes of a party have often had less to do with the strength of its social base or the credibility of its programmatic appeal than with the advantages or disadvantages derived from the electoral system. Under the proportional representation system that prevailed in the early years of the Fourth Republic, in theory, each party had equal chances. The antisystem PCF, the Catholic MRP, and the anticlerical and republican SFIO each had approximately 20 to 25 percent of the parliamentary seats from 1945 to 1951, the number of mandates faithfully reflecting the proportion of the popular vote received by each party. In the parliamentary elections of 1951 and 1956, new electoral laws provided that if any party or combination of parties obtained an absolute majority of the vote in a multimember constituency, that party could take all the seats allocated to the constituency and divide them among various components of the electoral alliance on the basis of prearranged formulas. This measure was intended to favor the prosystem parties near the center—the SFIO, the Radicals, and the MRP—among which electoral alliances were easily possible, and to reduce the representation of the antisystem parties, the PCF and the RPF, which could not easily combine (*s'apparenter*) with "neighboring" parties. Thus, although in the election of 1951, the popular vote of the PCF was nearly twice as large as that of the MRP, the parliamentary representation of the PCF was only slightly larger.[116]

In 1958, France returned to the parliamentary electoral system that had prevailed during most of the Third Republic: the single-member-district system of elections with two rounds. Under that system, which is in force today, a candidate is elected in the first-round ballot if he or she has received an absolute majority of the votes; if no one has received such a majority, there is a runoff a week later in which a candidate has merely to obtain a plurality of the votes. Since 1976, regulations have provided that any candidate who gets at least 12.5 percent of the total first-round votes may stay in the race for the second round; but this cannot benefit the vast majority of parliamentary candidates (of whom there were 8,458, or more than 14 per constituency, in 2002). Therefore, realism has demanded the withdrawal of relatively weak candidates in favor of a candidate whose second-round prospects are better and whose party is not too distant ideologically.

Withdrawals are, in principle, based on prior agreements between parties on a national level. Thus, since the early 1970s, agreements between the PS and the PCF provided that whichever of the two parties got the larger first-round vote could expect the other to withdraw in its favor. As noted, before the 1993 Assembly elections, the PS, conscious of its poor electoral outlook and of the loss of many of its traditional electorate to the environmentalist parties, had proposed mutual-withdrawal agreements with those parties but was rebuffed by their national leaders. In the 1980s and 1990s, numerous agreements were made between the PS and other parties of the Left for joint first-round candidates. Often, however, each party has made its own decision on the constituency level, and on many occasions the Socialist candidate, for personal or ideological reasons, has preferred to stay in the race, thus enhancing the electoral chances of a conservative candidate. There have also been withdrawal agreements between the Gaullist and the Giscardist camps, but the emergence of strong parliamentary candidates of the National Front has introduced a new problem. Although the leaders of both the RPR and the UDF have refused to make deals with the FN on a national level, decisions about how to react to a strong first-round showing of the FN in individual constituencies have been left to the local candidates.[117] Because candidates of the RPR and UDF have often appealed to a similar electorate and have not differed radically in regard to policy, the first round has served much the same purpose as a "primary" in the United States, in which candidate choices tend to be made on the basis of personality. In fact, the French have increasingly come to refer to the first election rounds as *"primaires."*

The method of electing the president is similar. If none of the several presidential candidates receives an absolute majority of all the votes in the first round, there is a runoff two weeks later in which only the two candidates with the largest number of first-round votes are the final competitors.[118]

Under the voting system as described above, the preelectoral aggregation process that has traditionally characterized Anglo-American politics has also been at work in France, with the result that the party preferences of French citizens are revealed even less precisely than before by the parliamentary representation of various political parties. The PCF's popular vote was relatively stable from 1951 to 1973, ranging from about 4 million to about 5.5 million, its registered membership remaining stable, too, at about 400,000; its Assembly representation, however, fluctuated from a high of 193 in 1946 to a low of 10 in 1958. Had the proportional representation (PR) system of the Fourth Republic been in effect in the November 1958 elections, the PCF would have received 88 seats instead of 10; the SFIO, 72 instead of 40; and the UNR, 82 instead of 189. Had the PR system of 1986 been continued for the Assembly elections of 1988, the PCF would have obtained 43 seats instead of 27; the PS and allies, 233 instead of 276; the FN 32 instead of 1; and the URC (the RPR and UDF combined), 267 instead of 271. Had such a system been in effect in 1997, the RPR-UDF would still have captured control of the Assembly, but with no more than 55 to 60 percent of the representation, and the environmentalist parties and the National Front would also have gained seats. It should be borne in mind that in the first round of the parliamentary election of 1993, the RPR-UDF got only 44.2 percent of votes (2.8 points more than in 1988 and 4.6 points less than in 1986) and that the size of its victory—85 percent of the seats—was due solely to the nature of the electoral system. In 1997 the relationship was somewhat less unbalanced, with the combined Left getting 48 percent of the popular vote and 55 percent of the seats; still, had the PR system been in effect, the National Front would have obtained 86 seats instead of 1.

Because there was a general conviction that the electoral system of the Fifth Republic was, until the mid-1970s, heavily weighted in favor of the Gaullists, most of the non-Gaullist parties favored a modification of that system. While in the opposition, the Radicals and Centrists advocated a return to proportional representation, as did the Socialists and Communists. Giscard, too, had favored such a return, but on becoming president, gave up the idea, especially after the creation of the UDF, a "presidential-election machine" that, he hoped, would utilize the second-round bipolarization tendency to his advantage—that is, keep the Radicals, Centrists, and Republicans in the fold and force the Gaullists to support him against a leftist alternative.

As leader of the main opposition party, Mitterrand had favored a return to proportional representation, in the belief that under such a system, the voters would be able to opt more freely for parties tied to neither the Gaullists nor the Communists, and hence that a democratic changing of the guard (*alternance*) from the Right to the Left would be facilitated. But when the elections of 1981 proved that the Socialists could capture the presidency and the Assembly, Mitterrand's position and that of most Socialists wavered.

The bipolarizing effect works more effectively in presidential elections than in parliamentary ones. To be nominated, a candidate needs 500 signatures from elected officials at any level—Parliament, regional assemblies, general councils, territorial assemblies of overseas departments, mayors, or municipal councils—spread over at least 30 departments. Extremist parties appeal especially to mayors of small towns and villages who have no clear partisan attachments, with the argument that democracy benefits from the expression of a great variety of political opinions. This explains why presidential candidates of very minor parties are able to get the 500 required signatures.

An electoral law passed in mid-1982 provided for a partial return to proportional representation for the election of municipal councils in towns of over 3,500 inhabitants[119] (see Table 4.7). Under the new system, first applied in 1983, Mayor Chirac's party won a massive victory in Paris and the Socialists incurred losses in several cities. The loss of seats to the majority party was not significant enough to be attributed to any specific factor; nonetheless, the law served in a sense as a precedent for a parliamentary act of 1985 that—temporarily—restored the proportional representation system on a national level.

As pointed out earlier, the Socialists had revived the system of proportional representation for the election of 1986 in the hope of reducing the scope of the anticipated victory of the RPR and UDF. Under the new system, which was based on department party lists, with seats allocated on the basis of the "highest average,"[120] the National Front was able to enter the Assembly and the Communist party to maintain its presence in it with reasonable representation. As soon as the RPR and UDF gained control of the Assembly, they returned the country to the single-member system, but as it turned out, neither by this change nor by gerrymandering several constituencies were these parties able to secure victory in the 1988 legislative elections. In any case, it was possible for a "center" party—the CDS—to gain seats even under the restored system.

The French electoral system has been changed more often than the systems of other major countries.[121] At the beginning of the Fifth Republic, the abandonment of proportional representation was justified on the grounds that it encouraged the existence of a multiplicity of parties, including powerful extremist ones that threatened the

TABLE 4.7
Electoral Systems in France

Election	Method of Election	Term of Office (years)	Constituency
President of Republic	Two rounds; majority	5	Whole country
National Assembly	Two rounds: 1st round, absolute majority; 2nd round, plurality	5	577 single-member constituencies
Senate	Indirect:[a]	9	*Département*
	1. For *départements* providing 4 or fewer senators: 2-round majority system		
	2. For *départements* providing more than 4 senators: proportional representation by party lists[b]		
European Parliament	Proportional representation by party lists	5	Whole country
Regional council[c]	Proportional representation by party lists	6	*Département*
Département council[d] (*Conseil général*)	Two rounds: 1st round, absolute majority; 2nd round, plurality	6	Canton
Municipal council[e]	1. For cities of fewer than 3,500 inhabitants, 2-round majority "list" system;[f] 50% to winner	6	Commune (except for Paris, Lyons, Marseilles)[g]
	2. For cities of more than 3,500, 2 rounds: 50% to winner; 50% proportional		

SOURCE: Adapted from *Institutions et vie politique: Les Notices* (Paris: Documentation Française, 1991), p. 70.
[a]Chosen by an electoral college composed of the Assembly deputies, departmental councillors, and delegates of municipal councils.
[b]"Staggered" elections; one-third of Senate renewed every three years.
[c]Total number 26 (of which 4 are in overseas regions); size varies from 41 to 197.
[d]Total number 100 (96 metropolitan France, 4 overseas); size varies from 15 to 76.
[e]Total number (rounded off): 36,760 (1992); size varies from 9 (communes of under 100 inhabitants) to 163 (Paris); total number of municipal councillors: 496,700 (1992).
[f]For cities of fewer than 2,500, there may be individual (i.e., nonlist) candidates.
[g]Divided into *arrondissements*, each with its own council, elected at the same time as the municipal council.

republic. But that threat is no longer credible: The Communist party has been "tamed" and marginalized, and the National Front (which has been unable to reach 20 percent electoral support) has not openly challenged the legitimacy of the system. Because of these developments, there has been a growing demand for a return to proportional representation on the grounds of fairness. This demand continues to be made by all the minor parties, ranging from left to right; and in recent years, there has been growing support for it within the PS as well.[122] A return to proportional representation, however, is not likely to be supported by the UMP, which has benefited from the present system.

The effect of the electoral system on voter participation is a matter of controversy. It would be logical to assume that the frequency of elections at various levels, the diversity of electoral modalities, and the constant changes of election laws tend to *discourage* voter participation. Conversely, the predominance of proportional representation in elections for subnational office facilitates multiple-party choices and would therefore *encourage* greater participation. In the most recent (1998) regional elections, for example, numerous political groups outside the mainstream parties presented candidates.[123] Electoral abstention, however, is relatively high in most local elections, because decision-making powers of elective bodies are weak, as in cantonal elections, and in cases where the policy impact is not clearly understood, as in European Parliament elections and in referenda (see Tables 4.8 and 4.9). Electoral behavior in subnational elections is different from that which obtains in national elections also because the issues are different, and because, despite decentralization, subnational decision-making powers are not nearly so important as national ones. Furthermore, in many communes, issues may be less important than personal acquaintance with the candidate, who often happens to be the mayor. All these factors explain why a national government's popularity is no guarantee of victory for its party in local elections. Thus, the Socialist victory in the legislative elections of 1997 was not translated into victories of the Left in the municipal elections of 2001, in which the Right made impressive gains at the expense of the Left (except in Paris and Lyons). In 2002, while the Left did poorly in the parliamentary elections, it captured the majority of the constituencies in Paris.

The rate of abstentions is not the same for all categories. In the regional elections of 1998, for example, abstentions were highest for the unemployed (44 percent); wage earners in low-paid and insecure jobs (37 percent), and industrial workers (32 percent); people without religion (36 percent) and nonpracticing Catholics (34 percent); and lowest for farmers (21 percent) and practicing Catholics (15 percent); the rate was low for people on the left, and high for those who were neither Right nor Left (43 percent).[124] In the presidential elections (first round) of 2002, the greatest abstention rate was found among young people, workers, and persons with weak family ties. In all these cases, the rates of abstention were similar to the proportion of votes for Le Pen.[125] In sum, the steady increase in voter abstention in presidential and parliamentary elections, a phenomenon found in other Western democracies as well, is due, not to the electoral system as such, but to the imprecision of programs and the absence of realistic policy choices.

The aggregative effect of the electoral system on the number and performance of political parties is much more obvious. It has now, however, been the only factor influencing the campaigning and the fate of political parties. Under existing laws, the number of campaign posters (which are printed at government expense) that may be affixed to public buildings is limited, as is the number of hours (these are cost-free) allocated for party publicity on radio and television. A series of laws enacted between 1988 and 1993 (supplemented by several decrees and regulations) limited the contributions of individuals and corporations for each candidate (to 2,000 and 50,000 francs, respec-

TABLE 4.8
Abstentions in Elections, 1978–2002
(percentage of total votes cast in metropolitan France)

	Presidential	National Assembly	European Parliment	Regional	Cantonal	Municipal
1978 (1)*		16.68				
(2)		15.34				
1979			32.29			
1981 (1)	18.91					
(2)	14.14					
1982					31.57	
1983						21.63
1984			43.24			
1986		21.90		22.07		
1988 (1)	18.62	34.26			50.87	
(2)	15.93	30.05				
1989			51.11			27.18 (1)
1992				31.30	29.34 (1)	
1993 (1)		30.80				
(2)		32.44				
1994			47.24		39.60 (1)	
1995 (1)	21.62					30.06
(2)	20.34					
1997 (1)		30.04				
(2)		28.87				
1998				41.95	39.60 (1)	
1999			53.24			
2000					•	
2001						32.71 (1)
2002 (1)	28.40	35.58				
(2)	19.86	39.68				

SOURCE: *Le Monde* (1978–2002).
*(1) = first round; (2) = second round.

tively). The law allowed a maximum expenditure of 500,000 francs per parliamentary-election candidate and limited the expenditure for first-round presidential candidates to 120 million francs and for second-round candidates to 160 million francs.[126] All parliamentary candidates who receive at least 5 percent of the votes are reimbursed for 10 percent of their expenditures; and presidential candidates, for 25 percent. In addition, each presidential candidate may print and distribute one campaign brochure at government expense.[127] Television time cannot be bought; any party with 20 deputies in the outgoing Assembly can get three hours of free time; other parties get seven minutes.[128] There is also a system of government subsidies to parties, under which (according to a law enacted in 1990) allocations to the various parties are based in equal measure on the votes

TABLE 4.9
National Referenda (percentage of total votes cast and abstentions)

	Referendum	Yes	No	Abstentions
1958	Adoption of Constitution	85.14	14.85	19.51
1961	Algerian self-determination	74.99	25.00	26.24
1962	Evian Accords	90.80	9.19	24.66
	Direct election of president	62.25	37.74	23.02
1969	Reform of regions and Senate	47.58	52.41	19.86
1972	Enlargement of European Community	68.31	31.68	39.75
1988	Autonomy statute for New Caledonia	79.99	20.00	63.10
1992	Adoption of Treaty of Maastricht	51.05	48.95	29.49
2000	Reduction of presidential mandate	73.21	26.79	69.81

SOURCE: Ministry of Interior.

they received in the preceding national elections and the number of incumbent senators and deputies. Under this formula, the government granted 1.66 € (about $1.60) for each vote in the legislative elections (as of 2002).[129] This subsidy has encouraged a number of politicians to put up candidates despite poor prospects for them, not so much for the purpose of electing them, but to build a nest egg for their own political ambitions. Despite these contributions, parties are hard-pressed to meet the cost of campaigning, which has constantly gone up, owing in part to the growing use of campaign aides. Because of the reduced number of registered party members, campaign costs can no longer be easily met with regular party funds (despite the salary contributions from their deputies),[130] a condition that has contributed to party corruption.

In 1990, business gifts to parties were legalized, but the amounts were limited to 10 percent and 500,000 francs from corporations or institutions, and from individuals (clearly identified), to 30,000 francs total for each election. A national commission on campaign expenditures was created. In 1993, the limit was reduced to 5 percent for each election; a law was enacted providing for a public listing of all firms providing financial support to political parties and to provide for complete reimbursement of a campaign if the party gets at least 5 percent of the vote. In 1995, electoral campaign support by enterprises or foundations (other than political parties) was forbidden—but in exchange, the government was to reimburse 50 percent of authorized campaign expenditures.[131] In 2002, candidates for the presidential election could not go beyond a ceiling of 14.8 million euros each for the first round and 19.7 million euros each for the second round. Each of the first-round candidates got an advance sum of 1 million euros; candidates *not* receiving at least 5 percent of the popular votes got a lump-sum payment of almost 740,000 euros (i.e., one-twentieth of the maximum) each. These measures have not been sufficient. One solution to the problem of declining membership has been money laundering; officials of most of the parties have resorted to that tactic, which has resulted in their indictment.

It has often been said that despite their mass dues-paying-membership figures (which are often inflated), all French parties are parties of notables. This aspect of French politics is buttressed by the *cumul* system—the simultaneous holding of several elective offices by individuals. Under this system (as pointed out in Chapter 7), national politicians are, in most cases, also mayors, a fact that gives them a certain degree of electoral security. *Cumul* is a politician's protection against electoral loss in one contest or another, a protection of fiefdom; at the same time, it constitutes a kind of political insurance for the local electors, who believe that their mayor is in a better position to speak for their interests if he occupies a national office as well. Most of the deputies and mayors would like to retain *cumul* at least in part, and they have largely succeeded. In 1956, 27 percent of the deputies were mayors; at the beginning of the Fifth Republic, 49 percent; and in 1988, 96 percent. Under a reform enacted in 1985, a person was permitted to combine his position as deputy in the Assembly with that of representative in *one* of the following bodies: European Parliament, general council of a department, Paris city council, regional council, city council of a commune of more than 3,500 inhabitants, or as mayor of a commune of more than 20,000, or deputy mayor of a commune of more than 100,000. But the law has been encumbered with exceptions and has not been fully adhered to.[132]

The 1985 reform did not go far enough for Jospin. Upon becoming prime minister, he required that politicians appointed to his cabinet abandon their mayoral positions in large cities. According to a law of April 2000, the *cumul* policy underwent further restrictions. Membership in Parliament could no longer be combined with more than one of the following elective offices: regional or departmental councillor, Paris city council, mayor of a commune of more than 20,000 inhabitants, deputy mayor of a city of more than 100,000 inhabitants, member of Corsican Assembly; or municipal councillor of a commune of at least 3,500 inhabitants.[133] A politician could no longer combine two subnational executive offices (e.g., mayor of a city and president of a general or regional council). The law also provided that the position of member of Parliament is incompatible with that of member of the European Parliament (which brings France into line with the legislation of Belgium, Greece, and Spain); an executive office in a territorial unit or membership in the Economic and Social Council. The Assembly had approved a much more stringent law, but the Senate watered it down.

POLITICAL FRINGE GROUPS, CLUBS, AND MOVEMENTS

On the periphery of the system of major political parties are numerous political grouplets *(groupuscules)*, minor parties, protest movements, and "clubs." Clubs occupy a position midway between parties and interest groups: Like parties, they are purveyors of ideologies and programs, and their leaders may harbor political (and occasionally electoral) ambitions. Like interest groups, they are not primarily interested in capturing political power but in influencing policies.

Clubs are part of an old tradition in France, going back to the Revolutions of 1789, 1848, and 1870. Clubs were relatively weak in the Fourth Republic, probably because the proportional representation system then in operation made it easy to establish polit-ical parties. The club phenomenon reasserted itself during the Fifth Republic when, in the face of the new electoral law that produced aggregative parties, the (temporary) mass support of de Gaulle, and the weakness of Parliament, parties proved inadequate vehi-cles for the promotion of specific ideas or programs. Thus, clubs arose for such purposes as criticizing the permissive society resulting from socioeconomic modernization, fight-ing Gaullism, combating fascism, promoting laicism, spreading Catholic doctrine, advo-cating revolution, suggesting a variety of institutional and social reforms, and providing forums for discussion or serving as instruments of political education.[134]

The differences and relationships among clubs, parties, movements, and interest groups are not always precise. Some clubs are structural components of parties or elec-toral coalitions, as was the case with *Perspectives et réalités* and the *Mouvement démocrate-socialiste de France*, both of which were part of the UDF. Some clubs are instrumental in the creation of new parties or electoral coalitions: for example, the *Convention des institu-tions républicaines* (CIR), which, in the 1960s, helped to create unity within the noncom-munist Left and was eventually fused into the new *Parti socialiste*; the *Fédération des réformateurs*, which, in the early 1970s, attempted to unite the Radicals and Democratic-Centrists; and *Démocratie nouvelle*, founded in 1974, which helped to reunite the major-ity and opposition Centrists and to create the CDS. Some groups, although formally separate from political parties, are used by them to recruit supporters, such as the *Union des jeunes pour le progrès*, which tried to capture young people for Gaullism in the 1980s; *Jeunes avec Chirac*, which was formed early in 1995 in order to provide electoral support for the mayor of Paris and included youths from the RPR as well as other right-wing groups; and *Solidarité et liberté*, founded after the 1981 elections by individuals from the RPR and the UDF in order to fight socialism. Other clubs may be the political instru-ments of individual politicians: Among these clubs were *Club 89*, a group of Parisian Gaullists supporting Chirac; the *Comité d'études pour un nouveau contrat social*, estab-lished in 1969 by Edgar Faure to create a "majority of ideas," to combine radical-socialism with Gaullism, and to keep Faure himself in the limelight; and a miscellany of groups formed to promote the presidential ambitions of individual politicians. Simi-larly, there are organizations that are combinations of clubs, parties, factions within par-ties, and "movements." Examples of such hybrids were *Alternative rouge et verte*, which was founded in 1989 as a fusion of the supporters of the presidential campaign of re-form Communist Pierre Juquin in 1988, dissident environmentalists, and militant femi-nists; and *France unie*, formed at the same time by Giscardist Jean-Pierre Soisson when he decided to support the Socialist government of Michel Rocard. Several of the *courants* in the Socialist party have considered themselves as *"clubs de réflexion,"* and have pub-lished their own newsletters, such as *Solidarités modernes* by Fabius's supporters and *Convaincre* by Rocard's supporters. One of the more dynamic clubs was *Agir*, a leftist "idea group" (founded in 1995 by Martine Aubry, the daughter of Jacques Delors), which included PS politicians as well as former Communists and a number of indepen-dent intellectuals; another was *Réunir*, a left-of-center club that served to advance the po-litical ambitions of Bernard Kouchner, a charismatic left-wing politician. Two organiza-tions that combined features of clubs and movements but transformed themselves into political parties or movements were Chevènement's *Mouvement des citoyens* and, more recently, the *Mouvement action égalité*, formed in October 1992 by Harlem Désir, the former leader of *SOS-Racisme*, as the political expression of poor urban-slum dwellers.[135] Other clubs include *Fondation Jean-Jaurès*, a "think tank" close to the PS; and *Idées-action*, founded in 1994 by Alain Madelin to expound the ideology of laissez-faire liberalism.

Still other clubs, although not formally associated with parties, have included politicians from various parties and have furnished them with ideas: for example, the *Club Jean Moulin*, formed in 1958 and now defunct, which included left-wing Catholics, Radicals, and nonpolitical civil servants and published widely respected monographs on institutional reform; the right-wing *Club de l'Horloge*, created in 1974, which appeals to businessmen and technocrats (and maintains ties to the National Front);[136] *Échange et projets*, founded in 1973 by Jacques Delors (Mitterrand's first minister of economics) as a link between "productivist" Socialists and the business community; *Espaces 89*, a group of intellectuals who analyze sociopolitical questions from the perspective of the democratic Left; and the *Groupe de recherche et d'étude sur la civilisation européenne* (GRECE), an extreme right-wing, elitist, and racist "study group." The clubs have ranged in membership from several tens of thousands spread over various parts of France (e.g., *Perspectives et réalités*) to only a few dozen members resident in Paris. Some clubs function primarily as organizations of support for ambitious politicians. One of the more recent, for example, is the club *Dialogue et initiative*, which is close to Chirac; it examines approaches to specific policy issues (e.g., law and order).

An organization that appeared recently on the horizon is *Atelier*. Founded in April 2001, it resembled a social movement more than a club; it included individuals who did not accept the pragmatism of Jospin's pluralist-Left coalition, opposed globalization, and fought for policies that, they believed, Jospin's coalition neglected, such as the effective integration of undocumented immigrants. It hoped to revive the antiliberal Left and attracted younger and more radical elements from among the Greens, the Communists, and the Socialists.[137] In addition, there are political organizations whose purpose is neither to promote a program nor to assist in the development of an ideology or advance the electoral prospects of a politician. An example is the *Association des amis de l'Institut François Mitterrand*, which is concerned with promoting a positive image of the legacy of this former president.

In addition to the organizations just mentioned, there are numerous small parties that are so diminished that they may become mere clubs. Among these are the CNIP, which has barely a handful of deputies; and the MDC, whose leader, Chevènement, has been disavowed. In the municipal elections of 1989, 1995, and 2001, there were candidates running under a bewildering variety of leftist, rightist, centrist, regionalist, and unclassifiable labels. Some of these parties have articulated ethnic claims (e.g., the *Union démocratique brétonne*); some are politically so extremist as to exist on the fringes of the political spectrum. Others, like the Trotskyist *Lutte ouvrière* and *League communiste révolutionnaire*, have run candidates for national office; some are single-issue parties, difficult to distinguish from interest groups (e.g., the environmentalists until a few years ago); and others have been promoters of purely local politicians and interests (e.g., the various *groupes d'action locale*). What distinguishes these parties from national ones is that their organization is weak, their membership ephemeral and unreliable, their electoral appeal limited, and their impact on national politics negligible.[138]

SUMMARY AND CONCLUSION

The major theme that emerges from the foregoing analysis is the gradual transformation of the party system. There has been a gradual convergence of positive views about the existing constitutional system and a lessened divergence on policies, so that a changeover from a right-wing (or right-of-center) to a left-wing (or left-of-center) coalition does not cause a disastrous jolt to the polity. The evolution from a multiparty system toward a four-party system—extreme Right, mainstream Right, mainstream Left, extreme Left—divided, for national electoral purposes, into two mainstream camps (if one still counts the PCF and the UDF and does not count the FN) has been the result of changes in the class system, the bipolarizing effect of the single-member-constituency method of elections, the reduced relevance of old ideologies, and the factor of presidential coattails.

These changes have been accompanied by changes in the position and character of the individual parties that are components of the system: The Socialist party has become more centrist, more receptive to the orientations of the bourgeois segments of its electorate, and less dogmatic.[139] The PCF (or what is left of it) has become more moderate or has for tactical reasons pretended to moderation. The Gaullist party, long bereft of its wartime hero, has become more institutionalized, whereas its ideology has become banal and diffuse; and the remainder of the UDF, itself the product of a presidential bandwagon effect and a reflection of a lessened antagonism between clerical and anticlerical elements, has become ideologically disoriented.

The emerging bipolarism has been manifested in a number of ways: (1) the increasing tendency, since the late 1970s, of each of the two major camps on the Right and Left to agree on single lists of candidates for the first rounds in many local and parliamentary constituencies, or (in the case of the PS and PCF) at least to more cooperation; (2) the acceptance of common platforms or "understandings"; and (3) more or less cohesive voting in the Assembly. At the same time, one should keep in mind that this bipolarization is neither smooth nor immune to rivalries and other fissiparous influences. Within each group, too, there are conflicts: among conservative, populist, Jacobin, neoliberal, and pragmatic Gaullists; among Marxist, social-democratic, "humanist," and "productivist" Socialists. There are conflicts even among the minor parties: between hard-line and moderate Marxists in the PCF, and among the dogmatic and pragmatic environmentalists.[140] At this point, none of these differences are likely to have an impact on the overwhelming control of the decision-making arrangement dominated by the UMP. It is possible to envisage changes in the future that might sharpen these internal differences and arrest or reverse the current unevenly bipolar arrangement. Economic difficulties or the personal failures of its leaders might discredit the recently victorious Right, just as it had discredited the PS and before it, the RPR and UDF; the enfranchisement of poor immigrant workers might introduce a new radicalism into political life. It is also possible that clubs, movements, or other extraparliamentary forces might grow and upset the existing party lineup, either by propelling themselves into Parliament or by influencing one or the other of the major parties to change its direction in ways that cannot be envisaged at this time.

NOTES

1. Jacques Fauvet, *La France déchirée* (Paris: Fayard, 1957), p. 22.
2. *Changer la vie: Programme de gouvernement du parti socialiste* (Paris: Flammarion, 1971).
3. For a discussion of the founding of the PS, see G. A. Codding, Jr., and W. Safran, *Ideology and Politics: The Socialist Party of France* (Boulder, CO: Westview Press, 1979), pp. 211–34. On the evolution of the PS, see D. S. Bell and Byron Criddle, *The French Socialist Party: The Emergence of a Party of Government*, 2d ed. (Oxford: Clarendon Press, 1988).
4. In the spring of 1980, *L'Express*, a weekly newsmagazine, revealed that Marchais had gone to work in Germany as a volunteer during World War II and not as a forced laborer, as he had been claiming.
5. On the wartime leftist connections of de Gaulle and his selective postwar leftist policies, see Henri Lerner, *De Gaulle et la gauche* (Limonest: L'Interdisciplinaire, 1994).
6. In 1971, UDR came to stand for *Union des démocrates pour la République*.
7. For a concise analysis of the rise of Gaullism and its condition during the first decade of the Fifth Republic, see Jean Charlot, *The Gaullist Phenomenon* (New York: Praeger, 1971). For an analysis of the connections between Gaullism and the traditional Right, see same author, "Le Gaullisme," in Jean-François Sirinelli, ed., *Histoire des droites en France* (Paris: Gallimard, 1992), vol. 1, pp. 652ff.
8. A clear expression of this "natalist" orientation is found in Michel Debré, *Lettre ouverte aux Français sur la reconquête de la France* (Paris: Albin Michel, 1980), esp. pp. 47–62.
9. In addition to Chirac, the Gaullist candidates in 1981 were Marie-France Garaud, a lawyer who had been Chirac's major advisor during his premiership and had been a cofounder of the RPR but had quit the party in 1979, and Michel Debré, an intimate collaborator of the General's.
10. At the same time, Chirac tried to project the image of a person interested in selflessly rallying the people for their own socioeconomic welfare. See his *La Lueur de l'espérance* (Paris: La Table Ronde, 1978), esp. pp. 13–14. See also Albert Lebacqz, *Les Droites et les gauches sous la Ve République* (Paris: Éditions France-Empire, 1984), pp. 147–59, which describes "Chiraquism" as a combination of Gaullist legitimism, pseudoliberalism, "neo-Bonapartism," and "*républicanisme d'autorité.*" See also Thierry Desjardins, *Les Chiraquiens* (Paris: Table Ronde, 1986), for a portrait of 16 politicians who began to rally around Chirac—not so much for his Gaullism as for their optimistic assessment of his future; N. Domenach and M. Szafran, *Le Roman d'un président* (Paris: Grasset, 1999); and J. M. Colombani, *Le Président de la République* (Paris: Stock, 1998).
11. In the past three decades, many writings about the "Giscard phenomenon" have appeared. These have covered the personality and policies of Valéry Giscard d'Estaing, the various parties he courted and co-opted in order to promote his presidential ambitions, and the system of government over which he presided. A statement of Giscard's pragmatic and pluralistic thinking is his *Démocratie français* (Paris: Fayard, 1976), trans. as *French Democracy* (Garden City, NY: Doubleday, 1977), and his more recent *Deux Français sur trois* (Paris: Flammarion, 1984). Books written by others include Daniel Séguin, *Les Nouveaux Giscardiens* (Paris: Calmann-Lévy, 1979), a sympathetic discussion of personalities and of relations between Giscardists and Gaullists; and Olivier Todd, *La Marelle de Giscard* (Paris: Laffont, 1977), which stresses Giscard's alleged talents as a political manipulator. Books about the Giscard system include Roger-Gérard Schwartzenberg, *La Droite absolue* (Paris: Flammarion, 1981); and J. R. Frears, *France in the Giscard Presidency* (London: Allen & Unwin, 1981), an informed effort; and Anne Nourry and Michel Louvois, *Le Combat singulier* (Paris: Denoel, 1980), which focuses on the complex relationship between Giscard and Chirac (and is hostile to both).

12. For a study of the complicated relations among the centrists, see William Safran, "Centrism in the Fifth Republic: An Attitude in Search of an Instrument," in William G. Andrews and Stanley Hoffmann, eds., *The Fifth Republic at Twenty* (Albany, NY: SUNY Press, 1981), pp. 123–45.

13. In 1959, Giscard was appointed secretary of state (i.e., junior minister) in the Finance Ministry and, three years later, full minister of finance. See William Safran, "Valéry Giscard d'Estaing," in David Wilsford, ed., *Political Leaders of Contemporary Western Europe* (Westport, CT: Greenwood Press, 1995), pp. 170–76.

14. The group of cofounders and leaders of the RI (later, the Republican party) included Prince Michel Poniatowski, Count Michel d'Ornano, and Prince Jean de Broglie.

15. For René Rémond, author of *La Droite en France*, trans. as *The Right Wing in France from 1915 to de Gaulle*, 2d ed. (Philadelphia: University of Pennsylvania Press, 1969), Gaullism, in its plebiscitary orientations and populist pretensions, represented the Bonapartist Right; and Giscardism, in its being based on middle-class (especially business) support, represented the Orléanist Right (i.e., evoked the reign of Louis-Philippe between 1830 and 1848, a reign allegedly noted for the self-enrichment propensities of the grande bourgeoisie). Another scholar, Colette Ysmal (author of "Nature et réalité de l'affrontement Giscard-Chirac," *Politique aujourd'hui*, nos. 3–4 [1978], 11–23), rejects the notion that Giscardism represents the political Right. She argues that Giscardism is "liberal" in its quest for consensus and its belief in social and economic pluralism. But note that to many French politicians and intellectuals, "liberalism" (viewed in its economic aspect more frequently than in its constitutional one) is by definition a right-wing ideology.

16. These included *Perspectives et réalités*, a club founded by Giscard and composed of businessmen, politicians, technocrats, and a few intellectuals, which had been an "idea-monger" for the Republican party; and the *Mouvement démocrate-socialiste de France* (MDSF), composed of anticommunist former Socialists and other supporters of Giscard. In 1995, *Perspectives et réalités* became a political party in the formal sense.

17. Among them many farmers who were upset because of a steep decline in farm incomes; and environmentalists, who objected to his excessive reliance on nuclear power.

18. See "Notre Espoir à 20 ans," *Tribune socialiste*, no. 11 (March 1980); and W. Safran, "The French Left and Ethnic Pluralism," *Ethnic and Racial Studies* 7:4 (October 1984), 447–61. For a well-documented recent study of the early years of the PSU, see Marc Heurgon, *Histoire du PSU*, vol. 1 (Paris: La Découverte, 1994).

19. See Frédéric Bon, *Les Élections en France* (Paris: Seuil, 1978). According to this source (pp. 189 and 193), which is based on SOFRES polls, during the elections of 1974, 780,000 industrialists, big businessmen, and *cadres supérieurs* voted for Mitterrand, as did more than 1 million practicing Catholics (compared to the 1.3 million in the first three categories who voted for Giscard).

20. Jean Mitoyen, *C'est dur d'être de gauche* (Paris: Syros, 1985), p. 75. On the euphoria of the new government and subsequent developments, see Julius W. Friend, *Seven Years in France: François Mitterrand and the Unintended Revolution, 1981–1988* (Boulder, CO: Westview Press, 1989).

21. See Michel Charzat, Ghislaine Toutain, and Jean-Pierre Chevènement, *Le CERES: Un Combat pour le socialisme* (Paris: Calmann-Lévy, 1975), for an authoritative statement of CERES ideas. CERES was founded by ENA graduates prominent in the Paris federation of the PS. For a profile of the CERES activist, see David Hanley, *Keeping Left? CERES and the French Socialist Party* (Manchester, UK: University of Manchester Press, 1986).

22. See Club de l'Horloge, *L'Identité de la France* (Paris: Albin Michel, 1985); Jean-Yves Le Gallou and Club de l'Horloge, *La Préférence nationale* (Paris: Albin Michel, 1985); Jean-Marie Le Pen, *Les Français d'abord* (Paris: Carrère-Michel Lafon, 1984); Dominique Schnapper, *La France de l'intégration* (Paris: Gallimard, 1991); Patrick Ireland, "Vive le jacobinisme: Les Étrangers and the Durability of the Assimilation Model in France," *French Politics and Society* 14:2 (Spring 1996), 33–46; and Riva Kastoryano, "Immigration and Identity in France: The War of Words," *French Politics and Society* 14:2 (Spring 1996), 58–66.

23. See Martin A. Schain, "The National Front in France and the Construction of Political Legitimacy," *West European Politics* 10:2 (April 1987), 229–52; Pierre Bréchon and Subrata Kumar Mitra, "The National Front in France: The Emergence of an Extreme Right Protest Movement," *Comparative Politics* 25:1 (October 1992), 63–82; and William Safran, "The National Front in France: From Lunatic

Fringe to Limited Respectability," in Peter H. Merkl and Leonard Weinberg, eds., *Encounters with the Contemporary Radical Right* (Boulder, CO: Westview Press, 1993), pp. 19–49. See also Nonna Mayer and Pascal Perrineau, eds., *Le Front national à découvert* (Paris: PFNSP, 1989); Guy Birenbaum, *Le Front national* (Paris: Balland, 1992); and Michael S. Lewis-Beck, "French Electoral Theory: The National Front Test," *Electoral Studies* 12:2 (1993), 112–27. Lewis-Beck emphasizes the "materialist" values of the National Front. For a more recent study, emphasizing both the evolution of this party and its relationship to other political formations, see Harvey G. Simmons, *The French National Front* (Boulder, CO: Westview Press, 1996).

24. The *Rénovateurs*, who were supported by an odd assortment of Trotskyists, anti-Stalinists, and elements of the PSU, focused on the environment, women's rights, education, and liberal naturalization laws. At the end of 1988, the Reform Communists transformed themselves into a *groupuscule*, the *Nouvelle gauche*, which was to be a "green and red" movement and was joined by the last remnants of the PSU after the latter had dissolved.

25. The National Front did manage to seat a single deputy (Yann Piat) from a Bouches-du-Rhône constituency (Marseilles area), but she was expelled from the party soon thereafter for publicly taking exception to a remark by Le Pen that the gas chambers used by the Nazis to liquidate Jews were a mere "detail of history." In November 1989, the National Front regained a seat in the Assembly when its candidate, Marie-France Stirbois (the widow of the party's second in command), won in a by-election in Dreux.

26. Léotard (a politician then in his forties whose relationship with Chirac was strained) did not join the "young Turks," or rejuvenators; he sided with the "old guard" reportedly because he was promised that he would inherit the leadership of the UDF from Giscard if the latter succeeded in becoming president of the European Parliament. See "Giscard-Chirac: Le Crépuscule des deux?" *Le Point*, 10 April 1989, pp. 42–43. See also "Droite: Le Plan secret des rénovateurs," *Le Point*, 17 April 1989, pp. 42–49. At the same time, a liaison *(intergroup)* including the RPR, UDF, *and* Centrists (UDC) was formed in the Assembly, largely for the purpose of restraining the rejuvenators.

27. The platform of the Greens in 1981 included, inter alia, a wider use of the popular referendum, a return to proportional representation, the granting of increased power to mayors, the reduction of the workweek to 35 hours, and a boycott of South Africa.

28. These newly elected environmentalists disturbed the "normal" political arrangements in the regional councils because they refused to align reliably with the major Right or Left parties. This behavior gave the environmentalists considerable influence on these subnational levels, despite their small number. See Daniel Boy, Vincent Jacques Le Seigneur, and Agnès Roche, *L'Écologie au pouvoir* (Paris: PFSNP, 1995), pp. 28–40 et passim.

29. See *Valeurs, principes et propositions des verts* (St. Brieuc: Parti écologiste, November 1991).

30. For a study of the political culture and electoral behavior of the environmentalists and the relationships among the rival formations, see Brendan Prendiville, *L'Écologie: La Politique autrement?* (Paris: L'Harmattan, 1993). On the "Lalonde comedy," see pp. 70–80. Because of Lalonde's socialist orientations and Waechter's "openness" toward selective support of FN politicians on local levels, some cynical French observers distinguished between the "red" Greens and the "brown" Greens (or *"écolos fachos"*).

31. He was widely thought to have mishandled French policy with respect to German reunification and to have misjudged developments in the Soviet Union; he failed to prevent the breakup of Yugoslavia, to change GATT rules, to influence Middle East negotiations, and to exert significant influence in postcommunist Eastern Europe.

32. Jean-Michel Apathie, "Le PS face à son identité perdue," *Revue politique et parlementaire*, 95 année, no. 964 (March–April 1993), 64–66.

33. For an analysis of the "big bang" speech, see Alain Bergounioux and Gérard Grunberg, "Quel Refondation pour le socialisme français?" *Le Monde*, 3 March 1993. See also Jean-Marie Vincent, "La Dégradation de la politique sous Mitterrand," *Futur antérieur*, no. 28 (1995/2), 51–68. This article argues that when Mitterrand came to power in 1981, the *100 Propositions* of the Socialist party, based in large part on the Common Program of 1972, were already irrelevant because both Keynesianism and socialism had been "conquered by events." Rocard admitted as much in 1988.

34. Patrick Jarreau, "Un Entretien avec M. Chevènement," *Le Monde*, 3 March 1993.

35. *Le Monde*, 21 February 1991, p. 10. See also Chevènement's own (self-serving) political statement, *Le Temps des citoyens* (Paris: Éditions du Rocher, 1993), in which he criticizes France's "capitulation to the European Union and to the U.S.A. and the PS's sellout to capitalism and the abandonment of its leftist vocation."

36. *Le Monde*, 4–5 July 1993, p. 8.

37. "Les Courants majoritaires du PS préconisent la rupture avec l'orthodoxie économique," *Le Monde*, 23 July 1993.

38. Including ministers Georgina Dufoix (the transfusion of contaminated blood and blood products) and Roland Dumas (the Habbash affair and improper gifts from the family of a Middle Eastern dictator), Bérégovoy (an interest-free loan), and former Assembly speaker Emmanuelli (the "Urba" affair, involving funds for the PS). See Michel Poniatowski, *La Catastrophe socialiste* (Paris: Bertrand, 1991), and the more neutral Alain Bergounioux and Gérard Grunberg, *Le Long Remords du pouvoir: Le Parti socialiste français* (Paris: Fayard, 1993).

39. Guy Bedos, quoted by Julius W. Friend, "Mitterrand's Legatee: The French Socialist Party in 1993," *French Politics and Society* 11:3 (Summer 1993), 1–11.

40. A tactically related matter was the conflict between the UDF and the RPR over who should head the list for the European Parliament elections of June 1994. In mid-1993, Balladur entertained the possibility of leading the RPR-UDF list in these elections, but this idea was opposed by Giscard, who thought of doing so himself, even though he had just resigned as deputy from the European Parliament because it conflicted with his other two elective mandates.

41. Later that year, Lalonde aligned himself on the side of Barre and Giscard—and against Balladur and Mitterrand—with respect to their positions on the WTO negotiations. At about the same time, however, he accepted an offer from Balladur to head a "study mission" on the environmental aspects of foreign trade.

42. See *L'Année politique 1991*, pp. 56 and 73. Giscard's article, which stressed kinship (as opposed to naturalization) for entitlement to citizenship, appeared in *Figaro-Magazine*, 21 September 1991.

43. This was the first time that an incumbent president of the Fifth Republic did not participate in a presidential election campaign. See Jean-Claude Zarka, "François Mitterrand et la campagne présidentielle," *Revue politique et parlementaire*, no. 978 (July–August 1995), 51–59.

44. See W. Safran, "The Socialists, Jospin, and the Mitterrand Legacy," in Michael Lewis-Beck, ed., *How France Votes* (New York: Chatham House, 2000), pp. 14–20.

45. This slogan became the title of a book published by Chirac during the campaign (Paris: NiL, 1995). Balladur's slogan, *"Croire en la France"* (Believe in France) was not exactly antisocial; nonetheless, it reminded some observers of Ronald Reagan's emphasis on "What's Right with America."

46. In many ways, Philippe de Villiers's rhetoric resembled that of Patrick Buchanan, the right-wing populist politician of the U.S. Republican party.

47. In his book, *Communisme: La Mutation* (Paris: Stock, 1995), Robert Hue referred to the bankruptcy of the Soviet model of communism but also argued that "social democracy has not made capitalism better" (p. 10). He asserted that the survival of party activism in the context of more intraparty pluralism would reflect the "profoundly French character" of the PCF (pp. 45–46).

48. After her selection as leader of the Greens, Voynet initiated a rapprochement with the *Alternative rouge et verte* (AREV), a left-wing environmentalist group that included former members of the PSU as well as dissidents from GE and the Communist party. In reaction to Voynet's nomination as the Greens' presidential candidate, Antoine Waechter tried to become a candidate of the *Mouvement écologiste indépendant*, a secessionist group, but failed to receive the necessary 500 signatures of elected politicians.

49. Another candidacy, that of Jacques Cheminade, is difficult to explain, because his ephemeral "party," the *Fédération pour une nouvelle solidarité*, was neither right-wing nor left-wing. A former civil servant, he was a conservative populist, who (like the American Lyndon LaRouche, from whom he received some support) had been convicted of a criminal offense. He received less than 1 percent of the popular vote.

50. Jean-Claude Colliard, "Le Processus de nomination des candidats et l'organisation des campagnes électorales," in Nicholas Wahl and Jean-Louis Quermonne, eds., *La France présidentielle: L'Influence du suffrage universelle sur la vie politique* (Paris: PFNSP, 1995), pp. 67–89.

51. For example, Hughes Portelli, *La Ve République* (Paris: Grasset, 1994).
52. For one of the few accurate predictions of the election outcome, based on a rational-choice model in which economic factors play a large role, see Christine Fauvelle-Aymar and Michael Lewis-Beck, "L'Iowa donne l'opposition gagnante," *Libération*, 23 May 1997, p. 15.
53. Alain Madelin had replaced François Léotard as leader.
54. The membership estimates are as follows: *Force démocrate*, 30,000; PPDF (formerly *Perspectives et Réalités*), 15,000; Radical party, 9,000; a handful of Republicans who chose not to follow the departure of *Démocratie libérale*; and 10,000 direct adherents of the UDF. See Stéphanie Abrial, "Entre libéralisme et centrisme," in Pierre Bréchon, ed., *Les Partis politiques français* (Paris: Documentation Française, 2001), pp. 61–83.
55. *L'Année politique 1995*, pp. 84, 148, 164. The leader of the PPDF was Hervé de Charette, Juppé's foreign minister.
56. *Que chacun vive bien, que nous vivions mieux ensemble*, a 90-page monograph prepared by Martine Aubry after the Grenoble party congress (Paris: Parti Socialiste, 2002).
57. See Jacques Rupnik, "Dead Center," *New Republic*, 10 June 2002, pp. 12–14.
58. Cf. Cécile Cornudet, "Législatives: La Campagne se focalise sur la question de la cohabitation," *Les Echos*, 27 May 2002.
59. For a recent revisionist study of de Gaulle's family and Gaullist ideology, see Serge Berstein, *Histoire du gaullisme* (Paris: Perrin, 2001).
60. Another indication of the UMP's self-assurance during the legislative elections was the refusal of Serge Lepeltier, the vice-president of RPR, to commit to the withdrawal of a Gaullist in favor of a PS candidate in case of "triangulars," i.e., a three-person race, with the National Front candidate coming into the second round with the largest number of votes, followed by a Socialist candidate. See Jean-Baptiste de Monvalon and Jean-Louis Saux, "Face au Front national, la stratégie de la droite reste hésistante," *Le Monde*, 23 May 2002.
61. In Calais, a traditionally Communist city, Le Pen came in first and Hue in fifth place. Jean-Paul Dufour, "Les Enfants perdus de la classe ouvrière," *Le Monde*, 25 April 2002; see also Alain Chouraqui, "Ce Monde du travail qui choisit l'extrême droite," *Le Monde–Économie* (Supplement), 30 April 2002. Recent estimates of PCF membership are as follows: 520,000 in 1978; 330,000 in 1987; 270,000 in 1996; under 200,000 in 2001. Fabienne Greffet, "Le PCF: Combattre le déclin par la mutation?" in Pierre Bréchon, ed., *Les Partis politiques français* (Paris: Documentation Française, 2001), p. 111.
62. *Le Monde*, 27 June 2002, p. 8. Meanwhile, the PCF was broke; its failure to reach the threshold of 5 percent of the popular vote in the presidential elections cost it 8.38 million euros (nearly $8 million). Its headquarters had to lay off 44 of its 104 employees, and the party was selling flowers on the street.
63. Chevènement's nationalism had even appealed to a number of royalists. See the interview with Paul-Marie Coûteaux, "Les Français souhaitent un nouveau legitimisme," in *L'Express*, 31 January 2002.
64. E.g., for the FN: *Alliance générale contre le racisme et pour le respect de l'identité française; Cercle chasse, pêche et nature; Cercle national des rapatriés; SOS enfants d'Irak*; for the MNR: *Terroir et ruralité; Sécurité pour les Français; Association française de défense de la famille*. See Gilles Ivaldi, "Les Formations de l'extrême droite: Front national et Mouvement national républicain," in Bréchon, ed. *Les Partis politiques français*, pp. 15–37.
65. Pascal Perrineau (interview), *Le Monde*, 12 June 2002, p. 6.
66. See Patrice Lestrohan, "Pasqua-Villiers: L'Affrontement national," *Canard Enchaîné*, 24 May 2000.
67. With an estimated 1.5 million hunters in France, the CPNT is a powerful enough group to pressure the mainstream parties. In 2000 a law was enacted creating a National Hunting Office, which tries to find a middle ground between accommodating the CPNT and adhering to EU law. See Paul Havet, "Les Enjeux de la loi sur la chasse," *Regards sur l'actualité*, no. 266 (November–December 2000), 25–36.
68. European Union rules provide for periods during which migratory birds may not be shot on their southward flight. The Left has not been immune to CPNT pressure: While the Greens opposed the CPNT on the issue of hunting, the Communists voted to support them and the Socialists abstained. See Jean-Michel Bezat, "La Gauche a abandonné Dominique Voynet lors du vote sur la chasse au Sénat," *Le Monde*, 27 May 2000.

69. The CPNT is strong in the southwestern part of the country (especially Gironde).
70. In a poll conducted just before the first round of the 1997 elections, 32 percent had confidence in the PS and its allies; 35 percent, in the UDF and RPR; and 31 percent in neither camp. See *Le Monde, Élections législatives, 25 mai–1er juin 1997, Dossiers et Documents*, p. 20.
71. The membership of the SFIO in 1945 was 340,000 (the high point); in 1969, it was ca. 70,000; in 1975, the PS had 150,000; in 1982 (when Mitterrand was in office), 213,000; and somewhat under 120,000 in 1999. See Hughes Portelli, "Le Parti socialiste: Une Position dominante," in Bréchon, ed., *Les Partis politiques français*, pp. 85–103.
72. Among them are Jack Lang, who functioned as minister of culture for a decade, and Martine Aubrey, the daughter of Jacques Delors and a former minister of labor.
73. The PRG, formerly the MRG, not to be confused with the *Parti radical-socialiste*, the "Radical" component of the UDF.
74. Michael Hastings, "Philippe de Villiers ou la croisade inachevée," in Pascal Perrineau and Colette Ysmal, eds., *Le Vote de crise: L'Élection présidentielle de 1995* (Paris: PFNSP, 1995), pp. 127–40.
75. On these points, see Pierre Martin, *Le Vote Le Pen: L'Électorat du Front national*, Notes de la Fondation Saint-Simon, no. 84 (Paris: October–November 1996), esp. 43–45. In a poll conducted before the first round of the 1997 elections, 75 percent considered the FN a danger to democracy; 76 percent disagreed with Le Pen's ideas, including 2 percent of those who were inclined toward the FN. See Gérard Courtois, "Trois Français sur quatre perçoivent le Front national comme un danger," *Le Monde*, 20 March 1997, p. 6.
76. Robert de Jouvenel, *La République des camarades*, 8th ed. (Paris: Grasset, 1914), p. 17.
77. This practice is probably facilitated by the semicircular arrangement of the parliamentary chambers, in which a deputy's slight move to the right or left is not nearly so dramatic an exercise as "crossing the aisle" in the British House of Commons.
78. There is also the case of Maurice Duverger, the prominent political scientist who, having been rejected as a candidate for the European Parliament in 1989 by the PS, arranged to have himself put on the slate of the Italian Communist party! The PS had originally wanted to put Duverger on its list, but had changed its mind as a result of letters of protest that recalled his pro-Vichy activities during the Occupation. See *Le Point*, 8 May 1989, p. 65.
79. Mayor of a small town in Brittany, Lalonde became president of *Génération écologie* and served as minister for the environment in the Socialist government between 1988 and 1992. In the early 1990s he competed with Rocard in proposing a "green-pink-blue" (i.e., environmentalist, socialist, and European) party, over which he would preside; he supported Chirac in the 1995 presidential elections; but in December 1998 he made an electoral agreement with Madelin (chief of *Démocratie libérale*). In 2001, Lalonde announced his candidacy for the forthcoming presidential election but failed to get the necessary 500 signatures. After Chirac's reelection and the installation of the Raffarin government, Lalonde indicated his readiness to "help" that government, despite his suspicion about Chirac himself; and while suggesting that he might support Chirac's UMP, Lalonde tried to present 380 candidates of the GE for the legislative elections. After his failure to get any GE candidates elected to the Assembly, he announced that he would quit politics and was replaced as president of the GE.
80. *Libération*, 16 May 1999, p. 14.
81. Mitterrand was a leader of the *Union démocratique et socialiste de la Résistance* (UDSR), a prosocialist but independent party of former Resistance members; the *Convention des institutions républicaines* (CIR), a collection of democratic-socialist clubs in the early and middle 1960s; the FGDS (1965–1969), the democratic-leftist electoral federation; and finally, the Socialist party—all these different vehicles for an essentially consistent ideological-tactical position. On Mitterrand's maneuverings from the Fourth Republic on, see Cathérine Nay, *Le Noir et le rouge* (Paris: Grasset, 1984), and her equally critical *Les Sept Mitterrand ou les métamorphoses d'un septennat* (Paris: Grasset, 1988). For a more recent discussion of Mitterrand's partisan ambiguities, see Alistair Cole, *François Mitterrand: A Study in Political Leadership* (London and New York: Routledge, 1994), pp. 1–31.
82. See Jean-François Revel, "La Droite en mal de doctrine," *Le Point*, 10 November 2000, p. 72.
83. An interesting example of the dominance of tactics over principle is the positioning of the relatively progressive *Force démocrate* (the former CDS) behind François Léotard, then leader of the UDF, who used to preside over the *Parti républicain*, the "neoliberal" party of the UDF. See Cécile Cham-

braud, "Les Centristes de Force démocrate s'engagent derrière François Léotard," *Le Monde*, 12 March 1996, p. 7.

84. The Right has argued that the Muslims adhere to a religion that does not accept the principle of separation of religion and state and, hence, that their massive presence may undermine the principles of French republicanism.

85. Emmanuel Todd, *La Nouvelle France* (Paris: Seuil, 1988), p. 11.

86. Emmanuel Todd, "Le Grand Recyclage européen," *Le Point*, 12 June 1989, pp. 44–45.

87. Alain Duhamel, *Le Complexe d'Astérix* (Paris: Gallimard, 1985), chapter 1.

88. For details about the institutional, socioeconomic, environmental, and "law-and-order" aspects of the programs of the 2002 presidential candidates, see "Demandez le programme!" *Le Monde*, Supplement, 11 April 2002.

89. See tables "Les Mots préférés des Français" and "Les Valeurs selon la préférence partisane," in Gérard Le Gall, "Le Front national à l'épreuve du temps," SOFRES, *L'Etat de l'opinion 1998*, pp. 72–73.

90. *L'Année politique 1998*, pp. 45–46.

91. See Alain Touraine, "Gauche-Droite," *Le Monde*, 8 July 1993; Alain Duhamel, "Les Deux Droites," *Le Point*, 11 September 1993, p. 23; and Olivier Duhamel and Jérôme Jaffré, "Un Paysage politique dévasté," SOFRES, *L'État de l'opinion 1993*, pp. 11–17.

92. Oliver Duhamel and Gérard Grunberg, "Référendum: Les Dix France," SOFRES, *L'État de l'opinion 1993*, pp. 79–86. See also Pascal Perrineau, "La Logique des clivages politiques," in *France: Les Révolutions invisibles*, ed. Daniel Cohen (Paris: Calmann-Lévy, 1998).

93. Although this change was inspired by partisan politics, it was passed with the support of Jospin's leftist allies as well as about 30 UDF deputies (supported by Valéry Giscard d'Estaing and Raymond Barre) and, after a second reading in Parliament, approved by the Constitutional Council. See Pascal Virot, "Calendrier électoral: Les Sages vont trancher," *Libération*, 9 May 2001. In the end, Chirac won, and so did the UMP, which confirmed the law of unintended consequences.

94. The question of "continuity" figured heavily during the trial of Maurice Papon in 1998 for crimes against humanity. Elements of both the Right and the Left opposed the trial; for many Gaullists, the trial of a person who had held high office not only under the Vichy regime but also in the Fifth Republic (as Paris police chief and member of the cabinet under Giscard d'Estaing's presidency) called into question two of the myths carefully cultivated by de Gaulle (subsequently, by Mitterrand as well), namely, that the deportation of Jews to death camps was the work of the German occupiers alone and that there was no continuity between the Vichy State and the republics that followed; and the trial was therefore an implied attack on the memory of de Gaulle and of Gaullism itself. This critique was embraced by Chevènement and other nationalist socialists. See Gérard Guicheteau, *Papon Maurice ou la continuité* (Paris: Éditions Mille et une Nuits, 1998).

95. Perrineau, "La Logique des clivages politiques," pp. 289–300.

96. Jacques Julliard, "Gauche: Du progressisme social au libéralisme moral," *Le Débat*, no. 110 (May–August 2000), 202–16.

97. See Roland Hureaux, "Les Trois Âges de la gauche," *Le Débat*, no. 103 (January–February 1999), 29–30.

98. See Jacques Capdevielle, Elisabeth Dupoirier, Gérard Grunberg, Étienne Schweisguth, and Colette Ysmal, *France de gauche, vote à droite* (Paris: PFNSP, 1981), pp. 217–27 and Table 122.

99. IFRES exit poll of 24 April 1988, cited in Philippe Habert and Colette Ysmal, eds., *L'Élection présidentielle 1988* (Paris: Le Figaro/Études Politiques, 1988), p. 31.

100. *L'Élection présidentielle 1995*, *Le Monde, Dossiers et Documents*, pp. 47–48.

101. According to a SOFRES poll, 56 percent of respondents in November 1989 (compared to 33 percent in March 1981) considered the Right-Left labels irrelevant to the positions of parties and politicians. *Le Point*, 27 November 1989, pp. 44–45.

102. IFOP, SOFRES, and BVA polls of end of September 1993, reported by *Antenne 2*. See also *Figaro-Magazine*, 2 October; *Le Monde*, 6 October; and *Paris Match*, 7 October 1993.

103. See Mathieu Brugidou, *L'Élection présidentielle: Discours et enjeux politiques* (Paris: L'Harmattan, 1995). Not all electoral results should be attributed to considerations of economic rationality: The results of the parliamentary elections of 1968 were due to "backlash" against the rebellions of that year; those of the presidential elections of 1974, to unhappiness about the bipolarization of French

political life; those of the parliamentary elections of 1993, to negative reaction to the scandals associated with a government too long in power. The reelection of Chirac in 2002 was due to the fear that the election of his opponent would threaten the democratic order.

104. Based on exit poll. See Stéphane Courtois, "La Victoire de Jacques Chirac et la transformation des clivages politiques," in Perrineau and Ysmal, *Le Vote de crise*, pp. 164–66.

105. Jean Charlot, *Pourquoi Jacques Chirac?* (Paris: Éditions de Fallois, 1996), esp. pp. 207–71.

106. In another poll (Capdevielle et al., *France de gauche, vote à droite*, Table 31, p. 257), 8 percent of PCF voters classified themselves as belonging to the center or center-right on an ideological spectrum ranging from extreme Left to extreme Right; 19 percent of PS-MRG voters classified themselves as belonging in the center and 4 percent in the center-right; 10 percent of the PSU electorate labeled itself as being in the center, and 3 percent in the center-right; and 45 percent of UDF voters labeled themselves as belonging to the center or center-left (as contrasted with 37 percent of Gaullist voters who labeled themselves as centrist or center-left!). These outcomes raise some questions regarding the existence of sufficiently objective criteria for ideological self-classification.

107. According to a public opinion poll conducted in the beginning of 1981 by the *Institut français de démoscopie*, when asked to choose between economic security and liberty, 26.4% of the respondents chose the former and 70.3%, the latter. See *Le Monde (Dimanche)*, 1 March 1981, p. xviii.

108. A poll conducted on 24 April 1988 on the "ideological profile" of the Right and the Left revealed that 78 percent of those identified as being on the left and 51 percent of those identified as being on the right had a positive view concerning the right to strike. Other positive views were as follows: the role of trade unions: Left, 69 percent, Right, 41 percent; nationalization: Left, 57 percent, Right, 33 percent; privatization: Left, 29 percent, Right, 70 percent; employers: Left, 38 percent, Right, 71 percent; private schools: Left, 36 percent, Right, 76 percent. Based on Elisabeth Dupoirier, "Changement et persistance du clivage gauche-droite en 1988," *L'Élection présidentielle 1988, Le Monde, Dossiers et Documents*, p. 49.

109. One scholar, Alain Leroux, in *La France des quatre pouvoirs* (Paris: PUF, 1989), argued that since 1981, all major parties in France have abandoned programmatic orientations in favor of various kinds of pragmatism: political (in the case of the PS); charismatic (the Gaullists); technocratic (Giscardists); and populist (Le Pen).

110. For instance, during Giscard's presidency, deductions of all kinds *(prélèvements obligatoires)* went up from 36.3 percent of GNP in 1974 to 41.6 percent in 1980; investments in nationalized industries went up from 16.9 percent of total industrial investment in 1974 to 27 percent in 1981. See Denis Jeambar, "La Pieuvre étatique," *Le Point*, 16–22 February 1981, pp. 36–42.

111. According to Alain Touraine, "Rocardism [could] not be explained in terms of its ideological content" but rather in terms of a variety of favorable (though conflicting) images. Cited in Hervé Hamon and Patrick Rotman, *L'Effet Rocard* (Paris: Stock, 1980), p. 337.

112. According to a SOFRES poll in February/March 1988 concerning the qualities of the three major presidential candidates, Mitterrand (with 40 percent) was judged more competent than Chirac (with 30 percent), while Chirac (with 26 percent) was judged more aggressive than Mitterrand (with 3 percent). On the eve of the presidential elections a year later, the gap between the two had widened. See SOFRES, *L'État de l'opinion 1989*, pp. 102–3. Note, however, that there were great fluctuations in Mitterrand's popularity as president: from 48 percent in 1981 to 32 percent in 1984, 51 percent in 1986, 56 percent just before the 1988 elections, 60 percent in 1989, between 30 and 40 percent in 1992, about 35 percent just before the 1993 elections, and 47 percent in August 1993, that is, four months after the parliamentary elections.

113. The strong point of Chirac was his personality for 52 percent of those interrogated, and his weakest points were his program (7 percent) and his achievements (6 percent); Jospin's strongest points were his program (16 percent) and his accomplishments (19 percent), and personality, his weakest point (16 percent as well). SOFRES poll, 21 April 2002, cited in *Le Monde*, 17 April 2002, p. 10. In a much earlier poll (IPSOS–*Le Point*, October 2000), Jospin had come out well ahead of Chirac on several items: inspiring greater confidence; understanding the needs of society; and representing moral vigor; but Chirac was ahead of Jospin in being considered closer to the people. For that reason alone, the Socialists expressed lack of assurance about Jospin's prospects. See Eric Perrandeau, "La Gauche française face aux élections de 2002," *Revue socialiste*, April 2002, pp. 130–42.

114. In the words of Catherine Pegard, "Les Français sont 60% à juger le bilan [de Jospin] positif. . . . Pour Chirac, son bilan va de pair avec sa popularité: le bilan du president, c'est lui tel qu'il est à l'Elysée." See Pegard, "La Guerre des bilans n'aura pas lieu," *Le Point*, 11 January 2002, pp. 20–21.

115. See Jérôme Jaffré, "France de gauche, vote à gauche," *Pouvoirs* 20 (1982), 13.

116. For a treatment of the technicalities of electoral systems from the Third to the Fifth Republics, see Edmond Jouve, ed., *Modes de scrutin et systèmes électoraux, Documents d'Etudes, Droit constitutionnel et institutions politiques*, no. 1.05, nouvelle édition (Paris: Documentation Français, 1986).

117. In November 1996, in the second round of a municipal by-election in Dreux, the Socialist candidate withdrew in favor of the Gaullist in order to prevent the FN candidate (who had come in ahead in the first round) from winning. But such behavior in the name of "republican defense" is not necessarily reciprocal. In the municipal elections of June 1995 in a small town (Vitrolles), the UDF candidate refused to pull out in the second round in favor of the runner-up PS candidate, thus making it possible for the FN candidate to be elected. However, in a special election in the same town in February 1997, the Gaullist candidate did withdraw in favor of the PS candidate in the second round, in a vain attempt to block the FN candidate from gaining victory.

118. Various requirements concerning presidential candidacies are established by law, which provides that candidates must be at least 23 years old, must not have been convicted of a felony, and must have been placed in nomination with the signatures of 500 politicians (deputies, senators, general councillors, or mayors). Since 1981, naturalized citizens have been eligible to be presidential candidates.

119. The law provides for a mixed, single-member/proportional-representation system with two ballots. The party list that receives an absolute majority of the votes on the first ballot gets 50 percent of all seats plus one, the remainder of the seats being divided proportionally among all lists that receive at least 5 percent of the vote. In this way, a majority party or coalition is doubly rewarded, but minor parties still obtain *some* representation.

120. For a detailed description of the "highest average" system, see Jouve, *Modes de scrutin*, pp. 7–8.

121. In addition to changes in the method of elections, there have been several postponements, by act of Parliament, in dates of elections on municipal, cantonal, and regional levels. The two most recent were the postponement of the municipal elections of 1995, so as not to have them take place too close on the heels of the presidential elections; and the switching of the electoral calendar for 2002, so that the presidential would precede the parliamentary elections.

122. See *L'Année politique 1991*, pp. 78–79. The Vedel Commission on constitutional reform, in its report in February 1993, suggested a possible compromise: electing 10 percent of the Assembly deputies on the basis of proportional representation. Under such a system (roughly modeled on that of the German Federal Republic), each voter would be able to cast two ballots, one for an individual candidate as at present and one for a party list. In the fall of 1996, the government put forth for study a proposal to add a "dose" of proportional representation to the system of Assembly elections, especially in heavily urbanized departments. Under the proposed system, parties coming out first on departmental lists would get a bonus of 25 percent. One of the consequences would be increased representation of smaller parties (including the PCF, the environmentalists, and the FN). But it might also weaken the UDF (by enabling its components to be represented separately) and strengthen the relative position of the RPR. See Olivier Biffaud and Cécile Chambraud, "Alain Juppé met à l'étude une réforme du mode du scrutin," *Le Monde*, 7 September 1996, p. 6.

123. The list included regional parties such as *Moins d'impôts maintenant, Combat pour l'emploi, Parti de la loi naturelle, Parti humaniste, Ligue nationaliste*, etc., most of them ad hoc groups getting less than 1 percent of the vote.

124. Claude Dargent, "Participation et actions politiques," *La Société française contemporaine*, ed. Jean-Yves Capul, *Cahiers français*, no. 291 (May–June 1999), pp. 68–74.

125. Hervé Le Bras, "FN-abstention: Même profil," *Libération*, 11 June 2002. The various reasons for abstentions are explored by Jérôme Jaffré and Anne Muxel, "S'abstenir: Hors du jeu ou dans le jeu politique?" in *Les Cultures politiques des Français*, ed. Pierre Bréchon, Annie Laurent and Pascal Perrineau (Paris: Presses de Sciences-Po, 2000), pp. 19–52. For explaining abstentions in the first round of the legislative elections of 2002, see Gérard Courtois, "L'Abstention du 9 juin révèle plus de désintérêt que de mécontentement," *Le Monde*, 15 June 2002.

126. A law passed in 1995 (which forbade corporate contributions to presidential candidates) limited the total for each candidate to 250,000 francs plus one franc for each person in the constituency, so that the contribution to a candidate in an average constituency was about 350,000 francs (ca. $60,000). See François Chirot, "Certains Candidats dépasseraient les coûts de campagne autorisés," *Le Monde,* 31 March 1995, p. 6.

127. A candidate for a seat in Parliament at that time had to deposit 1,000 francs for advertising, which was reimbursed if he or she got a minimum of 5 percent of the vote.

128. Since 1974 there have been television debates between the two or three major presidential contenders. Before the parliamentary elections of 1997, there was a "debate about a debate" between the leaders of the Right and the Left: Jospin wanted a one-on-one debate with Juppé, but the latter preferred a two-on-two formula, with himself and another leader of the RPR-UDF coalition face to face with Jospin as well as Communist leader Hue, but the Socialist leader declined.

129. There were two qualifications: A party had to put up at least 50 candidates and had to receive at least 5 percent of the national popular vote.

130. Deputies must give up part of their salaries to their parties. Communist deputies transfer their entire salaries to the party, which returns less than 30 percent to them. In contrast, Socialist deputies (in 1988) gave up only 8,000 francs.

131. *Le Point,* 8 December 2000, p. 70.

132. An extreme case is that of Michel Delebarre. Formerly minister of urban affairs, he was elected mayor of Dunkerque, and reelected in 1995 and 2001. In the latter year he held 30 elective offices, including the presidencies of a regional council, a *syndicat mixte,* the urban community (i.e., metropolitan district) of Dunkerque, and the national union of moderate-rent housing units (HLMs).

133. See Philippe Augé, "La Nouvelle Législation sur le cumul des mandats électoraux et des fonctions électives," *Regards sur l'actualité,* no. 270 (April 2001), 19–32.

134. Frank L. Wilson, "The Club Phenomenon in France," *Comparative Politics* 3 (July 1971), 517–28. For a historical treatment, see Jean-André Faucher, *Les Clubs politiques en France* (Paris: Didier, 1965). See also Janine Mussuz, *Les Clubs et la politique* (Paris: Colin, 1970). Mussuz distinguishes between clubs that are *sociétés de réflexion* and those engaging in *combat politique.*

135. After being replaced as leader, Désir left the party, joined *Génération écologie,* and subsequently (in 1993) became a member of the Socialist party.

136. The *Club de l'Horloge* also maintains links to the Heritage Foundation, a conservative "think tank" in the United States.

137. Pascal Virot, "Les Juniors de la gauche s'unissent," *Libération,* 27 April 2001.

138. One illustration of the tendency for the formation of ad hoc miniparties was provided during the elections to the European Parliament in 1994. Candidates were put up under the following lists in addition to those of the mainstream parties and smaller existing ones: (1) *Pour l'Europe des travailleurs et la démocratie,* a proworker party hostile to a "capitalist" European Union; (2) *L'Autre Politique,* a leftist anti-Maastricht list headed by Jean-Pierre Chevènement; (3) *Sarajevo,* a list initiated by the philosopher Bernard-Henri Lévy to call attention to the European Community's abandonment of the Bosnian Muslims; (4) *Énergie radicale,* an independent leftist pro-European list intended to promote the political fortunes of Bernard Tapie, a Left-Radical deputy whose parliamentary immunity had been lifted when he was indicted for the misappropriation of funds; and (5) *L'Autre Europe,* a conservative anti-Maastricht party led by Philippe de Villiers, then a Gaullist deputy.

139. On the "post-socialism" of the PS, see Alain Touraine, *L'Après-Socialisme* (Paris: Grasset, 1980), and the much more critical book by Alain Peyrefitte, *Quand la rose se fanera* (Paris: Plon, 1983). Other studies include Jean Poperen, *Socialistes, la chute finale?* (Paris: Plon, 1993), written by a left-oriented insider; and Marc Sadoun, *De la démocratie française: Essai sur le socialisme* (Paris: Gallimard, 1993). Sadoun, a political scientist, argues that the PS adapted its rhetoric too readily to that of the PCF, although it was unable to produce results expected by the working class. For a critique of "postsocialism" and a demand for a renewal of an ideology of a state-directed socialism stressing the public good, see Pierre Moscovici, *À la recherche de la gauche perdu* (Paris: Calmann-Lévy, 1994).

140. On the attitudes and behavior of the environmentalists, their internal divisions, their relations with the different traditional parties, and their electoral fortunes, see Florence Faucher, *Les Habits verts de la politique* (Paris: Presses de Sciences-Po, 1999).

CHAPTER 5

Interest Groups

Interest groups occupy an important position in France. At present, there are thousands of associations, ranging from trade unions and business organizations with large memberships to small groups of students, and from nationally organized professional groups to purely local fellowships.[1] They play a crucial role in shaping political attitudes, in policy formulation, and even in the support of republican institutions. Groups are involved politically through their linkage to the formal decision-making organs, their alliance with political parties, and their direct "colonization" of Parliament and the civil service.

TRADE UNIONS

Among the most significant interest groups, in terms of age, connections to parties, mass membership, and the ability to mobilize support for or against government policies, are the trade unions. The oldest trade union "umbrella" organization, the General Confederation of Labor (*Confédération générale du travail*—CGT), was founded in 1895. As a union of anarcho-syndicalist, Marxist, and revolutionary inspiration, it used to be as much concerned with general political goals (e.g., changing the whole political system) as with bread-and-butter issues. After World War I, workers inspired by Catholic principles split from the CGT to form their own union, the French Confederation of Christian Workers (*Confédération française des travailleurs chrétiens*—CFTC). In 1947, many workers who disliked the growing dependence of the CGT on the Communist party and the union's preoccupation with politically inspired general strikes created a new organization, the Workers' Force (*Confédération générale du travail–Force ouvrière*—CGT-FO, or simply FO). The CGT was by far the largest union in the 1960s and 1970s, and despite the loss of about half its membership in the past several years, it remains powerful; its present membership has been estimated at about 650,000. Although today only a minority of CGT members are Communists, the fact that most of its top leaders have also been prominent in the PCF used to make the CGT appear like an obedient "transmission belt" for the party.[2] The FO has about 400,000 members; during the Fourth Republic, it was a significant union because many of its members (and some of its leaders) were ideologically linked to the Socialist party (SFIO). Unlike the CGT, the FO firmly supported the regime and was convinced that benefits could be gained for workers through collective bargaining and lobbying. The FO has resembled the Anglo-American type of trade union in its acceptance of the (capitalist) political system, its pragmatic approaches to labor-management relations, and its staunch anticommunism.

The CFTC was closely allied to the Christian Democratic party (MRP). This alliance, coupled with the CFTC's rejection of the class struggle and the deeply held conviction that "man does not live by bread alone," enabled that union to recruit many traditionalist members of the working class. But the CFTC lacked dynamism and was in danger of losing much of its membership to the CGT, which never tired of pointing out that clericalism could not be credibly combined with the promotion of workers' interests. In response to this claim, the bulk of the CFTC's membership and leadership "deconfessionalized" the union in the 1960s and renamed it the French Democratic Confederation of Labor (*Confédération française démocratique du travail*—CFDT). The bylaws of the CFDT do not mention Christianity but merely refer to man's "spiritual needs."[3] A rump of the old CFTC remains in existence, with about 100,000 members.[4]

The CFDT, whose membership is estimated at about 500,000, has become the second-largest trade union federation.[5] In the late 1960s, this union began an ideological evolution that gradually led it to endorse three principles: the nationalization of the means of production; democratic planning; and factory self-management *(autogestion)*. These positions brought most of the CFDT's leadership, and much of its membership, close to the Socialist party. The existence of several ideologically fragmented trade unions has made for a certain amount of competition, which has often forced one union or another to adopt radical rhetoric in order to appeal to potential members, to keep its own members from deserting, or otherwise to outbid its rivals.[6]

Ideological conflict has not been the only factor in the fragmentation of the employee sector. In France, as elsewhere in Western Europe, the white-collar segment has organized separately in order to maintain its status distinctions. The *Confédération française de l'encadrement–Conféderation generale des cadres* (CFE-CGC)[7] is such a union, and it counts among its approximately 180,000 members supervisory or managerial personnel and technicians. Not all white-collar employees belong to the CGC; many are, in fact, found within the three major trade union federations. In order to keep the white-collar segment within their ranks, the latter have insisted that salary differentials between white- and blue-collar workers ought to be retained; this is true even of the CGT, which has tried to combine its egalitarian ideology with opposition to a policy of complete leveling of wages. One must not, however, exaggerate the meaning, or the political implications, of the distinctions between blue- and white-collar employees, as differences in outlook exist within the white-collar sector as well.[8] There are a number of additional trade unions, whose membership may be highly specific or mixed. Among them is the *Union nationale des syndicats autonomes* (UNSA); established in 1993, it is an umbrella organization including a number of specialized unions, for example, associations of tax collectors, nurses, bank clerks, journalists, and police officers.

The prospect of unity among the various trade unions is uncertain. During Gaullist-Giscardist rule, the ideological divisions among the unions, which had been exacerbated by their relationships to different "patron" parties, began to weaken, in part because the representation of leftist parties in Parliament had declined, and in part because Parliament, the traditional arena for the promotion of labor interests, had become a less effective decision maker. This situation provided an incentive for the unions to be self-reliant and to combine forces to promote their common interests. All major industrial unions have shared a commitment to higher wages, expanded fringe benefits, higher levels of public welfare spending, more-secure protection of the right to organize in the factories, the reform of the tax system, and a general hostility to Gaullism and Giscardism.

However, there has been disagreement on important matters. Although all three industrial unions have favored *some* form of factory democracy, the CFDT was most insistent about promoting worker self-management, the CGT was hostile to the idea, and the FO indifferent to it. There have also been differences in approach to general politics, with the CGT and CFDT favoring direct political involvement and the search for parliamentary and other allies, and the FO proclaiming its independence from political forces. The commonalities have resulted in (more or less ritualistic) interunion collaboration, especially (until the mid-1990s) between the CGT and CFDT, as in joint demonstrations, interunion bargaining committees (e.g., in nationalized industries), common deputations to government officials, common demands, and sometimes common strikes.

The nature of interunion relationships has not been static and has not been based merely on ideological differences. Thus, all three unions took part in the massive strikes of railroad workers at the end of 1995 in opposition to the government's economic policies, including its privatization measures and its efforts at reducing the public deficit by retrenchments in the welfare state. The unions were particularly united in opposing Prime Minister Juppé's proposal to raise the retirement age (then 55) of railroad workers, part of an overall reform of the social security system. In this instance, the FO took a more radical position than the CFDT (and was generally supported by the CGT), because the FO, which had been administering the health insurance funds like a fiefdom for more than two decades, did not want to give up its position.

Whatever their basis, the diversities among unions and the personal rivalries among their leaders have been persistent and have been reflected in competing union lists in factory-council and social security elections, in the union leaders' periodic trading of insults, and in the failure to promote organizational mergers. The elections to social security boards, labor tribunals, and parity-based personnel committees attached to government ministries, which take place every three years, and to the factory-committee elections, which occur every two years, provide rough indicators of relative union support among the rank and file.

In many polls conducted among workers, most of the respondents have expressed the view that unions should not mix in politics, but that view has not been dominant among union leaders (except those of the FO). In fact, union leaders have supported leftist political candidates and have worked actively for their election, although the support of such candidates has been neither unified nor consistent, and it has not necessarily mirrored the preferences of rank-and-file members.[9] In the presidential contest of 1981 (first round), however, the unions were divided: The CGT came out publicly for the Communist candidate, Marchais; the CFDT for Mitterrand; the CFTC for Giscard; and the FO for no one in particular. In 1981 and 1988, the leaders of all three unions and most of their members opted for Mitterrand in the second round. The behavior of these unions in the 1995 presidential elections was more complex. All of them were officially neutral; their leaders insisted that their support of one or another candidate would depend on the candidate's economic and social policy proposals. Even the CGT would not come out clearly for the PCF candidate in the first round (as it had done in 1988). Before the second round, however, the three major unions actively supported Socialist candidate Jospin. The trade unions were less directly involved in the parliamentary election campaign of 1997, although the leaders of most of the unions were hoping for the victory of the Left (except, perhaps, for Nicole Notat of the CFDT, who reputedly got along well with Juppé). In 2002, the trade unions played a prominent role on the eve of the second round of the presidential elections when they called upon their members to help defeat Jean-Marie Le Pen.

A politically activist approach by unions has been unavoidable because autonomous bargaining in the Anglo-American sense—leading to collective contracts with employers—has not been very effective. The ideological splits in the labor movement have weakened the trade unions' position in bargaining with a relatively unified employer. In the case of factories in which workers' membership is split among several unions, the National Labor Relations Board (*Commission nationale de la négociation collective*—CNNC), which includes union and management representatives, may in theory certify one union as the bargaining agent for all the workers in the plant; in practice, however, the workers are represented at the bargaining table by several unions. There is no union shop in France, and until the early 1980s, union recruiting activities on the factory level were forbidden; if workers wished to join a union, they had to register at a local branch office. Since 1981, collective bargaining at the plant level has been legalized, but the local unions have been so weak that they have tended to rely on national union-management agreements *(accords-cadres)*. Since these agreements have often involved the government as a third party, it has, in effect, been a co-negotiator whose goodwill is crucial.

In France, in contrast to the United States, there is no automatic payroll deduction system for union dues. These have had to be collected (with dismal success) by the local union officials, and the union coffers have been relatively empty. This situation is a consequence of a steady decline of union membership *(désyndicalisation)*. In 2001, only 8 to 9 percent of the labor force was unionized (compared to about 28 percent in Germany and Britain). This decline must be attributed to the loss of industrial working-class jobs: from 8,207,000 workers (out of the active labor force of 21,775,000, i.e., 37 percent) in 1973–1974 to 7,634,000 workers (out of an active labor force of 25,755,000, i.e., 29 percent) in 1998.[10] In the steel industry alone, the loss of jobs between 1980 and 1988 was 43 percent. The threat of further job losses in industry makes union leaders hesitant about exerting union pressures. The result has been a loss of working-class dynamism and a weakening of interunion collaboration.[11] This does not mean, however, that unions should be counted out altogether. Despite smaller membership, some unions—for example, that of the railway workers (for the most part, affiliated with the CGT), are still potent enough when they strike—in part because of the importance of rail transport, and in part because of overall public support.

In the past, conservative governments, because they felt that the political system might be threatened by the unions' historical "revolutionary" ideology, often discriminated against them; for their part, the unions could not easily replace their belief in the politics of *confrontation* with a politics of *accommodation* (i.e., a businesslike bargaining outlook) so long as they were convinced that bargaining opportunities and fruitful access to government were restricted. Under Presidents Pompidou and Giscard d'Estaing, unions resented the government because, in its preoccupation with productivity, it did little to moderate the traditional resistance of organized business to collective bargaining (and the tendency of employers to renege on collective contracts).

For these reasons, most of the unions welcomed the election of a Socialist president and a Socialist Assembly majority in 1981. Their optimism was not misplaced: During the Socialists' first year in power, they raised the wages of workers (especially the lowest paid) significantly; expanded social security benefits; increased the taxes on the incomes of wealthy individuals and firms; and introduced legislation (the Auroux laws) that made it obligatory for management and workers to conduct wage negotiations annually at the plant level and strengthened the unions' representation in factory councils.[12] In addition, a number of union officials were given ministerial posts or were placed on the staffs of individual ministers.

Unfortunately, these legal improvements were counterbalanced by growing unemployment and the loss of jobs, particularly in the "smokestack" industries, in which unions had been relatively strong. It has even been argued that the unions were worse off under Mitterrand's Socialist governments than under previous (Gaullist-Giscardist) governments, whose leaders were sensitive to charges that their policies were antisocial. The Socialist government's austerity program, put into effect early in 1983, could not be attributed to any inherently antisocial attitudes, especially in view of the generosity of the social reforms just cited. However, the nationalization policies initiated by the Socialist government had a restrictive effect on the unions' freedom of action, because it was more difficult to denounce a Left-dominated state and make tough claims against it than against a private employer. Although under the Mauroy government the major unions had their separate axes to grind, they voiced only relatively low keyed criticisms of government policy because they did not wish to give too much ammunition to the Gaullist-Giscardist opposition. Under subsequent Socialist governments, too, the unions' power was limited by three major factors: the frequent closing of factories, the declining public image of the unions, and pressures on the government to promote productivity and keep the currency stable. Although the majority of union members considered themselves to be on the left, had voted for Mitterrand in 1981 and 1988, and had a generally favorable view of Socialist policy (at least until 1983), they complained about the "politicization" of the union leadership, that is, its nearly automatic support of Socialist governments.[13]

It was partly in order to improve the image of the unions and renew their energy that the leadership of two of the major union federations was replaced in the past several years. The new leaders made it a point to stress their independence from political parties. For example, Louis Viannet, the secretary-general of the CGT, although still a member of the PCF, resigned from the party's executive committee in 1996. His successor, Bernard Thibault, went even further. For example, in 1999 he refused to join a Communist-organized march in favor of employment because of its "political" nature, arguing that the union was not a member of the governing coalition. The reasons for that distancing could be explained by two developments: PCF leader Hue had become too accommodating to the government's "moderate" policies; and the CGT, with more than double the membership of the PCF, no longer wished to be the union tail of the party dog.[14] Meanwhile, the CFDT under the leadership of Nicole Notat continued its moderate position with respect to its public behavior and its claims. In contrast, the FO has became more radical since the election of Marc Blondel as president.

BUSINESS ASSOCIATIONS

The business community, possessing greater wealth and organizational unity, has usually been in a better position than the trade unions. This is especially true of big business, which after 1946 was organized in the National Council of French Employers (*Conseil national du patronat français*—CNPF), an umbrella organization of about 900,000 industrial, commercial, and banking firms belonging to some 400 constituent associations, which are, in turn, grouped into 85 federations. During World War II, the business community (then represented by another organization) discredited itself by its collaboration with the Vichy regime. The weak Resistance record of industrialists, and their virtual absence from de Gaulle's London entourage, prevented a rapprochement between organized business and postwar governments that were dominated by left-wing political parties.[15] The poor image of business was in some measure reflected in the nationalization of many industries and in the enactment of numerous laws in favor of workers.

Nevertheless, throughout most of the Fourth Republic, the CNPF proved to be an effective interest group. The government's commitment to capitalist planning transformed the business community into a crucial partner in economic-policy making; the disunity of organized labor frequently permitted business to ignore collective contracts; and the *pantouflage* relationship of business and the higher civil service gave business favorable access to the authorities. This relationship enabled bureaucrats who had proved their goodwill toward business to slip (*pantoufler*) into lucrative positions in that sector.

With the establishment of the Fifth Republic, the CNPF acquired much greater power, and the relationship between business and the upper-level civil service intensified. Furthermore, the government had committed itself to a number of goals favored by big business: consolidation, productivity, and exports. This was particularly the case under the premiership of Barre, who was in frequent contact with the CNPF president, François Ceyrac, an older man who personified almost perfectly the conservative, gerontocratic leadership of organized business (and who stepped down in 1981 after a 20-year tenure). In the past two decades, the CNPF tried to improve its image and "rejuvenate" its leadership.[16] Under the prodding of the Young Employers (*Jeunes patrons*), a group of dynamic businesspeople vaguely affiliated with the CNPF,[17] the CNPF became more sympathetic to free-market competition, collective bargaining, and even a modicum of worker participation in industrial decisions, if only in order to weaken the class-struggle approach of some unions and get workers to identify with firms. Nevertheless, differences of opinion on all these matters—and on the "correct" reactions to government policies—continued to exist within the CNPF.[18] For example, Jean Gandois, the president of the CNPF (1994–1998), frequently expressed himself in favor of the welfare state and, more specifically, of the social and wage demands of the workers, and encouraged bilateral union-management discussions. However, he also favored Juppé's privatization measures and (after the legislative victory of the Left) called upon Jospin to pursue a "realistic" government policy, under which taxes and social charges on business would be reduced, in order to make French industry more competitive and help to create employment.[19]

In 1999, Ernest-Antoine Seillière became president of the CNPF, and the name of the organization was changed to *Mouvement des entrepreneurs de France* (MEDEF). Under Seillière's leadership, the MEDEF has become more politically active; it successfully opposed a number of government policies,[20] and engaged more openly in the electoral campaigns of 2002. The MEDEF is technically open to both big and small business; however, the latter is separately organized in the General Confederation of Small- and Medium-Sized Enterprises (*Confédération générale des petites et moyennes entreprises*— CGPME), an association that, although formally linked to the MEDEF, has acted independently in an effort to maintain traditional family business in the face of international competition and industrial modernization. The CGPME is a federation of 400 constituent federations representing 1.5 million firms, including more than 350,000 commercial establishments, about 100,000 manufacturing firms, and nearly 1 million service enterprises. Additional associations have been trying to speak for the interests of the small shopkeeper and artisan. Some of these date back to the Fourth Republic, when France began to commit itself to economic modernization policies. One of the most vocal of these groups was the Union for the Defense of Shopkeepers and Artisans (*Union pour la défense des commerçants et des artisans*—UDCA); founded in 1953, it attracted a membership of more than 350,000, and as a political party (the Poujadists) it attained considerable electoral success in 1956 (see Chapter 4). Another organization was the *Confédération intersyndicale de défense–Union nationale des artisans et travailleurs indépendants* (CID-UNATI), whose main strength was in the provinces. Unlike other small-business associations (such as the CGPME, which has tried to lobby in Parliament and to cultivate good relations with conservative or centrist parties), the CID-UNATI became quite radicalized and preferred violent forms of political expression—which, in 1970, led to the imprisonment of its founder and leader, Gérard Nicoud. The "martyrdom" of Nicoud may have accounted for the fact that in the early 1970s, the membership of that group grew from 23,000 to 189,000. Since then, the CID-UNATI declined and became hardly more than a political club. Still other organizations are the *Confédération nationale de l'artisanat et des métiers*, whose 1,000 affiliated associations encompass about 100,000 individual firms, and the *Union professionnelle artisanale* (UPA), which represents about 350,000 artisans.

Adding up the membership of all the small-business associations results in a statistically impressive figure. However, organizational fragmentation has compounded this sector's problems in promoting its interests, given the weakness of the center parties to which it has been ideologically linked, and given the pressures for the consolidation of enterprises, which have contributed to a constantly increasing number of bankruptcies.

In addition to these voluntary, or "associational," business groups, there is a network of 153 chambers of commerce and industry, organized into 21 regional chambers. The existence of these chambers, which are bodies of public law (*établissements publics*), goes back to the seventeenth century (although their status was redefined by a law of 1898). The chambers, which represent local business firms and derive a part of their budget from dues imposed on the firms, are under the supervision *(tutelle)* of the state (specifically, the minister of industry) and are charged with a number of public tasks, including the administration of ports and airports (and business concessions in them), warehouses, private business schools, and vocational-training institutes. In order to coordinate the activities of the chambers and to improve their function as intermediaries between the business community and the state, the government in 1964 established the *Assemblée permanente des chambres de commerce,* which represents the business organizations by means of periodic elections. A parallel system of chambers exists for artisans and craftsmen (carpenters, plumbers, bakers, and so forth), which are topped on a national level by an *Assemblée permanente des chambres de métiers.* But because of the artisans' organizational fragmentation and their generally precarious economic position, neither their chambers nor the permanent assembly has been very effective in representing their interests vis-à-vis the government.[21]

AGRICULTURE

The weakness of small business is paralleled in the agricultural sector, which has had some difficulty in preserving its position. Whereas until the end of the Fourth Republic, agriculture was a dominant economic force and several political parties in Parliament represented farmers' interests, today agriculture must rely largely on its own organizational strength. Agriculture, however, like labor, suffers from fragmentation and internal competition. The largest farmers' organization is the National Federation of Farmers' Unions (*Fédération nationale des syndicats des exploitants agricoles*—FNSEA), an umbrella organization of 38 specialized farmers' groups. With its 600,000 members (grouped in more than 30,000 local associations and 94 department federations), the FNSEA includes only half of the 1.2 million farmers in France, a poor showing compared to the 90 percent of British farmers included in the National Farmers' Union. The FNSEA embraces primarily independent farmers and is generally thought to be conservative in political outlook, although one of its constituent groups, the Young Farmers (*Centre national des jeunes agriculteurs*—CNJA), originally led by the Christian Agricultural Youth (*Jeunesse agricole chrétienne*—JAC),[22] has tried to infuse "progressive" (in addition to Catholic) attitudes into the FNSEA.

The CNJA, with its 80,000 members, is formally "attached" to the FNSEA but maintains organizational autonomy. The FNSEA tries to reconcile the interests of proprietors of small and large farms. In the 1960s, the CNJA charged the FNSEA with being more interested in representing large-scale farmers (especially of cereals) and food-processing companies rather than family farms and selectively boycotted its activities; but in the 1970s, the CNJA became more influential when one of its leaders, Michel Débatisse, took over the direction of the FNSEA, became active in the UDF, and eventually (in 1979) became a cabinet minister.

The decline in the number of small landholdings reduced the numerical weight of the peasantry. Conversely, the adding of land to nearly 300,000 existing farms and the establishment of about 100,000 large farms created a new (American-style) category of agricultural producers whose entrepreneurial attitudes enhanced the position of the CNJA within the FNSEA even further and facilitated closer cooperation with the CNPF.

Fragmentation of agriculture along ideological lines was fairly widespread before World War II, when the *Société nationale d'encouragement à l'agriculture* was close to the Radicals, and the *Confédération générale de l'agriculture* related well to the SFIO. Today, there are still agricultural associations that are ideologically oriented. The FNSEA tends to be Catholic and right of center; the *Confédération nationale de la mutualité, de la coopération, et du crédit agricoles* has links to the center-left and Socialist parties; and the *Mouvement de coordination de défense des exploitants agricoles familiaux* (MODEF), which represents the very poorest farmers, is sponsored by the Communists. The newest agricultural association—formed in the 1980s—is the *Confédération paysanne* (resulting from the merger of several left-wing farmers' organizations). Led by José Bové, it gained considerable public attention in fighting against the creeping "globalization" of agriculture (and the growth of supermarkets), demanding more government aid to small farmers, and opposing the import of genetically altered products.[23]

The ideological identification of agricultural associations has been declining, however, and fragmentation is increasingly based on agronomic specialization: single-crop producers, such as wheat growers or winegrowers; and economic groups, such as credit or cooperative-marketing associations.[24] The various agricultural associations are united—if that is the word—under "corporatist" auspices, in the sense that they all elect representatives to the 94 departmental agricultural chambers (with half the members of each chamber elected every three years for six-year terms). These chambers are "bodies of public law" that the government calls on for expert advice and the performance of selected public administrative tasks, such as marketing, the implementation of farm price and credit policies, and training programs.[25] At the apex of this organizational pyramid is the *Assemblée permanente des chambres d'agriculture*, which consists of delegates chosen by each of the departmental chambers.

The decline of the farming sector and the fragmentation of agricultural organization have greatly reduced the pressure potential of agriculture. Other reasons for the weakness of agriculture as an interest group, however, have been even more important. One of them is the fact that the two-round, single-member electoral system has greatly weakened the centrist parties, which had traditionally been most sympathetic to agricultural interests. Another is the EU Common Agricultural Policy, which has "supranationalized" decisions concerning farmers and forced organized agricultural interests to relocate their lobbying efforts from Paris to Brussels. Nevertheless, the domestic political weight of the agricultural sector cannot be completely discounted; by means of lobbying with the minister of agriculture and massive public protests in the mid-1990s, that sector stiffened the government's resolve to halt the importation of British beef that was thought to be infected with "mad cow" disease.

STUDENTS AND TEACHERS

Organizational fragmentation is also found among teachers and students. There are separate Socialist, Communist, Catholic, Gaullist, and liberal student associations. For many years, the largest student organization was the *Union nationale des étudiants de France* (UNEF), which was founded in 1907. Generally leftist, it was weakened in 1960 when the Gaullist government, in response to the UNEF's critique of the government's

Algerian policies, cut off the UNEF's subsidy and refused to have dealings with it. Resentment of this governmental behavior was one of the reasons for the important role played by the UNEF in the rebellions of 1968. Today, the UNEF is divided into two rival organizations, *UNEF–Solidarité étudiante*, which is close to the Communist party, and *UNEF–Indépendante et démocratique*, whose membership is more diverse and includes Trotskyists and socialists of various hues.

The largest and most important teachers' organization for many years was the *Fédération d'éducation nationale* (FEN). Counting about 500,000 members during the 1970s and 1980s, it comprised more than 40 separate subgroups for a variety of educators, the largest of which was the *Syndicat national des instituteurs et professeurs d'enseignement général de collège* (SNI-PEGC), with 300,000 members, mostly elementary- and lower-secondary-school (or "junior high") teachers. Another large affiliated group was the *Syndicat national d'enseignement supérieur* (SNESup), which represented university teachers. The FEN was also divided internally on the basis of several ideological tendencies (e.g., Socialist, Communist, Trotskyist, and self-management-oriented *[autogestionnaire]*), but what held them all together was a common commitment to *laïcité*, that is, a secular public school system. Some teachers' unions are affiliated not with the FEN but with the various industrial unions (e.g., the *Syndicat général d'éducation nationale* [SGEN], a component of the CFDT). Sometimes these teachers' unions compete with one another in elections to the consultative bodies attached to lycées, universities, or the *Conseil supérieur d'éducation nationale*, which is attached to the Ministry of Education; at other times, they collaborate in lobbying for the promotion of *laïcité* or for higher teachers' pay. In the past several years, FEN lost more than half its membership as a result of internal fragmentation over the question of educational reforms—specifically, about the extent to which the increasing official openness toward the rival system of private schools *(écoles libres)* should be tolerated. In 1992, the FEN nearly collapsed and was eclipsed by other associations, the most important of which is the *Syndicat national unitaire des instituteurs, professeurs d'école et professeurs de collège* (SNUipp), which includes teachers at all levels from elementary school to university. This new association is egalitarian, "maximalist" in its demands for more teachers, and resolutely opposed to government measures authorizing the expenditure of public funds locally for private schools. In 1993, SNUipp joined with others to create a new umbrella organization, the *Fédération syndicale unitaire de l'enseignement, de l'éducation, de la recherche et de la culture* (FSU). In the elections to professional representative bodies in 1996, the FSU eclipsed the FEN as the largest teachers' association.[26] In order to increase its relative weight and improve its bargaining position, the FEN, now reduced to 140,000 members, joined with other associations representing a variety of interests in the *Union nationale des syndicats autonomes* (National Federation of Independent Unions—UNSA).[27]

The above listing is far from exhaustive, for there are teachers who belong to organizations that are subcomponents of the major "comprehensive" trade unions. All these organizations compete with one another in elections to the administrative councils of educational institutions.[28] Still another educational association is the National Union of Parents of Students in Private Schools (*Union nationale des parents d'élèves de l'enseignement libre*—UNAPEL), which speaks for more than 800,000 families. It has joined with teachers' associations and school administrators to lobby for increased government subsidies to parochial schools.[29] The prospects of both the FEN and the FSU improved considerably with the installation of the Jospin government. Jospin, a former minister of education, restored several thousand public-school teachers' positions that had been eliminated under the Juppé premiership.

MISCELLANEOUS INTEREST GROUPS

In addition to the major economic actors—labor, business, farmers, and teachers—there are numerous other interest groups that fall under a variety of classifications: They include a complex set of medical associations; religious groups; charitable organizations; *Médecins sans frontières,* a group of volunteer physicians and healthcare workers operating globally; and ad hoc "promotional" associations that focus on single issues, such as *Pour le mandat unique* (PMU), formed in 1997 to fight for the abolition of simultaneous multiple elective office *(cumul).*

In addition, one observes a growth of extrainstitutional activities—including anomic action—on the part of interest groups, especially by sectors that are insufficiently organized: the unemployed, the homeless, illegal immigrants. Some groups are hastily organized in response to a specific public policy, such as the group that, early in 1999, organized a big demonstration in Paris of nearly 100,000 people demanding, in the interest of "protecting the family," the withdrawal of a government bill that affirmed the rights of same-sex couples. Another example is the *Front anti-tunnel* (FAT), formed in 2001 to oppose the movement of trucks through an Alpine tunnel to Italy. By far the larger number of such groups are on the left; they include *Droit au logement,* which speaks for the homeless; *Mouvement national des chômeurs et des précaires* (National Movement of the Unemployed and Distressed); SCALP *(Section carrément anti–Le Pen),* which fights against the extreme Right; the *Organisation révolutionnaire anarchiste;* and what is left of the radical nucleus of the PCF. One of the growing social movements is the *Association pour une taxation des transactions financières pour l'aide aux citoyens* (Association for Taxation and Financial Transactions in Favor of Citizens—ATTAC). Its 30,000 members (1998), many of whom have come from the trade unions and left-wing parties, have been fighting against globalization and excessive market liberalism.[30]

THE ACCESS AND INPUT OF INTEREST GROUPS

The preceding list of interest groups, although far from complete, indicates that organizational frameworks exist for the important economic sectors in France. But such existence does not, by itself, indicate a group's position and power in French political life. In terms of its pluralistic reality, and in conformity with the freedom of association found in all democratic regimes, France (under republics) has been receptive to vigorous interest-group politics. However, in modern French political history, there has always been a school of thought, inspired in particular by Rousseau and the early Jacobins, that considered any political role for interest groups, secondary associations, or even political parties unnecessary interpositions between the people and the government and therefore destructive of the "general will." In consonance with that doctrine, the Le Chapelier law in 1791 declared intermediary bodies *(corps intermédiaires)* such as artisans' guilds (or trade unions) illegal, and their reestablishment was not permitted until 1884, when that law was rescinded. A law on associations passed in 1901 allowed the formation of interest groups without prior government authorization. Since that time, interest groups have flourished, and they have made their political influence felt in a variety of ways. In 2000–2001, on the occasion of the centenary of the 1901 law, numerous writings appeared celebrating the evolution of *"la vie associative"* and its contribution to democracy.[31]

The importance of interest groups can be shown statistically. In 2001, according to one count, there were about 880,000 associations embracing 20 million members; they employed over 1.6 million (full- and part-time) people, and spent 308 billion francs—or 3.7 percent of the gross domestic product—on their activities.[32] Although interest groups are an important aspect of civil society, it was evident that the government was not absent. During the celebration of the above-mentioned centenary, the government issued a charter of "reciprocal engagements," in which it "recognized the importance of the contribution of the associations to the general interest, of which [the State] is the guarantor," and via the *Fonds national pour le développement de la vie associative* (National Fund for the Development of Associational Politics) promised to increase government subsidies to interest groups.[33]

The evolution of interest-group politics has been complex. In the Third and Fourth Republics, various economic, professional, and ideological groups were strongly linked to political parties and exerted considerable influence on these parties or were at least close to them. In the Third Republic, the Freemasons considered the Radical party their voice in Parliament; in the Fourth Republic, the MRP was seen as echoing the views of the Catholic church, and the veterans' organizations supported the RPF because it was thought to represent their interests. Linkages to parties enabled interest groups to colonize the Parliament directly by having their spokespersons elected as deputies. By the end of the Third Republic, the Senate had begun to establish its reputation as the "chamber of agriculture," and in the Fourth Republic, trade union officials were elected to the National Assembly under Communist or Socialist party labels. Interest-group input was facilitated by the specialized legislative standing committees, with trade unionists securing squatters' rights in the Committee on Labor, and representatives of the farmers' associations in the Committee on Agriculture. This input was supplemented by the easy access of some interest groups to their "patron" ministry, and by the acceptance of ministerial portfolios by a leader of a client group; for example, the minister of agriculture was usually linked to an agricultural association. In addition, interest-group representatives were often recruited to serve on a minister's staff *(cabinet ministériel)*. The pervasive presence of interest groups, whether real or imagined, made political institutions, from Parliament to the bureaucracy, appear as a complex of fiefdoms. To the extent that this situation blurred the distinction between the public and the private domains, it helped to bring the Fourth Republic into disrepute.

After 1958, the power of interest groups declined considerably. This was due in part to the etatist philosophy of de Gaulle, who had as little use for interest groups as for political parties; he viewed both as particularistic and out of harmony with the public interest. Since the concept of *concertation* (translated, for lack of a better word, as "harmonization") was a favorite with de Gaulle and his followers, it has been argued that the general's views regarding groups were proto-fascist.[34] But whereas the Nazis had terminated the independent existence of groups by aligning them with the official authority structure, thereby creating the "corporate" (or corporative) state, de Gaulle did not wish to destroy the associational (i.e., voluntary) organizational basis of groups; rather, he wished to disarm the trade unions by making them part of a "capital-labor association" and depoliticizing them. It should be noted that *concertation* has also been a catchword of non-Gaullist planners and post-Gaullist and Socialist politicians, and that it was viewed as a device for technocratic decision making even during the Fourth Republic.

In the Fifth Republic, interest groups could not be removed from the political scene, even if political leaders had so wished, but the institutional framework could be rearranged so as to minimize or channel their influence. Parliament has not been a consistently reliable access point for interest groups; throughout most of the Fifth Republic, the legislative efforts of organized labor and agriculture have often been hampered by the underrepresentation or fragmentation of their "patron" parties in the Assembly.

The electoral system based on proportional representation that existed in the Fourth Republic had permitted the parties to articulate the views of fairly narrowly defined interests; in contrast, the single-member-constituency system of the Fifth Republic has forced the parties to become more aggregative and hence to be less reliable echoes of the demands of particular interest groups. To be sure, the PCF still represents the workers' point of view—*if* such a representation does not conflict with the party's general strategy at a given period. The PS still reflects the views of such "promotional" groups as the League of Human Rights *(Ligue des droits de l'homme)* and the interests of selected industrial workers, but it must also represent teachers, civil servants, and other interests that compose its electorate.

The ideological affinities between a political party and an interest group may sometimes be more useful to the former than to the latter. If a group's ideological orientation is too sharply defined, a rival association that does not share that orientation may be formed, with the result that a specific or "objective" interest can no longer be effectively articulated. This situation has obtained especially in the case of educational groups.

It is difficult, however, to determine the primary beneficiary of the linkage between party and interest group in the array of unions, circles, and associations affiliated with the National Front.[35] Some of these organizations are used by the National Front for purposes of electoral mobilization; others are in the process of claiming official recognition as "representative" bodies in order to be placed on advisory councils or participate in elections to labor relations tribunals.

PLURALIST, CORPORATIST, AND OTHER MODELS OF INTEREST-GROUP POLITICS

In their variety, organizational features, methods of action, and pursuit of specific policy aims, interest groups in France are in many ways comparable to those in the United States. In both countries, workers, industrialists, businesspeople, farmers, and members of various professions discover their common interests, freely organize, and try to protect and promote these interests by bargaining with one another and by seeking access to, influencing, or "lobbying" the political parties, the legislature, the executive, and other official decision-making agencies.

French legalistic-formalistic tradition makes a distinction between "lobbies," whose existence was deplored, and even denied, for many years, and "social partners" *(partenaires sociaux)* such as trade unions and business associations, who participate in the definition of the public interest.[36] Practice, however, is quite different. Interest groups lobby intensively with ministers and higher civil servants. Attempts are also made to influence individual legislators, especially those in charge of the dossiers that are of direct concern to the groups in question, despite the fact that party discipline and streamlined decision making in Parliament do not encourage such attempts. However, lobbying with central and local party headquarters is quite common. The fact that bribery often accompanies the lobbying is evidenced by the growing number of indictments of national and subnational politicians for "money laundering." Furthermore, there are constant attempts by interest groups to bring their cases before presidential candidates. During the 1995 election campaign, Chirac—sometimes at the request of the interest groups and sometimes on his own initiative—received delegates of veterans' organizations, environmentalist groups, the National Council of Women, and associations of repatriates, pensioners, and defenders of the homeless.[37] In recent years, the reality of lobbying as a professional political "marketing" activity has been grudgingly recognized, especially on the level of European Union institutions.[38]

Yet the structure and context of interest-group politics in France have diverged in several respects from those in the United States, a country that is said to conform to the *pluralist* model. In the United States, interest groups are organized on a purely voluntary basis; they determine their own organizational structures, define their goals, choose their leaders freely, and have their own sources of funds; and while pursuing these goals, which are usually concerned with concrete but limited policy issues, they maintain complete autonomy, distance from the public authorities, and freedom of action.[39] In France, by contrast, we observe the following: (1) Interest groups and political parties are often linked, sometimes in a formal structural sense and sometimes ideologically. (2) Interest groups may pursue goals that go far beyond single issues and that touch on the very nature of political institutions, if not the constitutional system as a whole. (3) There is a formal legitimization of the role of interest groups. Unlike the U.S. Constitution, which is silent on the matter of groups, the Fifth Republic Constitution (Art. 4) states that "political parties and groups shall be instrumental in the expression of the suffrage; they shall be formed freely and carry on their activities freely." This legitimization is also reflected in laws granting interest groups official status, providing for their representation in public bodies, and devolving on them certain tasks of policy implementation. (4) There is an institutionalized pattern of consultation of interest groups by governmental authorities, so that it is often difficult to determine the source of a set of policies or the boundaries between the public (the state) and the private (civil society).

Because of these divergences, some scholars have suggested that France cannot be considered pluralist but conforms to another model—the *corporatist* one—in which the state plays a much more important role. Originally, the term *corporatism* referred to the position of groups in authoritarian regimes of the fascist type, where group autonomy was severely limited (if not eliminated), lobbying and collective bargaining did not take place, strikes were forbidden, and all socioeconomic sectors were formally *incorporated* into the state. In recent years, the term has come to be used to refer to almost *any* kind of institutionalized relationship between interest groups and the public authorities that departs from the U.S. ideal type. In the American *pluralist* system, the "public interest" is a myth: There is only a plurality of interests that sometimes compete and sometimes conflict, complement one another, or converge. Public policy is piecemeal rather than comprehensive and is essentially the outcome of "the legislative struggle"; and the state is little more than a clerk registering the various demands or an umpire who sees to it that the rules are properly observed.[40]

In *corporatist* systems, however, the relationship between interest groups and the public authorities is characterized by some or all of the following: (1) the existence of a limited number of interest groups, organized in a hierarchical fashion; (2) special recognition by the state of the representational monopoly of a group through licensing or guaranteed access; (3) compulsory membership; (4) a highly formalized and institutionalized access to the public authorities; (5) governmental subvention of interest-group activities; and (6) state control over the selection of leaders and the articulation of demands.[41]

It is possible to find evidence of several of these features in France. Thus, the structured nature of interest-group access to the formal decision makers is reflected in a variety of institutions. Among them is the Economic and Social Council (*Conseil Economique et Social*—CES), which the government is constitutionally obligated to consult in the preparation of bills involving domestic issues. This agency of "functional representation" includes delegates of trade unions, farmers' organizations, business associations, professional groups, cooperative and mutual societies, and nationalized industries, in addition to unaffiliated experts and civil servants. The CES (whose members are appointed for five-year terms) is supplemented by numerous advisory bodies that have proliferated around ministries, the "modernization committees" that have helped to shape French economic plans, and (since decentralization) regional economic and social advisory councils. In addition, there are countless consultative bodies attached to departmental administrative offices.

The CES is organized into nine permanent sections, or "standing committees": simple labor, social affairs, finances, foreign relations, production, research and technology, food and agriculture, town and country planning, and living standards. The work of the CES includes input to the Assembly and Senate regarding pending bills as well as the four-year economic plan. The CES may not be called into session by Parliament, and may not examine finance bills. Between 1994 and 1999 the CES was called upon 20 times by the government, and it furnished more than a hundred reports or advisory opinions. These reports have dealt, inter alia, with educational reform, the railroads, poverty, and the supply of energy. In addition, the CES has decided upon its own studies in such areas as part-time work, mental illness, and biotechnology. There has been some debate about the (limited) effectiveness of the CES. The president of the CES (Jacques

Demange, elected in 1999), said that he hoped to improve the situation, and he expected that the CES would be the place where "civil society would be heard by the politicians."[42]

French governments have exercised a certain discretion in giving some interest groups favorable representation in advisory councils and in choosing others as privileged interlocutors. In the name of democracy and fairness, the government ought to give all important interests access to decision-making organs; but the fragmentation of and competition among interest groups have strengthened the government's power to determine which association is the "most qualified" defender of a particular socioeconomic sector.

Qualification is an important criterion for interest-group consultation. French bureaucrats, who have a highly developed sense that they alone represent the public interest, have tended to view the excessive involvement of interest groups in the decision-making process as endangering the "objective" resolution of a problem.[43] Since the civil servants' principal aim is to obtain accurate information, they tend to make a distinction between pressure groups, which they regard as selfish, and professional associations, which, in the civil servants' view, have expertise.[44] This distinction was greatly exaggerated during the Vichy regime when, in a manner characteristic of fascist systems, the government refused to acknowledge "private" groups and dealt only with chambers and other bodies of public law. Today, the existence of privately organized groups is so thoroughly recognized that trade unions, business associations, and other groups are considered de facto participants in government. Nevertheless, all governments have their own hierarchies of organizations with which they prefer to deal. Most governments (or at least the higher civil servants) have preferred to consult professional orders (ordres professionnels) where possible rather than pure interest groups (syndicats).[45] These "orders" have many tasks: the maintenance of intraprofessional standards and discipline, the control of access to the profession, the supervision of training, and the administration of selective government policies.

Where the criterion of professionalism is inadequate, the question of whether this or that association shall represent a particular interest may be decided by such measures of "representativeness" as an association's inclusiveness, its internal democracy, or even the extent to which a group's outlook is in tune with the public interest. Thus, the Ministry of Social Affairs has bargained on the matter of doctors' fees with the Federation of French Medical Associations (Confédération des syndicats médicaux français—CSMF) rather than with another medical association, because of the CSMF's "professionalism." (Although the Ordre des médecins is even more professional in outlook and membership in that it is compulsory for all practicing physicians, it has been less cooperative.)[46] Similarly, the Ministry of Education bargained with the FEN because it was more inclusive and not oriented toward a particular ideology (except laicism); and the Ministry of Education chose to recognize a secularly oriented rather than a religiously oriented parents' association because it considered the former more "qualified" than the latter. The government's recognition may be influenced by developments within a particular interest. Thus, when the FSU won out over the FEN in elections to representative councils in educational institutions at the end of 1993, it demanded legitimization as an official interlocutor; such recognition would give the FSU the right to representation in public bodies (e.g., the Superior Council of Civil Servants—*Conseil supérieur de la fonction publique*) and the right to be invited to participate in negotiations on educational policy. Such legitimization could not be withheld for long, because a large membership, and the "mobilizing capacity" that it implies, creates a "moral obligation" for the government to grant the requisite legitimacy to a group.[47]

Frequently, when the government does have a choice, it selects representatives of the more tractable and less radical trade unions as spokespersons of organized labor. Since the establishment of the Fifth Republic, the number of union delegates in the Economic and Social Council has been approximately equal for the FO and CGT, although for many years the latter had twice as many members as the former. Both labor and agricultural associations have periodically complained about being underrepresented in the CES, particularly in relation to business and the civil service. In the mid-1980s, the size of the CES was increased from 200 to 230 and subsequently to 231, and the number of trade union representatives was increased from 50 to 69, while the number of representatives of farmers' associations was reduced from 30 to 25 (see Table 5.1). The growing "governmentalization" of the CES is indicated by the fact that, whereas in 1946, 8 percent of the CES's members were individuals nominated by the government, the proportion had risen to 30 percent in the Fifth Republic (67 of the 231 in the CES in 1992).[48] But that governmentalization has not been a bad thing: Because of it, spokespersons of relatively weak interests such as environmentalist and parent-teacher associations have been seated on the CES.[49]

TABLE 5.1
Membership in the Economic and Social Council, by Sector, 1979, 1984, and 1998

	1979	1984	1998
Wage earners' representatives (trade unions)	50	69	69[a]
Employers' associations	27	27	27
Agricultural associations	30	25	25
Cooperatives and mutual societies	11	19	19
Family, renters', and savers' associations	8	10	17
Public enterprises	6	8	10
Artisans	10	10	10
Free professions	0	3	3
Others	8	7	11[b]
Other "qualified" individuals appointed by the government	50	48	40
Total	200	226	231

Sources: *Quid 1996* (Paris: Robert Laffont, 1995), p. 84, and *Quid 2001* (Paris: Robert Laffont, 2000), p. 739.
[a]In 1998, the breakdown of the 69 trade union representatives was as follows: CFDT, CGT, FO, 17 each; CFTC, 6; CFE-CGC, 7; UNSA, 3; FSU, 1; agricultural workers' association, 1.
[b]Includes representatives of associations of departments and overseas territories and of French citizens living abroad.

(In any case, the change in the composition of the CES has not had a decisive effect on its overall public-policy impact, which, in the view of many observers, has been very modest.) In the modernization committees dealing with the Economic Plan, trade unions have been chronically underrepresented, in part because the plan has tended (except for the period 1981–1984) to adhere to a business rather than a union outlook and to concentrate on growth and productivity rather than wages or social policy.

Even where interest-group representation is more equitable, its input can be minimized by the governmental practice of ignoring recommendations that do not fit into a preconceived policy framework. Thus, in the late 1950s, the advice rendered by the *Conseil supérieur de l'éducation* was ignored because it differed from the ideas of the minister of education; in the early 1960s, the government ignored the recommendations made by the multipartite committee of inquiry (the *Commission Toutée*) regarding an "incomes policy" for the public sector. The *Comité supérieur de l'emploi*, in which trade unions could in theory make recommendations regarding manpower training, met only once a year. The National Labor Relations Board, which advised the government on minimum wages and other labor-contract issues, met more often; but during Gaullist-Giscardist rule, the unions claimed that the government representatives on that body usually confronted organized labor with a fait accompli that was not in the interest of the worker. After Mitterrand's election, it was the turn of management to complain: Although the new president gave audiences to the chief of the CNPF, that organization realized that it could not deflect the government from its nationalization and wage policies (at least in the beginning).

The access and effectiveness of an interest group have depended on a number of factors: the size of its membership, the extent to which it can project an image as an effective agent for an economic or professional sector, the cohesion between the leadership and the rank and file, and the degree to which intrasector divisions can be overcome. These divisions are particularly apparent in the competing slates of candidates put up by agricultural associations, labor unions, and teachers' groups for elections to agricultural chambers, factory councils, university councils, boards of nationalized industries, social security organs, and labor-relations tribunals. On the one hand, divisions and rivalries may be exploited by a determined government; on the other hand, they are a manifestation of a pluralism *within* interests that the public authorities try to compensate for, if not overcome. They do so by encouraging the hierarchical organization (in the form of chambers, assemblies, and *ordres professionnels*) that is said to be a symptom of corporatism. Moreover, hierarchical organization is a reflection of the reality of professionalization and hence is found in large institutions in every advanced society.

Neither hierarchical organization nor equal (or favorable) and formalized access to the public authorities is a sufficient guarantee that an interest group will be taken seriously, for the scope of decision making in a public body in which interest groups are represented may be limited by outside forces or by policy constraints. The administrative councils of most public or mixed enterprises are multipartite in composition, with the workers, the consumers, and the management represented equally. However, the spokespersons of the consumers may vote on the side of the management, and the workers' interests may be slighted by the meddling of the minister of finance, who is concerned with ensuring "budgetary equilibrium" in the nationalized industries.[50]

Similar limitations apply to the *conseils de prud'hommes,* the functional tribunals (resembling the labor courts in Germany) that decide disputes arising in connection with labor legislation.[51] These tribunals (separately organized for industry, commerce, and agriculture) include representatives of trade unions, employers' associations, and other interested organizations, who participate in rendering verdicts. It is not clear, however, whether this participation is meaningful for interest groups, except in the most perfunctory sense, for the following reasons: Each group has only minority representation; the scope of decision is narrowed by codes of labor law; the presiding judge (who is not a spokesperson of any interest group) has considerable prestige and can often sway the lay members; and decisions rendered by the tribunals can be appealed to ordinary courts (see Table 5.2). Hence it is not surprising that workers' participation in the elections to the *conseils de prud'hommes* is seldom higher than 60 percent.[52]

Participation in the elections of trade union representatives to the social security boards *(caisses),* which administer health insurance programs and family subsidies, is somewhat higher, but the elections do not generate great interest. This was particularly true between 1967 and 1982, when the representation ratio favorable to trade unionists was abolished and parity of representation was granted to the employers, in effect giving the latter control over the boards. Under the Mitterrand presidency, the trade unions regained their formal majority status on the boards, but such a status is not enough: If trade union input is taken seriously within these boards, as was the case during much of the Fourth Republic, it may be because unions have privileged access to political parties that are well represented in Parliament and that can help to alter the conditions under

TABLE 5.2
Trade Unions and Elections to Labor Relations Tribunals
(Conseils de Prud'hommes)

	1979	1982	1987	1992	1997
Voters (in thousands)	12,323	13,547	12,256	13,913	14,568
Percent of participation	63.1	58.6	45.9	40.4	34.4
Abstentions (in thousands)	4,539	5,608	6,624	8,297	
Percent of abstentions	36.8	41.3	54.0	59.6	
Trade unions' shares of employees' votes[a]					
CGT	42.4	36.8	36.3	33.3	33.1
CFDT	23.1	23.5	23.0	23.8	25.3
FO	17.4	17.8	20.4	20.5	20.6
CFTC	6.9	8.5	8.3	8.6	7.5
CFE-CGC	5.2	9.6	7.4	7.0	5.9

SOURCES: Based on Jean Magniadas, "Elections prud'homales et syndicalisme de classe," *La Pensée,* no. 263 (May–June 1988), 13; Dominique Labbé, "Les Principales Confédérations syndicales de salariés," *L'État de la France, 95–96* (Paris: La Découverte, 1995), p. 110; *L'Année politique, 1993,* p. 479; and *Quid 2001,* p. 1641.
[a]In percent.

which the social security boards operate. However, Parliament may constrict the parameters of action of administrative agencies for all interest groups. The most recent example is the constitutional amendment of 1996, which took the power to decide on expenditures away from the social insurance funds and "returned" it to Parliament. Moreover, the actual work of the complex social security apparatus, which consists of national, regional, and local organisms, is done by 180,000 semipublic professional agents whose wages and working conditions are fixed by collective contracts between the state and the *Fédération nationale des organisations de sécurité sociale* (FNOSS), an "institutional" interest group created in response to the existence of the social security system.[53]

The trade unions also play an institutionalized role in the various social security organisms—such as the *Caisse nationale d'assurance maladie* (CNAM); the *Caisse nationale d'assurance vieillesse,* and *the Caisse nationale des allocations familiales.* Each of them is supervised by an administrative council representing the "social partners"—that is, trade unions, employers' groups, and family associations, the first two enjoying representational parity—and presided over by an official belonging to one of them. Thus, the president of the CNAM comes from the CFDT; and the president of the *Union des caisses nationales de securité sociale* (UCANSS) comes from the MEDEF. Among the powers of these councils is the appointment of professional social security specialists, most of whom have received training in a specialized school (set up by a decree in 1960), the *Centre national d'études supérieurs de la sécurité sociale* (CNESS). The councils are not free to do what they want; they are subject to the supervision *(tutelle)* of a national cabinet minister.[54]

Nevertheless, despite the powers of the government and the limits of pressure groups, the term *corporatism* is misleading.[55] In France, institutionalized relationships between groups and the government are still essentially *pluralist* because (1) the groups themselves have asked for, and helped to develop, the regulations regarding the formalized relationship (and they tend to complain about its "corporatist" nature only if their input does not result in policies they like);[56] (2) there is hardly an economic or professional interest that is articulated by a single organization, so that it is difficult for the government to grant representational monopoly to this or that organization; (3) the leadership of organized interests, including those that enjoy a relatively privileged access to the authorities, is chosen, not by the authorities, but by the rank and file; (4) "incorporated" groups may freely boycott the arena of formalized group-government intercourse; (5) privileged links between selected interest groups and official decision makers are found in *all* industrial societies, including the American "pluralist" one, and interest-group representatives may sometimes dominate the boards of public institutions on which they sit (as is often the case in the United States); (6) most groups, including highly "incorporated" ones, exhibit *plural* forms of behavior, for example, cooperative, co-optative, contentious and claims-asserting *(contestataire),* and uncooperative *(conflictuelle),* depending on the policy issue; and (7) groups continue to engage in such "pluralistic" activities that supplement "neocorporatist" representation in advisory councils and other kinds of official access points. These activities include lobbying with Parliament (albeit limited by party discipline), collective bargaining, and strikes, depending on the issue at hand.[57]

The fact that an interest group has official government connections may sometimes constrain it to the kind of "careful" behavior that does not jeopardize its privileged position. A major reason why the FO was ousted in 1996 from its administrative leadership of the medical insurance funds was its excessively radical opposition to the government's proposals to reform the social security system; but that ouster and the replacement of the FO by the CFDT was accomplished largely by the collusion of rival unions and the CNPF, which cooperated in the elections to the boards of the health insurance and unemployment agencies. In the same year, the cooperation of the CSMF, the largest and most "authoritative" medical association (which threatened to strike), and the organization of social security officials, an "institutional" interest group, forced the government to moderate its proposals regarding medical services.[58] These examples suggest that "corporatist" patterns should be looked on not as substitute but as supplementary methods of interest-group action.[59]

Moreover, none of the mainstream political parties is avidly promoting a "corporatist" relationship, and recent governments—of the Right and the Left—seem to have tried to move interest-group relations with the public authorities in a more "pluralist" direction, sometimes against the wishes of the interest groups themselves. Thus, the Socialist government in the early 1980s relinquished the power to regulate several aspects of labor-management relations (e.g., the reduction of the workweek) to the unions and employers; furthermore, it deprived the FNSEA of its monopoly status, in the face of that organization's loud protests, by granting equal recognition to three other agricultural associations,[60] and it invited the FNSEA to assert its claims in competition with the other associations. It may be true that the Gaullists had "corporatized" the agricultural sector's relations to the state in the 1960s,[61] but the evolution of the Gaullist party and its ally, the UDF, toward neoliberalism has implied a commitment to an "Anglo-American" kind of pluralism.

The corporatist model, once widely cited, is now increasingly admitted as not really (or no longer) applying to France, yet it is thought to have continued utility as a heuristic model.[62] But the concept of corporatism has been stretched to cover so many different political situations[63] that its usefulness has been questioned. That is why a new paradigm has recently been used to differentiate among industrial democracies—specifically, to distinguish France from the United States—that of *statism*. The statist (or "state-centered") model is said to apply to France and other countries where effective decision making is possible, because in its confrontations with private interests the state almost always seems to win. Unfortunately, the *state*, since its "rediscovery" by U.S. scholars several years ago,[64] has not been much more useful than corporatism as an orienting concept, because there has been no agreement on what is meant by it.[65] Ironically, the concept is being applied to France (especially by American scholars) at a time when French politicians, having rediscovered civil society and the market, are increasingly trying to reduce the role of the state and to "degovernmentalize" *(désétatiser)* a range of activities.

An examination of selected conflicts in France reveals that the policy process in that country involves a complicated interplay of reciprocal pressures between interest groups and a variety of (sometimes divided) public authorities, in which neither side possesses full autonomy. There have been many policy issues in which the government prevailed because it was willing and able to use the powers at its disposal in the face of considerable protest by interest groups. In the early years of the Fifth Republic, de Gaulle succeeded in granting independence to Algeria despite heavy resistance from military officers, nationalist organizations, and a variety of conservative political parties. Under several presidents, agricultural associations failed to obtain sufficient support for family farmers because of governmental emphasis on agricultural competitiveness, a failure that provoked farmers into blocking roads, dumping produce, and threatening violence; the alcohol lobby failed to secure tax exemptions because of the government's concern about alcoholism; the anticlerical associations failed to prevent the passage of the Debré law (in 1959), by which the government could make educational "contracts" with parochial schools, because of the Gaullists' interest in retaining the loyalty of the Catholic electorate; and the trade unions failed to secure wage increases commensurate with the rise in the cost of living and, until the early 1970s, to obtain the right to organize in factories because Parliament was dominated by conservatives. After the 1981 elections, the CNPF was demoralized by its failure to persuade the government to abandon its policies of nationalization, wage increases, and supplementary corporate taxes.

Conversely, there are instances in which the government has had to give in to the determined opposition by organized interests. The capital-gains tax bills introduced by the government during the Giscard presidency (in 1976–1977) were effectively blocked by both big and small business, as was a meaningful extension of factory democracy; the bill introduced by the Mauroy government in 1983 to integrate the private schools into the national school system was withdrawn in response to opposition by a coalition of Catholic educators, parents' associations, and conservative parties;[66] under the same government, the proposals for strengthening the role of workers' councils in factories and reducing the workweek to 35 hours foundered in the face of opposition by the CNPF (although the 35-hour workweek was successfully enacted in the 1990s). Under Chirac's cohabitation government, the bill introduced by the minister for universities, which proposed to make entry into universities more selective, was shelved because of massive student protests. In response to public protests by *SOS-Racisme,* an antiracist organization, the *Ligue des droits de l'homme,* and related groups in 1989 and 1993, the government was forced to modify bills concerning the entry and residence of foreigners. Between 1991 and 1993, the government modified or withdrew a number of educational reform measures in response to protest demonstrations by students' and teachers' organizations. In 1993, the new Gaullist-Giscardist government was forced to abandon part of a medical insurance reform bill that provided for cost sharing for drugs, because the RPR-UDF parliamentary group (which included most of the 55 deputies identified with the medical profession) opposed the provision.[67] In 1994, a government bill to increase the financial support of parochial schools was abandoned in the face of massive demonstrations and the determined opposition of trade unions and left-wing parties. In 1995, the Juppé government yielded to the combined pressures of the trade unions and to the massive strikes they instituted and abandoned a number of crucial elements in its proposals to cut the operating costs of the railroads. In 1996, the same government abandoned the *loi Debré,*[68] a bill to increase the surveillance of illegal immigrants, as a result of hunger strikes by them and anomic action by their supporters. Several months later, mass protests by associations of recipients of family-income supplements forced the newly formed Jospin government to rethink its proposal to apply a means test for such supplements.

In 1996, the government actively intervened to settle the strike of the teamsters' union, which represented workers in the private trucking industry. This episode confirmed the interventionist nature of the French political system and was an outward sign of a strong state; but since the settlement was achieved only after the government yielded to the demand of the unions for earlier retirement of truck drivers by assuming the cost associated with it, the intervention signified a victory of the "market" and brought to the surface the *weakness* of the state!

It would normally be expected that "institutional" groups who serve the state directly are particularly constrained by a corporatist embrace. Such expectation, however, was called into question in 2001 when the national gendarmerie organized a massive strike, demanding higher wages, better working conditions, and increases in manpower. Although such action was illegal, the government yielded, meeting all the gendarmes' demands—in part because, in view of the forthcoming national elections, it could ill afford to alienate a sector that was supported by the general public. In any case, the gendarmes' action was soon followed by strikes of municipal police forces, teachers, and other professionals (including those serving the state).

If recent trends toward a more independent role of Parliament continue (see Chapter 7) and the cohesion and discipline of parliamentary parties weaken, one may expect the influence of interest groups on the legislative process to grow. This will be true in particular for groups whose electoral weight is significant. A case in point is the *Bureau de liaison des organisations des retraités* (BLORE), the umbrella organization for eight associations of retired persons. As an articulator of the interests of more than 2 million pensioners, who account for nearly one-third of the electorate, it is likely to influence most Assembly election outcomes and, eventually, to demand formal representation in official organs.[69]

There are times when the government wins against an interest group, but its victory may be at least partially the result of help it has received from other interest groups. Premier Rocard's ability to stand his ground during the Paris transport strikes at the end of 1988 was enhanced by the growing opposition to the behavior of the CGT on the part of the public at large, as well as the other trade unions.[70] Conversely, a coalition of private interests may win against one component of the public authority structure because it is supported by another component of that structure. The victory of the unions, immigrant groups, churches, and left-wing organizations in opposing the nationality and citizenship bill introduced by Chirac's government in 1986 was achieved with the encouragement of President Mitterrand. In fact, one of those organizations, *SOS-Racisme*, had been formed in 1984 with the backing of the Socialist government in order to fight racism.[71]

The public transport workers' strike in 1995 gained additional effectiveness because its leaders were supported by student and teachers' organizations (who used the occasion to voice their own complaints) as well as by the public at large, which, although inconvenienced, was sympathetic to the strikers.[72] This support compensated for the numerical weakness of the trade union membership as well as the interunion conflicts.[73] In this instance, the public shared the union's annoyance with the behavior of Premier Juppé, who had introduced the reform proposals in the Parliament without prior consultation with union leaders.

Finally, there are policy decisions that are difficult to attribute clearly to the state or the private sector. This is increasingly true of agricultural policies, which may be made by a combination of forces: private interests, the national government, and the (now partly autonomous) institutions of the European Union. Moreover, both the power of the state and the influence of important interest groups have weakened as a consequence of globalization.

In any case, the policy process in France has become more pluralistic and incremental, the result of an interplay of a plurality of public and private preferences. As a consequence of these developments, a mutual adjustment has taken place. On the one hand, Socialist governments, sensing their dependence on business, became more sympathetic to it and more open to its policy suggestions, despite the (often harsh) ideological rhetoric of Socialist politicians about big business *(le grand patronat)*;[74] and even Mitterrand, despite impressive proworker legislation during the first three years of his presidency, reflected the evolution of the Socialist party in response to "postindustrialism" and had no working-class representatives in his entourage.[75] On the other hand, the Gaullists (during the election campaigns of 1988, 1993, and 1995) vowed to retain the social achievements of the working-class community. Meanwhile, the trade unions have become more realistic in that they no longer expect the government to bring about full employment, and business has become more socially oriented and less hostile to Socialist governments (realizing that these governments are quite helpful on occasion, as, for instance, in bringing about the "de-indexation" of salaries). These things have happened because of a recognition of the fact that the power of government is not absolute, or even "autonomous."

More often than not, policy making (e.g., on issues such as working conditions, wages, and productivity) is a tripartite affair, involving government, labor, and business. Governments need the input of interest groups in order to lend legitimacy to a public policy, and, occasionally, to pass the buck and spread the blame. Conversely, interest groups obtain some of their power from being called upon by governments. Both explain the resort to meetings between government ministers and spokespersons of interest groups. A recent example is the meeting, in 2001, called by Elisabeth Guigou, minister of social affairs, with representatives of medical associations, medical insurance funds, the CFDT, and Parliament for the purpose of arriving at measures to reduce medical expenditures.

The interest groups are the "social partners" of the government, which acts as a coordinator. However, it is increasingly difficult for the government to play that role, for, as a French planning commissioner put it, "it has become practically impossible to assemble in a single place and around a few tables the principal economic and social decision makers. The industrial texture has become diversified; the financial institutions have multiplied . . . in short, our system is much richer but also more complex than it was yesterday, while the [patterns of] behavior have become more and more individualistic."[76] The diversification of the business sector has been accompanied by three related symptoms: *désétatisation, désyndicalisation,* and *déplanification* (degovernmentalization, the decline of unionization, and the reduction of planning).

The role of interest groups is likely to grow in the future, if only because many French people question the excessive role of the state, and because the state has itself been attempting to hand over some of its weaponry to the civil society and the market. To be sure, the state still defines the parameters of discussion, but that is also true of the United States and other "pluralist" systems; otherwise, it would not even be possible to speak of states and governments.

NOTES

1. Bernard Stasi, in *Vie associative et démocratie nouvelle* (Paris: PUF, 1979, pp. 47–58), mentions the following as examples of the tens of thousands of associations registered with local prefectures: a group of unpublished authors; organizations of amateur surfers; associations of pedestrians, retirees, and apartment renters; former residents of the Suez Canal Zone; and consumers', stockholders', and environmental groups. According to Stasi, 25,000 *new* associations were registered in 1977 alone, that is, more than five times the annual average for the period immediately following World War II. Frank L. Wilson, in his *Interest-Group Politics in France* (Cambridge: Cambridge University Press, 1987), lists over 70 nationally organized interest groups whose officials he interviewed (Appendix B, pp. 291–92). See also Martine Barthélémy, "Les Associations dans la société française: Un État des lieux," *Cahiers du CEVIPOF,* no. 1 (1994). According to this source (pp. 12–17), 60,000 interest groups were formed annually in the 1990s, and more than 700,000 associations were in existence in 1994. These statistics must be interpreted with care, for they include both active and long-lasting and passive and ephemeral organizations. Moreover, their growth does not necessarily correlate with an increase in number of active members. Nevertheless, it is estimated that in 1992, nearly 50 percent of French adults belonged to at least one association.
2. See André Barjonet, *La CGT* (Paris: Seuil, 1968), pp. 124–29. According to this source, the CGT was not a complete transmission belt, yet relationships between the leadership of the CGT and that of the PCF were so close that the CGT often neglected concrete economic policies in favor of general antisystem policies. For a personal view of these relationships, see Georges Séguy, *Lutter* (Paris: Stock, 1975), esp. chapter 12. See also René Mouriaux, *La CGT* (Paris: Seuil, 1982), esp. pp. 190–206, for a discussion of the changes in this union's relations to the political parties.
3. According to W. Rand Smith, in *Crisis in the French Labor Movement* (New York: St. Martin's Press, 1987), pp. 64–67, the influence of the Catholic subculture was very strong among the original membership of the CFDT who had broken from the CFTC but has been much less significant for those who joined subsequently.
4. In the past few years, this union has been "invaded" by National Front activists, especially in the south.
5. The membership figures cited in the text, which include those still active in the labor force, are based on a variety of sources, among them the following: Pierre Rosanvallon, *La Question syndicale* (Paris: Calmann-Lévy, 1988); Dominique Labbé, "Les Principales Fédérations et confédérations syndicales de salariés," *L'État de la France 96–97* (Paris: La Découverte, 1996), pp. 115–23; *L'Année politique 1995,* p. 115; and Jean-Claude Boual, ed., *Syndicalisme, quel second siècle?* (Paris: Éditions Ouvrières, 1995), pp. 14–15. For the most recent figures, see *Quid 2001* (Paris: Laffont, 2000), pp. 1622–23. But these statistics, like those of party memberships, are unreliable. The figures issued by an organization for its own membership tend to be inflated (usually by the inclusion of retired members) and those issued for its rivals are usually understated. For the most recent statistics concerning the size,

evolution, and internal structure of union membership, see Dominique Labbé, *Syndicats et syndiqués en France depuis 1945* (Paris: L'Harmattan, 1996), pp. 7–29.

6. There are several additional union confederations (each claiming about 100,000 members), among them the *Confédération des syndicats libres*, which is anti-Marxist and believes in class collaboration; the *Union française du travail*, which favors "pure" collective bargaining; and the *Confédération nationale des salariés de France*, which represents certain white-collar employees as well as truck drivers.

7. Refered to as the CFE-CGC or simply the CGC.

8. A somewhat dated (but still valid) study done more than two decades ago has distinguished, on the one hand, between the legitimist white-collar workers, who are hostile to unionization and close to the boss, and those who are close to the boss but favor unionization (preferably separate), for example, most members of the CGC; and, on the other hand, between individualists, who are hostile to unionization but close neither to the boss nor to (blue-collar) wage earners, and the *solidaristes*, that is, those who favor unionization in common with blue-collar workers. The first two are generally on the right politically, and the latter two on the left. See Gérard Grunberg and René Mouriaux, *L'Univers politique et syndical des cadres* (Paris: PFNSP, 1979).

9. For the preferences of workers in the 1995 presidential elections, see Chapter 4. On the relationship between union leaders and rank-and-file members, see Labbé, *Syndicats et syndiqués*, pp. 74–85. Labbé argues that the gap between the two has grown since the 1970s because the decrease in the number of activists has led to a "greater bureaucratization of the leadership, so that disagreements among union leaders tend to be fights between ideological clans to which the ordinary unionist cannot relate."

10. It is estimated that the three major union confederations lost half of their members between 1978 and 1988, and in 1990 only 12 percent of wage earners were unionized, compared to 28 percent in 1981. See Rosanvallon, *La Question syndicale*, p. 14; and Dominique Labbé, Maurice Croisat, and Antoine Bévort, *La Désyndicalisation: Le Cas de la CFDT* (Grenoble: CERAT, 1990). According to the latter source (p. 7), the departure from the union was a "silent flight": Rather than quitting in a formal sense, members simply stopped paying dues. Among other reasons for the decline of union membership is the refusal to take into account new concerns of workers that go beyond wages and threats of unemployment. See Boual, *Syndicalisme, quel second siècle?* While the membership of the CGT (like that of other unions) has declined, the number of full-time paid officials has increased. A similar situation prevails among other unions; see Dominique Andolfatto and Dominique Labbé, "Sociologie des syndicates français," unpublished monograph of the Association internationale des sociologues de langue française, Québec, July 2000.

11. See Jacques Capdevielle, "Les Opinions et les comportements politiques des ouvriers: Une Évolution inévitable? Irreversible?" *Cahiers du CEVIPOF*, no. 21 (January 1999), 78–79.

12. For a summary of the Auroux laws, see Smith, *Crisis in the French Labor Movement*, esp. pp. 209–19.

13. Labbé, Croisat, and Bévort, *La Désyndicalisation*, pp. 40, 81ff.

14. See Andrew Appleton, "France: Party-Group Relations in the Shadow of the State," in *Political Parties and Interest Groups: Shaping Democratic Governance*, Clive Thomas, ed. (Boulder and London: Lynne Rienner, 2001), pp. 45–62.

15. Henry Ehrmann, *Organized Business in France* (Princeton: Princeton University Press, 1957), pp. 58–100, 103.

16. Among other things, the CNPF set up new rules providing that the maximum age of the organization's president and vice-president be 70 years, and it encouraged younger entrepreneurs to take a more active part in the organization's executive. Still, in the late 1970s, the average age of the typical firm's *président-directeur-général* was 60.

17. The *Jeunes patrons* also joined with associations of managing directors, Christian employers *(Centre du patronat chrétien)*, and young managers *(Jeunes dirigeants)* to form *Entreprise et progrès*, itself a subgroup of the CNPF (MEDEF since 1999).

18. For an interesting journalistic treatment of the diversity of attitudes within the business community, see Alain de Sédouy and André Harris, *Les Patrons* (Paris: Seuil, 1977). For a later, and more scholarly, study, see Henri Weber, *Le Parti des patrons: Le CNPF 1946–1986* (Paris: Seuil, 1986), in which

the author discusses the "modernization" of attitudes of French business leaders, from Malthusian, protectionist, and paternalistic orientations to a growing readiness for global competition and social responsibility.

19. Alain Faujas, "Le Patronat juge que le principe de réalité s'imposera au gouvernement de Lionel Jospin," *Le Monde*, 4 June 1997, p. 12.

20. For example, in 1999, Martine Aubry, the minister of employment, gave in to MEDEF pressure and abandoned a proposal to take money out of the national employment insurance fund (UNEDIC) to finance the reduction of the workweek to 35 hours.

21. Wilson, *Interest-Group Politics in France*, pp. 105–07.

22. The JAC (which dates back to 1936) is a movement concerned with organizing educational and leisure-time activities and the diffusion of Catholic values among rural youth. In the mid-1980s, it formed the agricultural component of the *Mouvement rural de jeunesse chrétienne* (MRJC) and accounted for about 20 percent of the latter's membership of 250,000.

23. In 1999, Bové was indicted for sacking a McDonald's restaurant in Brittany.

24. On the multitude of farmers' groups, see Yves Tavernier et al., *L'Univers politique des paysans dans la France contemporaine* (Paris: Armand Colin, 1972); and Jacques Lachaud, *Les Institutions agricoles* (Paris: MA Editions, 1987).

25. For a detailed study of the relationship between agriculture and the public authorities, see John T. S. Keeler, *The Politics of Neocorporatism in France* (New York and Oxford: Oxford University Press, 1987).

26. Béatrice Gurrey, "Les Enseignants du premier degré détrônent la FEN au profit de la FSU," *Le Monde*, 20 December 1996, p. 10.

27. The UNSA encompasses about 360,000 members.

28. In 1994, the election results (in percent, for all levels of education and various types of educational personnel put together) were as follows: FSU, 30.8; FEN, 29.7; CFDT, 12.4; FO, 9.3; CGT, 5.6; CGC, 1.7; CFTC, 0.9; others, 9.5.

29. See Jean-Michel Dumay, "Grandes Manoeuvres dans l'enseignement catholique," *Le Monde*, 14 May 1992; and same author, "Un Lobby redouté," *Le Monde*, 16–17 January 1994 (supplement, "Les Français et leurs écoles," p. v).

30. Bernard Poulet, "À gauche de la gauche," *Le Débat*, no. 103 (January–February 1999), 39–59.

31. See, for example, Jean Michel Belorgey, *Cent Ans de vie associative* (Paris: Presses de Sciences-Po, 2000).

32. Pascale Robert-Diard and Laetitia Van Eeckhout, "Le Président de la République et le premier ministre courtisent le monde associatif," *Le Monde*, 1–2 July 2001.

33. In 2001 these subsidies amounted to 54 percent of the budget of associations. See ibid.

34. See Alexander Werth, *De Gaulle: A Political Biography* (Baltimore: Penguin, 1967), pp. 197, 203–6.

35. These groups include the *Front national de la police*; the *Force nationale des transports en commun*; the *Fédération nationale d'entreprise moderne et libertés*; the *Mouvement pour un enseignement national*; the *Association de défense des intérêts des Antilles françaises*; and the *Renouveau étudiant*, among many others. See "Le Pen hésite sur le choix de sa stratégie syndicale," *Le Monde*, 29 March 1997, p. 6.

36. Marie-Christine Vergiat, "Groupes de pression ou partenaires socio-professionnels," *Après-Demain*, no. 373 (April 1995), 22–23.

37. Michel Noblecourt, "Les Lobbys dans la cour des grands," in *L'Élection présidentielle 1995, Le Monde, Dossiers et Documents*, p. 29.

38. Gilles Lamarque, *Le Lobbying* (Paris: PUF, 1994), esp. pp. 3–5, 68–74. See also Frank J. Farnel, *Le Lobbying: Stratégies et techniques d'intervention* (Paris: Éditions d'Organisation, 1994).

39. For representative presentations of the (American) pluralist "ideal type," see Robert A. Dahl, *Who Governs* (New Haven: Yale University Press, 1961); *Polyarchy, Participation, and Opposition* (New Haven: Yale University Press, 1971), and "Pluralism Revisited," *Comparative Politics* 10 (January 1978), 191–204. See also Gabriel A. Almond, "Research Note: A Comparative Study of Interest Groups and the Political Process," *American Political Science Review* 52:1 (March 1958); and G. A. Almond and G. B. Powell, Jr., *Comparative Politics: A Developmental Approach* (Boston: Little, Brown, 1966), pp. 72–79. See also the summary in Wilson, *Interest-Group Politics in France*, pp. 18–25.

40. See Arthur F. Bentley, *The Process of Government: A Study of Social Pressures* (Evanston, IL: The Principia Press, 1949 reissue), p. 163; Earl Latham, *The Group Basis of Politics* (Ithaca, NY: Cornell University Press, 1952), pp. 1–16; and Bertram M. Gross, *The Legislative Struggle* (New York: McGraw-Hill, 1953).

41. This is a paraphrase of Philippe C. Schmitter, "Modes of Interest Intermediation and Models of Social Change in Western Europe," *Comparative Political Studies* 10:1 (April 1977), 9.

42. Jean-Claude Zarka, "Le Conseil économique et social," *Regards sur l'actualité*, no. 225 (November 1999), 39–45 (44).

43. Ezra Suleiman, *Politics, Power, and Bureaucracy in France* (Princeton: Princeton University Press, 1974), pp. 316–51.

44. Henry W. Ehrmann, "French Bureaucracy and Organized Interests," *Administrative Science Quarterly* 5 (1961), 534–55.

45. Bernard Chenot, *Organisation économique de l'État* (Paris: Dalloz, 1965), pp. 257ff.

46. Cf. Jean Meynaud, *Les Groupes de pression* (Paris: PUF, 1962), p. 16. The *Ordre des médecins* suffered from the stigma of having been created during the Vichy regime and hence of being a vestige of fascist corporatism. This fact and the *Ordre*'s attempt to scuttle the implementation of birth control led the government to suggest internal reforms and the Socialists to encourage the establishment of a rival medical association.

47. The government promised to be "reasonable" but seemed to be in no hurry because of the FSU's negative position regarding public support of parochial schools; see Valérie Devillechabrolle, "Les Syndicats réclament une clarification des règles de représentativité dans la fonction publique," *Le Monde*, 22 December 1993, p. 21. On the government's "fiddling" with formulas of representation, see Rafaële Rivals, "Bataille entre syndicats autour de nouvelles règles de représentativité," *Le Monde*, 17 October 1996, p. 6.

48. Jack Hayward, *Private Interests and Public Policy: The Experiences of the French Social and Economic Council* (New York: Barnes & Noble, 1966), pp. 23–24. See also Jean Frayssinet, *Le Conseil économique et social*, Notes et études documentaires, no. 4807 (Paris: Documentation Française, 1986).

49. Wilson, *Interest-Group Politics in France*, p. 161.

50. Alain Bockel, *La Participation des syndicats ouvriers aux fonctions économiques et sociales de l'État* (Paris: LGDJ, 1965), pp. 237–38.

51. The use of the word *prud'homme*, signifying a valiant, honest, and accomplished master of a craft, goes back to the late Middle Ages, when autonomous "corporations" existed in which craftsmen chose their representatives. Elections to the modern tribunals were instituted by Napoleon. Women were given the right to vote in those elections between 1898 and 1908, more than a generation before general women's suffrage. See Dominique Andolfatto, *L'Univers des élections professionnelles* (Paris: Éditions Ouvrières, 1992), pp. 13–17, 68. The workload of the *conseils de prud'hommes* has grown steadily. In 1990, they dealt with more than 190,000 cases. See V. Carrasco and A. Jeammaud, "Relations du travail," *Droit Ouvrier*, June 1992, pp. 204–07.

52. See François Subileau, "Les Élections prudhomales: Participation, représentativité, légitimité," *Politix*, no. 47 (3d trimestre, 1999), 151–66.

53. There are 129 primary funds, 16 regional funds, and 5 national organs, one each for special purposes (health insurance, retirement benefits, general insurance, income supplements for children, etc.). FNOSS is an umbrella organization that embraces several associations of specialists administering the various funds. In addition there are several thousand medical controllers.

54. Marie-Thérèse Join-Lambert, "L'Intervention croissante de l'État," in *La Crise du paritarisme*, Gilles Nezosi and Dominique Labbé, eds., *Problèmes Politiques et Sociaux*, no. 844 (September 2000), 21–25; and Philippe Frémeaux, "Le Paritarisme: Entre théorie et réalité," ibid., pp. 27–31.

55. Note that "corporatism" has not had the same meaning in France as in other countries, namely, the role of the state in controlling the access and influencing the behavior of interest groups. On the contrary, it has connoted the habit of interest groups of selfishly protecting their own interests against the public interest and thus in weakening the power of the state. See Ezra Suleiman, *Private Power and Centralization in France: The Notaires and the State* (Princeton, NJ: Princeton University Press, 1987), pp. 20–22.

56. Police officers, hospital nurses, and other public employees have been uncertain whether they preferred an "autonomously bargaining" union (which may give them more freedom) or a "corporatized" one (which would put them into a more advantageous salary category). See Valérie Devillechabrolle, "Les Dérives corporatistes," *Le Monde*, 23 June 1993, p. 32.

57. According to one observer of parliamentary life, the Assembly is constantly exposed, in one way or another, to the pressures of organized interests. See Marc Abélès, *Un Ethnologue à l'Assemblée* (Paris: Odile Jacob, 1999).

58. Jean-Michel Bezat, "Les Négociations caisses-médecins s'engagent dans un climat tendu," *Le Monde*, 10 October 1996, p. 5.

59. Among the endless stream of writings on the corporatist or "neocorporatist" paradigm, the following should be mentioned: Gerhard Lehmbruch and Philippe Schmitter, *Patterns of Corporatist Policy-Making*, Sage Modern Politics Series, vol. 7 (Beverly Hills, CA: Sage Publications, 1982); Suzanne Berger, ed., *Organizing Interests in Western Europe: Pluralism, Corporatism, and the Transformation of Politics* (Cambridge: Cambridge University Press, 1981); and Reginald J. Harrison, *Pluralism and Corporatism* (London: Allen & Unwin, 1980). For a critique of the use of this paradigm, see William Safran, "Interest Groups in Three Industrial Democracies: France, West Germany, and the United States," in F. Eidlin, ed., *Constitutional Democracy: Essays in Comparative Politics*, Festschrift in honor of Henry W. Ehrmann (Boulder, CO: Westview, 1983), pp. 315–43; and Wilson, *Interest-Group Politics in France*. For an attempt to "mediate" between the corporatist and pluralist views, see Yves Mény, "Interest Groups and Politics in the Fifth Republic," in Paul Godt, ed., *Policy-Making in France* (London: Pinter, 1989), pp. 91–101.

60. Keeler, *The Politics of Neocorporatism in France*, p. 5.

61. Ibid., p. 4.

62. Keeler himself (ibid., pp. 3–10), despite the title of his excellent book, seems to be drawing back from the "corporatist" paradigm when he speaks of a "weak corporatism" in France, which is becoming a "structured pluralism."

63. See Dominique Colas, ed., *L'État et les corporatismes* (Paris: PUF, 1988). This book, based on a colloquium, contains a bewildering variety of approaches to, and definitions of, corporatism, including an increased role of professional associations in politics, the growing role of politics in social organization, a more orderly pattern of labor-management relations, and a policy-making partnership between the private and public sectors.

64. See, for example, Eric Nordlinger, *On the Autonomy of the Democratic State* (Cambridge: Harvard University Press, 1981); and Peter B. Evans, Dietrich Rueschemeyer, and Theda Skocpol, *Bringing the State Back In* (Cambridge: Cambridge University Press, 1985).

65. The term *state* has been variously used to refer to a strong government, to government as such, to all or most political institutions (hence the "new institutionalism"), to particular institutions (such as the bureaucracy), to the public interest, and to effective decision making.

66. John S. Ambler, "French Education and the Limits of State Autonomy," *Western Political Quarterly* 41:3 (September 1988), 469–88.

67. Jean-Michel Normand, "Simone Veil face au lobby médical," *Le Monde*, 1 July 1993. In this instance, the medical lobby was supported by the trade unions.

68. Jean-Baptiste de Montvalon, "M. Juppé renonce au système de contrôle des étrangers voulu par M. Debré," *Le Monde*, 20 February 1997, p. 5. This bill, named after Jean-Louis Debré, the minister of the interior, is not to be confused with the (Michel) Debré law of 1959, which provided for subsidies to parochial schools.

69. See Jean-Michel Normand, "Le 'Lobbying' préélectoral des retraités," *Le Monde*, 13 March 1993.

70. There was a widespread feeling that the CGT's tough wage demands (if not the strike itself) had been instigated by the PCF in order to convince the Socialist government to take the PCF more seriously.

71. A mass demonstration in 1985 against the racist propaganda of the National Front was said to have been orchestrated by Jack Lang, the minister of culture. See W. Safran, "The French State and Ethnic Minority Cultures," in J. R. Rudolph and R. J. Thompson, eds., *Ethnoterritorial Politics, Policy, and the Western World* (Boulder, CO: Lynne Rienner, 1989), p. 146.

72. Jean-Marie Pernot, "Les Syndicats à l'épreuve du mouvement social," *Regards sur l'actualité*, no. 222 (June 1996), 5. This public support paralleled that of many other massive strikes in the past 30 years but was, however, not accompanied by sympathy for the unions!

73. As a journalist put it, "the three unions (CGT, FO, CFDT) have never counted for so little in terms of membership but never, since 1968, counted so heavily in face of the government." Romain Gubert, "Syndicats: L'Été de la Saint-Sylvestre," *Le Point*, 30 December 1995, pp. 36–37.

74. See Michel Bauer, "La Gauche au pouvoir et le grand patronat," in Pierre Birnbaum, ed., *Les Elites socialistes au pouvoir, 1981–1985* (Paris: PUF, 1985), pp. 266–68.

75. Except for Bérégovoy, who had ceased years earlier to identify with his working-class origins. See Guy Groux and René Mouriaux, "François Mitterrand et les ouvriers," *French Politics and Society* 9:3–4 (Summer–Fall 1991), 43–62.

76. Interview with Pierre-Yves Cossé, in "Le Xe Plan, pour quoi faire," *Regards sur l'actualité*, no. 148 (February 1989), 3–9.

CHAPTER 6

Instruments and Patterns of Decision Making: The Executive

Western democratic regimes usually conform to one of two models. The first is a parliamentary system in which there is an executive composed of two "units": a monarch or a figurehead president, and a prime minister (or premier) and his or her cabinet, the latter two selected by, and ultimately responsible to, a parliament. The alternative is a presidential system in which a popularly elected president functions as both chief of state and head of government and is independent of the legislative branch of government; in such a system, both branches cooperate with and balance each other.

In terms of both tradition and the political institutions mentioned in its Constitution, the Fifth Republic is a hybrid, embodying features of standard continental parliamentary democracies and of various types of presidential systems. Parliament was retained; but in conformity with de Gaulle's preferences, the president is mentioned first and the legislature second, a reversal of the order of the Fourth Republic's Constitution.

THE POSITION OF THE PRESIDENT

Much of the power of the French president is derived from the fact that he or she is virtually independent of other branches of government. The president's term of office was seven years (as it had been in the two previous republics) from the beginning of the Fifth Republic until 2000, when it was reduced to five years. Whereas in the Fourth Republic a president was limited to two terms, today there is no such limitation. In previous republics, the president was elected by Parliament and was subject to its controls and pressures, and therefore did not possess an independent popular mandate. In the Fifth Republic until 1962, the president was chosen by an electoral college composed of members of Parliament and municipal councils; since then, the president has been elected by direct popular vote. The president appoints the prime minister, or premier, presides over the cabinet, initiates referenda, and has the authority to dissolve the National Assembly and thereby bring about a new election of that body.

A number of labels have been used to describe the special character of the Fifth Republic, among them *principate, elective monarchy,*[1] and *plebiscitary democracy.* The system bears some resemblance to that which prevails today in Austria, Finland, Ireland, and Iceland, in the sense that the president is popularly elected. But in these countries, the president is in fact much weaker than their respective constitutions would suggest, because his role is circumscribed by his being subject to ouster by Parliament (as in Iceland) or because the Parliament possesses strong legislative powers (as in Austria, Finland, and Ireland). The French president has none of these limitations. He or she is like the president of the Weimar Republic in possessing special emergency powers. The French president is like the U.S. president in that he or she "reigns" and "rules." The president's role is like that of a monarch, possessing in practice all the powers that the English queen now possesses only in theory.

The president is the head of state—in fact, "the highest authority of the state"; the guarantor of national independence; the individual chiefly responsible for seeing that the Constitution is observed; the person who (under Art. 5) ensures "the functioning of governmental authorities"; the "arbiter" of political and institutional conflicts; the principal appointing officer and diplomatic negotiator; and the commander in chief of the armed forces. The president is also the "guide of France"; "in charge of the destiny of France and the Republic"; and "the inspirer and orienter of national actions."[2] The president conveys general principles of policy to the people and Parliament through formal and informal messages; the president has the right of pardon and reprieve; and the president's signature is necessary in order for acts of Parliament to be valid. Although not granted the right to veto legislation in a formal sense, the president may ask Parliament to reconsider a bill he or she does not like. Like a monarch, he or she may choose to be aloof and above political battles—in theory, presidents do not demean themselves by overt identification with political parties.

The presidential "mediation" role was intended to apply primarily to the areas of defense and foreign affairs. The Third Republic Constitution specifically granted the president the initiative in foreign affairs (e.g., in the negotiation of treaties), and early Third Republic presidents had a voice in choosing the foreign minister. Gradually, presidential power to make foreign policy atrophied, especially after World War I. The Fourth Republic Constitution merely stipulated that the president was to be "informed" about international negotiations and that the president was to sign treaties.

In the Fifth Republic, the president negotiates *and* signs treaties (Art. 52). Because (under Art. 15) the president is commander in chief of the armed forces, presidents have always taken defense *policy* as their own domain. For a number of reasons, most of the French accepted de Gaulle's predominance in the areas of defense and foreign policy. In the first place, the precedent of continuity in foreign affairs had already been set in the Fourth Republic, when in the face of constant reshuffling of cabinets and premiers, there was remarkable stability in the Foreign Ministry: Whereas there were 17 premiers (in 23 governments), there were only 8 foreign ministers. Second, de Gaulle came to power largely because the premiers under the Fourth Republic's institutional arrangements had been unable to solve the problem of Algeria. If one of the principal reasons for calling on de Gaulle was to solve that problem, he had to be given a relatively free hand. Third, implicit in de Gaulle's political philosophy was the reassertion of the international role of France, a position that would necessitate a strong executive.

Although the presidency is associated with other institutions, these were for many years underdeveloped and unable to balance presidential power. The Constitution states that the president chooses the premier and then ratifies or confirms the premier's selection of his or her cabinet colleagues. In fact, under "normal" conditions—that is, if the majority of the National Assembly, and hence the premier, belongs to the same political party as the president—it is the president who selects most, if not all, the members of the government. A rigid interpretation of the Constitution would have it that once the cabinet is chosen, only Parliament can dismiss it. However, parliamentary dismissal of the cabinet has been difficult and fraught with political risk to the deputies because the Assembly itself is subject to dissolution by the president. Constitutional amendments, referenda, and the invocation of emergency powers require consultation with the Constitutional Council (see Chapter 7), but three of its nine members, including its presiding officer, are appointed by the president. One of the few national institutions that would seem to be independent of the president is the Economic and Social Council (see Chapter 5); that body, however, has only consultative powers.

Many of the powers the premier possessed in the Fourth Republic were allocated to the president in the Fifth Republic. In the former, the president presided over cabinet meetings during ceremonial occasions, but the premier was the real chairperson. In the Fifth Republic, the premier is merely "head of government," or, more formally, chair of the Council of Ministers, whereas the president is the actual decision maker. The president has left to the premier the role of being a link between the presidency and the Parliament, particularly on matters that are of little interest to the president. Thus, the premier's position has been almost analogous to that of the provincial prefect in France (until 1982), who provided a link between the national government, on the one hand, and the city council and mayor, on the other. Presidents, rather than premiers, have tended to make all decisions in the "reserved domain" (foreign policy, defense, and constitutional matters), and they have attempted to include in their domain whatever else has been of importance to them, such as sensitive social and economic problems. When such problems have ceased to be headline issues, they have devolved upon the ministers.[3] Significant policy decisions made by presidents have included granting Algeria independence in 1962; blocking British entry into the Common Market in 1963 and 1967; initiating constitutional amendments in 1962 and 1969; withdrawing France from the integrated command of NATO in 1966; placing an embargo on military supplies to certain Mideast countries in 1967; devaluing the franc in 1969 and 1971; reducing petroleum imports in 1974; suspending the construction of nuclear power stations in the early 1980s; participating in the Gulf War in 1990; deciding to hold a referendum on the Treaty of European Union in 1992; and deciding in 1995 to abolish the military draft.

Presidents have specific responsibilities in the domestic arena as well. These include choosing members of the government; accepting resignation of cabinet members; setting the agenda of cabinet meetings; signing ordinances and decrees issuing from government; nominating civilian and military officers; issuing pardons; promulgating laws; asking for reconsideration of bills; calling Parliament into special session; and nominating members of the High Council of the Magistrature.

Finally, there is a list of implied presidential powers and actual decisions that is so exhaustive that the notion of the "dual executive" came to be regarded as a myth, at least until 1986. True, the Constitution allows a degree of independence to the premier once he or she has been appointed, because according to a strict interpretation, only the National Assembly can dismiss the premier. Moreover, according to the Constitution, the premier has a respectable number of powers and responsibilities. The premier is expected to manage government bills and see them safely through Parliament, but that task is facilitated by the streamlined sessions of Parliament, the government's control over the agenda, and the president's threat of dissolution. The premier prepares budget bills, defends government policy in Parliament, and answers parliamentary questions. The premier (in cooperation with the other cabinet members) supervises the work of the ministries and departments and of the civil servants who staff them; and he or she also issues regulations for the ministries. But these regulations can be vetoed by the president. In addition, the premier's control over the ministries is somewhat limited by the fact that the president may take a direct interest in the work of certain ministries or ignore the recommendations of the cabinet.

Some presidential decisions do not require cabinet input at all, such as the dissolution of the Assembly and the invocation of Article 16 (see below). Although in these two cases consultation with the premier is mandatory, the consultation would probably have little meaning beyond the requirement that the premier be informed of the president's intentions: If the premier should object, the president might react in the same way that President Lincoln was said to have reacted when his seven-member cabinet unanimously voted against a policy he had embraced: "Seven nays, one aye; the ayes have it."

At a press conference in January 1964, de Gaulle said that "it cannot be accepted that a diarchy exist at the top."[4] He was free to listen to or to ignore his premier and, in fact, to replace him. It has been asserted that this attitude about presidential monopoly, which prevailed from 1958 to 1963, was subsequently modified by the development of a more genuine *"copilotage"* between president and premier, in the sense that de Gaulle withdrew from clearly articulated leadership in domestic affairs and gave his premier a freer hand in that area.[5] It has also been argued that the role of the premier under de Gaulle's immediate successor increased because Pompidou lacked de Gaulle's charisma and did not face the same domestic and foreign policy problems (e.g., the Algerian crisis or the "May Events"). But Pompidou fully shared his predecessor's attitude toward the premier. At a press conference in 1972, Pompidou outlined in the following way what he required of his premier:

1. He must have ideas that correspond as closely as possible to those of the President.

2. He must completely accept the institutions of the Fifth Republic, meaning the preeminence of the chief of state in matters of general policy direction and in the most important decisions.

3. "He must be capable of carrying out his own duties—a heavy load . . . since it means not only directing daily policy, but also . . . being responsible for government policy before the Assembly and the Parliament; and, finally, carrying out relations with the Majority."[6]

In the mid-1960s, as finance minister, Giscard d'Estaing had criticized de Gaulle's "lonely exercise of power"; but upon assuming the presidency himself, he endorsed the ideas of his predecessors unreservedly. In a number of interviews and speeches he argued that "the French do not want a president for [receiving] chrysanthemums and for inaugurations . . . [but one who is] responsible for the policy orientations of the country";[7] and he viewed the premier as a "loyal and active" spokesperson for him.[8] It has been suggested that under Giscard, *all* policy matters had become part of the "reserved domain," and that Premier Barre behaved, not like a chief of government, but like a minister of economic affairs.[9] One of the manifestations of Giscard's unmediated governmental leadership was his practice of issuing to the premier monthly written directives in which details on policy matters, and even the timetable for their discussion, were spelled out.[10]

When Mitterrand assumed the presidency, there was hope that he would be more responsive to Parliament. That hope was based on the fact that, as leader of the opposition for many years, he had fully identified with the Socialist party's call for a chief of state who would not be authoritarian and would respect the other institutions of government, and whose term of office would be reduced.[11] But during the first five years following his election, he behaved much like his predecessors in insisting that "the premier and the ministers must execute the policies defined by the president, since the president has the duty to put into effect the program for which he had contracted with the nation. The role of the premier is important . . . but when it comes to making decisions at a crucial moment, it is my responsibility to decide."[12]

Chirac largely followed these interpretations, at least until the cohabitation with a Socialist government. In his inaugural remarks, he promised to see to it that "our democracy be firmed up and better balanced by an equitable division of competences between the executive and legislative branches, as General de Gaulle . . . had wanted it. The president arbitrates, determines the principal directions [of policy], assures the unity of the nation and preserves its independence. The government conducts the policies of the nation, [and] the Parliament makes law and controls the action of the government."[13]

THE PREMIERS

As appointees of the president, premiers oscillate between obeying the president, taking their cues from Parliament, reacting to the pressures of interest groups, and occasionally hiding behind the recommendations of *comités de sages* (committees of experts). Some premiers may bring a particular vision or plan to their jobs, as, for example, Raymond Barre and his emergency plans for fiscal restraints or Juppé and his prescriptions for saving the social security system; but most others have not presided over government policies that could be called their own. Under normal circumstances, premiers interpret the president's messages to Parliament (where the latter may not appear in person) and translate his general "orientations" into government bills. In the view of Raymond Barre, this translation implies the following tasks: "to direct the governmental team . . . to implement regulatory powers . . . to organize the relations of government with the National Assembly and the Senate . . . to establish contacts with representatives of public opinion, of the economic and social partners and of scientific, cultural, and intellectual activities . . . and finally, to make contact with [ordinary] French people."[14]

From the lack of independence of the premier's office that has prevailed—under normal circumstances—one should not infer that premiers of the Fifth Republic have been political nobodies. All premiers thus far have been prestigious individuals with wide experience in elective office or the civil service. They have been selected because of their qualifications, their political backgrounds, their suitability to the presidential temperament, and (even before 1986) their acceptability to the Assembly (see Table 6.1).

The original party allegiances of the premiers have been diverse. Michel Debré and Jacques Chaban-Delmas had been Radical-Socialists in the early years of the Fourth Republic; Georges Pompidou and Pierre Messmer had been briefly affiliated with the Socialist party; the backgrounds of Maurice Couve de Murville, Jacques Chirac, and Raymond Barre could be considered more or less "nonpolitical." Pierre Mauroy and Pierre Bérégovoy had been well-established members of the old Socialist party (the SFIO) and played prominent roles in the creation and leadership of the new Socialist party (the PS) in 1969–1970. Michel Rocard had been a leader of the PSU and, after his entry into the PS in the early 1970s, controlled an important faction within that party; in late 1980, he briefly vied with Mitterrand for the nomination as the party's candidate for the presidency. Edith Cresson had been active in the Convention of Republican Institutions (CIR), a political formation led by Mitterrand, and a few years after he assumed the leadership of the PS, she became a member of that party's secretariat.

Debré had been a senator, a civil servant, an important ideologist of Gaullism, and one of the chief architects of the new Constitution. Pompidou had been, by turns, a lycée professor of literature, de Gaulle's presidential chief of staff, a member of the Council of State, and a director of the Rothschild banking house. Couve de Murville had been a respected civil servant and had served as de Gaulle's foreign minister for several years. Chaban-Delmas had been a hero of the Resistance, mayor of Bordeaux, and speaker of the Assembly. Messmer had been a civil servant, cabinet minister, and colonial troubleshooter. Chirac had held a number of important civil service positions and, after 1968, a variety of cabinet posts. Barre, a professor of economics, had been minister of foreign trade, and Mauroy had been mayor of Lille. Laurent Fabius, appointed in 1984—at age 37, the youngest French premier in the twentieth century—had been a professional civil servant who had begun his political career in 1974 when he joined the Socialist party; in quick succession he had become Mitterrand's economic adviser, chief of staff, and manager of his successful presidential election campaign. Subsequently, Fabius had served as Economics Minister Delors's deputy for the budget and had been credited (or blamed) for much of the government's austerity policy; later, as minister of industry, he had been responsible for cutting the budgetary allocations to the public sector and for promoting efficient private industry. Edith Cresson had served as minister of agriculture and, subsequently, as minister of foreign trade and minister in charge of European Community affairs. Bérégovoy had been secretary-general of the Presidential Office when Mitterrand assumed the presidency, subsequently becoming minister of social affairs, finance, and, finally, a "superminister" of economic affairs, finance, and budget. Edouard Balladur had held a number of high administrative positions (including membership in the Council of State) and had served as secretary-general of the Presidential Office under Pompidou. After an interlude of activity in the private sector, he had been appointed minister of finance in the first "cohabitation" government, headed by Chirac. Alain Juppé had been an inspector of finances and a deputy mayor of Paris; in the first cohabitation government, he had served, by turns, as deputy minister for the budget, deputy

TABLE 6.1
Fifth Republic Premiers

President	Prime Minister	Month/Year of Appointment	Length of Tenure (in months)	Cumulative
de Gaulle	Debré	January 1959	39	39
	Pompidou I	April 1962	7	
	II	December 1962	37	
	III	January 1966	15	
	IV	April 1967	15	74
	Couve de Murville	July 1968	11	11
Pompidou	Chaban-Delmas	June 1969	36	36
	Messmer I	July 1972	8	
	II	April 1973	11	
	III	March 1974	3	22
Giscard d'Estaing	Chirac	June 1974	27	27
	Barre I	August 1976	7	
	II	March 1977	12	
	III	April 1978	15	
	IV	July 1979	22	56
Mitterrand	Mauroy I	May 1981	1	
	II	June 1981	21	
	III	March 1983	16	38
	Fabius	July 1984	20	20
	Chirac	March 1986	25	25
	Rocard I	May 1988	1	
	II	June 1988	35	36
	Cresson	May 1991	10	10
	Bérégovoy	April 1992	12	12
	Balladur	March 1993	26	26
Chirac	Juppé I	May 1995	6	
	II	November 1995	19	25
	Jospin I	June 1997	34	
	II	April 2000	25	59
	Raffarin	June 2002	current[a]	

NOTE: Months are rounded off.
[a]Named interim premier following Chirac's reelection in April 2002 and reconfirmed after parliamentary elections.

minister of foreign affairs, and government spokesman, and he became foreign minister in the Balladur government. Lionel Jospin had been by turns a member of the diplomatic service, a professor of economics, the first secretary of the Socialist party, and minister of education. The six premiers before August 1976 had been loyal Gaullists at one time or another: They had been prominent in either the Resistance or the Free French movement (except for Pompidou, who sat out World War II and the Occupation in Paris, and Chirac, who was too young) or had close personal relations with de Gaulle; and all but one had experience in the government bureaucracy. Before the 2002 elections twelve premiers had had parliamentary experience—Debré, Chaban-Delmas, Messmer, Chirac, Mauroy, Fabius, Rocard, Cresson, Bérégovoy, Balladur, Juppé, and Jospin—and three, Pompidou, Couve de Murville, and Barre, had not, although in 1968 Couve de Murville had run unsuccessfully for an Assembly seat.

Jean-Pierre Raffarin's background is altogether different: Unlike most of his predecessors, he is not a Parisian, but a man from the provinces; he is not an *Enarque* (a graduate of the National School of Administration [ENA]), but the product of a business school; his political experiences derived not from being an Assembly deputy, but a senator and president of a regional council. In order to protect small shopkeepers, Raffarin, as a member of the government, sponsored a law in 1996 to freeze the expansion of supermarkets. He is not a Gaullist, but a member of *Democratie libérale*, formerly a component of the UDF, a formation he once served as secretary-general. In 1998, however, he switched his loyalties from the UDF to Chirac, via *Dialogue et initiative*, an ultra-Chiraquist political club.[15]

All premiers, except those in office during "cohabitation" periods, have possessed a quality considered politically desirable by the president. Debré had helped to launch the new regime whose ideas he had done much to shape; Pompidou represented a technocratic outlook and a business orientation; Couve de Murville, clearly an interim premier, stood for nonpartisanship; Chaban-Delmas was chosen to appeal to progressive centrist forces with his quest for a "new society"; Messmer was chosen largely for the purpose of retrieving the support of orthodox adherents of Gaullism; and Chirac was appointed (to his first term) because he combined a background of Gaullism and technocracy and had the wisdom to prefer Giscard d'Estaing over Chaban-Delmas in the first round of the presidential elections of 1974. Barre was chosen because of his professional orientation and his seeming lack of political ambition. Mauroy was selected because of his nearly ideal background: Born into the working class (and for a time employed as a teacher in a vocational school), he maintained close ties with the industrial unions of the northeast region; as a moderate, he got along easily with the leaders of the various party factions. Fabius was chosen partly in order to help rejuvenate the image of Mitterrand, whose popularity had slipped badly in public opinion polls, because of dissatisfaction over the unresolved unemployment problem. Fabius was not only brilliant (he was a graduate of the ENA and the *École Normale Supérieure*, the two most prestigious schools of France) but was also identified as a competent pragmatist who was closely associated with the national effort at industrial modernization. Rocard was appointed in part to appease his numerous supporters within the Socialist party and in part because his nonideological approach to problems would facilitate the building of bridges to the political Center—

and in so doing, would help to weaken the political Right.[16] Edith Cresson was selected because of her loyalty to the president as well as her identification with a policy of industrial competitiveness, and Bérégovoy was chosen as an interim premier identified with fiscal responsibility.[17] Juppé was chosen because of his reputation as an able civil servant —he was a graduate of both ENA and the *École Normale Supérieure*—and because of his long association and personal friendship with Chirac. Raffarin was selected because—in contrast to Juppé, who had a reputation for arrogance—of his moderation and modesty.

Despite their qualifications, most premiers have had a subservient relationship to their presidents, especially if such behavior has helped to promote their ambition of someday succeeding to the presidency (as Pompidou had done). However, that subservience has been uneven, even during "normal"—that is, noncohabitation—periods. A recent study of the French premier includes a "typology of presidential–prime ministerial relations" that distinguishes among premiers who were subordinates, rivals, and opponents of the president.[18] The nature of the relationship has depended on a variety of factors: the "chemistry" of personal interaction, the cohesion within the cabinet, the nature of policy issues, the electoral factor, and the composition of Parliament.

COHABITATION I: PRECEDENT-SETTING PATTERN OR POLITICAL PARENTHESIS?

The relationship between president and premier changed dramatically after the parliamentary election of 1986, which produced a Gaullist-Giscardist antipresidential majority in the National Assembly. Some politicians argued that this result should be interpreted as a popular disavowal of Mitterrand's conduct as president and that he should resign.[19] Mitterrand (whose term of office still had two years left) refused to do so. However, he was obliged to appoint a premier and cabinet to the Assembly's liking rather than his own and had to relinquish most of the decision-making power, at least in domestic matters, to the premier.

The obligation to share power, or "cohabit," with a hostile premier and Assembly transformed a hitherto powerful president into a constitutional semimonarch. In effect, Mitterrand considered his main task "to be watchful that the decisions of the government or of the [parliamentary] majority not be detrimental to that which is good, sane, and necessary in [the spirit of] national unity."[20] Like the British queen (who, in the words of Walter Bagehot, retained "the right to be consulted, to encourage, and to warn"),[21] Mitterrand thought that he retained "in domestic politics [the right], when necessary, to make known his judgment and to warn the public against that which . . . was dangerous for national unity and the public interest."[22]

The precise method of power sharing had to be determined in an ad hoc fashion because there was no precedent for it in the Fifth Republic. Cohabitation was an experiment in terms of both government appointments and policy making. Although it was clear from the beginning that the new government would be led by a person who would be supported by the Assembly, it was not certain that it would be Chirac. Mitterrand probably chose the latter as premier because in so doing he averted the possibility of the Assembly's *imposing* him on the president. He left the nomination of ministers to Chirac almost entirely, but rejected his original choices for the posts of minister of foreign affairs and defense, the two areas considered presidential domains. Once the government was constituted, Mitterrand's contact with it was confined to the weekly cabinet meetings: These were run by the premier, with Mitterrand confining himself on most occasions to words of admonition and wise council.

Driven by ambition, Chirac attempted to "invade" the presidential foreign-policy domain, or at least to achieve a kind of co-management of it. Thus, he insisted on accompanying Mitterrand to the economic summit meeting in Tokyo in 1986; subsequently, he appeared at a French-Spanish summit meeting in Madrid and took the credit for the improvement of relations between the two countries, only to be publicly "corrected" by Mitterrand.

Conversely, although Mitterrand left domestic matters largely in Chirac's hands, he was not above interfering in that domain to the extent that he was able to do so and when it suited his political purposes. Thus, Mitterrand did nothing to stop the promotion of Chirac's major policies, among them the denationalization of more than 60 state-owned enterprises, tougher laws to fight terrorism and illegal immigration, and a return to the single-member-constituency system that had been abandoned only a year earlier by the Socialists. But he refused to sign government decrees providing for selected policy changes (e.g., changing the boundaries of election districts), thereby forcing the government to put these measures through the "normal" (though accelerated) parliamentary processes.[23] Furthermore, Mitterrand publicly expressed his reservations about projected government policies regarding the treatment of immigrants and changes of the naturalization laws, thereby forcing the government to seek wider consensus for these reforms by means of a specially appointed "committee of experts."

Mitterrand got away with these forays into policy making because the Chirac government was not a monolithic bloc. The government was weakened by its lack of internal unity; it was itself an experiment in "cohabitation" between Gaullist and Giscardist ministers.[24] Between 1986 and 1988, the relations between the RPR and the UDF were embittered by policy differences and by feelings that the latter did not get enough consideration from Chirac and that the former was taking the lion's share of top ministerial and other political jobs. In addition, there were arguments *within* the ranks of the Gaullist ministers. This lack of government solidarity made presidential intervention easier and sometimes even provoked it.

Mitterrand's withdrawal from most of the domestic policy arena enhanced his presidential stature in the eyes of the public. Conversely, Chirac's increased policy-making responsibilities served as a long rope with which he could, so to speak, hang himself. Chirac's standing was weakened, not merely because he was unable to bring unity to his government, but also because he was not firm enough to maintain his policy directions in the face of public pressures. Whereas in the beginning of Chirac's premiership in 1986, cohabitation had worked fairly smoothly—in part in response to public opinion, which seemed to be solidly in favor of the experiment—at the end, it had deteriorated to a strained relationship between president and premier.

COHABITATION II: A "CIVILIZED" WAITING GAME

With the overwhelming victory of the combined Gaullist-Giscardist forces in the parliamentary elections of 1993, it became clear that the cohabitation experiment would have to be repeated. Even before the elections, Mitterrand had prepared himself for renewed power sharing by announcing that he would continue to serve out his presidential term no matter who won the elections and no matter who was prime minister. He reminded his audience at a press conference that the Constitution provided for a division of responsibilities and that "it is not the task of the president of the Republic to govern."[25] The appointment of Edouard Balladur, a moderate Gaullist, to head the new conservative government was a compromise: It was in accord with the wishes of both the RPR and the UDF. Given the competing presidential ambitions of Chirac, the leader of the RPR, and Giscard d'Estaing, the leader of the UDF, neither would have been tolerated by the other. As the RPR had by far the largest number of seats in the new Assembly, Chirac could have insisted on the premiership despite the misgivings of both Giscard and Mitterrand; but he preferred (wisely, as it turned out) to have someone else take on the job. Thus he could avoid a replay of the first cohabitation episode, that is, avoid taking direct responsibility for unpopular political decisions that might alienate the voters during the next presidential elections.

The second cohabitation proved to be a relatively smooth one. Not only did Mitterrand and Balladur respect each other, but each also had an interest in continuing a working relationship as long as possible, for if that relationship broke down, Mitterrand might resign and an accelerated presidential election would take place, in which Chirac would be the likely winner. For his part, Balladur wished to be prime minister long enough to solve important problems, prove his ability to govern, and come to be regarded as capable of becoming president someday. Balladur did not openly avow any presidential ambitions, and Chirac continued to be regarded as the presumptive presidential candidate of the RPR. Balladur's presidential appetite, however, was whetted as his popularity rose.

Mitterrand and Balladur differed on a number of issues, such as the right to asylum, constitutional reform, and socioeconomic policies, and periodically the president voiced his policy preferences and his concern for social justice. But the two had similar views on foreign policy, defense, and international trade negotiations, a circumstance that made it easier for the premier to accept Mitterrand's continued involvement in these matters and permitted both the president and the prime minister to test the limits of the presidential "reserved domain." The president and the premier held frequent consultations, avoided public criticism of each other, and often appeared together at international meetings. In fact, Balladur sometimes consulted with the president *before* he met with his cabinet. Their collaboration was facilitated by the harmonious relationship of their respective chief executive officers.[26]

As premier, Balladur had to perform multiple balancing acts: to avoid needlessly antagonizing the president without incurring the accusation of being his mouthpiece; to ensure a smooth relationship between the Gaullist and Giscardist members of his government; and to prevent policy disagreements within his coalition and within the Gaullist leadership group itself (e.g., between the pro- and anti-Europeans and the social progressives and conservatives) from getting out of hand. In addition, he had to make sure that he would not be too openly criticized by Chirac from his safe perch outside the national government. For his part, Chirac, too, had to perform a balancing act: to pretend to support the policies of Balladur lest he be accused of undermining the solidarity of the RPR-UDF coalition *and* to hope that Balladur's performance would deteriorate and his popularity decline, while he, Chirac, would escape the blame.[27]

COHABITATION III: CO–DECISION MAKING OR A NEO-PARLIAMENTARY REGIME?

The cohabitation inaugurated in June 1997 sparked a debate about whether a new intra-executive relationship had been introduced that changed the institutional setting of the Fifth Republic. During the first two cohabitation periods, Mitterrand had been both president of the Republic and, with the Socialist party behind him, chief of the opposition. The third cohabitation, because it was unnecessary, self-inflicted, and the result of a tactical blunder committed by Chirac, weakened his presidential authority, so that he became little more than titular chief of state.[28] Furthermore, since the election of Philippe Séguin as official leader of the RPR, Chirac was deprived of control of his own party and thus of his role as leader of the opposition. Chirac was, in short, subjected to a double cohabitation—on the one hand with Jospin, a Socialist prime minister, and on the other hand with Philippe Séguin, who had been a rival of Juppé's, Chirac's trusted former prime minister. Almost from the beginning of the new government, it became clear that decision-making power was being effectively transferred to the prime minister. This transfer was the result of an implicit acknowledgment by Chirac that for the first time in the Fifth Republic, a prime minister had been chosen, not by the president, but by the people.

At his first meeting with the new government, Chirac expressed the hope that the cohabitation between Jospin and himself would take place "in a dignified manner, with mutual respect and a constant concern for France's interests." The precise nature of the division of labor, however, remained ambiguous. During a news conference on 14 July (the major French national holiday), Chirac alluded to a "modest" presidency when he suggested that he would not oppose the government, which he expected would govern for five years (that is, until the end of his presidential term) "in its own manner and according to its own convictions." At the same time, he would reserve the right to comment on major domestic issues. Whether this was a French variant of the classic role assigned to the British constitutional monarch was open to question, for Chirac not only advised the RPR-UDF to get closer to the people and forget its internal differences, but also launched into a critique of a number of Jospin's policies, ostensibly because of their implications for foreign policy.

The constitutional text stipulates that "the *government* determines the foreign policy of the nation"; most of de Gaulle's successors, however, have followed him in arrogating this domain to themselves. In a speech in 1997 (just after the parliamentary elections) Chirac echoed this belief when he said, "Today it is my duty to fight every inch of the way everywhere in the world so that France retains its rank, assures its security, affirms its influence, increases its share of the market . . . preserves its European achievements . . . and continues to advance toward a united, strong, and just Europe."[29] During periods of cohabitation, however, that interpretation has been challenged by prime ministers, who have insisted that foreign policy was a "shared domain." This has been particularly true of Jospin, who has frequently articulated his positions on international affairs.[30]

Jospin lost no time in reminding Chirac of the policy-making prerogatives conferred by the Constitution on the premier. Jospin admitted that the president, as head of the armed forces, was responsible for defense and that foreign policy continued to be part of the reserved domain of the president; nevertheless, the premier's prerogative extended to the domain of foreign policy insofar as it was connected with domestic policy. Chirac seemed to admit as much; a few days after being installed as premier, Jospin accompanied Chirac to a European Union summit in Amsterdam almost as a matter of course (just as during previous cohabitations, the premier had accompanied the president to the great European rendezvous). At a joint news conference, Jospin suggested that such appearances together reflected a unity of views with respect to, for example, the Treaties of Amsterdam and Nice, the admission of new members to the European Union, the institutional restructuring of the latter, and other matters pertaining to Europe; but that did not mean that there was a "fusion" of outlooks between the prime minister and the president, to which the president retorted that there was no "fission" either, and that on foreign policy, "France speaks with a single voice."[31]

Shortly after assuming office, Jospin began to concern himself with relations with Africa, North-South cooperation, *francophonie*, international human rights, and, of course, European Union affairs. Conversely, Chirac envisaged his role as chief of state to encompass, not only "guarding the rank of France in the world" and "protecting the European achievement," but also protecting the French place in high technology and "guaranteeing the social solidarity and social protections" of French citizens.[32]

Whether the new intraexecutive relationship was fated to become a permanent institutional change was uncertain, for the president still had the power to dissolve the Assembly, which he could exercise after a proper interval (of perhaps two years). But such a move would have been a departure from tradition, for no president had ever dissolved Parliament twice during a single term of office. Nevertheless, Chirac might have gotten away with a second premature dissolution—and produced a majority to his liking—but only if the Jospin government could be charged with policy failures so grave as to destroy its popular support.[33] Failing this, a second rebuff would probably have forced the president to resign.

The third cohabitation proceeded with the prime minister assuming the dominant position. Jospin's schoolmaster's tone and his evocation of the need for "civic morality" suggested that he had the qualifications of a president and that he competed with the latter in his use of the premier's office as a "bully pulpit."[34] Jospin's authority, however, was not unlimited, for it had to be shared with several left-wing parliamentary parties that were not in complete agreement on crucial issues.[35]

Gradually, the Chirac-Jospin relationship deteriorated, and expressions of open hostility became more frequent as the presidential election of 2002 approached and the two prepared to confront each other as candidates. In this confrontation, as it turned out, Chirac had the advantage: The blame for policy failures was focused on the premier, while the relative powerlessness of the president brought him a degree of public sympathy.

THE GOVERNMENT

In size if not power, the typical Fifth Republic government resembles those of earlier French regimes. It has ranged from 24 members under the provisional premiership of de Gaulle in July 1958 to 49 under Premier Rocard in June 1988 (see Table 6.2). The nature

TABLE 6.2
Party Composition of Fifth Republic Governments

President	de Gaulle				Pompidou		Giscard d'Estaing		
Prime Minister	Debré	Pompidou		Couve de Murville	Chaban-Delmas	Messmer	Chirac	Barre	
	January 1959	April 1962	April 1967	July 1968	June 1969	July 1972	June 1974	August 1976	July 1979
Gaullists	6	9	21	26	29	22	12	9	12
Republicans	—	3	3	4	7	5	8	10	11[a]
UDF	—	—	—	—	—	—	—	—	—
Centrists	3[c]	5[c]	—	—	3[d]	3[d]	2	2[e]	4[e]
Radicals	1	1	—	—	—	—	6[g]	5	1[h]
Left Radicals	—	—	—	—	—	—	—	—	—
Socialists	—	—	—	—	—	—	—	—	—
Communists	—	—	—	—	—	—	—	—	—
Miscellaneous	7[j]	—	—	—	—	—	—	—	3[k]
Nonparty	10	11	5	1	—	—	8	10[t]	10[t]
Totals[v]	27	29	29	31	39	30	36	36	41

[a]Known until 1977 as Independent Republicans.
[b]*Démocratie libérale* (DL).
[c]*Mouvement républicain populaire* (MRP).
[d]*Centre pour la démocratie et le progrès* (CDP).
[e]*Centre des démocrates sociaux* (CDS).
[f]*France unie*, a coalition formed in the Assembly of Left Radicals and Centrists to enlarge the presidential majority toward the center and support Michel Rocard.
[g]*Réformateurs* (Reformers).
[h]"Democratic Left."
[i]*Mouvement des radicaux de gauche* (MRG), which also belonged to *France unie*.
[j]Includes 5 Independents.
[k]Includes 1 "Social Democrat," 1 member of CNIP, and the prime minister.

and distribution of ministerial portfolios have reflected the problems and pressures of the day. In the Fourth Republic, ministerial posts were established for veterans' affairs, colonies, and Algerian affairs. Under de Gaulle's presidency, the Ministries of Cultural Affairs, Scientific Research, Information, and International Cooperation were created. President Pompidou established a Ministry for Craftsmen and Small Businessmen, and President Giscard d'Estaing added a Ministry for the Quality of Life. Under the Socialist governments of President Mitterrand's first term, a new Ministry for the Economic Plan was formed (both to stress the revival of interest in planning and to satisfy the ambitions of Michel Rocard); the Ministry of Interior was given the added task of decentralization; and the name of the Ministry of Repatriates was changed to Ministry of Immi-

Mitterrand								Chirac				
Mauroy		Fabius	Chirac	Rocard		Cresson	Bérégovoy	Balladur	Juppé		Jospin	Raffarin
May 1981	June 1981	July 1984	March 1986	May 1988	June 1988	May 1991	April 1992	March 1993	May 1995	November 1995	June 1997	June 2002
—	—	—	20	—	—	—	—	14	21	17	—	16
—	—	—	7[a]	—	1	—	—	6	8	4	—	6[b]
								2	1	1		8
—	—	—	7[e]	—	1[f]	2[f]	—	5[e]	7	5	—	—
—	—	—	2	1	1	—	—	1	1	1	—	1
3	2	3	—	2	3	2[i]	2	—	—	—	3	—
39	37	36	—	26	25	32	31	—	—	—	18	—
—	4	—	—	—	—	—	—	—	—	—	3	—
1[l]	1[l]	1[m]	—	2[n]	3[n]	1[o]	—	1[p]	2[q]	4[r]	2[s]	—
—	—	3	6	11	15	9	9	1[u]	3	1	1	8
43	44	43	42	42	49	46	42	30	43	33	27	39

[l] *Mouvement des démocrates,* an ex-Gaullist group supporting Mitterrand in the presidential elections of 1981.
[m] *Parti socialiste unifié* (PSU).
[n] Direct (nondifferentiated) members of UDF.
[o] Environmentalist movement.
[p] *Club Perspectives et réalités* (a component of UDF).
[q] Includes 1 *Parti populaire pour la démocratie française* (PPDF), formerly known as *Perspectives et réalités;* 1 former member of *Génération écologie* (GE).
[r] Includes 2 PPDF; 1 ex-GE; 1 miscellaneous conservative.
[s] Comprising 1 from Greens *(Verts)* and 1 from *Mouvement des citoyens* (MDC).
[t] Collectively designated as "presidential majority."
[u] Simone Veil, a centrist close to Giscard d'Estaing.
[v] Totals include prime minister.

grants. Later, under the premiership of Chirac, the Ministries of Culture and of Communication were merged, and a "superministry" of Economic Affairs, Finance, and Privatization was set up. Under the premiership of Balladur, Social Affairs, Health, and Urban Affairs were put under the authority of a single minister of state. In the first Juppé government, a number of new portfolios were created, presumably for specific tasks, among them Ministries for Work, Social Dialogue, and Participation; Integration and the Fight Against Exclusion; and Intergenerational Solidarity. These ministries, which corresponded to some of Chirac's presidential campaign themes, were dropped six months later when Juppé reorganized his government, and their functions (if any) were merged with those of other ministries. Under Jospin, the Ministry of Environment dealt with regional development as well; the Ministry of Education was transformed into a "superministry"; the Ministry of Employment was given expanded responsibilities; and a new junior ministerial post was created, that of "secretary for economic solidarity" (attached to the Ministry for Employment), whose occupant was to be concerned with the unemployed and the needy.[36] Under Raffarin, the most important position in the cabinet hierarchy is that of Nicolas Sarkozy, who heads the Ministry of Interior, Internal Security, and Local Freedoms (see Table 6.3), formerly the Ministry of Interior, renamed to trumpet the government's commitment to fighting criminal violence.

France does not have a "patron" ministry for Bretons, Basques, or Alsatians that would be analogous to the British Ministries for Scottish or Welsh affairs. As noted earlier, gender equality has not been part of French political tradition. The first government appointed by Juppé included a relatively large number of women, probably in order to reward them for contributing significantly to Chirac's election victory in 1995, but when the government was restructured six months later, most of them were left out. It was under Jospin that the government was genuinely "feminized," as women accounted for 5 out of 14 cabinet ministers. In Raffarin's government, too, women are well represented, with 10 out of 39 ministers, of whom 3 (out of 15) are full cabinet ministers. One of these, Michèle Alliot-Marie, is the first woman to be in charge of the Ministry of Defense. She was given that important post essentially to reward her for allowing the RPR, of which she was secretary-general, to be "absorbed" by the UMP, Chirac's electoral machine.

An interesting innovation in the Raffarin government was the appointment of two "Beurs," descendants of Muslim immigrants from North Africa.[37] This was a symbolic move to "outdo" the Left, which, despite its frequently articulated commitment to the integration of immigrants, had never appointed people of such a background to its governments.

Occasionally a person may be co-opted from the world of business or banking, as is the case at this writing: The Ministry of Economy, Finance, and Industry is headed by Francis Mer, who had been chief executive of a steel corporation. Still, a cabinet like that of President Eisenhower, which consisted of "nine millionaires and a plumber," would be unthinkable in France. Whereas in the United States an intellectual as a cabinet member is a rarity, the typical French cabinet since the Third Republic has included a high proportion of university and lycée professors, as well as assorted intellectuals.[38] Fifth Republic cabinets have contained a significant number of professional civil servants, many of them graduates of ENA and other elite schools. For example, Chirac's second (i.e., the

TABLE 6.3
The French Government in June 2002

Prime Minister: **Jean-Pierre Raffarin** (DL)

Ministers
Interior, Internal Security, and Local Freedoms: **Nicolas Sarkozy** (RPR)
Social Affairs, Labor, and Solidarity: **François Fillon** (RPR)
Keeper of the Seals, Minister of Justice: **Dominique Perben** (RPR)
Foreign Affairs, Cooperation, and Francophonie: **Dominique de Villepin** (no party)
Defense: **Michèle Alliot-Marie** (RPR)
Youth, National Education, and Research: **Luc Ferry** (no party)
Economy, Finance, and Industry: **Francis Mer** (no party)
Infrastructure, Transportation, Housing, Tourism, and Maritime Affairs: **Gilles de Robien** (UDF)
Ecology and Sustainable Development: **Roselyne Bachelot-Narquin** (RPR)
Health, Family, and Disabled: **Jean-François Mattei** (DL)
Agriculture, Food, Fisheries, and Rural Affairs: **Hervé Gaymard** (RPR)
Culture and Communication: **Jacques Aillagon** (RPR)
Civil Service, Administrative Reform, and Regional Planning: **Jean-Paul Delevoye** (RPR)
Overseas Departments and Territories: **Brigitte Girardin** (no party)
Sports: **Jean-François Lamour** (no party)

Deputy Ministers (**ministres délégués**)
Budget and Budgetary Reform [Economy]: **Alain Lambert** (UDF)
Industry [Economy]: **Nicole Fontaine** (UDF)
Local Freedoms [Interior]: **Patrick Devedjian** (RPR)
European Affairs [Foreign Affairs]: **Noëlle Lenoir** (no party)
Cooperation and Francophonie [Foreign Affairs]: **Pierre-André Wiltzer** (UDF)
Primary and Secondary Education [National Education]: **Xavier Darcos** (RPR)
Research and New Technologies [National Education]: **Claudie Haigneré** (no party)
Foreign Trade [Economy]: **François Loos** (UDF-Radical)
City and Urban Renewal [Social Affairs]: **Jean-Louis Borloo** (UDF)
Family [Health]: **Christian Jacob** (RPR)
Professional Parity and Equality [Social Affairs]: **Nicole Ameline** (DL)

State Secretaries (**secrétaires d'État**), *not in cabinet*
Relations with Parliament and Government Spokesperson [Prime Minister]: **Jean-François Copé** (RPR)
Sustainable Development [Ecology]: **Tokia Saïfi** (DL)
Action Against Social Insecurity and Exclusion [Social Affairs]: **Dominique Versini** (RPR)
Handicapped Persons [Health]: **Marie-Thérèse Boisseau** (UDF)
Small and Medium-Sized Enterprises, Trade, Artisan Activities, Free Professions, and Consumer Affairs
    [Economy]: **Renaud Dutreil** (UDF)
Transport and Maritime Affairs [Infrastructure]: **Dominique Bussereau** (DL)
Administrative Reform [Civil Service]: **Henri Plagnol** (UDF)
Tourism [Infrastructure]: **Léon Bertrand** (RPR)
Veterans [Defense]: **Hamlaoui Mekachera** (no party)
Aged Persons [Social Affairs]: **Hubert Falco** (DL)
Real Property and Justice [Justice]: **Pierre Bédier** (RPR)
Foreign Affairs [Foreign Affairs]: **Reynaud Muselier** (RPR)

SOURCES: *News from France*, vol. 2.06 (15 May 2002); *Le Monde*, various issues.
NOTE: Brackets [ ] indicate principal or supervising ministry.
RPR = *Rassemblement pour la République* (Gaullist party)
UDF = *Union pour la démocratie française* (center-right party)
DL = *Démocratie libérale* (neoliberal, formerly a part of UDF)

cohabitation) government contained 12 ENA graduates *("Enarques")* and one graduate of the *École Polytechnique.* Although the Balladur government contained only 8 *Enarques* (the premier among them), it included no one from outside the "political class": All had been elected to Parliament at least once (4 of them to the Senate). Most of Jospin's cabinet ministers had had parliamentary experience; seven of them were graduates of ENA, and only one (the Communist minister) had been a member of the working class.

Cabinet ministers have the specific roles of supervising the civil servants in their particular ministries (which may include several departments or agencies), developing policy in their domains, helping to draft bills and steer them through Parliament, and defending government policy touching on their jurisdictions. The cabinet reflects a complex hierarchy of titles and positions, indicating both the importance of a portfolio and the political position of the minister. At the top are the full ministers, among them the ministers of finance, defense, foreign affairs, justice, interior, and education. Occasionally, the title "Minister of State" may be granted to a full minister in order to indicate his or her special relationship to the president or (as in 1986 and 1993) the premier, as in the cases of André Malraux, de Gaulle's minister of culture; three ministers under Giscard; five in the first Socialist government under President Mitterrand;[39] one each in the Fabius government and in Chirac's cohabitation government; four in the second Rocard government; four in the Balladur government. Below the ministers are the "deputy ministers" *(ministres délégués),* who are usually attached to the office of the premier or a full minister but may participate in the weekly cabinet sessions, and the state secretaries *(secrétaires d'État),* who attend cabinet meetings only when invited to do so.[40]

The principle of collective cabinet responsibility—that is, the notion that individual ministers must publicly agree with the general cabinet position on all issues—has been retained. This principle was often violated in the Fourth Republic, because cabinets were coalitions of great ideological diversity and political parties frequently insisted that their representatives in the cabinet stand by the parties' positions on specific issues. Ambitious ministers were sometimes interested in deliberately creating cabinet disunity so that a government would collapse and they would, they hoped, be able to move up when it was reconstituted—for example, from the Ministry of Finance or Labor to the premiership. If, after a reshuffle, ministers did not get any cabinet post, they did not lose everything, since they retained their parliamentary seats. In the Fifth Republic, an ousted minister, even though he or she may have been recruited from Parliament, has no formal right to return to it (see Chapter 7 for a discussion of the "incompatibility" rule).

Although cabinet making no longer *completely* depends on party alignments in Parliament, factionalism within the parties supporting the president (or, during cohabitation, the government) has remained significant, with the result that ideological or programmatic divergences within the cabinet cannot altogether be avoided. Within the Mauroy government, for example, there were disagreements regarding the inclusion of Communists in the government, the nationalization of industries, and administrative decentralization; within the second Chirac government, there were differences of opinion regarding collaboration with the National Front, immigrants, and civil liberties. Within the Balladur government, there were differences of opinion within both the RPR and the UDF regarding the European Union, social security, and law-and-order issues; in the Juppé government, there were serious differences between deputies and ministers over employment and fiscal policy. Within the Jospin government differences existed between ministers concerned with fiscal responsibility and those dedicated to economic redistribution.

What power does the cabinet have? In the Fourth Republic, the cabinet was as powerful as the premier, however, the premier's position was insecure because Parliament was so jealous of its prerogatives that it was hesitant to grant meaningful decision-making powers to him. It tended to oust premiers who asserted themselves too much. In the Fifth Republic, premiers and cabinet members have been less powerful because the president is jealous of *his* prerogatives; hence the constitutional provision (Art. 20) stipulating that "the government shall determine and direct the policy of the nation" is not a reliable prescription for power sharing with the president, unless (as during periods of cohabitation) the premier is fully supported, and the president is opposed, by the National Assembly. Since under normal conditions premiers and cabinets depend more on the support of the president than Parliament, the role of the cabinet is frequently that of a sounding board for presidential ideas. This is especially true of foreign affairs, which are seldom fully discussed in cabinet meetings.

Furthermore, the cabinet and premier share whatever power they have with other bodies, such as the staff of the Presidential Office, or with personal friends of the president who are part of a "kitchen cabinet." The Presidential Office (the Elysée Palace staff) is headed by a secretary-general and includes a growing number (now well over 500) of legal, financial, military, technical, and political counselors, secretaries, liaisons with other agencies (e.g., the Planning Office, the Economic and Social Council, the Parliament), and a correspondence department.[41] The kitchen cabinet has been institutionalized in the personal staff of the president *(cabinet du président)*. Some of the individuals heading this personal staff have been self-effacing; others have been very much in the limelight.[42] Most of the special counselors have been ambitious, as have the secretaries-general of the Elysée, who have used their office as a stepping-stone to a higher position.[43] Some of the staffers have been recruited from the higher civil service (often via ENA); others from Parliament; still others from the universities or even from interest groups. The president may also consult with individuals who have no official position at all. Giscard would often meet with leaders of business; Mitterrand had consultations with officials of trade unions and teachers' associations, business leaders (to the chagrin of some leftist Socialists), and assorted intellectuals. He also frequently consulted the secretary-general of the Socialist party and the leader of that party's parliamentary group (though Mitterrand did this less often after his election to a second term).

The frequency of cabinet meetings is in itself no indication of the extent to which the president consults his ministers when he makes a decision. Meetings of the full cabinet, which take place every Wednesday morning, are not always conducive to thorough discussions of issues. Therefore, the custom of appointing smaller bodies in which only selected ministers participate has arisen: These include interministerial committees, usually chaired by the premier, and restricted committees *(conseils restreints)*, presided over by the president. There have been many more meetings of interministerial committees than of the cabinet. In 1994, for example, 1,808 such meetings were held at Hôtel

Matignon, the premier's residence. Some of these committees, such as the Committee on National Defense or the Committee on Foreign Affairs, took on a permanent character, whereas others, such as the Committee on Urban Affairs, formed by Balladur, were ad hoc.

Under Pompidou, a slight upgrading of the cabinet took place, and it met more frequently than it had under his predecessor. This upgrading was probably due to two circumstances: (1) The relative absence of international conflicts involving France turned the president's attention more to domestic problems, in which *arbitrage* functions were less important than economic and other technical expertise (often found in the cabinet). (2) The cabinets contained certain old Gaullists or pro-Gaullists whose stature was too great for Pompidou to ignore them—notably Michel Debré, the first premier under de Gaulle, and Valéry Giscard d'Estaing, minister of finance and leader of a political party (the Independent Republicans) that was of growing importance. But even under Pompidou's presidency, there was no reliable evidence indicating that consultation with the cabinet as a basis of presidential decisions occupied a more prominent place in relation to other consultative mechanisms than it did under de Gaulle.

Under Giscard, the full cabinet ministers met weekly to discuss policy, with the secretaries of state called on to participate only occasionally. Moreover, Giscard was in almost daily contact with his premier and consulted frequently, and informally, with selected cabinet ministers (notably Michel Poniatowski, a personal friend, who was minister of interior from 1974 to 1977).

Mitterrand continued this pattern, in addition to the practice of convoking, on a weekly basis, an "inner cabinet" chaired by himself and composed of the secretary-general of the Presidential Office, the premier, and a few ministers. One of Mitterrand's innovations was the creation in 1982 of a *conseil restreint* for economic policy, which included the premier and a small number of ministers and met weekly. Although Mitterrand determined the major direction of policy, he allowed his ministers a great deal of discretion on specific issues. Thus, at least until early in 1983, Premier Mauroy had overall responsibility for promoting legislation regarding economic policies and for justifying them to the public. The ministers of interior, justice, and education were given considerable freedom to develop measures concerning, respectively, administrative decentralization, penal reforms, and the modernization of secondary-school curricula. Mitterrand would, of course, intervene in case of disaccord among the ministers, especially if it could not be resolved by the premier.[44] During the first cohabitation interlude, decision making shifted in the direction of the premier and the cabinet, as Article 20 (which gives the government policy-making power) acquired new significance. This shift applied to some extent even to military and foreign affairs (e.g., matters relating to the European Community and defense spending), to which the president, the premier, and the cabinet developed a more or less collaborative approach.

With Mitterrand's reelection in 1988 and the installation of Rocard's Socialist government, a growing understanding between the president and the premier could be discerned. As Mitterrand's status of Socialist politician evolved toward that of nonpartisan statesman, the implementation of his preferences, as outlined in his "Letter to All the French," was increasingly left in the hands of Premier Rocard.[45] He was given the credit for the successful handling of delicate problems, among them the crisis in New Caledonia (a French overseas territory), the claims of Corsican civil servants for increased financial support from Paris, and the strikes of transport workers. It was reported that at cabinet meetings, Mitterrand carefully (and even ostentatiously) solicited the advice of Rocard on every question of policy under discussion.

Whether this was done voluntarily is a matter of debate, for the president and the premier did not always agree. Mitterrand favored a more liberal policy vis-à-vis immigrants and a more benevolent attitude toward the less-privileged classes than Rocard; and Mitterrand wanted to keep the flame of leftist unity burning and tried to maintain a bridge to Communists (as if he were still running for the presidency), while Rocard concentrated on developing openings to the Centrists, in part in order to cultivate support for his policies in Parliament and improve his ability to govern.

In the eyes of some observers, the relationship between Mitterrand and Rocard was a "paper marriage" marked by a thinly cloaked tension.[46] In any case, the growing civility of that relationship translated into an approval rating of 60 percent for both in the spring of 1989. This result attested to the improved position of the premier, but it was unclear whether that increased the power of the cabinet as a whole. In a letter addressed to his ministers, Rocard promised to "govern differently" by according greater respect to the Constitution, to Parliament, and to "civil society" outside the political establishment. But he seemed to give little scope to his fellow ministers; in fact, he envisaged a "rigorous definition of the role of the premier vis-à-vis his team: [He] would not merely arbitrate [interministerial] disputes but would make decisions." Above all, he would insist on governmental solidarity, as reflected in "a strict discipline with respect to public declarations."[47] In accordance with that principle, he dismissed the minister of health, whom he had appointed only a week earlier, because the minister had made a number of public policy pronouncements without clearing them with the premier. This scenario was repeated in 1995, when Premier Juppé dismissed Alain Madelin, his minister of economics and finance, for having criticized the government's socioeconomic policies. Juppé, in justifying this action, asserted that "the government is not a debating society where everyone can play his little music. . . . There is a score and a conductor."[48]

In such instances, however, it is not clear whether the premier is the conductor or merely the enforcer of policy discipline for the president, nor is it always easy to know which decisions arrived at by the cabinet owe their inspiration to the president, the premier, or individual ministers. All presidents have stretched the definition of the "presidential" domain and have made decisions about matters that might well have been left to the discretion of ministers. In the case of de Gaulle, these decisions included the refusal to lower the retirement age of workers; opposition to the reforms of the *baccalauréat* examination; the decision to raise the minimum wage by 3 percent; and frequent intervention in budget making. Under Pompidou, presidential intrusions involved raising the height limits for buildings in the Paris area, vetoing an appointment to the *Académie Française*, and deciding to lower the value-added tax on foodstuffs. In the case of Giscard, presidential decisions involved prices, wages, the floating of the franc, and many other economic matters. He went beyond the practice of his predecessors in scrutinizing the texts of ministerial communiqués and personally editing the language of bills prepared by civil servants (thus bringing the bureaucracy more directly under presidential control).[49] It is unclear whether some of the decisions of the Mauroy government should be attributed primarily to President Mitterrand or to the cabinet, among them the decisions to seek the abolition of capital punishment, to replace the holdover administrators of the national radio and television offices, or (under the Cresson government) to move the National School of Administration from Paris to Strasbourg. But the decisions to include Communists in the government and to press ahead with legislation to nationalize certain industries—both of which were favored by some ministers and opposed by others—were doubtlessly the president's alone. That was also true with respect to a decision to appoint a program director of a newly built opera house in Paris.

Presidents have shown their independence of the premier and cabinet in other ways as well. De Gaulle undertook periodic *tours de France* in order to "consult" the people—he visited every department on the French mainlaind—a practice continued by succeeding presidents. Moreover, both de Gaulle and Pompidou used the referendum, which allowed them to bypass the cabinet and obtain legitimation of a purely presidential decision. Although Article 11 of the Constitution specifies that a referendum must be "proposed" by the government before it is submitted to the people, in 1962 de Gaulle announced to the cabinet that *he* would propose to it a referendum on the direct election of the president. Similarly, it was Pompidou, rather than the cabinet, who initiated the referendum on the question of Britain's membership in the Common Market in 1972.[50] Under Giscard, consultation with the people did not involve referenda. Instead, it took the form of "walking tours" through Paris, frequent meetings with spokespersons of national economic organizations, and highly publicized encounters with ordinary citizens. Mitterrand's attitude toward referenda was ambiguous. In mid-1984, Mitterrand announced that he would introduce a constitutional amendment that would provide for the holding of public referenda on questions of civil liberties—in addition to their original use for questions pertaining to "the organization of public powers." There was no follow-through in this instance. However, as we have seen, Mitterrand resorted to a referendum to ratify the Treaty on European Union in 1992, although he left it up to Parliament to pass a constitutional amendment made necessary by that treaty. It must be assumed that the decision to replace the military draft by a professional army was made by President Chirac alone; however, given the close relationship between Chirac and Juppé, it is probable that most domestic policies, and many of the presidential "orientations" on which they were based, were the result of joint deliberations.

During the most recent cohabitation arrangement, foreign and defense policies were based on shared decision making but domestic policies were made exclusively by Jospin and his government. Such a division of labor was reflected in a new pattern of cabinet meetings. As before, regular cabinet meetings, including all important ministers and chaired by the president, were held every Wednesday at the Elysée Palace; these took up generalities, constitutional formalities, and nominations of high officials requiring the signatures of the president and the premier. In addition, meetings of the full cabinet were held every two weeks at Hôtel Matignon, the premier's office, and chaired by the premier, for concrete policy discussions. Meetings of *conseils restreints* were held more often. In order to ensure that his ministers devoted their fullest attention to their tasks, Jospin insisted that they resign from their positions as mayors. At the behest of Chirac,

Raffarin adopted a similar approach to *cumul*—and for that reason, a number of people who were offered ministerial posts declined them because they did not want to give up their positions as mayors in important cities.

THE CONSTRUCTION AND RESHUFFLING OF CABINETS

The Constitution requires a ministerial countersignature of a presidential action, a provision that seems to harness individual ministers more precisely to a decision-making role. But ministers have owed their positions to the president in one way or another. Although they are, in theory, chosen by the premier after he has been selected by the president, many ministers have, in fact, also been chosen by the president. At a press conference in 1964, de Gaulle referred to "the president who chooses the premier, who has the possibility of changing him, either because he views his task as accomplished, or because he no longer approves of him."[51] De Gaulle's successors have clearly agreed with this interpretation of presidential discretion. Pompidou's position was articulated by Premier Messmer, who announced on television that after the parliamentary elections of 1973, the president would form a government on the basis of policies he wished to pursue and not on the basis of the ensuing parliamentary lineup. Although Giscard's first premier, Chirac, resigned of his own volition, Giscard admitted that he himself had decided two months earlier to choose a new government.[52]

It is reported that most of the premiers who resigned while still enjoying the support of the Assembly—Debré in 1962, Pompidou in 1968, Chaban in 1972, Chirac in 1976, Mauroy in 1984—had agreed in advance to resign whenever the president wished it.[53] Whether there is any basis to the rumor that every minister deposits on the president's desk an undated letter of resignation is difficult to confirm. But there is no doubt that all Fifth Republic presidents have had considerable discretion in regard to the selection and retention of cabinet members—except, of course, during periods of cohabitation.

De Gaulle personally selected a number of ministers for the Debré and Pompidou cabinets and was said to have totally constructed the cabinet of Couve de Murville.[54] It has been asserted that Messmer's cabinet colleagues were chosen by a confidant of Pompidou's and that the governments of Chirac and Barre were entirely selected by Giscard. In 1981, Mitterrand made the crucial decisions regarding cabinet appointments, although in some cases he did so on the advice of his friends, particularly that of Premier Mauroy. In 1982 (long before power sharing was envisaged), Mitterrand asserted that he "was not sure" whether he would want to keep the same ministers until 1988.[55] Even in 1986, Mitterrand exercised a certain veto power over ministerial appointments.

The foregoing should not be taken to mean that presidents have been entirely willful in the construction of cabinets. Despite the independence of the presidential role, all the chiefs of state in the Fifth Republic have taken into account the political composition of the Assembly (even during normal, i.e., noncohabitation, periods), the electorate at large, or both. The first Fifth Republic cabinet, which was installed in January 1959, reflected an attempt to strike a balance between a few old Gaullists, who had to be rewarded for their political loyalties, and leaders of non-Gaullist parties, whose support of the Fifth Republic during its initial phase was considered important. However, as if to illustrate de Gaulle's contempt for party politicians, more than one-third of the cabinet members were nonparty technicians or civil servants, a proportion that was retained until the end of 1962. The depolitization of the cabinet during those years was also reflected in the *cabinets ministériels* (the ministers' staffs); whereas in the Fourth Republic they were composed largely of the ministers' party associates or personal friends, there has been a tendency in the Fifth Republic to co-opt civil servants for these positions.

Between the parliamentary elections of 1962 and 1967, the number of civil servants in the cabinet was reduced, and the number of Gaullists was increased, roughly in proportion to the growth of the Gaullist majority in the Assembly. After the parliamentary elections of 1968, the cabinet assumed an even more Gaullist coloration, clearly corresponding to the overwhelming majority of the UDR in the new Assembly. The repolitization of the cabinet was balanced by the choice of a nonparty technician (Couve de Murville) as premier.

Under Pompidou, the repolitization of the cabinet was virtually complete; more than three-fourths of his ministers were Gaullists, and nonpartisan technocrats were almost totally excluded. Although Pompidou shared de Gaulle's notions about presidential independence and owed his election to a new presidential majority, he was in fact less independent than de Gaulle had been vis-à-vis the Gaullist party establishment. No deputies had been elected on his coattails; although he openly asserted his leadership over the UDR (as the Gaullist party was then labeled), his Gaullist credentials were being challenged, and he was forced to silence these challenges with political payoffs. Moreover, he had to reward a certain number of non-Gaullists who had supported him during the presidential election of 1969 with cabinet positions. After the parliamentary election of 1973 and the collapse of the Gaullist majority in the Assembly, Pompidou's sensitivity to Parliament increased. Although the idea of presidential continuity was conveyed in the retention of a genuine Gaullist as premier, most of the other important holdovers were nonorthodox Gaullists, Independent Republicans, and Centrists.

With the election of Giscard, the cabinet was recast in a manner reflecting at once the composition of the Assembly, the new president's penchant for technicians,[56] and his rather centrist presidential majority. One-quarter of the cabinet seats were assigned to nonparty people, and Gaullist representation was reduced to one-third of the total. After the parliamentary elections of 1978, the number of Gaullist ministers was reduced in favor of Independent Republicans and the cabinet was progressively "Giscardized."

In the first government headed by Mauroy, the great majority were Socialists, two-thirds of them recruited from the outgoing Parliament. Mitterrand and Mauroy were careful to include the leaders of all the important Socialist party factions, whose support might be needed for government bills taken up in the Assembly. Nevertheless, the presidential dependence on Parliament should not be exaggerated. Even if, at some future time, the president in constructing a cabinet should be oblivious of party alignments in the Assembly, that body is not likely to take great risks in opposing him, because he is able to distribute favors (including political offices and pork barrel), censure motions are (under normal conditions) difficult to pass, and he maintains the power of dissolution.

The composition of the government under Juppé reflected both party representation in the Assembly and the circumstances surrounding the presidential election campaign. Most of the prominent Gaullist and UDF politicians who had supported Balladur before the first round of the election were studiously excluded from the government immediately after Chirac's election as president. When the government was recast six months later, however, the number of "Balladurians" was increased, largely in order to reduce the mounting criticism of government policy on the part of UDF deputies in Parliament.

During periods of cohabitation, the construction of cabinets clearly depends much less on the president than on the premier. Nevertheless, the premier operates under certain constraints. In view of the president's visibility and involvement in foreign and military affairs, premiers are not likely to insist on the appointment of foreign and defense ministers to whom the president is hostile. Furthermore, in making his or her ministerial appointments, the premier must satisfy the various factions in the coalition. Chirac's weakness during the first cohabitation period stemmed in part from the belief of his UDF partners that their camp was underrepresented in the cabinet. Balladur's strength during the second cohabitation period derived in part from the fact that he divided ministerial portfolios neatly between the RPR and the UDF. During the third cohabitation, Jospin carefully crafted his cabinet to provide an image of technical competence, relative youth, and political probity. Most of the familiar faces associated with the Mitterrand presidency (in particular those implicated in ethically questionable political behavior) were left out, at least in the beginning. At the same time, the apportionment of ministerial portfolios reflected the factionalism within the Socialist party as well as the ideological and gender pluralism of the leftist coalition in the Assembly.[57]

Given the fact that presidential discretion applies equally to cabinet appointments and dismissals, and that there have been only five presidents in the Fifth Republic, with four of them representing a continuity of political outlook, there has been much greater cabinet stability in the Fifth than in the Third and Fourth Republics. But this stability has not been absolute. Thus far (1959–2002), there have been only 16 prime ministers (if Chirac is counted only once) and 30 "governments," but there has been a significant turnover of ministers and a corresponding lateral movement of the ministers' higher civil service staffs.[58] Since 1959 there have been 26 ministers of education and 24 ministers of justice; in contrast, greater stability has prevailed in the Ministries of Foreign Affairs and Defense, largely because of overall consensus between president and premier and across the Right-Left divide on matters of foreign policy. Many foreign ministers have been chosen not from the parliamentary pool but from the diplomatic service, as in the case of the two most recent foreign ministers, Hubert Védrine (1997–2002) and Dominique de Villepin (since April 2002). The former was a Socialist in Jospin's government, and the latter is a nonparty person in that of Raffarin; both, however, had served as chief of staff in the Presidential Office.

There have been over 50 cabinet reshuffles, but not all of them involved the appointment of new faces. By virtue of their stature or political connections, a number of individuals have been extremely *ministrables* and were moved from one ministry to another (e.g., Michel Debré, who served as premier, finance minister, and defense minister; Edgar Faure, who had been a premier in the Fourth Republic and served in the Social Affairs and Education Ministries in the Fifth; Jacques Chirac, who held the interior and agriculture portfolios before becoming premier—and who was mayor of Paris from 1977 until his election as president; and Jean-Pierre Chevènement, who was successively minister of industry, education, defense, and interior).

After the first election of Mitterrand, there was a complete turnover of ministers. This was paralleled by a replacement of the staffs of *cabinets ministériels,* often by union officials, journalists, and party hacks—not a surprising move by a party that had been out of power for more than 20 years. The element of continuity was not absent, however; one cabinet member (Gaston Defferre, interior) had occupied two ministerial posts during the Fourth Republic; another (Claude Cheysson, foreign affairs) had been the *chef de cabinet* of Premier Mendès-France (1954). One minister in the Rocard government (Jean-Pierre Soisson) had been a leader of the Republican party and had held several ministerial posts under Premiers Chirac and Barre.

Whereas in the Fourth Republic, cabinet reshuffles were usually the result of shifting parliamentary party alignments and disagreements among coalition partners, changes in the Fifth Republic have taken place mostly because of disagreements between ministers and the president. To cite several examples: In 1959, the Socialist and Radical ministers left the cabinet because of disenchantment with de Gaulle's domestic policies; in 1962, five ministers close to the MRP resigned in disagreement with de Gaulle's anti-European policies; in 1969, the minister of justice quit after de Gaulle's resignation because he was convinced that no successor could maintain a genuinely "Gaullist" policy. In 1985, Rocard resigned from the cabinet because he opposed Mitterrand's decision to reinstitute proportional representation for the forthcoming parliamentary elections; and in 1991, Chevènement resigned as minister of defense because of his opposition to French participation in the Gulf War; in 2002 he resigned again (as minister of interior) in opposition to Jospin's government bill to grant increased autonomy to Corsica.

Sometimes, the president may oust the premier or a cabinet minister because of the need for a scapegoat on whom blame can be fixed for a policy failure. De Gaulle replaced several ministers of education in the wake of public criticism of university reforms, and he replaced Premier Pompidou after the Events of May 1968. In 1975, Giscard sacked the minister of posts because he had mishandled a mail strike (and had insulted postal workers by calling mail sorting "idiots' work"); in the same year, the defense minister was replaced because of unrest in the army over low pay. In 1984, the foreign minister was replaced for having mishandled relations with countries in the Middle East and misleading the president; and in 1985, the defense minister was replaced because of the president's embarrassment over the *Greenpeace* affair (in which the French navy sank a foreign vessel in New Zealand waters). In 1992, Bernard Tapie was suspended from his duties as minister of housing when he faced indictment for a questionable business deal. In 1995, Elisabeth Hubert was removed as minister of health because she had caved in to the pressures of physicians who resisted cuts in medical fees (thereby impeding Juppé's proposals to reform the medical insurance system). In 2000, Dominique Strauss-Kahn was suspended from his job as finance minister because of allegations of improper involvement in an insurance scandal.

There are occasions when the sacking of ministers over a policy blunder may be more embarrassing to the president than keeping them. A case in point was the Habbash affair in 1992, in which a Palestinian terrorist was secretly allowed to come to France for medical treatment. When this incident was made public, Mitterrand dismissed, not the responsible ministers of foreign affairs and interior, but their directors-general.[59]

Sometimes a minister resigns of his or her own free will for personal or political reasons. Thus Martine Aubry, the popular minister of employment, resigned in order to become mayor of Lille, to help prepare the PS for the elections of 2002, and to provide herself with a foothold for the pursuit of a more important national office subsequently—perhaps that of prime minister.

Cabinet changes may also occur if the president or (during cohabitation) the prime minister decides to give the government a new orientation or image, as when Pompidou appointed Chaban-Delmas as premier in 1969 in order to veer the Gaullists toward the center, and conversely, when he appointed Messmer in 1972 in order to return them to the right, and when Giscard replaced Premier Chirac with Barre in 1976 because the former had demanded too much power and had questioned Giscard's move toward an economic policy of "neoliberalism" (i.e., greater reliance on market forces, a policy that Chirac himself was later to embrace). In 1984, Premier Mauroy was replaced by Fabius in order to signal a shift from a policy of welfare statism to one of productivity and austerity. The president may revamp the cabinet in order to make room for politicians whose party has moved from the opposition to the government side, as when the Communists gave their unqualified support to Mitterrand in the second round in 1981 and, after the parliamentary elections, were rewarded with four ministerial posts.

In 1983, Mitterrand undertook a major restructuring of the cabinet, largely in response to the worsening economic situation. The total number of ministers was only slightly diminished, but the number of full cabinet members was reduced from 35 to 14. This "battle cabinet" was more conservative than the previous one and better suited for carrying out a policy of austerity. Most of Mitterrand's close collaborators retained their positions; but one of his most severe critics (Chevènement, leader of the radical CERES faction of the Socialist party) was dismissed, and another (Rocard) was "demoted" from minister of planning to minister of agriculture. Although Mauroy continued as premier, Jacques Delors (a conservative [Catholic] Socialist and a proponent of tighter fiscal policies) became the "superminister" of economic affairs, finance, and budget and given the major responsibility for economic policy.

The government's shift to the center was a political *necessity* in view of the fact that in the 1983 municipal elections, the parties of the Left had lost control of 31 major cities to the Gaullist-Giscardist opposition; it was a political *possibility* because the Communists, having lost more seats than the Socialists, were too weak to resist. A subsequent restructuring of the cabinet in 1984 signaled even more clearly the shift to the center. Although the Communist ministers had been invited to remain in the government, and although several leftist Socialists who had been ousted (including Chevènement) returned to the government, the identification of the new premier, Fabius, with the austerity policy that was vehemently opposed by the PCF made it difficult for Communist ministers to remain in the government. Conversely, the departure of the Communists caused a number of centrist politicians within the UDF to express greater interest in supporting the government.

In 1991 Mitterrand suddenly replaced Rocard with Edith Cresson in order to provide the government with a new dynamism and thus to reverse his own decline in popularity. Mitterrand hoped that Cresson, a loyal ally, would devote greater attention to domestic policies and restore a sense of unity to the Socialist party, whose left wing had been somewhat alienated by Rocard. After 11 months, Cresson was in turn replaced by Pierre Bérégovoy. This move was occasioned by her failure to govern effectively, her combative public remarks,[60] and—most important—the poor performance of the Socialist party in the regional and cantonal elections of 1992. A year later Bérégovoy had to be replaced by a Gaullist premier in the wake of the Socialists' defeat in the Assembly elections. During the first two years of his presidency, Chirac continued to rely on his premier and to proclaim that he fully supported his domestic policy agenda; nevertheless, given the low public opinion ratings of both the president and the premier and the growing opposition to government policies within the ranks of the majority in the Assembly, Chirac would have served himself better if, in 1997, he had replaced Juppé as premier in order to redynamize his government and improve his image instead of calling for early parliamentary elections.

When Jospin became premier in 1997, he began with a fresh team representing a mixture of left-wing parties. The new government was supposed to be a collegial rather than a hierarchical one; in addressing his ministers, Jospin said that "here one doesn't impose [positions] but one seeks to convince."[61] But after three years, his government was weakened by internal division and had lost its luster. That was the reason why, in the spring of 2000, he decided to "re-Mitterrandize" his government by reappointing Jack Lang, Laurent Fabius, and other "elephants" of the PS.

The foregoing discussion suggests that the tenure of the premier has been as dependent on the president's goodwill as has the rest of the cabinet. According to the record so far, most of the replacements of premiers have been at the discretion of the president, and only one has occurred as a result of the decision of the premier himself.[62] In the event that the premier should refuse to resign at the president's behest, the president could "persuade" the Assembly to oust the premier on a vote of censure; if the president lacked Assembly support, he could accomplish the same purpose by the threat of dissolution. But that can happen only if the president has a parliamentary majority behind him or is reasonably certain that after a new election, he will have such a majority.

THE EXECUTIVE AND PARLIAMENT

The fact that about half of the premiers have been recruited from Parliament, that many ministers have had parliamentary origins, and that most premiers have found it desirable to go before Parliament to be invested (i.e., voted into office by the deputies) may make it seem as though the Fifth Republic has been evolving from pure presidentialism to a more traditional parliamentary democracy. But investiture by Parliament is not legally required. Sometimes the cabinet is presented to the Assembly quite a few days or even weeks after it has already been functioning. The decision to seek investiture is normally made by the president, although it may be influenced by the premier-designate's prior relations with Parliament and the extent to which the president or the premier wishes to show respect for that institution.

For nearly three decades, it was considered almost axiomatic that parliamentary support of the premier, while it might be desirable, was not a precondition for his or her retention. As Pompidou said, "[T]he President . . . takes the composition of the Assembly into consideration . . . [but] he is not its slave."[63] Whereas in the Fourth Republic, a president had to accept the resignation of a premier when the latter lost the confidence of Parliament, a Fifth Republic president can retain the premier despite a no-confidence vote in the Assembly—as de Gaulle did when he retained Pompidou as premier in 1962—as if to demonstrate his indifference to, or even contempt for, the collective preferences of Parliament.

Conversely, the president could dismiss the premier because the latter enjoyed *too much* confidence in Parliament. Pompidou's dismissal of Chaban-Delmas in July 1972 was prompted in part by the latter's receipt of a massive vote of confidence in the Assembly. In contrast, the low turnout of the electorate (only 60 percent voted, including 7 percent who cast blank ballots) in the referendum earlier that year on Britain's entry into the Common Market had been interpreted as an indicator of President Pompidou's waning popularity. Chaban's dismissal may therefore have been prompted by Pompidou's jealousy of his premier's own strong showing. Chaban's popularity, as measured by public opinion polls, was consistently higher than that of Pompidou. In the words of Pompidou, the retention of Chaban would have created a situation in which "the premier . . . ends up becoming too powerful and reducing the president of the Republic to a symbolic role . . . or else to . . . a kind of director of the cabinet."[64] Political jealousy was not the only reason for Chaban's dismissal. Negative feelings toward the premier had been developing because of revelations of his failure to pay taxes and because of his inability to implement his "new society" program, which had promised more telephones, more money to students, and more housing. As the campaign for the forthcoming parliamentary elections approached, Pompidou needed to restore the image of the Gaullist party, and to do so he had to purge a government in which there had been instances of corruption and scandal. Moreover, he wished to remind the country that in addition to a parliamentary majority, there was also a presidential one, and he wanted to make the former dependent on the latter. Such a position was not a Gaullist monopoly. In a television debate with Giscard before the presidential election of 1974 and again before the elections of 1981, Mitterrand also affirmed his belief in the dominance of the presidential over the parliamentary majority and indicated that if elected, he would dissolve the Assembly.

All this was before the legislative election of 1986: Its outcome—power sharing—set against the *presidential* mandate a competing *parliamentary* mandate, the more recent expression of popular sovereignty. To be sure, that majority was neither overwhelming nor particularly disciplined, and Mitterrand might have been tempted to manipulate or undermine it, using the weapons in the presidential arsenal. But it is doubtful whether public opinion would have supported him, for at that time he was not sufficiently popular to set himself against Parliament, which (especially since the mid-1970s) had been asserting its role with increasing confidence.

In 1988 much of the president's power was restored; yet Mitterrand's relationship to Parliament remained ambiguous. This was due in part to the fact that two years of being reduced to a figurehead had taught him to take Parliament more seriously, and in part to the fact that the premier, Rocard, appeared on occasion to enjoy greater public confidence than the president.

Between 1995 and 1997 the Assembly was controlled by a comfortable "presidential majority" of Gaullists and Giscardo-centrists. This situation made it possible for the government to get several bills through Parliament by making them matters of confidence. However, the premier had to face increasing criticism from UDF deputies, Gaullist deputies who had been left out of Juppé's government, and Philippe Séguin, the Gaullist speaker of the Assembly, who worked hard to upgrade the power of that body and who hoped to become premier himself.

The victory of the Left in the parliamentary elections of 1997 strengthened the power of Jospin, the new premier, at the expense of the president; but Jospin's power gradually diminished because of increasing disunity within the government between the PS and the other components of the "pluralist Left."

As a consequence of the presidential and parliamentary elections of 2002 the executive-legislative relationship returned more or less to what it had been in the first decade of the Fifth Republic. Like de Gaulle before him, Chirac became the unchallenged master of decisions: He was chief of state, de facto chief of government, effective leader of a new political formation in total control of the parliamentary agenda (although formally, its secretary-general was Chirac's friend Juppé). The cabinet gave the superficial impression of being pluralistic, insofar as it contained people from a variety of right-of-center parties; however, it was thoroughly "Chiraquist," because all its non-Gaullist members had been the president's personal friends or had been co-opted to his cause.

Irrespective of such developments, the president's relationship to Parliament has remained uncertain. Some have argued that the new five-year presidential term strengthens the hand of the president vis-à-vis Parliament because both are elected at more or less the same time—but that is the case only if the latter is elected on the coattails of the former and both are on the same side of the political spectrum,[65] as happened in 2002. On the one hand, the position of the president is comparable to that of a constitutional monarch: He is politically powerless in the sense that he cannot formally veto bills, does not engage in parliamentary debates, and does not appear in Parliament—with which he is expected to communicate only by means of messages.[66] On the other hand (as the foregoing discussion clearly shows), the president retains several powerful weapons normally associated with the executive in presidential regimes.

ARTICLE 16

One of the most powerful instruments possessed by Fifth Republic presidents is Article 16 of the Constitution. It provides that "when the institutions of the Republic, the independence of the nation and the integrity of its territory . . . are threatened in a grave and immediate manner, and when the regular functioning of the constitutional governmental authorities is interrupted, the president shall take the measures commanded by these circumstances." The constitutions of several other democratic countries have contained similar emergency provisions, which have been aimed, not at destroying constitutional government, but at preserving it. Article 16 provides that whenever the president invokes emergency powers, he must inform the nation in a message, and it stipulates that the steps he undertakes "must be inspired by the desire to ensure to the constitutional governmental authorities, in the shortest possible time, the means of fulfilling their assigned functions." The Constitution also provides that the Constitutional Council be consulted with regard to any measures taken by the president and that Parliament meet during the emergency period. Article 16 has been invoked only once, during the generals' abortive putsch in Algeria. That putsch began on 23 April 1961, and was put down a few days later; yet the state of emergency remained in effect until 29 September, that is, for more than five months.

Article 16 leaves open a number of questions. Is it necessary at all, in view of the existence of Article 36, which deals with martial law? That article provides that martial law be decreed by the cabinet but can be extended beyond 12 days only by Parliament. It is therefore not a weapon of the president, and it may have seemed too restrictive to de Gaulle. Article 16, however, may be too open-ended, because it is not clear whether any meaningful checks exist against its abuse or excessively prolonged application. If Parliament is in regular session, it cannot be dismissed during the exercise of Article 16; if it is not, it must be called into special session. But what is Parliament entitled to do while sitting? When de Gaulle invoked Article 16, he told Parliament that, in its special session, it had legislative and surveillance powers, but in a communication to the premier (Debré), he said that Parliament could *not* legislate, and that motions of censure would not be allowed. It is difficult in any case for Parliament, in special session or otherwise, to legislate against the wishes of the president, as the government would continue to control the major agenda items (and the president would, under normal conditions, be able to influence the government).

Furthermore, what are the protections against an unwarranted interpretation of "danger" to the republic? What measures are allowed, or forbidden, to the president? Can he suspend civil liberties? The Weimar Constitution's emergency powers clause (Art. 48) authorized the president to suspend only *some* of the rights guaranteed by that constitution, and these were specifically named. But there is no specific bill of rights in the Fifth Republic Constitution; ergo, can the president suspend the rights that exist by statute law or custom? The provision that the measures taken by the president must be inspired by a desire to return to a "normal" state of affairs is not very helpful. What if there is a will to return to normal constitutional government, but no way (as the president sees it) to do so? And what is considered a "regular functioning of . . . institutions"?

De Gaulle's actions during his presidency raised some doubts about the extent to which he was interested in "guaranteeing" the Constitution. He violated Article 11 a number of times in bypassing Parliament and submitting a bill directly to a referendum—the most notorious case being the referendum of 1962 that amended the Constitution by providing for the direct election of the president. He violated Article 29 by refusing to accede to the Assembly's demand for a special session in 1960; Article 38, by asking for special decree powers in 1967; and Article 50, by refusing to dismiss Pompidou as premier in 1962, after the latter had been ousted by a vote of censure in the

Assembly. Although de Gaulle adhered to the letter of Articles 23 and 16, he interpreted them so as to violate their spirit or intent. Although emergency powers have traditionally been designed for use during civil disorders, insurrections, or wars, Presidents de Gaulle and Pompidou hinted on a number of occasions that Article 16 might be used for political purposes, especially in order to overcome a hostile parliamentary majority.[67]

Most of the Socialists, Communists, and miscellaneous anti-Gaullists, who eventually adjusted to other features of a powerful presidency, have favored the elimination of Article 16, and Mitterrand, as president, on several occasions proposed such action. The opponents of Article 16 are reminded of how a similar provision in the Weimar Constitution was abused by an antirepublican president and contributed to the downfall of democratic government in Germany.

It appears unlikely that Article 16 will be invoked in the foreseeable future. Wars or invasions are not on the horizon; in the past three decades, terrorism and other domestic disturbances have been handled well enough by normal legislative and executive means; and after the departure of de Gaulle, both Parliament and the Constitutional Council became more assertive and more interested in both protecting civil liberties and promoting an institutional division of power.[68]

In the final analysis, the decision to invoke Article 16 depends on the degree of public support a president enjoys. With public opinion on his side, he would be less hesitant to dissolve a Parliament that might obstruct his efforts at dealing with emergencies without resorting to Article 16; if public opinion were solidly against the president, the use of Article 16 would not save him. Conversely, it is doubtful whether the elimination of the article would be sufficient to reduce the power of the president, which, after all, depends also on structural factors: specific constitutionally defined powers and the patronage associated with them; a weak Parliament; and a weakened party system.[69] Finally, the elimination of formal emergency provisions would not greatly diminish presidential power so long as a strong executive—whether king, emperor, or charismatic leader—is in consonance with a certain strain in French political tradition.

THE PRESIDENT AND CHARISMA

The periodic eruption of charismatic rule in French political history has already been noted. It is useful to recall that Bonapartism has always appealed to a wide ideological spectrum, and that Napoleon I, Napoleon III, Boulanger, and de Gaulle were supported by both the Right and the Left (although not necessarily at the same time and to the same degree) because these "heroes" were expected to rectify the disorders and evils perpetrated by parliamentary bodies.[70] To be sure, the Right and the Left have been Bonapartist for different reasons: the former because it hoped that a charismatic authority figure would help maintain the existing socioeconomic order and temper a Parliament in which the underprivileged classes were represented; and the latter because it expected such a figure to counterbalance a Parliament that was regarded as the preserve of the privileged classes, and also, perhaps, because the "psychic income" of vicarious glory and national greatness radiating from a hero-executive was a substitute for economic wealth.

According to Michel Crozier, "the conception of authority that continues to prevail in France is universal and absolute, and retains something of the tradition of absolute monarchy with its mixture of rationality and entertainment."[71] Stanley Hoffmann has remarked that most of the French have been socialized to the acceptance of an authority figure who is abstract, impersonal, and removed from the people, yet at the same time embodies personal charisma.[72] Perhaps the reason is that for many years republican constitutions, and the institutional relationships they define, did not enjoy sufficient legitimacy and were not stable enough to serve as reliable foci of identification; or perhaps the relationship of the French to authority is a survival of monarchic nostalgia. Nothing illustrates this better than the pomp—the state funeral, the mass observances, the eulogies, and the veneration in the printed media—following the death of Mitterrand several months after his term of office ended.[73]

The factors just cited do not quite explain why the French—who have a reputation for rationalism and political skepticism and a preference for institutional orderliness— accepted for more than a decade de Gaulle's suprainstitutional assertions of omnipotence, his claim that he had "embodied national legitimacy for twenty years," and his position (reminiscent of Louis XIV) that "the indivisible authority of the State is confided entirely to the president . . . that there is no [authority]—ministerial, civil, military or judicial—except that which is conferred and maintained by him"; and that it was up to him whether to share with others that supreme power.[74]

Personalization of power is, of course, not confined to France. In the United States, the presidential election has become a political popularity contest in this age of television, and the president's collaborators in Congress often owe their election to the presidential coattails; moreover, the way in which the vast powers of the presidency are exercised and expanded depends on the incumbent's unique view of presidential "stewardship." In Britain, the leader of a party is elected or reelected as prime minister, nowadays in a largely plebiscitary fashion, because of his or her views on public policy and the leadership image projected to the British people. However, in both the United States and Britain, "countervailing" powers are found that may be significant: In the United States, Congress can effectively block presidential legislative programs, and even in Britain it is possible for backbenchers to rebel against the leadership. In France, by contrast, countervailing powers are not yet strong enough—even with the experiences of cohabitation.

Nevertheless, the personalization of power under de Gaulle should not be compared to that of Hitler, Stalin, or absolute monarchs of an earlier age. In the first place, the office of president in France is nonhereditary and fallible. Like Hitler and Stalin, de Gaulle wished to be judged by history (as have his successors); but unlike these two, he was also judged by public opinion polls, a relatively free press, and unfettered plebiscites, whose outcome was not always predictable and which in the end caused him to abandon the presidency peacefully. De Gaulle, like imperious rulers in nondemocratic regimes, virtually monopolized the mass media and used the press conference to appeal for national unity, provide drama, and demand support for his policies. But that support was not a foregone conclusion. He had to submit to elections, the outcome of which would affect his decision-making powers or serve as political weather vanes and, on occasion, inflect his policies.[75]

In France, as in other democracies, the extent to which personal power can be exercised depends on the support of the political parties and, ultimately, the people. Some of the personalization of power is no doubt due to the *vedettisation de la politique* (i.e., the orientation of politics around a celebrity) by the mass media,[76] which capitalize on the average citizen's need for excitement, an emotional focus, and a flesh-and-blood symbol of national aspirations. De Gaulle filled that need more than any corresponding figure in other Western countries because of his towering personality, his martial figure and background, his Resistance leadership, and his image as the prophet of legitimacy— all of which were enhanced even more by comparison with the premiers of the Fourth Republic, most of whom were relatively colorless political birds of passage. However, in the end, none of de Gaulle's qualities proved sufficient to overcome the "antiexecutive itch"—a characteristic found especially among the French Left—that helped to secure his departure from the political scene in 1969.[77]

Pompidou had all the constitutional weapons of his predecessor, and in his press conferences he repeatedly emphasized his desire to affirm presidential authority. But he did not inherit the political crises that had brought about de Gaulle's accession to the presidency; although he was the heir of a "president-king,"[78] Pompidou showed by his frequent outbursts of temper that he possessed neither the royal hauteur nor the "institutional" qualities of de Gaulle. (It was unlikely that Pompidou could perpetuate de Gaulle's Caesarian habit of referring to himself in the third person.) Instead, Pompidou portrayed himself as an ordinary French citizen. In an appeal to the voters during the presidential election of 1969, he said, "As President of the Republic, I would constantly remind myself that I am only one Frenchman among many, and therefore that I am able to understand them and their problems."[79]

Pompidou's efforts at identification with the people failed. In his election to the presidency, the abstention rate was 31 percent in the second round (abstention rates were less than 16 percent in the case of de Gaulle and less than 13 percent in the case of Giscard). What authority Pompidou had was essentially derived from the fact that he wore de Gaulle's mantle and from his ability to make crucial decisions. Unfortunately, the final two years of his presidency were marked by a politics of drift and indecisiveness, which was exemplified when in April 1972, he relinquished part of the presidential domain by using the referendum on a foreign-policy issue—British entry into the Common Market. The public disavowal of his rule (and the temporary eclipse of the presidency) was demonstrated the following year by the UDR's loss of its parliamentary majority.

In the beginning of his term, Giscard's authority rested largely on the image he projected of a modern-minded and competent technocrat, who had less need than his predecessors for full-dress uniforms, parades, and other political prostheses. But there was no question that he believed in a strong presidency. At his first press conference after acceding to the office, he asserted that "as a product of universal suffrage," he was committed to a presidential regime in which the president initiates policies and "propels" them by means of the government he appoints.[80] However, he promised to grant a larger role to the Constitutional Council in safeguarding public liberties and to give a greater role to Parliament and, in particular, the opposition within it. Many of his promises were not kept, among them the reduction of the presidential term of office and meaningful de-centralization. Giscard later justified his inaction by saying that he, as the guardian of the Constitution, was obligated to leave the political institutions to his successor in the same condition as he had inherited them. In fact, he had accumulated more power than any of his predecessors, but he failed to use it for solving urgent economic problems. That failure contributed to Giscard's increasing preoccupation with the politics of sym-bolism: trips abroad, appearances at international conferences, stage-managed press conferences, and carefully packaged addresses to "my dear television viewers." By the end of his tenure, Giscard had become almost imperial in his behavior: contemptuous of Parliament, overly sensitive to the press, yet indifferent to critiques of his egocentric conduct.[81]

Perhaps it is the *role* of the French presidency that imposes a certain kind of behav-ior or rhetoric on the incumbent, irrespective of his personality or ideology. Mitterrand, who got his political start in the antiexecutive climate of the Fourth Republic, came to power in the Fifth Republic on a platform of change and democratization, one that os-tensibly rejected Gaullist policies and style. Unlike de Gaulle, who was uncomfortable as a political candidate and as a party politician, Mitterrand did not cease to identify as a party leader and did not abandon the role of a political candidate until developments of the second cohabitation made his "lame-duck" status obvious.[82] But several months after assuming office, Mitterrand began to behave in a manner at least in part reminis-cent of his predecessors. His call for a policy that would "place France at the head of industrial nations" echoed the slogans used earlier by Giscard; in his insistence that "France would not be worthy of its history" unless it played a global role, and in his commitment to a national nuclear force, he echoed de Gaulle's preoccupation with "grandeur."[83] To be sure, his views regarding the balance of institutions were more democratic; he wanted to replace the authoritarianism under previous chiefs of state by an "authentic republic," which meant that "each institution must be put back in its place: The government governs; the Parliament legislates and participates in the debate without constraints. As for me, while I intend to exercise to the fullest the responsibili-ties that the sovereign people have entrusted to me, I do not wish to substitute myself for one [institution] or the other."[84]

Nevertheless, Mitterrand, at his first press conference, announced the domestic and foreign policies the government and Parliament were to follow. In his appointments, he used presidential patronage to the fullest. His predecessor had "Giscardized" the execu-tive, the prefectures, the nationalized industries, and the media; Mitterrand systemati-cally "de-Giscardized" them. Even in his style, he followed in the footsteps of those who had preceded him. His press conferences, conducted from the presidential palace, were heavy with pomp and ceremony: Flanked by his cabinet ministers, Mitterrand carefully selected (and grouped together into categories) the questions submitted to him by jour-nalists before answering them, just as de Gaulle and Giscard had done. It has been sug-gested that the temptation to monarchical behavior on the part of a president is difficult to resist because he is the heir of kings who have embodied historic continuity as well as popular sovereignty;[85] this temptation is increased because of the absence of *political* (as distinct from moral) responsibility on his part: the lack of reliable checks and balances, the practical difficulty of a Parliament pitting itself against the president, and the government's dependence on his confidence (and his whims).[86]

Before these constraints were removed (albeit temporarily) in 1986, and circumstances forced Mitterrand to put into practice his ideas concerning the division of powers, presidents were free to choose their particular brand of monarchy. De Gaulle was a Bonapartist monarch in the sense that he publicly downgraded Parliament and parties and had his rule confirmed periodically by the masses directly by means of referenda. Giscard was an "Orléanist" monarch in the sense that his rule was supported—and much of his policy determined—by the wealthy business sector, the free professionals, and the upper- and middle-echelon technocracy. The beginning of Mitterrand's first term was somewhat prematurely labeled a "social monarchy" in the sense that it was a strong presidential rule supported by leftist mass parties and predicated on the expectation that "popular," redistributive policies would be promoted. The first cohabitation experiment, of course, reduced Mitterrand's power, but it gave him practice in acting like a monarch who transcended politics.[87] By playing the role of unifier (rassembleur) who fought against selfish (i.e., mostly Gaullist) factions, he acquired a charisma associated with maturity, openness, and avuncular solicitude that enabled him not only to be easily reelected but also to assert his power as an "arbiter" of conflicts between the government, the Socialist party, the administration, and the Parliament.[88] However, he did not always want to assert that power. His political longevity had been such that even before the second cohabitation period, he showed an increasing preference for the role of constitutional monarch—aloof from the technical concerns of daily politics, interested in grand architectural projects, acting as the great impresario of public celebrations (such as the bicentennial of the Revolution), and surrounding himself with intellectual courtiers who helped to give his "reign" a kind of legitimacy.[89]

During the final two years of his presidential term, Mitterrand functioned more like a ceremonial chief of state than a decision maker. He had little choice; many of the policies he had once stood for had been made irrelevant by events.[90] In addition, his presidential image (and his place in history) had deteriorated as a result of revelations of details about his close relationship with elements of the extreme Right during the last years of the Third Republic and his subsequent role in the Vichy regime.[91] He regained a certain degree of public sympathy when the fact that he had incurable cancer became known.[92] After the election of Chirac, Mitterrand retrieved part of his positive image when he chose not to follow Giscard's unsportsmanlike example and facilitated a smooth transfer of power to his successor.[93]

The presidential stature of Chirac so far is difficult to assess. He does not display the aloofness of de Gaulle, the semiaristocratic aura of Giscard, or the dignity and political finesse of Mitterrand. He has been compared to U.S. President Bill Clinton in his seemingly perpetual campaigning style, his easy relationship with the populace, and his occasional displays of political courage.[94] He has been impatient with ideology and has tried to combine a concern with social justice with the traditional themes of his conservative supporters—a tendency that has raised doubts about whether he has a consistent vision.[95] He has had to reconcile his impetuousness with the need to behave in a more "presidential" fashion. Being a proper chief of state in the context of the Fifth Republic has implied the articulation of certain Gaullist themes, such as the involvement in a global statesmanship that is often more symbolic than substantive. The symbolic aspect of the presidency as the embodiment of national unity was apparent when Chirac's popularity ratings increased by more than 15 percent immediately following the attack on the New York World Trade Center (to which Chirac reacted with "statesmanlike" speeches).

The reelection of Chirac in 2002 gave rise to an intensive debate about his presidential legitimacy. A few months before the elections his presidential stature had been damaged by charges of improper, even illegal, actions both as mayor of Paris and as president of the Republic, and he was saved from indictment only by last-minute rulings by the highest court. Presidential legitimacy, however, is circumstantial; on the one hand, Chirac was elected by more than 80 percent of the voters in the second round, a higher percentage that was received by any preceding Fifth Republic president; on the other hand, his vote in the first round—20 percent—was lower than that of any other president, and lower even than he had himself obtained in 1995. Moreover, he won finally with the massive support of the Left, which saw him as the only alternative to Le Pen, whose election might have threatened the existing republican order. For that reason, it was argued in leftist circles that the legitimacy of Chirac's rule would depend on the extent to which his policies reflected the will of the majority of the *whole* electorate, and that he had insufficient authority to ignore the opposition. Others, however, insisted that Chirac's presidential authority was reconfirmed during the ensuing parliamentary election, which produced an overwhelming victory of the candidates of the UMP, the electoral alliance he had himself created.

SUMMARY

The Fifth Republic is equipped with a powerful and stable executive. Yet, as the preceding discussion indicates, the *intraexecutive* relationship is not always clearly established. Although the Constitution makes the president chief of state and entrusts the government to the premier, the distinction between heading a state and leading a government, and between ceremonial duties and decision-making responsibilities, is not as precise as it might be. Presidents are sometimes tempted to intervene forcefully in the decision-making process and at other times to leave the onus for risky policies to someone else, in particular, the premier. Most of France's presidents have managed to find their own delicate balance between their "dignified" and "efficient" roles (to use Bagehot's terminology). But there is no guarantee that future presidents will achieve such a balance. Therefore, some have suggested that France rectify the situation by opting for a U.S. type of president who would be both chief of state and head of government and by abolishing the post of prime minister; others have advocated a return to a more conventional parliamentary model (perhaps a combination of the Fourth Republic, the British, and the German Federal Republic systems), under which the president's role would be more precisely defined as a figurehead one. However, the first option is likely to make the president too strong and resented by an electorate that wants a greater diffusion of power; the second option might be rejected because it would make the executive too dependent on the Parliament and hence introduce the danger of government instability and weakness. A third option has been that of "aligning the presidency and Assembly by giving both the same five-year terms. That approach, adopted in 2000 when the presidential term was reduced from seven to five years, reduced the likelihood of premature dissolution, but did not eliminate it.[96] In any case, thus far there have been no political crises, popular demands, or parliamentary challenges serious enough to necessitate a constitutional redefinition of the position of the executive.

NOTES

1. See Pierre Miguel, *Les Rois de l'Elysée* (Paris: Fayard, 2001), a study of the monarchical attributes of French republican presidents, from the Third Republic to the Fifth; and Serge Berstein, *Chef de l'État* (Paris: Armand Colin, 2002), esp. chapters 18–22, on Fifth Republic presidents.
2. Radio address by General de Gaulle, 20 September 1962.
3. It is the president, not the premier, who represents French interests in the European Union. The interests of other member countries, by contrast, are represented by their respective prime ministers. The French premier or other ministers may speak for their country in more technical negotiations. See Jean-Louis Quermonne, "Le Président de la République: Acteur des politiques publiques," in Nicholas Wahl and J. L. Quermonne, eds., *La France présidentielle* (Paris: PFNSP, 1995), pp. 184–93.
4. *Major Addresses, Statements, and Press Conferences of General de Gaulle, 1958–1964* (New York: French Embassy, 1964), p. 248.
5. Michel-Henri Fabre, *Principes républicains de droit constitutionnel*, 2d ed. (Paris: LGDJ, 1970), p. 347. For another interpretation, see Roger-Gérard Schwartzenberg, *La Droite absolue* (Paris: Flammarion, 1981). He argues (pp. 37–40) that between 1965 and 1968, most decisions (except for foreign affairs) were made, not by de Gaulle, but by Premier Pompidou, who even suggested to the president the idea of dissolving Parliament in 1968.
6. Ambassade de France, Service de Presse et d'Information, *Bulletin* 72/65, p. 13. See also *Le Président de la Cinquième République*, Documents d'études (Paris: Documentation Française, November 1977), esp. pp. 25–39.
7. Interview in *La Croix*, 4 May 1974.
8. *New York Times*, 17 June 1976.
9. Schwartzenberg, *La Droite absolue*, p. 37. On Barre's subservience, see Robert Elgie, *The Role of the Prime Minister in France, 1981–1991* (New York: St. Martin's Press, 1993), pp. 142–43.
10. *Le Monde*, 8–9 June and 15 November 1980.
11. In 1973, President Pompidou had announced his intention to reduce the presidential term to five years. He even saw to it that an amendment bill to that effect was introduced in Parliament (which passed the bill), but then he failed to convoke Parliament for a joint session, a procedure required for the ratification of the amendment. President Giscard d'Estaing, after *his* election (May 1974), had also promised that an amendment would be introduced for the same purpose, but nothing came of that promise. And Mitterrand, as a presidential candidate, had repeatedly endorsed the notion of a reduction of the presidential term of office to five years and a two-term limitation—or, alternatively, the retention of the seven-year term, but without the possibility of reelection. He did so also in his "Lettre à tous les Français" ("Letter to All the French"), issued just before the presidential elections of 1988. See *Libération*, 7 April 1988.
12. *Le Monde*, 11 December 1981.
13. *L'Année politique 1995*, p. 183.
14. Barre's statement to the press, 1978, quoted in Christian Bigaut, *Le Président de la Cinquième République*, Documents d'études, Droit constitutionnel et institutions politiques (Paris: Documentation Française, 2000), p. 50.
15. Gérard Courtois, "Les Atouts de Jean-Pierre Raffarin," *Le Monde*, 9 May 2002.
16. For a favorable portrait of Rocard by his chief of staff, see Jean-Paul Huchon, *Jours tranquilles à Matignon* (Paris: Grasset, 1993). On his own quest for government by consensus, see M. Rocard, *Le Coeur à l'ouvrage* (Paris: Odile Jacob, 1987).

17. For detailed political biographies, see Arthur Conte, *Les Premiers Ministres de la Ve République* (Paris: Le Pré au Clercs, 1986). On the "political styles" of Socialist premiers and the relations between Mitterrand and his premiers, see Thierry Pfister, *À Matignon au temps de l'union de la gauche* (Paris: Hachette, 1985). For a discussion of the economic policies of Barre, Bérégovoy, and Balladur, see Véronique Auger, *Trois Hommes qui comptent* (Paris: Pluriel, 1993).
18. Elgie, *The Role of the Prime Minister in France*, p. 167. According to this typology, Chaban-Delmas, Chirac (under Giscard), and Rocard were rivals of the president; Chirac (under Mitterrand) and Jospin were opponents; and the rest played subordinate roles.
19. See Raymond Barre, *Question de confiance* (Paris: Flammarion, 1988), esp. pp. 238, 249–51.
20. *Le Monde*, 20 May 1986.
21. Walter Bagehot, *The English Constitution* (Garden City, NY: Doubleday, n.d.), p. 124.
22. *Le Monde*, 11 December 1986.
23. Under the Constitution, the president cannot *veto bills* duly enacted by Parliament, and has to sign them within 15 days. But he can refuse to *sign decrees*, thereby nullifying them.
24. Among the pettier episodes was a conflict between Minister of Culture François Léotard, who had been promised that the large wing of the Royal Palace then occupied by the Giscardist Ministry of Finance would be made available to house additional art treasures of the Louvre, and Edouard Balladur, the Gaullist minister of finance, who refused to vacate the premises and move into a newly built ministerial complex. Chirac chose not to intervene in this matter.
25. "Les Cérémonies des voeux à l'Elysée," *Le Monde*, 7 January 1993. See also Alain Rollat, "Le Second Tribunat de M. Mitterrand," *Le Monde*, 30 January 1993.
26. Hubert Védrine, the secretary-general of the Elysée, and Nicolas Bazire, Balladur's chief of staff. The latter presided over a *cabinet* of 27 *conseillers techniques* and other advisers of various ranks in charge of economic, cultural, budgetary, legal, and parliamentary affairs, relations with the press, and even military affairs (handled by a rear admiral).
27. An interesting and partly chronological comparative treatment of the first two cohabitation periods can be found in Arnaud Teyssier, *La Ve République de de Gaulle à Chirac* (Paris: Pygmalion, 1995), pp. 383–415 and 485–519. See also Jacques Attali, *Verbatim*, vol. 2: *Chroniques des années 1986–1988* (Paris: Fayard, 1995), for a highly personal and critical account by one of Mitterrand's major advisers. For descriptions of the relationship between Chirac and Balladur, see Nicholas Domenach and Maurice Szafran, *De si bons amis* (Paris: Plon, 1994); and Catherine Nay, *Le Dauphin et le Régent* (Paris: Grasset, 1994). According to the last source (pp. 372–78), the strain in the relationship between Chirac and Balladur began a year before the latter made known his interest in running for the presidency.
28. "Les Pouvoirs de Chirac plus faibles que ceux de Mitterrand en 86 et 93," interview with René Rémond, *Les Echos*, 3 June 1997, p. 5.
29. Bigaut, *Le Président de la Cinquième République*, p. 48.
30. During a visit to Israel and the West Bank in 2000, Jospin referred to the Hezbollah organization as "terrorists," thus upsetting the president and the Foreign Office and creating difficulties for their pro-Arab policies. Note that Chirac's own forays into global policy making, however, have frequently been clumsy and unsuccessful.
31. To some observers, the "unity of tone" was only a show intended to reassure France's European Union partners.
32. Jean-Michel Bezat, "Le Chef de l'État veut être le protecteur des acquis européens," *Le Monde*, 8–9 June 1997, p. 6.
33. On this point, see Guy Carcassonne, "La Tentation du quinquennat," *Le Point*, 14 June 1997, p. 19.
34. Jospin was perhaps in a better position to speak for public morality than Chirac, whose political friends, including Juppé, Paris mayor Jean Tiberi, and other prominent Gaullists, had been implicated in scandals of various sorts.
35. For example, disagreements between Minister of Justice Guigou and Interior Minister Chevènement on the use of the police; between Finance Minister Strauss-Kahn and Employment Minister Aubry on the 35-hour week; between Transport Minister Gayssot and Environment Minister Cochet on permitting heavy trucks to use an Alpine tunnel.
36. This position, which was intended to convince the government's more leftist supporters that it had a "social" orientation, turned out to be largely symbolic, because it remained unclear how these needs

were to be addressed. Given the "penny-pinching" outlook of the Ministry of Finance, the aforementioned secretary soon began to emphasize local, private sector, and voluntary initiatives.

37. One of these, Hamlaoui Mekachera, as secretary of state for veterans, was to be a middleman between the government and the Harkis (North African Arabs who had fought on the side of France and opted for French citizenship).

38. The intellectual image of a large proportion of ministers is attested by the numerous books they have written (or commissioned others to ghostwrite).

39. These included Gaston Defferre, long-time mayor of Marseilles, leader of the Socialist group in the Assembly, and minister in charge of decentralization; Michel Rocard and Jean-Pierre Chevènement, leaders of rival factions in the PS; Charles Fiterman, a Communist; and Michel Jobert, formerly a prominent Gaullist.

40. The "pecking order" established by protocol (and not necessarily based on relative political power) has remained virtually the same as in the Fourth Republic: president of the Republic, premier, president of the Senate, speaker of the Assembly, and, finally, the rest of the cabinet.

41. The correspondence department, which grew from 40 under Giscard to more than 80 under Mitterrand, is charged with answering (or forwarding to other units of the executive) an annual average of 200,000–300,000 greetings, complaints, petitions, and invitations from individuals and associations. On the growth of citizen communications to the president, see Yves Agnès, "Cher M. le président," *Le Monde*, 13 September 1981. On the precise breakdown of the Elysée staff and expenditures, see Jean Massot, *La Présidence de la République en France*, Notes et Études Documentaires, no. 4801 (Paris: Documentation Française, 1986), esp. pp. 49–66. For a list of the higher civil servants in the president's office under Mitterrand, see République Française, Secrétariat Général du Gouvernement, *Présidence de la République: Gouvernement et Cabinet Ministériels* (Paris: Journal Officiel, 15 June 1994).

42. As in the case of General Lanxade, a member of the Elysée staff, who before and during the Gulf War was consulted by Mitterrand more often than his minister of defense, and (to a lesser extent) Claude Chirac, who has been a constant adviser to her father on matters of politics and policy.

43. Thus, Michel Jobert, who had been secretary-general of the Elysée under Pompidou, was later (in 1973) promoted to foreign minister. Among the secretaries-general who subsequently became premiers are Pompidou, Bérégovoy, and Balladur.

44. On the position of the president in relation to his advisers, see also Maurice Duverger, *La République des citoyens* (Paris: Ramsay, 1982), esp. pp. 145–89.

45. For "Letter to All the French," see note 11, this chapter. On Rocard's duties, see Jean-Louis Andréani, "Un Premier Ministre au long cours," *Le Monde*, 10 May 1989.

46. On this and other points, see Elijah Kaminsky, "The Contemporary French Executive: Stable Governments, Unstable Institutions," paper presented at meeting of American Political Science Association, Atlanta, GA, 30 August–3 September 1989, p. 26. See also Jean-Marie Colombani, "Tirs croisés contre M. Rocard," *Le Monde Hebdomadaire*, 12–18 October 1989.

47. "Gouverner autrement: La Circulaire Rocard du 25 mai 1988," *Le Monde*, 27 May 1988; and *Regards sur l'actualité*, no. 143 (July–August 1988), 15–18.

48. *Journal RFI*, 28 August 1995.

49. Bertrand Fessard de Foucault, "Le Grand Conducteur," *Le Monde*, 28–29 July 1974.

50. In addition to the referendum of September 1958, on the Fifth Republic Constitution, there have been eight popular consultations: January 1961, on self-determination for Algeria; April 1962, on the Evian Accords, granting independence to Algeria; October 1962, on changing the method of electing the president; April 1969, on amending the Constitution so as to reform the Senate—a referendum that resulted in a negative vote and culminated in de Gaulle's resignation; the referendum of April 1972; November 1988, on autonomy agreements in New Caledonia; September 1992, on the (Maastricht) Treaty on European Union; and in October 2000, the reduction of the presidential term to five years. For rates of abstention see Table 4.9.

51. Massot, *La Présidence de la République*, p. 137.

52. Didier Maus, *Les Grandes Textes de la pratique institutionnelle de la Ve République*, Notes et Études Documentaires, no. 4786 (Paris: Documentation Française, 1985), pp. 39–40. For Chirac's letter of resignation, see 1995 edition of the same book, p. 127.

53. Massot, *La Présidence de la République*, p. 137.

54. Fabre, *Principes républicains*, p. 367n.
55. Massot, *La Présidence de la République*, p. 137.
56. The 43 members of Chirac's cabinet, as reconstituted in January 1976, included 31 with professional civil service backgrounds. Under de Gaulle, 44.6 percent of the ministers were chosen from outside Parliament; under Pompidou, 43.9 percent; under Giscard, 32.6 percent; and during the precohabitation period (1981–1986) of Mitterrand's first term, 25.8 percent. See Olivier Duhamel, "The Fifth Republic Under François Mitterrand," in George Ross, Stanley Hoffmann, and Sylvia Malzacher, eds., *The Mitterrand Experiment* (New York: Oxford University Press, 1987), p. 146.
57. In the case of the two appointments that required Chirac's approval, those of the ministers of foreign affairs and defense, there were no problems. This was particularly true of Hubert Védrine, the foreign minister, who had been a friend of Balladur's and was well respected by Chirac.
58. On the lateral movement of prime ministers' civil service staffs under three presidents from and to the Council of State, the Court of Accounts, the prefectoral corps, and private business, see Bertrand Badie and Pierre Birnbaum, "L'Autonomie des institutions politico-administratives: Le Rôle des cabinets des présidents de la République et des premiers ministres sous la Cinquième République," *RFSP* 26 (April 1976), 286–322.
59. Presidential protection does not extend to former members of the government. In 1992, Mitterrand refused to intervene when three former ministers (including former premier Fabius) faced indictment for their alleged roles in a scandal involving blood transfusions.
60. By March 1992, confidence in her leadership had fallen to between 19 percent and 27 percent. She had started her premiership with a confidence level of 49 percent.
61. Renard Dely, "Jospin: Le Discours de la méthode (tome 2)," *Libération*, 31 March 2000.
62. Of the 16 replacements of the premier, 6 have been made on the basis of the president's discretion, 7 have followed presidential elections, 2 have been forced on the president as a consequence of legislative elections, and 1 (that of Chirac in 1976) was based on the premier's voluntary resignation. Not a single resignation has resulted from a motion of censure. On the evolution of the relationship between president and premier, see Jean Massot, *Chef de l'État et chef du gouvernement*, Notes et Études Documentaires, no. 4983 (Paris: Documentation Française, 1993), esp. pp. 43–52, 82.
63. Press Conference of 9 January 1972, Ambassade de France, Service de Presse et d'Information, *Bulletin* 72/12/H.
64. *Le Monde*, 23 September 1972.
65. See Georges Vedel, "Le Quinquennat contre les risques de cohabitation," in Philippe Tronquoy, ed., *La Ve République, permanence et mutations, Cahiers Français*, no. 300 (Paris: Documentation Française, January–February 2001), pp. 33–37.
66. Presidential messages to Parliament have been resorted to relatively infrequently. They were used 15 times between 1959 and 1991: 5 times by de Gaulle, 3 by Pompidou, once by Giscard, and 6 times by Mitterrand. See Maus, *La Pratique institutionnelle*, 1995, p. 116. There have been only two occasions when presidents were permitted to appear personally in Parliament: in 1975, when Giscard appeared at the Senate for the celebration of the centenary of its founding; and in 1982, when Mitterrand came to the Assembly to participate in a ceremony honoring Pierre Mendès-France.
67. Maurice Duverger, "L'Article 16," *Le Monde*, 19 November 1966.
68. Perhaps for these reasons, academic discussion of Article 16 has lessened. In a book on the Constitution (Olivier Duhamel and Jean-Luc Parodi, eds., *La Constititution de la Cinquième République* [Paris: PFNSP, 1985]), the article is not discussed at all; and in a book on the presidency (Massot, *La Présidence de la République*), it is dealt with in two pages. For a more recent discussion of the uncertainties surrounding Article 16, see Guy Carcassonne, *La Constitution*, 5th ed. (Paris: Seuil, 2002), pp. 109–13.
69. For an analysis of structural and institutional factors, see Robert Elgie, "The French Presidency: Conceptualizing Presidential Power in the Fifth Republic," *Public Administration* 74 (Summer 1996), 275–91.
70. Cf. Jacques Fauvet, *The Cockpit of France* (London: Harvill House, 1960), pp. 80–81. See also Philip Thody, *French Caesarism from Napoleon to Charles de Gaulle* (New York: St. Martin's, 1989), which (with some exaggeration) traces the historical roots of de Gaulle's authoritarian inclinations.
71. Michel Crozier, *Le Phénomène bureaucratique* (Paris: Seuil, 1963), p. 288.

72. Stanley Hoffmann, "Heroic Leadership: The Case of Modern France," in Lewis Edinger, ed., *Political Leadership in Industrialized Societies* (New York: Wiley, 1967), pp. 108–54.

73. For a typical series of articles, see "Vénération Mitterrand," *Le Point*, 17 February 1996, pp. 51–57.

74. Press conference of 31 January 1964, cited in Jean Lacouture, ed., *Citations du Président de Gaulle* (Paris: Seuil, 1968), p. 39.

75. Although the president is politically "irresponsible" in that his "ordinary" political actions are not subject to legal challenge, he may be indicted for high treason by the two chambers of Parliament and tried by a special court under Article 67.

76. Léo Hamon and Albert Mabileau, eds., *La Personnalisation du pouvoir* (Paris: PUF, 1964), p. 375.

77. Stanley Hoffmann, *Decline or Renewal? France Since the 1930s* (New York: Viking, 1974), p. 103. To be sure, de Gaulle brought his departure on himself because he had threatened to resign if the 1969 referendum (reforming the Senate) did not pass. But the failure of the referendum was itself a reflection of the people's growing disenchantment with de Gaulle.

78. The expression of Pierre Viansson-Ponté, "Un Dimanche tous les sept ans," *Le Monde*, 1 November 1972.

79. Quoted in Robert Rocca, *Pompi-deux* (Paris: Éditions de la Pensée Moderne, 1969), p. 55.

80. *Le Monde*, 27 July 1974.

81. One critic, Roger-Gérard Schwartzenberg, in *L'État-spectacle* (Paris: Flammarion, 1977), p. 64, cites Giscard's remark (in an interview in October 1974): "I attach a great deal of importance to style: Style is the esthetics of action." The same author labeled Giscard's system as a "techno-profitariat" (p. 59).

82. Biographies of Mitterrand are numerous. Among controversial ones, see Catherine Nay, *Le Noir et le rouge* (Paris: Grasset, 1984), and her equally hostile *Les Sept Mitterrand* (Paris: Grasset, 1988); Franz-Olivier Giesbert's critical *Le Président* (Paris: Seuil, 1990); Pierre Favier and Michel Marin-Roland, *La Décennie Mitterrand*, vol. 1: *Les Ruptures, 1981–1984* (Paris: Seuil, 1990); and Wayne Northcutt's detailed but too chronological *François Mitterrand: The Centrist Revolutionary* (New York: Holmes & Meier, 1991). For an interesting comparison of de Gaulle and Mitterrand, see Alain Duhamel, *De Gaulle–Mitterrand: La Marque et la trace* (Paris: Flammarion, 1991).

83. See "Mitterrand: Le Nouveau Ton," *Le Point*, 28 September 1981, pp. 64–69.

84. Press conference of Mitterrand on 24 September 1981. See also "De Gaulle? Non, Mitterrand," *Le Monde*, 26 September 1981.

85. Jacques Julliard, "La Tentation du Prince-Président," *Pouvoirs*, no. 41 (1987), 27–28.

86. Guillaume Bacot, "Ni se soumettre, ni se démettre," *Revue politique et parlementaire*, January–February 1978, pp. 27–33; and Michel Béranger, "La Responsabilité politique du chef de l'état," *Revue du droit public* 95:5 (September–October 1979), 1265–314, which compares the president's "arbitrage" to the moral leadership of the British queen.

87. On the monarchic behavior of de Gaulle and his successors, see Charles Zorgbibe, *De Gaulle, Mitterrand, et l'esprit de la constitution* (Paris: Hachette, 1993).

88. In 1988, before Mitterrand had officially decided to seek reelection, French citizens (including non-Socialists) appealed to him with the slogan "Uncle, do not leave us!" (Tonton, ne nous quitte pas). See Jean-Yves Lhomeau, "1987–1988, la gloire de 'Tonton,'" *Le Monde*, 22 March 1988.

89. Stanley Hoffmann, "Mitterrand: The Triple Mystery," *French Politics and Society* 6:2 (April 1988), 3–6.

90. For a particularly critical assessment, see Jean-Marie Vincent, "La Dégradation de la politique sous Mitterrand," *Futur antérieur*, no. 28 (1995/2), 51–68.

91. See Pierre Péan, *Une Jeunesse française: François Mitterrand, 1934–1947* (Paris: Fayard, 1994); and Emmanuel Faux, Thomas Legrand, and Gilles Perez, *La Main droite de dieu* (Paris: Seuil, 1994). Many French people were shocked by revelations that Mitterrand had continued to maintain friendly relations with René Bousquet, a notorious Vichy collaborator who had shared responsibility for the deportation of Jews, and they had difficulty accepting his "explanations." See SOFRES, *L'État de l'opinion 1995*, p. 43; and *L'Année politique 1994*, pp. 82–83.

92. At the same time, it was revealed that Mitterrand had failed to inform the public of the fact that he suffered from cancer for most of his second term, a failure that came to be referred to as "a lie in the national interest" *(mensonge d'État).* See Sophie Coignard and Marie Thérèse Guichard, "14 Ans d'intrigues à l'Elysée," *Le Point*, 20 January 1996, pp. 38–45.

93. See "François Mitterrand, artisan de son destin," *Le Monde* (special issue), 11 May 1995 (supplement); "François Mitterrand sous l'oeil du 'Monde,'" *Le Monde*, 12 January 1996 (supplement). For biographies, see Alistair Cole, *François Mitterrand: A Study in Political Leadership* (London and New York: Routledge, 1994), and the monumental work by Franz-Olivier Giesbert, *François Mitterrand: Une Vie* (Paris: Seuil, 1996).

94. For example, shortly after his assumption of the presidency, he departed from the mythology of his predecessors by acknowledging the active role of the French state in the deportation of Jews.

95. For a statement of that vision, see Jacques Chirac, *Une Nouvelle France* (Paris: NiL Éditions, 1994). This essay contains references to often contradictory policy preferences, for example, a belief in a strong state and a viable market; and a solid currency and an expansion of social expenditures. See also Siwaim Alizzi, *Chirac ou les états d'âme d'un président* (Paris: Apogée, 2001), on Chirac's adapt ability; and Raphaëlle Bacqué, *Chirac ou le demon du pouvoir* (Paris: Albin Michel, 2002), which focuses on Chirac's policy inconsistencies and his preoccupation with power for its own sake.

96. See Vedel, "Le Quinquennat contre les risques de cohabitation."

CHAPTER 7

Instruments and Patterns of Decision Making: The Parliament

The conception of republicanism that was traditional in France from the 1870s until 1958 rested on parliamentary supremacy. The Parliament, as the main expression of popular sovereignty, occupied the central role in the French decision-making structure. Parliament was supreme in that it had, at least in a formal sense, a monopoly on legislative power; it elected the president of the Republic; it invested and dismissed prime ministers and cabinets at will; it controlled the budgetary process; it regularly exercised its power of surveillance over the executive by means of questions, interpellations, and votes of censure; and it was the absolute master over such matters as special sessions, internal parliamentary rules, and the dissolution of the Assembly prior to the calling of new elections. Parliamentary legislative monopoly, in principle, did not permit "delegated legislation" (i.e., the granting of power to the executive to issue decrees), and parliamentary decisions were not subject to judicial review.

The formal dominance of Parliament during the Fourth Republic did not, however, mean that Parliament was an *adequate* decision maker. The legislature was unable to use its powers, because it lacked effective management; none of the parties in Parliament had an absolute majority, and few of them were disciplined. Coalition cabinets were unstable, in part because of the personal ambition of the deputies. Many members of Parliament considered themselves capable of being ministers, and deputies were easily persuaded to express lack of confidence in an existing government in the hope that, as a result of the next cabinet "replastering," they would get portfolios.

In order to hasten the resignation of a cabinet, the bills initiated by the government were often sabotaged in Parliament. The legislative standing committees (of which there were 19 in the Fourth Republic Assembly) were particularly adept at gutting a government bill. If a committee, which tended to be the preserve of special interests, did not pigeonhole a government bill, its *rapporteur* (the committee member assigned as the principal "steering" person for the bill) would report a "counter-bill" *(contre-projet)* that embarrassed the government and sometimes led to its resignation. In order to stay in power, the government sometimes refrained from introducing controversial bills. Budgetary and other crucial measures were frequently dealt with by cabinet decree, based on a broad framework law *(loi cadre)* that Parliament enacted in order to grant the executive full powers and to enable deputies to escape responsibility for unpopular legislation. Yet in the Third and Fourth Republics, it was still meaningful to speak of a parliamentary system; the very existence of a government depended on parliamentary approval, for Parliament could prevent the *permanent* dominance of political leaders by cutting short their terms of office. Despite the fact that in the Fourth Republic many premiers enacted decree laws even after losing the confidence of Parliament (that is, while they were acting as mere chairpersons of "caretaker" governments), they did so with the implied permission of Parliament and in the clear knowledge that they would soon be replaced.

Rightly or wrongly, many French citizens attributed the failures of the Fourth Republic—and not its achievements—to the excessive power of Parliament. They developed a measure of cynicism owing to the deputies' frequent manifestations of opportunism, their endless perorations, and their fruitless ideological quarrels. These tendencies made the deputies appear to be the enemies of the electorate and reinforced the substratum of antiparliamentary thinking prevalent in France.[1]

PARLIAMENT IN THE FIFTH REPUBLIC

Despite their critical view of Parliament, the Gaullist drafters of the Constitution knew that such an institution must be preserved because it was the sine qua non of republicanism. But the new Parliament would be rationalized and harnessed for efficient collaboration with the executive. Accordingly, the Fifth Republic Parliament emerged as a mere shadow of its predecessor. The forms are observed: Parliament still has a legislative function, and the government is still responsible to the National Assembly. In terms of its size, structure, and procedures, the Fifth Republic Parliament does not differ radically from parliaments in earlier regimes. The Palais Bourbon, the venue of the Assembly, is an intimate club in which the traditional esprit de corps of politicians, though somewhat weakened since 1958, is still present and occasionally transcends party labels.[2] The deputies spend their working week much in the same way as they might have done during the Fourth Republic. A typical week of a deputy is as follows:

Tuesday	A.M.:	Arrival in Paris by train. At office in Assembly, reading mail accumulated since Saturday; telephone conversations; discussions with officials of a government ministry or agency.
	NOON:	Lunch with delegation of mayors from constituency.
	P.M.:	Meeting with parliamentary party *(groupe politique)*. Legislative working group; legislative standing committee. In office, meeting with experts and representatives of organizations. Dinner with former residents of constituency now living in Paris.
Wednesday	A.M.:	Meeting with parliamentary party. Working in legislative committee.
	NOON:	Quick lunch. Preparing notes for Assembly session.
	P.M.:	Assembly session; posing questions to government; participating in debate of a government bill. Return to office to read mail. Dinner at Assembly restaurant. Return to Assembly for continuing debate of a government bill.

Thursday	A.M.:	At office, meeting with interest-group representatives. Visit to a government ministry. Meeting with parliamentary party or subgroup; examining a private member's bill. Return to office for mail and telephone calls.
	NOON:	Lunch with delegation of foreign legislators.
	P.M.:	Meeting with a political group. Preparing remarks for a colloquium. Checking train reservations. Return to constituency. Dinner at home.
Friday	A.M.:	Office hours at constituency headquarters, meeting with local residents and officials.
	NOON:	Lunch with local officials.
	P.M.:	Visit to a local housing project. Meeting with a director of a vocational school. Discussions at the prefecture. Inauguration of an artisans' exhibit in a neighboring locality. "Dinner debate" with a visiting politician.
Saturday	A.M.:	Office hours at one or two cantons (subdistricts) of the constituency.
	NOON:	Lunch with mayors and other officials of the canton(s).
	P.M.:	Addressing a meeting of a local or regional social service association. Visits with local shopkeepers. Discussions with representatives of interest group. Buffet dinner. Concert at local cultural center.
Sunday	A.M.:	Attending commemorative mass at local church.
	NOON:	Lunch at gathering of war veterans.
	P.M.:	Attending soccer match. Visit to a local fair. Visit to a festival in a nearby canton. At home.
Monday	A.M.:	Meeting with officials of agricultural association. Meeting with department officials. Meeting with the president of the local chamber of commerce.
	NOON:	Lunch with president of local chamber of commerce and directors of local firms.
	P.M.:	Meeting with officials of the departmental legislature (*conseil général*). Reading mail, telephone conversations. Meeting with department officials. Quick dinner. Meeting with local party officials.[3]

The present Parliament has retained the bicameralism traditional in French politics. The Assembly's 577 members are elected for a five-year term on the basis of universal suffrage;[4] the 321 senators are elected for nine years by an electoral college composed of deputies and local politicians. Each chamber is headed by a speaker, elected by its respective membership. The speaker is assisted by a "steering committee," known as the Presidents' Conference. (The speakers of both chambers are called *présidents,* as are the chairpersons of parliamentary parties.) The Presidents' Conference consists of the leaders of the various parliamentary parties and is responsible for the allocation of committee seats and the allotment of time for debate on most legislative items. The management of the Assembly and the Senate is the respective *bureau,* which consists of the speaker, 6 deputy speakers, 14 secretaries (who take minutes and count votes), and 3 *questeurs* (who are in charge of supplies). In addition, there are nearly 2,000 parliamentary functionaries, who are concerned with purely administrative or technical-managerial tasks.[5]

Formal parliamentary procedure basically follows the pattern established in previous French republics (see Figure 7.1). A distinction is made between government bills *(projets de loi)* and private members' bills *(propositions de loi)*, the former traditionally accounting for most of the bills passed in the Assembly. When a bill is introduced, it is sent first to the *bureau;* the speaker, who heads that unit, transmits the bill directly to a legislative committee. After the committee has done its work, the *rapporteur* reports the bill to the floor for what is technically the initial "reading." The ensuing debate, which provides an opportunity for the introduction of amendments, is followed by a vote. After its passage in the Assembly, the bill is transmitted to the Senate. If that chamber accepts the original version of the bill, it is sent to the government (i.e., the prime minister) for signature. If the Senate rejects the bill, the subsequent procedure varies. (1) There can be a resort to the shuttle *(navette),* the sending of a bill back and forth between the two chambers until a common version is achieved; (2) the government may request the appointment of a conference committee *(commission mixte paritaire)* of seven members from each chamber, which is the method used for about half of the bills; (3) the government may ask each chamber for a "second reading" (i.e., a reconsideration and new vote on the original bill); and (4) if disagreement persists, the government may ask the Assembly to determine the final version of the bill by simple majority vote (as happened in the case of the 35-hour workweek, enacted in 2000).

THE COMMITTEE SYSTEM

The Fifth Republic's legislative committee system is a compromise between the systems found in the U.S. Congress and the British House of Commons. There are only six standing committees in the Assembly (and six in the Senate), and they are specialized. Their size ranges from 72 members (foreign affairs, defense, finance and economic affairs, and constitutional and administrative matters) to 144 (cultural and social affairs, production and exchange). Deputies are assigned to committees on the basis of the proportional representation of parliamentary parties. The chairperson of a committee, who has little power, is elected by committee members and does not necessarily belong to the largest party. When the new Assembly met after the legislative elections of 1981, the Socialists offered to share the chairs of legislative committees with the opposition parties, but the latter refused. The parties belonging to the majority assumed all the chairs but, in so doing, followed a kind of *internal* spoils system.[6] After the Assembly elections of 1988, the opposition was offered the chair of the foreign affairs committee, which was assumed by Giscard d'Estaing (who had reentered the Assembly in 1986). When the UMP became the dominant parliamentary group in 2002, it was careful to take into account the various parties that helped to constitute that group; thus important committee chairmanships were allocated to politicians belonging not only to the RPR but also to the UDF and the DL.

Only deputies who belong to a parliamentary party *(groupe parlementaire)* are allocated membership in committees (and only such parties are given office space, ready access to reference materials, and miscellaneous administrative benefits).[7] Formerly, a parliamentary party, in order to be recognized as such, had to have at least 30 deputies, a requirement that forced "loose" deputies to align themselves *(s'apparenter)* with larger

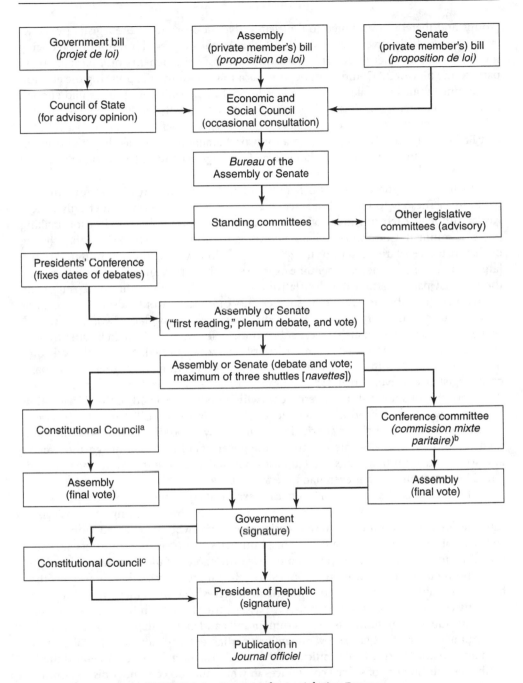

FIGURE 7.1   Steps in the Legislative Process

Source: Based on Jean-Charles Maoût and Raymond Muzellac, *Le Parlement sous la Ve République* (Paris: Colin, 1971), pp. 68–69.

[a]In case of disagreement between the government and either chamber on the constitutionality of a bill.
[b]In case of disagreement between the two chambers.
[c]For organic law.

groups and thereby contributed to the aggregative process within the legislature. However, after the legislative elections of 1988, the Assembly passed a resolution reducing the minimum number to 20. This was done to accord the benefits of a parliamentary party to the bloc of 27 Communist deputies as a reward for their supporting the election of Laurent Fabius as speaker. After the elections of 2002, only four groups had enough members to be recognized as parliamentary parties: the UMP, the PS, the UDF, and the PCF. There were not enough deputies belonging to smaller left-wing parties, such as the Left Radicals and the Greens, to form a joint parliamentary party, as they had done in 1997; instead, they can "attach" themselves (s'apparenter) to the PS for organizational purposes.

In the beginning of the Fifth Republic, legislative committees met four times a week, from Tuesday to Friday, but since 1969, many committees have met only once a week. Although each bill must be sent to a committee, that body's decision-making power is minimal. Committees are not permitted to produce substitute bills that change or distort the legislative intent of the government. In any case, the committees are too large and unwieldy to develop genuine expertise. In the early years of the Fifth Republic, the Gaullist party insisted that legislative committees had no authority to subdivide themselves, probably for fear that smaller subcommittees would develop into anti-Gaullist power centers. But such subdivision has in fact taken place; "working groups" (groupes de travail), which are de facto subcommittees, have been formed frequently, and in recent years they have been more or less officially sanctioned. Neither the subcommittees nor the full committees, however, can function meaningfully other than as parts of the legislative conveyor belt, for a committee must report back to the chamber within three months, or sooner if the government (which under Article 48 of the Constitution has the power to assign priority status to a bill) has labeled a bill "urgent." (Between 1959 and 2000, that label was attached to a bill well over 100 times in the Assembly and even more often in the Senate.) At times, the government has so arranged the agenda and so rushed a bill that it has come up for floor debate before the committee has prepared its report on it or has even had time to discuss it.

The weakness of standing committees is exemplified by the committee on finance. The internal regulations of the Assembly provide that at the beginning of each legislature the finance committee appoints special *rapporteurs*, who are charged with the surveillance of the expenditures of the various ministries. However, the ministers are often unwilling to provide full information; moreover, the choice of the *rapporteurs* is made by the majority party, and ambitious deputies are reluctant to exercise their power, for they hope to be able to enter the government themselves.[8] Despite these handicaps, the standing committees have not been totally passive; they have been increasingly successful in introducing amendments to government bills and getting them passed.

At the request of either the government or a parliamentary chamber, a special committee may be named to consider a particular bill. In the past, the government tolerated the Assembly's establishment of special committees in which the subjects under discussion were not highly partisan (e.g., subsidies for repatriates from North Africa, birth control). After 1968, the government became more amenable to the creation of special committees dealing with a broader scope of problems, because the absolute majority that the Gaullists enjoyed in the plenum of the Assembly (see Table 7.1) was reflected in the makeup of the

TABLE 7.1
Composition of the National Assembly, 1956–2002

Parliamentary Elections	Communists	Socialists & Allies	Radicals & Allies	MRP & Center	Conservatives, Moderates, & Independents	Gaullists & Affiliates	Miscellaneous & Unaffiliated	Total Seats
1956	150	99	94	84	97	22	50	596
1958	10	47	40	56	129	206	64	552
1962	41	66	43	55	268[a]		9	482
1967	73		121[b]	41[c]	242[a]		10	487
1968	34		57[b]	34[c]	344[d]		18	487
1973	73	100[e]	34[f]		270[d]		13	490
1978	86	105	10[g]		123[h]	9[i] 153	5	491
1981	44	286[e]			62[i]	88	11	491
1986	35	214[e]			132[j]	158	38[k]	577
1988	27	277[e]			130[j]	129	14[l]	577
1993	23	57[e]			215[j]	257	25[m]	577
1997	36	250	33[n]		113[j]	140	5[o]	577
2002	22	141[p]			29[q]	365[r]	20[s]	577

SOURCES: *Bulletin de l'Assemblée nationale*, 10e législature, no. 1 (13 April 1993); and *Le Monde*. 4, 5, and 7 June 1997 and 18 June 2002.

[a] Gaullists and Independent Republicans.
[b] Socialist and Radical alliance.
[c] Progress and Modern Democracy.
[d] Gaullists, Independent Republicans, and progovernment Centrists.
[e] Socialist and Left Radicals.
[f] Reformers (Radical-Socialists and opposition Centrists).
[g] Left Radicals (MRG).
[h] UDF and "presidential majority" (Giscardists).
[i] Independents and Peasants (CNIP).
[j] UDF (Republicans, CDS, and Radical-Socialists).
[k] Includes 32 National Front and 6 unaffiliated.
[l] Includes 13 miscellaneous Right and 1 National Front deputy.
[m] Includes miscellaneous right-wing deputies.
[n] Includes 13 Left Radicals, 8 environmentalists, 7 Citizens' Movement.
[o] Includes 1 National Front and 1 Movement for France.
[p] Includes 1 *apparenté*.
[q] UDF.
[r] *Union pour la majorité présidentielle* (UMP), includes 9 *apparentés*.
[s] Includes 7 Left Radicals, 6 miscellaneous Left, 3 Greens, 5 miscellaneous Right.

special committees. Between 1959 and 1995, more than 90 demands for special committees were made in the Assembly, and two-thirds of them were approved; all 35 demands for such committees made during the same period in the Senate were approved.

After his election as president in 1981, Mitterrand called on Parliament to do its share to "rebalance" the relationship between the executive and the legislature by developing its means of investigation and control. The setting up of parliamentary committees of inquiry into, or investigation of, general problems and of control of government operations (including nationalized industries) had been authorized by an ordinance of November 1958. But major restrictions have been imposed on the conduct of such inquiries. The investigative committees are limited by a set time period and a narrow frame of reference. They cannot be created if the problems they are to deal with may give rise to judicial proceedings—a prohibition intended to obviate interference in the work of the Ministry of Justice. Members of committees of inquiry are selected by vote of the majority, which may decide the rules of conduct of the committee and exclude deputies belonging to minority parties who are likely to be interested in embarrassing the government. The results of the inquiry must be reported to a permanent (standing) committee, which might reject the report. Finally, the committee meets only in closed session (unlike the standing committees, which since 1988 may be open to the public), with the result that government mismanagement can be exposed only by means of leaks (and the parliamentarians' disregard for the pledge of secrecy). In spite of such restrictions, the executive has tended to discourage the appointment of committees of inquiry, and only a small proportion of the deputies' requests for these committees has been satisfied.

The issue of parliamentary investigative powers became particularly important in 1973 after revelations about government wiretapping. French parliamentarians were impressed by the Watergate hearings conducted in the U.S. Senate and wanted to use them as a model. The wiretapping issue, referred to in France as "Watergate-on-the-Seine," had come before the Senate and the Assembly, and in both chambers the government's response had been unsatisfactory. Calls by left-wing deputies for an Assembly investigative committee were rejected; the Senate succeeded in appointing such a committee, but the government refused to cooperate with it (and the Senate, in turn, took revenge by cutting appropriations for wiretapping). After the election of Giscard to the presidency, the Senate had a freer hand and formed committees to investigate the television authority, price fixing by nationalized petroleum companies, and the management of the telephone system.

However, the handful of investigative committees set up by the Assembly during Giscard's presidency remained ineffectual. Thus, the committee of inquiry into the electronic media, set up in 1979, concluded its work six months later with a report of 15 lines—after 38 meetings and after questioning 96 witnesses. A special committee set up (on the demand of the Socialists) in 1980 to look into the unsolved murder of a Giscardist politician met for nine months and presented a short report that was ambiguous.[9] A committee of inquiry into the problems of the textile industry, set up the same year, made detailed recommendations, but these did not lead to any legislation, because the government did not like them. These results were due in part to the self-denying behavior of the deputies belonging to the Giscardist-Gaullist majority, who did not want to embarrass the president.

After the 1981 elections, the Assembly formed three committees of inquiry. The government took the work of these committees seriously, largely because the problems they unearthed (among them alleged police brutalities) were identified with the previous government. During both the period of Socialist domination and the first cohabitation period that followed, the Assembly was a cooperative partner of the government and was careful not to upset it with unnecessary investigations. In 1988, rules were changed to allow any parliamentary group to request the appointment of a committee of inquiry on any topic once a year, although not all requests have been approved.[10] Since 1989, the Assembly has set up a variety of committees, a development that has signified an enlarged role for Parliament. The investigation committees formed since 1991 have been partly or fully open to the public (except for the committee investigating the Mafia). In 1991, the Assembly passed a bill (introduced by Laurent Fabius, the Assembly speaker) to permit the publication of the hearings of committees of investigation. At the same time, the distinction between committees of inquiry and committees of control was abolished. Since then, the number of special committees has averaged about two a year in the Assembly and fewer in the Senate, and they have dealt with diverse subjects (see Table 7.2).[11]

TABLE 7.2
Assembly Committees of Inquiry, Investigation, and Control, 1989–2002 (selected)

1989	Privatization of industries and banks
	Integration of immigrants
1990	Bioethics
1991	Financing of parties and election campaigns
	Decentralization of national education
1992	Fighting the Mafia
1993	Condition of the railroad system
1994	Financial condition of *Crédit Lyonnais*
1996	Illegal immigration
1998	Rights of children
	Functioning of tribunals of commerce
	Use of public funds in public services in Corsica
	Superphénix and nuclear reactors
1999	Financial condition of religious sects
	Protection against physical violence
	Industrial groups
	System of social security for students
	Functioning of police in Corsica
	Condition of prisons
	Safety of food products
2000	Use of animal products as feed
2001	Incidence of floods
2002	Safety of industrial plants

SOURCE: *Le Monde*, 1998–2002, various issues.

Speakers of the Assembly have used such ad hoc committees in order to enhance the power of that chamber. Yet despite its increasing assertiveness, the Assembly's ability to go against a determined executive is limited. This applies both to legislation and the control over government activities. Such constraint is due in part to the frequent movement of legislators to executive positions. Thus Laurent Fabius, when he was speaker between 1997 and 2000, established a *Mission d'évaluation et de contrôle*, which would exercise surveillance over public expenditures.[12] But two years later, having been appointed minister of economic affairs, he wanted to weaken parliamentary surveillance over budgetary matters.

There are other constraints that override the desire of individual deputies to assert themselves against the executive. In 1992 the opposition deputies, convinced that the government would be whitewashed, refused to participate in a special committee to investigate the government's responsibility in the use of AIDS-infected blood for transfusions. In 2001, a Socialist deputy collected 30 parliamentary signatures to impeach President Chirac for corruption; but Prime Minister Jospin objected, and the Assembly's support for this effort went no further.

Nevertheless, the Assembly continued to be more active than previously, enacting significant legislation. Between May 1997 and February 2002 it sat for 4,536 hours and 498 days; during that period it adopted 261 bills, of which 45 percent were of private member origin (see Table 7.3), and voted on 173 international agreements. During that period, the Assembly met jointly with the Senate in Versailles on four occasions to ratify constitutional amendments. While Jospin was premier, the Assembly set up 24 committees of inquiry or investigation, 14 of which were followed by legislation.[13]

TABLE 7.3
Activities of the National Assembly, 1997–2002

	1997–1998	1998–1999	1999–2000	2000–2001	2001–2002
Hours of meetings	1,015	1,129	984	858	550
Number of days of session	120	115	104	96	63
Number of meetings	269	295	244	224	143
Government bills adopted[a]	30	34	37	25	17
Private members' bills adopted	23	19	43	16	17
Number of amendments proposed	10,709	13,835	12,326	8,479	4,885
Number of amendments adopted	2,722	3,472	4,182	3,754	2,237
Motions of censure introduced	1	1	0	0	0
Oral questions with debate	756	719	762	678	426
Oral questions without debate	452	450	254	295	268
Written questions	15,559	15,521	16,058	11,568	7,124
Responses to written questions	12,926	13,721	13,779	9,827	5,515

SOURCE: *Bulletin de l'Assemblée Nationale–Statistiques*, 1997–2002.
[a]Does not include government bills authorizing approval of treaties or conventions (most of them related to the European Union).

THE SENATE

Physically and institutionally, the French Senate has not changed much through various republican regimes. Senators are elected, not by the people directly, but by an electoral college composed of the Assembly deputies, more than 3,000 departmental councillors, and more than 100,000 delegates of city councils. Thus, more than 95 percent of the electors are representatives of localities.

During the Third Republic, the Senate was a powerful legislative chamber. It was virtually equal to the Assembly in the sense that the Senate could render an absolute veto over an Assembly decision. The Senate, like the Assembly, could produce a vote of censure, and it competed with the Assembly as a body from which cabinet members were recruited. In the Fourth Republic, the Senate was abolished; in its stead was a "Council of the Republic," which had only a delaying veto. The founders of the Fifth Republic wished to restore the Senate to the position it had occupied in the Third Republic because they expected that chamber, composed largely of conservative local politicians, to be a guardian of conservative views against the more-left-wing views traditional in the Assembly, and thus to be an institutional supporter of de Gaulle's presidency. The writers of the Constitution lengthened the senators' term of office from six to nine years, added to the legislative powers of the Senate, and made its speaker the acting president of the Republic in case of a vacancy of that office.

Throughout most of the Third and Fourth Republics, the Senate had been an "agricultural chamber." During the first two decades of the Fifth Republic, it continued to be conservative (see Table 7.4), but it was often hostile to Gaullist-dominated governments because their economic policies tended to discriminate against the provincial and more "backward" makeup of the Senate. Thus, while the Assembly's complexion reflected that of the president more or less precisely in 1958, 1968, 1981, 1988, 1995, and 2002 and adapted its views to presidential policy preferences, the Senate retained an independent outlook, at least until 1974, when most of its members rallied to the Giscardist "presidential majority." The Senate's independence was expressed, not only in repeated requests for the appointment of committees of inquiry, but also in appeals to the Constitutional Council to review government bills it did not like. Even during the Giscard years, the Senate functioned as a forum in which disagreement with government policy was expressed more freely, and more often, than in the Assembly, occasionally even obliging a cabinet minister to appear before the Senate to defend government policy.

Many of the Senate's legislative positions have related to matters about which that body, by virtue of its origins, is quite sensitive: for example, policies relating to regions and localities, the protection of farmers, and the privileges of shopkeepers and artisans. In 1972, the Senate amended government bills on regional reform (in order to give greater fiscal powers to regional councils) and attempted to alter a social security bill (in order to raise old-age pension payments to shopkeepers). In 1982, the Senate voted against a government bill on social security because it objected to one of the bill's provisions, the reimbursement of the cost of abortions. In the mid-1990s, senators took an active interest in shielding small shopkeepers against competition from supermarkets. Of course, when the government is adamant about a bill or any of its features (as in the case of the 1982 bill), the Assembly can be asked to override Senate objections to it in a

TABLE 7.4
Composition of the Senate, 1959–2001 (selected years)

	Gaullists	Independents	Peasants	MRP/ Democratic Center	Democratic Left (mainly Radicals)	Socialists	Communists	Unaffiliated	Vacant	Total
1959	41	92		34	64	51	14	11		307
1965	30	79		38	50	52	14	11		274
1968	29	80		40	50	54	17	13		283
1973	36[a]	60[b]	16[c]	46[d]	38[e]	48	18	21		283
1980	41	52[f]		67[d]	39[g]	69	23	13		304
1987	77	52[f]		70[d]	35[g]	64	15	4	1	319
1989	91	52[f]		68[d]	23[h]	66	16	5		321
1992	90	47[f]		66[d]	23[h]	70	15	10		321
1995	92	48[f]		63[d]	28[h]	67	15	8		321
1998	98	45[f]		51[d]	23[h]	76	18[i]	8	2	321
2001	96	40[f]		53[d]	23[j]	83	19[j]	6	1	321

SOURCES: *L'Année politique* (1959–2001), *Le Monde*, and *Regards sur l'actualité*.

NOTE: Figures for each party include affiliated senators (*apparentés*).

[a]UDR.
[b]Independent Republicans (RI).
[c]Independents and Peasants (CNIP).
[d]Center Union.
[e]Reformers.
[f]Republicans and Independents.
[g]Includes Left Radicals (MRG).
[h]*Rassemblement démocratique et européen*.
[i]Includes supporters of Chevènement's *Mouvement des citoyens*.
[j]Since 1999, includes supporters of both Radical-Socialist and Left Radical parties.

definitive "second reading," thus reducing the action of the Senate to a mere suspensive veto.

Because of the Senate's independent attitude, it has been widely viewed as an institutionalized opposition and "censor" of the government.[14] During de Gaulle's presidency, this oppositionist attitude—attributable both to the Senate's resentment of its reduced status as a participant in the legislative process and its hostility to Gaullist ideology—was aggravated by de Gaulle's decision to ignore the Constitution and bypass the Parliament as a whole when, in 1962, he introduced the referendum to institute the system of direct election of the president. As a result, Gaston Monnerville, the Senate speaker, stopped speaking to de Gaulle. Later, Alain Poher, the centrist who succeeded to the speakership in 1968 (and held the office until 1993), ran against Pompidou for the presidency in 1969.[15]

Unable to dissolve the Senate, de Gaulle tried to neutralize it by "reforming" it. The constitutional amendment bill prepared by the government in the fall of 1968 proposed to have only half the members of future Senates elected by the usual method, by regional and local politicians, and the other half in a corporative fashion (i.e., by organized socioeconomic sectors such as trade unions, farmers' associations, and business groups) and to permit the Senate to co-legislate only on clearly enumerated social, economic, and cultural matters. That chamber would be totally excluded from decision making in "general" political affairs, as defined by the government. To sweeten the pill, the government associated the dismemberment of the Senate with a popular reform: greater regional autonomy. Most people favored such reform but opposed the reform of the Senate. The referendum lost, and de Gaulle resigned from the presidency. Opposition to the referendum occurred in part because the reform was an affront to those who had always associated republicanism with the existence of a viable Senate, and in part because of objections to the *procedure* chosen for the reform (i.e., the referendum).

Having been saved as an institution, the Senate's weakness remained; Edgar Faure, the Gaullist speaker of the Assembly in the mid-1970s, contemptuously described the activities of the Senate as *"litanie, liturgie, léthargie."*[16] In fact, between 1959 and 1977, fewer than 20 percent of the bills passed by Parliament that had a private member (as opposed to governmental) origin had originated in the Senate. After 1981, the Senate became more active in introducing amendments to government bills, and it has been the source of many private members' bills.

A symptom of the Senate's weakness, especially under the Gaullists, was the relatively small number of meetings: Between 1959 and 1974, the Senate held an average of 66 meetings a year, compared with the Assembly's 91 meetings. In contrast, in the 2000–2001 session, the Senate held 95 days of meetings (and 668 hours), and in 2001–2002, 66 days (and 464 hours); in each case, about one-fourth of the hours were during the evening. It should be noted, moreover, that in 2000–2001, 30 government bills were introduced in the Senate before they were presented to the Assembly; in 2001–2002, 62 bills.

The legislative influence of the Senate has in large measure depended on the role permitted (or assigned to) it by presidents and prime ministers. Under Gaullist-dominated governments, the Senate was distrusted. During Giscard's presidency, it was viewed more positively because it was more favorably inclined to Giscardism. This change brought about an increase in the Senate's decision-making role: There was a significant growth in the number of both government and private members' bills originating in that chamber.[17] Finally, the executive's perception of the cooperative mood of the Senate was such that in 1975, the government of Premier Chirac presented its general political program to the Senate and asked that body for a vote of approval, and in 1977 Premier Barre, having reshuffled the cabinet, asked the Senate for a vote of confidence; Juppé did the same in 1995.[18]

During the period of Socialist dominance, the Senate asserted itself even more frequently, to the point of obstructing the government's reform efforts (and, in fact, was encouraged to do so by Gaullist members of the Assembly). That assertiveness, which contributed to a "conflictual bicameralism,"[19] was attested by the growing difference of opinion between the two chambers on specific bills: The proportion of bills on which conference committees achieved agreement, which had been 71 percent before 1981, fell to 30 percent during the period 1981–1986 and was about the same in 2000–2001 (see Table 7.5)[20] Moreover, the number of Assembly overrides of Senate "vetoes" increased from 61 for the entire period 1959–1981 to 140 for the period 1981–1986.[21] After the elections of 1997, which returned the Assembly to Socialist control, the largely right-of-center Senate became particularly oppositionist and sided increasingly with the president.[22] It opposed government bills on a variety of issues: gender parity, the legalization of unions of same-sex couples, changes in the electoral calendar, judicial reform, and the enlargement of autonomy for Corsica.[23] Also, in 2001, the Senate modified the budget considerably. Most of the Senate vetoes were quickly overturned by the Assembly, which has the final word. It is not surprising that the Left continues to view the Senate in a negative light; it complains about the provincial composition of that chamber, which is based on the census of 1975. It argues that the term of office of senators should be reduced from nine to six years.[24]

LIMITS ON PARLIAMENTARY DECISION MAKING

Despite the survival of the Senate, President de Gaulle left in the wake of his departure a Parliament that had been devalued and put under such effective tutelage of the government that many observers wondered whether France could still be considered a parlia-

TABLE 7.5
Use of Conference Committees, 1994–2001

	1994	1996	1998	1999	2000	2001
Bills adopted without conference committee	37	39	28	32	21	18
Bills going to conference committee	26	30	18	19	29	25
Successful	25	29	5	8	10	8
Unsuccessful	1	1	13	11	19	17

SOURCE: *L'Année politique 2001*, p. 172.

mentary democracy. Parliament no longer participates in the election of presidents or in the selection of premiers and their cabinets (except indirectly, and on rare occasions); it no longer enjoys a monopoly in lawmaking but must share legislative power with the executive and the people (via the referendum); and it has lost its power of dissolution. Parliamentary officials no longer determine most of the agenda; instead, a priority agenda is established by the government, which "informs" the Presidents' Conference about matters to be taken up, and a complementary agenda is determined by the speaker of each chamber and approved by it. (The latter agenda, in the Assembly at least, is strongly influenced by the government majority.) The original text of the Constitution limited the duration of ordinary parliamentary sessions to five and one-half months a year: two and one-half months in the fall (October–December) and three months in the spring (April–June). Special sessions may be called by the premier or by a majority of deputies for a specific agenda, but for no more than 12 days. (De Gaulle refused all requests for special sessions.) In July 2002, shortly after the National Assembly elections, Chirac convoked a special session of Parliament to "invest" the new government and to enact urgently needed measures. Of the more than 50 special sessions so far, only 2 were convoked on the request of the deputies.[25] No opposition input or obstruction is allowed when budget bills are considered.

In 1995, Articles 28 and 48 of the Constitution were amended to reform the position of Parliament. To what extent these amendments (most of them responding to the wishes of Assembly Speaker Philippe Séguin) increased the power of that institution is a matter of controversy.[26] On the one hand, the two ordinary sessions of Parliament were replaced by a single continuous session of nine months, from early October to the end of June; on the other hand, the maximum number of days of meetings was reduced from 170 to 120. In any case, the efficiency of Parliament has been increased, because an unnecessary interruption of several weeks between two sessions is avoided. The intersession break tended to disrupt the activities of Parliament in the following sense: If a government bill had not been adopted by the end of the fall session, the legislative process often had to be started over again in the spring, causing the government to force the chambers to deal with a bill at breakneck speed. The reform also provided that Parliament had to be consulted by the premier if he or she wished to hold supplementary meetings, and that one meeting a month had to be reserved for an agenda to be fixed by the respective chamber. One amendment (Art. 11), which extended the scope of referenda beyond institutional matters to economic and social policy, seemingly reduced the legislative power of Parliament (as stipulated in Art. 34); however, the amendment provided that such a referendum had to be submitted by the government to both houses of Parliament, which could debate the issue.

Whereas in the Fourth Republic, Parliament's legislative competence was absolute, the Fifth Republic Constitution spells out in detail what falls into the domain of "laws" requiring parliamentary participation. Article 34 enumerates civil rights, military conscription, criminal law, taxation, education, social security, the nationalization of industries, property rights, employment, and the jurisdiction of local communities. In 1996 three articles (34, 39, and 47) of the Constitution were amended to refer specifically to the *funding* of social security expenditures. Until then, many details pertaining to revenues and disbursements had been decided by the various social security organisms and the "social partners" that managed them, a situation that contributed to the growth of deficits; henceforth, all financial aspects of social security came under the jurisdiction of Parliament.

Presumably, all matters not enumerated can be decided by the president and/or the government. Such decisions are decrees or ordinances rather than laws, yet they have the force of a law enacted by Parliament. Virtually the entire area of foreign and defense policy has been preempted by the executive. There may be debates in the legislative committees of Parliament on aspects of foreign policy, but often these debates are in closed session and do not cause the government to modify its decisions. The Assembly does vote to ratify treaties, most often on European Union matters, where parliamentary ratification is stipulated, but it rarely rejects a treaty.

The Parliament's role regarding war and other military matters is particularly uncertain. Article 35 provides that Parliament is empowered to authorize a declaration of war. The preamble of the 1946 constitution (which, according to the preamble of the Fifth Republic Constitution, is still valid) forbids France to use "its arms against the liberty of any people." Technically, this provision was not violated when France's forces participated in the Gulf War (1991), in Bosnia (1994), and in Kosovo (1999), because these wars were waged under the aegis of international organizations. In the case of the Gulf War, Michel Rocard, then prime minister, employed Article 49, Section 1, during a special session of Parliament to engage the government's responsibility in using French forces to help liberate Kuwait. In October 2001, in order to commit French troops to Afghanistan, Jospin chose another method, Article 132 of the Parliament's own rules, which provides for separate debates in the Assembly and the Senate without a vote following. He could do so because the French action was not, strictly speaking, a declaration of war.

Even areas that are constitutionally within the competence of Parliament can be "invaded" by the executive. Article 38 of the Constitution provides that the government may ask the legislature to delegate to it the power to issue decrees (albeit for a limited period and purpose). By their nature, such legislative grants are not much different from British "statutory instruments." French governments have resorted to delegated legislation on numerous occasions. In 1960, for example, Parliament authorized the government to make ordinances to deal with alcoholism and prostitution and, in the same year, to control disturbances in connection with the government's policy in Algeria. During the last years of Giscard's presidency, Article 38 was not used, but it was revived under Mitterrand, whose government invoked it in 1981 for enacting 40 measures, including reducing the workweek, lowering the retirement age, and lengthening the period of paid vacations. Premier Chirac also used that article several times, but he was prevented from doing so by Mitterrand on three occasions. Premier Jospin did not resort to delegated legislation.

By virtue of its power to determine the agenda, the government can ensure that its bills have priority over private members' bills. In the case of a particular bill, it can stipulate what the extent of debate shall be, what sections of the bill shall be open to amendments, and how much time shall be allocated to specific sections of a bill, often on its integral, unamended text. This procedure, the "blocked vote," as provided for by Article 44 of the Constitution, effectively eliminates parliamentary input on detail (except for those changes, often made by deputies informally, that the government decides to accept). Since the beginning of the Fifth Republic, the blocked-vote procedure has been used several hundred times. Governments under de Gaulle and Pompidou resorted to the blocked vote frequently; until the late 1960s, over 100 bills were introduced in this fashion in each chamber. Despite Giscard's professed respect for Parliament, Premier Barre resorted to the blocked vote on many occasions, sometimes in an openly contemptuous manner.[27] Under the Socialist governments between 1981 and 1985, the blocked vote was used only three times in the Assembly and six in the Senate, but Chirac's cohabitation government used the procedure with a vengeance,[28] possibly because of the belief that it did not have reliable enough parliamentary majorities to resort to ordinary legislative procedures.

Blocked-vote bills have not always had a smooth passage in the Senate, which has rejected a sizable number of them. But the Senate's opposition has been easily overcome because the degree of legislative involvement of that chamber has depended to a large extent on the government's discretion. Because most of the blocked votes relate to financial matters, the Senate's lack of cooperation with the government may be of little consequence. On the annual budget bill, the government is virtually complete master. According to Article 47 of the Constitution, the Assembly is limited to 40 days in which to process a finance bill, the Senate to 15 days. If, within a 70-day period, the two chambers of Parliament have not approved a budget bill submitted to them by the government, the latter may enact the budget by decree. Because of the invocation of that article, or the threat of its use, comprehensive budget bills have gone through the legislative process in both houses of Parliament very quickly almost every year.

The prohibition against private members' bills on appropriations may be extended to virtually any public matter. For example, if a deputy introduced a bill to reintroduce the death penalty, this bill could be declared inadmissible, inasmuch as guarding a prisoner under a life sentence costs more than executing him. Such an interpretation may be extreme, but it may be assumed that the possibility of the government's use of its various trump cards has had a chilling effect on the introduction of bills by private members. In 1957, at the end of the Fourth Republic, 71 of the 198 bills passed by Parliament were private members' bills. In contrast, in 1959, during the first legislature of the Fifth Republic, only 1 of the 52 bills passed was a private member's bill. Less than 9 percent of about 500 bills passed in the seventh legislature (1981–1986) had been introduced by private members, whereas 18 percent of the 179 laws passed in the eighth (the first "cohabitation") legislature (1986–1988) were of private member origin. Of the 40 bills enacted by Parliament between April and July 1993, none was of private member origin. Of the 108 bills enacted in 1995–1996, only 14 were of such origin. There has been considerable improvement since then, with 43 private members' bills out of the 80 adopted in 1999–2000 and 17 out of 34 in 2001–2002 (see Table 7.3).

Even if a law that significantly reflects the ideas of parliamentarians is passed, it may not take effect. The executive may express contempt for parliamentary lawmaking by failing to implement the legislation. For example, Parliament passed a law on birth control in 1967, but the law was not implemented until 1975. An act legalizing abortion passed in 1975 (substantially confirming a similar act passed earlier), but although it stipulated that implementing regulations had to be passed within six months, the minister of health refrained from doing so as long as possible. Many laws dealing with immigrants have been enacted since the 1960s, but not all of them have been equipped with the appropriate regulations or applied by the public authorities. In order to reduce the time lag between the passage of laws and their implementation, the government in 1981 appointed an official charged with "pushing" for follow-up regulations as soon as possible, and in 1988, the Assembly adopted a procedure whereby various committees would report on the implementation of laws. However, such efforts (which are continuing) are likely to prove insufficient because the regulations, decrees, and ordinances flowing from the legislation are either inadequate or overreaching.[29]

THE CONSTITUTIONAL COUNCIL

The power of Parliament was to be further reduced by the creation of a new institution, the Constitutional Council, which was assigned certain functions that had once been exercised by the legislature. In the Fourth Republic, Parliament could deal with any nonfinance bill or resolution it wished; today, the French Constitution distinguishes among several types of laws, or "rules," as follows:

1. Ordinary laws, relating to social, economic, and other matters enumerated in Article 34, which are enacted by Parliament.

2. Organic laws, relating to the organization of public powers and their relationship to each other (Art. 46), which are also passed by Parliament, but only after the Constitutional Council has certified that they are in accord with the Constitution.

3. Constitutional amendments, which the executive proposes, the Parliament advises on, and the people may ratify.

4. Regulations (*règlements complémentaires*), which are made by the president or the premier in order to implement parliamentary law.

5. Decrees (*règlements autonomes*), which are made by the president or the premier without any reference to Parliament whatsoever, as long as the Constitutional Council certifies that the matters dealt with by decree have a regulatory character.

Regulations of all kinds may be submitted to the Council of State, which determines their scope and legality and may modify them (see Chapter 8). But it is the Constitutional Council that decides which problems are subsumed under the various laws or rules; in short, it determines what is within the purview of government or Parliament. The council must be consulted whenever the government decides to invoke Article 16 and whenever there is a question about the constitutionality of any bill (*before* it is officially enacted) or an international treaty (*before* it is ratified). Finally, the council is responsible for certifying election results.

During the first decade of the Fifth Republic, most of the Constitutional Council's decisions tended to favor the government, even to the point of permitting a government decision to violate constitutional procedures. The most famous case was the constitutional amendment of 28 October 1962, providing for the direct election of the president, in which the government had decided to use the popular referendum, bypassing

Parliament. The council, in an advisory opinion, originally held that the procedure chosen by the government was unconstitutional: It violated Article 89, which stipulated that a referendum could be used only *after* each chamber of Parliament had passed the amendment bill by simple majority. (An alternative method of amendment, which obviates a referendum, requires a vote of three-fifths of the members of both houses sitting jointly.) After its advisory opinion had been ignored and the referendum had taken place, the Constitutional Council, impressed by the popular verdict in favor of the amendment, declared itself unable to judge on the issue.

For many years, the Constitutional Council was not expected to function as a checks-and-balances device in relation to the executive. Between 1958 and 1975, the council made 484 "decisions," which included 35 certifications of election and referenda results. During the same period, it examined the constitutionality of organic laws only 20 times, of Assembly regulations 22 times, of ordinary laws 11 times, and of international treaties only once. Since then, the council has become much more active, largely as a consequence of an amendment to the Constitution in 1974 that permitted the council to examine a bill's constitutionality (after parliamentary passage, but before signature by the president), not only on the request of the president, the premier, or the speakers of the two chambers, but also on the petition of 60 deputies or senators.[30] During the period from 1975 to 2002, the council made countless decisions (apart from more than 1,000 decisions on challenges to election results). It ruled on 75 organic laws, well over 250 ordinary pieces of legislation, and numerous regulations relating to laws, and it approved several pieces of legislation relating to international treaties.[31] In 2001 alone, the council examined 15 bills already voted on and promulgated (including 4 organic laws). Eleven of those had been referred to it by Parliament. Still, the council has practiced considerable judicial self-restraint, which must be attributed in part to the fact that it is given only one month to rule on a piece of legislation. More important, that self-restraint derives from the absence of a tradition of constitutional review (in the U.S. sense) as well as from the council's method of appointment. Of its nine members, who serve nine-year terms, three are chosen by the president, three by the speaker of the Assembly, and three by the speaker of the Senate.[32] Members of the Constitutional Council do not have to be lawyers; they may be higher civil servants, seasoned elected politicians, or academicians.[33]

Despite the proexecutive (and, until 1981, the pro-Gaullist or conservative) bias of many of its members, the Constitutional Council gradually widened the scope of its interpretations and came to be seen as the protector of the rights of citizens against the claims of the state. In 1971, the government introduced a bill that would infringe on the right to form associations (confirmed by statute in 1901) by permitting prefects to block the formation of groups whose aims were viewed as subversive. The bill was passed by the Assembly but rejected by the Senate; the Senate speaker (Alain Poher) referred the bill to the Constitutional Council, which declared it unconstitutional. In this landmark case, the council based its decision on the contention that the bill violated one of the rights of French citizens. This right was not explicitly stated in the body of the Constitution of 1958; the preamble of the Constitution, however, referred to the Declaration of the Rights of Man and of the Citizen of 1789, which contained a detailed catalogue of civil rights. In giving operational validity to the preamble, the council in effect "inserted" a bill of rights into the Constitution.

The Constitutional Council's preoccupation with civil liberties became more or less institutionalized after 1974, when members of Parliament began to take advantage of their ability to appeal to that body. Before the election of Mitterrand, the council took up 38 bills at the behest of parliamentarians, in most cases Socialist or Communist deputies. Although the council upheld the government on 24 bills, there was a spate of decisions that had the effect of enlarging or "creating" a catalogue of rights. In 1977, the council voided a government bill that would have allowed the police to search parked cars without securing a warrant, because such a search would contravene a constitutional provision (Art. 66) designed to protect against arbitrary detention. In 1979 and again in 1993, the council rejected as contrary to the right of asylum a government bill that would have restricted clandestine immigration. In 1980, it nullified a bill providing for special surveillance of foreign workers and parts of a bill that would have allowed them to be deported without judicial action, on the grounds that the bills violated the principle of equality before the law (Art. 2). In 1993, it voided part of a bill to increase the subsidies for private schools because it violated the principle of equality for public schools. The council also widened the powers of the Assembly by a series of rulings, from the mid-1960s through the 1970s, according to which Parliament's legislative competence was based, not only on Article 34 (which listed areas of ordinary legislation), but on other articles as well.[34] Furthermore, the council voided several finance bills for not following proper procedure.

Occasionally, the government may ask the council to judge on the constitutionality of a bill or treaty in order to depoliticize an issue. For example, in 1992, President Mitterrand referred the Treaty of European Union to the council after the government had signed it; the council's ruling that its provisions conflicted with the Constitution set in motion a process that resulted in a formal constitutional amendment (Art. 88).

This "quasi-judicial review" falls far short of the U.S. or German practice. Unlike the U.S. Supreme Court or the German Constitutional Court, the French Constitutional Council does not judge "cases and controversies" arising under a law already in the statute books; pending legislation can be referred to the council only by official agents of the state (i.e., the legislative or executive branch), not by private individuals (as in the German "constitutional complaint"); and the council cannot meet by its own volition (as in the American writ of certiorari).[35] Nonetheless, the council's *potential* as a genuine constitutional review mechanism and as a means of checking a reactionary or autocratic executive was valued by the Left in opposition. Conversely, it was condemned by the Gaullists and their allies, who regarded the council as "a supreme oligarchy, totally irresponsible."[36] But after the Socialists came to power, it was the turn of the right-of-center parties (especially in the Senate) to invoke the Constitutional Council against the Left on several occasions. Thus, at the end of 1981, the opposition appealed to the council in an effort to fight the government's nationalization policies. The effort was partly successful in that the council judged the indemnification payments to the private shareholders too low (hence, an unconstitutional deprivation of property) and forced the government to modify the legislation, thus delaying the implementation of nationalization. Early in 1982, the opposition used the council again, in order to fight against the decentralization policies, in particular a bill granting partial autonomy to the island of Corsica. In this instance, the council upheld the bill, interposing only minor procedural objections. In both cases, however, the government and its obedient Assembly majority complained that the council's activities amounted to an undemocratic "meddling" in the work of duly elected representatives of the sovereign people.[37] In 1990, the council nullified a section of a bill to increase the autonomy of Corsica; that section referred to "the Corsican people, a component of the French people." The council did so on the grounds that the Constitution refers to France as an "indivisible" republic.

After the resumption of parliamentary control by the Right in 1993, it was again the turn of the Left to look to the council for recourse. However, although there was an increasing acceptance of judicial review, the corresponding growth of judicial self-restraint led to a greater selectivity on the part of opposition parliamentarians in sending bills to the council. For example, only 9 of the 25 bills passed by the new majority in the spring of 1993 were sent to the council for review; of these, only one was declared unconstitutional, the others being subjected to partial invalidation or reserved interpretation.

The impartiality of the Constitutional Council has been questioned because of the "political" composition of its membership. Both the Right and the Left, when in power, have tried to "pack" the council with politically reliable people.[38] In any case, it is clear that the council has been equally active under left-wing and right-wing governments.[39] There is no doubt, however, that the Constitutional Council has taken root as a French institution and that its members have become more sure of themselves and more independent, a development that has been reflected in its increased pace of activities. The council would probably be even more active but for the fact that its very existence—and the probability of its intervention based on precedent—has produced a certain amount of legislative and executive self-restraint. For example, in the spring of 1993, the new conservative government, in its effort to curb illegal immigration, introduced a bill permitting the police to check the identity papers of suspicious-looking people; the government's acceptance of an amendment to that bill eliminating its racist features was no doubt due to the desire to avoid its submission to the council.[40]

When Parliament has succeeded in opposing or modifying government bills, it has done so less by resorting to the Constitutional Council than by utilizing external, non-juridical forces. This was the case in the "Anti-Breakers" bill of 1970 and the "Security and Liberty" bill of 1980. These bills, as finally passed—in the one case, providing for punishment of participants in an assemblage that results in disorder or damage to property, and in the other, making the sentencing for violent crimes more uniform—were less harsh than the original versions, as a result of modifications introduced by the Assembly. Behind the modifications of these bills, and of bills on agriculture, shopkeepers, and education, were the pressures exerted from outside of Parliament by interest groups.

QUESTIONS AND CENSURE MOTIONS

In conformity with French republican tradition and with Article 48 of the Constitution, members of Parliament have the right to ask questions of the government in written and oral form. Written questions may be addressed at any time to a minister, whose reply is also written (and published, together with the question, in the *Journal officiel*). Oral questions take place once a week.

During the first two decades of the Fifth Republic, doubts were expressed about the effectiveness of the question procedure. There were complaints that most written questions were not answered within the required time period (one month after submission); that ministers often delayed answering in order to blunt the immediacy of a particular problem; that they sometimes refused to respond at all; or that they delegated junior ministers to provide vague replies prepared by the ministry, on which the reader was unable to elaborate orally.[41]

Since the mid-1970s, the situation has improved. The number of written questions has increased dramatically, as has the number of written responses, and the oral exchanges have become somewhat more informal and more important. One hour each week (before the "ordinary" questions may be asked) has been devoted to "questions on current topics" *(questions d'actualité)*—half of them posed orally by majority deputies and half by the opposition—a practice that has resulted in somewhat more relaxed exchanges of views. Oral questions have become more frequent as a consequence of the constitutional amendment (to Article 48) of 1995, which stipulates that *at least* one meeting per week is to be reserved for questions by members of Parliament and responses by the government. This change has made it possible to have questions on Tuesdays as well as the customary Wednesdays in the Assembly.[42] The result has been impressive: During 1997–2002, the period of Jospin's premiership, members of the Assembly were able to ask 5,059 oral questions (see Table 7.3). Jospin answered 186 of them personally.[43]

In sum, however, the question period has not proved an effective means of controlling or embarrassing the government (despite the fact that the question period can now be shown on television). In the Fourth Republic, inadequate ministerial answers would often lead to an enlargement of the scope of "innocent" factual questions—that is, to a debate on the general policy of the government. The debate might be followed by an "interpellation," a vote on the question of confidence in the conduct of the government, and might lead to its resignation. Today, oral questions (which are still far outnumbered by written questions) are of two types: with debate and without debate. The number of questions with debate has been declining since the 1980s, because the debates following a question cannot culminate directly in a vote of censure (or "no confidence"); questions without debate have their limitations as well, because the deputy is confined to two minutes per question.[44]

Theoretically, distinct procedures are available to Parliament for ousting a government. Under Article 49, the Assembly may, on its own initiative, make a motion of censure (Sec. 2); alternatively, the premier may "provoke" a censure motion by pledging the responsibility of his government to a general policy or program (Sec. 1) or the text of a bill (Sec. 3)—that is, the bill will be considered adopted unless the Assembly produces a motion of censure within 24 hours after the government has pledged its responsibility. In either case, if the motion passes, the government must resign. But the procedure in the case of an Assembly-initiated censure motion is cumbersome: The motion must be cosigned by at least 10 percent of the members of the Assembly. The vote on the motion can occur only after a "cooling-off" period of 48 hours, and the motion must be adopted by an absolute majority of *all* members of the Assembly. Any deputy may cosponsor an Assembly-initiated censure motion only once during each parliamentary term.

Since the founding of the Fifth Republic, more than 40 censure motions have been introduced in the Assembly (motivated for the most part by discontent over policy in general or economic policy), but only one of them was successful or, to put it more accurately, *would* have been successful if the president had adhered to the Constitution. De Gaulle's unconstitutional procedure in connection with the change in the method of electing the president had provoked a storm of protest in both houses of Parliament; the Assembly, in 1962, produced more than the required absolute majority for censure of the government headed by Pompidou. However, instead of dismissing Pompidou, de Gaulle expressed his lack of confidence in the Assembly by dissolving it. After the parliamentary elections that followed, the Gaullists had an absolute majority in the Assembly, and Pompidou was appointed premier of a "new" government.

The "provocation" approach (Art. 49, Sec. 3) has been an effective tool of the executive. Between 1958 and 1996, the government engaged its responsibility more than 70 times, on each occasion successfully.[45] The fact that the article was used 39 times during the ninth legislature (1988–1993) alone can be explained easily: During this period, the government did not enjoy a disciplined majority that could be relied on to enact without difficulty bills considered important by the premier. Balladur also used the article during the tenth legislature; for although he had a solid majority that was confronted with too many amendments, especially to privatization and employment bills, introduced by Gaullist and Giscardist deputies. Juppé used the procedure several times, despite the fact that he had an overwhelming majority in the Assembly composed of two relatively disciplined parties. However, there was increasing criticism from their ranks (especially the UDF) of his domestic policies, a criticism often encouraged by the Assembly speaker himself. Nevertheless, the difficulty surrounding the formal process of censure has served to make the premier's position, both as a legislative initiator and as an "enforcer" of party discipline, somewhat more secure.[46] Between 1993 and 1997, the government engaged its responsibility on a legislative text three times; but during the period 1997–2002, Jospin chose not to use Article 49, Section 3, at all, preferring to hint that he would resign if certain bills were not adopted.

In sum, Article 49, Section 3, undoubtedly facilitates the legislative process, but as one scholar has observed, it "denies the Parliament its deliberative function and imposes silence where there should be discussion and decision."[47] In any case, the Parliament has thus far failed to oust a single premier (though the Assembly would no doubt have had the votes to do so if, in 1986, Mitterrand had appointed a Socialist premier). That failure has made it easier for governments to rule by decree or to make policy by simple declaration. The ineffectiveness of the censure procedure must be largely attributed to the fact that the opposition has lacked the necessary votes. Moreover, even opposition deputies can sometimes be dissuaded from voting for censure by possibilities of executive co-optation (i.e., the promise of favorable policy consideration or participation in future governments).[48]

THE INCOMPATIBILITY RULE

The position of government vis-à-vis Parliament has been strengthened by the "incompatibility" clause, Article 23 of the Constitution, which provides that no person may simultaneously hold a parliamentary mandate and a cabinet or other national government position. The clause was introduced, not to provide for separation of powers in the

U.S. sense, but to reduce the dependence of members of the government on Parliament. Such a dependence prevailed under the Fourth Republic: If a deputy had a reasonably good chance of getting a cabinet post in the event that a government was voted out and a reshuffling took place, then he might be tempted to hasten such a process by doing everything possible to embarrass the government and cause its resignation. If a government in which he served would, in turn, fall a few months later, the deputy would still retain his parliamentary seat. Nowadays, the political future of a deputy who becomes part of a newly constituted cabinet is more uncertain. If a cabinet minister offends the legislature, he risks little, in view of the difficulty of passing censure motions; if he loses the president's support and is ousted from the cabinet, he cannot automatically return to the legislative chamber from which he came.

The incompatibility clause has not prevented the government from recruiting many ministers from the Assembly. A deputy who is asked to join the government has a 15-day period in which to make up her mind. If she opts for a ministerial position, her alternate *(suppléant)* takes over her parliamentary mandate. The system whereby each candidate for an Assembly seat runs with an alternate, whose name also appears on the election ballot, precludes the necessity of frequent by-elections. A by-election must, of course, be held if a vacancy is created by the resignation or death of an incumbent alternate. Nothing prevents a deputy from having a prior understanding with the alternate that in case the deputy wishes to return to Parliament after a stint in the cabinet, the alternate will resign, thus forcing a by-election and (presumably) facilitating the parliamentary reentry of the deputy (though the evidence thus far does not provide many instances of such deals). About one-fourth of the more than 100 by-elections held so far under the Fifth Republic have taken place as a result of the resignation of the *suppléant*.[49]

The spirit, if not the letter, of Article 23 has been repeatedly violated. Many members of the cabinet have run for seats they have no intention of occupying. President de Gaulle himself encouraged his ministers to seek parliamentary seats, perhaps in order to enhance the image of a government consisting of members enjoying support in the country at large, or at least in important constituencies. But why do electors vote for a candidate for the Assembly if they have reason to believe that he or she will resign the seat right after the elections? The voters are aware of the weakness of Parliament; hence they would rather strengthen their bonds with a person who is closer to power—and who therefore can do much more for the constituency than a mere member of Parliament—and they may even hope that the deputy they elected will be "promoted" out of Parliament. That the transfer from Parliament to the cabinet has become a normal procedure in the Fifth Republic is demonstrated by the fact that between 1958 and 1967—the period of de Gaulle's unchallenged dominance, during which the reputation of parliamentarians was at an all-time low—73 cabinet ministers were recruited from among the membership of the National Assembly. So far, more than 500 deputies and senators have given up their parliamentary seats in order to accept ministerial appointments, many of them after having just been formally elected.

Whereas it has clearly become desirable for the president to use Parliament as a pool of competent ministers, the political risk to the deputy limits both the deputy and the president. To minimize that risk, the incompatibility rule is circumvented: The government may select several deputies or senators as "parliamentary delegates"

(parlementaires en mission [temporaire]), who are attached to ministries or who participate in interministerial committees but retain their parliamentary seats (thus becoming,
in effect, part-time ministers) provided that their "ministerial" service does not exceed
three months. In order to resolve the problem of incompatibility, the first Chirac government supported a constitutional amendment that would have permitted ministers to
resume their parliamentary seats automatically six months after relinquishing their cabinet posts. The amendment failed when (in 1974) it fell short of the necessary three-
fifths vote in a joint session of Parliament.[50] Since then, more than 80 parliamentarians
have served as *parlementaires en mission*.

THE ROLE OF THE DEPUTY

Members of Parliament have themselves been aware of the state of weakness to which
the Gaullist regime reduced them. Polls of Assembly deputies conducted in the past 20
years reveal that only a small proportion of legislators believed the role of Parliament to
be very important or even satisfactory, although as expected, members of the majority
party attached a greater significance to Parliament than did opposition party members.
In view of this negative institutional self-image, why do deputies choose their political
profession, and why has the number of candidates for election to the Assembly steadily
increased, in 2002 reaching 8,456—that is, an average of nearly 15 for each of the 577
constituencies.[51] One scholar has distinguished among four "typologies of motivation":
status (social prestige), program (influencing public policy), mission (giving meaning to
one's life), and obligation (the fulfillment of a moral duty to society).[52] (Curiously,
power or material payoffs are not listed among the motivations.) The "program" orientation was evident in the case of the Socialist deputies of the seventh legislature
(1981–1986), 193 of whom were elected for the first time. They brought with them a
youthful enthusiasm, a feeling of solidarity with a brand-new government, and a recognition that a great number of reforms were overdue and had to be enacted quickly. For
that reason, many of them were willing to be docile tools of Mitterrand's presidential
majority, cogs in a well-oiled parliamentary machine. After the Assembly elections of
1993, an equally impressive rejuvenation of the parliamentary contingent could be observed; and—at least at the beginning—there was a willingness among Gaullist and UDF
deputies to help Chirac and his government to achieve their policy goals. Among many
deputies, there continued to be a selfish element in their cooperation with the government: the hope of the ultimate reward of ministerial appointment.

Still, the "mission motivation" of French legislators must play a larger role than it
does in the case of U.S. legislators, because the payoff is more limited. Although the staff
of Palais Bourbon has been growing—in 2002 it comprised 4,177 people, of whom
1,300 were civil servants, 2,100 assistants to deputies, and 100 employed by the various
parliamentary parties[53]—French deputies do not have the large individual staffs and
salaries of their U.S. congressional counterparts and they enjoy fewer fringe benefits.
Their monthly net salary (in 2002, about $4,900—a sum calculated on the scale for se-
nior civil servants) is not particularly large. They receive additional allowances of about
$5,500 a month for housing and miscellaneous expenses; a reduction in telephone

rates; 40 first-class train tickets and a large number of free airline trips annually to their constituencies; and an allocation of about $6,500 monthly for assistants.[54] Yet many deputies are financially hard-pressed, for (in addition to having to give up part of their salary to their party) they must maintain two residences (and sometimes employ two secretaries) and entertain frequently.

Most deputies are not wealthy; in fact, in terms of their social and professional backgrounds, they do not differ greatly from the French bourgeoisie as a whole. The contingent of deputies elected to the National Assembly in the past 20 years has included a sizable number of public officials, many schoolteachers and university professors (especially among the Socialists), and a modest number of lawyers, physicians, pharmacists, and businesspeople. The number of farmers has been insignificant, as has the number of blue-collar workers (except, on occasion, for the Communists). In the Assembly elected in 2002, this occupational breakdown has been more or less continued (see Table 7.6). There has been equally little change with respect to gender (as pointed out in Chapter 2) or ethnic minority representation. In 1997 there was one deputy of sub-Saharan African origin, a Socialist, but in 2002, none.

Most deputies enjoy compensatory prestige and emoluments as active local politicians—mayors or departmental or regional councillors. This multiple-office holding (cumul des mandats), which has been traditional in France (and which was not affected by the incompatibility clause), has served the purpose of "connecting" a politician's national and local concerns.[55] It has also provided a modicum of job security to the deputy in case he or she loses the parliamentary seat, and it has compensated the deputy for a reduced status in a weakened Parliament.[56] Conversely, the weakness of Parliament has, in part, been abetted by the cumul insofar as it has contributed to the deputies' tendencies toward absenteeism.

The regulations providing for a reduction in the per diem pay of deputies for excessive absence have not reversed such tendencies, as these regulations are not consistently

TABLE 7.6
Professions of Members of the Twelfth Assembly, 2002

Farmers	18
Cadres and engineers	96
White-collar employees	29
Teachers	76
Owners/directors of business	55
Civil servants	100
Journalists	8
Liberal professions	115[a]
Miscellaneous	78
Workers	2

SOURCE: <http:www.assemblée-nat.fr/12 tribun/csp2asp>.
[a]Including 36 lawyers, 6 physicians, 8 dentists, 1 architect, and 8 pharmacists.

implemented.[57] An attempt was made a few years ago to counteract a vestige of the Fourth Republic—when an absent deputy could have his vote cast for him by proxy—by instituting a system of electronic voting. This led to a new practice, that of having colleagues press the buttons for absent deputies. That practice is officially banned, but it has continued nonetheless. In 1987, a group of deputies asked the Constitutional Council to nullify an Assembly vote that had involved proxy voting, on the grounds that it violated Article 27, which states that "the right [of a deputy] to vote is personal." The council refused to rule, arguing that the outcome of the vote would have been no different had the absent deputies been present. In 1991, Assembly Speaker Laurent Fabius on several occasions withheld per diem pay from deputies who voted by proxy, but he dropped the practice in the face of hostile reactions by many deputies.[58] In 1993, Philippe Séguin, newly elected as speaker, reintroduced the application of the *vote personnel*, but his success was limited. Several deputies, including members of his own party, accused the speaker of "galloping megalomania" and suggested that his approach discriminated against deputies from the provinces.[59] Except for censure motions or the government's pledging its confidence on a particular bill (where the roll call is used), the various other methods of voting in the Assembly—by raising of hands, rising and sitting, or secret ballot (as for the election of the speaker)—have had equally little impact on attendance.

Another measure intended to reduce absenteeism and to increase the attention span of deputies with respect to their parliamentary business was a bill passed at the end of 1985 to limit to *two* the number of elective offices that could be held at the same time.[60] The law became operational in 1987, but its effect has not been as dramatic as was hoped. Neither the decentralization measures (giving local communities and regions much greater power) nor the enhanced ambitions of Parliament have brought about a sufficient disjunction of a deputy's position from that of a mayor; in fact, in the mid-1990s, at least 90 percent of Assembly deputies continued to hold an elective local mandate, most often that of mayor (see Chapter 8).[61] Thus, 202 of the 577 deputies elected in 1993 were (and continued to be) mayors, 14 were members of regional councils, and 24 were members of general (departmental) councils. This pattern continued in the eleventh legislature, elected in 1997, where one out of every four deputies was (simultaneously) head of a regional assembly or a general (departmental) council or mayor of a city of more than 20,000 inhabitants.[62] In the interest of lengthening the attention span of deputies, proposals have been advanced—initially by Socialists but subsequently by right-wing party leaders as well—to limit the *cumul* even more than had been done by the 1985 law, specifically, to bar a deputy from continuing to be mayor of a sizable city or executive of any regional or departmental legislature.

The absenteeism of deputies is also a reflection of their sense of frustration. That condition is due largely to the deputies' own awareness of the streamlined nature of the legislative process; but it is also due to the recognition that Parliament must contend with rival arenas of deliberation and decision. Among these rivals are the "committees of experts" (*comités de sages*), which, paradoxically, have proliferated in recent years—when the executive has been expressing a willingness to give Parliament an enlarged role. These committees, which may be compared to the royal commissions in Britain or Sweden, are appointed by the cabinet; they are composed of nonparliamentarians such as academicians, higher civil servants, independent lawyers, and members of other professions.[63] The committees conduct lengthy hearings, taking testimony from representatives of interest groups and from individual experts. When the committees are finished with their investigations, they submit a report (often quite detailed) with policy recommendations to the appropriate minister, who then submits it to the whole cabinet. On the positive side, these committees can be viewed as able to gather information from a variety of sources in an unhurried manner, free from partisan pressures. But they can also be seen as attempts to depoliticize a delicate public issue, that is, as a means of buck-passing used by the government (and tolerated by Parliament). Under the presidency of Mitterrand, "committees of experts" were appointed for (among other problems) university reform, ethics in government, AIDS, the cultures of ethnic minorities, the rehabilitation of slums, nationality and naturalization, social security, and the construction of a new national library; and since Chirac has been president, such committees have been set up to deal with the funding of private schools, the reform of the tax system, and changes in criminal investigation procedures.[64] It should be noted, however, that the prime minister does not necessarily adopt the recommendations of a *comité de sages*, especially if they do not agree with his or her own ideas.[65]

The weakening of Parliament, particularly of the power of individual deputies, was not entirely a Gaullist invention. As we have seen, Parliament's immobility in the Fourth Republic had provoked measures to streamline the legislative process. These measures were sufficient neither to save the Fourth Republic nor to satisfy the growing number of French citizens who criticized, and wished to reduce, the role of Parliament. Among these critics were not only adherents of the (Gaullist and non-Gaullist) Right, but also liberal Anglophiles who envied the tight management of the House of Commons and certain leftists who (although as a matter of principle or tactics, wished to have *no* effective decision-making institution) criticized Parliament's failure to resolve urgent problems. Even a number of politicians most strongly identified with traditional parliamentary government occasionally voiced doubts about a strong, uncontrolled legislature. For example, Mendès-France, the Radical leader of the Fourth Republic, argued that Parliament could not function alone and ought to be aided by a specialized, quasi-corporative chamber (representing, not geographic units, but economic and professional groups).[66] It could even be said that those who were skeptical about the dominant role of Parliament spoke for the majority of the French. In the past 100 years, French citizens often voted for opposition parties that were undemocratic or whose commitment to parliamentary government was questionable or parties that could not (for lack of discipline) effectively transform Parliament into an instrument of government. On occasion, the people voted for a charismatic leadership that was antiparliamentary, or they participated in periodic "happenings" (e.g., mass demonstrations or strikes) that were intended to supplement the decision-making work of Parliament.

The negative views of Parliament evinced by politicians in the past have been reflected by the general public in somewhat ambivalent fashion. According to a poll conducted in 1972, 59 percent of French respondents thought Parliament should determine basic policies, while 27 percent thought the president should.[67] According to an earlier poll (1969), 52 percent found Parliament useful, as against only 15 percent who did not.[68] Over the years, the public confidence in Parliament improved concurrently with the growing consensus about Fifth Republic institutions; in a poll taken in mid-1989, 68 percent said that the National Assembly played a useful role (against 24 percent who disagreed and 8 percent who had no opinion).[69] Among specific political institutions or positions, that of the deputy has engendered relatively low confidence. According to another poll in which respondents were asked what profession they would choose if they were to do so at that point, 32 percent wanted to be heads of enterprises; 24 percent, physicians; 9 percent, lawyers; and only 4 percent, deputies.[70] According to an opinion survey conducted in 2000 about the degree of corruption among various occupational categories, members of Parliament took first place.[71] The growing incidence of misbehavior on the part of legislators explains, in part, the amendment of the Constitution (Art. 26) in August 1995 that facilitates the lifting of their parliamentary immunity by the *bureau* of the chamber to which they belong.

Many French citizens who vote for a deputy doubt not only the latter's efficacy as a legislator but also his or her ability to intervene on behalf of the constituency with the higher civil service. The reputation for relative powerlessness of deputies may be attributed to the appropriation of legislative functions by the executive, as well as to the fact that many political debates have been "delocalized" from the national to the supranational and infranational levels—to the Commission of the European Union (for instance, on agricultural legislation) and, since the decentralization laws of 1982, to municipalities and regional councils.[72] But there is a paradox: The negative image citizens have of deputies as a categoric group does not necessarily apply to "their" deputy, whom they may know personally as mayor.[73]

The negative view of the importance of the French deputy is not endorsed by all political scientists. Some would argue that deputies today have nearly as much opportunity to participate meaningfully in debate as they had in previous republics, particularly on domestic issues; others suggest that Article 34, which enumerates the areas of parliamentary jurisdiction, has not taken any powers away from Parliament that it possessed previously. They assert that as many important bills are passed by the Assembly today as were passed during the Third Republic.[74] However, although deputies are now accorded less time for debate than in the past, they *need* less time because the new system has obviated onerous and fruitless debates on government competence. Because parliamentary investiture of newly constituted governments is no longer required, there is no call for a discussion of their merits. Moreover, owing to the consolidation of parliamentary parties and the diminished importance of ideology, there is less scope for long-winded oratory about matters of principle.

One should not equate the formal weakness of Parliament with lack of participation in decisions. Many government bills, especially since the early 1970s, have been subjected to important changes by deputies. The role of the Assembly has continued to grow: The number of private members' bills has steadily increased; and many government bills have been successfully amended in committee. Government bills on farm prices, social security, and educational reforms have been extensively modified during the parliamentary process; the penal reform bill of 1980 was subjected (in both chambers) to numerous alterations; and the land transfer and inheritance tax bill of 1976 was virtually "gutted" in Parliament. Statistically, the success rate of deputies' amendments (introduced in the plenary session) to government bills between 1970 and 1977 was impressive, ranging from 27 percent for amendments introduced by Gaullists to 5 percent for those introduced by Communists. The rate was equally good between 1986 and 1988, when 24 percent of the more than 9,000 amendments introduced in the Assembly that were of parliamentary origin were adopted.[75] The ninth legislature (1988–1993) was particularly active. It passed 455 bills (60 of parliamentary origin) and several thousand regulations connected with the European Community and voted on 18 motions of censure. It made significant contributions to legislation concerning immigration, environment, education, minimum wages, and the reform of the penal code.

Many bills have been successfully amended in committee; others have been subjected to changes by the government itself in response to *informal* suggestions by deputies, who in turn sometimes responded to the external pressures of interest groups.[76] This increased involvement has not necessarily improved the quality of the laws; it has, however, resulted in the growth of the average size of bills (from 93 lines in 1950 to 220 lines in 1990) and of the bulk of the *Journal officiel* (from 7,070 pages in 1976 to more than 17,000 pages in the mid-1990s).

Much of the success of deputies in the legislative process depends on the goodwill of the executive: Many of the private members' bills or amendments have made it through the legislative process because they have been accepted (and occasionally even encouraged) by the government, especially if they have dealt with such politically innocuous topics as the limitation of imports of household pets, the medical coverage of domestics, and so on. Occasionally, private members' bills are of greater importance, and the government endorses them because opposing them might be embarrassing.[77] Most often, however, the deputy's role seems to be that of processing requests from local constituents to the government. The "pork barrel" concerns of the deputy have been to some extent forced on him by the single-member-district system of elections, under which he tends, in Anglo-American fashion, to be the victor in a local popularity contest. He continues to justify his popularity, and assures his future reelection, by securing the help of the national government in solving local problems. But in order to do this, he must cooperate with the government and not alienate it by being a parliamentary troublemaker. This explains why some opposition deputies whose parties have no realistic prospects of assuming control over the Assembly or blocking the majority steamroller break ranks and vote for certain government bills.[78]

Parliament was impotent in the first decade of the Fifth Republic because until 1969, the chief of state was General de Gaulle, who regarded himself (and was regarded) as an institution eclipsing all others and who reinforced the special legitimacy of his position by periodic popular mandates, and also because there was usually a cooperative majority of Gaullists in the Assembly. After the collapse of that majority in 1973 and its replacement by more-disparate "presidential majorities" (except for the cohabitation interludes), a number of Assembly speakers—of whom two (Chaban-Delmas and Fabius) had once served as premiers[79]—have demanded "structural changes" that would enhance the role of legislators, and a succession of premiers, particularly at the beginning of their terms of office, have avowed their intention to support such demands. Perhaps they did so for the sake of public relations or to ensure that their government programs would receive a resoundingly affirmative vote. But lest the premiers create illusions among deputies—and irritate the president of the Republic—they have accompanied their promises to Parliament with the reminder that the executive (during cohabitation, the premier) remains the chief decision maker.

The inauguration of Giscard d'Estaing in 1974 had raised new hope that Parliament would be called on to participate in legislative activity more meaningfully than under the first two presidents. The blatant violations of the Constitution in regard to Parliament that had occurred under de Gaulle were not repeated under Giscard.[80] On the contrary, the restricted options available in an economy beset by difficulties had rendered many policy initiatives politically risky and tempted Giscard to share the onus with Parliament. Indeed, between mid-1974 and the end of 1975, the formal input of the legislature on important government bills—divorce, abortion, budget, education, and employment in the public sector—was significant. However, this burst of activity did not transform the deputies into genuine co-decision makers, particularly on financial matters. Moreover, it was short-lived, for by the end of 1978, the government increasingly ignored Parliament. Although nearly half the hours of discussion in both chambers were devoted to an examination of the budget, one deputy (a Communist), complained in the mid-1970s that "the budget [still] leaves the Assembly in practically the same condition in which it entered"; and even the Assembly speaker admitted that Parliament did little more than perform an "autopsy" on the budget.[81]

When in opposition, the Socialist party repeatedly complained about the contempt shown for Parliament by Gaullist and conservative presidents and premiers; the party's platforms called for an enlarged role for that institution, and Mitterrand advocated such a role both before and after his election to the presidency. One measure of that enlarged role has been the growth of the operating budget for both chambers. However, the newly elected and Socialist-dominated Assembly that met in 1981 was held to a very tight schedule by a government determined to see a speedy enactment of legislation it considered urgent. The government allocated only three days for debate on a bill concerning administrative decentralization. The government may have resorted to this "railroading" tactic because of its inexperience or because decentralization was a "hot" topic on which Parliament (especially the Senate) had dragged its feet some years earlier. In any case, several Socialist deputies, although approving the substance of the bill, voted against it because of their resentment of the procedures used.

For many years, much of the submissive behavior of the majority deputies could be attributed to their belonging to a disciplined party that had been elected on the presidential coattails; in addition, there was the psychological impact of the bipolar situation: If deputies did not support their party, they gave aid and comfort to the other side. But gradually this bipolar situation changed because of the existence of factions within each party, the transpartisan interest-group connections of individual deputies, and the support groups *(amicales)* containing both majority and opposition deputies favoring specific causes. In 1988, bipolarity was modified by the fact that many deputies did not owe their Assembly election to the presidential coattails; lacking an absolute Socialist majority, Premier Rocard had to construct ad hoc majorities for different policy issues by depending on the supplementary votes of Centrists, Communists, and occasionally even Gaullists.[82] In 1993, although the Right achieved a decisive victory in the parliamentary elections, its Assembly majority remained fragile, given the conflicts between and within the RPR and the UDF.

Such fragility, which characterized the Left and the Right during cohabitation periods, gave deputies more freedom to express themselves, especially since during the past two decades, the number of hours devoted annually to plenary sessions in the Assembly has nearly doubled. However, the government retains tight control of the calendar; and in a situation in which deputies are given five or six working days for examining a score of government bills (and sometimes only three days during special sessions) and opposition deputies are allowed two minutes each for a discussion of farmers' benefits, the problems of artisans, or overall economic policy, the Parliament cannot make the most informed contributions.

The election of former premier Laurent Fabius as speaker of the Assembly in 1988 was a promising sign for that chamber. Under his leadership, the Assembly's national and international prestige and its general atmosphere improved, and it became the destination of visits by prominent personalities. In addition to this "politics of reception,"[83] Fabius suggested other innovations, among them (besides the abortive attempt to eliminate proxy voting) the right of the speaker to call a meeting of a standing committee during periods when the Assembly was not in session.

The speaker of the tenth legislature (1993–1997), Philippe Séguin, reiterated the demand for interim sessions of standing committees. He also continued the "politics of reception" by (unsuccessfully) inviting British Prime Minister John Major to the National Assembly, subsequently (and successfully) inviting King Juan Carlos of Spain to address the plenum of that chamber,[84] and, as if to snub the Foreign Office, notifying President Mitterrand of the visit before notifying the foreign minister. (For his part, René Monory, the speaker of the Senate, had earlier invited German Chancellor Helmut Kohl to *his* chamber). In addition, Séguin took up the demand, first made by Fabius, to lengthen ordinary parliamentary sessions from five and a half to nine months. He also called for the automatic meeting of a special standing committee of the Assembly during periods when the full Parliament was not in session. Such a committee, composed of members of various parties, would be able to call on ministers to answer questions on current topics. (Fabius had proposed such a standing committee, but one that could be convoked only at the president's request.) By the end of the eleventh legislature, such a committee has not been established.

Among other concrete measures announced by Séguin were the following: (1) the right of chairpersons of standing committees to demand the appearance of ministers to defend specific provisions of government bills; (2) the requirement that the text of bills to be debated in plenary session be the amended version that had been adopted by the *standing committees* rather than the original text submitted by the government;[85] and (3) the rebroadcasting of parliamentary debates on television. There is no doubt that the efficiency of Parliament has improved in the past several years and is likely to improve even further, both as a consequence of Séguin's prodding and in response to the Treaty of European Union, which stipulates the specific involvement of the Parliament in future adaptations to European legislation.

Premier Balladur expressed himself in favor of strengthening the decision-making role of Parliament, but he envisaged such efforts as part of a package of constitutional

reforms, some of which had been suggested by the president and a blue-ribbon committee on the subject.[86] He repeatedly assured the deputies that he wanted a continuing dialogue with them and eagerly looked forward to private members' bills on social policy
matters. Both President Chirac and Premier Juppé echoed such assurances; but the
meaning of these assurances was unclear, because Séguin used the office of speaker to
demarcate his policy preferences from those of the premier in an attempt to transform
the Assembly into a counterpower to the executive.[87]

Under Laurent Fabius, who regained the speakership of the Assembly in June 1997,
efforts at upgrading that chamber's involvement in decision making continued. The
number of hours of plenary meetings was increased, as was the number of bills and
amendments introduced in the chamber. In 1997 alone, a third of the texts voted on in
the Assembly were sponsored by deputies rather than the government.[88] Under Raymond Forni, who succeeded Fabius as speaker in 2000, the Assembly achieved a significant degree of independence, if only because the divisions within the pluralist Left made
it increasingly difficult for Premier Jospin to secure coherent parliamentary support for
his policies, many of which the Communists and the Greens opposed for ideological
reasons.

It is doubtful whether the Assembly elected in 2002 will assert itself meaningfully.
The speaker, Jean-Louis Debré, is a committed Gaullist and friend of the president's; the
opposition, with less than 30 percent of the seats, is divided and hopelessly underrepresented; and the presidential majority is likely to be too disciplined, and too realistic, to
go against the wishes of the president.

NOTES

1. On the French tradition of antiparliamentarism, see Philippe Lavaux, "Récurrences et paradoxes:
   Une Histoire contrapuntique," *Pouvoirs*, no. 64 (February 1993), 5–22.
2. See André Soury, *L'Envers de l'hémicycle*, 3d ed. (Paris: L'Harmattan, 1995). In this highly personal account, the author, a former Communist deputy, admits that the deputies address one another in familiar terms (*se tutoyer*) but hardly ever socialize with members of other parties.
3. Daniel Garrigue, ed., *Le Député aujourd'hui*, Collection Connaissance de l'Assemblée, no. 6 (Paris: Assemblée Nationale, 1992), pp. 114–17. "Mail" may now include E-mail. The expansion of the high-
   speed-train network has made the departure of deputies from their constituencies to Paris early Tuesday morning much easier.
4. As shown in Table 7.1, the number of Assembly members has varied over the years, depending on
   the nature of the electoral system and the splitting up of constituencies.
5. They include secretaries, stenographers, word-processor personnel, drivers, supply agents, guards,
   and so forth, to whom the rules for the ordinary civil service do not apply. They are politically neutral, though many of them are unionized (for the most part in the CFDT). See Jacques Klein, "Une
   Carrière administrative peu connue: Le Fonctionnaire parlementaire," *Revue administrative* 33:194
   (March–April 1980), 131–38; and *Le Monde*, 14 July 1989. For an overall treatment, see Pierre
   Servent, *Le Travail parlementaire sous la Ve République* (Paris: Montchrestien, 1995).
6. Thus, in 1981, Socialist deputies belonging to the Mitterrand faction got the chairs of the finance and
   defense committees; an adherent of the Mauroy faction became chief *rapporteur* for the budget; the
   chair of the committee for cultural and social affairs was given to a supporter of Rocard, and that of the
   committee on laws to a member of CERES. A Left Radical, ally of the Socialists, got the chair of the foreign affairs committee, and a Communist, that of production. Furthermore, the division of chairs
   aimed at a regional and generational balance. In the Assembly elected in 1997, internal factionalism

was much less significant than it had been before: The majority of newly elected PS deputies did not have much use for the system of various factions within the party. Nevertheless, the party as such predominated in the assignment of committee chairs. Thus five of the six committee chairs were given to Socialists (three of them to the Fabius faction), one to a Communist, and none to the smaller leftist parties, which prompted the leaders of those parties to allude to the partisan "imperialism" of the PS leadership. After the victory of the Right in the parliamentary elections of 2002, Balladur was given the chair of the committee on foreign affairs, in compensation for his failure to get the Assembly speakership (for which he had competed with Chirac's friend Jean-Louis Debré).

7. However, deputies who belong to a *groupe parlementaire* pay a certain price: Not only are they subject to party discipline (although this is less strict in some parties [e.g., the UDF] than in others [e.g., the PCF]), but they must also give up part of their salaries to their *groupe parlementaire* or to the party as a whole.

8. Christian Goux, "Le Rôle du Parlement: Comment contrôler l'argent public?" *Après-Demain*, no. 379 (December 1995), 24–26.

9. The politician, Jean de Broglie, had been murdered in 1977. It was alleged that Michel Poniatowski, a former interior minister and (like the victim) a friend of Giscard's, had covered up the matter.

10. In 1995 there were 15 requests for special committees, but only 2 were accepted. Guy Carcassonne, "L'Indicateur démocratique," *Le Point*, 12 October 1996, p. 16.

11. Between 1960 and 1997, more than 45 investigation or control committees were set up in the Assembly, and more than 35 in the Senate. See Bernard Chantebout, ed., *Le Contrôle parlementaire*, Documents d'études, no. 1.14 (Paris: Documentation Française, 1998), pp. 8–16.

12. Virginie Malingre, "Les Députés affirment leur pouvoir d'investigation dans le contrôle des dépenses publiques," *Le Monde*, 9 July 1999.

13. Ariane Chemin and Clarisse Fabre, "Lionel Jospin utilise l'Assemblée comme tremplin vers l'Elysée," *Le Monde*, 21 February 2002.

14. See Jean-Pierre Marichy, *La Deuxième Chambre dans la vie politique française* (Paris: LGDJ, 1970); Jean Mastias, *Le Sénat de la Ve République: Réforme et Renouveau* (Paris: Economica, 1980), for a discussion of that body's legislative and control functions; and Didier Maus, "Le Sénat, l'Assemblée nationale et le Gouvernement," *Pouvoirs*, no. 44 (1988). Also see the highly detailed, though somewhat formalistic, *Le Sénat* (Paris: Documentation Française, 1993), preface by René Monory.

15. In 1988, Poher was reelected (at the age of 80) to the speakership, an office to which both Charles Pasqua and Jean Lecanuet aspired but that was finally (in 1993) won by René Monory, a prominent centrist (and UDF politician).

16. *Le Monde*, 11 July 1989. The Senate's continued reputation as a relatively relaxed body explains why Michel Charasse decided in 1992 to quit as minister of the budget (a role that, in his opinion, required too much work) and renew his political career in that chamber.

17. Specifically, in 1969 only 1 government bill was introduced in the Senate, and in 1975 (the high point), 59 bills.

18. Of course the Senate approved; but it is not clear what, if any, effect a disapproval would have had on the legitimacy and continuation of the government, since the Constitution (Art. 49) makes no provision for a vote of censure by that chamber.

19. The expression of Olivier Duhamel, "The Fifth Republic Under François Mitterrand," in George Ross et al., eds., *The Mitterrand Experiment* (New York: Oxford University Press, 1987), p. 152.

20. Between 2000 and 2002, about 40 bills were adopted as a result of shuttles between the two chambers.

21. Didier Maus, *Les Grands Textes de la pratique institutionnelle de la Ve République*, Notes et Études Documentaires, no. 4864 (Paris: Documentation Française, 1988), p. 162. Note that 20 of the bills thus overridden were subsequently voided by the Constitutional Council.

22. See Marie-France Verdier, "La IIIe Cohabitation ou le retour aux sources du Sénat?" *Revue politique et parlementaire*, no. 997 (November–December 1998), 74–88.

23. Most of the government bill on Corsica was passed by the Assembly, but at the end of 2001 it was saddled with so many amendments by the Senate that the bill was in effect undermined.

24. Jean-Jack Queyranne, "La Réforme ne peut s'arrêter aux portes du Sénat," *Le Monde*, 13 April 2002.

25. Forty-three special sessions were called by the premier, one was convoked automatically in connection with the use of emergency powers (Art. 16), and three met on the election of a new Assembly after dissolution of the old one. One special session was convoked at the behest of the president in

June 1992 when he decided that the amendment of the Constitution (made necessary by the [Maastricht] Treaty on European Union) should be ratified by joint session of Parliament rather than by referendum. A special session convoked (June–July 1992) by the deputies dealt with minimum wages.

26. Christian Bigaut, "La Révision constitutionnelle du 4 août 1995," *Regards sur l'actualité*, no. 214 (September–October 1995), 3–15.

27. Note that once (in 1980) the Assembly actually *rejected* a blocked-vote government bill that would have provided increased subsidies to families with numerous children, when the Gaullists broke majority discipline and voted together with the Socialists against the bill. Although the Gaullists claimed to favor the substance of the bill, they did not like the blocked-vote procedure invoked for it. The Communists, although objecting to the procedure, voted for the measure because of its socially progressive content.

28. The Chirac government of 1986–1988 used the blocked vote 36 times in the Assembly and 32 times in the Senate.

29. According to one estimate, 1 piece of legislation produces an average of 10 regulations, and the 8,000 laws under which France is governed are complemented by 100,000 decrees. These include numerous European Union directives. Christian Bigaud, "Parlement: Les Offices d'évaluation de la législation et des politiques publiques," *Regards sur l'actualité*, no. 224 (September–October 1996), 27–34.

30. As part of the amendment bill, the government had proposed that the council be permitted to examine cases on its own initiative *(auto-saisine)* if its members felt that bills (or laws) violated public liberties. But that part of the amendment was withdrawn when the Assembly opposed it on the grounds that it would result in a "government of judges" and undermine the powers of Parliament even further. See François Luchaire, *Le Conseil constitutionnel* (Paris: Economica, 1980), p. 30. On *auto-saisine*, see also *Le Monde*, 6 September 1986, pp. 10–11. For an exhaustive analysis of judicial policy making, see Alec Stone, *The Birth of Judicial Politics in France: The Constitutional Council in Comparative Perspective* (New York: Oxford University Press, 1992).

31. Louis Favoreu and Loïc Philip, "La Jurisprudence du conseil constitutionnel," *Revue du droit public* 91 (January–February 1975), 165–200; and Didier Maus, *Les Grands Textes de la pratique institutionnelle de la Ve République* (Paris: Documentation Française, 1995), passim. Updated from <www.conseil-constitutionnel.fr/tableau/tabdc.htm>.

32. In addition to the nine appointed members, former presidents of the (Fourth and Fifth) Republic are ex-officio members of the Constitutional Council. However, only Vincent Auriol (a Fourth Republic president) participated in council sessions (regularly until 1960 and once in 1962), the other ex-presidents (René Coty and all the Fifth Republic presidents) choosing not to do so. For a discussion of judicial self-restraint and the "autolimitation" effect, especially under the Socialist government of 1981–1986, see John T. S. Keeler and Alec Stone, "Judicial Political Confrontation in Mitterrand's France," in George Ross, Stanley Hoffman, and Sylvia Malzacher, eds., *The Mitterrand Experiment* (New York: Oxford University Press, 1987), pp. 161–81.

33. The most recent appointee (chosen by the Senate in 2001) is Dominique Schnapper, a prominent sociologist (who replaced Alain Lancelot, a political scientist). Schnapper has a pronounced "Jacobin" view of nation and state, and her view is likely to influence the council's action regarding Corsican autonomy and the question of minority languages.

34. Including various articles (72–74, and 76) that related to the administration of overseas departments. For the full text of 46 decisions from 1958 to 1991, see Louis Favoreu and Loïc Philip, *Les Grandes Décisions du Conseil constitutionnel*, 6th ed. (Paris: Sirey, 1991).

35. In 1989, Mitterrand came out in favor of a constitutional amendment that would permit ordinary citizens to appeal to the Constitutional Council, an idea that has since been supported by other politicians of both the Left and the Right. Meanwhile, one innovation has already taken place: In January 1996, the council departed from its tradition of admitting only written arguments by permitting the personal appearance of an applicant (and his lawyers) in the case of a contested senatorial election. See Guy Carcassonne, "La Voie de l'oral," *Le Point*, 27 January 1996, p. 20.

36. René Lacharrière, "Opinion dissidente," *Pouvoirs*, no. 13 (1980), 133–50.

37. Cf. Loïc Philip, who points out (in "La Loi et les principes," *Le Monde*, 17 December 1981) that *no* French government that has happened to control the legislative process has been enthusiastic about the idea of constitutional supremacy.

38. Early in 1986, anticipating a Socialist defeat in the forthcoming Assembly elections, Mitterrand appointed Robert Badinter, his minister of justice, to the presidency of the Constitutional Council. However, Badinter's decisions did not always favor the Socialist position.

39. The average number of signatures for each submission of a case to the Constitutional Council has been 80—far more than the 60 required. Note that between 1974 and 1994, 15 percent of all bills (other than those authorizing ratification of treaties) were submitted to the council by members of Parliament.

40. See Philippe Bernard and Erich Inciyan, "Délit de faciès," *Le Monde*, 22 June 1993. Nevertheless, the council declared the amended bill unconstitutional, holding it "incompatible with respect to individual liberty." See *Le Monde*, 7 August 1993.

41. Cf. Philip Williams, *The French Parliament* (New York: Praeger, 1968), pp. 19, 46–51; *Le Monde*, 9–10 February 1975; and Michel Ameller, *Les Questions instruments du contrôle parlementaire* (Paris: LGDJ, 1964), pp. 80–81.

42. In the Senate, the customary day for questions has been Thursday. Typical Tuesday questions posed in the Assembly in 1996 related to the consequences of the abolition of the draft; bank credits; problems in Corsica; the operation of employment services; hunting legislation; human rights in Russia; privatization policies, and so forth. See *Bulletin de l'Assemblée Nationale*, Xe législature, no. 79 (28 February 1996), 21–27.

43. Chemin and Fabre, "Lionel Jospin utilise l'Assemblée."

44. Senators have five minutes per question. In each chamber, the questioner has the right of rebuttal to a minister's response.

45. Data are from Jean-Louis Quermonne and Dominique Chagnollaud, *Le Gouvernement de la France*, 4th ed. (Paris: Dalloz, 1991), pp. 707–09. On some bills, the government engaged its responsibility more than once, that is, during several readings. On more than a dozen occasions, the "engagements" were not even followed by censure motions.

46. Cécile Chambraud, "Alain Juppé veut obliger l'UDF à lui confirmer son soutien," *Le Monde*, 26 September 1996, p. 6; and Caroline Monnot and Jean-Baptiste de Montvalon, "Alain Juppé tente de passer la bride à la majorité parlementaire," *Le Monde*, 1 October 1996, p. 8.

47. Joël Boudant, "La Crise identitaire du Parlement français," *Revue du droit public*, September–October 1992, pp. 1322–402.

48. In 1972, the "moderate" Radicals, led by Jean-Jacques Servan-Schreiber, did not support a censure motion, because they anticipated continued Gaullist control of the Assembly after the 1973 Assembly elections, and they wished to keep the door open to the UDR in the hope of being asked to join a postelection coalition. Between 1984 and 1986, and again in 1988, the Communists refrained from supporting the Gaullists and their allies in censure motions against Socialist governments despite growing disagreements with these governments over economic policy.

49. The following former ministers, for example, reentered the Assembly upon the resignation of their *suppléants*: Edgar Faure in 1969, Pierre Messmer in 1974, and Jacques Chirac in 1976. *Suppléants* who replace deputies who have become ministers may not be candidates against them in the next regular election. However, they may be candidates for the Senate; between 1980 and 1995, in fact, 98 "replacers" subsequently became Senators.

50. On this occasion, most of the deputies who had entered the Assembly as *suppléants* understandably voted with the opposition and signed a statement refusing to resign and thus bring about a by-election. Georges Morin, "L'Impossible Réforme du statut des suppléants parlementaires," *Revue du droit public* 95:6 (November–December 1979), 1559–90.

51. In 1993, there were 5,167 candidates for the 555 legislative constituencies in metropolitan France, an average of 9.3 candidates for each constituency. This compares to 8.3 in 1986 and 5 in 1988. In Paris alone there was an average of 13 candidates for each constituency in 1993.

52. Oliver H. Woshinsky, *The French Deputy* (Lexington, MA: Lexington Books, 1973), esp. chap. 1. The author's findings: 38 percent, mission motivated; 28 percent, program; 20 percent, status; 14 percent, obligation. The interview responses about the *effect* of deputies on public policy are inconclusive.

53. Total budget of the Assembly was 466 million euros in 2002. See Christine Ducros, "L'Assemblée Nationale, une 'usine' qui ne dort jamais," *Le Figaro Entreprises*, 27 May 2002, p. 11.

54. See Christoph Candelier, "Le Salaire d'un député," *Le Point*, 5 July 1997, p. 15; updated in *Le Figaro Entreprises*, 27 May 2002, p. 11.

55. On the background and effects of *cumul*, see Jean-Philippe Colson, ed., *Le Cumul des mandats et des fonctions* (Paris: Documentation Française, 1999). See also J. Becquart Leclerq, "Multiple Office-holding in Local and National Elective Positions," *Tocqueville Review* 9 (1987–1988), 221–41; and Stéphane Dion, "Le Cumul des mandats en France," *French Politics and Society* 13:3 (1992), 99–126.

56. Support for this argument may be the fact that in the Fourth Republic (when Parliament was relatively powerful) only 36 percent of the deputies had one or more local mandates, whereas in the Fifth Republic, the proportion has averaged between 65 percent and 95 percent. See Guy Carcassonne, "Cumul des mandats: L'Anachronisme," *Le Point*, 6 February 1993, p. 36.

57. According to a complicated formula (based on an ordinance issued in December 1958), a deputy loses one-third of his allowance for being absent during more than one-third of the meetings, and one-half of his allowance for being absent half of the time.

58. In effect, Fabius compromised by accepting the rule that voting in person would be mandated only for bills considered important by all the parliamentary parties.

59. Pascale Robert-David, "Philippe Séguin persiste et signe," *Le Monde*, 6 October 1993. See also "Fronde contre Philippe Séguin," *Le Monde*, 30 September 1993. For an overall analysis of Séguin's role, see Muriel de l'Écotais, "Les Innovations de Philippe Séguin, président de l'Assemblée Nationale," *Pouvoirs*, no. 74 (1995), 169ff.

60. The anti-*cumul* law provides that politicians may hold no more than two of the following positions simultaneously: deputy or senator; member of the European Parliament; regional councillor; general (departmental) councillor; member of a Paris municipal council; mayor of a town of more than 20,000 inhabitants; deputy mayor of a city of more than 100,000. The anti-*cumul* law does not affect important nonelective positions; a deputy might continue to be an important party official, a member of a (transpartisan or nonpartisan) "friendship society" (*groupe d'amitiés*), or a member of the executive of a professional association.

61. This is also true of cabinet ministers. Thus Juppé, shortly after becoming premier, became mayor of Bordeaux. In most cases, the 1985 law induced deputies to relinquish the least important elective offices. For example, Giscard, having been reelected to the National Assembly in 1993, decided to resign as a member of the European Parliament, while retaining his positions as president of the regional council of Auvergne and president of the UDF. See Pierre Bitoun, *Voyage au pays de la démocratie moribonde* (Paris: Albin Michel, 1995), p. 49.

62. More specifically, 18 were presidents of general councils; 6, presidents of regional assemblies; and 121, mayors of towns of over 20,000 inhabitants. See Cécile Chambraud, "Un Député sur quatre est à la tête d'une région, d'un département ou d'une grande ville," *Le Monde*, 4 June 1997, p. 8.

63. A committee on defense, named by Balladur shortly after he became prime minister, had 9 high-ranking military officers among its 27 members. The committees are often chaired by prominent individuals. Among those who have been asked on several occasions to fulfill this task are Marceau Long, vice-president of the Council of State; Georges Vedel, former member of the Constitutional Council; and René Rémond, historian and president of the *Fondation nationale des sciences politiques*.

64. See Pierre Servent, "La République des commissions," *L'Express*, 3 July 1987, pp. 10–13; "Les Commissions parlementaires jalouses de la multiplication des comités de 'sages,'" *Le Monde*, 1 August 1987; "Les Hommes-providence de la République," *Le Point*, 11 September 1993, p. 9; Pierre Merle, "Le Rapport Fauroux et le Café du Commerce," *Le Monde*, 28 June 1996, p. 14.

65. For example, in part because of the strong opposition of teachers' unions, in 1996 Juppé rejected most of the recommendations made by the Fauroux committee on educational reforms, which he had appointed.

66. Pierre Mendès-France, *La République moderne* (Paris: Gallimard, 1962), pp. 73–108.

67. SOFRES poll, May 1972, cited in Edouard Bonnefous, "Crise des institutions: Restaurer le côntrole parlementaire," *Revue politique et parlementaire* 74 (October 1972), 16.

68. SOFRES poll, November 1969.

69. SOFRES poll, cited in *Le Monde*, 15 July 1989.

70. Poll conducted for *Figaro* in October 1986. Cited in SOFRES, *L'État de l'opinion 1988*, pp. 222–23.

71. Corruption among deputies was considered very frequent or frequent by 72 percent of the respondents, and rare by 25 percent. SOFRES poll, October 2000, cited in Gilles Corman, "L'Image de la politique dans le contexte de l'Affaire Méry," in SOFRES, *L'État de l'opinion 2001*, p. 220. According

to a poll taken the same month, only 36 percent had confidence in deputies, compared to 42 percent in senators, and 70 percent in mayors. Cited in Olivier Duhamel, "Confiance institutionnelle et défiance politique: La Démocratie française, in SOFRES, *L'État de l'opinion 2001*, p. 81.

72. See Pierre Mazeaud, "Le Parlement et ses adversaires," *Pouvoirs*, no. 64 (February 1993), 109–22.

73. See Boudant, "La Crise identitaire du Parlement français," pp. 1349–51.

74. See François Goguel, "Parliament Under the Fifth French Republic: Difficulties of Adapting to a New Role," in *Modern Parliaments: Change or Decline?* ed. Gerhard Loewenberg (Chicago: Aldine-Atherton, 1971), pp. 81–109. For another optimistic view, see Didier Maus, "Parliament in the Fifth Republic: 1958–1988," in Paul Godt, ed., *Policy-Making in France from de Gaulle to Mitterrand* (London: Pinter Publishers, 1989), pp. 12–27.

75. Cf. J. R. Frears, "Parliament in the Fifth Republic," in *The Fifth Republic at Twenty*, ed. William G. Andrews and Stanley Hoffmann (Albany: State University of New York Press, 1981), pp. 60–62; and Christian Bigaud, "La Pratique parlementaire sous la cohabitation," *Regards sur l'actualité*, no. 141 (May 1988), 10–11. In 1987 alone, 404 amendments were introduced in the Assembly by the government, 990 by the standing committees, and 3,637 by private members, for a total of 5,031. Of these, 1,394 were adopted.

76. This pressure seems, on occasion, to be actively solicited by deputies. For example, in December 1995, Assembly Speaker Séguin held meetings with the striking railroad workers, thereby encouraging them to persist in their demands (which Séguin supported but Premier Juppé opposed).

77. One such bill, successfully introduced in 1990 by Communist deputies, provided for punishing those who publicly question the historicity of Nazi crimes with a year in prison and a heavy fine.

78. For example, in 1981, 16 Gaullist and 21 UDF deputies voted with the Socialist majority in favor of the bill to abolish capital punishment, despite the fact that public opinion continued to be in favor of its retention.

79. The list of Fifth Republic Assembly speakers is as follows: Jacques Chaban-Delmas, Gaullist (1958–1969, 1978–1981, and 1986–1988); Achille Peretti, Gaullist (1969–1973); Edgar Faure, pro-Gaullist (1973–1978); Louis Mermaz, Socialist (1981–1986); Laurent Fabius, Socialist (1988–1991 and 1997–2000); Henri Emmanuelli, Socialist (1991–1993); Philippe Séguin, Gaullist (1993–1997); Raymond Forni, Socialist (2000–2002); and Jean-Louis Debré, Gaullist (2002–).

80. Examples of violations under de Gaulle are the government's refusal to call a special session demanded by Parliament in accordance with Article 29 in 1960, and its refusal (in violation of Art. 49) to permit a vote on foreign policy in 1962.

81. Patrick Francès, "Les Leçons et promesses de l'année parlementaire," *Le Monde*, 24 December 1975.

82. The greater independence of deputies explains why the Assembly involved itself in lengthy debate on matters of foreign policy (especially on the Gulf War and the Maastricht Treaty) and why it (jointly with the Senate) initiated impeachment procedures against three cabinet ministers involved in the affair of the AIDS-contaminated blood.

83. The expression used by Thierry Bréhier, "Radioscopie de l'Assemblée," *Le Monde*, 14 July 1989.

84. This was the first time since the Second Empire that the head of a foreign state was given this privilege.

85. See Pascale Robert-Diard, "Philippe Séguin persiste à vouloir réformer le travail parlementaire," *Le Monde*, 6 October 1993. On the overall view of Séguin about the crisis of Parliament and ways of overcoming it, see his article, "Pour une révolution culturelle du Parlement," *Revue politique et parlementaire*, no. 986 (November–December 1995), 7–12.

86. The Vedel Commission, which was appointed in 1992 and submitted its recommendations to the president in February 1993.

87. In this endeavor he has had the help of Balladur and others who had opposed the presidential ambitions of Chirac. See Gérard Courtois and Jean-Louis Saux, "Philippe Séguin conforte son statut de rival d'Alain Juppé," *Le Monde*, 28–29 January 1996, p. 5.

88. Laurent Fabius, "L'Assemblée de l'an 2000 sera-t-elle celle de 1999?" *Revue politique et parlementaire*, no. 997 (November–December 1998), 54–59.

The Administrative System

BACKGROUND, STRUCTURE, AND RECRUITMENT

The bureaucratic tradition in France, as in Italy and Germany, antedates the republican system. In the fifteenth century, the French monarchs appointed *intendants*, officials who served as tax collectors or commissioners in the provinces. (They were precursors of the modern prefects.) The sixteenth century witnessed the creation of technical corps, such as the Forest Administration and the Bridges Authority. The function of the bureaucracy was "modern" in that it was an instrument of "forceful national integration."[1] But the basis of its recruitment was distinctly ascriptive. Because they had to buy or inherit their positions, most high administrative recruits came from the nobility. As a result of the Revolution of 1789, hereditary office was abolished, and during Napoleon's reign, the criteria of professionalism and merit were introduced, under the dictum of "careers open to talent"; during the July Monarchy, the principles of political independence and permanent tenure of bureaucrats became more generally accepted. Still, bureaucrats were expected to be supporters of the regime and proponents of its ideology. Each change of political system was accompanied by a "purge" of the civil service, for which there existed no overall national organization and no coherent recruitment standards. Hence, each minister had full discretion in matters of appointment, promotion, and dismissal of civil servants. In the 1830s the Bourbon bureaucracy, composed mainly of landed aristocrats, was replaced by an Orléanist one, consisting largely of the upper bourgeoisie; and in 1848, middle-class prefects were chosen to help fight revolutionary activities in the provinces.

In the Third Republic, the social base of recruitment was expanded. The growth of public education provided greater opportunities for the petite bourgeoisie to find places, particularly in the middle echelons of the civil service. Many prestige positions did remain the preserve of the upper and upper-middle classes, especially in the foreign service and finance; and even middle-echelon bureaucrats tended to reflect the traditional values of statism and conservatism. But the bureaucracy gradually accepted the two dominant values of laicism and republicanism. With the assertion of supremacy by Parliament, the civil service ceased in theory to be a major decision maker. In practice, however, it was as powerful as ever. Because Parliament was disparate in its composition and relatively disorganized, and because the ministers responsible to it held too brief a term to familiarize themselves with their departmental domains, higher civil servants were often left to their own devices. Parliament implicitly recognized its own weaknesses and its unwillingness to make detailed administrative decisions by adopting the custom of passing framework laws *(lois cadres)* under which ministers were given vast powers to issue decrees and regulations. These powers in fact devolved upon the civil servants.

Many French citizens did not view this lack of political supervision as an evil. In contrast to the American notion of a federal bureaucrat as a hired hand, an individual employed to implement public policy, the French have considered the civil servant to be one who pursues a respected vocation and who is a member of a superior class, who may be following a family tradition, and whose job, especially at the higher levels, includes policy making. French higher civil servants have represented an awesome entity known as the State—at one time equated with the monarch and later with the republic.

Prior to World War II, relatively little uniformity and cohesion existed in the civil service. The division of grades was imprecise and differed somewhat from one ministry to another because each ministry was in charge of its own organization and recruitment. The *Conseil d'État* (Council of State), the pinnacle of the bureaucracy, provided only general supervision. In 1945, the civil service acquired the form it has today: It was unified; a Civil Service Commission *(Direction de la fonction publique)* was created and put under the supervision of the prime minister or (in later years, as under the Rocard government) that of a separate minister; hierarchical grades were set up; training and recruitment methods were standardized; and fiscal responsibility for the bureaucracy was delegated to the Ministry of Finance.

Today, about 2.6 million people are employed by the state—12 percent of the total labor force—compared to 135,000 in 1845. The 2001 figure includes some 900,000 teachers from elementary to university levels, 450,000 employees of the postal and telecommunications services, 200,000 employees of the Finance Ministry (among them tax collectors), 420,000 employees of the Defense Ministry (among them 300,000 military personnel), and the full-time local agents of the national government (e.g., prefects and subprefects).[2] If one adds the officials or "public service agents" of departments (100,000) and communes (about 600,000), and the employees of public hospitals (650,000), the railroads (250,000), gas and electricity (140,000), and other public corporations, one arrives at a figure of well over 5 million.[3]

There are four basic categories of civil servants, which are roughly similar to those that prevail in the British Civil Service:

Category	Class
A	Administrative *(fonctionnaire de conception et de direction)*
B	Executive *(fonctionnaire d'application)*
C	Clerical *(fonctionnaire d'exécution spécialisée)*
D	Custodial *(fonctionnaire d'exécution simple)*

Within each category there are corps (e.g., *grand corps* or prefectoral corps), indicating the type of work or agency of the civil servant, and echelons, determining the nature of the position, the rank, and the salary. The most complicated differentiation obtains in the upper ranks of the administrative civil service, the approximately 10,000 higher bureaucrats *(hauts fonctionnaires)* who are technically above category A *(hors échelle)*. This class is itself divided into several categories and includes, in ascending order of importance and status: (1) *fonctionnaires principaux* (e.g., attachés to central administrative offices, the revenue service, and prefectures); (2) *fonctionnaires supérieurs* (e.g., engineers and most of the civil administrators); (3) *hauts fonctionnaires* (e.g., inspectors of finance, officials of the Court of Accounts, members of the diplomatic and prefectoral corps); and (4) *grands fonctionnaires* (e.g., secretaries-general of ministries, ambasssadors, the director of the budget, the chief of the Planning Commission, and the top members of the Council of State).

Recruitment to the French civil service is tied to the educational system. Thus for category D, very little formal schooling is required; for C, the requirement is the completion of elementary school; for B, a *baccalauréat* (secondary-school diploma); and for category A, a university education. Prior to 1945, training for the civil service was generally provided by the *Ecole Libre de Science Politique* (a private institution founded in 1871) and by the law faculties of universities. These institutions prepared the bulk of the recruits either for immediate entry into the higher bureaucracy or for "postgraduate" studies in the *Ecole Polytechnique* or other *grandes écoles*. Most of these schools are run by individual ministries. Thus the Ministry of Finance has maintained the *Ecole Nationale des Impôts* for training tax officials, and the *Ecole des Mines* has been maintained by the Ministry of Industry for the training of geologists. After World War II, a number of additional *grandes écoles* were opened in order to prepare civil servants for the specialized technocratic functions that were gaining in importance in a growing welfare state.

The most interesting postwar innovation in the education of the bureaucracy is the National School of Administration (*Ecole Nationale d'Administration*–ENA), established in 1946. The original purpose of this "superinstitution" was to deemphasize the legal curriculum that had been traditional for the majority of civil servants in favor of more modern subjects such as sociology, economics, statistics, and public administration. (However, a large proportion of the entrants to ENA have been graduates of law faculties.) The curriculum provides for a unique combination of the practical and the theoretical. The three-year program begins with a year of work in an administrative office, often in the provinces. The second year is devoted to academic study. The third year consists of further on-the-job training in the particular ministry that the student hopes to enter.[4]

ENA is unique in many other ways. Unlike ordinary university faculties supervised by the minister of national education or the minister of universities, ENA is under the authority of the premier; it is politically neutral, in contrast to the ideological tendencies still found in various law faculties; it offers mostly seminars rather than the formal lectures to large audiences typical of the ordinary institution of higher education. Furthermore, it has virtually no permanent faculty; professors are lent to ENA from universities, from the civil service, and occasionally from business. ENA graduates choose their own careers, that is, determine which part of the civil service they wish to enter. A large number of ENA graduates—there are now well over 5,000—have gone into the upper echelons of the Council of State, the Inspectorate of Finances, the diplomatic services, and the prefectoral corps. Many ENA graduates, or *Enarques* ("Enarchs"), have joined the staffs of prestigious ministries;[5] some have become prominent politicians; others have gone into the planning technocracy; and still others, into business.[6] The *Enarchie* has occupied a particularly prominent place among government ministers. In the Jospin government (in 2002) 12 out of the 33 ministers were graduates of ENA, but only 4 out of 38 in the Raffarin government (June 2002). Two presidents of the Republic have been Enarques.[7]

Under the Third and Fourth Republics, most graduates of the *grandes écoles* were from the upper or upper-middle classes and hailed from Paris. ENA was intended to provide for less ascriptive and more democratic recruitment, not only by means of competitive entrance examinations, but also by a system of financial subsidies (in effect, salaries) paid to the students. The attempt to broaden recruitment did not succeed as anticipated. At the end of the 1970s, no more than 2 percent of the students were from the working or peasant class. A large proportion of the approximately 100 applicants admitted annually have been Parisians, or at least graduates of a Parisian lycée and a Parisian university, and have tended to be children of civil servants or other professionals.[8] During recent decades, the recruitment pool has been somewhat enlarged in favor of the "popular" classes, but has by no means become representative of society as a whole.[9] Under the Socialist governments of 1981–1986, special efforts were made to seek out ENA graduates who had come from the petite bourgeoisie and had been active in Socialist party politics and give them important appointments.[10] In 1983, in an attempt to make the higher civil service more egalitarian, the government introduced legislation providing for an alternative path of entry into ENA: Competitive examinations would be open to members of general (departmental) councils, mayors and deputy mayors of medium-sized and larger towns, and officials of mutual societies and social security agencies.[11] These measures were rescinded by the Chirac government in 1987 but (in the spring of 1989) were restored by the Rocard government.[12] Such measures have been only partly successful, and even under the Socialists, ENA "dynasties" were found: A significant proportion of entrants to that prestigious institution had fathers who were themselves members of the political establishment.[13] In 1991, in an effort to dilute the Parisian bias of ENA and to further the decentralization of governmental functions, Premier Cresson decided to move that institution to Strasbourg.[14] Such a step was highly unpopular with the Parisian elite; nevertheless, when Balladur became prime minister, he reconfirmed the decision, which had already been partly implemented. During the past two decades, the prestige of ENA has declined; and many an ambitious young person choses education in (private) business school and becomes a *présidént-directeur-général* (PDG), or CEO.

THE POLITICAL COMPLEXION OF CIVIL SERVANTS

The social selectivity of *Enarques* has led to the impression that they share not only a high degree of intelligence and technical competence but also outlook and manners and that they feel a certain contempt for other members of the political apparatus, if not for society at large. This perception is widespread among the general public and extends beyond the *Enarchie* to the administrative and political elite as a whole.[15] In turn, the non-ENA elite and outside observers hold ambiguous impressions of ENA: as a place for ambitious but not necessarily cultured young people, where education is practical in orientation but not particularly technical or "professional" and where students learn above all to cultivate useful social relations and to become part of a tightly knit elite network.[16] It may be true that many higher civil servants have an overblown self-image that has expressed itself in a disdain for Parliament, because that body contains a large number of nonexperts. Even though the educational and cultural backgrounds of parliamentarians and *Enarques* are often similar, the bureaucratic orientation of the latter leads them to exaggerate the facile distinctions commonly made in modern democratic systems between politics and administration. In a democracy, the elected representatives are expected to make the political decisions, and the civil servants to implement them. The former are by necessity partisan, whereas the latter are (ideally) politically neutral; the former are instruments of change, whereas the latter are supposed to provide stability and continuity, while always remaining responsible to the politicians and therefore responsive to demands for change.

However, although the French civil service has often thought of itself as an "objective" counterweight to the parliamentary party system, it has never been completely dissociated from the ideological arguments that often inform politicians. This is illustrated by the fact that most of the premiers of the Fifth Republic have been higher civil servants, and that many of its prominent politicians, both on the right and the left, have been ENA graduates.[17] Higher civil servants in France, unlike their colleagues in Britain, are not expected to be completely nonpartisan. They may join political parties, express their ideological preferences, and even run for seats in Parliament (if they win, they receive a leave of absence without loss of seniority). In short, the political and bureaucratic orientations of higher civil servants are intertwined, as politicians are bureaucratized and bureaucrats abandon their political neutrality. This applies in particular to members of ministerial staffs *(cabinets ministériels)*.[18] It has been argued that partisan identification may even protect a civil servant's position better than political neutrality. This was particularly the case during the Chirac-Jospin cohabitation, when prefects on each side were protected by their respective "patrons" in the executive.[19]

Occasionally there may be restrictions regarding the civil servants' partisan commitments, as in 1945 when there was a purge of collaborationist bureaucrats, but the purge occurred because they had adhered to the ideology of a regime regarded as illegitimate.[20] During the middle years of the Fourth Republic, some ministers attempted to block the appointment or promotion of Communist civil servants; however, in 1954 the Council of State ruled such discrimination illegal. Nonetheless, certain political parties have almost always enjoyed a preferred status in the civil service.

In the Third and Fourth Republics the staffs of national ministries reflected the ideological diversity of parliaments, and there were many bureaucrats who identified themselves as "leftist," irrespective of the etatist outlook implicit in their roles. In the Fifth Republic, the diminished position of Parliament has tended to fortify both the conservative and the technicist orientation of civil servants. They have attained a higher status and greater autonomy in relation to Parliament than they possessed in previous republics, but their political dependence on the executive has increased because the premiers (and sometimes the presidents directly) have asserted their own authority more effectively, as most of them have had civil service backgrounds. Under President de Gaulle, many civil service positions were "politicized"; he often preferred his Resistance companions to young ENA graduates whose political reliability was an unknown factor. At the same time, he contributed to the professionalization *(fonctionnarisation)* of the political apparatus by preferring to appoint civil servants rather than politicians. This trend has continued, as is illustrated by the dominance of cabinets by members of the higher civil service.[21]

Conversely, there has been a continuation of the Fourth Republic practice of appointing parliamentarians of the favored party, after they have failed in their attempts at reelection (or in anticipation of electoral defeat), to positions in the public sector;[22] however, many of these appointees have a background in the civil service. A good number of higher civil servants, including about half the directors of the central administration, have owed their positions to political collaboration with a minister, and their appointments and promotions have not been justified by merit or seniority alone. Partisan criteria have been particularly important in the staffing of "sensitive" agencies such as the Foreign Ministry and the television networks, because great importance has been attached to the civil servant's reliability in voicing the official viewpoints. Until 1974, with a strong Gaullist executive and a weakened and Gaullist-dominated Assembly, many higher civil servants (including prefects) were blatantly Gaullist and participated in UDR activities.

Between 1974 and 1981, the upper echelons of the civil service were increasingly staffed with Giscard's supporters and friends (a significant proportion of whom happened also to be *Enarques*); indeed, the governmental bureaucracy was said to have been so effectively "Giscardized" that Socialist leaders after 1981 rationalized some of their own policy-making failures in terms of alleged roadblocks erected against them by ideologically hostile bureaucratic holdovers. But the Socialists, too, changed the coloration of the civil service: Many appointments to the Elysée staff, the *cabinets ministériels,* the management of railroads and other public enterprises, and the television agencies were made on the basis of a balanced representation of different Socialist party factions, electoral and personal fidelity to Mitterrand, and even family ties.[23] The growth of patronage in the civil service was reflected in the replacement of 350 *directeurs d'administration* by more reliable people during the first five years of the Mitterrand presidency (compared to nearly 300 during the Giscard presidency).[24]

A significant ideological diversity and, as a result, a certain ideological "blending," if not neutrality, have existed for a long time in the (non-policy-making) middle and lower echelons of the civil service, which are characterized by fragmented unionization. The more than one million unionized civil servants have belonged to a variety of unions—with public transport workers generally opting for the (pro-Communist) CGT and teachers for the (pro-Socialist) FEN.[25]

While the civil servants' ideological orientations may influence their general political conceptions, ideology does not necessarily determine the bureaucratic behavior of civil servants. In the highly institutionalized system of France, the roles of civil servants have been so well defined that they have tended to use technical arguments and to identify with their official roles rather than with partisan outlooks. The behavior of members of the Socialist-oriented bureaucratic elites was not much different from that of their more conservative predecessors. As they pursued their careers, they gradually shifted to the right. Moreover, the conflict between the ideology of the ENA and that of the Socialist party has been reduced as that party has itself become partly "Enarchized."[26] That explains why in the 1980s an increasing number of Socialist officials "discovered the virtues of [market] liberalism," just as certain modern-minded directors of private enterprises wanted a larger dose of "the rationalizing action of the state."[27]

At the same time, conservative attitudes have been fortified by extrabureaucratic influences, particularly from the law schools and *grandes écoles* and their faculties, with which higher civil servants are bound to have continuing contact. Although "in France the aroma of political reaction which aspirants for the higher administrative career acquired during their preparation for entrance [into prestige schools] as late as the 1930s has gone out of style," and although ENA has fostered the idea of opposition to a government that acts on behalf of special interests,[28] the civil service is constantly influenced by interest groups and indeed even seeks their input. But that influence is unequal, because the civil service does not represent the kind of broad cross-section of the population that is organized into competing socioeconomic associations, and therefore does not always reflect the most progressive or democratic ideologies (and sometimes not even the interest of the state). Higher civil servants tend to be close to business executives because both groups are bound to the existing order (the former for professional reasons and the latter because the system has favored the economic advantages of the owning classes). The shared background and (since the end of World War II) a shared commitment to rationalized economic decision making (including planning [see Chapter 10]) have strengthened the institutional ties between big business and the higher civil service, and both sectors have used the planning machinery to head off the "unrealistic" demands of the trade unions. The emphasis on productivity has been as characteristic of the *Enarques* of the higher civil service as of the bureaucrats in the technical services (e.g., electricity, railroads, and nationalized manufacturing industries).

Many of the specialized civil servants who staff these technical services are trained in the *Ecole Polytechnique*, which was set up in 1795 as a combined civilian-military school and was to be open to the talented of all social classes. The *Polytechniciens*, like the *Enarques*, respect efficiency and technological (rather than legal or partisan) approaches to problems, and some hope to get jobs in the private business sector. In addition, the rapport between the technical civil servants and private entrepreneurs is strengthened by the fact that occasionally there are close ties between private and nationalized industries—and sometimes virtual mergers of production and marketing, as, for example, between the public Renault and the private Peugeot automobile-manufacturing firms.

To what extent, then, is the French civil service an instrument of democracy? Administrative careers are not quite so open to the masses as are political careers. The sons of artisans and others of modest circumstances could become prime ministers in the Third and Fourth Republics and in the Fifth as well, as illustrated in the case of Bérégovoy, but such people are not likely to enter the higher civil service, because it would be relatively difficult for them to climb the educational ladder (and gain admission to the *grandes écoles*) required for an administrative career.[29] When Parliament was supreme, this upper-class bias of the civil service was moderated by the lower-class ideological orientation of many parliamentarians and cabinet ministers, who theoretically furnished the "political" input into the bureaucracy and also provided an antidote to the conservative and antipopulist extra-administrative influence of law professors and business leaders.

Now the only effective counterforce to bureaucratic conservatism is the president, who appoints the politicians who supervise the civil service. Presidents are products of popular majorities, but not all presidents have interpreted the "public interest" in the same fashion. De Gaulle equated the public interest with the promotion of France's greatness and global influence; and Giscard (as one scholar has argued) so confounded the public interest with that of big industries that the autonomy of the state was called into question.[30] It has been contended that the notion of the public interest is largely a myth used by administrators and by governments to perpetuate the existing nonegalitarian social order.[31] But that contention did not quite apply to President Mitterrand and his Socialist government officials, who sponsored many egalitarian policies. In addition, over the past 50 years, the internal reshuffling of civil service positions has shown a certain democratic trend, in that the staffs of ministries concerned specifically with upward mobility and egalitarian resource allocation—for example, the Ministries of Education, Public Health, Social Affairs, and Labor—have increased dramatically, compared with those of the Foreign Affairs and Defense Ministries.[32]

CONTROLS OVER THE CIVIL SERVICE

The French civil service is not unlimited in its power. In the first place, civil servants can administer only on the basis of laws. During the heyday of parliamentary supremacy, particularly under the Third and Fourth Republics, the laws on which administrative regulations were based emanated from Parliament, and therefore one could say that Parliament exercised control over bureaucratic behavior. This is less true today, as most parliamentary activities are inspired, directed, and controlled by the government (itself often a product of presidential discretion), and under the present Constitution the executive is given sweeping decree powers.

The second limitation on bureaucratic absolutism traditionally resulted from the "checks and balances" provided by the ideological diversity of civil servants. This diversity was the result of the coalition governments, which ensured that bureaucrats affiliated with a variety of parties be rewarded for loyal service, placed in key positions, and promoted. Diversity can still be found, but it has been reduced as a consequence of the simplification of the party system and the narrowing of the ideological gap between the Right and the Left.

The third limitation on bureaucratic absolutism is provided by the input of expertise from social and economic sectors via the ever-expanding consultative machinery. This machinery is of three distinct types. The most widespread consultative bodies are the advisory councils attached to ministries and composed of representatives of interest groups, technicians, and prominent personalities, the latter chosen by the government. The second type is made up of the multipartite boards attached to national and local social security organisms, and composed of spokespersons of trade unions, employers, and other economic or professional sectors. The third type of consultative machinery is found in the regional economic development commissions. There are today over 15,000 councils and committees with which the bureaucracy deals, and they are of widely divergent character.[33] These include the Superior Council on Education, the Central Commission for Marketing, the National Committee for the Control of Real Estate, and regional employment and retraining committees. However, it is a matter of controversy whether these consultative bodies provide adequate checks on the administration, because many of them are either ad hoc in nature or have restricted competence.

Bureaucratic regulations are based on framework laws *(lois cadres)*, and the input of interest groups on these laws (except indirectly through the Economic and Social Council) may not be decisive. Interest-group influence is limited by several factors: the ego of civil servants, which does not easily lend itself to the notion that nonprofessional outsiders can make valuable contributions to administrative decisions; the unequal representation of social sectors; and the principle of central government supervision *(tutelle)*, which permits civil servants to restrict the parameters of consultative input. Moreover, a committee's recommendations may be ignored by the civil servants (even when consultation is obligatory), may merely provide the façade of public participation, or may be cited to promote unpopular regulations, thus permitting the civil servants to escape the blame for these.

A fourth check on bureaucratic absolutism is provided by the administrative court system, in which a citizen may question the legality of bureaucratic regulations or behavior. At the top of this system is the Council of State *(Conseil d'État)*. This body is not "independent" in the Anglo-American sense, as it is officially a component of the civil service. The Council of State was established in 1799 by Napoleon as a mechanism for resolving disputes *within* the civil service, to advise the government on legal matters, and to protect the government from challenges on the part of citizens by hearing (and heading off) grievances. One important reason for the creation of the Council of State was to prevent interference by ordinary courts in administrative acts (i.e., to shut off juridical and political surveillance of the civil service).[34]

The independence of the Council of State was strengthened when in 1875 its members obtained security of tenure and when, subsequently, appointments to it were based not on political considerations but on competitive examinations. These changes led to the transformation of the nature of the Council of State. During the early part of the Third Republic, the council was one of the main pillars of authority, whereas Parliament was the arena of partisan controversy and opposition to the executive. Gradually the council developed a degree of detachment from the executive and concerned itself with protecting citizens against administrative arbitrariness.[35] But because the council is formally still part of the executive elite (in the juridical sense), there is considerable lateral movement between it and a variety of political positions. Some councilors run for Parliament (obtaining a leave of absence when elected); others are detailed to service as ambassadors, ministers of state, cabinet secretaries, or members of "blue ribbon" commissions *(comités de sages)*; and still others may serve as officials in public corporations.

The Council of State still resolves intrabureaucratic disputes and advises the government on the language of draft bills. It examines, not the constitutionality of laws (this role belongs to the Constitutional Council), but the legality of regulations and the behavior of the executive in implementing them. The Council of State, meeting in

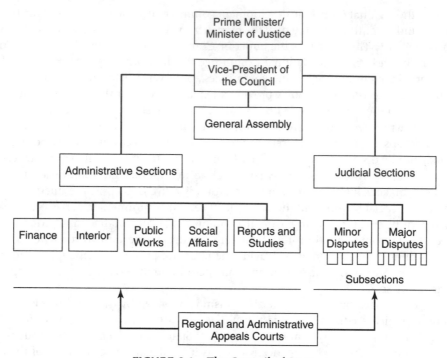

FIGURE 8.1 The Council of State
SOURCE: Based on Ambassade de France, Service de Presse et d'information, *France*, May 1975, updated.

general assembly, is presided over by the prime minister (or, in his absence, the minister of justice) (see Figure 8.1), but that official is only the nominal head (president) of the council and does not interfere in its activities. The actual chairperson, the vice-president, is chosen from among the councillors. Nearly half of the councillors are members of the judicial or redress *(contentieux)* section, which operates separately from the other five sections, which deal with administrative and advisory matters. (There are more than 200 higher civil servants in the Council of State, of whom only about one-third are councillors of state, the remainder being the subordinate *maîtres de requêtes* and auditors.) Despite the size of the redress section of the Council of State and despite the fact that only five councillors are required to sit in judgment on a case, it may take several years for a case to be decided by the council, because the "judicial explosion" has been such that the docket is often full, and auditors and *maîtres de requêtes* may need a great deal of time to complete an investigation.[36] The judicial explosion is in turn a consequence of the rapid growth of laws, regulations, and decrees.[37] The Parliament has enacted many of these laws in haste and has demanded equal haste of the Council of State in examining their proper formulation.

In the early 1950s, the burden of the Council of State was lightened when the original jurisdiction of the two dozen inferior courts *(tribunaux administratifs)* was enlarged and the council was transformed into a largely appellate court. At the end of 1987, in another attempt to deal with the "asphyxiation" of the council, Parliament passed a law creating five interregional administrative appeals courts (located in Paris and other large cities).

Although councillors have come mainly from the upper-middle class, there has not been in France the kind of class justice one frequently finds in the administrative courts of Germanic countries; and although the Council of State is said to have a highly developed "sense of state" and a sympathetic understanding of public authority and to be reticent about interfering in acts of government, that body has been at least as likely to find in favor of the citizen as of the government (especially since the end of World War II). The council has enriched the concept of civil liberties by inferring them from existing laws. Thus, its decisions have contributed to promoting sexual equality before the law, limiting the administrative internment of foreigners, and affirming civil servants' right to strike, freedom of the press, the principle of public trials, and the equality of access of candidates to state examinations regardless of their political orientation.[38]

Nevertheless, the council is not completely effective as an instrument for safeguarding the individual against governmental excesses or arbitrariness. Many a seemingly harsh or undemocratic decision or regulation is based on laws whose constitutionality can hardly be challenged and whose lack of wisdom can be questioned only by Parliament. Also, the government has a hand in nominating councillors, whose tenure is a specified number of years;[39] and finally, the council's decisions may be ignored by the executive.

It was perhaps for these reasons that the French instituted an "ombudsman," or mediator *(médiateur)* system.[40] In accordance with a law of 1973, the government appointed the first mediator (Antoine Pinay, a Fourth Republic prime minister) to a six-year, nonrenewable term.[41] Unlike the Swedish ombudsman, the French mediator receives complaints not directly from the citizen but through the "filter" of a deputy or senator. The mediator's competence extends to all areas of administration: ordinary, social security, nationalized industries, and justice. The mediator can request from administrative agencies any information he or she considers pertinent and can initiate proceedings against malfeasant civil servants. The mediator submits an annual report to the president and Parliament that contains a summary of cases dealt with as well as recommendations for legislative and administrative reforms. If possible, the mediator tries to find amicable solutions to problems, but may, if necessary, issue injunctions and initiate litigation. The number of complaints received by the mediator has grown steadily— from 1,600 in 1974 to more than 51,000 in 2000; the budget more than quintupled during that period to 27 million francs, or $4 million), and the staff increased correspondingly, so that the mediator's office had nearly 100 employees by the end of that period. In addition to the national staff, there are 123 departmental delegates, who deal with the public at prefectures.[42]

The office of mediator, which was modeled largely on that of the British parliamentary commissioner, represents an institutional grafting that is not entirely appropriate to the French context. Theoretically, the administrative court system already provides the French citizen with a redress mechanism against illegal bureaucratic actions, and checks against maladministration (the proper province of the mediator) are provided (albeit with mixed success) by the government itself in the form of committees of inspection and inquiry. Thus far, the mediator has not been spectacularly successful, because neither civil servants nor their ministers have been very cooperative in revealing information.

In order to remedy this situation, Parliament in 1978 passed legislation enabling citizens to find out whether or what compromising personal data about them is contained in official computerized files and guaranteeing them access to documents. In order to implement these rights, two special bodies were created: the *Commission nationale de l'informatique et des libertés* (CNIL) and the *Commission d'accès aux documents administratifs* (CADA).[43] Other legislation (of 1979) obliged bureaucrats to justify their decisions to the citizens. But it is doubtful whether these reforms have rendered the civil service responsive enough to the citizenry.

The less than perfect redress machinery is a minor matter compared to what many perceive to be the structural deficiencies and lack of modernity of the French civil service. Some of the problems of that civil service are endemic to government bureaucracies everywhere, such as the rivalry among different agencies; the conflict between the Finance Ministry, which allocates money, and the ministries that are on the fiscal receiving end; the tendency toward duplication of services; the political interference in administrative work; and the question of the efficiency of bureaucrats.

Despite a growing belief to the contrary (pointed out above), there is relatively little corruption among higher administrative bureaucrats, not only because of their professional self-esteem, but also because they are well paid and therefore are not tempted to supplement their incomes by taking bribes. Traditionally, certain civil servants, in particular those recruited to the administrative staff of a minister (the *cabinet ministériel*), retained their connections with, and derived additional income from, their private business or professional activities, but in the course of the past three decades (owing to various scandals) the regulations concerning such connections have been progressively tightened.[44]

The prestige of the lower-echelon civil servants is not high enough to compensate for their relatively low pay, and consequently their unions engage in tough bargaining and occasionally call strikes.[45] But even among higher civil servants there is sometimes a problem of salary inequities. A "pecking order" exists not only among administrative grades but also within a particular grade. Thus, an ENA graduate who works for the Ministry of Finance receives more pay than one who works for the Ministry of Culture. Despite the postwar organizational reforms that created greater unity within the civil service, it is difficult to move a higher civil servant from one ministry to another against his will, a situation that has resulted in the overstaffing of some ministries and the understaffing of others. The proliferation of administrative staff is in part a response to the pressure to create enough positions to employ bureaucrats in the service grades to which their educational attainments entitle them.

Another problem that has affected the morale of civil servants is the threat of a reduction in force of the national bureaucracy. This threat was articulated a few years ago in a proposal by Premier Juppé that included a restructuring of the civil service corps for greater efficiency and the elimination of 7,000 positions.[46] Such a reduction is a response to a number of developments that have themselves been reflections of supranationalism, decentralization, and neoliberalism: (1) the pressures (emanating in part from the European Union) to reduce the governmental deficit; (2) the transfer of selected central government tasks to regional and local authorities; and (3) the transfer of state responsibilities to "civil society" by the privatization of selected state enterprises—

for example, telecommunications, civil aviation, and certain sectors of mass transportation. There has been a resistance to privatization on the part of the employees of public corporations, who fear that the transfer of their activities to the market would result in a reduction of wages and retirement benefits, and on the part of the public, who believe that privately supplied utilities would cost more. Furthermore, there has been opposition by some intellectuals and politicians who have argued that these measures, in removing the civil service from its pedestal, would also undermine the mystique of the state itself.[47]

SUBNATIONAL ADMINISTRATION

During the final century of the *ancien régime*, local government was severely circumscribed by the Bourbon monarchy's policy of centralizing control over localities and provinces in the hands of the Crown and its emissaries. After the Revolution of 1789, the old provinces were replaced by smaller units; later, Napoleon established a pattern of centralization of administrative functions that prevailed well into the middle of the twentieth century and is still, mutatis mutandis, in effect today. Under this system, the communes, cantons, districts *(arrondissements)*, and counties or departments *(départements)* are not independent decision-making centers possessing "original jurisdiction" as clearly spelled out in the constitutions of federal regimes; rather they are subnational units existing for national administrative convenience. Each of the units has a specific purpose. In the commune, the citizen is dealt with most directly; the canton contains a police squad of the national gendarmerie and functions as the constituency for general (i.e., departmental) council elections; the district serves as the basic (single-member) constituency for National Assembly elections; and the department is the most important subdivision of the national government and the locus operandi of its chief agent, the prefect.

Although some units—the commune, with its council and mayor, and the department, with its assembly (the *conseil général*)—contain elected bodies, locally generated decision-making power has been relatively limited. The prefects, who administer the 96 metropolitan departments, are neither elected by the local constituency nor directly responsible to it. Rather, they are national civil servants appointed by the minister of the interior and responsible to him. The prefect is assisted by a subprefect and a cabinet composed of specialists for public works, agriculture, water supply, public health, housing, and so on. Until 1960, the prefect's task of supervising *all* local services was rendered difficult because the specialists not only had to take orders from him but also had to clear their activities with the relevant national ministries. After 1960, the prefect was empowered to deal with these ministries himself, a change that facilitated his coordinating efforts.

As the chief liaison between the national government and local administrative units, the prefect is expected to maintain good relations with mayors and members of regional and local councils and to process local complaints and demands. Prefects can fulfill their roles as liaisons only as long as they enjoyed the confidence of the minister of the interior, who can shift them from one department to another or even dismiss them. After the end of the purges of the immediate post–World War II years, the suspension of prefects became a rare occurrence. However, during the year following the inauguration of Giscard in 1974, 27 prefects were suspended by the interior minister for "inadequate" performance of their functions; in 1981–1982, the new Socialist government replaced 103 of the 124 prefects in metropolitan and overseas departments; and the "cohabitation" government of 1986–1987 replaced 69. By mid-1995, shortly after Chirac's election as president, more than 30 prefects had been replaced, most of them leftist ones, while certain Gaullist prefects were transferred to the staffs of cabinet ministers.[48]

THE COMMUNE

The commune is the basic administrative unit. Originating in the prerevolutionary parish, the commune was established in 1789. Each commune has a municipal council elected for a six-year term (the elections for a partial renewal of the council taking place every three years). The number of councillors varies with the size of the commune: For localities of fewer than 100 souls there are 9 councillors; for towns of 5,000 to 10,000 there are 29; for cities of between 150,000 and 200,000, 59; for cities of more than 300,000, 69; and for Lyons there are (since 1983) 73; Marseilles, 101; and Paris, 163. The council selects one of its members as mayor and supervises his governmental activities. In 2001 there were about 500,000 communal councillors.

Just as the prefect is the chief executive of the department, the mayor is the chief executive of the commune in addition to being the major elected spokesperson of the people. The mayor and municipal council have a number of responsibilities, including the control of traffic; fire protection; trash disposal; nursery schools, elementary-school buildings, and sports facilities; and the provision of welfare services for the poor, the aged, and others in need. Not all of the responsibilities of the mayor can be associated with local self-government: He or she is charged with implementing national laws; the registration of births, marriages, and deaths; the maintenance of electoral lists; and the issuing of building permits. The mayor keeps order, but the police service is financed and controlled by the national government. He or she drafts the budget, but many of the expenditures of the commune have been made mandatory by the national government. Just as the laws pertaining to the election of municipal councillors and the selection of the mayor are made by the national government (which bears the cost of printing ballots and posters in the elections of most communes), so the national government was for many years empowered to veto acts of the mayor and even to dismiss him or her from the post, although the latter step has been resorted to rarely.

Controversy has continued about the extent to which the mayor is a genuine decision maker, a symbol of local electoral legitimacy, or a figure of folklore. One scholar has emphasized the strong leadership of the mayor: his control over the political machine, initiative in local improvement projects, and role in obtaining for his community the necessary financial assistance from the national government. That scholar insisted that "local governments [were] in fact free to make numerous choices," that they "determine[d] policy," and that "the particular choices made by local government [had] consequences for the commune." But he also admitted that local governments "[were] relatively inactive and [did] not play a vital role in meeting local needs."[49] After the family, the commune is perhaps the most important socialization agent in France, but it has not been an important decision-making unit. Rather, it has been an administrative unit created and maintained for the purpose of carrying out policies decided by the national government. Its legal powers have been determined by that government, and to the extent that the mayors had significant power, they derived it not merely from their position as head of the city administration or chief local notable, but—especially if their commune was large—from the fact that they could use their position in order to exert influence on a political party on the national level and get elected to Parliament.

According to another scholar, the fact that mayors have often also been deputies has not reduced their dependence on the prefect. In interviews conducted in 1973, it was revealed that 47.9 percent of the mayors received special favors through the prefectural system, as against 11.1 percent through ministerial offices.[50] The position of the mayor in his or her relationship to the prefecture—specifically, his or her ability to function as "a 'policy broker' between the national government and the town, and between the bureaucracy and the politicians"[51]—might be strengthened if the mayor had an additional public office, such as the chairmanship of a mixed (public-private) construction agency or housing office. Furthermore, the prefecture could sometimes be bypassed, particularly in large towns whose mayors had direct dealings with the Finance Ministry via the Delegation for Space Planning and Regional Action (*Délégation à l'aménagement du territoire et à l'action régionale*—DATAR), which helped to secure funds for regional and local economic projects.

Still another scholar stresses (and exaggerates) the hereditary ("dynastic") elements in the mayor's (and the commune's) politics,[52] whereas a fourth scholar suggests that strong mayors often derive part of their power (and their ability to confront the national government) from the support of trade unions, teachers' associations, and other well-organized interest groups.[53] (Mayors may be pressured into action by local voluntary associations; conversely, they may encourage the formation of such associations, sometimes in order to relieve themselves of tasks for which they have insufficient funds or personnel.) Finally, it should be noted that mayors of large towns would have had less need for the intercession of the prefecture if they had been appointed to the cabinet. Among the numerous examples of mayors simultaneously holding national cabinet office are former premiers Chaban-Delmas, Chirac, and Mauroy, who were mayors respectively of Bordeaux, Paris, and Lille; and the late minister of the interior Gaston Defferre, who was mayor of Marseilles for four decades.

To a large extent, the administrative powerlessness of local governmental units was caused by their relative poverty. Budgetary options were limited by the lack of financial resources of the locality and by its underdeveloped revenue-generating powers. Some of the locally collected taxes, voted on by the municipal council, were quite petty, such as dog-license charges, hunting and fishing fees, and surtaxes on the income tax. Other, more important taxes (e.g., assessments on property, on rents, and on shops, which were collected by the local government) were based on the national government's calculation of the taxable worth of each community, a calculation that local economic developments rendered unrealistic in many communes. These revenues covered little more than half the expenses incurred in the administration of required services, the rest coming from the national government in the form of grants-in-aid. Much of this national subsidy came from the value-added tax, which was collected locally, transferred to the national government, and then reallocated by the central government to local communities. In 1975, about 85 percent of the personal-income taxes collected by the national government was in fact paid out to localities, but the localities' share of the total governmental expenditures remained quite small (below 20 percent in 1970, or proportionally less than in West Germany and especially the United States).[54] In the 1970s both local revenue collection and national government allocations experienced growth, but it was not enough to enable local governments to provide the services increasingly demanded of them.

The ineffectiveness of municipalities was due also to the character of their locally recruited administrative personnel, which has been described as "top-heavy, bureaucratic, and archaic" and as "reproducing and often multiplying the faults of the national bureaucracies." In many of the smaller towns, the municipal employee was "aged, not well educated, [and] lethargic," and had little job mobility.[55] According to one estimate, 62 percent of the mayors in 1980 were more than 50 years old; and 55 percent were farmers or pensioners.[56]

Finally, the lack of viability of local communities stemmed from their multiplicity and archaic nature. There are still more than 36,500 communes in France, compared to 1,350 in Britain, 8,000 in Italy, and 16,000 in Germany.[57] The large number in France was realistic about 150 years ago when much of the country was rural and the extent of local services was limited. Gradually, many communes were rendered inadequate as administrative units because of their depopulation, loss of an economic base, and consequent inability to maintain basic services efficiently. In 1975, about 10 percent of the communes were settlements of more than 2,000 inhabitants, while 22,700 communes (i.e., nearly two-thirds of the total) had fewer than 500 inhabitants (and in 2000 about 4,000 communes had fewer than 100 inhabitants). Many residents of rural communes have moved to the cities, a move that spurred the growth of metropolitan areas that spilled over into several traditional administrative subdivisions. Grenoble, for example, increased in population from 80,000 in 1950 to 150,000 in 2000 and its metropolitan area to more than 400,000. Some "bedroom" suburbs of Paris grew even faster; Sarcelles, for example, increased from 8,400 in 1954 to about 60,000 in 2000.

Raymond Marcellin, who was minister of the interior until 1973, seemed to be interested in giving greater authority to the communes. In 1970 he declared at a meeting of the National Association of Mayors: "The city hall *(la mairie)* is the most perfect symbol of an administration accessible to those who are being administered and the most responsive to human concerns. The commune is also the most natural arena for civic training."[58] That civic training, unfortunately, was likely to result in anticentralistic and antistate attitudes as long as local administrative units possessed only phantom powers.

ADMINISTRATIVE REFORM AND DECENTRALIZATION

The preceding discussion refers in part to an ongoing situation and in part to the past, because the relationship between the national and local governments is in a state of flux. That relationship has been a subject of debate for two centuries; from the early nineteenth century on, numerous proposals were advanced to modify the extreme centralization of government.

After World War II the debate quickened; French governments seemed to have become more seriously concerned with the reform of subnational administration for a variety of reasons: (1) population movements and inequalities;[59] (2) the need for new forms of functional administration for which old units were insufficient; (3) the problems of duplication and inefficiency; (4) the recognition of the fact that provincial attitudes had survived strongly in some areas (e.g., Alsace, Brittany, and Provence) and that these attitudes (and the localism of political parties) had become inconsistent with existing patterns of overcentralization; and (5) the popular desire to participate in a more meaningful type of grassroots politics. All these trends contributed to an awareness of the need for decentralization. Similar developments can be found in other European countries with unitary political structures, and it is quite probable that the attempts by France's neighbors—Italy and the Low Countries—to devise new administrative formulas have inspired French politicians and technocrats.[60]

In France, decentralization does not mean the establishment of federalism, for that would constitute too drastic a departure from the country's administrative tradition. In addition, various sectors have been opposed to meaningful decentralization of any kind: the "Jacobin" Left and the Communists, who have feared that it would encourage reactionary particularism and social (Catholic) conservatism; orthodox Gaullists, who have argued that it would undermine the unity of the nation and the authority of the state and lead to separatism; the prefectoral corps, which has feared a loss of power; and even certain local politicians, who have themselves been part of the national elite and therefore apprehensive about the creation of rival subnational centers of power.[61] In view of this, the record of decentralization, was, until recently, largely one of campaign rhetoric and half-measures.

Decentralization implies the creation of better and more realistic instruments for the regional or local execution of centrally conceived policies. An instance of this approach to decentralization was the ill-fated proposal (couched in the form of a constitutional amendment) by de Gaulle in April 1969 to establish (or reestablish) the *region* as a formal territorial unit of the French state. In the popular referendum, the amendment was rejected (an event causing de Gaulle's resignation) for several reasons, among them not only the uncertainty about the actual powers attributed to the regions but also (and perhaps primarily) the growing unpopularity of de Gaulle, with whom the referendum was intimately associated.

One approach to administrative reform was the creation of economic regions. These were first established during the Fourth Republic to provide the means for local, and therefore more relevant, input of economic information necessary for economic planning and to have more realistic units to which to apply regional plans *(plans nationaux d'aménagement du territoire)*, containing a catalogue of needs and resources for the purpose of deconcentrating industry and population. In 1964, the government gave greater recognition to those regions by naming as a "superprefect" one of the department prefects of each region (see Figure 8.2). The superprefect did not replace the department prefect; rather, he was a coordinator: He "stimulate[d] and [held] conferences."[62] The superprefect was assisted in this task by Regional Economic Development

FIGURE 8.2 The 22 Regions of France
SOURCE: French Embassy, Press and Information Division.

Commissions (*Commissions de développement économique régional*—CODERs), bodies in which local politicians, deputies and senators, interest-group spokespersons, and technicians participated, not in the making of policy, but in advising the superprefect about regional needs and prospects.

The hope that the CODERs would provide an arena of regional economic policy inputs was not fulfilled; they were abolished at the end of 1974, and their tasks were vested in the regional councils. These councils, established by Parliament in 1972, were given the power to obtain revenues from driver's license fees and taxes on real estate transfers, to be used to finance regional investments. But the 1972 reforms fell short of instituting meaningful provincial self-government;[63] they were seen as providing for only a symbolic transfer of financial resources to subnational units and as constituting merely "a caricature of decentralization."[64] Giscard had been one of the critics, and he was elected under a widely held assumption that he would make decentralization a major policy priority.[65] But owing to a variety of constraints, including pressure from his Gaullist allies, he failed to live up to these expectations. As president, Giscard said: "The role of the region is not to administer, but to provide an [additional] coordinating echelon. France is not rich enough to have four echelons of administration—local, departmental, regional, and national. It is too divided to wish to introduce new political games."[66]

THE REFORMS OF 1981–1983

The most significant institutional innovations since the French Revolution were undertaken after the Socialist electoral victories of 1981. For the Socialists, decentralization, as an essential step toward bringing government closer to the people, was a major policy objective—"la grande affaire du septennat"—and was seen as being associated with industrial "self-management" and the recognition of ethno-regional peculiarities.[67]

A law passed in the spring of 1982—the culmination of a year-long parliamentary debate—set the tone in affirming that "the communes, departments, and regions shall administer themselves freely by means of elected bodies."[68] The office of prefect was abolished, and replaced by that of "commissioner of the Republic" (commissaire de la République). The effective executive powers of the department were relocated in the hands of the president of the general council (elected by direct popular vote, with cantons serving as single-member constituencies).[69] Furthermore, members of regional councils were to be elected for six-year terms by universal suffrage beginning in 1986. Both the city councils and the general councils were to be given increased power to collect revenues (including corporate taxes). The decisions of all three types of councils were to be self-enforcing; in abolishing the a priori veto of these decisions by the commissioner (who would henceforth be merely a "delegate" of the central government), the new legislation intended to reduce the scope of national tutelle (supervision). In 1987, the title commissioner was changed back to prefect, but the old functions were not restored; rather the role has been transformed from that of an executive to that of a "negotiator" between the mayor, the department, and the regional authorities.[70]

Under Jospin, new energy was put into decentralization efforts, in part to respond to the diversities of the French regions and the special needs of communes (including the modernization of local finances), and the need to bring government closer to the people.[71] Part of this process, promoted by Jean-Pierre Chevènement, then minister of the interior, was the expansion of the size and functions of local and municipal police forces. Introduced in 1984, these forces now number well over 13,000, spread over some 3,000 communes. They are appointed by the mayor and, ranging from a single agent per commune to more than 20, work together with the ordinary (national) police and are sometimes in competition with them.[72] They are auxiliaries of the national police, not substitutes for it; they do not normally carry arms; and their appointment by the mayor must be formally approved by the state prosecutor *(procureur)*. Nevertheless, they function as a sort of neighborhood police *(police de proximité)*; they show a special interest in the clientele they serve and have closer relations with it. Their responsibilities vary widely; they may include public order in housing projects, security in public schools, and patrolling dangerous neighborhoods.

At this writing—two decades since the enactment of the first decentralization laws—there are still differences of opinion about the scope of actual decentralization, its success, and its impact on the political system as a whole. The powers of local governments have been enlarged in a variety of areas, including the construction and maintenance of school buildings, urban transport, and the control of commercial transactions (see Table 8.1). There have been diverse local and regional initiatives in economic development. Concurrently, there has been an undeniable growth of local budgets, based on both locally collected revenues and increased allocations received from the national government. In 1995, the localities collected nearly 730 billion francs ($140 billion), but in the eyes of many that is insufficient, in view of the pressure of local needs, the demands of higher wages by local officials, and the obligation to implement decisions taken on the level of the departments and regions (which collect their own relatively limited funds).[73]

To some extent, the growth of activities of subnational authorities has been the consequence of buck-passing by the national government, especially during years of austerity policies. The increased responsibilities of local authorities have led to a greater professionalization and an improvement of the quality of regionally and locally elected officials. Many of them continue to come from the ranks of physicians, dentists, pharmacists, and educators; but there are now more professional civil servants, and fewer local notables.

Although there is still a large proportion of farmers among the mayors, the professional backgrounds of the latter have become more diverse. One effect of decentralization has been the rise of a new kind of mayor, especially in the big cities—more dynamic, more managerial, and more charismatic.[74] The charisma of these mayors is often based on excessive ambition, which is reflected in grandiose building projects (e.g., subways and convention centers) that lead to greater indebtedness. In order to cover the costs of such projects, mayors may seek loans from the national government, private sources, and even the European Union (with which mayors sometimes negotiate directly).[75] Furthermore, they may apply pressure on the national government to increase the staffs of prefectures. A mayor is helped in this effort if he is also a deputy (preferably belonging to the political party that governs).

Most communities, however, are not very successful in such efforts. Because of their relative poverty, their resources are strained by increased pressures on social services; and because of their relatively low political weight, they are less able to appeal to the national government. The fiscal strain has been particularly severe in smaller communities, of which there are still too many. Some of them cannot even pay the salaries of their regular personnel and turn in desperation to their prefecture.[76] They also band together to engage in common lobbying efforts by means of organizations such as the *Association des petites villes de France*. In order to alleviate the fiscal problem of small communes, a law was enacted in 1992 to encourage intercommunal collaboration in the collection of

TABLE 8.1
Subnational Authorities and Jurisdictions (selected tasks)

	Commune	Department	Region
Social action	Application, intake; supplementary benefits; public health office	Services to child-maternity care; shelters for handicapped and aged; social services; preventive care	
Education	Primary	Junior high (collèges)	High school (lycées); special education; continuing (vocational) education
Economic and local development	Indirect assistance; direct supplementary assistance; intercommunal space planning	Direct assistance; direct supplementary assistance; rural development	Research centers; economic development; direct and indirect assistance; space and other planning; regional parks
Transport	Urban	Nonurban; school transport	Regional liaisons
Culture	Archives; municipal museums, libraries, conservatories	Departmental archives, museums, central lending libraries	Regional archives and museums
Environment	Drinking water; drainage; waste disposal	Planning and maintenance of hiking/riding trails	Environmental protection
Road maintenance	Communal; resorts	Departmental; fishing and commercial harbors	

SOURCES: Based on *L'Administration territoriale II: Les Collectivités locales*, Documents d'études, no 2.03 (Paris: Documentation Française, October 1984); *Cahiers français*, no. 220 (March–April 1985); *Institutions et vie politiques, Les notices* (Paris: Documentation Française, 1991), pp. 55–60; and Gaëlle Dupont, "Les Pouvoirs locaux s'emancipent," Les Cles de l'Info, *Le Monde, Dossiers et Documents*, March 2001, p. iv.

taxes and (after a certain number of years) a common tax structure for clusters of communes. There is a specialized national agency, the *Direction générale des collectivités locales*, which facilitates this process.[77]

Since 1982, there has been a steady growth of the subnational civil service, which in 1995 employed more than 1.2 million people and has grown apace since (see Table 8.2). There is insufficient professional competence especially within the ranks of the local civil service, in part because of relatively low salaries. This explains the increasing resort to outside "consultants," in particular by the larger cities that can afford to hire them.

TABLE 8.2
Civil Service and Other Public Employees on Subnational Levels

	Number
Departmental and regional organisms	
Regional bodies	8,657
Departmental bodies	165,999
Establishments of public law	43,178
Total	*217,834*
Communal and intercommunal bodies	
Communes	1,011,440
Communal organizations	98,478
Intercommunal organizations	111,550
Total	*1,221,468*
Private "local action" organizations in large part publicly funded	*108,439*

SOURCE: *Annuaire Statistique de la France,* vol. 103, (Paris: INSEE, 2000), p. 144.

Despite the growing fiscal responsibilities of subnational authorities, local spending (as compared to national-government spending) has remained lower in France than in other Western democracies.[78] Such spending continues to be conditioned by national resource allocations, which remain significant (see Table 8.3). Thus, while in 1995 Chirac called upon the prefects to help mobilize local resources to fight unemployment, his government initiated a complex series of measures to wage that fight. These measures included both investment contracts between the central government and the regions (in the context of the Eleventh Plan—see Chapter 10) as well as "start-up" pacts with cities.[79] Because the extent and reliability of such measures are uneven, citizens relate more easily to their mayors and think of the central government as more distant than they did before decentralization.[80] However, because citizens also believe that the state should continue to concern itself with the economic life of local communities, their relationship to the mayor—and the mayor's democratic legitimacy—is affected by his relationship to the national authorities.

National political parties play a role in this relationship in the sense that they serve as the instrument of recruitment to both local and national elective positions. Local elections are orchestrated by the major national parties (which operate along the traditional Right-Left axis), but the parties are not such important local actors once the election is over, and that is perhaps why voters do not replicate their national party behavior when they vote locally. The national parties' involvement varies from commune to commune, and sometimes national partisan relationships may be reflected on subnational levels;[81] but as the responsibilities of local governments and the authority of mayors increase, relations (and coalitions) between parties on a subnational level are increasingly determined by local considerations.[82] According to a poll conducted in 1989, 86 percent of the mayors thought that they were judged in municipal elections on the basis of

TABLE 8.3
Sources of Revenue and Expenses of Subnational Units, 1999
(in billions of francs)

	Communes	Departments	Regions	Total
Receipts				
Taxes	225.7	137.9	42.3	474.9
Contributions of national government	96.5	30.0	19.4	145.4
Endowments	32.3	12.7	7.6	36.0
Borrowing	32.9	9.5	5.1	65.2
Other[a]	70.5	28.9	1.5	98.5
Expenditures				
Administration	298.3	139.5	33.6	482.5
Investments	105.5	57.8	35.0	205.3
Annuities and interest payments	56.1	20.8	7.4	117.6

SOURCES: Based on Jean Luc Boeuf, "Les Finances locales," in "Les Collectivités locales en mutation,"
  Cahiers français, no. 293 (October–December 1999), p. 48. For a different set of figures, see *Quid*
  2001 (Paris: Robert Laffont, 2000), p. 1830.
NOTE: The added statistics of the receipts and expenditures may be lower than the total sums indicated,
  because the former do not necessarily include the figures for intercommunal structures.
[a]Including user fees and sale of equipment.

their municipal management, and only 7 percent thought that they were judged according to their political label.[83]

The mayors' growing prestige has been a consequence not only of their enhanced power but also of the limit on multiple-office holding (discussed in Chapter 7), which tends to force politicians to choose between national, supranational, and subnational offices. In 1986, Alain Carignon, the mayor of Grenoble and president of a general council (Isère), showed the way by giving up his National Assembly seat in order to devote greater attention to the interests of his city. That action has so far not served as an example to many other mayors; however, the defeat in the municipal elections in 2001 of a number of cabinet ministers who were also mayors was widely attributed to the citizens' expectation that their mayors would pay full attention to municipal affairs and not be distracted by national office or national ambitions.

One of the problems of mayors is the fact that despite the increasing tempo of decentralization, many tasks of communes are prescribed by the national government. The state provides subsidies for such tasks, but these rarely cover the whole cost. Some cities, in particular larger and more dynamic ones, can well afford to undertake these tasks; but many others, especially small rural communes, lack the means to do so. One way in which local government has been modernized has been the passing of laws permitting the merger of communes that have become too small and inefficient to perform mandatory services by themselves. (By 1977, 838 fusions, involving 2,045 communes, had taken place.) As an alternative to mergers, a law passed in 1971 permitted the formation of commune associations for the joint administration of selected public services, and laws passed subsequently extended the communes' powers in financial matters. In 2001 there were 20,000 such associations serving more than 23,485 communes.[84]

Many communes have shifted responsibilities for selected municipal jobs to *groupements de communes* or—as in the case of trash collection—have contracted with *syndicats intercommunaux* to perform them.[85] Intercommunal cooperation is not new; it dates back to 1890, when a law was passed permitting the creation of *syndicats intercommunaux à vocation unique* (SIVU), which enabled groups of rural communes to perform joint services (e.g., water supply). These were later followed by the *syndicats intercommunaux à vocation multiple* (SIVOM), which deal with several types of service. These *syndicats* are not "interest groups"; rather, they are gatherings of municipal councillors whose recommendations must still be approved by the national government.[86] Further reforms followed in due course, among them a law of 1992 that permitted the creation of different kinds of *établissements publics de coopération intercommunale* (EPCI). These bodies, designed especially for cooperation among cities of more than 20,000 inhabitants, now serve an urban population of more than 32 million.[87] Under legislation introduced in 1999 by the minister of the interior (Chevènement), communes were encouraged to adopt a common tax system in exchange for getting higher state subsidies. If they refused, the law required wealthier communes to subsidize poorer ones in the name of "regional solidarity."[88]

What one hand giveth, the other taketh away. In 2000, the automobile license tax, which had been collected by regional authorities, was abolished, and the collection of local taxes on business (as well as part of the property tax in the Paris region) was transferred to the national government. The lost revenue was to be replaced by government grants.[89] Such measures place the mayor at the mercy of national budgetary constraints.

The increased aid given by the national government, which has been associated with the (re)imposition of national standards, has resulted in the regain by prefects of some of the powers they had possessed before the mid-1980s. For example, according to a law enacted in July 1999, prefects share with the municipal councils the right to initiate the creation of intercommunal associations. In these cases, prefects must consult an advisory body, the *commission départementale de coopération intercommunale*, but they are not obligated to follow its advice. Furthermore, prefects may limit the perimeter of such associations.

Where does that leave the mayor? Traditionally, mayors, although lacking power, had a certain psychic income derived from their local prestige, but today, many of them are disillusioned. According to an IPSOS poll conducted at the end of 1999, only a third of the incumbent mayors intended to be candidates for reelection; many of the latter wanted to remain in office out of a sense of duty to their constituents and the (often slim) hope of being able to lobby on their behalf with the authorities in Paris. Most of the rest intended to devote their time to their own professions.[90]

The Jospin government tried to make the mayors' task easier by increasing their salaries very slightly and by changing the laws covering the legal liability of the mayor: henceforth (as a result of an act passed in 2000), the mayor's failure fully to perform a mandated task will not result in criminal penalties against him if it is not his fault. The salaries earned by mayors depend on the size of their communes. In 2000, the gross salaries of mayors ranged from 3,882 francs (592 euros) a month for the mayor of a commune of under 10,000 inhabitants to 33,113 francs (5,048 euros or about $4,900) for mayors of cities of more than 100,000. Considering the fact that more than 25,000 communes (out of 36,773) had fewer than 700 inhabitants (while only 40 cities had more than 100,000) the income of the typical mayor has been rather limited; and most of them have been unable to supplement it from their own resources. In 1995, more than 30 percent of mayors were retired persons.

The continuing uncertainties about the role of mayor are surpassed only by those concerning the general and regional councils. There is confusion especially about the role of the presidents of these bodies: Are they the spokespersons of their subnational geographic constituents or do they control these constituents? Do these councils bring citizens closer to government, or are they unnecessary fiefdoms, as is charged by traditional Jacobin centralizers?[91]

An equally controversial matter is the relationship between decentralization and local democracy. The fact that there is one local councillor for every 100 inhabitants (as compared to every 1,000 in Britain) and that the rate of participation in local *elections* (75 percent between the end of World War II and the end of the 1980s) is high does not mean that citizens participate in local *administration* more meaningfully than before. The mayor makes the decisions (which are of course more important than they were prior to decentralization) and often merely informs the councillors.

FUNCTIONAL DECENTRALIZATION

One of the areas to be affected by the recent reforms is the system of functional decentralization. Since the end of World War II, the various agencies for the administration of health insurance, family subsidies, and retirement benefits have been based on "activity" (as opposed to geographic) subdivisions. These agencies, or funds *(caisses)*, which are essentially mutual-aid societies that have acquired legal personalities because they have been co-opted for certain administrative tasks and put under the supervision of a national ministry, operate on various subnational levels that do not exactly match the usual administrative units. Thus, whereas there are 22 ordinary regions in metropolitan France (and 4 regions overseas), there are only 16 regional social security offices *(caisses régionales de sécurité sociale)*; and whereas there are 96 departments in metropolitan France, there are 114 family-allowance offices and 121 primary social security offices.

Another kind of "functional decentralization" has been the creation of 25 school districts *(académies)* in which the rector of a particular university is responsible for the administration of the district's entire educational system, including secondary and elementary schools. The university-reform laws of 1968–1970 empowered these school districts and the district councils of education to make many decisions (e.g., about changes in curricula, the restructuring of academic departments, and the disbursement of certain day-to-day expenditures) without direct prior approval by the national Ministry of

Education. In practice, however, this kind of decentralization has been implemented with hesitation. The overlapping of territorial and functional administrative subdivisions is symptomatic of the problems of the French administrative system. This overlapping may provide flexibility, but the jurisdictional rivalries and confusions it introduces must be a nightmare for the specialist in administrative law.

THE ADMINISTRATION OF PARIS

The government of Paris has always been exceptional, and the national government has taken a special interest in it because the capital is the pride and property of the French nation. By special statute promulgated by Napoleon in 1800, the city of Paris was divided into 12 administrative districts (*arrondissements*). During the Second Empire, 8 more districts were added, to form the 20 subdivisions existing to this day. For many years, each *arrondissement* had its own mayor (but no separate council). The mayor's area of competence was quite restricted, encompassing hardly more than the keeping of personal registers and electoral rosters and the performance of marriages. There was an elected municipal council for all 20 *arrondissements*, which had the power to change street names, to recommend budgets, and to issue traffic regulations. The real government of Paris was concentrated in the hands of *two* prefects: the prefect of the Seine and the prefect of police, who were both under the authority of the Ministry of the Interior and whose jurisdictions sometimes overlapped.

Such a centralized administration proved inadequate in view of the urban sprawl around the capital. In order to take into account suburban growth and population shifts, some departments surrounding Paris were subdivided in the early 1960s; in addition, a Paris regional government was set up, with its own appointed council that was concerned with certain types of public services and urban planning. In 1975 Parliament passed a bill providing (for the first time since 1870) for a mayor for Paris as a whole (to be elected by an at-large municipal council for a six-year term) and for an enlargement of the capital's municipal-service bureaus. (The two prefects, however, remained in place.)[92]

From a fiscal perspective, the relationship between Paris and the national government has been much more productive than the relationship between large U.S. cities (including the capital) and the federal government. Paris mayors are much better off than mayors of capitals in other countries: In 2000 the city had a budget of 32 billion francs, which it used not only to pay the salaries of 40,000 officials (including phantom employees) and maintain more than 100 official vehicles but also to subsidize artistic performances and host several hundred official receptions.[93]

Most of the funding for museums, libraries, universities, theaters, and public transport in Paris comes from the national government. Nevertheless, the relationship is not immune to partisan politics. The fact that from 1977 to 1995 the mayor of Paris was Gaullist leader Chirac did not make the mayor's dealings with the national government easier (except, of course, between 1986 and 1988 when Chirac concurrently held the prime ministership). Relations with Giscard were strained because of Chirac's tendency to use his office to promote his presidential ambitions; relations with Mitterrand and his Socialist prime ministers were difficult because the Socialists constituted a minority in the Paris city council.

In mid-1982 the government introduced legislation ostensibly intended to bring Paris government closer to the people (and incidentally also to reduce the power of Chirac). The government proposed to transform the city's *arrondissements* into independent municipalities, each equipped with its own legislative council, mayor, and budget—with the mayor of Paris demoted to the role of a mere presiding officer with ceremonial functions. The modified reforms for Paris enacted by Parliament that went into effect in 1984 provided that the mayors of the *arrondissements* be consulted by the mayor of Paris on such matters as the demolition and construction of buildings, street maintenance, and the municipal investment budget. In addition to retaining their traditional functions (e.g., the registration of births and deaths), the *arrondissements* were to have their own civil servants—an average of 40 for each—and put in charge of allocating subsidized housing, administering child-care centers and old-age homes, and establishing industrial zones, and were empowered to make their own "mini-budgets." (Parallel provisions were enacted for Marseilles and Lyons, cities that are also divided into *arrondissements*. The practical impact of these reforms is not clear, as the budget allocated to each of the arrondissements has been quite small.) Since the election of Chirac to the presidency, relations between the mayor of Paris and the national government improved considerably because of party alignments, official connections, and personal friendships.

CORSICA AND OVERSEAS TERRITORIES

An important aim of decentralization policy has been to breathe new life into the regions. The first beneficiary of this policy was Corsica; its island status, its relative economic underdevelopment, its special cultural-linguistic heritage, and its sociopolitical traditionalism (marked, inter alia, by power struggles among rival clans)—all made for a particularism (expressing itself in political movements of various kinds as well as violence) that Paris could not ignore.

Since it was ceded to France by Genoa in 1768 (a year before Napoleon's birth there), Corsica has been a special problem. Neglected by Paris in the nineteenth century (when many Corsicans migrated to the mainland), it has been heavily subsidized since the end of World War II, with a large proportion of the population working in the public services. Since 1970, the population has become increasingly radicalized, with some (led by the *Front de libération nationale de la Corse* [FLNC]) demanding independence, and others greater autonomy. Still others, in particular the immigrants from the mainland, fear that any relaxation of control by Paris would increase the power of local notables and revive clan rule.[94]

In 1982 Parliament passed special autonomy laws for Corsica. These provided for a regional council, to be known as the "Corsican Assembly," elected for a six-year term under a direct proportional-representation system. The assembly would have wide powers of decision making in agriculture, transport, housing, and education; it would be able to formulate economic-development policies; and it would collect part of its own revenue (from taxes on vehicles and tobacco, for example), to be supplemented by financial allocations from Paris.[95] Corsican civil servants have periodically complained about the inadequacy of such allocations, and in the spring of 1989 threatened to strike in order to obtain salary supplements. In 1990 the government introduced a bill to expand Corsican autonomy; it was passed after the Constitutional Council forced the government to eliminate as unconstitutional the original reference to "the Corsican people, component of the French people." It was doubtful whether the Corsican statute would serve as a prototype for autonomy arrangements for the other French regions. Although decentralization has helped to revive the expression of certain regionally specific cultural identities (in particular in Alsace, Brittany, and the Catalan and Basque areas), this expression has not been accompanied by violence or threatened the unity of the state. The Corsican difference, however, has challenged the central government, which has responded (so far with limited success) with an inconsistent combination of economic incentives and repressive measures (the latter designed especially to stem the growth of separatist movements).[96]

In 2000 the Socialist government introduced another bill that would grant not only increased legislative power to the Corsican regional assembly "in its specific areas of competence" (e.g., space management, environmental protection, tourism, professional training, transport) but also the power to mandate instruction in the Corsican language as a normal part of the curriculum in kindergartens and elementary schools (unless parents specifically oppose it). Some politicians and writers supported the bill, and even suggested that France liberate itself from the "archaic yoke of the Jacobin state" and return to a "Girondin" (i.e., a more decentralized, but not quite federal) conception of France.[97] Former prime minister Michel Rocard insisted that "in our devotion to uniformity . . . it is history that speaks rather than the law . . . [and] that it is better to have a [duly] recognized difference than a false and oppressive uniformity."[98] There were, however, opponents of autonomy for Corsica on both the right and the left. They argued that such a grant would open the door to demands by other regions and lead to the disintegration of the French state; others pointed out that the Jacobinism of 1789 ended in the decade following the 1980s,[99] and still others insist that France already has special regimes that take into account the unique situations of Alsace and Corsica, as well as New Caledonia and other overseas departments or territories, and that the legislature has many options without violating the constitution and endangering "the republican pact of 1792" under which France would be "one and indivisible.[100] Finally, there were those who suggested that the island has been causing so much trouble for Paris that it might perhaps be best to grant it complete independence.

The administration of overseas departments and territories has constituted a different challenge owing to their diversity and their distance from the French mainland. Some overseas possessions, like New Caledonia, have been granted considerable autonomy; others (Guadeloupe, Martinique, Guyana, and Réunion) were transformed into regular departments after World War II and are therefore administered in the "normal" fashion. However, their cultural peculiarities and economic problems have made necessary the introduction of special administrative regimes that are still evolving.[101]

BUREAUCRACY, TECHNOCRACY, AND ECONOMIC ADMINISTRATION

It has long been recognized that the reform of administration goes beyond geographic decentralization. Many governments since the end of World War II have shared an intellectual commitment to address themselves to the following "constant themes": the reduction of the number of ministries; better training and more democratic recruitment of civil servants; better coordination of administrative work; the deconcentration of administrative responsibilities; and the reduction of tensions between administrator and administered. One should also note the existence in France of multiple obstacles to reform: the lack of financial resources, the rivalries among administrative offices, and the virtually automatic (seniority-based) advancement of civil servants, which renders them resistant to change. A decade and a half ago, Michel Rocard committed himself to reform when (in a circular issued shortly after his appointment as premier) he called for a greater respect by civil servants for the needs of civil society, promised to explore possibilities of reorganizing bureaucratic agencies, and (in the interest of cost-effectiveness) recommended the rescission of "obsolete and unduly constraining" regulations.[102] The Balladur government, too, had promised greater openness of the administrative apparatus and a limit to *pantouflage* (see Chapter 5). Premier Juppé, as we have seen, made the streamlining of administration one of his principal aims, but had little success.

One approach to dealing with these problems has been to resort to specialized agencies or "technostructures." The people involved in economic administration (that part of the administrative system concerned with nationalized industries and public corporations) fall outside the ordinary civil service categories. The economic-industrial sector of the administrative apparatus has been important in France for several generations; its increased significance since the end of World War II is a reflection not only of French *dirigisme* but also of the importance of left-wing political parties during the Fourth Republic and in the Fifth Republic between 1981 and 1993, which committed France to a policy of nationalization of industries and a plethora of welfare-state schemes, the administration of which required the creation of novel technocratic agencies. Recruitment of personnel to these agencies is according to nonpolitical criteria, at least in theory, which gives the nationalized industries considerably greater flexibility in hiring than is found in the ministries.

In the administration of the economic-industrial sector there are, however, a number of problems. First, there is a lack of uniformity even greater than that which now prevails in the regular bureaucracy. A multitude of legal forms and institutional typologies exist, ranging from the (commercial or industrial) *établissement public* to the *régie autonome* (e.g., the Paris transport authority). Although many of these agencies are supposed to be "autonomous" and to follow purely business or technical rather than political methods in their management, each of the enterprises is in fact under the control of a particular minister. Nevertheless, there is relatively little democratic supervision of these public corporations. Whereas in the Fourth Republic there were special parliamentary "watchdog" committees in charge of specific public corporations, today there is no effective parliamentary control over them, despite the growth of the number and importance of committees of investigation (see Chapter 7). Moreover, the redress mechanism that one finds in the ordinary civil service is lacking; the Council of State has virtually no jurisdiction in cases involving the nationalized industries.

The government's policy on strikes, already confusing with respect to civil servants, appears to be even more unclear for the economic sectors of the public service. In the Fifth Republic various laws or ordinances have been passed forbidding strikes: In 1963, *grèves tournantes* (staggered strikes of short duration by successive segments of the workforce in a particular plant or office) were forbidden to all sectors of the nationalized economy; and in 1964, strikes by airline controllers were outlawed; but these measures have not been strictly enforced. In 1988, during a prolonged strike of Paris subway workers, Premier Rocard hinted that no-strike clauses regarding public service workers might be enforced and strengthened, but he had no time or inclination to follow up. In 1993, there was a strike of employees of *Air France*, the national air carrier, in response to massive layoffs, but the government responded by replacing the director of the airline; and in 1995, there was a massive strike of railroad workers, to which the government responded by yielding to the demands of the latter.

A certain kind of formal "democratic" input is provided by the multipartite advisory councils attached to the various nationalized industries and composed of representatives of consumers, officials, business managers, and trade unions, but these councils have limited power, owing to their disparate composition, their lack of expertise and information, and their purely consultative nature. The modernization of the administrative structure that has occurred has often been the consequence of pressure from the business sector and has been in the interest of economic expansion; more recently, such modernization has been speeded up in connection with selective deregulation and privatization.

Finally, there is the technocracy of the French Planning Commission, which is in many ways quite different from the traditional civil service. Like many higher civil servants, most of the planning technocrats are graduates of ENA and are subject to supervision by a guardian ministry, in this case the Prime Minister's office (in a formal sense) as well as the Ministry of Economy and Finance (in practice). But the relatively small number of economic planning officials (about 150–200 in all) are economists and statisticians; they are likely to be younger than higher civil servants elsewhere, and they have worked under an aura of scientific mystique. Whereas ministerial civil servants have tended to be etatist and *dirigiste*, many of the planners have been nonideological and willing to accept both interventionist and liberal principles if these help to promote the objectives of growth and efficiency. But like the traditional civil servants, French planning officials have distrusted Parliament and hoped for the decline of interference from that quarter. The administration of economic policy therefore tends to remain a collaborative effort of managers of big business and higher civil servants rather than a partnership between government and a diversity of social and economic sectors. When the Socialists came to power in 1981, the trade unions were promised a somewhat enlarged role in economic planning, but in subsequent years the fulfillment of that promise was impeded both by the reduction of the plan's relevance in the face of pressures of the market and by the steady decline of the power (and membership) of unions.

NOTES

1. John A. Armstrong, "Old Regime Administrative Elites: Prelude to Modernization in France, Prussia, and Russia," *International Review of Administrative Sciences* (hereafter cited as *IRAS*) 38:1 (1972), 21–40. See also Marceau Long, "The Civil Service in France," in *Civil Service Systems*, ed. Louis Fougère (Brussels: International Institute of Administrative Sciences, 1967), pp. 67–68.

2. These figures are approximate. They are based on the following sources: Dominique Quarré, "Les Agents de l'État," *L'État de la France 95–96* (Paris: Éditions de la Découverte, 1995), pp. 167–72; and various issues of *News from France, Le Monde,* 1988–2001; and *Quid 1999, 2000, 2001* (Paris: Laffont).

3. During the first few years of Mitterrand's first presidential term, about 80,000 government employees were added—in part to the educational system, and in part to the sector of nationalized industries, but (under the Chirac government) the number of public employees was reduced as a consequence of the denationalization policies.

4. On the curriculum of ENA, see Jean-Michel Gaillard, *L'ENA, miroir de l'État de 1945 à nos jours* (Paris: Éditions Complexe, 1995), pp. 41f.

5. The percent of ENA graduates among the ministerial staffs of various governments has been as follows (in percent): Fabius 24.3; Chirac 2: 34.3; Rocard 1: 28.2; Rocard 2: 26.9; Cresson 22.0; Bérégovoy 22.4; Balladur 32.4; Juppé I, 36; Juppé II, 30.3. See Luc Rouban, "Les Enarques en cabinets, 1984–1996," *Cahiers du CEVIPOF*, no. 17 (June 1997), 9–10. The largest number of *Enarques* (47.9%) have been in the Ministry of Finance; the smallest (7.8%) in the cabinets of the minister for relations with the Parliament and in Ministry of Veterans' Affairs (8.2%).

6. Examples of ENA graduates who embraced careers outside the government include the presidents of Saint-Gobain, an industrial conglomerate; Peugeot; ELF-Aquitaine, a formerly nationalized petroleum corporation; and Crédit Agricole. See Jean-François Kesler, *L'ENA, la société, l'État* (Paris: Berger-Levrault, 1985), p. 468.

7. Valéry Giscard d'Estaing and Jacques Chirac. Giscard was a graduate of both ENA and the *École Polytechnique*. On the whole, *Polytechniciens* have not done well in electoral politics: They are considered to "abstract," too rigid, and even more arrogant than *Enarques*. See Benjamin Neumann, "Les X peinent à jouer du corps électoral," *Libération*, 20 August 2001.

8. On the social and geographic origins of entrants to ENA, see Pierre Birnbaum, *La Classe dirigeante française* (Paris: PUF, 1978), pp. 55–63; and see also Samy Cohen, *Les Conseillers du président* (Paris: PUF, 1980), esp. pp. 51 and 187 (table). In a highly critical book (Jacques Mandrin, *L'Enarchie*, 2nd ed. [Paris: La Table Ronde, 1980]), it is argued that the *Enarchie*, originally envisaged as a nonpartisan, neutral, and professionally competent elite holding aloft the mystique of the state, was corrupted by Giscard, who transformed it into a combination of managers close to big business and consisting of his personal friends.

9. There are conflicting appraisals of the origins of ENA entrants. According to Michel Euriat and Claude Thélot, "Le Recrutement social de l'élite scolaire en France," *Revue française de sociologie* 36:3 (July–September 1995), 403–36, only 7.1% of entrants into the three most prestigious *grandes écoles* (*Polytechnique, École Normale Supérieure,* and ENA) in 1993 were from the "popular" classes (i.e., shopkeepers, the working class, and the peasantry), but this represents a *decrease* compared to 15.4% in 1965, 13.6% in 1975, and 8.9% in 1985. According to Gaillard, *L'ENA,* that institution was more bourgeois and more Parisian in the 1990s than 30 years earlier.

10. See Pierre Birnbaum, *Les Élites socialistes au pouvoir* (Paris: PUF, 1985). For a critique of this pattern, see Michel Poniatowski, *La Catastrophe socialiste* (Paris: Rocher, 1991), pp. 14–15.

11. *Le Monde,* 28 April and 12 November 1983. Applicants for the alternative path (*troisième voie*) had to be at least 41 years old. For earlier attempts to make entrance to ENA more democratic and to modernize its curriculum, see Pierre Racine, "L'École National d'Administration et son évolution," *Revue administrative* 26 (March–April 1973), 131–41.

12. See "La Création d'un troisième concours d'entrée à l'ENA," *Le Monde,* 16–17 April 1989. According to Gaillard, *L'ENA* (p. 153), the maximum authorized proportion of entrants via the "third way" was 20%, but in fact the number of openings was less than 10% in a typical year. In 1995, the

104 entry places were divided as follows: 47 for "external" applicants, most of them graduates of the *Institut d'Études Politiques* in Paris; 47 for civil servants with at least 5 years of job experience; and 10 for elected officials and others under 40 years old. Rafaële Rivais, "L'État est de nouveau accusé de discriminations sociales," *Le Monde*, 25 July 1996, p. 6.

13. Thierry Pfister, *La République des fonctionnaires* (Paris: Albin Michel, 1988), p. 46; and Michel Schifres, *L'Enaklatura* (Paris: Lattès, 1987), pp. 20ff.

14. The decision, which followed a recommendation by an interministerial committee, also affected other administrative services, which were to be transferred to 73 cities. It was envisaged that by the end of the decade, 30,000 public employees would be transferred.

15. According to a 1995 poll, a majority of the public no longer trusts the "ruling elite": 58% think of it as not very honest; and 53%, that they do not meet their responsibilities. Airy Routier, "La France contre sa classe dirigeante," and Michel Bauer, "Choisir autrement," *Nouvel Observateur*, 21–27 December 1995, pp. 40–43. See also Claude Goasguen, "Un Divorce consommé entre les technostructures et le peuple," and Colette Ysmal, "Les Élites politiques: Un Monde clos?" *Revue politique et parlementaire* 980 (November–December 1995), pp. 20–22 and 27–34. Both of these authors speak of the fracture between the elite and the people and of the lack of confidence of the majority in the former.

16. See Schifres, *L'Enaklatura*, pp. 15–23 et passim. See also Gaillard, *L'ENA*, according to which that institution is "a business school marked by a mystique of the state" (pp. 65f).

17. Among them Giscard, Chirac, Fabius, Rocard, Balladur, Juppé, Jospin, and Séguin.

18. See Jean-Patrice Lacam, *La France, une république de mandarins? Les Hauts Fonctionnaires et la politique* (Paris: Complexe, 2000).

19. Rafaële Rivais, "La Cohabitation fait la part belle aux préfets 'engagés,'" *Le Monde*, 10 August 1999.

20. The purge was not complete; one of the most notorious cases was that of Maurice Papon, who served both the Vichy state (and played a crucial role in the deportation of Jews to the death camps) and the subsequent republics as a high official.

21. For a statistical breakdown, see Jean-Louis Quermonne and Dominique Chagnollaud, *Le Gouvernement de la France sous la Ve République*, nouvelle édition (Paris: Fayard, 1996), pp. 643–47.

22. For example, Mitterrand appointed Robert Badinter, the minister of justice, to the presidency of the Constitutional Council just before the anticipated defeat of the Socialist party in the parliamentary election of 1986. For a similar reason he appointed Pierre Joxe, the minister of defense, to the national audit office (*Cour des comptes*, or Court of Accounts) early in 1993; and just before the presidential elections he appointed Roland Dumas, his old friend and former foreign minister, to head the Constitutional Council. Mitterrand's patronage appointments included numerous ambassadorships. See Michel Colomès, "Les Verroux de Mitterrand," *Le Point*, 27 February 1993, pp. 36–39.

23. Maurice Szafran and Sammy Ketz, *Les Familles du président* (Paris: Grasset, 1982). See especially chapter 1, "La République des fidélités," pp. 7–32. Of the 27 rectors of academies (the chief administrators of the school districts), 14 were replaced in 1981, mostly by reliable Socialists. The Paris subway authority (RATP) was put under a Communist director—no doubt because the new minister of transport was a Communist. On the French "spoils system" under Giscard, Chirac, and the Socialists, see also Christiane de Brie, "La Très Réélle Politisation des hauts fonctionnaires," *Le Monde Diplomatique*, April 1987.

24. Marie-France Toinet, "La Morale bureaucratique: Perspectives transatlantiques et franco-américaines," *International Political Science Review* 9:3 (1988), 193–203.

25. For statistics, see Jeanne Siwek-Poudyesseau, "Le Syndicalisme des fonctionnaires, 1900–1981," *Vingtième Siècle*, January–March 1993, p. 122.

26. According to Pfister (*République des fonctionnaires*, pp. 22–23), 19 percent of the members of the PS executive bureau in 1977 were *Enarques*.

27. Birnbaum, *Les Élites socialistes au pouvoir*, pp. 202–3. A more recent study of the ideology of *fonction publique* has revealed that professors and other public educators tend to vote on the left; others, e.g., *cadres* in areas other than education, tend to vote more in the center. All public servants tend to be etatist (which lead them to the right) but also public service oriented (which leads them to the left). Luc Rouban, "Les Attitudes politiques des fonctionnaires: Vingt Ans d'évolution," *Cahiers du CEVIPOF*, May 1999, pp. 32–34, 55–86.

28. F. M. Marx, "The Higher Civil Service as an Action Group in Western Political Development," in *Bureaucracy and Political Development*, ed. J. La Palombara (Princeton: Princeton University Press, 1963), p. 79.

29. In addition to Bérégovoy there have been other "self-made men" who have achieved high-profile elective office, among them Bernard Tapie, who was a left-wing deputy and political leader in Marseilles, and Alain Carignon, who was a Gaullist mayor of Grenoble. Some have argued that one reason for their ultimate imprisonment in the mid-1990s for the misappropration of public funds (as for the suicide of Bérégovoy) was that they were not educated enough to "finesse" the legal system and received little support from the traditional political elite.

30. Pierre Birnbaum, *Les Sommets de l'État: Essai sur l'élite du pouvoir en France* (Paris: Seuil, 1977), pp. 151ff.

31. Jacques Chevallier, "L'Intérêt général dans l'Administration française," *IRAS* 41:4 (1975), 325–50.

32. Gabriel Mignot and Philippe d'Orsay, *La Machine administrative* (Paris: Seuil, 1968), p. 8. See also Jean Montheu, "Un Château-fort médiéval: Le Ministère de l'économie et des finances," *L'Esprit*, n.s., special issue, January 1970, p. 147. According to this source, the staff of the tax office (Ministry of Finance) grew from 48,900 in 1963 to nearly 60,000 in 1970. It continued to grow from the 1970s to the 1990s, but there are still not enough tax inspectors to resolve the persisting problem of tax evasion.

33. See Georges Langrod, *La Consultation dans l'administration contemporaine* (Paris: Cujas, 1972). This massive work on "consultative administration," although dated, is still useful because it lists more than 300 *comités, commissions,* and *conseils* on the national level alone.

34. See Jean-Paul Costa, *Le Conseil d'État dans la société contemporaine* (Paris: Economica, 1993), and the briefer Marie-Christine Kessler, *Le Grand Corps de l'État* (Paris: PUF, 1994), esp. chap. 1.

35. Most of the work of the Council of State concerns *excès du pouvoir* (i.e., overstepping of responsibilities by an official in such a way as to damage a private citizen's interest). There are actually four grounds of challenge to bureaucratic action: (1) lack of authority *(ultra vires)*, (2) failure to observe procedures called for by an existing law, (3) abuse of power *(détournement de pouvoir)*, and (4) violation of the law.

36. The number of cases brought before the Council of State averaged about 4,000 annually from 1973 to 1976 but grew to about 11,000 in 1992. Blandine Barret-Kriegel, *L'État de la démocratie: Rapport à François Mitterrand* (Paris: Documentation Française, 1985), p. 202; and *Le Monde*, 8 October 1987 and 9 September 1993.

37. In its annual report of 1992, the Council of State mentions 7,500 laws, 82,000 decrees, 22,000 European Community regulations, and more than 10,000 *circulaires* for whose enforcement it is theoretically responsible. See Thierry Bréhier, "Le Conseil d'État critique la 'logorrhée législative et réglementaire,'" *Le Monde*, 21 May 1992; and Guy Braibant, "Qui fait la loi," *Pouvoirs*, no. 64 (1993), 47. For other statistics, see Philippe Guilhaume, *La République des clones* (Paris: Albin Michel, 1994), pp. 71–73; and Pierre Bitoun, *Voyage au pays de la démocratie moribonde* (Paris: Albin Michel, 1995), p. 101.

38. Gérard Soulier, *Nos Droits face à l'État* (Paris: Seuil, 1981), pp. 33, 88–90, 124. In 1962, when the Council of State challenged the legality of an ordinance creating a military court of justice, de Gaulle was so enraged that he briefly thought of curtailing the power of the council.

39. The recruitment of members of the Council of State is complicated, involving competitive examinations given by ENA (for auditors), promotion from below, based on seniority (for *maîtres de requêtes*), and pure discretion of the government (for a third of the councillors).

40. The bill to provide for a mediator was introduced in 1972 by Premier Pierre Messmer; however, the idea can be traced to Michel Poniatowski (an intimate friend of Giscard's) who in 1970 (as an Independent Republican deputy) introduced a bill in 1970 to create a "High Commission for the Defense of the Rights of Man" (composed of members of the Council of State and the Court of Cassation [see Chapter 9 herein]). See Bernard Maligner, *Les Fonctions du médiateur* (Paris: PUF, 1979), p. 13.

41. The current mediator, appointed in 1998, is Bernard Stasi, a progressive former deputy belonging to the *Force démocrate*, the Christian Democratic wing of the UDF.

42. Recently a special delegate of the national mediator was installed in a post office in an industrial suburb of Paris. See Hervé Guénot, "Un Médiateur face á l'administration," *Figaro*, 30 May 2000, p. 13.

43. The CNIL is composed of 17 members, of whom 3 are named by the government, 2 by the speakers of the two chambers of parliament, 6 by the members of the chambers, and 6 by various national judicial bodies. The CADA is named by the premier, and composed of 19 people, including (in 1988) 4 deputies, 2 municipal councillors, 2 university professors, and higher civil servants. Cf. J. Robert, "Le Giscardisme et les libertés," *Pouvoirs*, no. 9 (1979), 95. See also J. Lemasurier, "Vers une démocratie administrative: Du refus d'informer au droit d'être informé," *Revue du droit public*, no. 5 (1980), 1239 ff; and *L'Accès au documents administratifs*, 5th Report of CADA (Paris: Documentation Française, 1988).

44. On conflicts of interest (relating to politicians and officials of public corporations to a much greater extent than to ordinary civil servants), see Yves Mény, *La Corruption de la République* (Paris: Fayard, 1992), esp. pp. 20–21, 66.

45. In 1946, civil servants obtained the right to join unions. Their right to strike has remained unclear; striking is not forbidden, but neither is it specifically permitted (although the Council of State affirmed that right).

46. Rafaële Rivais, "Le Gouvernement propose une réforme tous azimouts pour modernizer l'État," *Le Monde*, 8 March 1996, p. 7; and same author, "Les Hauts Fonctionnaires veulent conserver leurs privilèges," *Le Monde*, 6–7 October 1996, p. 5.

47. Jean-Luc Bodiguel and Luc Ruban, *Le Fonctionnaire détrôné? L'État au risque de la modernisation* (Paris: Presses de la Fondation Nationale des Sciences Politiques, 1991), esp. chap. 1 ("La Fin du pouvoir d'État?"). One indication of the relinquishment of functions of the state has been the transfer of certain police protection activities to private security personnel (see Sebastian Roché, "Le Marché de la sécurité," *L'État de la France 95–96*, pp. 80–82); another has been the reduction of the personnel of the ministerial offices dealing with social affairs, health, and labor (see Quarré, "Les Agents de l'État," pp. 167–72; and *L'Année politique 1995*, p. 474).

48. This was done despite Chirac's promise that his state would be "impartial." See Rafaële Rivais, "Plus de trente préfets ont été déplacés depuis l'élection présidentielle," *Le Monde*, 14 July 1995, p. 7.

49. Mark Kesselman, *The Ambiguous Consensus* (New York: Knopf, 1967), p. 8. See appendix B of that work (pp. 171–84) for a description (now somewhat dated) of the legal powers of communes.

50. Sidney Tarrow, "Local Constraints and Regional Reform: A Comparison of France and Italy," *Comparative Politics* 7:1 (October 1974), 1–36.

51. Sidney Tarrow, *Between Center and Periphery: Grassroots Politicians in Italy and France* (New Haven: Yale University Press, 1977), pp. 111–41.

52. Edgar Morin, *Commune en France* (Paris: Fayard, 1967).

53. Philippe Garrard, "Le Recrutement des maires en milieu urbain," *Pouvoirs*, no. 24 (January 1983), 29–43. See also Yves Mény, "Le Maire, ici et ailleurs," *Pouvoirs*, same issue, pp. 19–27, who argues that because of his local popularity, the mayor in effect "chooses" the city council and dominates whatever agent the national government might send.

54. Gabriel Mignot and Philippe d'Orsay, *La Machine administrative* (Paris: Seuil, 1977), p. 48. Cf. Jean de Savigny, *L'État contre les communes?* (Paris: Seuil, 1971), p. 64, which cites 8 percent for departments and 20 percent for communes.

55. Pierre Gaudez, "La Réforme des collectivités locales," *Le Monde*, 4 June 1975.

56. Odon Vallet, "D'abord, entre dans la vie des communes," *Projet*, no. 142 (February 1980), 149–55.

57. See "La Décentralisation en marche," *Le Monde, Dossiers et Documents*, no. 164 (March 1989), for conflicting comparative statistics.

58. *Le Monde*, 8 April 1970.

59. An example of such inequality: At the end of the 1960s the department of Basses-Alpes had 83,354 inhabitants, and the department of Nord, 1,917,452.

60. For a history of decentralization attempts, see Michel Phlipponeau, *Décentralisation et régionalisation* (Paris: Calmann-Lévy, 1981). For an excellent comprehensive work, see Vivien A. Schmidt, *Democratizing France: The Political and Administrative History of Decentralization* (Cambridge, MA, and New York: Cambridge University Press, 1991).

61. See Tarrow, "Local Constraints and Regional Reform." It has also been argued that the following prevailing ideologies (shared by local politicians) have militated against meaningful decentralization: individualism (which does not tolerate geographic intermediaries between citizen and state), the "logic of capitalism," and the "ethnocentrism of the bourgeoisie" (both of which have justified the traditional suppression of the provinces). Claude de Vos, "La Région: À la recherche d'un sens," in *Annales de la Faculté des Lettres et Sciences Humaines de Nice* (issue on "Urbanisation, développement régional, et pouvoir public"), no. 26 (1975), 137–51. See also Club Moulin, *Les Citoyens au pouvoir* (Paris: Seuil, 1968).

62. P. B. M. Jones, "The Organisation of Regional Economic Planning in France," *Public Administration* (London) 45 (Winter 1967), 358. For a more detailed treatment, see François Damiette, *Le Territoire français et son aménagement* (Paris: Éditions Sociales, 1969).

63. Jacques Baguenard, "L'Organisation régionale (loi du 5 juillet 1972)," *Revue du droit public*, 89 (November–December 1973), 1405–65. See also Dominique Henry, "La Région et l'aménagement du territoire," *Revue administrative*, January–February 1976, pp. 73–75; for a general treatment, see Jérôme Monod and Philippe de Castelbajac, *L'Aménagement du territoire* (Paris: PUF, 1971); and (on regional reform), see William G. Andrews, "The Politics of Regionalization in France," in *Politics in Europe*, ed. Martin Heisler (New York: David McKay, 1974), pp. 293–322. For a more recent (heavily historical and legal) treatment of the region, see Bruno Rémond, *La Région* (Paris: Montchrestien, 1995).

64. François Grosrichard, "Renouvellement politique et ouverture régionale," *Le Monde*, 28 March 1973. See also same author, "Le Crépuscule des régions," *Le Monde*, 28 November 1975.

65. See "Enfin, la décentralisation," *Regards sur l'actualité*, no. 74 (September–October 1981), 22–23; and "La Décentralisation," *Cahiers français*, no. 204 (January–February 1982), 44–45.

66. *Le Monde*, 26 November 1975. See also Alain Peyrefitte, "Régionalisation ou décentralisation?" *Le Monde*, 22 November 1975; and Mark O. Rousseau, "President Valéry Giscard d'Estaing and Decentralization," *French Review* 54:6 (May 1981), 827–35.

67. As Premier Mauroy put it, the reforms were intended to lead to a selective "degovernmentalization" *(désétatisation)* of decision making by "[strengthening] the structures of civil society. . . [building] a new citizenship . . . [and giving] the state back to the citizen." "La Décentralisation en marche," p. 52.

68. Article 1 of the law of 2 March 1982, cited and discussed in Paul Bernard, *L'État et la décentralisation*, Notes et Études Documentaires, nos. 4711–12 (Paris: Documentation Française, 1983), pp. 121ff.

69. Eventually, the elections of general councillors were to take place simultaneously with those of municipal councillors.

70. If the commissioner felt that local governments violated the laws or exceeded their budgetary authority, he would no longer be able *himself* to nullify these local acts; instead, he would be empowered to submit them for a judgment to an administrative tribunal or to a newly constituted regional fiscal control tribunal, or Court of Accounts. On the further refinement of the prefect's role, see Jean-Jacques Gleizal, ed., *Le Retour des préfets?* (Grenoble: Presses Universitaires de Grenoble, 1995), esp. chap. 1.

71. See Lionel Jospin, "Décentralisation: Les Six Priorités du gouvernement," *Revue politique et parlementaire*, January–February 2001, pp. 4–11.

72. See Jérôme Ferret, "Les Polices municipales en France, une perspective socio-politique," *Déviance et société* 22:3 (1998).

73. Patrice Joly, "L'Évolution des compétences communales," *Après-Demain*, May–June 1995, pp. 5–8. Some transfers of resources have also been undertaken as part of the "deconcentration" policy, a term that refers to the shifting of selective national tasks from Paris to the regions or departments. A number of (sometimes overlapping) interministerial and interprefectoral committees exist for that purpose. But with the policies of decentralization, the distinctions between the latter and deconcentration have become increasingly irrelevant. See Olivier Diederichs and Ivan Luben, *La Déconcentration* (Paris: PUF, 1995), esp. pp. 55–72. The transfer of funds to communes is partly nullified by local expenditures resulting from the imposition not only of Parisian tasks but also of European Union directives, such as those relating to environmental protection. Claude Francillon, "Des Nouvelles Charges pèsent sur le budget des petites villes," *Le Monde*, 23 October 1996, p. 11.

74. See Jean-Michel Gaillard and Catherine Rambert, *La Fête des maires* (Paris: Lattès, 1993); and André Chandernagor, *Les Maires de France* (Paris: Fayard, 1993). Examples of younger mayors of larger cities who are frequently mentioned are Georges Frêche of Montpellier and Catherine Trautmann of Strasbourg. Nevertheless, more than 11,000 mayors were over 61 years old in 1995 and fewer than 4,000 were under 40. Jean-François Merle, "Le Métier de maire," *Après-Demain*, May–June 1995, pp. 36–39.

75. Gérard Fayolle, *Des Élus locaux sous la Ve République* (Paris: Hachette, 1989), p. 52. On the increasing pressure on mayors to initiate projects and seek funds, see Paul J. Godt, "Decentralization in France: Plus ça Change . . . ?" *Tocqueville Review* 7 (1985/86), 191–203.

76. See "Contrats clochemerlesques," *Le Monde (Heures Locales)*, 5–6 September 1993, which discusses the financial dilemmas of "Podunks."

77. See "L'État de la décentralisation," *Cahiers français*, no. 256 (May–June 1992), 87ff. See also Marie-Christine Bernard-Gélabert and Patrick Labia, *Intercommunalités—Mode d'Emploi* (Paris: Economica, 1992).

78. From 1978 to 1985, total local revenues and expenditures grew by only 29 percent; in the latter year the proportion of local spending in France was only 8 percent of the gross national product and 16 percent of public expenditures, compared to 19 percent of GNP (and 37 percent of public expenditures) in the United States and 13 percent (and 26 percent) in Britain. Figures from Vincent Hoffmann-Martinot and Jean-Yves Nevers, "French Local Policy Change in a Period of Austerity: A Silent Revolution," in *Urban Innovation and Autonomy: The Political Implications of Policy Change*, ed. Susan Clarke (Newbury Park, CA: Sage, 1989).

79. See Philippe Chain, "Les Contrats de plan État-régions," *Regards sur l'actualité*, no. 215 (November 1995), 32–46; and Francis Idrac, "Le Pacte de relance pour la ville," *Regards sur l'actualité*, no. 222 (June 1996), 19–34. Under that pact, "enterprise zones" *(zones franches)* would be set up in three dozen cities, which would benefit from tax concessions for local enterprises and lower social security deductions. The burden for this "affirmative action," which includes funding supplements for schools, new public service posts, and increased police, would be shared by the state in the form of subsidies and low-interest credits.

80. According to SOFRES polls, in 1990, 22% of respondents thought of the state as being close to them (compared to 41% in 1970), while 74% thought of the state as being distant (compared to 51% in 1970). Thierry Bréhier, "L'Opinion des Français," in *Dix Ans de décentralisation, Le Monde, Dossiers et Documents*, no. 202 (September 1992), 4. In contrast, 63% of respondents in a recent poll were satisfied with the actions of their mayor. CSA poll of 11–13 June 1996, cited in *Figaro*, 26 June 1996, p. 7.

81. For example, in 1996 the UDF, frustrated in its relationship with the RPR in Parliament, was engaged in attempts to reduce Gaullist dominance in the legislative organs of the Paris region. Cécile Chambraud, "L'UDF se prépare à disputer au RPR son hégémonie en Ile-de-France," *Le Monde*, 26 October 1996, p. 7.

82. See Stéphane Dion, *La Politisation des mairies* (Paris: Economica, 1986), pp. 202–7 et passim.

83. "La Nouvelle Vie locale," *Le Monde, Dossiers et Documents*, March 1989, p. 2. For a contrary view, see Pierre Martin, "Existe-t-il en France un cycle électoral municipal?" *RFSP* 46:6 (December 1996), 961–95. Martin notes that municipal elections serve as political "weather vanes" in the sense that the outcome reflects the popularity of the national government and may constitute a preliminary "mobilization of dissatisfied voters."

84. "L'Allègement de la tutelle administrative," *Revue administrative*, July 1971, pp. 459–62. See also Yves Madiot, *Fusions et regroupements de communes* (Paris: LGDJ, 1973); and Christine Brémont, "La Réorganisation des territoires en marche," *Territoires 2020: Etudes et prospective*, no. 2, DATAR, December 2000, pp. 37–45.

85. Catherine Bernard, "Le Mal de maire des élus de la terre," *Libération*, 23 February 2001.

86. Elisabeth Zoller, "La Création des syndicats de communes: Une Décision des communes ou de l'Etat?" *Revue du droit public* 92 (July–August 1976), 985–94.

87. For a statistical breakdown of intercommunal organizations and the populations they serve, see Didier Lallement, "Intercommunalité: Les Enjeux d'une nouvelle réforme," *Regards sur l'actualité*, no. 247 (January 1999), 3–14.

88. Nathalie Raulin, "Communes: Difficile solidarité," *Libération*, 13–14 February 1999. By 2000, 1,849 "intercommunal" fiscal systems had already been created, involving more than 21,000 communes with a total of 37 million inhabitants.

89. Renaud Dely, "Les Élus locaux pleurent leur vignette," *Libération*, 1 September 2000.

90. Nicole Gauthier, "Malgré le blues, les édiles sont prêts à rempiler," *Libération*, 23 February 2001.

91. See Jean-Pierre Chevènement, "Dangers et limites," *ENA mensuel*, no. 214: "La Décentralisation" (August 1991), 13.

92. The prefect of police is not only under the authority of the Ministry of the Interior but also under that of other ministries whose responsibilities relate to the various tasks of city government. The prefect of police is responsible, inter alia, for public order, the control of strikes, the maintenance of prisons, the protection of houses of worship, the security of embassies, and the control of the movement of foreigners. In contrast, the prefect of Paris (formerly, prefect of the Seine) has very limited powers; he "represents" the state, but he has given up most of the real power to the mayor of Paris, who is also the president of the general council of the Paris department. The prefect of police has two budgets: one allocated by the state for executing national tasks, and another voted by the municipal council of Paris for local tasks. For a discussion of the evolution of the government of Paris and current details of its politics and administration, see Christian Bigaut, "Histoire municipale de la ville de Paris," and same author, "La Mairie de Paris," *Regards sur l'actualité*, no. 272 (June 2001), 17–43.

93. Fabien-Roland Lévy, "Le Train de vie de Tibéri," *Le Point*, 6 October 2000, pp. 75–82.

94. See Jean-Louis Briquet, *La Tradition en mouvement: Clientélisme et politique en Corse* (Paris: Belin, 1997).

95. The Corsican Assembly was expected to work closely with two advisory councils—a social and economic council and a council for culture, education, and the quality of life—each composed of representatives of interest groups.

96. Vanessa Schneider and Pascal Virot, "La Majorité demande au gouvernment," *Libération*, 13 March 1996, p. 6; and Caroline Monnot, "M. Juppé veut un débat public sur la politique du gouvernement en Corse, *Le Monde*, 24 May 1996, p. 6.

97. Claude Imbert, "Une Révolution annoncée," *Le Point*, 1 September 2000, p. 7. See also Jean-Marie Colombani, *Les Infortunés de la République* (Paris: Grasset, 2000).

98. M.R., "Pour en finir avec le jacobinisme," *Le Monde*, 31 August 2000. The concept of Jacobinism originated at the beginning of the Revolution, in a discussion group composed of individuals from various provinces who met in Versailles under the name of *"Club breton."* This group developed the most important revolutionary theses later adopted by the Assembly, such as the unity of nation and state and a centralized government to which the citizen could relate directly without intermediaries. The group later moved to Paris, where it was known as *"Société des amis de la Constitution."* But since it met regularly in the refectory of the Convent of the Jacobins (a former monastery), it soon came to be referred to as the *Club des Jacobins.* Michel Voyelle, *Les Jacobins de Robespierre à Chevènement* (Paris: Plon, 1999), pp. 157–78.

99. Voyelle, *Les Jacobins*, pp. 157–78.

100. Gérard Bélorgey, "Ni République strictement unitaire, ni Fédération de régions: Un État composé," *Revue politique et parlementaire*, 103 année, no. 1009/1010 (November–December/January–February 2001), 166–71. This article is part of a whole special issue titled "Quel État pour les régions?" devoted to the debate on whether Corsican autonomy is compatible with republican unity.

101. Paul Cousseron, "De la Polynésie à la Corse: Vers 'l'autonomie évolutive'?" *Le Monde*, 28 January 1996, p. 12. See also Marc Janus, *Les Départements d'outre-mer et la CEE* (Paris: L'Harmattan, 1995). This book describes how the overseas departments, despite their geographic disadvantage, have created informal networks of influence by mobilizing their political and administrative connections in Paris and utilizing the autonomous powers given to them as a result of decentralization to conduct special economic relations with European Union and Caribbean countries.

102. "Gouverner autrement: La Circulaire Rocard du 25 mai 1988," *Regards sur l'actualité*, no. 143 (July–August 1988), pp 15–18.

CHAPTER 9

Law, Justice, and Civil Liberties

THE JUDICIAL SYSTEM

The French judicial system shares many features with those of Britain and the United States: the belief in procedural due process, the principle that no action is punishable except on the basis of law (*nulla poena sine lege*), the rejection of ex post facto law, the presumption of the innocence of the accused, and the independence of the judiciary. Some of these principles were articulated in the Declaration of the Rights of Man and the Citizen of 1789 and reaffirmed and extended by the preamble to the Constitution of 1946, and they have become part of republican constitutions; others have been embraced by political practice through legislation and judicial interpretation. The French system of legal norms is based on abstract principles (code law) as compared with the Anglo-American tradition of judicial precedents (common law, or case law). However, this distinction has in reality become somewhat obscured. Much common law in Anglo-American democracies has been superseded by statute law; conversely, French code law allows for rules of custom and precedent in cases where codes are insufficient as guides for judicial decisions.

French civil and criminal codes date back to the Romans, but they were revised by the Napoleonic Civil Code of 1804, followed by the Criminal Code of 1810. Code law, in principle, has the merit of providing uniformity, of ensuring that in a given case the same principles apply throughout the country and that decisions are not dependent on diverse judicial temperaments. In practice, however, there is a great regional diversity of sentencing patterns.[1] Nevertheless, code law may be regarded as more rigid than common law, and its assumptions may quickly become antiquated. The French Parliament began to modernize the Criminal Code in 1959 and continued that process by fits and starts. After 18 years of effort, the first thorough overhauling of the Criminal Code since Napoleon was completed early in 1994. Under this reform, new delicts were added, among them sexual harassment, crimes against humanity (with no statute of limitations), and computer crimes.

France's judicial system has been widely imitated because it has many admirable features. There is a wide geographic distribution of courts at various levels and, therefore, easy accessibility to justice for most of the population. Courts of first instance are found in every *arrondissement*, and there are many higher courts (see Figure 9.1). In addition to the civil and criminal courts, a network of functionally specialized tribunals exists. The best known are the administrative courts, in which citizens can bring a suit against civil servants for violations of laws and regulations and for arbitrary behavior (see Chapter 8). There are also separate regional tribunals for labor relations *(conseils de prud'hommes)*, social security matters, commercial disputes, children's courts, and conflicts between tenant farmers and landlords *(baux ruraux)*.[2] Some of these tribunals date back to the First Empire and even to the *ancien régime*, but they are still relevant for disputes engendered by the administration of the contemporary welfare state. Traditionally, the specialized tribunals were structurally separate from the civil and criminal courts. In 1970, legislation was passed to bring these tribunals into the ordinary appellate court system. The law provided for setting up, within every court of appeal, "social chambers" to deal with labor relations and collective contracts. Each of these chambers is composed of one judge and four lay assessors, two from trade unions and two representing employers, chosen by the government from lists submitted by the appropriate associations. (This method differs from that of the *conseils de prud'hommes*, where the assessors are elected by trade unions and employers' associations.)

The corps of judges in France represents a distinct segment of the legal profession. A privately practicing attorney cannot, after he or she is well established, decide to become a judge. A person who is interested in a judicial career must, after completing studies at a faculty of law, enter a special law school, the *École Nationale de la Magistrature* (ENM), which was set up in Bordeaux in 1958 and which, in terms of its study program and its social selectivity, is patterned somewhat on the ENA.[3] Before completing studies at the ENM, students must opt for a specific part of the national judiciary—either the *magistrature* or the *parquet*, the former comprising the judges, and the latter, the prosecuting attorneys *(procureurs)* working on behalf of the Ministry of Justice. By 1992, 4,700 of France's 6,000 sitting judges were graduates of ENM.

Career judges are technically part of the civil service, at least in terms of their security of tenure, pay, promotions, and retirement benefits. Original appointments of judges are made, not by the minister of justice, but by the president, on the basis of recommendations by the High Council of the Magistrature. This body, which includes, ex officio, the president of the Republic and the minister of justice, is composed of two sections: one dealing with sitting judges, and the other with prosecuting attorneys, with their incumbents selected in a complicated fashion involving the president of the Republic, the Court of Cassation *(Cour de cassation)*, the Council of State, and the presiding officers of the two chambers of Parliament.[4]

The organization of the French legal profession appears inordinately complex when compared to the American one with its single class of lawyers, or the British one, with its two categories, barristers and solicitors. The French have several types of legal professionals in addition to judges: (1) *avocats*, attorneys who can plead in most trial courts; (2) *notaires* (notaries public), whose main responsibility is the preparation of contracts, wills, and property settlements;[5] and (3) *fiduciaires*, who are concerned with tax matters. There used to be another type of juridical profession, that of *conseiller*

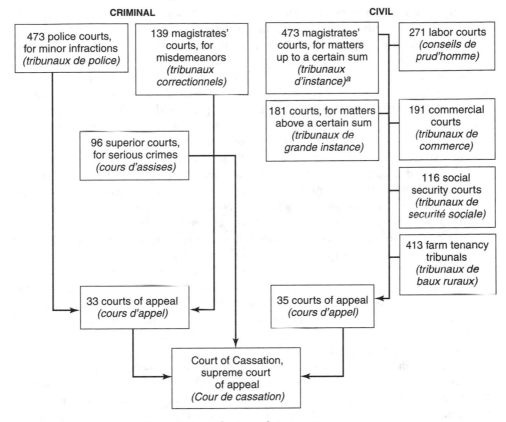

CRIMINAL   CIVIL

473 police courts, for minor infractions *(tribunaux de police)*

139 magistrates' courts, for misdemeanors *(tribunaux correctionnels)*

473 magistrates' courts, for matters up to a certain sum *(tribunaux d'instance)[a]*

271 labor courts *(conseils de prud'homme)*

181 courts, for matters above a certain sum *(tribunaux de grande instance)*

191 commercial courts *(tribunaux de commerce)*

96 superior courts, for serious crimes *(cours d'assises)*

116 social security courts *(tribunaux de securité sociale)*

413 farm tenancy tribunals *(tribunaux de baux ruraux)*

33 courts of appeal *(cours d'appel)*

35 courts of appeal *(cours d'appel)*

Court of Cassation, supreme court of appeal *(Cour de cassation)*

FIGURE 9.1 The French Court Structure

SOURCE: Figure adapted in part from François-Louis Coste, "Le Procés pénal," in Pierre Truche, ed., *Justice et institutions judiciaires* (Paris: Documentation Française, 2001), p. 110.

NOTE: The figures, which are for 2001, represent metropolitan France. The system of justice for minors *(tribunaux pour enfants)* is not included.

[a]Until 1958, there were about 3,000 justices of the peace—one for each canton—whose functions have since been taken over by the *tribunaux d'instance.*

juridique, who gave general legal advice (and who was often employed by corporations), but in 1992 this category was fused with that of *avocat.*[6]

At the top of the legal profession's hierarchy are the *avocats aux conseils,* of whom there are about 60, who may appear before the Court of Cassation—the highest court of appeal for civil, criminal, and socioeconomic cases—or the Council of State, its counterpart for administrative cases. The Court of Cassation is divided into six "chambers" or panels—five civil and one criminal—each composed of at least seven judges, who decide by majority vote. (Unlike U.S. courts, neither the Court of Cassation nor the other French courts publish dissenting opinions.)[7] This court does not determine the facts in the case, but rather the legality of the decision rendered by a lower court.[8] At the bottom of the judicial ladder are the *greffiers* (court clerks) and the *huissiers* (bailiffs). This functional differentiation goes back several centuries. The "medieval" aspects of the profession are manifested in the special gowns the *avocats* are required to wear in court, the hereditary nature of some of the categories (e.g., *greffiers* and *huissiers*), and the retention of the practice of setting fees by law for all but the *avocats*.

The judicial procedure itself differs in some important respects from Anglo-American patterns. There is the "inquisitorial" system of trial procedure, whereby the presiding judge intervenes actively in the trial by questioning the defendant, the witnesses, and the lawyers on both sides (in contrast with the "adversarial" system common in the United States and Britain, where the judge's primary duty is to ensure the orderly progress of the trial). Most verdicts in the lower courts are decided by a panel of judges. The number of judges needed to decide a case varies according to the level of the court and the nature of the charges. However, trial by jury is becoming more common, particularly in courts of appeal (where, typically, nine jurors and three judges sit together to decide a case and a two-thirds majority is needed to uphold a conviction).

There is a much greater tendency in French courts than in Anglo-American courts to convict a defendant, a phenomenon that has given rise to the notion that in France, the innocence of the accused is not safeguarded so well as it is in the Anglo-Saxon democracies, and that in a criminal trial, procedures favor the state. But not every case goes to a full trial; there is a lengthy pretrial investigation by an examining magistrate in which various due-process guarantees are applied and the suspect may be able to use counsel.

The pretrial investigation of a crime has two stages: the first is the preliminary police inquiry; this is followed by the magistrate's investigation *(instruction par le juge)*, which often used to be so protracted that the accused was held for a long time in detention before being indicted. There is no writ of habeas corpus per se in the Constitution of 1958; nevertheless, Article 66 provides that "no person may be detained arbitrarily," and there have been a series of piecemeal reforms to bring France closer to de facto habeas corpus protections. Thus, the Penal Code Reform of 1959 specified that "preventive detention is an exceptional measure"; and in 1970, 1974, and 1980, bills were passed that gradually limited preventive detention to four months. The culmination of this evolution was the Habeas Corpus Act of 1984, which provided that no one could be placed in temporary detention without argument by a state attorney, evidence by the accused, and challenge by defense counsel.[9]

One of the aims of legal reforms has been to bring French law into conformity with international and, more specifically, European norms—respectively, the International Court of Criminal Justice (created by the United Nations in 1998) and the European Court of Human Rights. Thus, France has had to alter its laws to conform to European Union rules in permitting women to work at night; granting paid paternity leave; and allowing parents to decide to have their children bear either the father's or the mother's family name. There have been over 600 complaints by French citizens to the European Court of Human Rights for violations of human rights. In 1999, France was sanctioned by that court for torture by the police and ordered to pay a fine to a plaintiff.[10]

JUSTICE AND THE DEMOCRATIC STATE

Among the charges leveled against the French judicial system is that it is unduly politicized. "Political justice" sometimes results from a combination of government action (or inaction) and ideologically conditioned judicial arbitrariness, as in the case of Paul

Touvier, a Vichy official whose indictment was temporarily thrown out in 1992 by a reactionary court of appeals.[11] More often, however, such justice arises from the tendency of a government to protect its own members and political friends against embarrassing judicial proceedings.[12] The apparent immunity of politicians to the application of ordinary criminal law has provoked public protests; it was partly in response to these protests that the Constitution was amended in 1993 to create a new tribunal, the Court of Justice of the Republic, in which members of the government could be judged (Art. 68). However, the majority (12 out of 15) of this court was to consist of members of Parliament, a fact that raises questions about their impartiality in trying individuals of their own kind.[13]

Yet reducing the intervention of the state (i.e., the executive and the legislature) in judicial proceedings does not by itself guarantee the independence of the judiciary and protect it against sources of undue influence, for example, that of interest groups or ideological movements. That is a major reason why many French citizens think that the state is *not active enough* in matters of justice.[14] Political approaches to justice go beyond the elite and are seen also in the matter of prosecuting young offenders: For example, between 2000 and mid-2002, in order not to offend a growing Muslim electorate, the government was slow in prosecuting individuals suspected of attacking Jewish targets.

There has been a continuing debate about whether judges in France, who influence the course of a trial so strongly, render justice democratically—whether their formal position predisposes them to favor the state against the citizen and whether their bourgeois background prejudices them against the lower classes. Since judges not only apply the law but also have a responsibility to reflect "the general will," it is widely believed that they tend to favor the government (as the repository of that will) against the individual.[15]

The problem of unequal justice had been particularly apparent in the imposition of what Anglo-Americans might call "cruel and unusual punishment." The death penalty (by guillotine) was imposed mainly on members of the lower classes. Since the end of the Third Republic, there have been no public executions, and presidents exercised their right of pardon in capital crimes with increasing frequency.[16] In 1982, capital punishment was abolished (despite the fact that, in the face of an increasing incidence of violent crimes, a large proportion of the public favored its retention).

Until three decades ago, the laws concerning abortion appeared to be much more discriminatory against the poor than the well-to-do. Abortion was considered a crime for which the patient was punished by a heavy fine and the physician was fined, imprisoned, or lost his or her license. However, in the early 1970s, sentences were imposed but suspended because of a public outcry and the issuance of a manifesto signed by several hundred physicians confessing to having performed abortions. As a result, in 1974, the government, in one of the steps undertaken by the Giscard presidency to liberalize aspects of French society, successfully proposed a bill to legalize abortion. The government under President Pompidou had already promoted two other liberal measures: the introduction of sex education in public schools and the granting of equal rights of inheritance to children born out of wedlock. These reforms were later extended by Socialist governments to cover the equal protection under law of women, homosexuals, and the handicapped and to legalize same-sex unions (*Pacte civil de solidarité*—PACS).

There is no doubt that in France, as in most highly stratified societies where legal counsel costs money and the judiciary tends to be recruited from the bourgeoisie, the judicial system favors the existing regime and the established classes (although the members of the judiciary deny this charge).[17] This was reflected in the fact that before 1978, juries were highly selective—for the most part they included mayors, city councillors, and other "respectable" citizens and excluded manual and domestic workers. Since that time, however, juries have been drawn by lot from lists of registered voters. There has been also a growing number of examining magistrates whose leftist ideologies have predisposed them to proworker decisions,[18] and there were indications that the appointment and promotion of such magistrates were encouraged under Socialist governments. Yet discrimination against the underprivileged has continued, despite a reform in the early 1970s that provided for free legal counsel for indigent defendants and a dramatic increase in budgetary allocations for such counsel.[19]

In recent years, however, judges more and more often have been pronouncing judgment in the name of the French *citizen* (as distinct from the *state*) and following "general principles of rights" in order to take into account individual cases.[20] They have done so in response to the growing belief that the state is not doing enough to advance the general welfare, promote equality, defend individual liberties, and even define issues properly. This has led to a gradual juridification of politics, a development reflected, inter alia, in interpreting commitments made by factories to employees in case of layoffs, the question of what is a religion, what constitutes a crime against humanity, and even what is historical truth.[21]

At the same time that French judges have become more sympathetic to the ordinary citizen, their own self-image as members of an elite has been blurred. Owing in part to an expansion of the judiciary and insufficient appropriations for the magistrature,[22] there has been an increase in the unionization of judges. The judges' and lawyers' associations have not only agitated for better pay but have also expressed concern for a liberalization of the penal code; the overhauling of the labyrinthine court structure; and the simplification of the legal language, which is often incomprehensible to the average citizen. In an attempt to relieve the burden on the courts, laws were enacted in the early 1990s to computerize certain operational aspects of the judiciary and to increase the number of judges and court clerks.[23]

There is the additional problem of increased crime and overloaded dockets, which (because of the absence of plea bargaining) cannot be effectively disposed of by the relatively small number of prosecuting attorneys and defense lawyers. This has resulted in the development of a sort of judicial rationing during the appeals process; for example, the various chambers of the Court of Cassation reject about 60 percent of the cases for "lack of interest."[24]

One approach to making access to justice speedier and less expensive (and to relieve the dockets of courts of first instance) was the creation in 1978 of a system of *conciliateurs.* These nonsalaried conciliators, appointed for one-year terms, are not professional judges but lay persons—members of the liberal professions, educators, sociologists, and officials of private associations. They attempt to settle by "amicable means" a variety of disputes, such as conflicts between landlords and tenants, breaches of contract, neighborhood quarrels, and interracial or interethnic conflicts. By 1981, the number of conciliators had grown to 1,200, but—owing to the hostility of Robert Badinter, the Socialist minister of justice, who did not want to "deprofessionalize" the judicial process—the appointments of many were not renewed, and their number fell to 400 in

1986. Albin Chalandon, the Gaullist minister of justice in Chirac's "cohabitation" government, proposed to revive the system and bring the number of conciliators up to 3,800 (roughly 1 for each canton) by 1989, but with the return of Socialist rule, this ambitious scheme was scaled back, so that in 1999 there were only 1,605, while the number of cases successfully dealt with was about 40,000.

One set of reforms that touched on the question of equal justice was the "Security and Liberty" bill introduced by the Giscard regime and passed early in 1981. Under the provisions of this legislation, criminal procedure was simplified, and the maximum allowable period of preindictment detention was reduced. The legislation also provided for mandatory minimum sentences for a number of infractions, especially crimes of violence, and thereby diminished the discretion of judges. This provision led to protest demonstrations, media publicity, and heavy lobbying by magistrates' and lawyers' associations and university professors. An equally controversial feature of the reform provided that certain criminals (e.g., pimps, drug pushers, and selected white-collar transgressors) could have their prison sentences reduced if they quickly paid compensation to their victims—a provision that was interpreted by some as instituting a preferential system of justice for those with money.[25] Finally, the reform provided that the police could ask any person on the street to show his or her identification and detain those unable to furnish it—ostensibly in response to the growing number of illegal aliens. In 1982, most of the illiberal provisions of the "Security and Liberty" law were rescinded by Parliament.

A persistent problem has been the overcrowding of prisons, which was aggravated by a variety of factors contributing to a growth of criminality: population growth, the rapid urbanization of society, the spread of drugs, and (with the modernization of the French economy) a steep increase in white-collar crimes. Based on the recommendations of a committee of experts, the Socialist government in the 1980s enacted a variety of measures, among them the improvement of prison conditions and the selective use of alternatives to prison, such as probation, fines, or community service. The Chirac government of 1986 in turn proposed to solve the problem by recommending the decriminalization of a number of acts usually leading to jail sentences and even toyed with the notion of setting up privately run prisons. Proposals to protect prisoners against abuses by prison guards have also been discussed.[26]

For a long time, there had been a feeling that the rights of the defendants needed additional protection. In 1996, President Chirac appointed a blue-ribbon group, the Truche committee, to examine ways to make justice more efficient, more impartial, and more independent of the executive.[27] The report of the committee, issued in July 1997 and endorsed by Chirac and the Jospin government, reaffirmed the principle of the presumption of innocence of the defendant and recommended a number of measures to protect his rights. The recommendations were reflected in a law passed in June 2000, which stipulated that a suspect had to be informed of the nature of the charges against him so that he could be indicted without delay. In addition, preindictment detention *(garde à vue)* would be limited to 24 hours unless extended to 48 hours with a warrant issued by an examining magistrate *(juge d'instruction)*. The law also provided for the right of a person arrested to refuse to answer questions (which was inspired by the U.S. tradition of protection against self-incrimination). A reform of 1993 had confirmed the right of a defendant to an attorney after 20 hours of police custody, even in serious cases (e.g., suspected terrorism or drug-related crimes) where such custody is extended;[28] it also provided that the Ministry of Justice be informed of any extension of police custody. The new law gives the suspect the right to have a lawyer immediately, so that the lawyer could participate in the examination of the facts. Furthermore, the law protected the suspect against attacks by the press on his dignity. It also stipulated that persons could not be tried twice for the same crime unless a judicial error had been committed or new facts had come to the attention of an examining magistrate after an acquittal, and that the power to indict be separated from the power to detain. Finally, the bill stipulated that remand into custody and prolongation of detention required the assent of two judges.[29]

A continuing problem dealt with by reformers has been the lack of adequate demarcation between the judiciary and the executive.[30] One of the most important recommendations of the Truche committee concerned the position of the prosecuting attorney (who, like the Anglo-American grand jury, decides whether a trial should take place). Traditionally, that person has been under the authority of the minister of justice, and as such might be subject to strong hints about how to proceed. The government, and especially ministers of justice, have tended to interfere in the work of prosecuting attorneys, a tendency sometimes reflected in light sentences or in a sudden closing of judicial proceedings (*classement sans suite*) against well-connected members of the "political class."[31] An example of such abuse was said to have occurred when Jacques Toubon, Juppé's minister of justice, interrupted the prosecution of Jean Tibéri, the mayor of Paris, a political friend, for the misuse of public funds. Henceforth, the minister of justice would no longer be able to order a *procureur* to refrain from prosecuting a case. While accepting the Truche recommendations in the name of the Jospin government, Elisabeth Guigou, the minister of justice, suggested that a "dialogue" between the minister of justice and the prosecuting attorney be maintained and that ways be found to prevent inaction or obstruction by the latter for his or her own political reasons.[32]

The law came into effect in January 2001, but its full implementation has been delayed, owing largely to the lack of judicial manpower and opposition by the police. There were calls for amending it, in part because many suspects were being released before trial. In fact, the law was modified: Provisional detention was facilitated, especially for recidivists. A major reason for that modification was foot-dragging by the judicial establishment. Early in 2001 judges struck in protest against overwork, and the police argued that its work was impeded in the face of increased threat of terrorism (especially since the bombing of the World Trade Center in New York in September 2001).

A widely debated instance of political justice was the judgment by the Court of Cassation (the supreme court of appeal) in October 2001 to grant immunity to Chirac, which permitted him to escape prosecution for his role in a kickback scheme when he was mayor of Paris.[33] The Court of Cassation decided that a president could not be brought to trial before an ordinary court during the exercise of his mandate (thus confirming a ruling of the Constitutional Council two years earlier), and could not even be called as a witness against his will. The court, however, held open the possibility of a trial after the expiration of his mandate.[34] Sitting presidents could be tried only for high treason, but in a specially constituted High Court of Justice.

The foregoing suggests that the French judiciary is not as independent as the Anglo-American one, because there is no separation of powers in the American sense. Nevertheless, the principle of separation of powers *does* exist in France insofar as it applies to the idea of an independent judiciary. In a textbook on judicial institutions, it is stated that "judges may not interfere in the legislative function" and "may not oppose the application of the laws"; and that "the legislator may not interfere in the judicial function." Furthermore, "a judge may not interfere in the executive powers" and "the executive power may not interfere in the judicial function." However, there is judicial control of administrative acts.[35] Judicial independence is implied in a constitutional reference to the president as guarantor of that independence and to the irremovability of judges (Art. 64).[36] In any case, sitting judges as well as prosecuting attorneys have behaved in an increasingly independent fashion in the past several years. Although the latter are part of the executive branch, they have become more fearless in their investigation and prosecution of members of the executive branch.[37]

THE LEGAL PROTECTION OF ALIENS AND MINORITIES

The French legal system has reflected an ambivalence between widespread xenophobia and a tradition of welcome to immigrants. The 4 million foreign workers and their families, while contributing to the labor force, have also contributed their share to the growth of crime. In response to this problem, a law was passed in 1979 (the *loi Bonnet*) that permitted the minister of the interior to expel foreigners without resorting to the customary legal procedures, not only for illegal entry and lack of proper documents, but also for violating public order. This provision had a chilling effect on the foreigners' freedom to join unions and participate in public demonstrations. In 1981, this law was rescinded; somewhat later, bills were passed granting foreigners the right to participate in elections to labor tribunals, giving them access to official documents pertaining to themselves, and providing for punishment of employers who underpaid them. In 1983, another bill gave naturalized citizens the same political rights as native-born citizens: They obtained the right to form associations, and they were permitted to run for political office, including the presidency of the Republic, without having to wait 10 years, as the previous law had stipulated.

Ambivalence is also shown in the still-unsettled conflict between the right to political asylum and the extradition of criminals. In 1986 and 1987, the Chirac government had laws passed (the *lois Pasqua*, so named after the tough-minded Gaullist minister of the interior) that made it more difficult than before for foreigners to enter France and obtain residence permits and easier for the Ministry of the Interior to expel them without judicial recourse. Under the subsequent Socialist governments, the right of asylum (implicitly guaranteed by the Constitution)[38] was reaffirmed; but when the RPR and UDF returned to power in 1993, that right was challenged. Charles Pasqua, who was again appointed minister of the interior, introduced a bill to restrict the right of asylum. Before this bill could pass, it was necessary to amend the Constitution (Art. 53) to reconcile it with the Schengen Accords of 1990, which provide for the free circulation of people within the European Community. Another "Pasqua bill" (passed in 1993 after much parliamentary debate) toughened the conditions of entry for immigrants and the acquisition of citizenship and gave the police increased power to make random identity checks.[39] At the end of 1996, the government introduced new legislation concerning immigrants. The status of selected illegal immigrants was to be normalized to prevent the splitting up of families; conversely, however, the conditions for many other immigrants were to be made more stringent, police searches of vehicles owned by foreigners were to be facilitated, and the power of judges to delay the deportation of illegal immigrants was to be reduced.[40] Not all these provisions passed muster with the Constitutional Council, and some others have not been implemented.

Many French citizens, especially on the left, have opposed such measures as discriminatory. At the same time, there has been a growing demand to deal with the many terrorist organizations that seem to have made France a major theater of operations. So far, the problem has been handled in an ad hoc fashion: In 1977, the French government (under pressure from Arab countries) refrained from prosecuting a PLO terrorist implicated in the murder of Israelis;[41] but in 1982, the government issued a decree making it a punishable offense to belong to *Action directe*, an extreme-leftist group that was held responsible for several bombings throughout France, and eventually (in 1987) convicted a number of its members. In the interest of good neighborly relations, the Socialist governments extradited Spanish Basque separatists who had fled to France. Nevertheless, laws were passed that lengthened the pretrial detention of suspected terrorists and abolished popular juries in terrorist trials. However, during the trial of an Arab terrorist in 1987, the Chirac government was widely accused of sacrificing due process in the national interest (i.e., maintaining good relations with Arab states) and of having pressured the prosecuting attorney to ask for a light sentence. (The court, however, showed its independence by imposing a life sentence.) In 1992, the judicial authorities, under pressure from the Foreign Ministry, refused to indict or extradite George Habbash, a well-known Arab terrorist who was implicated in the killing of civilians (see Chapter 6). During the final days of 1993, the French government, invoking reasons of state, released two Iranian assassins from prison and permitted them to return to their homeland in defiance of a Swiss request for extradition. In 1996, as a consequence of several terrorist attacks in Paris, the government again toughened its position and began proceedings against selected groups of Islamic fundamentalists. The increased concern with fighting internal terrorism in the wake of the September 2001 events led to the revival of *Vigipirate*, a national effort entailing enhancement of the powers of police, especially in searches, seizures, and checks of identity papers.[42] The extent to which this will limit existing civil liberties is, at this writing, uncertain. Working-class immigrants are particularly subjected to these measures, which have increased their resentment of the state and, in particular, of the police.[43]

THE POLICE

The poor are particularly exposed to the vagaries of the police, who have significant power in the judicial process. There have been many reports of police brutality, especially against workers, immigrants, and leftists. These categories of people not only form the class most likely to clash with the police force, which is recruited primarily from the petite bourgeoisie, but they are also the most likely to confront the police in situations judged to be provocative—in demonstrations and strikes.[44] In addition, the police must take orders from the government, the Ministry of the Interior, and the prefectures, all of which have been very concerned about threats to internal security.

The French obsession with law and order, which is understandable in a society that was, until fairly recently, given to periodic challenges to the regime, is reflected in the size and complexity of the police system. The various French police forces combined comprised more than 250,000 members in 1999—1 for about 250 inhabitants (compared to 1 for 454 inhabitants in Britain and 1 for 322 inhabitants in Germany). Approximately 60 percent of them—that is, 134,000—were in the National Police, of whom some 100,000 were in uniform. About half of the National Police are organized in the Urban Police, which operates in cities with more than 10,000 inhabitants; the rest are divided between the *Compagnies républicaines de sécurité* (CRS) and smaller specialized security services. The CRS maintains 10 regional centers, mobile units, and detachments for highways, beaches, and mountain areas, as well as several functional subdivisions (for intelligence, counterespionage, judicial business, and border surveillance). In addition, there is the Paris police, a specially organized force of some 25,000 men and women, about 16,000 of whom are under the immediate direction of the prefect of police. Finally, there is the *Gendarmerie nationale*, which is technically a component of the armed forces. The *Gendarmerie* (with about 100,000 members) has at least one company in each *arrondissement* and includes maritime, civil air, and riot police as well as the *Garde républicaine*, a group of honor guards and bodyguards of prominent politicians.[45]

This impressive police establishment has not transformed France into a police state: The structural subdivisions, the jurisdictional competition between the Ministry of the Interior and the Ministry of Defense, the possibility of redress in administrative tribunals, and the watchful eye of the French Left, the intellectuals, and other sectors have all contributed to moderating the power of the police. Moreover, the police have become concerned about their public image. Recruited largely from the lower-middle and the working class, the police are not "anti-populist"; in fact, during the Events of May 1968, there was evidence of fraternization between the police and the striking workers, and in 1971, the prefect of police of Paris was dismissed for not being tough enough on leftist demonstrators. During the past decade the image of the police has suffered because of instances of corruption and a widespread feeling that the police are not doing their job.[46]

In 1996, the *Fédération autonome des syndicats de police* (FASP), the largest (and most leftist) of the four police officers' unions, held public interviews and protest demonstrations in Paris and Lyons to counter the police's unpopularity, to inform the public about inadequate pay and working conditions and the government's reluctance to increase the number of recruits, and to complain about the intense pressures on officers on the beat that have led to a wave of suicides. During the demonstrations, a spokesperson for the *Fédération* declared that "cops are often regarded as clowns" by a society that expects them to be a shield against problems it cannot solve by itself and that holds them responsible for everything that goes wrong.[47] The most recent manifestation of unhappiness was a massive demonstration in 2001, in the wake of a successful strike by the national gendarmerie.

Governments under all presidents since de Gaulle have been torn by the conflict between demands by segments of the population (especially workers and immigrants) for a curbing of excessive powers of the police and the need to equip them with adequate means to do their job. Socialist governments were sympathetic to the idea of restraining the police, but they had to be aware of both the increase in violent crimes and corresponding increases in gun ownership and vigilantism. Under the pressure of events (including terrorist attacks), Socialist governments (both before 1986 and after 1988) shifted from a concern with sensitizing the police to democratic values to an interest in making them more efficient—by providing higher pay, better training, more up-to-date weaponry, and the use of computerized data files.[48] The emphasis on strengthening the police, which continued when the RPR-UDF returned to power in 1993, evoked mixed public reactions. On the one hand, there has been widespread belief that the police misbehave; on the other hand, there are those who sympathize with the growing feeling among police officers that they are given insufficient means to deal with criminals, a feeling that has accounted for the growth of the influence of the National Front among police officers.[49] Given the fact that under the Raffarin government law and order are a major policy priority, the police are slated to benefit from a significant increase in size and funding.

FREEDOM OF EXPRESSION

Many of the infringements of a citizen's substantive rights are caused not so much by the police as by existing legislative provisions and government attitudes that give rise to them. Although France is committed in its principles and statute law to freedom of speech, French regimes have found it necessary to infringe upon this freedom occasionally. Such infringement occurred especially after the Liberation, when the government had to deal with World War II collaborators, and during the Algerian crisis, when it was confronted with seditious elements. Between 1960 and 1962, a number of French military officers who had been arrested without warrant for plotting against the regime were tried by special tribunals rather than by ordinary courts, and the usual rights of the defendants (including protection against self-incrimination) were restricted. In 1963, such an approach was institutionalized with the creation of the controversial State Security Court for cases of conspiracy and treason. Any case that involved persons accused of subversion could be transferred, by decision of the minister of justice, from ordinary courts to the State Security Court. This power was used in more than 200 instances—at first to prosecute Maoists and other revolutionary leftists and later, leaders of Breton and other autonomist movements (but not international terrorists). In 1970, the Anti-Breakers Law, under which participants in public disorders, members of organizations instigating them, and even innocent bystanders could be punished, was enacted. Invoking this law, the government was able to ban public meetings of leftists, to suspend radical teachers, and to censor publications. During the first year of the Mitterrand presidency, the Socialist government abolished the State Security Court (as well as the military tribunals) and rescinded the Anti-Breakers Law.

Freedom of the press was guaranteed by a law passed in 1881, but the same law made it a felony to publish statements damaging to the president of the Republic *(lèse majesté)* or to public authorities in general. This law had been in disuse for many years, but the Gaullists revived it. In the Third Republic, the law was applied fewer than 10 times; in the Fourth Republic, 3 times; but in the early Fifth Republic (i.e., between 1958 and 1970), about 100 times.[50] As if this law were not enough, Article 30 of the Penal Code of 1959 gave departmental prefects (and the prefect of police in Paris) the right to "undertake all acts necessary with a view to preventing crimes and violations of the . . .

security of the state." These laws were used as the basis for seizures of newspapers and occasionally even the harassment and temporary detention of newspaper vendors. An illustrative case of governmental interference concerned *Le Canard Enchaîné*, a mass-circulation weekly of political satire. Early in 1974, following a typical "revelation" by the paper of scandals involving Gaullists, the journal's offices were raided and its staff phones wiretapped by government agents.[51] In 1980, the minister of justice instituted criminal proceedings against the editor of *Le Monde*, the most respected French daily newspaper, for having published a series of articles alleging a mishandling of some cases by the judiciary. The government based its case on an article of the Penal Code that made it a punishable offense for "any person who publicly tries in deeds, words, or writings to discredit a judicial act or decision in circumstances likely to affect the judiciary and its independence."[52] The government's wrath against *Le Monde* had been fed by that paper's criticism of Giscard's entanglement in a number of scandals.[53] When the Socialists came to power, the proceedings against the paper were dropped.

Another challenge to the free press occurred in 1987, when Interior Minister Pasqua issued an order forbidding the sale of several pornographic magazines to minors. The order was based on a law enacted in 1949, and previous governments (including Socialist ones) had invoked it to halt the distribution of numerous issues of periodicals; however, Pasqua's action was regarded as heavy-handed by several of his cabinet colleagues (especially the more liberal Giscardists).

In recent years, government interdiction has focused on two kinds of printed expression: group libel, that is, incitement to racial, ethnic, or religious hatred; and material that "causes danger to public order."[54] Thus, a number of individuals have had to pay fines for racist or anti-Semitic tracts, among them notably, and repeatedly, Jean-Marie Le Pen; and in 1995, a book on Islam written by an Arab imam was banned by the minister of the interior because of "its clearly anti-Western tone and theses contrary to republican laws and values."[55] In 1996, in response to Le Pen's widely publicized racist and xenophobic statements, the government pondered a bill that would tighten penalties for such statements. A debate in early 2002 concerning freedom of expression focused around a book written by a former general about his experiences during the Franco-Algerian war in which he discussed the use of torture and summary executions.[56] The general was fined and stripped of his honors—ostensibly for having committed illegal acts, but, perhaps more important, for justifying them and making embarrassing historical revelations.[57]

Another government proposal infringing on freedom of expression was to restrict the reporting of current police investigations.[58] Still another restriction on freedom of the press—it also applies to the electronic media—related to elections. In 1977 a law was passed forbidding the publication of vote projections or exit polls one week before or between balloting and until all polling stations had closed. But since the law did not apply to media outside France, and French citizens could get the poll results via the Internet, the ban was rescinded in early 2002.

Despite these instances, the French press has remained relatively free and unobstructed.[59] There is a great diversity and independence of opinion, and there are a number of highly respected newspapers (see Table 9.1). Most of the important newspapers are published in Paris (although there are some distinguished provincial newspapers). Journals are not the forums of expression of ordinary people that they are (ideally) presumed to be in the United States. Letters to the editor are not so common in French

TABLE 9.1
Important Parisian Newspapers, 1999

	Circulation (in 1,000s, rounded)	Orientation
Le Parisien	486	Conservative (lower middle class)
Le Figaro	367	Conservative
L'Équipe	393	Sports
Le Monde	391	Liberal
France-Soir	163	Conservative
Libération	172	Leftist
International Herald Tribune	235[a]	English language
L'Humanité	59	Organ of Communist party (PCF)
La Croix–L'Événement	92	Catholic
Les Echos	14	Economic and financial
Quotidien du Médecin	83	Physicians

Source: *Quid 2001* (Paris: Laffont, 2001), p. 1279.
[a]Circulation in France, 36,000.

newspapers as in American ones. The average person can contribute to weekly news-magazines, such as *L'Express* and *Le Point*; but *Le Monde*, which is noted for the regular commentaries written by France's foremost intellectuals (and for its general excellence), prints letters or responses largely from "established" individuals.

Theoretically, there are certain limits to the independence of newspapers, since they depend on a government-controlled news agency *(Agence-France-Presse)* for many of their sources of information and, more important, on the government's indirect financial subsidies. These subsidies involve reduced postal and rail-transport charges and reduced tax rates (including a waiver of value-added tax). Such reductions may amount to 10–15 percent of the total budget of a typical newspaper and may make the difference between the continuation or termination of publication. In addition, journalists receive tax deductions, but these are gradually being reduced.

There is little concrete evidence that the government has used its fiscal powers to control the content of newspaper articles; but—unlike the electronic media, which are under more direct government influence[60]—newspapers that disseminate positions favored by the government do so largely because they share official positions. Two top Parisian bourgeois dailies, *Le Figaro* and *France-Soir*, have generally been critical of Socialist governments, and a third newspaper, *L'Humanité*, has frequently been acerbic in its treatment of the domestic policies of both right- and left-wing governments. *Le Monde*, although often critical of the government, has tended in most cases to endorse it on foreign policy and other crucial issues.

Several important newspapers have ceased publication in the past two decades, including the Gaullist-oriented *La Nation*, the pro-Socialist *Le Matin*, and the Conservative *Quotidien de Paris*. Newspapers are beset by rising costs of newsprint (much of it imported) and rising wages of reporters. The decline in the number of dailies in metropolitan France has been significant: from 414 in 1892 to 203 in 1946 to fewer than 100 in 2000.

In contrast, the electronic media have gained in importance. For many years, the radio and television networks were government monopolies in France, as in many other countries. But whereas in Germany they are regionalized, in France they were centralized; whereas in Britain the BBC is an autonomous corporation rarely subject to government interference, in France all broadcasting was, until about two and a half decades ago, controlled by the *Office pour la télévision et la radiodiffusion françaises* (ORTF), which was never free of intervention by the ruling authorities. Cabinet control over radio and television during the Fourth Republic did not materially infringe on the independence and diversity of these media because there were so many cabinet reshuffles and several political parties were in a position to exert influence over broadcasts. In the early years of the Fifth Republic, the ORTF, although technically an autonomous agency, was a mouthpiece of the Gaullist government. TV and radio news broadcasts were highly selective and one-sided—except for the limited time made available to opposition candidates during election campaigns and the occasional TV and radio programs in which political differences were aired by means of a dialogue (e.g., *Aux armes égales*). News was frequently doctored by distortion or omission, and the government was almost always presented in a favorable light. In 1964, the role of the government was strengthened when the ORTF was put under the control of an interministerial committee including the premier and assisted by an advisory committee composed mainly of Gaullists. During the Events of May 1968, the failure to provide full and accurate information led to resentment by the public and the reporting staff of the ORTF. Many of the latter struck and were dismissed from their jobs. Periodic attempts by Parliament (especially by the Senate) to provide a truer measure of independence for radio and television failed.

In 1975, the ORTF was replaced by a number of independent units, each with its own budget. This change was intended to facilitate technical innovation and internetwork competition, but since the state continued to maintain a monopoly over broadcasting, the reform did not result in the media's gaining genuine freedom to criticize the government.[61] Partly for this reason, several private "pirate" stations broadcast between 1977 and 1981. One of these, *Radio Riposte*, was set up by the Socialist party; when that station's criticisms of the government became unbearable to him, Giscard had the Paris police raid the PS headquarters. In the case of other stations, the government resorted to jamming, arrests, and the confiscation of equipment.

When the Socialists assumed office in 1981, they replaced the directors of two television networks who were thought to have been dedicated Giscardists. The staffs were given greater autonomy in programming and were not subjected to direct government interference in news coverage. Furthermore, the government authorized the establishment of private radio stations; these must function on a nonprofit basis, limit their commercials, and confine their broadcasts to an area within a 20-mile radius. (In 2001 more than 1,500 private radio stations were in existence.) In 1982, the High Authority for Audiovisual Communication was created. Its mission was to guarantee the independence of broadcasting, the "respect for pluralism," "the promotion of [different] languages," and the "right to reply" to government pronouncements.[62]

The Chirac government repoliticized the electronic media when it replaced the High Authority with the *Commission nationale de la communication et des libertés* (CNCL). This body was to be an autonomous agency, but it soon became a transmission belt for government (i.e., Gaullist) preferences—for example, in the matter of deciding who would be awarded contracts for the purchase of two television channels that were to be privatized. Upon regaining power, the Socialists (in 1989) replaced the CNCL with a new body, the *Conseil supérieur de l'audiovisuel* (CSA), which was to be an autonomous administrative body less obedient to governmental wishes and subject to control by the Council of State.[63]

During the past two decades, four of the six television channels were privatized. In addition, regional cable television channels were gradually set up in several large cities. These innovations have led to a relentless commercialization of the media (and the "Americanization" of their programs).[64] Moreover, the competition between the various private television channels has led them to hire "superstar" anchorpersons at huge salaries. At the same time, these developments have contributed to a more genuine pluralism of the media, a pluralism reflected in the growing popularity of programs of political satire[65] as well as in the growth of investigative reporting, which has done much to expose the illicit behavior of public officials.[66]

Efforts at promoting pluralism in the electronic media were made by the Jospin government, whose minister of culture, Catherine Trautmann, wanted to encourage an increase in the number of private radio stations on local levels, some of them sponsored by ethnic and religious communities. She also called for rules to be enacted obligating public TV channels to "take into account the diversity of origins and cultures of the national community." In response, the CSA asked Canal+ (a private channel) to make its own programming team more diverse.[67]

One of the constraints on free expression is wiretapping. This practice, which rested on a questionable legal basis, was widely abused (especially under the presidency of Mitterrand, and by the Elysée Palace itself), as we have seen. Under pressure from the European Court of Human Rights, a law was passed in 1991 that permitted wiretapping for exceptional reasons (such as national security), but only if authorized by an examining magistrate. In order to prevent abuses, a special control committee was set up. So far, these measures have not been effective; governments have refused to abandon the practice for reasons of national security *(secret-défense)*, including the fight against terrorism.[68] It is possible, however, that wiretapping will decline as a consequence of the partial privatization of *France-Télécom*, the national telecommunications giant.[69]

NOTES

1. An inquiry revealed that judges in the Paris region, for example, are harsher in their sentencing for theft and drug dealing than provincial judges, but more lenient for homicide cases than judges in smaller towns. See "Le Tour de France des sanctions pénales," *Le Point,* 5 February 1994, pp. 44–51.
2. For a description of the competences of these various tribunals, see Hubert Pinsseau, *L'Organisation judiciaire de la France,* Notes et Études documentaires, no. 4777 (Paris: Documentation Française, 1985), esp. pp. 45–46.

3. In 1963, 24 percent of the entrants to the ENM (then known as the *Centre national d'études judiciaires*) had fathers who were magistrates or members of other legal professions; 24 percent were descended from civil servants, and only 3.5 percent from the working class. See Charles Laroche-Flavin, "Le Magistrat, la justice, et l'État," *Après-Demain*, no. 122 (March 1970), 11. In a typical year, ENM admits 200–300 students. In 1974, *L'École d'Application des Greffes*, a school for training court clerks, was opened (in Dijon), and more recently, *L'École Nationale de l'Administration Pénitentiare*, for training prison personnel, was opened (in the Paris region).

4. The composition and method of appointment were changed by a constitutional amendment in July 1993. The selection process of the *Conseil Supérieur de la Magistrature*, which is presided over by the president of the Republic, has involved considerable partisanship. See Maurice Zavaro, "Le Corporatisme menace la justice," *Libération*, 5 July 2000.

5. The *notaire* is the typical "village lawyer" who, in more traditional times, was one of the chief liaisons between the often illiterate peasant and the legal authorities, and he was therefore, together with parish priest *(curé)*, village teacher, and prefect, a part of the rural elite.

6. There had been other types of legal professionals, for example, the *avoué* (who was largely concerned with the preparation of legal briefs) and the *agréé* (who specialized in pleading before certain commercial tribunals), but these were abolished in 1972.

7. Laurent Cohen-Tanugi, *Le Droit sans l'État: Sur la démocratie en France et en Amérique* (Paris: PUF, 1985), p. 53.

8. If the legality of the lower court decision is in question, the case is sent back. The full complement of 25 Court of Cassation judges meets only on rare occasions.

9. See William Safran, "Rights and Liberties Under the Mitterrand Presidency: Socialist Innovations and Post-Socialist Revisions," *Contemporary French Civilization* 12:1 (Winter/Spring 1988), 1–35. The 1984 law also obliged the judge to inform the accused of his right to counsel.

10. Government responses in this case were not unanimous: The foreign minister promised that France would conform to European Union norms and obey the court's judgment; the minister of interior argued that the court lacked jurisdiction over France's internal affairs; and the minister of justice took no position. See "La Condamnation de la France pour 'torture' embarrasse le gouvernement," *Le Monde*, 30 July 1999.

11. Paul Touvier had been a high militia official of the Pétain regime in Lyons and had been responsible for the killing of Jewish hostages. Condemned to death in absentia during the purges in 1945 for war crimes, he was hidden by the Catholic church but reappeared in 1967 and was pardoned by President Pompidou in 1971. Fearful that he would be prosecuted again, he hid in a Catholic convent, but was rearrested in 1989 and indicted for crimes against humanity. His trial began in 1991 and he was convicted, but a year later, the appeals court reversed his conviction by quashing the indictment; it rendered a lengthy opinion that contained a virtual whitewash of the Vichy regime and of Marshal Pétain. In the wake of considerable public agitation, the Court of Cassation (upon request of the government) restored the indictment and ordered a new trial. He was sentenced to life imprisonment in 1994. See J. D. Bredin, "Affaire Touvier: L'Histoire et la justice malmenés," *Libération*, 23 April 1992; and Bertrand Poirot-Delpech, "Les Juges entre responsabilité et immunité," *Le Monde*, 10 June 1992.

12. This is illustrated by reluctance to indict the principals in the Urba affair, which involved the financing of the Socialist party, and the long delays in the prosecution of high officials implicated in the blood transfusion scandal.

13. As of 2002, the court has not been convened.

14. According to a public opinion poll of September 1999, 57% thought that the state did not intervene sufficiently in judicial matters; 15% that it intervened too much; and 25%, that its intervention was balanced. Olivier Duhamel, "Les Français et l'État," *L'État de l'Opinion 2000*, p. 138. According to a SOFRES poll conducted in 2000, 58% of the population found French justice unsatisfactory; 83%, too slow; 78%, too complicated; 66%, too expensive; and 46%, too lenient vis-à-vis politicians. However, only 17% thought that ordinary citizens were treated too harshly. Poll cited in Gérard Mermet, *Francoscopie 2001* (Paris: Larousse, 2000), p. 231.

15. See Georges Dupuis and Marie-Josée Guédon, *Institutions administratives et droit administratif* (Paris: Colin, 1986), and Cohen-Tanugi, *Le Droit sans l'État*. Both books emphasize the influence of the

statist philosophy on the French legal system and exaggerate the weakness of the citizen's legal remedies against the state. There are persistent complaints that examining magistrates tend to keep suspects in pretrial detention, not because of the gravity of the infraction, but because the suspect is prejudged to be a danger to public order. See Antoine Garapon, "L'Évolution du rôle du juge," *Cahiers français*, no. 251 (May–June 1991), 75–76.

16. There were 17 executions between 1956 and 1967, 1 between 1968 and 1971, and 5 between 1972 and 1981.

17. In a poll of judges in 1990, 61 percent insisted that rich and poor are treated equally. "La Justice déboussolée," *Le Monde, Dossiers et Documents*, no. 215 (November 1993), 1.

18. A director of a large firm interviewed more than two decades ago provided examples of leftist judges who were active in the *Syndicat de la magistrature* (which is said to be close to the CFDT) and who showed a clear antibusiness bias in their decisions. See André Harris and Alain de Sédouy, *Les Patrons* (Paris: Seuil, 1977), pp. 169–95.

19. In 1972 a law on public defenders was passed, and it has been amended several times. In 1999, those earning less than the equivalent of $10,000 a year were entitled to legal aid.

20. See Vincent Wright, "The Fifth Republic: From the droit de l'État to the État de droit," in *The Changing French Political System*, ed. Robert Elgie (London: Frank Cass, 2000), pp. 96–119.

21. Jerôme Favre and Boris Tardivel, "Recherches sur la catégorie jurisprudentielle," *Revue du droit public*, no. 5 (September–October 2000), 1411–40. See also Roger Perrot, *Institutions judiciaires*, 9th ed. (Paris: Montchrestien, 2000), p. 52.

22. In 1992, the judicial establishment employed 56,000, a figure that includes prosecuting attorneys, judges, and court clerks *(greffiers)*. The last category (85 percent of whom are women) is particularly underpaid.

23. In 1999, there were 6,721 magistrates in France. Altogether there was 1 judge per 10,000 inhabitants (compared to Germany—where there was 1 judge for each 3,800). See Perrot, *Institutions judiciaires*, p. 51.

24. *Faut-il avoir confiance en la justice de son pays?* (Paris: Les Dossiers du Canard, April 1992), p. 35.

25. See Jean Foyer, "Le Projet de loi 'sécurité-liberté' devant l'Assemblée Nationale," *La Nouvelle Revue des deux mondes*, November 1980, pp. 276–86. The government, in resorting to the "blocked-vote" procedure to get the bill passed, was seemingly inspired by an increase in crimes of violence and by a perception of a growing public sentiment in favor of a tough "law-and-order" approach.

26. There were also suggestions to shorten the period of provisional detention and to allow "preventive detention" only in exceptional cases. These and other proposals emanated from the report of a blue-ribbon committee *(Commission Rassat)* on penal code reforms. See Sophie Huet, "Toubon: Les Effets pervers de la détention provisoire," *Figaro*, 4 October 1996, p. 8.

27. The committee, chaired by Pierre Truche, the president of the Court of Cassation, consisted of 21 members, including judges, lawyers, journalists, university professors, and higher civil servants.

28. This reform brought French procedure in line with European Community norms.

29. *Rapport de la Commission de réflexion sur la justice*, 2 vols. (Paris: Documentation Française, 1997). See also *News from France*, 20 December 1999, p. 6; and Laure Bédier, "La Loi renforçant la protection de la présomption d'innocence et les droits des victimes," *Regards sur l'actualité*, no. 272 (June 2001), 3–16.

30. It has been argued that the lack of separation between the state (the bar) and the courts (the bench) is due to the Jacobin-Napoleonic tradition, which, like the Marxist one, doesn't fully accept judicial independence; and that prosecuting attorneys focus on protecting the state more than on promoting justice, because ministers of justice and court judges come from the same schools and follow the same career patterns. See Hubert Dalle and Daniel Soulez-Larivière, "Justice: À la recherche de la bonne coupure," *Le Monde*, 30 May 2002.

31. This is illustrated by the scandal concerning the transfusion of contaminated blood. In this affair, which began in the mid-1980s and continued beyond 2001, cabinet ministers were indicted but soon acquitted, and Fabius, who was prime minister at the time, was "rehabilitated" when he was named finance minister in 2000.

32. See Denis Demonpion, "Les Coulisses de la Commission Truche," *Le Point*, 12 July 1997, pp. 42–45.

33. Eric Halphen, the magistrate who investigated Chirac, was removed from the case and subsequently resigned his position.

34. In addition to the Constitutional Council, the state prosecutor *(procureur de la République)* also weighed in with his opinion. See Henri Leclerc, "Le Locataire de l'Elysée face à une béance juridique," *Libération*, 2 April 2001.

35. Perrot, *Institutions judiciaires*, pp. 27–31.

36. Jacques Robert, "De l'indépendance des juges," *Revue du droit public*, no. 1 (1988), 3–38; and Arlette Heymann-Doat, *Libertés publiques et droits de l'homme*, 3d ed. (Paris: LGDJ, 1994), pp. 195–98.

37. Denis Demonpion, Catherine Pégard, and Jean-Loup Reverier, "La Révolution des juges," *Le Point*, 20 July 1996, pp. 38–43.

38. The preamble to the Fifth Republic Constitution (which is held to have operative validity) embodies the catalogue of rights of the Fourth Republic Constitution, which stipulated in *its* preamble that "anyone persecuted because of his activities in the cause of freedom has the right of asylum within the territories of the Republic."

39. See *Le Monde*, 20–21 June, 12 and 15–16 August 1993; and Jacqueline Costa-Lascaux, "Les Lois 'Pasqua': Une Nouvelle Politique de l'immigration?" *Regards sur l'actualité*, no. 199 (March 1994), 19–43. Before these reforms, children born in France of foreign parents had become French citizens automatically upon reaching majority; henceforth, they were obliged, before reaching the age of 21, to make an express application for citizenship (which could be denied under certain conditions, e.g., if the applicant had a criminal record or had not learned the French language). By 1996, very few applicants had been rejected.

40. Philippe Bernard and Nathaniel Herzberg, "Le Gouvernement a décidé de modifier la loi Pasqua sur l'immigration," *Le Monde*, 9 October 1996, p. 9.

41. Abu Daoud, who had been a ringleader in the murder of Israeli athletes at the Munich Olympics in 1972.

42. *Vigipirate* had been launched in 1996 in response to terrorist bombings in the Paris transport system. Ultimately, soldiers of the Foreign Legion joined the regular police in patrolling public places.

43. See Pascal Ceaux, "L'Incompréhension police-population persiste dans les quartiers déshérités," *Le Monde*, 25 May 2000.

44. See Jean Claude Monet, "Police et inégalités sociales," *Regards sur l'actualité*, no. 117 (January 1986), 3–18.

45. An additional force that deserves mention is the *Police municipale*, which operates in small towns and is subject to a certain amount of local control. This force includes about 15,000 full-time and several thousand part-time constables and guards. See Georges Carrot, *Histoire de la police française* (Paris: Tallandier, 1992), which deals with changes in the structure of various police forces. For details about the different police forces and their responsibilities and budgets, see Jean-Loup Reverier, "La Police au scanner," *Le Point*, 30 April 1993, pp. 24–29.

46. In 1996, several police officers in Lyons were indicted for participation in an extensive theft ring. See "La Maigre Défense des ripoux lyonnais," *Figaro*, 16 January 1996, p. 30. Growing criticism of the performance of the police in general has led to a significant increase in the number of private security personnel.

47. Dominique Le Guilledoux, "La FASP estime que le 'divorce est consommé' entre l'État et la police," *Le Monde*, 31 May 1996, p. 12. The sensitivity of police officers to being the "unbeloved" of society has occasionally affected their performance, and once (in 1970) prompted the minister of the interior to initiate libel actions against several newspapers of the extreme Left that had been particularly critical of the police. A discussion of antipolice attitudes ("racisme anti-flic") is found in Rémy Halbwax and Jean-Charles Reix, *La Police assassinée* (Paris: Table Ronde, 1983). Another book suggests a countertheme: that there are numerous policemen who have little use for the democratically elected authorities that control them. See Alain Hamon and Jean-Charles Marchand, *P . . . comme police* (Paris: Éditions Alain Moreau, 1983). A middle position is taken by Bernard Deleplace, *Une Vie de flic* (Paris: Gallimard, 1987). Deleplace was the secretary-general of the FASP. See also Erik Blondin, *Journal d'un gardien de la paix* (Paris: La Fabrique, 2002), for a recitation of a policeman's problems with his colleagues, his superiors, and the public at large.

48. See "Une Police au service des citoyens," *Après-Demain*, no. 292 (March 1987), especially the articles by Pierre Joxe and Jean-Michel Belorgey.
49. The influence of the *Fédération professionnelle indépendante de la police*, a pro–Le Pen organization, has grown, particularly in the Paris region.
50. In 1965, a right-wing author, Jacques Laurent, was sentenced to prison by a criminal court for having written *Mauriac sous de Gaulle* (Paris: Table Ronde, 1965), a book that was critical of the general. The publisher, too, was fined. Between 1965 and 1970, the law was applied "only" three or four times a year. See François Sarda, "Offenses aux chef d'État," *Le Monde*, 8–9 March 1970.
51. According to a law of 1970, wiretaps (generally placed by security services or interministerial committees) can be used, with the premier's approval, only for reasons of national security. But the law was widely abused during the presidencies of de Gaulle and Pompidou, when the Paris telephones of union leaders, journalists, and left-wing politicians were bugged. See *Nouvel Observateur*, 7 March 1973. In the late 1980s and early 1990s, there were frequent press reports alluding to illegal wiretapping by the Mitterrand presidency as well. See Hervé Gattegno, "L'Elysée, les gendarmes et le journaliste," *Nouvel Observateur*, 11–17 March 1993, pp. 46–48. In 1991, a special committee (the *Commission nationale de contrôle des interceptions de sécurité*) was created to investigate and monitor wiretapping.
52. *Le Monde*, 9–10 November 1980.
53. One of the scandals revolved around the allegation that Giscard had accepted diamonds from ex-Emperor Bokassa of the Central African Empire.
54. In 1972 a law was enacted that made discrimination based on race, religion, or ethnicity or incitement to group hatred a felony. This legislation was extended by the Gayssot law, passed in 1990, which made the denial, in print or speech, of the Holocaust a punishable offense. See Jean-Claude Gayssot and Charles Lederman, "Une Loi contre l'antisémitisme militant," *Le Monde*, 26 June 1996, p. 14.
55. Nathaniel Herzberg, "Le Ministère de l'intérieur interdit un livre sur l'islam," *Le Monde*, 30 April–2 May 1995, p. 9.
56. Paul Aussaresses, *Services spéciaux: Algérie 1955–1957* (Paris: Perrin, 2001).
57. For a detailed analysis, see Tramor Quemeneur, "La Mémoire mise à la question: Le Débat sur les tortures dans la guerre d'Algérie, june 2000–septembre 2001," *Regards sur l'actualité*, no. 276 (December 2001), 29–40.
58. This was proposed on the official grounds that in reporting on a pending case, newspapers tend to imply a person's guilt and thus put in question the initial presumption of innocence. See Anne Chemin, "Le Rapport Rassat préconise un renforcement du secret de l'instruction," *Le Monde*, 3 October 1996, p. 8.
59. However, during the Gulf War, journals were asked by the Ministry of Defense to refrain from publishing information tending to endanger the security of military operations. This was paralleled by a directive asking TV commentators to behave similarly. Jean-Marie Charon, "Le Malaise des médias," *Regards sur l'actualité*, no. 173 (August 1991), 16–27.
60. See José Barroso and Antoine Jacob, "Les Radios communautaires face au conflit israélo-palestinien," *Le Monde*, 11 April 2002.
61. In 1974, a few months after his election, Giscard announced liberalization measures for the networks. In the same month, the government dismissed the director-general of Europe No. 1 because in his broadcasts he had not been "obsequious" enough to the government. See *Figaro*, 25 October 1974. Europe No. 1 is technically a "private" station in which the government has 37 percent of the shares.
62. *L'Année politique 1982*, pp. 115–16.
63. One of the responsibilities of the CSA was to ensure that the regulations concerning political pluralism be adhered to. Although the buying of TV time by political candidates during election campaigns is forbidden by law, and both the government (or parliamentary majority) and the opposition must get approximately equal amounts of time, the law is occasionally violated by both the public and the private networks. See Jacques Chevallier, "Les Instances de régulation de l'audiovisuel," *Regards sur l'actualité*, no. 149 (March 1989), 39–55; on the CSA, see esp. pp. 51ff. See also *News from France*, 15 April 1994, p. 2. On the role of the media in election campaigns, see Guy

Drouot, "La Politique sur les ondes," in G. Drouot, ed., *Les Campagnes électorales radiotélévisées* (Paris: Economica, 1995), esp. pp. 21–27.

64. The fear of the growing American influence on the audiovisual media has led the French government to limit the importing of U.S.-produced films and to require a minimum "European" content in TV programming.

65. These include *Les Guignols*, a political puppet show; and (until its cancellation in 1995) *Le Bébête Show*, in which public figures (including the president of the Republic) were portrayed as animal puppets.

66. The media have sometimes been accused of abusing their freedom. Thus, Bérégovoy (while in office) was made the object of repeated criticism for irregular financial dealings, a criticism that was said to have contributed to his suicide shortly after the Socialists' electoral defeat in 1993. See Alain Rollat, "La Machine infernale," *Le Monde*, 5 May 1993; and "Qui lynche qui?" *Le Canard Enchaîné*, 5 May 1993. The fear of irresponsible reporting probably explains the decision by the CSA in May 2002 (just before the legislative elections) to ban private "pirate" television stations from broadcasting during electoral campaigns.

67. Paul Gonzales, "Le Décompte des quotas en suspens," *Figaro*, 20 May 2000, p. xi.

68. Olivier Biffaud, "Alain Juppé ordonne une enquête sur l'affaire des écoutes," *Le Monde*, 10 April 1997, p. 6.

69. See Heymann-Doat, *Libertés publiques*, pp. 174, 237; and Anne Chemin, "L'Affaire des écoutes de l'Élysée sera-t-elle jugée ou enterrée?" *Le Monde*, 18 June 1996, p. 11.

CHAPTER 10

Political Changes
and Public Policies

How successful is the French political system, and in terms of what criteria? Some analysts of French politics have argued that the Fifth Republic has been relatively effective in policy making because the state has been so powerful that little is left to the private sector; others have suggested that the state machinery is so complex and over-institutionalized that it has produced bottlenecks and policy immobility.[1] The streamlining of institutional relationships that the Fifth Republic brought about helped to unblock the decision-making process and, if judged in terms of policy outputs, transformed the French polity into a relatively responsive one. Policies that had been inaugurated during the Fourth Republic were elaborated and reinforced, and others were initiated. This success has been particularly apparent in the production of public goods: comprehensive medical and unemployment coverage, retirement benefits, family income supplements, subsidies for university students, paid vacations, a constantly modernizing mass transport system, and the protection of the interests of small-scale farmers and businesspersons (to the extent possible in the European Union context). In terms of idealized (socialist, egalitarian, or Catholic) expectations, many of these policies have been judged inadequate; yet if measured against U.S. policies, they may be considered successful. French policies in the Fifth Republic have reflected a convergence of the demands of sectors with mass memberships, powerful organizations, and electoral weight: labor, schoolteachers, small business, war veterans, and agriculture—although as the numbers in the latter three categories have decreased, so has the attention paid to them by policy makers.

As suggested in Chapter 5, French policy making does not correspond strictly to the American model of pluralism, according to which conflicting demands are articulated mainly in the marketplace by private "countervailing powers," with the state acting as a registration agent; nor does it conform to what has been posited as a countermodel, that of "corporatism." Rather, it is the result of an interplay of market decisions, inputs by socioeconomic sectors, and autonomous governmental preferences—these last influenced by partisan political considerations and by the "rationality" of professional planners' cost-benefit criteria. The traditional ideology of Colbertism[2] has influenced the tendency of the public authorities to control a large part of the credit machinery; socialism has been reflected in minimum wage and nationalization policies; Catholic social doctrine is at least in part embodied in the benefits accorded to large families; and the "experto-cratic" orientation has revealed itself in the French approach to economic planning.

ECONOMIC POLICY FROM THE LIBERATION TO THE GISCARD PRESIDENCY

After the Liberation, French economic policy focused on the following objectives: recon-struction of a war-ravaged economy; modernization of the railroads; consolidation and mechanization of farms; gradual replacement of small firms by larger and more compet-itive ones; rationalization of industrial production; general economic growth; and a more egalitarian division of the economic pie. By the early 1970s, many of these goals had been achieved: For two decades, the growth of the gross national product had been impressive, averaging about 6 percent annually; the food supply was plentiful, the franc was relatively stable, unemployment was low, and the real income of workers had risen steadily.

In pursuing their policies, governments were helped by a growing consensus among political parties about the desirability of government intervention and about the need to build on the welfare-state legislation enacted by the Popular Front government of 1936, which included statutory medical coverage, old-age insurance, and minimum wages. There was also considerable popular support for the maintenance and expansion of the public sector by means of the nationalization of industries. These policies culmi-nated in the public or semipublic ownership of railroads, gas and electric companies, seaports and airfields, urban transport, civil aviation, several banks and insurance com-panies, and oil prospecting and marketing. The nationalized sector in France has been one of the most important among modern democracies and has helped the government to intervene effectively in domestic policy making.

CAPITALIST PLANNING

Many economic policies were pursued in the context of national plans, the first of which was unfolded in 1946. In arriving at such a plan, the government rejected the Soviet planning model, which was based on central government directives and depended on a totally socialized economy. However, in accordance with their interventionist traditions and in the interest of accommodating left-wing demands for welfare statism and social justice, the French authorities also rejected the pure free-market model. They compro-mised by devising an economic plan that tried to combine governmental fiscal interven-tion and official policy preferences with the decisions, commitments, and projections of the private sector.

Economic planning in France has been based on several assumptions and processes: (1) the notion of a total set of goals for society, (2) a rational and empirical approach to problem solving, (3) a process of information gathering, (4) a matching of data on available resources with a number of "options," (5) supplying information about projected government policies to private firms to help them make their own plans, and (6) the belief that the self-interest of the private sector can be reconciled with a common interest promoted by the public authorities. On the basis of a complex system of stocktaking and forecasting, the government makes long-range decisions affecting employment, production, consumption, the allocation of resources, growth, social spending, public works projects, and the like. These decisions are not binding on all private sectors; rather, they are guidelines that enable the government to coordinate, or "harmonize," its own decisions with those of business and the trade unions.

Planning has involved a variety of governmental, quasi-public, and private institutions. At the apex is the General Commission on Planning (*Commissariat général du plan*—CGP), which is staffed by 200 economists, statisticians, sociologists, and other specialists, and is normally attached to the premier's office. The government provides a catalogue of general objectives to the CGP, which in turn produces several alternative blueprints containing basic economic data, short- and long-range projections, and recommendations for resource allocation. These preliminary blueprints are then submitted to subunits for discussion and for additional input. In the course of time, many participating units or agencies have been set up; annually, more than 2,000 technocrats, local and regional politicians, industrialists, trade unionists, representatives of agricultural and other interests, and independent experts have provided these agencies with information supplementary to that already obtained by the CGP.

A variety of bodies of functional representation, or consultation, have been involved in French planning. These have included national and regional economic development, or "modernization," committees, consisting of representatives of big and small business, trade unions, agricultural associations, local politicians, and independent experts. These committees are divided into subcommittees, which meet occasionally with "working groups" set up by the CGP. These working groups have been concerned with such diverse matters as industrial strategy, agriculture, monetary policy, social policy, housing, education, and nationalized industries, and their input is "collected" by the CGP. A further aggregative process takes place during the final phases of the planning enterprise, when the economic plan is discussed in the Economic and Social Council before it is approved by the cabinet.

The public authorities have been involved in the planning process at virtually every stage. During the first stage, the information-gathering one, there are consultations with the Finance Ministry, the government-controlled credit institutions, and the National Statistical Office (*Institut national de la statistique et des études économiques*—INSEE). During the subsequent consultative phases, the Finance Ministry continues to be involved. In addition, there are the Delegations for Spatial Planning and Regional Action (DATARs), set up in 1963, which are composed of civil servants assigned by the premier's office to the various economic regions. The DATARs work closely with regional councils and a variety of economic advisory bodies. Technically, the DATARs are under the authority of the premier;[3] in practice, however, space planning, which embraces land use, urban planning, and environmental policies, has heavily involved the finance minister, who has strong influence or control over a variety of funds for socioeconomic, urban, and industrial development projects.

The planning methods of the governmental authorities are (1) the traditional "Keynesian" methods of fiscal intervention: manipulation of interest rates; use of government contracts; granting of tax concessions, export guarantees, and import licenses; and determination of wage and price levels; (2) the allocation of investment loans and grants; and (3) the use of nationalized industries in order to influence the price structure of private industry. The question whether the fiscal methods of the public authorities have been conservative or progressive is not easy to answer. On the one hand, some of the officials working for the CGP and the Finance Ministry have been suspicious of private sector activities and have been striving to "direct" them on behalf of the state's purposes and official notions of the public interest.[4] On the other hand, numerous higher civil servants have been inordinately receptive to the business viewpoint.

The initial fears of the business community that the economic plan might become a socialist device were overcome with the appointment in 1946 of the first planner, Jean Monnet, himself a businessman, who convinced the business community that French-style planning would help save capitalism.[5] Since then, most chief planners have been chosen because of their affinity for capitalist management or their ideological acceptability to business-oriented presidents, premiers, or finance ministers.[6] The industrial outlook of these planning directors has harmonized with the composite objectives of each of France's development plans. The First Plan (1946–1952) concentrated on reconstruction and quantitative growth; the Second Plan (1953–1957), on the modernization of industrial and agricultural production; the Third Plan (1958–1961), on fiscal stability and the improvement of the balance of payments; the Fourth Plan (1962–1965), on regional development and the creation of 1 million new jobs; the Fifth Plan (1966–1970), on a rise in productivity; the Sixth Plan (1971–1975), on a strong annual growth rate, the raising of the level of foreign currency reserves, and an improved highway system. Subsequent plans—the Seventh (1976–1979), Eighth (1980–1983), Ninth (1984–1988), and Tenth (1989–1993)—were all concerned with problems that began with the oil crisis of the mid-1970s: unemployment, inflation, and the loss of world markets. The Eleventh Plan (1994–1998) aimed at the solution of a variety of problems, chief among them unemployment and the government deficit. The Twelfth Plan (1999–2003) has had four major objectives: to create jobs, to adapt France to the European Union (EU) framework; to enhance social cohesion; and to make government more effective.[7]

All these plans contained a number of social elements, such as increased welfare-state benefits. But in view of the planners' closeness to the business community, the trade unions have had doubts whether the plans' social features would be actively promoted. To the trade unionist or the traditional socialist, whose ideal plan is primarily an instrument of a redistributive policy, the capitalist nature of French planning is marked, not only by its stress on productivity, but also by the chronic underrepresentation of trade unions in the various discussion committees.[8] In confronting the government and business sectors, unions have also been at a disadvantage because of their emptying coffers and their lack of technical expertise and industrial information.

Unions have (unsuccessfully) presented counterplans, periodically boycotted the planning bodies, or tried to appeal to Parliament to "rectify" the plans. Parliamentary involvement in the plans has been selective and uneven. Technically, parliamentary legitimation is required only for the "carrot-and-stick" aspects of economic policy contained in the plans (i.e., those involving taxing and spending); nevertheless, most plans have been debated in Parliament. During periods of domination by Gaullists and Giscardists, the National Assembly has been reluctant to disapprove the plans. In any case, the plans have periodically been subjected to modifications or additions by acts of Parliament, executive decrees, and central accords between government and the "social partners" in response to outside pressures (for example, the Grenelle Agreement of 1968 between the government, industry, and labor, as a result of which workers' wages were raised by around 30 percent). Some of these measures have been incorporated into subsequent plans.

The relevance and success of French economic plans have depended on a variety of factors: the realism of the plan; the thrust of supplementary policies (which might redound to the credit of the plan); external events (such as the disturbances of 1968, which upset the Fifth Plan almost completely); the degree of collaboration of the private sector; and the attitudes of presidents. De Gaulle had viewed planning as "an ardent obligation," not only because of his faith in the guiding hand of a wise state, but also because of his disdain for political parties and his distrust of Parliament as an economic decision maker.

Since de Gaulle's departure, there has been an avalanche of publications dealing with the decline or death of planning. What is meant by decline is not the absence of a multiannual plan, but the tendency of decision makers to follow its detailed recommendations less seriously (if at all) and to produce policies that are increasingly short-term. It has been widely suggested that Pompidou and Giscard were hostile to planning, because of their neoliberal ideologies or their personal connections with big business. For Giscard, "advanced liberalism" meant that instead of *directing* the economy, the state would limit its role to *facilitating* economic concentration, respecting competition, and helping to capture foreign markets. In conformity with this orientation, price controls on consumer goods were gradually abolished, as were licenses for the import of raw materials; unions were encouraged to secure improvements in wages and fringe benefits by means of collective bargaining (*contrats de progrès*); private business was encouraged to consolidate and expand by means of tax concessions; and the public sector (e.g., electricity, railroads, and the medical care system) was urged to strive toward financial self-reliance by raising prices or fees.

Giscard's neoliberalism had its limits: Electoral pressures, the threat of violence by workers and farmers, the growing insolvency of social security funds, and the scarcity of private investment capital forced Giscard and his premier, Barre, to raise the minimum wage and impose taxes on excess profits. Tax concessions, low-interest loans, and outright subsidies were to be awarded to certain "champion" industries, such as electronics, aeronautics, transport, and communications equipment. These sectors were considered to have global marketing potential on the basis of such criteria as existing know-how, available manpower and energy resources, and hard-currency earning capacity. To some extent, these policies were embodied in the Seventh Plan, but reliance on a single multiannual plan proved to be unrealistic with the onset of the worldwide economic crisis. What followed were the "Barre plans," a series of short-term emergency measures that included surtaxes on high incomes and on business profits that were not plowed back into investment, a freeze on high salaries, selective price controls, and supplementary government outlays for social security and unemployment payments and other welfare benefits—all of which increased the government's deficit and aggravated the pressure on the franc.

Planning still exists, both in terms of an institutional arrangement and a final document. For a number of reasons, however, it is no longer an effective basis of government policy. The state has lost much control over economic forces due to (1) the growth of supranational decision making, largely in the context of the EU; (2) increasing privatization of crucial economic sectors; and (3) globalization. These interrelated developments have been associated with others, including corporate corruption and an unstable stock market. What is left of planning, then, is a catalogue of measures considered desirable. Thus the Twelfth Plan has become a dead letter since the elections of 2002, which have brought to the fore new priorities embraced by President Chirac and his government: These include domestic security; protection against terrorism; income tax reductions; dealing with the growing social security deficit, especially in medical care; and employment.

ECONOMIC POLICY UNDER THE MITTERRAND PRESIDENCY

The Socialists assumed their governmental functions in 1981 full of optimism and committed to promoting truly "socialist" policies. They wished to make up for what they perceived to be the failure of their predecessors in the redistribution of incomes. It was expected not only that planning would be revived, but also that its processes and nature would change. The plan would be made in a more democratic fashion, on the basis of more equitable participation of trade unions, local authorities, and Parliament; and the final plan would pay as much attention to social justice as to growth.[9]

In their first year in office, the Socialists raised minimum wages by 10 percent, imposed surtaxes on the rich, enlarged social security benefits, increased total social spending by 20 percent, raised corporate taxes, and extended paid vacations to a fifth week for all workers. In an effort to reduce unemployment, the new government raised interest rates (hoping that this measure would attract investment capital), made low-interest loans available to business, reimbursed private firms for a large proportion of their expenditures for hiring and training young people, and created 50,000 additional public service jobs. Furthermore, the government pushed through a series of bills (the Auroux laws) that strengthened the union presence in factories and obliged employers to negotiate annually with union representatives at the plant level about wages and workplace democracy. Perhaps the most controversial policy was the nationalization of about a dozen industrial groups (including steel, electronics, and aeronautics firms) and 36 banks.

The Politics of Austerity

By the fall of 1982, the government had begun to shift its economic policy orientation in response to a deepening crisis. The number of unemployed was approaching 2 million (about 9 percent of the workforce) and threatened to surpass that figure, as nearly 20,000 firms were going bankrupt. The rate of inflation was 14 percent, and deficits in both the national budget and the balance of trade were increasing at dangerous rates. To some extent, the economic situation was the consequence of chronic problems in the French economy and the failure of previous governments to deal with them. These problems included a loss of global markets, insufficiently aggressive sales techniques, and inadequate investments by private firms—which could, in turn, be attributed to the habit of reliance on the state to provide capital. Between 1974 and 1981, nearly 700,000 industrial jobs had been lost, the number of unemployed had risen from 340,000 to about 1.7 million (from 2.3 percent to 7.5 percent), and prices had nearly doubled; however, despite grandiose rhetoric about the "restructuring" of industries and selective government allocations for this purpose, many obsolescent industries (such as steel) could be neither consolidated nor left to their own devices lest the ranks of the unemployed be expanded even further.

The Socialist government compounded the problem by a policy of nationalization that was soon perceived as ill advised. When they took office, some Socialist politicians thought that the firms intended for nationalization had a great deal of money and that once the government took them over, it would use the profits for public purposes. But the amount of money the government had to pay the expropriated shareholders was increased as a consequence of a ruling by the Constitutional Council. More important, several newly nationalized firms turned out to be close to bankruptcy and the government had to pay considerable sums to keep them afloat. Soon the government was forced to shift its policy from redistribution, job creation, and deficit financing to forced savings, curbs on public spending, and the fight against inflation. The extension of public sector jobs was to be limited; the franc was devalued; deductions for social security were permitted to go up; and a temporary freeze on wages and prices was imposed.

In 1983, after these measures had proved inadequate, the government inaugurated a policy of "rigor." This policy included a reduction of credit to industries and of loans to local communities; a levy of 1 percent on all incomes and the imposition of a forced loan on upper-income groups; supplementary taxes on large fortunes and new surtaxes on alcohol and tobacco, to be used to replenish the social security funds; an increase in patient fees for hospital stays; increases in charges on gas, electricity, telephones, and train tickets; a limit on the amount of currency French citizens could take out of the country; and cuts in public sector spending for roads and other projects.[10] In 1984, Premier Mauroy presented a new set of proposals to the cabinet for a "restructuring" of French industry. Under these proposals, obsolescent plants would be gradually phased out and more-dynamic and competitive industries would be encouraged by means of tax concessions and subsidies. These measures would apply to the "champion" industries mentioned earlier and would entail government investment of more than $500 million. To critics, these proposals, some of which were embraced by a new government headed by Laurent Fabius, were hardly distinguishable from the policies of Giscard and Barre and constituted a virtual abandonment of the "social" commitments (if not the socialism) with which the Socialists had come into office.[11] But that characterization was not entirely fair, for the proposals contained a number of measures designed to render economic modernization policy more humane: the encouragement of early retirement; the granting of leaves of absence to workers in the shipbuilding and steel industries and coal miners so that they could be retrained; and the payment of part of their salaries by the government.

Some of these proposals had been embodied in the Ninth Plan, which was to go into effect in 1984. This plan had called for measures to foster industrial and educational modernization, the reduction of inequalities, the improvement of the regional equilibrium, and the expansion of scientific research. Yet one could argue that the multi-annual plan had been more or less sidetracked and replaced by interim "adjustment" policies in which interest groups, political parties, and Parliament were heavily involved. The government wished to make policies in an orderly and objective fashion, and it leaned heavily on the reports of study commissions *(comités de sages)* on labor relations, immigrant workers, and social security; it also tried to shift responsibility for creating jobs, increasing productivity, and controlling inflation to labor and management. At the same time, the government's interim plans had to be modified constantly because of pressures from business, farmers, and workers, who, if not appeased, had the potential to mobilize large numbers of voters against the government in future elections.

The Chirac Cohabitation Government and the Politics of Neoliberalism

What had been a matter of pragmatic adaptation for the Socialists had become a matter of ideology for Chirac. As a new convert to the principles of the free market, he proposed to limit the amount of state interference in the economy by lowering taxes; reining in public spending; and ending controls on prices, rents, and currency transactions. Laws were enacted to privatize 13 public industrial groups, to permit employers to lay off unneeded workers, and to allow firms to set up variable work schedules. Surtaxes on great wealth were annulled, added-value taxes on certain durable goods (e.g., cars) were lowered, corporate taxes were reduced, and tax allowances were provided for the start of job-creating businesses. Furthermore, a bill was passed to reduce the social security contributions by firms that undertook to employ and train young people. Nevertheless, the policies that the Chirac government adopted were a far cry from the supply-side economics associated with the Reagan presidency. Thus, the existing system of family income supplements was retained, and a significant sum of money was allocated for the integration of *pieds-noirs* (French citizens born in Algeria) into the French economy. Moreover, despite his embrace of the market and his disdain for state intervention, Chirac could not bring himself to abolish the planning machinery.

The Governments of Rocard, Cresson, and Bérégovoy: Prospects and Growing Constraints

The installation of a new government under Socialist Rocard in 1988 was greeted with optimism by those elements (the workers, the poor, and the unemployed) that had felt neglected under Chirac. However, by the end of 1989, there had been no drastic departures from preceding policies, because fiscal realities and external influences (e.g., the world market and the European Community) had limited Rocard's options and because the fact that his party had only minority representation in the Assembly had limited his political power. Rocard's policies were based not on grand designs but on a series of dialogues—between socialists and nonsocialists, state and local authorities, the "political class" and the citizens, and employers and workers. His policies reflected the needs of "everyday democracy": practical steps to improve education, housing, and the environment, and—consistent with the imperative of growth and productivity—measures to foster greater social justice. The budget for 1990 contained a number of traditionally "socialist" features: a surtax on high incomes, a reduction of taxes on rents, the creation of several thousand new civil service posts, and supplementary budgetary allocations to support the long-term unemployed. However, the budget did not call for a renationalization of privatized industries.

Both the content and the methods of Rocard's policies were in some measure reflected in the Tenth Plan. This "medium-term program of action," which was oriented heavily toward the modernization of French industry, confined the role of the state to taxation and selected subsidies (e.g., for retraining and research), the improvement of infrastructure (such as the railroads), and the enforcement of rules of competition.[12] The plan could be regarded as a series of intellectual exercises rather than as a "socialist" program of action, because both economic growth and wage increases were expected to be the consequence, not of government action, but of collective bargains between business and trade unions, in which both sides promised to behave responsibly (i.e., to postpone immediate gratification). The trade unions, middle-level public service workers, Communists, and many of the traditional Socialist politicians wanted a more activist and clearly redistributive policy, but they had little power and few realistic alternatives.

This applied equally to the governments that succeeded Rocard. Edith Cresson's priorities were to make French industry more competitive while preserving the achievements of the welfare state. The first priority, embraced under pressure of competition generated by the European Community, was incompatible with the second, formulated in order to recapture the support of workers and other traditional supporters of the PS who had been alienated by Rocard's "centrist" moderation. One of the concrete measures enacted in the spring of 1992 was the *Revenu minimum d'insertion* (RMI), a minimum family income (see Chapter 2). Another measure was a subsidy for the training of apprentices, destined primarily for small business. Under Pierre Bérégovoy, Cresson's successor, there were no major departures from that policy, except for an emphasis on protecting the stability of the franc.

The Balladur Government: Redressement and Rigueur

When he assumed office, Premier Balladur was faced with several major challenges: unemployment, nearly empty social security funds, a flight of industries, the pressures of competition generated by the European Community—it became the *European Union* in November 1993—and the negotiations under the World Trade Organization (WTO), which required a reduction of subsidies to farmers. Balladur's program was a hybrid of the policies of Chirac's cohabitation government and the continuation of existing "social" measures. Bills were introduced to provide for a reduction of social security charges on small business; funds were allocated for retraining; limited attempts were made to bail out farmers (and reduce their opposition to the WTO talks); greater cost sharing for hospital care was mandated, accompanied by a reduction in social security benefits; and laws were enacted to increase taxes on tobacco, alcohol, and gasoline. A major aspect of policy was privatization: Bills were passed to denationalize 21 large companies, embracing aerospace, maritime transport, electronics, automobiles (Renault), insurance, and banks. Some of these (including *Crédit Lyonnais*) had been offered for privatization in

1986–1988 but had not been sold before the Socialists recaptured control of the government. The privatization policy not only was in accord with the government's conservative ideology but also promised to bring in over $7 billion in 1993 alone and help to reduce the budget deficit.

There was a "stimulus" element in Balladur's policy as well: a program to spend $2.5 billion on construction and environment projects, intended mainly to create jobs for youth. Some of the reform proposals, such as the reduction of the workweek to 32 hours, were met with skepticism on the part of employers; others, such as the hiring of young people at 80 percent of the minimum wage, were opposed by the trade unions.[13] Still other reforms were symbolic, including a 10 percent cut in the salaries of ministers (who earned about $100,000 a year) and a ban on their official use of luxury cars. Although pressed by Gaullist hard-liners to reduce taxes on business, Balladur also listened to more socially oriented Gaullists and Giscardists, who urged him to preserve the achievements of the welfare state.

Balladur's popularity, based on his image as a pragmatic moderate, would serve him in good stead as he attempted to balance these conflicting aims. Some of these aims had been envisaged by the Eleventh Plan, which was supposed to encourage competitive industries and retraining of laid-off workers. The original plan was virtually abandoned and replaced by a new five-year "recovery plan" (1994–1998), largely inspired by a special commission appointed by Balladur. That plan, like earlier ones, was aimed at growth as well as social justice.[14] However, given the global pressures and the evolving policies of the European Union, these aims were diagnostic rather than absolute, qualitative rather than quantitative, and, except for contracts with regions, did not involve the state's fiscal resources.

ECONOMIC POLICY UNDER THE CHIRAC PRESIDENCY

The Juppé Plan

The election of Chirac took place in an aura of uncertainty about the economic system. On the one hand, there were some positive indicators: a stable currency, a low inflation rate, and a large trade surplus. On the other hand, France was buffeted by growing unemployment, continued housing shortages, an overburdened social security system, and pressures from students, teachers, and farmers. The government deficit, resulting from high social spending, was made up in part by selling off selected nationalized industries, but that solution was short-range and inadequate. Significantly increased public spending, one of the traditional solutions to the diverse sectoral demands, was no longer possible, since participation in a common European currency, which was originally projected to be introduced in 1997, required a reduction of the public deficit. Chirac had run on a platform that promised to combine a variety of goals: to save money by reducing expenditures for costly and inefficient public services; to salvage the health insurance system by increasing employee contributions and making the providers of medical services more responsible; and to motivate private firms, by tax incentives and a reduction of social security charges, to hire young people.

In the early 1980s, a number of French decision makers had looked with some admiration at the American market-oriented approach to economic policy, while others thought the German model (based on the "social market economy") might be applicable to France. But by the mid-1990s, neither the United States (with its "savage" liberalism) nor Germany (with its own growing unemployment) was deemed worthy of imitation.[15] This explains why the "republican pact" of the Gaullists, presented during the 1995 election campaign, was different from the "contract with America" proposed by congressional candidates of the Republican party in the United States in the sense that the pact was designed to retain existing welfare-state provisions.

The incompatibility of the Gaullist government goals became apparent soon after the election, when Premier Juppé began to try to implement them. The strikes of railroad workers and public service workers, the resistance of medical personnel, and the demands of teachers threatened to undermine the efforts at fiscal restraint. Despite Juppé's rhetoric about the responsibilities of the government, the latter proved too weak to ignore falling approval ratings and overcome the resistance of the public to any meaningful retrenchment in traditional entitlements. Thus, Juppé's policies throughout 1995 and 1996 became a series of trial balloons and half-measures of an ad hoc nature that were often contradictory. These included proposals to dismantle several thousand public service positions while protecting the jobs of incumbents and to reduce government expenditures while increasing government contributions to the pensions of transport workers in the public and private sectors whose retirement age had been reduced. Juppé oscillated between tax increases and decreases; and he promised to protect and promote the French language while reducing the budget of the Ministry of Culture. These contradictions reflected clashing priorities and values. On the one hand, the need to take into account the exigencies of the market, preached by a number of Gaullist politicians, was reflected in an increasing tempo of privatizations; in attempts to make it easier for employers to lay off workers; and in efforts aimed at encouraging citizens to subscribe to complementary private pension schemes (and to permit the insured to invest part of their social insurance deductions in the stock market). On the other hand, the fact that "neoliberal" solutions were rejected not only by the French Left but also by a number of majority politicians was manifested in the retention of a "solidarity tax" on wealth.

In any case, the economic recovery package *(plan de redressement)*—which included reducing the social security deficit (as part of a reduction of total government expenditures)—was hopelessly upset. The reduction of income taxes (which were already quite low in comparison with other industrialized countries)[16] announced by Juppé in 1996 was designed to boost the morale of the French, but this reduction (to be spread over five years) was almost certain to increase the deficit. Moreover, the decrease was nullified by other measures, such as a raise in salary deductions for social security and increased taxes on alcohol, tobacco, and fuel.

By the spring of 1997 it had become clear that Juppé's attempts at reducing unemployment and promoting growth could not be easily combined with the spending cuts required to qualify France for participation in a European monetary union. Juppé's failure was due not only to the incompatibility of these goals but also to the resistance of the unions, whose leaders were upset by Juppé's not consulting with them in a timely fashion. Although a majority of French citizens were in favor of European integration and, more specifically, the idea of a common European currency, they were not willing to make sacrifices for it.[17]

The Jospin Government: Squaring the Circle

The economic policies of the Jospin government, which took office in June 1997, were designed to respond to a variety of pressures: the Socialists' campaign promises to reduce unemployment, to retain the essentials of the welfare state, and to make France ready to participate in the European monetary union. The public was assured that these goals could be met without reducing public spending, without privatizations, and without increasing taxes. However, Jospin and his minister of economics, Dominique Strauss-Kahn, were hard-pressed to keep these promises. While reiterating their commitment to the euro, they were hoping that the EU would show flexibility and permit a somewhat higher deficit than 3 percent. Furthermore, they hoped that the EU leaders would add a "social" component—that is, the promotion of employment—to their concern with fiscal stability. At the end of 2001, Jospin proposed to give employers more freedom by making dismissals of workers easier, but his coalition partners would not agree.

Jospin and his government reiterated their commitment to create 700,000 new jobs, half of them in the public sector; to shorten the workweek from 39 to 35 hours without reductions in wages; to raise the minimum wages of the lowest-income earners; and to retain most of the existing socioeconomic entitlements—all this while bringing the deficit down. The cost of these policies would be met by a combination of measures that would bring in 32 billion francs (about $5 billion): an increase in capital-gains taxes (from 19 to 42 percent); an excess profits tax on corporations; and a temporary surtax on large fortunes. In addition, money (amounting to 10 billion francs) would be saved by a reduction of military expenditures. Pressed by business and subjected to the imperatives of competition, Jospin appeared to be willing to consider the privatization of certain enterprises (the giant Thomson industrial conglomerate as well as *France-Télécom* and *Air France*); but his left-wing coalition partners were uneasy about such a policy, in the belief that it would lead to large-scale dismissals. In the end, Jospin embraced a middle position: the opening up of certain enterprises (e.g., *Electricité de France*) to limited private stock purchases.

Minister of Economics Strauss-Kahn asserted that although the creation of jobs would remain a priority of the government, it needed the help of the private sector to achieve that goal; and he admonished the unions to become more flexible and warned the public that certain "corrections" of the welfare system might be unavoidable. One of the controversial proposals, introduced by Martine Aubry, the minister of employment and solidarity, was to apply a means test to recipients of family income supplements, a proposal that generated massive protests.[18]

Some of these policies were socialist, others neoliberal. Their eclectic nature was made possible by the evolution of attitudes of the pluralist Left, in which pragmatism moderated traditional ideological positions. This evolution was reflected in Aubry's cost-cutting proposals; Chevènement's grudging acceptance of European integration; and the "reasonable" behavior of Communist leader Hue, who was willing to give credit to the good intentions of Premier Jospin. The mixed, and contradictory, nature of the government's policies was also reflected in the introduction of the 35-hour workweek, which was favored by the labor unions, and tax reductions for small business.[19]

Raffarin's Policies: Pressures and Prospects

Upon taking office, Prime Minister Raffarin was saddled with a number of policy commitments handed to him by Chirac and reconfirmed by the victory of the UMP in the parliamentary elections. Among the most important of these commitments were tax reductions, the reinforcement of the police to reduce violence in the cities and fatalities on the highways, and the reduction of social security contributions by small firms in order to encourage them to create jobs. Some of the other commitments were not innovations but adaptations of policies of the outgoing Socialist government, among them the following: preserving the 35-hour workweek but making it more flexible by allowing adjustments on the basis of collective bargaining; speeding up the tempo of privatizations while protecting the interests of the state; reducing unnecessary welfare expenditures while raising wages of the lowest-income earners; reining in medical costs while maintaining the quality of health care; ending illegal immigration while keeping the door open to young, productive immigrants; and embracing selected reforms in the direction of greater decentralization by means of practical steps, such as intercommune cooperation (*intercommunalité*), but not the kind of autonomy the Socialists had envisaged for Corsica. Other commitments included protecting French agriculture while adhering as much as possible to Europe's Common Agricultural Policy; fighting terrorism while preserving the individual liberties of citizens; and adapting the country to globalization without adopting the American approach to unrestrained capitalism.

The more conservative features of this contradictory agenda would seem easier to pursue, since there is no need to worry about the reaction of a confused Socialist party and a terminally weakened Communist party. This applies above all to wages. Almost immediately upon becoming prime minister, Raffarin raised the minimum wage (SMIC), but did not go beyond a cost-of-living increase, thereby provoking the ire of the trade unions.[20] Nevertheless, the government, although dominating all the national decision-making institutions, cannot ignore the majority of the population, who want to preserve the welfare state, or the antiglobalization forces, whose appeal is growing.[21] One of the few areas in which the Raffarin government seems to have a freer hand than its predecessor is the continued reliance on nuclear energy.

The cost-cutting possibilities of French governments, whether right-wing or left-wing, have been limited by two major factors: (1) French political culture, which rejects the kind of unfettered market-driven capitalism often attributed to the United States; and (2) a large-scale dependence on the state. With more than 12 percent of the population receiving some kind of social security benefit, 25 percent of the labor force working for the state (which pays 40 percent of all salaries), and government transfer payments amounting to 50 percent of the GDP, 90 percent of the state budget is earmarked. Given an anticipated growth of the number of pensioners, these percentages are likely to increase, and the government will be under pressure to adjust retirement pensions of public employees downward to those of the private sector.

EDUCATION, RESEARCH, AND CULTURE

As was pointed out in Chapter 2, the reforms of education began more than three decades ago in the face of popular demands and the changing labor market. In 1981, the pace of reform quickened: The number of nursery schools was enlarged; many new teaching positions were created; and the salaries of lycée and university professors were raised substantially. These reforms must be attributed in part to the fact that many deputies (including about one-third of the Socialists) and a large proportion of the politicians in the executive branch, were educators. Many of the reform proposals that Parliament embraced originated with several study commissions dealing with education that were set up at the behest of the Socialist government. The reports issuing from these commissions advocated an expansion of vocational education; called for greater attention to scientific studies; pointed to the need for better teacher training; proposed more meaningful decentralization of school administration and curriculum planning; and suggested that admission to, and tracking within, the collèges (middle schools) be made more democratic and that "tutorials" be provided for students having difficulties.

In mid-1983, Alain Savary, then minister of education, made proposals that provoked unexpected resistance. The most controversial related to the place of parochial schools in the French educational system. When the Socialists came to power, they signaled their intention (largely due to pressure from the more dogmatic officials of the FEN) to integrate the private, largely Catholic,[22] schools into the public system by tightening government controls over the use of public funds, making public financial support they received subject to more stringent curriculum controls by the state, and granting the private-school teachers a more official status.[23] This issue has been difficult to resolve, as it has involved a clash of two conflicting but strongly held values: uniform national education and freedom of choice. Although only one-fifth of French pupils are enrolled in private schools, the majority of the French population favor the retention of the dual school system. In any case, public opposition was such that in 1984, the government withdrew this proposal (which had already been passed by the Assembly).

The controversy over the relationship between public and private schools was renewed in the fall of 1993 when the Balladur government introduced legislation to reform the Falloux laws of 1850. Under these laws, local authorities were permitted to subsidize up to 10 percent of the cost of maintaining the physical plant of private secondary, but not primary, schools. However, since many of these primary schools were in such precarious physical condition that they proved unsafe and since the local communities (which, under decentralization, had been given the responsibility to maintain school buildings) were unable to solve this problem, the government was forced to step in. A bill introduced in the Assembly by a Gaullist deputy, and subsequently incorporated in a government bill, provided that parts of the budgetary grants to departments and communes could be allocated to private elementary as well as secondary schools. Government support of private schools was not new; since the passage of the Debré law of 1959, subsidies had been gradually extended, so that by 1992, they covered private-school teachers and their training; moreover, the total proportion of the proposed allocation was not expected to be significant. But to the defenders of public secular education, the legislation reflected bad timing, especially in view of the budgetary stringencies that public schools were enduring and the periodic challenges to secular education posed by Muslim fundamentalists. The FEN (representing 100,000 members) and the SNESup (62,000), supported by Socialist opposition politicians (some of whom had children enrolled in private schools), protested energetically;[24] as a result, the bill was dropped, to be replaced by the promise of a sustained "dialogue" between the government and the interested parties—teachers' unions, parents' associations, and local authorities.[25]

An important problem has been the growing violence in public schools. In order to deal with it, a number of measures have been proposed, among them the expansion of "civic" education and the monitoring of school grounds by volunteers. Nevertheless, the violence has increased, with more than 200,000 cases recorded in 2000.[26]

Higher education also was the subject of several reform proposals introduced during the past decade. Among them have been the expansion of university autonomy; the simplification of the curriculum of the first two years; the creation of technology "branches" within existing universities, which would grant technological diplomas; and an increase in exchange programs with other European universities by providing for a "European semester." These proposals failed to address the problems of the majority of university students, namely, overcrowded lecture halls, underequipped laboratories, inadequate financial support, and insufficient job opportunities for graduates.

Premier Jospin, a former minister of national education, was sympathetic to students' concerns; this attitude explains the fact that between 1997 and 2001 the budget for education was increased by 19 percent, reaching 9 billion euros.[27] The number of teachers, especially at primary and secondary levels, was increased—but not enough, so that teachers periodically engaged in protest actions. The Jospin government continued its commitment to the democratization of education, specifically, to the goal of secondary-school diplomas for almost all students in the appropriate age group. Great progress has been made in this direction: In 2001, almost 62 percent of French 20-year-olds were lycée graduates, as compared to 25 percent in 1975, and in 2002, 78.8 percent of lycée students passed the baccalauréat examinations. A class bias remains, however: During the past five years, only 14 percent of children of workers were lycée graduates, compared to over 83 percent of children of families of liberal professions, university professors, and scientists.[28] An element of the commitment to democratization has been the uniform middle school (college unique); but this has been accompanied by a lowering of educational standards, especially in working-class suburbs. In 1996, a study commission (Commission Fauroux) appointed by the Juppé government had recommended that secondary schools in economically disadvantaged areas be given the means to encourage students to pursue a vocational curriculum. Those students would receive a diploma equivalent (theoretically) to a traditional academic diploma.

Related to both economic and educational policy was the Socialist government's approach to science and technology. Prompted in part by the ambitions of Chevènement, the minister of science and technology, the government committed itself to large increases in public funding for basic research. At least one-third of the total allocations for research were earmarked for the *Centre national de la recherche scientifique* (CNRS), a governmental institution employing over 25,000 individuals. Several hundred million francs would be spent annually for selected research projects, among them robotics, electronics, biotechnology, and energy conservation. The aim of these projects, which constituted a revival of efforts initiated by de Gaulle, was to make France the third global science center (after the United States and Japan). The global orientations of research and development policy were moderated by several interesting government proposals. One was to "democratize" research by giving labor a greater role in research councils; another was to "regionalize" research by dispersing research activities in a kind of pork barrel fashion; and the third was to require French scientists to use French, not English, in writing up the results of their government-supported research. A more controversial proposal was to reduce the funding of the deficit-ridden CNRS and gradually eliminate the distinction between nonteaching researchers and university teaching personnel.[29]

Since the mid-1980s, there have been few departures in the area of science policy, except that governments have attempted, with limited success, to encourage universities to make research contracts with private industries and with foreign institutions. An interesting symptom of the increasingly global orientation of French science (and of culture in general) was the governmental acquiescence in the decision of the prestigious Pasteur Institute in the spring of 1989 to publish its proceedings on biological research henceforth in English instead of French. Such acquiescence is not likely to be reversed, despite efforts by subsequent governments to insist on the exclusive use of French by civil servants and others representing France in international forums.

French governments have long taken an interest not only in enhancing the prestige of the French language and guarding its purity, but also in promoting the arts, music, theater, and literature. Since the time of the monarchs, most French citizens have accepted it as entirely proper that governments have a set of cultural policies. As we have seen, under de Gaulle, arts centers were set up in various cities, centers in which films and concerts were to be presented. Although the working class did not, in general, take advantage of these facilities, the Socialists continued their efforts at subsidizing theaters and the cinema. In deference to France's economic problems, the 1984 budget for culture and the arts represented an increase of only 15 percent over the previous year, but it still amounted to nearly $1 billion. By the end of 1992, the budget for the arts had more than doubled, and the amount allocated to the Ministry of Culture for 1993 was $2.8 billion, or 1 percent of the total state budget.[30] This money was used to subsidize theaters, opera, films, museums, art education, libraries, and the maintenance of historic monuments.

For many years, French culture was xenophobic and its purveyors (artists, writers, and professors, who were predominantly leftist) tended to complain about American cultural imperialism. Shortly after his appointment in 1981 as Mitterrand's minister of culture, such a complaint emanated from Jack Lang, who tried to put French art and literature on the world map and to prevent them from being "polluted" by un-French, and antisocialist, influences. Since then, the French establishment view of culture has become more open (even under Lang, who was reappointed to his old post in 1988), for, paradoxically, just as the Left was gaining ground politically, there was a simultaneous tendency on the part of many intellectuals to question Marxist assumptions about economics, politics, and culture.

An important innovation in cultural policy related to the legitimation of the claims of France's ethnic minorities. Between 1981 and 1986 the government not only legalized the teaching of Breton, Basque, and other "peripheral" languages in elementary and secondary schools but also allocated money for the training of teachers of these languages. Two landmark government reports recommended a more comprehensive "decentralization" of cultural policy, under which ethnically oriented museums, social studies, theater, and literature would be actively promoted.[31]

Under the Chirac government, and to a lesser extent under the succeeding Rocard government, French cultural policy was pulled in several directions: On the one hand, there was a lessening of interest in the culture of minorities; on the other hand, a kind of cultural pluralism was to emerge, as culture was increasingly privatized, the funding of a number of cultural institutions (e.g., the National Library and the *Comédie Française*) was reduced, and private corporations and individuals were encouraged to support libraries and museums and to "sponsor" musical, theatrical, and athletic events. At the same time, it was expected that French culture would become increasingly Europeanized as a result of developments in European integration[32] and "Americanized" as a result of the success of U.S. enterprises in appealing to the tastes of the French public.[33] But there were limits; indeed, the protection of the French cultural patrimony was an issue that went beyond the confines of party ideology. One of the issues that held up the WTO negotiations in 1993 was the insistence of the Balladur government (in this instance, supported by Mitterrand) that the importation of American films be restricted and continue to be subjected to heavy tariffs.

ASPECTS OF FOREIGN POLICY

The affective relationship of the citizen to the regime has been heavily influenced by France's position in the international system, its domestic self-image having depended on the image it could project abroad. Before World War I, France was one of the major global powers; its culture was imitated in foreign lands; and the French language was the lingua franca of international diplomacy. It was also the second-largest colonial empire, after that of Great Britain.

During the interwar period, France's position began to weaken, and its attempts to keep Germany in check ended in failure with the rise of Hitler, which culminated in the outbreak of World War II. Defeat by Germany in 1940 confirmed France's military weakness; the installation of the Vichy regime, a Nazi puppet state, was a heavy blow to the nation's self-image. After World War II, the old "European system" had been replaced by a bipolar balance in which the two main actors, the United States and the Soviet Union, were extra-European continental giants. France was permitted the appearance of great-power status by winning a permanent seat on the United Nations Security Council, securing an occupation zone in Germany, and regaining control over its colonies. But such prestige proved ephemeral, because the United Nations was immobilized, the occupation of Germany ended, and France was unable to retain its colonies.

In the mid-1950s, France began the process of decolonization. It granted independence to Morocco and Tunisia and, after a humiliating military defeat, disengaged itself from Indochina. Algeria was a different matter because about 1.5 million settlers in that territory regarded themselves as French and wished to retain a permanent political tie with the mainland. These settlers and the French military became embroiled in a protracted war against the indigenous Algerian population, and this conflict was the proximate cause of the collapse of the Fourth Republic in 1958.

When de Gaulle returned to power as first president of the Fifth Republic, he set out to achieve two main goals: the solution of the Algerian problem and the restoration of France to a position of importance in the international system. Under the Evian Accords of 1962, Algeria achieved independence. As for its sub-Saharan colonies, France in 1958 asked them to elect one of several options: to remain dependencies of France, to become French provinces (or overseas departments), to acquire membership in a "French Community" (somewhat analogous to the British Commonwealth), or to become completely independent. Although all chose independence (and therefore the French Community never developed), France's ex-colonies in Africa retain a degree of economic dependence on their former colonial overlord.

The problem of enhancing France's global role was more complex. At the end of World War II, a condition of inequality existed between France and the other two major Western powers, a condition that de Gaulle felt the Americans and the British wished to perpetuate. During the Fourth Republic, France had been content with its role as client state of the United States; the need for aid under the Marshall Plan and military weakness in the face of potential Soviet aggression had made France a willing junior partner in the North Atlantic alliance created in 1949. Moreover, France's recognition of its economic weakness had made it amenable to European integration.

By 1958, France was on the way to economic recovery and had made a start toward the development of a nuclear weapons system. It is possible that the Atlantic collaborative spirit would have been maintained if de Gaulle had felt that his country's national ego was accommodated by changes in the structure of NATO—specifically, the establishment of a military leadership triumvirate consisting of the United States, Britain, and France. But the United States rejected that idea because it did not want to slight a revived West Germany.

Because the NATO alliance frustrated French aspirations of prestige, de Gaulle pursued a policy of independence from the two blocs. In 1966, he withdrew French military forces from the integrated command of NATO and expelled its European headquarters from French soil. At the same time, he sought rapprochement with Communist regimes, in particular the Soviet Union (while simultaneously warning his compatriots of the danger of communism within France). He vetoed the British application for membership in the Common Market because he considered Britain a potential American "Trojan horse" in Europe and feared that Anglo-American influences would undermine a traditional French linguistic hegemony. De Gaulle's visits to Latin America, Romania, and Canada (where, to the dismay of many Canadians, he proclaimed the slogan "Long Live Free Quebec") were inspired by pan-Gallic pretensions to capitalize on a common Latin heritage.

De Gaulle was convinced that a nation's diplomatic independence was predicated on its ability to defend itself militarily. He disliked the fact that the nuclear umbrella over the NATO countries was controlled solely by the United States, not only because there was no assurance that nuclear weapons would be used to protect primarily European interests, but also because there was imperfect consultation on a joint Western policy. He therefore expended much effort on building France's own nuclear strike force. That force was frequently criticized as an expensive toy, which cut too deeply into the domestic budget while providing neither adequate defense nor significant spillover for nonmilitary technology. The nuclear deterrent might bring France prestige as a member of the nuclear club, but it was doubtful whether French stockpiles or delivery systems (even after considerable expansion by de Gaulle's successors) would be sufficient to inflict unacceptable damage on the Soviet Union.

While the likelihood of a new world war was receding, de Gaulle pursued a strictly "national" foreign policy. This policy was reflected in France's refusal to sign the test ban and nonproliferation agreements and (until 1981) the European Human Rights Convention. The policy also expressed itself in a pronounced hostility to the United Nations and in a reluctance to foster the evolution of the European Community toward greater supranationality.

Despite de Gaulle's abhorrence of purely ideological considerations in the conduct of foreign policy, his actual foreign-policy approach was subject to intrusions of ideology (and even irrationality) that cannot be clearly related to the promotion of national interest. Thus, in the late 1960s, de Gaulle demonstrated a rather surprising friendship with nondemocratic regimes. He declined to endorse the Council of Europe's denunciation of Greece's military dictatorship, refused to join a United Nations condemnation of South Africa's apartheid policy, and advocated the membership of (then fascist) Spain in the Common Market.

Four great achievements in foreign policy have been ascribed to de Gaulle or Gaullism: the liberation and economic revival of France; decolonization; a reconciliation with Germany; and the attempt to find an alternative to the bipolar conflict and to moderate it by the creation of a "third force." But it can be argued that these were not achievements of Gaullism at all or that they were, at best, phantom achievements; that France was liberated by the Anglo-Americans rather than by its own efforts; and that the economic recovery of France, for which the foundations were laid in the Fourth Republic, was made possible by U.S. aid. Decolonization was begun in the Fourth Republic and was pursued by de Gaulle because he had little choice: Continued involvement in Algeria proved an unbearable economic and psychological strain on the French people. Reconciliation with Germany, too, was begun when France committed itself to the Coal and Steel community (Schuman Plan) and signed the Treaty of Rome, which set up the Common Market; the Franco-German Treaty of Friendship of 1963, which formally ratified this reconciliation, was in a sense made necessary by de Gaulle's exclusion of Britain from the Common Market.

De Gaulle's reminder that Europe consisted of separate nations and national interests that could not easily be submerged into an Atlantic civilization was realistic, but his evocation of a Europe "from the Atlantic to the Urals"—embracing Western and Eastern European countries—ignored the postwar Soviet subjugation of Eastern Europe (whose reversal more than a decade ago could not have been predicted). The attempt to find an alternative to the bipolar conflict and to create an atmosphere of détente in Europe was a worthy one, but it succeeded only partially. It is ironic that to the extent that there was an East-West rapprochement in Europe, it was brought about, not by French efforts, but by Germany's *Ostpolitik* in the late 1960s on the one hand, and Soviet-American bilateral efforts and the domestic needs of the Soviet Union on the other; that the problems in U.S.-Canadian relations have been a consequence, not of Gaullist policy, but of disagreements over trade and the control of scarce natural resources; that the war in Vietnam, against which de Gaulle had railed so vehemently, was ended, not through French diplomacy, but by a concatenation of domestic developments in the United States; that the loss of American power in the United Nations was occasioned, not by French efforts at building a "third force," but by the skillful use of the oil weapon by Middle Eastern countries of which France, too, had been a victim; and that the Middle East crisis was, by turns, encouraged and "controlled" by the two superpowers, despite the long-held French illusion that the crisis would be resolved by a four-party agreement in which France would have a prominent role. (Middle East discussions today involve France only as part of the European Union, which tries to work together with three other partners—the United States, Russia, and the United Nations.) Yet in spite of doubts regarding the long-range significance of de Gaulle's foreign policy, there is no question that he restored the pride of the French and left an imprint on the world scene.

What is left of Gaullism in contemporary French foreign policy? To the extent that this policy was based on the vision of the United States as a bête noire, it was undermined by a number of developments: the receding memory of the McCarthyism of the 1950s; the end of the war in Vietnam, an event that showed the United States as a less than omnipotent, and therefore a less threatening, giant; the weakness of the dollar and the vulnerability of the U.S. economy to oil embargoes; and trade pressures (by Japan), which called into question old assumptions about American economic imperialism. Furthermore, the modernization of French society and economy had the effect of "Americanizing" many aspects of French social life and culture. Nevertheless, the essentials of de Gaulle's foreign policies were continued by Pompidou and Giscard, except that they were less stridently anti-American, more actively interested in promoting intra-European cooperation, more acutely aware of France's limited power, and more responsive to global pressures than de Gaulle had been.

It is doubtful whether French citizens expected dramatic departures in foreign policy with the election of Mitterrand. Some commentators detected distinctly "socialist" foreign-policy aims, which included the promotion of peace and disarmament, support for international organizations, a more circumspect approach to arms sales, expanded economic aid to poor Third World countries, and a refusal to join a military bloc led by a superpower.[34] The policies pursued under the Socialists and under the first two cohabitation governments in part corresponded to these aims; but, more important, they reflected a degree of continuity and a readiness to adapt to current realities.

The Gaullist features that were retained under Mitterrand included the promotion of *francophonie* (the spread of the French language by means of a network of French schools and cultural activities abroad), the refusal to rejoin the NATO military command, and the maintenance of a national nuclear strike force. At the same time, there was a more vocal condemnation of Soviet actions in Afghanistan and Poland; a greater sympathy for a strong American military presence in Western Europe; and an interest in selective Atlantic military collaboration. One could also detect signs of a rapprochement between France and the United States, although this was dampened by controversies over economic issues—rivalries over the sales of equipment to the Soviet Union, American monetary policy, and the occasional articulation of anti-American sentiments by intellectuals and politicians.[35]

With respect to the Middle East, French policy remained essentially the same: support for Israel's existence, but in the context of a recognition of the legitimacy of the PLO's claims to a Palestinian state. France played a less active role in the Arab-Israeli conflict; this change was accompanied by a less acerbic critique of Israel and several official visits by Mitterrand to that country.

Intellectuals have played a significant role in shaping French foreign policy.[36] This circumstance was once an obstacle to good Franco-American relations, but in recent years relations have been better because of the gradual displacement of the traditional humanistic (and nationally oriented) elite by a more technocratic (and often English-speaking) elite and because of the decline of Marxism and the banalization of Gaullism, two important anti-American ideologies.

However, the changes in French foreign policy had less to do with ideology than with evolving realities. The greater sympathy to the United States and the Atlantic alliance could be attributed to a variety of factors: discomfort over a growing West German neutralism; a partial displacement of the old fear of American economic domination by an anxiety about Japanese inroads into European markets; and a diminished concern about the critical reaction of the (greatly weakened) French Communist party. Similarly, the fact that French policy in the Middle East became less stridently pro-Arab than before was not merely a matter of sentiment: Mitterrand's personal sympathies for Israel were balanced by the continued anti-Israel attitudes of officials in the Foreign Ministry and of a significant number of ideologues on the left fringes of the Socialist party. Rather, the change had to do with the oil glut, the reduced power of OPEC, and finally, French manpower losses in Lebanon, a country to which France had sent a peacekeeping force in 1982, and the transformation of that country into a virtual protectorate of Syria.

In regard to Third World countries, Giscard's idea of a "trialogue" among OPEC countries, poor African states, and France, in which the last would play a dominant role, was given up by the Socialists as a delusion. Instead, France's relationships were determined by treaty commitments—as in the case of its continued, though reluctant, military intervention in Chad—and by economic considerations: Opposition in principle notwithstanding, France continued to sell arms to a number of dictatorial and unstable Third World regimes. France's involvements in the mid-1990s in Rwanda, Zaire, the Central African Republic, and other countries in sub-Saharan Africa, as well as its continuing presence in Algeria, have reflected a variety of motivations: an interest in restoring peace, a commitment to preserve the status of a francophone elite; and a desire to portray itself as an important global actor.

The response of France to the collapse of the Communist system in Eastern Europe and of the Soviet Union itself has been ambiguous. On the one hand, that collapse vindicated de Gaulle's convictions about the *national features of Russia* (as opposed to the transitory nature of *Soviet ideology*) and his notions of a Europe embracing East and West. On the other hand, the reunification of Germany (which the French government tried to prevent or delay) enhanced Germany's status and made the country more as-sertive. This assertiveness, reflected in demands for a permanent seat on the UN Security Council and an enlarged political role in the European Union as well as Germany's role in the disintegration of Yugoslavia, has revived traditional French fears of Germany (al-though French leaders have been reluctant to express these openly). Whether such fears are realistic is moot; nevertheless, the perception that these developments have dimin-ished the relative global status of France explains why France, while proclaiming the solidity of the Franco-German partnership, began to express greater interest in NATO and in a continuing U.S. involvement in Europe and joined the military committee of NATO.[37] In fact, France played a crucial role in activating the involvement of NATO (and of the United States) in Bosnia and Kosovo.

With the election of Chirac, France returned to the pro-Arab policies of de Gaulle, Pompidou, and Giscard. This was illustrated by Chirac's visit to the Middle East in the fall of 1996—a visit designed, not to represent the European Union position (as Chirac had claimed), or to make a positive contribution to Arab-Israeli negotiations that were then in progress, but to assert France's presence on the diplomatic stage.[38] Furthermore, although the president and government verbally condemned international terrorism, they favored a "critical dialogue"—a continuation and expansion of economic rela-tions—with states sponsoring such terrorism. As if to proclaim his Gaullist credentials, Chirac resumed nuclear testing soon after becoming president, but stopped it some weeks later in response to domestic and international opposition. Like his Gaullist pre-decessors, Chirac articulated selected anti-American positions: He opposed certain as-pects of U.S. actions in Africa and U.S. commercial policies that were ideologically in-spired (including the continuing U.S. boycott of Cuba). One important innovation that cannot be labeled Gaullist, however, was Chirac's decision to replace the military draft with a professional army of volunteers.

As if to compensate for their reduced weight in Europe, the French have explored various opportunities for participation in global affairs, whether military (as in their contribution to peacekeeping forces in Bosnia, Cambodia, and Somalia), economic (aid to Russia), humanitarian (the missions of the French "Doctors Without Borders" (*Médecins sans frontières*), or essentially symbolic (the French involvement in the Gulf War in 1991 and the campaign against Al Qaeda in Afghanistan in 2001–2002).[39]

Under cohabitation, President Chirac, having been largely factored out of domestic policy, concentrated on the symbolic aspects of foreign policy: ensuring that the global rank of France was duly recognized. In addition, Chirac made trips to various countries to promote French products and French culture. The major substantive elements of French foreign policy, however, were retained, except that expressions of hostility toward both the United States and Israel sharpened. In the wake of the bombing of the World Trade Center in September 2001, anti-Americanism was suspended for a few weeks in order to show French solidarity with the United States in its fight against global terror-ism. Among the major disagreements were American policy regarding the Arab-Israeli conflict and Iraq. While the United States was discussing ways of removing Saddam Hussein, possibly by military means, French decision makers, in view of their tradition-ally close relations with Iraq and in their self-designated role as "privileged interlocu-tors" between the Arab world and Europe, favored a rapprochement with that country.

FRANCE AND EUROPE

It is increasingly difficult to deal with the French polity in isolation from the European regional context. France was a crucial and often dominant partner in European integration efforts, from the inauguration of the Coal and Steel Community (the Schuman Plan) between 1950 and 1952 to the signing of the Treaty of European Union at Maastricht in 1992. It was due to France's insistence that a Common Agricultural Policy (CAP) was put in place in the late 1960s. With the progressive development of supranational European Union institutions and rules, many decisions made in Paris are no longer entirely national. This is particularly true in economic policy; laws on agriculture, social security, investment, added-value taxation, transport, and interest rates enacted in Paris must follow the guidelines and parameters set in Brussels.

These developments have had institutional and constitutional implications. The European Parliament, the legislative branch of the European Union, is located in Strasbourg, the capital of Alsace (which is also the venue of the Parliamentary Assembly of the Council of Europe). French politicians and civil servants have played prominent roles in European institutions. Simone Veil, a prominent member of the government during the Giscard presidency and, later, in the Balladur government, served as president of the European Parliament from 1979 to 1982, and another French woman, Nicole Fontaine, was elected to that post in 1999; Giscard d'Estaing, until recently a member of that body, long harbored the ambition to become "president" of the European Union. A Frenchman (Jacques Delors) was president of the European Commission until 1995; another (Jacques Larosière) directs the European Bank for Reconstruction and Development.[40] Within the French state, too, new agencies and positions have been created to deal with the European Union: an ambassador to the European Union, assisted by several high officials; a ministerial portfolio (the deputy minister for European affairs, under the foreign minister); a specialist in the premier's office; a presidential adviser; and an interministerial committee for problems of European economic cooperation. The French Constitution had to be amended (Art. 53) in order to make it conform to supranational norms on political asylum, and the role of the French Parliament has been enhanced (under amended Art. 88) in conformity to the stipulations of the Maastricht Treaty on European Union. A considerable amount of parliamentary activity revolves around European Union business: the discussion and approval of regulations issued in Brussels; questions in the Assembly and Senate relating to broadcasting, human rights, trade, agriculture, and other matters increasingly dealt with on Europe-wide levels. Reports of the National Assembly delegation for the European Union are incorporated into the *Journal officiel*.

An important institutional adaptation was the creation in 1993 of an autonomous French National Bank. Modeled on the German Federal Bank *(Bundesbank)*, this institution is expected to make monetary policy without direct interference by any national government. Another phenomenon has been the growth of transfrontier regional cooperation agreements (e.g., involving areas bordering on France, Belgium, and Germany). The stepped-up involvement of Parliament and of subnational authorities has not, however, undermined the executive. On the contrary: The frequent summit meetings of European chief executives have increased the power of the president vis-à-vis other parts of the French executive and his prestige within Europe.[41]

As we have seen (Chapter 4), conflicts over Europe have contributed to the factionalism within the mainstream parties of the Right and the Left, and one small party (Hunting, Fishing, Nature, and Traditions), formed specifically in protest against European Union directives affecting hunting, gained considerable support during the elections to the European Parliament in 1989. To be sure, the French party divisions or voting patterns relating to European Parliament elections (and party organization within that body) do not correspond exactly to those obtaining for national contests; nevertheless, such elections function as indicators of the popularity of national parties.

Most of the French did not object to the growth of European supranationalism and the corresponding sacrifice of state sovereignty as long as they gained symbolic as well as concrete benefits. The symbolic benefits were manifested in the choice of Strasbourg as the "legislative capital" of Europe; in the use of French as the major working language of the European Community (at least until the entry of Britain into the Community in the early 1970s); and in France's leading role in the European Union's political relations with the outside.

The concrete benefits of France's membership in the EU have been even more impressive. Because of the pressure of competition, firms have had to modernize and consolidate. A strong franc enabled French firms to invest increasingly in other European countries. French agriculture has been a particular beneficiary. Under the external tariff wall for agricultural imports, a cornerstone of the CAP, the French farming sector has enjoyed a privileged position in the European Union's agricultural markets. Despite the steep reduction in the number of farmers, agriculture remains an important sector of French production, and the European Union is the principal market for France's farm products (especially French wheat, which accounts for more than 35 percent of European Union consumption).

European Union membership has also benefited the French nonagricultural sector; it has contributed to French industrial dynamism and general prosperity and helped to transform France into the second major exporting country in Europe (after Germany). Some French durable products, such as automobiles, have become popular export items in Europe. The abolition of controls on prices and currency transactions in 1990 made it easier for French firms to invest in neighboring countries (including, after German reunification, in the newly privatized industries of eastern Germany); and France has become a participant in a number of European projects in aerospace industries *(Ariane)*, aircraft manufacture *(Airbus)*, and mass transportation (the Channel tunnel). There has been a partial "Europeanization" of the French electricity grid; and a joint (and bilingual) Franco-German TV channel *(Arte)* was created.

There are problems, to be sure. Large French businesses are much more Europe-oriented than small firms, but even many larger enterprises have not been able to match Germany's investments and sales to Eastern European countries. And although French agriculture is extensive and increasingly mechanized, it has faced stiff competition with Spain over fishing, Italy over citrus fruit, and Britain over meat imports. One of the most contentious recent issues revolved around French efforts at preventing the import of contaminated British beef.

Although many French citizens, especially the younger generation, think of themselves increasingly in European terms, there are those who complain that the European

Union has become too technocratic and who are worried about a growing loss of control over their own fate. Under pressure from the Commission of the European Union, the French government was forced to end its subsidies to the steel industry; the growth of multinational corporations (in part capitalized by France's European partners) reduced the possibilities of an autonomous national industrial policy; and lower costs of production in neighboring countries have led to the transfer of industries and aggravated France's unemployment problem.

The question of European integration became a matter of serious controversy with the signing of the Treaty of Maastricht. The extended debate before the referendum on the ratification of the treaty revealed a cleavage that cut across the various political parties. The pro-Maastricht forces insisted that France's economic well-being and European stability could best be safeguarded in the context of a united Europe. They also contended that the treaty contributed to democracy insofar as it called for an expanded involvement of national legislatures in policy decisions made by the EU. Opponents of the treaty (especially on the left) argued that the European Union was essentially a capitalist enterprise concerned more with profits than employment and that the decision makers in Brussels were too far removed from local needs. Other opponents (especially on the right) warned that the EU spelled the end of French independence and therefore constituted "a crime against the nation" (as Le Pen put it).[42] They pointed to various threats to the French way of life and to the country's environment and to a possible disruption of traditional French political patterns.[43] And Séguin, then Assembly speaker, while not condemning European unity in general, referred to the Maastricht Treaty as "a historic stupidity."[44]

Chirac, Juppé, and Jospin were committed to the European Union, and more specifically the euro, the common European currency, which replaced the franc and several other national currencies in January 2002. The introduction of the euro, to which the majority of the French adjusted with surprising rapidity, was welcomed for a number of reasons. It ended the competition between states regarding changes in interest rates and created some order with respect to investments; resulted in a common monetary approach vis-à-vis the dollar; stimulated investments by lowering interest rates; eliminated costs of transactions of enterprises involved in trade across frontiers; and simplified the life of citizens in their travels from one country to another. These advantages were not of particular interest to disprivileged sectors of French society—those who do not invest or travel across frontiers—or to the left-wing politicians who speak for those sectors, and those politicians have been among the most vocal opponents of monetary integration.[45]

In any case, the arguments in favor of the euro *were* convincing to most of the business community as well as to the president, the premier, and the leaders of the major opposition parties. The imminent prospect of a common currency acted as an incentive to decision makers, much of whose economic policy was informed by the need to meet several major conditions for joining the system: (1) a government budget deficit under 3 percent of the GDP; (2) relatively low interest rates; (3) a maximum public debt of 60 percent of GDP; (4) a low rate of inflation; and (5) no currency devaluation above the norm of 2.25 percent allowed under the European Monetary System.

Some French politicians believe that the euro puts France in a policy straitjacket; others are convinced that the euro places France at the economic mercy of Germany; and still others think that increasing integration, which has permitted both private industry and local authorities to make deals with their counterparts outside the country, has already caused the state to lose its identity. In the eyes of still others, the "federalist" tendencies within the European Union are at odds with the centralism that has been part of the Jacobin heritage. Finally, there are those who insist that the neoliberalism implicit in much of the European integration effort is incompatible with the statism of France and the "social" orientation of its policies. They argue that the European Union has not been helpful in compensating for the losses of jobs in France or in guaranteeing the achievements of the welfare state (despite the European "Social Charter" adopted in 1989, which stipulates minimum supranational norms of social protection).[46] It was partly for that reason (and in order to silence the criticism of anti-Maastricht critics on the left) that Chirac called for a more "social" Europe at a summit meeting in Turin (Italy), early in 1996. He hoped that the European Union would help to create employment in various countries by sponsoring and financing large public works projects. That hope was expressed again when, in June 1997, Chirac and Jospin appeared together at a European Union summit in Amsterdam and, while subscribing to a "stability accord," reiterated their demand for a common effort at expanding employment (without, however, obtaining specific commitments) from their European partners.

No incumbent president can be against the EU, because many of its rules and norms have a direct impact on French domestic legislation. Thus, the creation of "enterprise zones" *(zones franches)* in 38 French communes experiencing serious economic difficulties required the approval of Brussels. The communes in question could be exempted from business taxes; however, under European Union rules, tax concessions may not apply to more than 1 percent of the population. In fact, the commitment to the monetary policy of the European Union was a proximate cause of the premature dissolution of the National Assembly in 1997.

The above discussion is not meant to suggest that the European Union is omnipotent. Many of its rules are not automatically adhered to—there is cheating by all member governments—and some of its programs serve as norms or guidelines for domestic policy rather than as enforceable law. For example, in 1995 the European Commission adopted a "social action program" that covered health, job retraining, workplace safety, and other matters; but the implementation of this program, which is an elaboration of the "social chapter" of the Maastricht Treaty, depends on the individual states. As another example, rules already agreed on may be breached in the name of national interests. Thus, the Schengen Accords of 1990, which provided for the free movement of people across the frontiers of individual European Union countries, was "frozen" for a number of years in response to increasing international terrorism. A more recent illustration is the decision of the Raffarin government shortly after its installation in June 2002 to ignore European Union regulations limiting the shooting of migratory birds. Finally, even if a number of European countries agree on a particular policy, they may do so for divergent reasons. The French have agreed with the Germans on the question of expanding the European Union eastward; but for the latter, it has been largely a question of economic opportunities, while for the former (who cannot match the Germans in the matter of investment capital), it has been a matter of prestige and of renewing the cultural ties that existed during the interwar period.

Although the Maastricht Treaty calls for common foreign and defense policies, such policies have not yet been achieved. French attempts to promote a "European" approach to global issues have so far failed, because the major European states have been marked by divergent orientations: Germany, with its Eastern European interests; Britain, whose policies are often considered too closely aligned with those of the United States; and France, with its Mediterranean and African involvements and its tendency to project itself globally and articulate its own national foreign policy while pretending that it speaks for Europe. In the view of Hubert Védrine, who was foreign minister from 1996 to May 2002, France is in an ideal position to speak for the European Union—and in so doing to counterbalance the United States, which is regarded as a "hyperpower" but whose foreign policies are considered naïve and simplistic. France, Britain, and Germany remain "world powers with legitimate global interests"; but Britain is too "Anglo-Saxon" and Germany has its history.[47] In order to play a more convincing role, France—and the European Union—would have to spend a larger part of its domestic resources on defense; but this can be done only by cutting into social expenditures, a step France has so far been unwilling to take.

What is true of foreign policy is true, a fortiori, of defense policy. Earlier attempts at creating a European defense system (such as the European Defense Community of the 1950s) had foundered because of fear of Germany's military potential. The Western European Union (formed in 1948 in a feeble attempt to produce a strictly European defense policy) has been unable to function as a substitute for NATO (although the utility of the latter organization has itself been called into question with the end of the Cold War). The creation of a joint Franco-German military contingent of 30,000 soldiers has been little more than symbolic; and the European Union provides no guarantee against either its political domination by Germany or future attempts by that country to engage in adventures tending to destabilize Europe. It was perhaps for that reason that Chirac began to think seriously about reintegrating French forces into the NATO military command while acknowledging that the U.S. nuclear umbrella is the ultimate guarantor of European security. At the same time, however, the French were arguing for a distinct "European pillar" within NATO that would concern itself with purely European tasks. This pillar would be composed of the original Western European Union countries.[48] Within this European group, France and Germany would play a special role and would closely coordinate their military policies. All this remained in the discussion stage; however, talks aimed at the creation of a common European frontier police, which are related to a common hardening of positions on immigration, have been taking place.[49]

In the meantime, however, the French have been forced to think in increasingly European terms and to redefine their notions of citizenship on the basis of less Jacobin and less "national" criteria.[50] One manifestation of this development was the adoption by the Jospin government of a bill that would make it possible, at last, for citizens of other European Union countries resident in France to vote in French municipal elections, thus putting into effect a constitutional amendment (Art. 88) that had been adopted in 1992.

European thinking has had a growing impact on elections. Although some of the candidates in the 2002 presidential elections (Le Pen, Chevènement, Saint-Josse, Hue, and the Trotskyists) were anti-European, the pro-European candidates together (Chirac,

Jospin, Bayrou, Mamère, Madelin, and Lepage) captured two-thirds of the first-round votes. To be sure, the French still worry about their national identity; in a poll conducted in 1999, 7 percent considered themselves only as Europeans, 35 percent considered themselves as French exclusively, but 58 percent regarded themselves as French *and* European (a higher percentage of combined national and European self-identification than found among the British, Swedes, Germans, and Portuguese.[51]

CONSTITUTIONAL AND INSTITUTIONAL ISSUES: CONCLUSIONS

In contrast to the continuing arguments about socioeconomic policy, educational reform, and European integration, there has been a growing consensus about the political system. The major developments in the past two decades have been the end of the legitimacy crisis and the acceptance of the Fifth Republic and its institutions, the weakening of extremist ideological thinking (despite the first-round score of Le Pen in the presidential elections of 2002), and the gradual abandonment of the traditional Jacobin approach to defining French politics and society (marked by the poor electoral performance of Chevènement).[52]

In a poll conducted in 2000, the majority of respondents held a positive view of the functioning of the Fifth Republic Constitution.[53] Attitudes seem to be very favorable toward certain specific aspects of the political system, such as the direct election of the president, the role of the Constitutional Council, and the use of popular referenda. These attitudes are inevitably mirrored in the acceptance of Fifth Republic institutions by the leaders of all the major parties to the extent that they entertain serious electoral ambitions. This is particularly noticeable among the Socialists, who have shown that they, too, can gain and maintain power in the context of the system established by and for de Gaulle. On the basis of the Communist party's regular electoral participation, its official commitment to such bourgeois institutions and values as competitive elections and civil liberties, its tacit acceptance of the patterns of presidential decision making, and its willingness to serve as a coalition partner of the Socialists, it may be argued that the PCF, too, has accepted the Fifth Republic. This change suggests a departure from the traditional extremism of that party, a departure that is also associated with the continuing questioning of Marxism by France's intellectuals (especially since the disintegration of the Soviet Union). Although more critical of selected institutions than the other parties are, the National Front also accepts (or pretends to accept) the overall institutional arrangements of the Fifth Republic. The Gaullist party has been, of course, the party most closely identified with the Fifth Republic. However, apart from having lost its monopoly as the defender of Fifth Republic institutions, the RPR came to be identified with themes not specifically associated with Gaullism, such as neoliberalism, Europeanism, international cooperation, and a growing pro-American orientation.

These developments do not imply that political disagreements have been eliminated. The French are divided about how to deal with problems such as the violence in the cities, the stridently racist pronouncements of Le Pen; and the necessity and speed of European integration. There are still significant differences of opinion about the extent of decentralization policies, notably with respect to Corsica; about whether the systems of national and subnational elections should be retained or modified in the direction of proportional representation (an issue that became particularly important after the 2002 elections); and about the role of the Senate. For several years there had been a debate about the length of the president's term of office, but it was resolved in 2000 with a constitutional amendment providing for a five-year term. This change met with widespread public approval, for it "harmonized" the functioning of the major decision-making institutions and reduced the likelihood of a president's being confronted with a hostile Assembly. Most of the French also seem to favor coordinating the presidential and parliamentary elections. There are differences of opinion about what balance should exist between the rights of citizens and the protection of the community and what kind of diffusion of power there ought to be between the state and the local authorities and between the legislative and executive branches. There is some concern about the independence of the judiciary (see Chapter 9) and the accumulation of elective offices (cumul); but on most other specific institutional details there does not seem to be much negative sentiment (see Table 10.1). Among the reforms that appear to enjoy wide support and are likely to be enacted are those proposed by a blue-ribbon commission appointed in 1992;[54] they include abolishing Article 16, granting ordinary citizens the right to appeal to the Constitutional Council, and enhancing the powers of Parliament.

Although the majority of French people are dissatisfied with existing socioeconomic policies, pessimistic about their prospects, and confused about developments in the European Union, they are reasonably satisfied with the overall structure of the political system. At the same time, the French are uneasy about what they perceive to be widespread corruption with the "political class," which, they believe, tends to be ignored or covered up.[55] But these attitudes have more to do with policies associated with institutions or the behavior of officeholders than with the institutions as such.

Despite occasional arguments to the contrary, presidential succession has proved to be quite orderly and has not provoked institutional crises so far, because the policy con-

TABLE 10.1
Public Opinion Survey on
Needed Institutional Reforms (percentages)

Increased independence of the judiciary	51
Simultaneous accumulation of elective mandates (cumul)	39
Criminal responsibility of elected officials	39
Greater autonomy for the regions	22
Balance of power between executive and legislative branches	21
Enlargement of possibilities of use of referendum	18
Reduction of the powers of the president of the Republic	9
System of elections of Assembly deputies	6

SOURCE: Olivier Duhamel, "Confiance institutionnelle et defiance politique: L'A-démocratie française," in SOFRES, L'État de l'opinion 2001 (Paris: Seuil, 2001), p. 75.

NOTE: Responses to the question: "In what institutional domains do you believe reforms are most urgent in the years to come?"

sequences of the shift from one president to another have not been so drastic as one might have feared. This was true even of the changeover from Giscard to Mitterrand, regardless of the rhetoric about "revolutionary" changes: Many of Mitterrand's reforms—decentralization, the penal code, the organization of the media, and steps to consolidate and modernize industry—had been conceived or launched by Giscard, if not earlier. Succession crises have been avoided in part by the exercise of the dissolution power, in part by the continuities of bureaucratic structures, and in part by a *"decrispation"* (loosening) of interparty discourse on matters of social, economic, and institutional policies.

The growing consensus about the political system, which is one of the symptoms of the end of French "exceptionalism," was reflected in the 1988 reelection of Mitterrand— less as a Socialist than as a figure who was both an architect and a beneficiary of the decline of ideology. An indication of this is the fact that public opinion polls from 1986 on gave Mitterrand high marks, not for pursuing specific economic policies, but for maintaining social peace, safeguarding individual liberties, and ensuring the smooth functioning of political institutions.[56] French consensus was reflected above all in a widespread feeling that France had become "dull and banalized."[57] The people's relative lethargy on political issues allowed Mitterrand to occupy himself with matters that, during more difficult and divisive periods, would be considered trivial: glittering international festivities, pronouncements about art and literature, and a series of grandiose building projects in Paris. When Chirac was elected president for the first time, he did not have that luxury; he could not hide behind symbolic gestures or relegate problem solving to the market. In fact, he admitted that despite the continuing talk about "civil society" and neoliberalism, he was responsible for leading a state that was not expected to be modest.[58] However, because he was held liable for the failures in the domain of real policy making, he was forced to give up power to a prime minister he had not chosen, and to become a figurehead president—a position that proved ultimately to his advantage.

The third cohabitation experiment began fairly smoothly but ended in bitterness and immobility, so that most of the French wanted no more of it. The 2002 elections revealed a disenchantment with both major "mainstream" candidates, which was reflected in high abstention rates and in the votes received by marginal candidates and the unexpected score of Le Pen. However, in overwhelmingly rejecting Le Pen in the second round, the French proved that they wanted to maintain the existing republic, despite its shortcomings.

Nevertheless, there still exist a number of political and institutional problems. Some of them are transitory and likely to be resolved with the passage of time. This is true of the periodic discoveries and trials of French war criminals, events that serve as reminders that the issue of French collaboration during World War II remains a sensitive one. It is also true of the presence of a large number of foreigners, a problem that serves as a reminder of France's erstwhile colonial involvements, but one that is likely to be settled as the children of many of the immigrants become integrated into French society.

Other problems are older and likely to be more persistent either because they are by nature more intractable or because their solutions are not voiced with sufficient clarity or conviction. For example, the political role of the bureaucracy has been a factor of continuity and stability, but even if the civil service were perceived as too powerful or too partisan, attempts at depoliticizing it and at weakening its decision-making role would be resisted by the beneficiaries of the status quo. Decentralization has been viewed positively, both as a principle and as a process, but old habits and expectations, as well as the uncertain resources of local communities, make it difficult to determine the ideal balance between national and local responsibilities. Many of the French are convinced that the judicial system is too partisan, too class-oriented, and too dependent on the political executive, but reforms of this system will be slow and piecemeal, because the problem does not threaten stability (despite suspicions of government interference in trials of politicians involved in corruption) and because alternatives (such as those found in Anglo-American judicial processes) are not coherently articulated.

Whether the acceptance of institutions and the emerging pragmatism on a variety of policy issues have become permanent features on the French political scene—whether, in short, the "post-Gaullist" era inaugurated by Giscard's election and the "post-Socialist" era heralded by Mitterrand's reelection in 1988 will continue, under Chirac and Raffarin, to be reflected in a nonideological approach to pressing problems—is difficult to predict. The present president, aided by a government of his choosing, has all the major institutional means at his disposal to enact policies to his liking. If he succeeds, the current French political system will have justified itself; if he, or his political program, fails, ideologically extreme thinking might become more significant—in the instrumental rather than the expressive sense—than it has been in the recent past, and economic frustrations might lead to the revival of a xenophobia that would threaten the fragile patterns of pluralism. There are pessimists who believe that the existing French political system is in need of an institutional overhaul because it has become too "tired" to handle increasing pressures from within and without. Some French politicians and intellectuals even assert that the Fifth Republic is dying of old age and is in need of replacement, and they are calling for a Sixth Republic.[59] In fact, just after the presidential elections of 2002, a *Convention pour la VIe République* was founded. That, however, is a minority position; it is not shared by the optimists, who point out that France has been remarkably successful in maintaining democratic stability, personal liberty, and prosperity.

NOTES

1. See Michel Crozier, *The Stalled Society* (New York: Viking Press, 1973); and Alain Peyrefitte, *The Trouble with France* (New York: Knopf, 1981).
2. So named after Jean-Baptiste Colbert, the chief financial adviser (or "finance minister") of Louis XIV (17th century). Colbert was a mercantilist under whose direction the state promoted industrialization and economic self-sufficiency by means of protective tariffs, taxes, subsidies, and price controls.
3. Except in 1981–1983, when Planning Minister Rocard was given authority over them.
4. Crozier, *The Stalled Society*, p. 97. Gaullist ministers (at least until the mid-1980s) generally endorsed the notion of the primacy of the public authorities over the private sector in economic affairs. However, as Ezra Suleiman points out in *Politics, Power, and Bureaucracy in France* (Princeton, NJ: Princeton University Press, 1974), pp. 173–77, certain ministers have felt that the higher civil service's hold over the business community was excessive and favored a more rapid devolution of economic initiatives to the private sector.
5. Stephen S. Cohen, *Modern Capitalist Planning: The French Model* (Cambridge, MA: Harvard University Press, 1969), p. 4. Though dated, this work remains one of the most detailed on the subject.

6. For example, Etienne Hirsch (1952–1959), who had once been director of a private chemical firm; Pierre Massé (1959–1966), a director of the French Electricity Board; François-Xavier Ortoli (1966–1967) and Pierre Monjoie (1967–1974), both friends of Pompidou; and Jean Ripert (1974–1978), an agricultural engineer, an official with the CGP, and subsequently director of INSEE. The director of the CGP for the tenth plan, Pierre-Yves Cossé (appointed in 1988), had once been a major adviser of Jacques Delors, a conservative Socialist who had been Mitterrand's first finance minister. However, Cossé had also worked closely with Rocard in 1981–1982, when the latter was minister of planning. Jean-Michel Charpin, the current director (appointed in 1998), is a professional econometrician who (in 1983–1984) served as chief of staff for Jean Le Garrec, the minister in charge of the plan under Socialist premier Mauroy.

7. See Commissariat general du Plan, *Rapport sur les perspectives de la France.* Rapport de Jean-Michel Charpin au Premier Ministre (Paris: Documentation Française, 2000).

8. In the mid-1990s, the 576 members of the various committees included 130 higher civil servants, 119 business and financial leaders, and only 106 representatives of the "social partners," of whom unions accounted for less than half.

9. In mid-1981, the government set up an ad hoc study committee on the reform of planning, consisting of deputies, civil servants, academics, businesspersons, party leaders, and local politicians. Its report, submitted to Planning Minister Rocard and to Parliament, recommended greater administrative centralization, greater regional involvement in planning, and a more "social" orientation of the plan. See *Commission de réforme de la planification* (Paris: Documentation Française, June 1982). For a discussion of what planning came to mean under the Socialists, see Howard Machin, "Economic Planning: Policy-Making or Policy-Preparation?" in Paul Godt, ed., *Policy-Making in France: From de Gaulle to Mitterrand* (London: Pinter, 1989), pp. 127–41.

10. See William Safran, "The Socialist Alternative in France: Mitterrand's Economic Policies," in Norman J. Vig and Steven E. Schier, eds., *Political Economy in Western Democracies* (New York: Holmes & Meier, 1985), pp. 200–27.

11. There was a pronounced shift from rhetoric about social responsibility to slogans about individual responsibility, productivity, and creativity.

12. Still, the plan entailed a projected state expenditure of 55 billion francs annually.

13. Under pressure from unemployed sectors of the lower-middle class, the Balladur government subsequently modified this proposal (the *"SMIC jeunes"*) by suggesting that young diploma holders be hired at 80 percent of the *average wage*.

14. Alain Minc, *La France en l'an 2000: Rapport du Commissariat Général du Plan* (Paris: Odile Jacob/Documentation Française, 1994), esp. pp. 85–92. The report called for a reduction of social contributions of employers in order to create 600,000 jobs; the modernization of the civil service, more regionally oriented planning, and greater attention to the environment; and while it also called for a fight against social exclusion, it recommended selective access to social benefits—a kind of "affirmative action" approach.

15. See Michel Albert, *Capitalisme contre capitalisme* (Paris: Seuil, 1991), which expresses admiration for the German model; and Jean-Pierre Chevènement, *France-Allemagne* (Paris: Plon, 1996), which contains a serious critique of it. For a discussion of the need to "rethink" the nature of the welfare state (while rejecting uncontrolled market liberalism), see Bruno Jobert and Bruno Théret, "France: La Consécration républicaine du néo-libéralisme," in B. Jobert, ed., *Le Tournant néo-libéral en Europe* (Paris: L'Harmattan, 1994), pp. 21–82; and Pierre Rosanvallon, *La Nouvelle Question sociale* (Paris: Seuil, 1995).

16. Ronald Tiersky, *France in the New Europe* (Belmont, CA: Wadsworth, 1994). According to this source (pp. 224–25), French income taxes had gone down steadily as a proportion of total government revenues since 1970, so that in the early 1990s they accounted for under 18 percent, compared to about double that proportion in West Germany and Britain.

17. According to a poll of early 1997, 61 percent of the French respondents were in favor of the euro (compared to 44 percent of Germans). See *News from France,* 17 February 1997, p. 5. See also Christian de Brie, "Resister à l'insécurité sociale," *Le Monde Diplomatique,* January 1996, p. 8.

18. The proposal provided for the suppression of family income supplements *(allocations familiales)* to couples with two children and combined incomes of 25,000 francs (ca. $4,800) a month.

19. On the contradictions of Jospin's economic policy, see William Safran, "The Socialists, Jospin, and the Mitterrand Legacy," in Michael Lewis-Beck, ed., *How France Votes* (New York: Chatham House, 2000), pp. 38–41; and Christine Mital and Erik Izraelewicz, *Monsieur Ni-Ni: L'Économie selon Jospin* (Paris: Laffont, 2002).
20. Virginie Malengre and Isabelle Mandraud, "Jean-Pierre Raffarin exclu tout 'coup de pouce' au smic," *Le Monde*, 23–24 June 2002.
21. Among these forces are the *Confédération paysanne*, headed by José Bové, and ATTAC (see Chapter 5).
22. There are also non-Catholic schools, including well over 50 Jewish schools and a number of Protestant and nonsectarian private schools.
23. For a detailed analysis of this issue, see Frank R. Baumgartner, *Conflict and Rhetoric in French Policymaking* (Pittsburgh, PA: University of Pittsburgh Press, 1989), pp. 178–83. On various postwar attempts to weaken the secular character of the French school system, see Philippe Raynaud and Paul Thibaud, *La Fin de l'école républicaine* (Paris: Calmann-Lévy, 1990), esp. chapter 2.
24. A protest march in Paris in January 1994 involved more than 300,000 participants, including the leaders of the major trade unions and of all the left-wing parties.
25. Christine Garin, "Le Report de la discussion sur la révision de la loi Falloux, *Le Monde*, 7 September 1993. See also *Le Monde*, 29 June, 2 July, 2 August, and 6 November, 1993. In an initial attempt to appease the defenders of secular education, the government had promised an extra 500 million francs, spread over a five-year period, to communes to repair public-school buildings. Subsequently, it decided to create 2,500 new jobs in public elementary and secondary schools.
26. *L'Année politique 2001*, p. 365.
27. Ibid., p. 488.
28. Marie-Laure Phelippeau, "Des cursus scolaires à plusieurs vitesses," *Le Monde*, 10–11 March 2002.
29. Jean-François Augereau and Jean-Paul Dufour, "La Rigueur budgétaire appliquée au CNRS inquiète les chercheurs," *Le Monde*, 13 March 1996, p. 8.
30. This compares to the combined outlay for 1993 of $363 million by the National Endowment for the Arts and the National Endowment for the Humanities. It is estimated that the per capita expenditure for culture in France is $41, compared to $1.43 in the United States. See John Rockwell, "French Culture Under Socialism: Egotism or a Sense of History?" *New York Times*, 24 March 1993.
31. Henri Giordan, *Démocratie culturelle et droit à la différence: Rapport au ministre de la culture* (Paris: Documentation Française, 1982); and Jean-Jack Queyranne, *Les Régions et la décentralisation culturelle: Rapport au ministre de la culture* (Paris: Documentation Française, 1982). See also William Safran, "The French State and Ethnic Minority Cultures: Policy Dimensions and Problems," in J. R. Rudolph, Jr., and R. J. Thompson, eds., *Ethnoterritorial Politics, Policy, and the Western World* (Boulder, CO, and London: Lynne Rienner, 1989), pp. 115–57.
32. For example, the ERASMUS program, which provides for the exchange of students and teachers among members of the European Union, the support of multinational research projects, and the equivalence of diplomas.
33. An illustration was the opening of "Disneyland" east of Paris in 1991.
34. See *Changer la vie: Programme de gouvernement du parti socialiste* (Paris: Flammarion, 1971), pp. 183–207; *Projet socialiste* (Paris: Club Socialiste du Livre, 1980), pp. 337–60. See also "Le Vrai Programme de Mitterrand," *Nouvel Observateur*, 15 June 1981, pp. 22–23. For less recent but more comprehensive treatments, see Edward Kolodziej, *French International Policy Under de Gaulle and Pompidou: The Politics of Grandeur* (Ithaca, NY: Cornell University Press, 1974); and Michael M. Harrison, *The Reluctant Ally: France and Atlantic Security* (Baltimore: Johns Hopkins University Press, 1981). For other analyses, see the critical Gabriel Robin, *La Diplomatie de Mitterrand ou le triomphe des apparences* (Paris: Éditions de la Bièvre, 1985); and Stanley Hoffmann, "Mitterrand's Foreign Policy, or Gaullism by Any Other Name," in George Ross et al., *The Mitterrand Experiment* (New York: Oxford University Press, 1987), pp. 294–305.
35. For example, statements by Michel Jobert, minister of foreign trade in the first Mauroy government; Pierre Chevènement, minister of technology; Jack Lang, minister of culture; and Claude Cheysson, foreign minister.
36. See Dominique Moïsi, "Franco-Soviet Relations and French Foreign Policy," in Godt, *Policy-Making in France*, pp. 211–25.

37. See Michel Drain, "La Sécurité européenne," *Regards sur l'actualité*, no. 179 (March 1992), 3–32. For a well-reasoned study of post–Cold War French foreign policy, see Philip H. Gordon, *A Certain Idea of France: French Security Policy and the Gaullist Legacy* (Princeton, NJ: Princeton University Press, 1993). The recent foreign-policy adaptations can be called "Gaullism" if one considers that a generic term for French foreign policy as such, and if one believes that de Gaulle, were he alive, would have pursued the policies currently pursued. On the gradual warming of France toward NATO under Mitterrand after the end of the Cold War, see Anand Menon, "From Independence to Cooperation: France, NATO, and European Security," *International Affairs* 71:1 (January 1995), 19–34.

38. See Pascal Chaigneau, "Le Tropisme afro-arabe de la diplomatie française," *Revue Politique et Parlementaire*, April 2002, pp. 200–5.

39. Pia Christina Wood, "François Mitterrand and the Persian Gulf War: The Search for Influence," *French Politics and Society* 10:3 (Summer 1992), 44–62. See also Franz-Olivier Giesbert, *Mitterrand: Une Vie* (Paris: Seuil 1996). According to that book (pp. 616–17), a major reason for Mitterrand's decision to participate in the Gulf War was to secure France's role in subsequent negotiations on the Arab-Israeli conflict. Among the more concrete "fruits of participation" was, it was hoped, an improvement of France's ability to sell military equipment to Middle Eastern countries.

40. The first president of the bank (whom Larosière replaced) was Jacques Attali, who had been a close political adviser of President Mitterrand's for many years.

41. Patrick Jarreau, "La Construction européenne a contribué à accroître la présidentialisation du régime," *Le Monde*, 28 March 1995, p. 8.

42. Robert Ladrech, "France in the European Community: Implications for Domestic Politics and Institutions," paper presented at the annual meeting of the American Political Science Association, Chicago, 1992, p. 9. See also Daniel Carton, "À la recherche de la dimension européenne," *Le Monde*, 8–9 March 1992, p. 7; Hughes Portelli, "Le Référendum sur l'Union européenne," *Regards sur l'actualité*, no. 184 (September-October 1992), 3–12; Elisabeth Guigou, "Les Français et l'Europe, regard d'une pro-Maastricht," and Philippe Séguin, "Les Français et l'Europe, regard d'un anti-Maastricht," in SOFRES, *L'État de l'opinion 1993*, pp. 87–97.

43. Examples of the first two: in 1991, a European Commission ruling banning the use of unpasteurized milk in cheese, which would have made the production of Camembert illegal; and in 1992, the shipment of German industrial waste to France. The first problem was resolved when the commission reversed itself, and the second was dealt with by bilateral negotiations. An example of the third is the right of residents of France who are citizens of other European Union countries to vote in municipal elections, which is stipulated by constitutional amendment (Art. 88, Sec. 3). The amendment specifically excludes the right of foreigners to select senatorial electors or to vote in Senate elections.

44. *Le Monde*, 19 January 1996, p. 6.

45. See Colette Ysmal, "Face à l'extrême droite, la droite existe-t-elle?" in Pierre Bréchon, ed., *Les Cultures politiques des Français* (Paris: Presses de Sciences-Po, 2000), p. 159.

46. Jean-Marc Ouazan, "La Dimension sociale de la construction européenne: Étapes, perspectives, et réalités," *Revue des affaires européennes*, no. 3 (1995), 53–70.

47. See Hubert Védrine, *Les Cartes de la France à l'heure de la mondialisation* (Paris: Fayard, 2000).

48. That is, the original six Common Market countries and Britain.

49. Jean-Pierre Stroobants, "L'Europe cherche les moyens de durcir sa politique d'immigration," *Le Monde*, 30 May 2002; and Pierre Bocev, "Une Police anti-clandestins pour les Quinze," *Figaro*, 31 May 2002.

50. See William Safran, "State, Nation, National Identity, and Citizenship: France as a Test Case," *International Political Science Review* 12:3 (July 1991), esp. 235–36.

51. Eurobarometer poll, 1999, cited in Gérard Mermet, *Francoscopie 2001* (Paris: Larousse, 2000), p. 241. According to an IPSOS poll taken in March 2002, Europe evoked a positive reaction in 80% of the respondents, compared with 50% for religion, 47% for the United States, and 39% for globalization. Cited in *Le Point*, 19 April 2002, p. 29.

52. William Safran, "Institutional Pluralism and Multiculturalism in France: Post-Jacobin Transformations," *Political Science Quarterly*, forthcoming.

53. In a SOFRES poll taken in August 2000 on the question whether the Fifth Republic Constitution has functioned well, 71% said yes. This compared to 56% in 1978, 57% in 1983, 61% in 1992. Cited in Olivier Duhamel, "Confiance instititionnelle et défiance politique," in SOFRES, *L'État de l'opinion 2001*, p. 75.

54. The *Commission Vedel.*

55. Cover-ups are less common today than 20 years ago. Between 1989 and 2001, more than a dozen major scandals involving politicians of the Right and Left have led to convictions. Moreover, the revelation of the existence of slush funds for politicians has led to a change in the law. For a list of the scandals, see Piotr Smolar and Fabrice Lhomme, "Affaires politiques, vingt ans d'enquêtes et condemnations," *Le Monde*, 7–8 April 2002.

56. See SOFRES poll of April 1987 on "Mitterrand six ans après," SOFRES, *L'État de l'opinion 1988*, p. 23, in which 66% gave Mitterrand a positive evaluation of his performance (since 1981) with respect to civil liberties; 65%, with regard to social peace; 55%, with regard to the smooth functioning of institutions; 48%, information and television policies; and 40%, the reduction of inequalities.

57. Olivier Duhamel and Jérôme Jaffré, "Dix Leçons de 1988," in SOFRES, *L'État de l'opinion 1989*, p. 240.

58. Rafaële Rivais, "Jacques Chirac estime que l'État n'a pas à être modeste," *Le Monde*, 5 January 1996, p. 6. Before the start of the 2002 presidential election campaign, the RPR affirmed that "wanting to reform the state did not mean a lesser state but a better state." Quoted in Luc Rouban, "La Réforme de l'État," *Regards sur l'actualité*, no. 277 (January 2002), 20.

59. See the articles in *Revue Politique et Parlementaire*, special issue on "Constitution: 40 Ans après, la nécessaire révision?" November–December 1998. See also the following: Yves Mény, "La Double Mort de la Ve République," *Le Monde*, 24 April 2002; and Eric Dupin, "La Fin de la monarchie républicaine," and Olivier Duhamel, "Osons la VIe République," both in *Le Monde*, 5–6 May, 2002.

The French Constitution of 1958[1]

Preamble

The French people solemnly proclaim their attachment to the Rights of Man and the principles of national sovereignty as defined by the Declaration of 1789, confirmed and complemented by the Preamble to the Constitution of 1946.

By virtue of these principles and that of the self-determination of peoples, the Republic offers to the overseas territories that express the will to adhere to them new institutions founded on the common ideal of liberty, equality and fraternity and conceived with a view to their democratic development.

Article 1. France shall be an indivisible, secular, democratic and social Republic. It shall ensure the equality of all citizens before the law, without distinction of origin, race or religion. It shall respect all beliefs.[2]

Title I—On Sovereignty

Article 2. The language of the Republic shall be French.[3]

The national emblem shall be the blue, white, and red tricolor flag.

The national anthem shall be "La Marseillaise."

The motto of the Republic shall be "Liberty, Equality, Fraternity."

Its principle shall be "government of the people, by the people, and for the people."

Article 3. National sovereignty shall belong to the people, who shall exercise it through their representatives and by means of referendum.

No section of the people nor any individual may arrogate to itself, or to himself, the exercise thereof.

Suffrage may be direct or indirect as provided by the Constitution. It shall always be universal, equal, and secret.

All French citizens of either sex who have reached their majority and are in possession of their civil and political rights may vote as provided by statute.

Statutes shall promote equal access by women and men to elective offices and positions.[4]

Article 4.   Political parties and groups shall contribute to the exercise of suffrage. They shall be formed and carry on their activities freely. They must respect the principles of national sovereignty and democracy.

They shall contribute to the implementation of the principle set out in the last paragraph of Article 3 as provided by statute.[5]

Title II—The President of the Republic

Article 5.   The President of the Republic shall see that the Constitution is observed. He shall ensure, by his arbitration, the proper functioning of the public authorities and the continuity of the State. He shall be the guarantor of national independence, territorial integrity, and observance of treaties.

Article 6.   The President of the Republic shall be elected for five years by direct universal suffrage.[6] The manner of implementation of this article shall be determined by an organic law.

Article 7.   The President of the Republic shall be elected by an absolute majority of the votes cast. If such a majority is not obtained on the first ballot, a second ballot shall take place on the second following Sunday. Only the two candidates who received the greatest number of votes in the first ballot, account being taken of any withdrawal of candidates with more votes, may stand in the second ballot.[7]

Balloting shall be begun by a writ of election issued by the Government.

The election of the new President shall be held not less than twenty days and not more than thirty-five days before the expiry of the term of the President in office.

Should the Presidency of the Republic fall vacant for any reason whatsoever, or should the Constitutional Council on a reference from the Government rule by an absolute majority of its members that the President of the Republic is incapacitated, the duties of the President of the Republic, with the exception of those specified in Articles 11 and 12, shall be temporarily exercised by the President of the Senate or, if the latter is in turn incapacitated, by the Government.

In the case of a vacancy, or where the incapacity of the President is declared permanent by the Constitutional Council, the ballot for the election of the new President shall, except in the event of a finding by the Constitutional Council of force majeure, be held not less than twenty days and not more than thirty-five days after the beginning of the vacancy or the declaration that the incapacity is permanent. If, in the seven days preceding the last day for lodging presentations of candidature, any of the persons who, less than thirty days prior to that day, have publicly announced their decision to be a candidate dies or becomes incapacitated, the Constitutional Council may decide to postpone the election.

If, before the first ballot, any of the candidates dies or becomes incapacitated, the Constitutional Council shall declare the election postponed.[8]

In the event of the death or incapacitation of either of the two candidates in the lead in the first ballot before any withdrawals, the Constitutional Council shall declare that the electoral procedure must be repeated in full; the same shall apply in the event of the death or incapacitation of either of the two candidates remaining standing for the second ballot.

All cases shall be referred to the Constitutional Council in the manner laid down in the second paragraph of Article 61 or in that laid down for the presentation of candidates in the organic law provided for in Article 6.

The Constitutional Council may extend the time limits set in the third and fifth paragraphs, provided that polling takes place not later than thirty-five days after the decision of the Constitutional Council. If the implementation of the provisions of this paragraph results in the postponement of the election beyond the expiry of the term of the President in office, the latter shall remain in office until his successor is proclaimed.

Neither Articles 49 and 50 nor Article 89 of the Constitution shall be implemented during the vacancy of the Presidency of the Republic or during the period between the declaration that the incapacity of the President of the Republic is permanent and the election of his successor.

Article 8.   The President of the Republic shall appoint the Prime Minister. He shall terminate the appointment of the Prime Minister when the latter tenders the resignation of the Government. On the proposal of the Prime Minister, he shall appoint the other members of the Government and terminate their appointments.

Article 9.   The President of the Republic shall preside over the Council of Ministers.

Article 10.   The President of the Republic shall promulgate Acts of Parliament within fifteen days following the final adoption of an Act and its transmission to the Government.

He may, before the expiry of this time limit, ask Parliament to reconsider the Act or sections of the Act. Reconsideration shall not be refused.

Article 11.   The President of the Republic may, on a proposal from the Government when Parliament is in session or on a joint motion of the two assemblies, published in either case in the *Journal officiel*, submit to a referendum any government bill which deals with the organization of the public authorities, with reforms relating to the economic or social policy of the Nation and to the public services contributing thereto, or which provides for authorization to ratify a treaty that, although not contrary to the Constitution, would affect the functioning of the institutions.

Where the referendum is held in response to a proposal by the Government, the latter shall make a statement before each assembly which shall be followed by a debate.[9]

Where the referendum decides in favor of the government bill, the President of the Republic shall promulgate it within fifteen days following the proclamation of the results of the vote.

Article 12.   The President of the Republic may, after consulting the Prime Minister and the Presidents of the assemblies, declare the National Assembly dissolved.

A general election shall take place not less than twenty days and not more than forty days after the dissolution.

The National Assembly shall convene as of right on the second Thursday following its election. Should it so convene outside the period prescribed for the ordinary session, a session shall be called by right for a fifteen-day period.[10]

No further dissolution shall take place within a year following this election.

Article 13.   The President of the Republic shall sign the ordinances and decrees deliberated upon in the Council of Ministers.

He shall make appointments to the civil and military posts of the State.

Councillors of State, the Grand Chancellor of the Legion of Honor, ambassadors and envoys extraordinary, senior members of the Audit Court, prefects, government representatives in the overseas territories, general officers, rectors of academies, and heads of central government services shall be appointed in the Council of Ministers.

An organic law shall determine the other posts to be filled in the Council of Ministers and the manner in which the power of the President of the Republic to make appointments may be delegated by him to be exercised on his behalf.

Article 14.   The President of the Republic shall accredit ambassadors and envoys extraordinary to foreign powers; foreign ambassadors and envoys extraordinary shall be accredited to him.

Article 15.   The President of the Republic shall be commander-in-chief of the armed forces. He shall preside over the higher national defense councils and committees.

Article 16.   Where the institutions of the Republic, the independence of the Nation, the integrity of its territory, or the fulfillment of its international commitments are under serious and immediate threat, and where the proper functioning of the constitutional public authorities is interrupted, the President of the Republic shall take the measures required by these circumstances, after formally consulting the Prime Minister, the Presidents of the assemblies, and the Constitutional Council. He shall inform the Nation of these measures in a message.

The measures must stem from the desire to provide the constitutional public authorities, in the shortest possible time, with the means to carry out their duties. The Constitutional Council shall be consulted with regard to such measures. Parliament shall convene as of right.

The National Assembly shall not be dissolved during the exercise of the emergency powers.

Article 17.   The President of the Republic has the right to grant pardon.

Article 18.   The President of the Republic shall communicate with the two assemblies of Parliament by means of messages, which he shall cause to be read and which shall not be the occasion for any debate.

Outside sessions, Parliament shall be convened especially for this purpose.

Article 19.   Acts of the President of the Republic, other than those provided for under Articles 8 (first paragraph), 11, 12, 16, 18, 54, 56, and 61, shall be countersigned by the Prime Minister and, where required, by the appropriate ministers.

Title III—The Government

Article 20.   The Government shall determine and conduct the policy of the Nation.

It shall have at its disposal the civil service and the armed forces.

It shall be responsible to Parliament in accordance with the terms and procedures set out in Articles 49 and 50.

Article 21.   The Prime Minister shall direct the operation of the Government. He shall be responsible for national defense. He shall ensure the implementation of legislation. Subject to Article 13, he shall have power to make regulations and shall make appointments to civil and military posts.

He may delegate certain of his powers to ministers.

He shall deputize, if the case arises, for the President of the Republic as chairman of the councils and committees referred to in Article 15.

He may, in exceptional cases, deputize for him as chairman of a meeting of the Council of Ministers by virtue of an express delegation of powers for a specific agenda.

Article 22.   Acts of the Prime Minister shall be countersigned, where required, by the ministers responsible for their implementation.

Article 23.   The duties of a member of the Government shall be incompatible with the exercise of any parliamentary office, any position of occupational representation at national level, any public employment, or any occupational activity.

An organic law shall determine the manner in which the holders of such offices, positions, or employment shall be replaced.

The replacement of members of Parliament shall take place in accordance with the provisions of Article 25.

Title IV—Parliament

Article 24.   Parliament shall comprise the National Assembly and the Senate.

The deputies to the National Assembly shall be elected by direct suffrage.

The Senate shall be elected by indirect suffrage. The representation of the territorial units of the Republic shall be ensured in the Senate. French nationals settled outside France shall be represented in the Senate.

Article 25.   An organic law shall determine the term for which each assembly is elected, the number of its members, their allowances, the conditions of eligibility, and the terms of disqualification and of incompatibility with membership.

It shall likewise determine the manner of election of those persons who, in the event of a vacancy, are to replace deputies or senators whose seats have become vacant, until the general or partial renewal by election of the assembly to which they belonged.

Article 26.   No Member of Parliament shall be prosecuted, investigated, arrested, detained, or tried in respect of opinions expressed or votes cast in the exercise of his duties.

No Member of Parliament shall be arrested for a serious crime or other major offense, nor shall he be subjected to any other custodial or semicustodial measure, without the authorization of the Bureau of the assembly of which he is a member. Such authorization shall not be required in the case of a serious crime or other major offense committed flagrante delicto or a final sentence. The detention, subjection to custodial or semicustodial measures, or prosecution of a Member of Parliament shall be suspended for the duration of the session if the assembly of which he is a member so requires.

The assembly concerned shall convene as of right for additional sessions in order to permit the preceding paragraph to be applied should circumstances so require.[11]

Article 27.   Any binding instruction shall be void.

The right to vote of Members of Parliament shall be personal.

An organic law may, in exceptional cases, authorize voting by proxy. In that event, no member shall be given more than one proxy.

Article 28.   Parliament shall convene as of right in one ordinary session, which shall start on the first working day of October and shall end on the last working day of June.

The number of days for which each assembly may sit during the ordinary session shall not exceed one hundred and twenty. The sitting weeks shall be determined by each assembly.

The Prime Minister, after consulting the President of the assembly concerned, or the majority of the members of each assembly, may decide to meet for additional sitting days.

The days and hours of sittings shall be determined by the rules of procedure of each assembly.[12]

Article 29.   Parliament shall convene in extraordinary session, at the request of the Prime Minister or of the majority of the members of the National Assembly, to consider a specific agenda.

Where an extraordinary session is held at the request of members of the National Assembly, the decree closing it shall take effect once Parliament has dealt with the agenda for which it was convened, or twelve days after its first sitting, whichever shall be the earlier.

Only the Prime Minister may request a new session before the end of the month following the decree closing an extraordinary session.

Article 30.   Except where Parliament convenes as of right, extraordinary sessions shall be opened and closed by decree of the President of the Republic.

Article 31.   Members of the Government shall have access to the two assemblies. They shall address either assembly whenever they so request. They may be assisted by government commissioners.

Article 32.   The President of the National Assembly shall be elected for the duration of the term for which the Assembly is elected. The President of the Senate shall be elected after each partial renewal by election.

Article 33.   The sittings of the two assemblies shall be public. A verbatim report of the debates shall be published in the *Journal officiel*.

Each assembly may sit in camera at the request of the Prime Minister or of one-tenth of its members.

Title V—On Relations Between Parliament and the Government

Article 34. Statutes shall be passed by Parliament.
Statutes shall determine the rules concerning:

- civic rights and the fundamental guarantees granted to citizens for the exercise of their public liberties; the obligations imposed for the purposes of national defense upon citizens in respect of their persons and their property;
- nationality, the status and legal capacity of persons, matrimonial regimes, inheritance and gifts;
- the determination of serious crimes and other major offenses and the penalties applicable to them; criminal procedure; amnesty; the establishment of new classes of courts and tribunals and the regulations governing the members of the judiciary;
- the base, rates, and methods of collection of taxes of all types; the issue of currency.

Statutes shall likewise determine the rules concerning:

- the electoral systems of parliamentary assemblies and local assemblies;
- the creation of categories of public establishments;
- the fundamental guarantees granted to civil and military personnel employed by the State;
- the nationalization of enterprises and transfers of ownership in enterprises from the public to the private sector.

Statutes shall determine the fundamental principles of:

- the general organization of national defense;
- the self-government of territorial units, their powers and their resources;
- education;
- the regime governing ownership, property rights, and civil and commercial obligations;
- labor law, trade-union law, and social security.

Finance Acts shall determine the resources and obligations of the State in the manner and with the reservations specified in an organic law.

Social security finance Acts shall determine the general conditions for the financial balance of social security and, in the light of their revenue forecasts, shall determine expenditure targets in the manner and with the reservations specified in an organic law.[13]

Laws pertaining to national planning shall determine the objectives of the economic and social action of the State.

The provisions of this article may be enlarged upon and complemented by an organic law.

Article 35. A declaration of war shall be authorized by Parliament.

Article 36. Martial law shall be decreed in the Council of Ministers.

Its extension beyond twelve days may be authorized only by Parliament.

Article 37.   Matters other than those that fall within the ambit of statute shall be matters for regulation.

Acts of Parliament passed concerning these matters may be amended by decree issued after consultation with the Council of State. Any such Acts which are passed after this Constitution has entered into force shall be amended by decree only if the Constitutional Council has declared that they are matters for regulation as defined in the preceding paragraph.

Article 38.   In order to carry out its program, the Government may ask Parliament for authorization, for a limited period, to take measures by ordinance that are normally a matter for statute.

Ordinances shall be issued in the Council of Ministers, after consultation with the Council of State. They shall come into force upon publication, but shall lapse if the bill to ratify them is not laid before Parliament before the date set by the enabling Act.

At the end of the period referred to in the first paragraph of this article, ordinances may be amended only by an Act of Parliament in those areas which are matters for statute.

Article 39.   The Prime Minister and Members of Parliament alike shall have the right to initiate statutes. Government bills shall be discussed in the Council of Ministers after consultation with the Council of State and shall be introduced in one of the two assemblies.

Finance bills and social security finance bills shall be presented first to the National Assembly.[14]

Article 40.   Bills and amendments introduced by Members of Parliament shall not be admissible where their adoption would have as a consequence either a diminution of public resources or the creation or increase of an item of public expenditure.

Article 41.   Should it be found in the course of the legislative process that a [private] Member's bill or amendment is not a matter for statute or is contrary to a delegation granted by virtue of Article 38, the Government may object that it is inadmissible.

In the event of disagreement between the Government and the President of the assembly concerned, the Constitutional Council, at the request of one or the other, shall rule within eight days.

Article 42.   The discussion of government bills shall pertain, in the assembly which first has the bill before it, to the text introduced by the Government.

An assembly which has before it a text passed by the other assembly shall deliberate upon that text.

Article 43.   Government and Members' bills shall, at the request of the Government or of the assembly having the bill before it, be referred for consideration to committees specially set up for this purpose.

Government and Members' bills concerning which such a request has not been made shall be referred to one of the standing committees, the number of which shall be limited to six in each assembly.

Article 44.   Members of Parliament and the Government shall have the right of amendment.

Once the debate has begun, the Government may object to the consideration of any amendment which has not previously been referred to committee.

If the Government so requests, the assembly having the bill before it shall decide by a single vote on all or part of the text under discussion, on the sole basis of the amendments proposed or accepted by the Government.

Article 45.   Every government or Member's bill shall be considered successively in the two assemblies of Parliament with a view to the adoption of an identical text.

If, as a result of a disagreement between the two assemblies, it has proved impossible to adopt a government or Member's bill after two readings by each assembly or, if the Government has declared the matter urgent, after a single reading by each of them, the Prime Minister may convene a joint committee, composed of an equal number of members from each assembly, to propose a text on the provisions still under discussion.

The text drafted by the joint committee may be submitted by the Government to both assemblies for approval. No amendment shall be admissible without the consent of the Government.

If the joint committee does not succeed in adopting a common text, or if the text is not adopted as provided in the preceding paragraph, the Government may, after a further reading by the National Assembly and by the Senate, ask the National Assembly to make a final decision. In that event, the National Assembly may reconsider either the text drafted by the joint committee, or the last text passed by itself, as modified, if such is the case, by any amendment or amendments adopted by the Senate.

Article 46.   Acts of Parliament that the Constitution characterizes as organic shall be passed and amended as provided in this article.

A government or Member's bill shall not be debated and put to the vote in the assembly in which it was first introduced until fifteen days have elapsed since its introduction.

The procedure set out in Article 45 shall apply. Nevertheless, in the absence of agreement between the two assemblies, the text may be adopted by the National Assembly on final reading only by an absolute majority of its members.

Organic laws relating to the Senate must be passed in identical terms by the two assemblies.

Organic laws shall not be promulgated until the Constitutional Council has declared their conformity with the Constitution.

Article 47.   Parliament shall pass finance bills in the manner provided by an organic law.

Should the National Assembly fail to reach a decision on first reading within forty days following the introduction of a bill, the Government shall refer the bill to the Senate, which must rule within fifteen days. The procedure set out in Article 45 shall then apply.

Should Parliament fail to reach a decision within seventy days, the provisions of the bill may be brought into force by ordinance.

Should the finance bill establishing the resources and expenditures for a financial year not be introduced in time for promulgation before the beginning of that year, the Government shall as a matter of urgency ask Parliament for authorization to collect taxes and shall make available by decree the funds needed to meet the commitments already voted for.

The time limits set by this article shall be suspended when Parliament is not in session.

The Audit Court shall assist Parliament and the Government in monitoring the implementation of finance Acts.

Article 47-1. Parliament shall pass social security finance bills in the manner provided by an organic law.

Should the National Assembly fail to reach a decision on first reading within twenty days following the introduction of a bill, the Government shall refer the bill to the Senate, which must rule within fifteen days. The procedure set out in Article 45 shall then apply.

Should Parliament fail to reach a decision within fifty days, the provisions of the bill may be implemented by ordinance.

The time limits set by this article shall be suspended when Parliament is not in session and, as regards each assembly, during the weeks when it has decided not to sit in accordance with the second paragraph of Article 28.

The Audit Court shall assist Parliament and the Government in monitoring the implementation of social security finance Acts.[15]

Article 48. Without prejudice to the application of the last three paragraphs of Article 28, precedence shall be given on the agendas of the assemblies, and in the order determined by the Government, to the discussion of government bills and of Members' bills accepted by the Government. At one sitting a week at least precedence shall be given to questions from Members of Parliament and to answers by the Government. At one sitting a month precedence shall be given to the agenda determined by each assembly.[16]

Article 49. The Prime Minister, after deliberation by the Council of Ministers, may make the Government's program or possibly a statement of its general policy an issue of its responsibility before the National Assembly.

The National Assembly may raise an issue of the Government's responsibility by passing a motion of censure. Such a motion shall not be admissible unless it is signed by at least one-tenth of the members of the National Assembly. Voting may not take place within forty-eight hours after the motion has been introduced. Only the votes in favor of the motion of censure shall be counted; the motion of censure shall not be adopted unless it is voted for by the majority of the members of the Assembly. Except as provided in the following paragraph, a deputy shall not sign more than three motions of censure during a single ordinary session and more than one during a single extraordinary session.[17]

The Prime Minister may, after deliberation by the Council of Ministers, make the passing of a bill an issue of the Government's responsibility before the National Assembly. In that event, the bill shall be considered adopted unless a motion of censure, introduced within the subsequent twenty-four hours, is carried as provided in the preceding paragraph.

The Prime Minister may ask the Senate to approve a statement of general policy.

Article 50. Where the National Assembly carries a motion of censure, or where it fails to endorse the program or a statement of general policy of the Government, the Prime Minister must tender the resignation of the Government to the President of the Republic.

Article 51.   The closing of ordinary or extraordinary sessions shall be postponed by right in order to permit the application of Article 49, if the case arises. Additional sittings shall be held by right for the same purpose.[18]

Title VI—On Treaties and International Agreements

Article 52.   The President of the Republic shall negotiate and ratify treaties.

He shall be informed of any negotiations for the conclusion of an international agreement not subject to ratification.

Article 53.   Peace treaties, commercial treaties, treaties or agreements relating to international organization, those that commit the finances of the State, those that modify provisions which are matters for statute, those relating to the status of persons, and those that involve the cession, exchange, or addition of territory, may be ratified or approved only by virtue of an Act of Parliament.

They shall not take effect until they have been ratified or approved.

No cession, exchange, or addition of territory shall be valid without the consent of the population concerned.

Article 53-1.   The Republic may conclude, with European States that are bound by commitments identical with its own in the matter of asylum and the protection of human rights and fundamental freedoms, agreements determining their respective jurisdiction in regard to the consideration of requests for asylum submitted to them.

However, even if the request does not fall within their jurisdiction under the terms of these agreements, the authorities of the Republic shall remain empowered to grant asylum to any foreigner who is persecuted for his action in pursuit of freedom or who seeks the protection of France for some other reason.[19]

Article 53-2.   The Republic may recognize the jurisdiction of the International Court of Criminal Justice as provided by the treaty signed on 18 July 1998.[20]

Article 54.   If the Constitutional Council, on a reference from the President of the Republic, from the Prime Minister, from the President of one or the other assembly, or from sixty deputies or sixty senators, has declared that an international commitment contains a clause contrary to the Constitution, authorization to ratify or approve the international commitment in question may be given only after amendment of the Constitution.[21]

Article 55.   Treaties or agreements duly ratified or approved shall, upon publication, prevail over Acts of Parliament, subject, in regard to each agreement or treaty, to its application by the other party.

Title VII—The Constitutional Council

Article 56.   The Constitutional Council shall consist of nine members, whose term of office shall be nine years and shall not be renewable. One third of the membership of the Constitutional Council shall be renewed every three years. Three of its members shall be appointed by the President of the Republic, three by the President of the National Assembly, and three by the President of the Senate. In addition to the nine members provided for above, former Presidents of the Republic shall be ex officio life members of the Constitutional Council.

The President shall be appointed by the President of the Republic. He shall have a casting vote in the event of a tie.

Article 57. The office of member of the Constitutional Council shall be incompatible with that of minister or Member of Parliament. Other incompatibilities shall be determined by an organic law.

Article 58. The Constitutional Council shall ensure the proper conduct of the election of the President of the Republic.

It shall examine complaints and shall declare the results of the vote.

Article 59. The Constitutional Council shall rule on the proper conduct of the election of deputies and senators in disputed cases.

Article 60. The Constitutional Council shall ensure the proper conduct of referendum proceedings and shall declare the results of the referendum.

Article 61. Organic laws, before their promulgation, and the rules of procedure of the parliamentary assemblies, before their entry into force, must be referred to the Constitutional Council, which shall rule on their conformity with the Constitution.

To the same end, Acts of Parliament may be referred to the Constitutional Council, before their promulgation, by the President of the Republic, the Prime Minister, the President of the National Assembly, the President of the Senate, or sixty deputies or sixty senators.[22]

In the cases provided for in the two preceding paragraphs, the Constitutional Council must rule within one month. However, at the request of the Government, if the matter is urgent, this period shall be reduced to eight days.

In these same cases, reference to the Constitutional Council shall suspend the time limit for promulgation.

Article 62. A provision declared unconstitutional shall be neither promulgated nor implemented.

No appeal shall lie from the decisions of the Constitutional Council. They shall be binding on public authorities and on all administrative authorities and all courts.

Article 63. An organic law shall determine the rules of organization and operation of the Constitutional Council, the procedure to be followed before it and, in particular, the time limits allowed for referring disputes to it.

Title VIII—On Judicial Authority

Article 64. The President of the Republic shall be the guarantor of the independence of the judicial authority.

He shall be assisted by the High Council of the Magistrature.

An organic law shall determine the regulations governing the members of the judiciary. Judges shall be irremovable.

Article 65.   The High Council of the Magistrature shall be presided over by the President of the Republic. The Minister of Justice shall be its vice-president ex officio. He may deputize for the President of the Republic.

The High Council of the Magistrature shall consist of two sections, one with jurisdiction for judges, the other for public prosecutors.

The section with jurisdiction for judges shall comprise, in addition to the President of the Republic and the Minister of Justice, five judges and one public prosecutor, one councillor of State appointed by the Council of State, and three prominent citizens who are not members either of Parliament or of the judiciary, appointed respectively by the President of the Republic, the President of the National Assembly, and the President of the Senate.

The section with jurisdiction for public prosecutors shall comprise, in addition to the President of the Republic and the Minister of Justice, five public prosecutors and one judge, and the councillor of State and the three prominent citizens referred to in the preceding paragraph.

The section of the High Council of the Magistrature with jurisdiction for judges shall make nominations for the appointment of judges in the Court of Cassation, the first presidents of the courts of appeal and the presidents of the Departmental courts. Other judges shall be appointed with its assent.

It shall act as the disciplinary council for judges. When acting in that capacity, it shall be presided over by the first president of the Court of Cassation. The section of the High Council of the Magistrature with jurisdiction for public prosecutors shall give its opinion on the appointment of public prosecutors, with the exception of posts to be filled in the Council of Ministers.

It shall give its opinion on disciplinary penalties with regard to public prosecutors. When acting in that capacity, it shall be presided over by the chief public prosecutor at the Court of Cassation.

An organic law shall determine the manner in which this article is to be implemented.[23]

Article 66.   No one shall be arbitrarily detained.

The judicial authority, guardian of individual liberty, shall ensure the observance of this principle as provided by statute.

Title IX—The High Court of Justice

Article 67.   A High Court of Justice shall be established.

It shall be composed, in equal number, of members elected from among their ranks by the National Assembly and the Senate, after each general or partial renewal by election of these assemblies. It shall elect its President from among its members.

An organic law shall determine the composition of the High Court of Justice, its rules of operation, and the procedure to be applied before it.

Article 68. The President of the Republic shall not be held liable for acts performed in the exercise of his duties except in the case of high treason. He may be indicted only by the two assemblies ruling by identical votes in open ballots and by an absolute majority of their members; he shall be tried by the High Court of Justice.

Title X—On the Criminal Liability of Members of the Government[24]

Article 68-1. Members of the Government shall be criminally liable for acts performed in the exercise of their duties and classified as serious crimes or other major offenses at the time they were committed.

They shall be tried by the Court of Justice of the Republic.

The Court of Justice of the Republic shall be bound by such definition of serious crimes and other major offenses and such determination of penalties as are laid down by statute.

Article 68-2. The Court of Justice of the Republic shall consist of fifteen members: twelve Members of Parliament, elected in equal number from among their ranks by the National Assembly and the Senate after each general or partial renewal by election of these assemblies, and three judges of the Court of Cassation, one of whom shall preside over the Court of Justice of the Republic.

Any person claiming to be a victim of a serious crime or other major offense committed by a member of the Government in the exercise of his duties may lodge a complaint with a petitions committee.

This committee shall order the case to be either closed or forwarded to the chief public prosecutor at the Court of Cassation for referral to the Court of Justice of the Republic.

The chief public prosecutor at the Court of Cassation may also make a reference ex officio to the Court of Justice of the Republic with the assent of the petitions committee. An organic law shall determine the manner in which this article is to be implemented.

Article 68-3. The provisions of this title shall apply to acts committed before its entry into force.

Title XI—The Economic and Social Council

Article 69. The Economic and Social Council, on a reference from the Government, shall give its opinion on such government bills, draft ordinances or decrees, and Members' bills as have been submitted to it.

A member of the Economic and Social Council may be designated by the Council to present, to the parliamentary assemblies, the opinion of the Council on such bills or drafts as have been submitted to it.

Article 70. The Economic and Social Council may likewise be consulted by the Government on any economic or social issue. Any plan or program bill of an economic or social character shall be submitted to it for its opinion.

Article 71. The composition of the Economic and Social Council and its rules of procedure shall be determined by an organic law.

Title XII—On Territorial Units

Article 72. The territorial units of the Republic shall be the communes, the departments, and the overseas territories. Any other territorial unit shall be established by statute.

These units shall be self-governing through elected councils and in the manner provided by statute. In the departments and the territories, the delegate of the Government shall be responsible for national interests, administrative supervision, and the observance of the law.

Article 73. Measures may be taken to adapt the legislative system and administrative organization of the overseas departments to their particular situation.

Article 74. The overseas territories of the Republic shall have a particular form of organization which takes account of their own interests with due regard for the general interest of the Republic. The bodies of rules governing the overseas territories shall be established by organic laws that define, inter alia, the jurisdiction of their own institutions; they shall be amended in accordance with the same procedure after consultation with the territorial assembly concerned.

Other provisions concerning their particular form of organization shall be defined and amended by statute after consultation with the territorial assembly concerned.

Article 75. Citizens of the Republic who do not have ordinary civil status, the only one referred to in Article 34, shall retain their personal status so long as they have not renounced it.

Title XIII—Transitional Provisions Relating to New Caledonia[25]

Article 76. The population of New Caledonia is called upon to vote by 31 December 1998 on the provisions of the agreement signed at Nouméa on 5 May 1998, which was published in the *Journal officiel* of the French Republic on 27 May 1998.

Persons satisfying the requirements laid down in Article 2 of Act No. 88-1028 of 9 November 1988 shall be eligible to take part in the vote.

The measures required to organize the ballot shall be taken by decree adopted after consultation with the Council of State and discussion in the Council of Ministers.

Article 77. After approval of the agreement by the vote provided for in Article 76, the organic law passed after consultation with the deliberative assembly of New Caledonia shall determine, in order to ensure the development of New Caledonia in accordance with the guidelines set out in that agreement and as required for its implementation:

- the powers of the State which are to be transferred definitively to the institutions of New Caledonia, at what time and in what manner such transfers are to be made, and how the costs incurred thereby are to be apportioned;
- the rules for the organization and operation of the institutions of New Caledonia, notably the circumstances in which certain kinds of instruments passed by the deliberative assembly may be referred to the Constitutional Council for review before publication;
- the rules concerning citizenship, the electoral system, employment, and personal status as laid down by customary law;
- the circumstances and the time limits within which the population concerned in New Caledonia is to vote on the attainment of full sovereignty;

Any other measures required to give effect to the agreement referred to in Article 76 shall be determined by statute.

Articles 78 to 87 *(Provisional articles, which have been repealed)*

Title XIV—On Association Agreements[26]

Article 88. The Republic may conclude agreements with States that wish to associate themselves with it in order to develop their civilizations.

Title XV—On the European Communities and the European Union[27]

Article 88-1. The Republic shall participate in the European Communities and in the European Union constituted by States that have freely chosen, by virtue of the treaties that established them, to exercise some of their powers in common.

Article 88-2. Subject to reciprocity and in accordance with the terms of the Treaty on European Union signed on 7 February 1992, France agrees to the transfer of powers necessary for the establishment of European economic and monetary union.

Subject to the same reservation and in accordance with the terms of the Treaty establishing the European Community, as amended by the Treaty signed on 2 October 1997, the transfer of powers necessary for the determination of rules concerning freedom of movement for persons and related areas may be agreed.[28]

Article 88-3.   Subject to reciprocity and in accordance with the terms of the Treaty on European Union signed on 7 February 1992, the right to vote and stand as a candidate in municipal elections shall be granted only to citizens of the Union residing in France. Such citizens shall neither exercise the office of mayor or deputy mayor nor participate in the designation of Senate electors or in the election of senators. An organic law passed in identical terms by the two assemblies shall determine the manner of implementation of this article.

Article 88-4.   The Government shall lay before the National Assembly and the Senate any drafts of or proposals for instruments of the European Communities or the European Union containing provisions which are matters for statute as soon as they have been transmitted to the Council of the European Union. It may also lay before them other drafts of or proposals for instruments or any document issuing from a European Union institution.

In the manner laid down by the rules of procedure of each assembly, resolutions may be passed, even if Parliament is not in session, on the drafts, proposals, or documents referred to in the preceding paragraph.

Title XVI—On the Amendment of the Constitution

Article 89.   The President of the Republic, on a proposal by the Prime Minister, and Members of Parliament alike shall have the right to initiate an amendment to the Constitution.

A government or a Member's bill to amend the Constitution shall be passed by the two assemblies in identical terms. The amendment shall have effect after approval by referendum.

However, a government bill to amend the Constitution shall not be submitted to referendum where the President of the Republic decides to submit it to Parliament convened in Congress; the government bill to amend the Constitution shall then be approved only if it is adopted by a three-fifths majority of the votes cast. The Bureau of the Congress shall be that of the National Assembly.

No amendment procedure shall be commenced or continued where the integrity of the territory is jeopardized.

The republican form of government shall not be the object of an amendment.

Notes

1. This English version is adapted by the author from a translation prepared under the joint responsibility of the Press, Information and Communication Directorate of the Ministry of Foreign Affairs and the European Affairs Department of the National Assembly.
2. Until the constitutional amendment of 4 August 1995, Article 1 dealt with the establishment of the French Community (meant to be the equivalent of the British Commonwealth of former colonies). The Community has been defunct since 1960. Before 1995, the present Article 1 was Section 1 of Article 2.

3. Amendment by Congress on 25 June 1992.
4. Amendment by Congress 8 July 1999.
5. Amendment by Congress 8 July 1999.
6. Election by universal suffrage adopted by referendum on 28 October 1962. Reduction to five-year term adopted by referendum on 2 October 2000.
7. Adopted by referendum on 28 October 1962.
8. This and the following four paragraphs were adopted by Congress on 14 June 1976.
9. Amendment by Congress 4 August 1995.
10. Amendment by Congress 4 August 1995 to conform with changes of Article 28.
11. Amendment by Congress 4 August 1995.
12. Amendment by Congress 4 August 1995.
13. Amendment by Congress 19 February 1996.
14. Amendment by Congress 19 February 1996.
15. Amendment by Congress 19 February 1996.
16. Amendment by Congress 4 August 1995.
17. Amendment by Congress 4 August 1995.
18. Amendment by Congress 4 August 1995.
19. Amendment by Congress 19 November 1993.
20. Amendment by Congress 8 July 1999.
21. Amendment by Congress 26 June 1992.
22. Amendment by Congress 21 October 1974.
23. From second paragraph to the end added by amendment by Congress 19 July 1993.
24. Amendment by Congress 19 July 1993.
25. Amendment by Congress 20 July 1998. Articles 76 and 77 replace an older Article 76.
26. Amendment by Congress 4 August 1995.
27. Amendment by Congress 25 June 1992.
28. Amendment by Congress 25 January 1999.

SELECTED BIBLIOGRAPHY

The following list includes a sampling of books that have been consulted by the author as well as a number of additional works of interest to the student of French politics. The periodical literature cited in the endnotes is not listed separately, nor are a number of French-language titles that are of use primarily to the specialist. However, the reader's attention is directed to the following periodicals, serials, and annuals that have been found most useful: French Embassy Press and Information Service, *News from France* (monthly and irregular bulletins); *L'Année politique; Cahiers français* (Documentation Française), irregular; *Contemporary French Civilization;* Documents d'études (Documentation Française); *L'État de la France* (La Découverte), annual editions; *French Politics and Society; Le Monde* (daily editions and *Dossiers et Documents*); *Pouvoirs; Problèmes politiques et sociaux* (Documentation Française), irregular; *Regards sur l'actualité; Revue administrative; Revue française de science politique; Revue française de sociologie; Revue politique et parlementaire;* SOFRES, *L'État de l'opinion* (Seuil), annual editions; *Tocqueville Review;* and the weekly newsmagazines *L'Express, Le Nouvel Observateur,* and *Le Point.*

The Historical and Constitutional Background and General Treatments

Allison, Maggie, and Owen Heathcote, eds. *Forty Years of the Fifth French Republic: Actions, Dialogues and Discourses.* New York: Peter Lang Publishing, 1999.

Andrews, William G., and Stanley Hoffmann, eds. *The Fifth Republic at Twenty.* Albany, NY: SUNY Press, 1981.

Avril, Pierre. *La Ve République: Histoire politique et constitutionnelle.* Paris: Presses Universitaires de France, 1987.

Beaucé, Thierry de. *La République de France.* Paris: Grasset, 1991.

Becker, Jean-Jacques. *Histoire politique de la France depuis 1945.* Paris: Armand Colin, 1988.

Bell, David S. *French Politics Today.* Manchester, UK: Manchester University Press, 2002.

Bell, John. *French Constitutional Law.* Oxford: Clarendon Press, 1992.

Blanquer, Jean-Michel, et al., eds. *Les 40 Ans de la Cinquième République.* Paris: Libraire Générale du Droit et de la Jurisprudence, 1998.

Carcassonne, Guy. *La Constitution,* 5th ed. Paris: Seuil, 2002.

Correa, M. Pio, ed. *The Dawn of the French Revolution.* East Sussex, UK: The Book Guild Ltd., 2000.

De Gaulle, Charles. *Major Addresses, Statements, and Press Conferences of General de Gaulle, May 19, 1958–January 31, 1964.* New York: French Embassy, Press and Information Division, 1964.

——. *The Complete War Memoirs,* 3 vols. New York: Simon and Schuster, 1972.

Denquin, Jean-Marie. *1958: La Genèse de la Ve République.* Paris: Presses Universitaires de France, 1988.

Duhamel, Olivier, and Jean-Luc Parodi, eds. *La Constitution de la Cinquième République.* Paris: Presses de la Fondation Nationale des Sciences Politiques, 1985.

Elgie, Robert, ed., *The Changing French Political System.* London: Frank Cass, 2000.

Elgie, Robert, and Steven Griggs. *French Politics: Debates and Controversies.* New York: Routledge, 2000.

Giles, Frank. *The Locust Years: The Story of the Fourth French Republic, 1946–1958.* New York: Carroll & Graf, 1994.

Goldstein, Marc Allan, ed. *Social and Political Thought of the French Revolution, 1788–1797: An Anthology of Texts,* abridged ed. New York: Peter Lang Publishing, 2001.

Hayward, Jack, Howard Machin, and Peter Hall, eds. *Developments in French Politics 2.* Hampshire, UK: Palgrave Macmillan, 2001.

Hazareesingh, Sudhir. *Political Traditions in Modern France.* New York: Oxford University Press, 1994.

——. *Intellectual Founders of the Republic: Five Studies in Nineteenth-Century French Republican Political Thought.* Oxford: Oxford University Press, 2002.

Hewlett, Nick. *Modern French Politics: Analysing Conflict and Consensus Since 1945.* Oxford, UK: Polity Press, 1998.

Hoffmann, Stanley. *Decline or Renewal? France Since the 1930s.* New York: Viking Press, 1974.

Hughes, H. Stuart. *The Obstructed Path: French Social Thought in the Years of Desperation, 1930–1960.* New York: Harper & Row, 1968.

Jeanneney, Jean-Marcel. *Que vive la constitution de la Ve République.* Paris: Arlea, 2002.

Jones, H. S. *The French State in Question.* Cambridge, UK: Cambridge University Press, 1993.

Lellouche, Pierre. *La République immobile.* Paris: Grasset, 1998.

Maier, Charles S., and Dan S. White, eds. *The Thirteenth of May: The Advent of de Gaulle's Republic.* New York: Oxford University Press, 1968.

Meny, Yves. *Le Système politique français,* 4th ed. Paris: LGDJ and Montchrestien, 1999.

Quermonne, Jean-Louis, and Dominique Chagnollaud. *Le Gouvernement de la France sous la Ve République,* new ed. Paris: Fayard, 1996.

Raymond, Gino G., ed. *Structures of Power in Modern France.* New York: St. Martin's Press, 2000.

Rohr, John A. *Founding Republics in France and America.* Lawrence: University of Kansas Press, 1994.

Saussay, François. *L'Héritage institutionnel français.* Paris: Hachette Education, 2002.

Shirer, William L. *The Collapse of the Third Republic.* New York: Simon & Schuster, 1969.

Teyssier, Arnaud. *La Ve République de de Gaulle à Chirac.* Paris: Pygmalion, 1995.

Thomson, David. *Democracy in France Since 1870,* 5th ed. New York: Oxford University Press, 1969.

Society, Economy, and Political Culture

Ardagh, John. *France Today.* London and New York: Penguin, 1987.

Bauberot, Jean. *Histoire de la laïcité française.* Paris: Presses Universitaires de France, 2000.

Borne, Dominique. *Histoire de la société française depuis 1945.* Paris: Armand Colin, 1988.

Braudel, Fernand. *The Identity of France,* 2 vols. New York: HarperCollins, 1992.

Bréchon, Pierre, Annie Laurent, and Pascal Perrineau, eds. *Les Cultures politiques des Français.* Paris: Presses de Sciences-Po, 2000.

Bukovansky, Mlada. *Legitimacy and Power Politics: The American and French Revolutions in International Political Culture.* Princeton, NJ: Princeton University Press, 2002.

Cook, Malcolm, and Grace Davie. *Modern France: Society in Transition.* New York: Routledge, 1999.

Crozier, Michel. *The Stalled Society.* New York: Viking Press, 1973.

——. *Strategies of Change: The Future of French Society.* Cambridge, MA: MIT Press, 1982.

Drake, David. *Intellectuals and Politics in Post-War France*. Hampshire, UK: Palgrave Macmillan, 2002.
Duhamel, Alain. *Le Complexe d'Astérix*. Paris: Gallimard, 1985.
——. *La Politique imaginaire*. Paris: Gallimard, 1995.
Dutu, Alesandru, and Norbert Dodille. *Culture et politique*. Paris: L'Harmattan, 2000.
Ezra, Elizabeth. *The Colonial Unconscious: Race and Culture in Interwar France*. Ithaca: Cornell University Press, 2000.
Fourastié, Jean. *Les Trente glorieuses ou la révolution invisible*. Paris: Fayard, 1979.
Giscard d'Estaing, Valéry. *Les Français: Réflexions sur le destin d'un peuple*. Paris: Pocket, 2001.
Grunberg, Gérard, Nonna Mayer, and Paul M. Sniderman, eds., *La Démocratie à l'épreuve*. Paris: Presses de Sciences-Po, 2002.
Hanley, David. *Party, Society and Government: Republican Democracy in France*. New York: Berghahn Books, 2002.
Hazareesingh, Sudhir, ed. *The Jacobin Tradition in French Politics*. Oxford: Oxford University Press, 2002.
Lehning, James. *To Be a Citizen: The Political Culture of the Early French Third Republic*. Ithaca: Cornell University Press, 2002.
Mendras, Henri, ed. *La Sagesse et le désordre*. Paris: Gallimard, 1980.
Mendras, Henri, and Alistair Cole. *Social Change in France: Towards a Cultural Anthropology of the Fifth Republic*. Cambridge, UK: Cambridge University Press, 1991.
Michelat, Guy, Julien Potel, Jacques Sutter, and Jacques Maître. *Les Français sont-ils encore catholiques?* Paris: Cerf, 1991.
Mossuz-Lavau, Janine. *Les Français et la politique*. Paris: Odile Jacob, 1994.
Noiriel, Gérard. *Le Creuset français*. Paris: Seuil, 1988.
Peyrefitte, Alain. *The Trouble with France*. New York: Knopf, 1981.
Saint-Robert, Marie-Josée. *La Politique de la langue française*. Paris: Presses Universitaires de France, 2000.
Tilly, Charles. *The Contentious French: Four Centuries of Popular Struggle*. Cambridge, MA: Harvard University Press, 1986.
Todd, Emmanuel. *La Nouvelle France*. Paris: Seuil, 1988.
Vincent-Legoux, Marie-Caroline. *L'Ordre public: Étude de droit comparé interne*. Paris: Presses Universitaires de France, 2001.
Weber, Eugen. *Peasants into Frenchmen*. Stanford: Stanford University Press, 1976.
Weil, Patrick. *Qu'est-ce qu'un Français? Histoire de la nationalité française depuis la Révolution*. Paris: Grasset, 2002.
Wylie, Laurence. *Village in the Vaucluse*, 2d ed. New York: Harper & Row, 1964.
——. *Chanzeaux: A Village in Anjou*. Cambridge, MA: Harvard University Press, 1967.
Zeldin, Theodore. *The French*. New York: Pantheon, 1982.

Political Parties and Elections

Algarrondo, Hervé. *La Gauche contre le peuple*. Paris: Robert Laffont, 2002.
Amar, Cécile, and Ariane Chemin. *Jospin et Cie: Histoire de la gauche plurielle, 1993–2002*. Paris: Seuil, 2002.
Bell, David S. *Parties and Democracy in France: Parties Under Presidentialism*. Brookfield, VT: Ashgate, 2000.
Bell, David S., and Byron Criddle. *The French Socialist Party: The Emergence of a Party of Government*, 2d ed. Oxford: Clarendon Press, 1988.
——. *The French Communist Party in the Fifth Republic*. Oxford: Clarendon Press, 1994.
Bihr, Alain. *Le Spectre de l'extrême droite. Les Français dans le miroir du front national*. Paris: Éditions de l'Atelier, 1998.
Birenbaum, Guy. *Le Front national en politique*. Paris: Balland, 1992.
Boursier, Jean-Yves. *La Politique du PCF, 1939–1945: Le Parti communiste français et la question nationale*. Paris: L'Harmattan, 2000.
Boy, Daniel, and Nonna Mayer, eds. *The French Voter Decides*. Ann Arbor: University of Michigan Press, 1993.

Bréchon, Pierre. *La France aux urnes: Cinquante Ans d'histoire électorale*. Paris: Documentation Française, 1998.

Bréchon, Pierre, ed. *Les Partis politiques français*. Paris: Documentation Française, 2002.

Cathala, Jérôme, and Jean-Baptiste Prédali. *Nous nous sommes tant haïs: 1997–2002, voyage au centre de la droite*. Paris: Seuil, 2002.

Cayrol, Roland. *La Nouvelle Communication politique*. Paris: Larousse, 1986.

Charlot, Jean. *The Gaullist Phenomenon*. New York: Praeger, 1971.

Cole, Alistair, and Peter Campbell. *French Electoral Systems and Elections Since 1789*, 3d ed. Brookfield, VT: Gower, 1989.

Comor, Jean Christophe, and Olivier Beyler. *Zéro politique: Les Partis, un monopole dans la crise*. Paris: Fayard, 2002.

Converse, Philip, and Roy Pierce. *Political Representation in France*. Cambridge, MA: Harvard University Press, 1986.

Declair, Edward G. *Politics on the Fringe: The People, Policies, and Organization of the French National Front*. Durham, NC: Duke University Press, 1999.

Dreyfus, Michel. *PCF: Crises et dissidences de 1920 à nos jours*. Paris: Éditions Complexe, 1990.

Dupoirier, Elisabeth, and Gérard Grunberg. *Mars 1986: La Drôle Défaite de la gauche*. Paris: Presses Universitaires de France, 1986.

Furet, François, Jacques Julliard, and Pierre Rosanvallon. *La République du centre*. Paris: Calmann-Lévy, 1988.

Gaffney, John. *The French Left and the Republic*. New York: St. Martin's, 1989.

Gaxie, Daniel, ed. *Explication du vote*. Paris: Presses de la Fondation Nationale des Sciences Politiques, 1985.

Hofnung, Thomas. *Georges Marchais: L'Inconnu du parti communiste français*. Paris: L'Archipel, 2001.

Johnson, R.W. *The Long March of the French Left*. New York: St. Martin's, 1981.

Laïdi, Zaïki. *La Gauche à venir: Politique et mondialisation*. Paris: Éditions de l'Aube, 2001.

Lancelot, Alain, ed. *1981: Les Élections de l'alternance*. Paris: Presses de la Fondation Nationale des Sciences Politiques, 1986.

Lewis-Beck, Michael, ed. *How France Votes*. New York: Chatham House Publishers, 2000.

Madelin, Philippe. *Les Gaullistes et l'argent*. Paris: L'Archipel, 2001.

Martin, Pierre. *Comprendre les évolutions électorales*. Paris: Presses de Sciences-Po, 2000.

——. *Les Élections municipales en France depuis 1945*. Paris: Documentation Française, 2001.

Mayer, Nonna, and Pascal Perrineau, eds. *Le Front national à découvert*. Paris: Presses de la Fondation Nationale des Sciences Politiques, 1989.

Molinari, Jean-Paul. *Les Ouvriers communistes: Sociologie de l'adhésion ouvrière au PCF*. Paris: L'Harmattan, 2000.

Nick, Christophe. *Les Trotskistes*. Paris: Fayard, 2002.

Orlow, Dietrich. *Common Destiny: A Comparative History of the Dutch, French, and German Social Democratic Parties, 1945–1969*. Oxford, UK: Berghahn Books, 2000.

Penniman, Howard, ed. *France at the Polls: 1981 and 1986: Three National Elections*. Durham, NC: Duke University Press, 1988.

Perrineau, Pascal, and Domininque Reynié. *Dictionnaire du vote*. Paris: Presses Universitaires de France, 2001.

Perrineau, Pascal, and Colette Ysmal, eds. *Le Vote de crise: L'Élection présidentielle de 1995*. Paris: Figaro and Presses de la Fondation Nationale des Sciences Politiques, 1995.

Pilbeam, Pamela. *French Socialists Before Marx: Workers, Women and the Social Question in France*. Montreal, Canada: McGill-Queen's University Press, 2001.

Pingaud, Denis. *L'Impossible défaite*. Paris: Seuil, 2002.

Poniatowski, Michel. *La Catastrophe socialiste*. Paris: Éditions du Rocher, 1991.

Rémond, René. *Les Droites en France*. Paris: Aubier, 1982.

Robrieux, Pierre. *Histoire intérieure du parti communiste*, 2 vols. Paris: Fayard, 1980–1983.

Schain, Martin. *French Communism and Local Power*. London: Pinter, 1985.

Simmons, Harvey. *The French National Front*. Boulder, CO: Westview, 1996.

Tribalat, Michèle. *Dreux, voyage au cœur du malaise français*. Paris: Syros, 1999.

Wahl, Nicholas, and Jean-Louis Quermonne, eds. *La France présidentielle*. Paris: Presses de la Fondation Nationale des Sciences Politiques, 1995.

Wilson, Frank L. *French Political Parties Under the Fifth Republic*. New York: Praeger, 1982.

Ysmal, Colette. *Le Comportement électoral en France*. Paris: La Découverte, 1986.

Interest Groups

Ansell, Christopher K. *Schism and Solidarity in Social Movements: The Politics of Labor in the French Third Republic*. Cambridge, UK: Cambridge University Press, 2001.

Baumgartner, Frank R. *Conflict and Rhetoric in French Policymaking*. Pittsburgh: University of Pittsburgh Press, 1989.

Berger, Suzanne D., ed. *Organizing Interests in Western Europe*. Cambridge, UK: Cambridge University Press, 1981.

Celestin, Roger, and Eliane Dalmolin. *Beyond French Feminism: Debates on Women, Culture and Politics in France 1980–2001*. New York: St. Martin's Press, 2002.

Cerny, Philip G., ed. *Social Movements and Protests in France*. New York: St. Martin's, 1982.

Femia, Joseph V. *Against the Masses: Varieties of Anti-Democratic Thought Since the French Revolution*. Oxford: Oxford University Press, 2001.

Gorrara, Claire. *Women's Representations of the Occupation in Post-'68 France*. Hampshire, UK: Palgrave Macmillan, 1998.

Hayes, Graeme. *Environmental Protest and the State in France (French Politics, Society and Culture)*. Hampshire, UK: Palgrave Macmillan, 2002.

Keeler, John T. S. *The Politics of Neocorporatism in France*. New York and Oxford: Oxford University Press, 1987.

Labbé, Dominique, and Maurice Croisat. *La Fin des syndicats?* Paris: L'Harmattan, 1992.

Mouriaux, René. *Le Syndicalisme face à la crise*. Paris: Armand Colin, 1988.

Rosanvallon, Pierre. *La Question syndicale*. Paris: Calmann-Lévy, 1988.

Sainteny, Guillaume. *L'Introuvable Écologisme français*. Paris: Presses Universitaires de France, 2000.

Sayès, Christian. *Heurs et malheurs du nationalisme français: Du radicalisme idéologique à la radicalisation du discours politique*. Paris: Pensée Universelle, 2000.

Slavin, Morris. *The Left and the French Revolution*. Amherst, NY: Humanity Books, 2001.

Smith, W. Rand. *Crisis in the French Labor Movement*. New York: St. Martin's Press, 1987.

Stasi, Bernard. *Vie associative et démocratie nouvelle*. Paris: Presses Universitaires de France, 1979.

Weber, Henri. *Le Parti des patrons: Le CNPF, 1946–1986*. Paris: Seuil, 1986.

Wilson, Frank L. *Interest-Group Politics in France*. Cambridge, U.K.: Cambridge University Press, 1987.

The Executive and the Legislature

Andrews, William G. *Presidential Government in Gaullist France: A Study of Executive-Legislative Relations, 1958–1974*. Albany: SUNY Press, 1982.

Angeli, Claude, and Stéphane Mesnier. *Chirac père et fille*. Paris: Grasset, 2000.

Auger, Véronique. *Trois Hommes qui comptent*. Paris: Pluriel, 1993.

Bacqué, Raphaëlle. *Chirac ou le démon du pouvoir*. Paris: Albin Michel, 2002.

Berstein, Serge. *Chef de l'État*. Paris: Armand Colin, 2002.

Cantier, Jacques, and Laurent Jalabert. *Chirac, Jospin, 1970–2002: Deux Vies politiques*. Toulouse: Éditions Privat, 2002.

Chalaby, Jean K. *The de Gaulle Presidency and the Media: Statism and Public Communications*. New York: St. Martin's Press, 2002.

Chevalier, Francois. *Le Sénateur français, 1875–1995: Essai sur le recrutement et la représentativité des membres de la seconde chambre*. Paris: LGDJ, 1998.

Cole, Alistair. *François Mitterrand: A Study in Political Leadership*. London & New York: Routledge, 1994.

Colombani, Jean-Marie. *Portrait d'un président.* Paris: Gallimard, 1985.

——. *Le Mariage blanc.* Paris: Gallimard, 1986.

Conte, Arthur. *Les Premiers Ministres de la Ve République.* Paris: Le Pré aux Clercs, 1986.

Derfler, Leslie. *President and Parliament.* Boca Raton: University Presses of Florida, 1983.

Duverger, Maurice. *Bréviaire de la cohabitation.* Paris: Presses Universitaires de France, 1986.

Elgie, Robert. *The Role of the Prime Minister in France, 1981–1989.* New York: St. Martin's Press, 1993.

Favoureu, Louis, and Loïc Philip, eds. *Les Grandes Décisions du Conseil constitutionnel,* 8th ed. Paris: Dalloz, 1995.

Frémy, Dominique. *Quid des présidents de la République et des candidats.* Paris: Laffont, 1987.

Giesbert, Franz-Olivier. *Mitterrand: Une Vie.* Paris: Seuil, 1996.

Giscard d'Estaing, Valéry. *State Secrets: A French President's Experiences with Power and Private Life.* New York: Random House, 1999.

Hollifield, James, and George Ross, eds. *Searching for the New France.* New York and London: Routledge, 1991.

Laurens, André. *Le Métier politique ou la conquête du pouvoir.* Paris: Alain Moreau, 1980.

Mage, Tristan. *Le Financement de la vie politique devant le Parlement français: L'Élection du Président de la République et celle des députés (13 juillet 1994–24 janvier 1995).* Paris: T. Mage, 2000.

Massot, Jean. *La Présidence de la République en France.* Paris: Documentation Française, 1986.

Maus, Didier, ed. *Les Grandes Textes de la pratique institutionnelle de la Ve République.* Paris: Documentation Française, 1995.

Morabito, Marcel. *Le Chef de l'État en France.* Paris: Montchrestien, 1995.

Nay, Catherine. *Les Sept Mitterrand.* Paris: Grasset, 1988.

——. *Le Dauphin et le Régent.* Paris: Grasset, 1994.

Northcott, Wayne. *Mitterrand: A Political Biography.* New York: Holmes & Meier, 1992.

Pfister, Thierry. *Dans les coulisses du pouvoir.* Paris: Albin Michel, 1986.

Ramsay, Raylene. *French Women in Politics: Writing Power.* Oxford, UK: Berghahn Books, 2002.

Rémond, René, et al. *Quarante Ans de cabinets ministériels: De Léon Blum à Georges Pompidou.* Paris: Fondation Nationale des Sciences Politiques, 1982.

Ross, George, Stanley Hoffmann, and Sylvia Malzacher, eds. *The Mitterrand Experiment.* New York: Oxford University Press, 1987.

Schrameck, Olivier. *Les Cabinets ministériels.* Paris: Dalloz, 1995.

——. *Matignon Rive gauche, 1997–2001.* Paris: Seuil, 2001.

Stone, Alec. *The Birth of Judicial Politics in France: The Constitutional Council in Comparative Perspective.* New York: Oxford University Press, 1992.

Thiollet, Jean-Pierre, *Les Dessous d'une présidence.* Paris: Anagramme Éditions, 2002.

Thody, Philip. *French Caesarism from Napoleon I to Charles de Gaulle.* New York: St. Martin's Press, 1989.

Thody Philip, and Malcolm Waller. *The Fifth French Republic: Presidents, Politics and Personalities.* New York: Routledge, 1999.

Victor, Barbara. *Le Matignon de Jospin.* Paris: Flammarion, 1999.

Administration and the Judicial Process

Bernard, Paul. *L'État et la décentralisation. Notes et Documents.* Paris: Documentation Française, 1983.

Birnbaum, Pierre. *Les Élites socialistes au pouvoir, 1981–1985.* Paris: Presses Universitaires de France, 1985.

Cohen-Tanugi, Laurent. *Le Droit sans l'État.* Paris: Presses Universitaires de France, 1985.

Dion, Stéphane. *La Politisation des maires.* Paris: Économica, 1986.

Fayolle, Gérard. *Des Élus locaux sous la Ve République.* Paris: Hachette, 1989.

Muller, Pierre. *L'Administration française est-elle en crise?* Paris: L'Harmattan, 2000.

Pfister, Thierry. *La République des fonctionnaires.* Paris: Albin Michel, 1988.

Pinsseau, Hubert. *L'Organisation judiciaire de la France.* Paris: Documentation Française, 1985.

Rémond, Bruno. *La Région,* 2d ed. Paris: Montchrestien, 1995.

Roussel, Violaine. *Affaires de juges: Les Magistrats dans les scandales politiques en France.* Paris: La Découverte, 2002.

Schmidt, Vivien A. *Democratizing France: The Political and Administrative History of Decentralization.* Cambridge, UK, and New York: Cambridge University Press, 1991.

Suleiman, Ezra. *Elites in French Society.* Princeton: Princeton University Press, 1978.

———. *Private Power and Centralization in France.* Princeton: Princeton University Press, 1987.

Tarrow, Sidney. *Between Center and Periphery: Grassroots Politicians in Italy and France.* New Haven: Yale University Press, 1977.

Economic, Social, and Foreign Policies

Aldrich, Robert, and John Connell, eds. *France in World Politics.* London and New York: Routledge, 1989.

Alexander, Martin S. *The Republic in Danger: General Maurice Gamelin and the Politics of French Defence, 1933–1940.* Cambridge, UK: Cambridge University Press, 2002.

Ambler, John S., ed. *France Under Socialist Leadership.* Philadelphia: Institute for the Study of Human Issues, 1983.

Ashford, Douglas E., ed. *Policy and Politics in France. Living with Uncertainty.* Philadelphia: Temple University Press, 1982.

Brenner, Michael, and Guillaume Parmentier. *Reconcilable Differences: US-French Relations in the New Era.* Washington, D.C.: Brookings Institution Press, 2000.

Chassaigne, Phillipe, and Michael Dockrill, eds. *Anglo-French Relations, 1898–1998: From Fashoda to Jospin.* Hampshire, UK: Palgrave Macmillan, 2002.

Christofferson, Thomas R. *The French Socialists in Power: From Autogestion to Cohabitation.* Newark: University of Delaware Press, 1991.

Dahm, Henrich. *French and Japanese Economic Relations with Vietnam Since 1975.* New York: Curzon Press, 1999.

Dutton, Paul V. *Origins of the French Welfare State: The Struggle for Social Reform in France, 1914–1947.* Cambridge, UK: Cambridge University Press, 2002.

Friend, Julius W. *Seven Years in France: François Mitterrand and the Unintended Revolution, 1981–1988.* Boulder, CO: Westview Press, 1989.

Friend, Julius Weis, and Simon Serfaty. *Unequal Partners: French-German Relations, 1989–2000.* Westport, CT: Praeger Publishers, 2001.

Godt, Paul, ed. *Policy-Making in France from de Gaulle to Mitterrand.* London: Pinter, 1989.

Gordon, Philip H. *A Certain Idea of France: French Security Policy and the Gaullist Legacy.* Princeton: Princeton University Press, 1993.

Gordon, Philippe M., and Sophie Meunier. *Le Nouveau Défi français: La France face à la mondialisation.* Paris: Odile Jacob, 2002.

Hall, Peter. *Governing the Economy: The Politics of State Intervention in Britain and France.* New York: Oxford University Press, 1986.

Harrison, Michael M., and Mark G. McDonough. *Negotiations on the French Withdrawal from NATO.* Lanham, MD: University Press of America, 2000.

Hayward, Jack. *The State and the Market Economy.* New York: New York University Press, 1986.

Howarth, David. *The French Road to European Monetary Union.* New York: St. Martin's Press, 2000.

Keeler, John T. S., and Martin A. Schain, eds. *Chirac's Challenge: Liberalization, Europeanization, and Malaise in France.* New York: St. Martin's Press, 1997.

Kolodziej, Edward A. *French International Policy Under de Gaulle and Pompidou.* Ithaca: Cornell University Press, 1974.

Levy, Jacques, ed. *From Geopolitics to Global Politics: A French Connection.* London: Frank Cass, 2001.

Machin, Howard, and Vincent Wright, eds. *Economic Policy and Policy-Making Under the Mitterrand Presidency.* New York: St. Martin's Press, 1985.

Mason, John G. *Mitterrand, the Socialists and French Security Policy: Left Elites and French Nuclear Politics.* Lanham, MD: Rowman & Littlefield, 2002.

Mital, Christine, and Eric Izraelewicz. *Monsieur Ni-Ni: L'Économie selon Jospin.* Paris: Robert Laffont, 2002.

Raffarin, Jean-Pierre. *Pour une nouvelle gouvernance.* Paris: L'Archipel, 2002.

Rivière, Franck. *Mondialisme: Un Défi pour les français.* Paris: Jean-Cyrille Godefroy, 1999.

Robin, Gabriel. *La Diplomatie de Mitterrand ou le triomphe des apparences.* Paris: Éditions de la Bièvre, 1985.

Schmidt, Vivien. *From State to Market: The Transformation of French Business and Government.* Cambridge, UK: Cambridge University Press, 1996.

Stern, Brigitte, ed. *United Nations Peace-Keeping Operations: A Guide to French Policies.* Brussels, Belgium: United Nations Publications, 1998.

Tiersky, Ronald. *France and the New Europe.* Belmont, CA: Wadworth Publishing Company, 1994.

Touraine, Alain. *Beyond Neoliberalism.* Malden, MA: Polity Press, 2001.

Touraine, Alain, et al., eds. *Le Grand Refus: Réflexions sur la grève de décembre 1995.* Paris: Fayard, 1996.

Trumbull, J. Gunnar. *Silicon and the State: French Innovation Policy in the Internet Age.* Washington, DC: The Brookings Institution, 2002.

Utley, R. E. *The French Defence Debate: Consensus and Continuity in the Mitterrand Era.* Hampshire, UK: Palgrave Macmillan, 2000.

Valance, Georges. *Histoire du Franc: 1360–2002.* Paris: Flammarion, 1998.

Veltz, Pierre. *Des Lieux et des liens: Le Territoire français à l'heure de la mondialisation.* Paris: Éditions de l'Aube, 2002.

Vinen, Richard. *The Politics of French Business, 1936–1945.* Cambridge, UK: Cambridge University Press, 2002.

Wilsford, David. *Doctors and the State: The Politics of Health Care in France and the United States.* Durham, NC: Duke University Press, 1991.

Académie Française, 197
Action directe, 306
Action française, 6
Affair of 16 May (1877), 6, 10
Affirmative action, 43, 49 n72, 350 n14
Africa, 8, 24, 35, 65, 92, 192, 226, 336, 339, 340. *See also* Algeria
Agence-France-Presse, 310
Agriculture, 26–28, 154–55, 170, 319, 331. *See also* Common Agricultural Policy; Farmers
Alcoholism, 52, 53
Algeria, 6, 8–9, 15(table), 46 n37, 64, 168, 179, 336
Alliot-Marie, Michèle, 110, 192
Allocations familiales (family allowances), 8, 24, 30, 330, 350 n18
Alsace and Alsatians, 37, 45 n25, 286
Alternate *(suppléant),* 244, 256 n49, n50
Alternative rouge et verte, 134, 140 n48
American culture, 37, 47 n45, 335, 340
Ancien régime, 3, 12, 28, 271, 298
Anticlericalism, 84, 119. *See also Laïcité*
Anti-Semitism, 34–35, 46 n31, 65, 70–71 n81, 92
Apparentement, 126, 244, 226
Arrondissements, 271, 284–85, 298
Artisans, 27, 124, 153, 163(table)
Assembly. *See* National Assembly
ATTAC *(Association pour une taxation des transactions financières pour l'aide aux citoyens),* 157, 351 n21

Aubry, Martine, 48 n65, 134, 142 n72, 173 n20, 203, 215 n35, 330
Auriol, Vincent, 255 n32
Auroux laws, 151, 324
Authoritarianism, 11–12
Autogestion (self-management), 88, 148, 149, 156
Avocats, 298, 299

Badinter, Robert, 256 n38, 290 n22, 302
Bagehot, Walter, 185
Balladur, Edouard, 215 n24, 254 n6, 287, 335
  cabinet and, 192, 194–95, 196, 201
  economic policy of, 327–28
  as premier, 42, 100, 182, 183(table), 184, 187–88, 191(table), 243, 252–53, 257 n63
  as presidential candidate, 78(table), 101–2, 103, 117, 123(table), 125, 140 n39, 140 n45
  as secretary-general, 82, 216 n43
Barre, Raymond
  cabinet and, 199
  as premier, 27, 124, 152, 181, 183(table), 184, 190(table), 203, 234, 237, 323–24
  as presidential candidate, 78(table), 92, 95, 96, 117
Barrès, Maurice, 46 n31
Basques, 36, 37, 286, 306, 335
Bayrou, François, 47 n53, 107, 109(table), 112, 123(table), 346

Bérégovoy, Pierre, 100, 140 n38, 182, 183(table), 184, 185, 191(table), 204, 216 n43, 317 n66, 327
Besancenot, Olivier, 109(table), 123(table)
Blanc, Jacques, 118–19
Blocked vote, 236–37, 255 n27, 255 n28
Blondel, Marc, 152
BLORE (Bureau de liaison des organisations des retraités), 169
Blum, Léon, 7, 42, 79
Bonapartism, 6, 12, 91, 138 n15, 208–9, 212
Bouchardeau, Huguette, 88
Boulanger, Georges, 6, 11, 208
Bourbons, 3–4, 5, 259
Bourgeoisie, 3, 6, 28, 79, 81, 83, 84, 89, 90, 113
Bousquet, René, 218 n91
Boutin, Christine, 109(table)
Bové, José, 155, 173 n23, 351 n21
Brittany and Bretons, 33, 36–37, 47 n43, 286, 335
Broglie, Jean de, 138 n14, 254 n9
Buddhism, 32
Budget, budgetary process, 10(table), 13, 237
  local, 277, 280, 281(table)
Buffet, Marie-George, 42, 112
Bureau, 223–24
Bureaucracy. See Civil service, civil servants
Business, organized, 152–54, 170. See also Shopkeepers, small business
  access of, to government, 152, 170
  civil service and, 261, 266, 279(table)
  Economic and Social Council and, 163
  economic planning and, 320, 321, 322, 323, 324

Cabinet, 10(table), 18(table), 44, 191–99, 260
  composition of, 193(table), 199–204, 217 n56
  Fifth Republic, 190–99
  Fourth Republic, 8, 195
  meetings of, 195–96, 198
  Parliament and, 195
  resignations of, 202–3
  role of, 194–95, 196, 197–98
  women in, 42
Cabinet ministériel, 190–99

CADA (Commission d'accès aux documents administratifs), 270, 292 n43
Cadres, 28
Caisses, 165–66
Campaign financing, 130–32, 146 n126
Cantons, 271
Capitant, René, 11, 83
Carignon, Alain, 281, 291 n29
Cartesian. See Descartes, René
Catholic church, 3, 7, 18(table), 120
Catholics, Catholicism, 32–35
  Catholic identity, 32–34
  FNSEA and, 185
  Fourth Republic and, 32
  French civic culture and, 53–54
  political parties and, 80, 82, 83, 90, 107, 122, 124, 138 n19
  schools and, 17, 33, 332
  social class and, 29
  voting and, 130
  See also CDS; Center, centrism, centrists; FD; MRP
CDP (Centre de la démocratie et du progrès), 76–77(fig.)
CDS (Centre des démocrates sociaux), 76–77(fig.), 87, 96, 99, 101, 103, 117, 118, 128, 134. See also FD
Censure, motions of, 21 n14, 241–43, 256 n48
Center, centrism, centrists, 73, 74–75(table), 83, 86–87, 91–92, 138 n12
CERES (Centre d'études, de recherches, et d'éducation socialistes), 90, 138 n21, 203, 253 n6
Ceyrac, François, 152
CFDT (Confédération française démocratique du travail), 42, 59, 148, 149, 150, 152, 165(table), 166, 167, 171 n3, 176 n73, 253 n5
CFE-CGC (Confédération française de l'encadrement–Confédération générale des cadres), 148
CFTC (Confédération française des travailleurs chrétiens), 147, 148, 165(table), 171 n3
CGC (Confédération générale des cadres), 163(table), 165(table), 172 n7
CGP (Commissariat général du plan), 321–22

CGPME *(Confédération générale des petites et moyennes enterprises)*, 153

CGT *(Confédération générale du travail)*, 31, 147, 148, 149, 151–52, 163, 165(table), 169, 171 n2, 176 n73, 264

CGT-FO *(Confédération générale du travail–Force ouvrière). See* FO

Chaban-Delmas, Jacques, 78(table), 83, 105, 117, 182, 183(table), 184, 190(table), 199, 203, 205, 215 n18, 250, 258 n79, 273

Chamber of Deputies (Third Republic), 5, 14, 73

Chambers, professional, 152–154, 170

Charasse, Michel, 254 n16

Charette, Hervé de, 141 n55

Charisma. *See* Heroic leadership

Charles X, 4

Charter of 1814, 4, 11

Cheminade, Jacques, 140 n49

Chevènement, Jean-Pierre, 98–99, 109(table), 112, 118, 123(table), 135, 141 n63, 143 n94, 146 n138, 202, 203, 215 n35, 216 n39, 277, 331, 333–34, 345, 346, 351 n35

Cheysson, Claude, 202, 351 n35

Chirac, Claude, 216 n42

Chirac, Jacques, 78(table), 123(table)
  background of, 298 n7
  cabinet and, 118, 192, 194, 198, 204
  economic policy of, 328–32
  European Union and, 343, 344
  foreign policy of, 340
  as Gaullist party leader, 83, 87, 108, 117
  Giscard d'Estaing and, 92, 96
  grant of immunity to, 304
  interest groups and, 160
  on immigrants, 102
  as leader of RPR-UDF, 100, 101–2, 187, 188
  as mayor, 273, 284
  media and, 312
  as minister, 201–2
  party composition of government, 191(table)
  party switching by, 118
  as premier, 27, 49 n74, 182, 183(table), 184, 186, 190–91(table), 192, 199, 203, 215 n18, 236, 256 n49, 326
  as president, 7, 34, 49 n74, 61, 105–6, 107, 110, 121, 181, 188–90, 206, 212–13, 215 n30, 220 n94, 230, 234, 237, 248, 253, 303, 324, 345, 348
  as presidential candidate, 94–95, 103–5, 108, 109(table), 125–26
  public opinion of, 144 n112, 144 n113
  voters for, 124–25
  See also Cohabitation

Christian Democrats, 12, 79. *See also* MRP

CID-UNATI *(Confédération intersyndicale de défense–Union nationale des artisans et travailleurs indépendants)*, 153

CIR *(Convention des institutions républicaines)*, 76–77(fig.), 80, 134, 182

Citizenship, 35, 46 n32, 66 n10, 92, 140 n42, 345

Citizens' Movement. *See Mouvement des citoyens*

Civil liberties, 18(table), 55, 85, 239–40, 308–12
  Council of State and, 269
  freedom of the press, 308–12, 317 n66
  freedom of speech, 308–12
  See also Constitutional Council

Civil service, civil servants, 3, 4, 192, 348–49
  administration of Paris, 284–85
  bureaucracy, technocracy, and economic administration, 287–88
  cabinets and, 192, 194, 200
  categories of, 260–61
  commune, 272–74
  composition and ideology of, 262–66
  controls over, 266–71
  Corsica and overseas territories, 285–86
  decentralization of, 274–77, 283–84
  executive and, 259
  history, 259–60
  image of, 56
  interest groups and, 162, 267
  limitations on, and citizen access to, 266–67, 277–78
  Parliament and, 264, 266
  recruitment of, 30, 259–62
  reform of, 274–83
  structure of, 259–62
  subnational, 271–72, 279, 280(table)
  women in, 41–42
  See also ENA

Civil Service Commission, 260
Civil society, 60. *See also* Interest groups
Classes, social, 28–32, 265–66, 333
Club 89, 134
Club de l'Horloge, 35, 135, 146 n136
Club Jean Moulin, 135
Clubs, 133–36. *See also individual clubs*
CNAM *(Caisse nationale d'assurance maladie)*, 166
CNCL *(Commission nationale de la communication et des libertés)*, 312
CNESS *(Centre nationale d'études supérieurs de la sécurité sociale)*, 166
CNIL *(Commission nationale de l'informatique et des libertés)*, 270, 292 n43
CNIP, CNI *(Centre national des independents et paysans)*, 76–77(fig.), 86, 115, 135, 227(table), 232(table)
CNJA *(Centre national des jeunes agriculteurs)*, 154
CNNC *(Commission nationale de la négociation collective)*, 150
CNPF *(Conseil national du patronat français)*, 152, 164, 167, 168, 172 n16, 172 n17. *See also* MEDEF
CNRS *(Centre national de la recherche scientifique)*, 334
Coal and Steel Community (Schuman Plan), 337, 341
CODERs *(Commissions de développement économique regional)*, 276
Cohabitation, 17, 101–2, 120, 184, 185–90, 196, 201, 237, 326, 348. *See also* Balladur, Edouard; Chirac, Jacques; Jospin, Lionel; Mitterrand, François
Colbert, Jean-Baptiste, 3, 349 n2
Comités de sages (blue-ribbon committees), 247–48, 267, 303, 304, 326
Commissaire de la République, 277. *See also* Prefect
Commission Fauroux, 333
Committees of inquiry, 228–30
Common Agricultural Policy (CAP), 27, 109(table), 331, 341, 342
Common Market, 8, 179, 336. *See* Europe, European Community, European Union
Common Program of the Left, 80, 82, 88, 125
Communards, Paris Commune, 6, 12, 21 n6

Communes, 54, 271, 272–74, 279(table), 280(table), 281(table), 281–82, 344
Communist party, Communists, 7, 48 n62, 55, 59, 63, 68 n32, 68 n43, 73, 74–75(table), 80–82, 88–89, 94, 105, 108, 109(table), 111(table), 112, 114(table), 119, 121, 124, 125, 126–27, 128, 136, 141 n68, 144 n106, 145 n122, 150, 151–52, 157, 159, 175 n70, 339, 346
  alliances, 79, 80, 81, 100, 116, 117
  decentralization and, 275
  de-Stalinization and moderation of, 80, 81, 82, 106
  in Fourth Republic, 81
  Fifth Republic constitution and, 81
  in Fifth Republic government, 81–82
  loss of power, 203
  Mitterrand and, 197
  in Parliament, 227(table), 232(table)
  presidential elections of 1995, 104
  Rénovateurs, 94
  Socialists and, 79, 80, 88–89, 90, 100, 110
  trade unions and, 147
Concertation, 158–59
Conciliateurs, 302–3
Confédération générale de l'agriculture, 155
Confédération nationale de l'artisanat et des métiers, 153
Confédération nationale de la mutualité, de la coopération, et du crédit agricoles, 155
Confédération paysanne, 155, 351 n21
Conference committees, 224, 225(fig.), 234(table)
Conseil général, 271
Conseil national des conventions collectives, 164
Conseil restreint, 196, 198
Conseils de prud'hommes. *See* Labor tribunals
Conseil superieur d'éducation nationale, 156
Conseil supérieur de l'éducation, 164
Conservatism, Conservatives, 13(table), 29, 42, 227(table)
Constitution, 1, 3
  of 1791, 6, 9, 10(table)
  of 1792, 9, 12
  of 1795, 12
  of 1799, 12
  of 1814, 9
  of 1830, 9
  of 1852, 4, 10(table), 11, 21 n2

of Fifth Republic, 10(table)
  adaptation of, 14–21, 37, 238, 371
  amendments to, 15(table), 16, 43, 238
  Article 1, 44, 355
  Article 2, 17, 37, 240, 355
  Article 4, 17, 356
  Article 5, 19, 356
  Article 11, 198, 207, 357
  Article 15, 19, 358
  Article 16, 12, 13, 19, 20, 180, 206–8,
    217 n68, 238, 358
  Article 20, 19, 359
  Article 21, 19, 359
  Article 23, 17, 19, 208, 243–44, 359
  Article 25, 19, 359
  Article 28, 16, 21, 235, 360
  Article 29, 207, 360
  Article 34, 235, 240, 249, 361
  Article 35, 236, 361
  Article 36, 19, 207, 361–62
  Article 38, 207, 236, 362
  Article 39, 235, 362
  Article 47, 235, 237, 363–64
  Article 48, 16, 226, 235, 241, 242, 364
  Article 49, 242, 243, 254 n18, 364
  Article 50, 16, 207, 364
  Article 52, 178, 365
  Article 53, 341, 365
  Article 66, 240, 367
  Article 67, 218 n75, 367
  Article 85, 15(table), 370
  Article 88, 341, 370
  Article 89, 239, 371
  guiding principle of, 20
  interpretation of, 14–21
  plebiscitary features of, 12
  preamble, 315 n38, 355
  text, 355–71
of Fourth Republic, 7–8, 10–11, 12, 14, 22
  n27
of Second Republic, 4, 10(table), 11
of Third Republic, 178
of Year I, 10(table)
of Year III (1795), 10(table), 11
of Year VIII, 10(table)
Constitutional Council, 15(table), 19, 20,
  47 n43, 53, 179, 207, 210, 238–41, 247,
  255 n32, n33, n34, n35, 256 n38, n39,
  325, 346
  civil liberties and, 239–40

constitutional provisions for, 365–66
  emergency rule and, 207
Constitutional principles, 18(table)
Consulate, 3, 19
Consultative Committee, 14
Convention pour la VIe République, 349
Corporatism, 160–61, 166, 167, 174 n55,
  175 n59, 319
Corruption, 55, 60, 140 n38, 249, 257–58
  n71, 270, 315 n46, 316 n53, 347
Corsica and Corsicans, 37, 47 n43, 121, 234,
  241, 254 n23, 285–86, 331
Coty, René, 9, 255 n32
Council of State *(Conseil d'État),* 14, 260,
  267–69, 291 n35, n36, n37, n38, 299
Council of the Republic, 8
Cour de cassation, 298, 299(fig.), 302, 313
  n8, 313 n11, 314 n27
Court of Justice of the Republic, 301
Courts. *See* Judicial system
Couve de Murville, Maurice, 182,
  183(table), 184, 190(table), 199, 200
CPNT *(Chasse, pêche, nature et traditions),*
  76–77(fig.), 109(table), 111(table),
  113–14, 114(table), 141 n67, 142 n69,
  342
Crépeau, Michel, 78(table)
Cresson, Edith, 42, 49 n74, 97, 102, 182,
  183(table), 184, 185, 191(table), 204,
  217 n60, 262, 327
Crozier, Michel, 209
CRS *(Compagnies républicaines de sécurité),*
  307
CSA *(Conseil supérieur de l'audiovisuel),* 312,
  316 n63, 317 n66
CSMF *(Confédération des syndicats médicaux
  français),* 162, 167
Cultural chauvinism, 36–38
Cultural diversity, 2–3
Culture
  politics and, 33–34, 36–38, 51–59,
    334–35. *See also* Political culture
  traditional, 33–34, 35, 37, 53, 55, 64, 67
    n26, 334–35, 351 n30
Cumul des mandats (accumulation of elective
  offices), 133, 157, 199, 247, 257 n60,
  347

DATAR *(Délégation a l'aménagement du territoire et a l'action régionale),* 273, 321–22

Débatisse, Michel, 154
Debré, Jean-Louis, 175 n68, 253, 258 n79
Debré, Michel, 11, 12, 117, 137 n9, 182, 183(table), 184, 190(table), 196, 199, 201
Debré law (1959), 33, 168–69, 333
Decentralization, 121, 274–77, 293 n73, 349
  functional, 283–84
  subnational administration and, 271–72, 279, 280(table). *See also individual subnational administrative units*
Declaration of the Rights of Man and the Citizen (1789), 3, 20, 239, 297
  Article 6, 43–44
Decolonization, 336
Deconcentration policy. *See* Decentralization
Decrees, 13, 238, 255 n29
Defense policy, 336–37, 338, 345
Defferre, Gaston, 78(table), 79, 202, 216 n39, 273
De Gaulle. *See* Gaulle, Charles de
Delors, Jacques, 103, 134, 135, 203, 341, 350 n6
Democratic Center, Centrists, 74–75(table), 85, 87, 88, 116. *See also* CDS
Démocratie libérale, 73, 74–75(table), 76–77(fig.), 78(table), 107, 109(table), 110, 111(table), 112, 113, 119, 121, 141 n54, 184. *See also* Republicans
Département council, 129(table)
Departments, 271, 277, 279(table), 281(table)
Depoliticization, 56–57
Deputies, 117–18, 133, 146 n130, 244, 278
  esprit de corps of, 116
  role of, 245–53
  weekly schedule, 222–23
  See also National Assembly; Parliament
Descartes, René, 21 n5, 55
Dirigisme, 23, 119
DLC *(Droite libérale chrétienne)*, 113, 119
Draft dodging, 52, 53
Dreyfus Affair, 6, 21 n8, 35, 86
Droit au logement, 157
Dual executive, 179
Duclos, Jacques, 78(table)
Dufoix, Georgina, 140 n38

Dumas, Roland, 140 n38, 290 n22
Durafour, Michel, 118
Duverger, Maurice, 142 n78

École des Mines, 261
École Nationale d'Administration. See ENA
École Nationale de la Magistrature. See ENM
École Normale Supérieure, 38, 47 n48, 184, 185
École Polytechnique, 38, 47 n48, 85, 261, 265
Economic administration. *See* Civil service, civil servants
Economic and Social Council (ESC), 10(table), 11, 161, 163(table), 164, 179, 321
  constitutional provisions for, 368–69
Economic growth, 23–28
Economic planning and policies, 63(table), 320–24, 341
  under Chirac presidency, 328–32
  four-year plans, 322–24, 326, 327, 328
  from liberation to Giscard, 320
  under Mitterrand presidency, 324–28
  regional, 275–76
Education, 3, 30, 38–40, 47 n54, 53, 332–33
  civil service and, 261–62, 265
  collège, 39
  democratization of, 30, 39–40, 333
  elitism in, 53
  lycée, 38, 40
  parochial and private, 17, 33, 332, 351 n21
  reform of, 39–40, 332–33
  school districts, 283–84
  See also Professors; Students; Teachers; Universities
Elections
  abstentions in, 131(table)
  to European Parliament, 129(table), 130, 146 n138
    1989, 96, 102, 342
    1999, 114(table)
    abstentions in, 131(table)
  European Union and, 345–46
  to labor tribunals, 57
  to social security boards, 165–66
  special (by-elections), 244
  system and method of, 126–33, 145 n121, 145 n122
  See also Referendum

Elections, local and regional, 114(table), 130, 131(table), 135, 145 n121, 203
  1992, 57, 97, 102
  2001, 43
  abstentions in, 131(table)
Elections, parliamentary
  1958, 74(table)
  1962, 74(table)
  1967, 74(table), 80
  1968, 74(table), 143 n103
  1973, 74(table)
  1978, 49 n77, 74(table), 80, 81, 87, 89
  1981, 74(table)
  1986, 74(table), 93–94
  1988, 48 n62, 74(table), 94–96
  1993, 75(table), 97–103, 144 n103, 187
  1997, 62–63, 75(table), 105–8, 150, 206
  2002, 75(table), 110–13, 254 n6
  abstentions in, 131(table)
Elections, presidential, 188, 124
  1965, 78(table), 81
  1969, 78(table), 80, 81
  1974, 78(table), 85, 143 n103
  1981, 48 n62, 78(table), 87, 89
  1988, 78(table), 94–96
  1995, 78(table), 103–5, 150, 172 n9
  2002, 57, 42–43, 78(table), 108–10, 123(table)
  abstentions in, 131(table)
Electoral college, 11
Electoral system, 126–33
  effect on political parties, 130–32
  effect on voters, 130, 131(table)
Electorate, 57–58, 62(table), 122, 126–27, 129(table)
Emmanuelli, Henri, 258 n79
ENA (École Nationale d'Administration), Enarques, 29, 41, 47 n48, 184, 185, 194, 261–62, 265, 288, 289 n5, n6, n7, n8, n9, n11, 289–90 n12
ENM (École Nationale de la Magistrature), 298, 313 n3
Environmentalists, 68 n32, 98, 102–3, 139 n28, 146 n140. See also Greens
EPCI (établissements publics de coopération intercommunale), 282
ESC. See Economic and Social Council
Etatism, 62–63(table), 98. See also State, statism

Ethnic minorities, 36–37, 43, 246, 305–6, 335
Euro, 66, 105, 328, 343, 350 n17
Europe, European Community, European Union, 2, 15(table), 65–66, 101, 141 n68, 155, 214 n3, 324, 327, 337, 340–46, 370–71. See also Common Agricultural Policy; Maastricht, Treaty of
European Court of Human Rights, 300, 312
European Parliament, 341. See also under Elections
Events of May 1968. See May 1968, events of
Evian Accords (1962), 15(table), 132(table), 336

Fabius, Laurent, 90, 96, 98, 99, 182, 183(table), 184, 191(table), 203, 204, 226, 229, 230, 247, 250, 252, 253, 257 n58, 258 n79, 314 n31, 325
Falloux laws, 332
Families, 24, 52, 54, 82, 320
Farmers, 29, 45 n19, 87, 89, 91, 154–55, 231, 278. See also Agriculture
Fascism, 3, 6, 52, 93
FASP (Fédération autonome des syndicats de police), 307
Faure, Edgar, 118, 134, 201, 233, 256 n49, 258 n79
FD (Force démocrate), 107, 116–17, 141 n54, 142 n83. See also CDS
Fédération des réformateurs, 134
Fédération pour une nouvelle solidarité, 140 n49
FEN (Fédération d'éducation nationale), 40, 156, 162, 264, 332, 333
FGDS (Fédération de la gauche démocratique et socialiste), 74–75(table), 76–77(fig.), 80, 84–85, 142 n81
Fiduciaires, 298
Finance, Ministry of, 260, 322
First Empire, 3–4, 13(table)
First Republic (1792–1799), 3, 12
Fiterman, Charles, 118, 216 n39
FLNC (Front de libération nationale de la Corse), 285
FN (Front national). See National Front
FNOSS (Fédération nationale des organisations de sécurité sociale), 166, 174 n53
FNSEA (Fédération nationale des syndicats des exploitants agricoles), 154, 155, 167

FO *(Confédération général du travail–Force ouvrière)*, 147, 148, 149, 152, 163, 165(table), 167, 176 n73
Fontaine, Nicole, 341
Foreign policy, 335–40
  European Union and, 345
  premier and, 188–89
Foreign workers, 24–26, 31–32
Forni, Raymond, 253, 258 n79
Fourth Republic (1946–1958), 7–9, 10(table), 12, 13(table), 18(table), 19, 126, 158
  accomplishments of, 8
  civil service and, 263, 264, 275, 287
  Constitution of, 7–8, 10–11, 12, 14, 22 n27
  freedom of press during, 308
  influence on Fifth Republic Constitution, 16
  interest groups under, 152, 158
  parliaments of, 221–22, 231
  parties of, 79, 81, 82, 84, 86
  power of cabinet in, 195
  prime minister, 17
Framework laws, 260, 267
France unie, 118, 134
French language, 53, 64, 66, 334, 338
French National Bank, 341
FSU *(Fédération syndicale unitaire de l'enseignement, de l'éducation, de la recherche et de la culture)*, 156, 162–63, 174 n47

Gandois, Jean, 152–53
Garaud, Marie-France, 137 n9
Garde républicaine, 307
Gaulle, Charles de, 78(table), 143 n94
  anti-Semitism and, 34
  cabinets and, 17, 191, 194, 197, 198
  Communist party and, 81
  constitutional ideas of, 7–8
  constitutional violations of, 19, 207–8
  domestic policies of, 17
  economic planning and, 323
  foreign policy of, 17, 336–38
  Fourth Republic and, 7–9
  heroic leadership and, 208, 209–10
  interest groups and, 158–59
  leftist policies, 137 n5
  notions of government, 11

party composition of government, 190(table)
  as premier, 9
  as president, 16, 17, 19, 30, 178, 180, 197, 198, 199, 207–8, 233, 237, 243, 244, 250, 264, 266, 275, 334
  presidentialism, 12
  resignation of, 202–3
  Socialist party and, 79
Gaullism, Gaullists, 11, 14, 19, 20, 44, 63, 67 n31, 68 n32, 68 n45, 73, 74–75(table), 82–83, 86, 88, 110, 117, 121, 124, 125, 127, 128, 134, 136, 137 n7, 200–1, 206, 338
  agriculture and, 170
  Bonapartism and, 138 n15
  civil service and, 264
  decentralization and, 275
  deputies, 245
  economic planning and, 323, 329
  foreign policy and, 346, 352 n37
  Giscardists and, 92
  media and, 308–9, 310, 311
  in Parliament, 227(table), 231, 232(table), 233
  See also RPF; RPR; UEM; UMP; UNR
Gayssot, Jean-Claude, 215 n35
Gayssot law, 316 n54
GE *(Génération écologie)*, 76–77(fig.), 97, 142 n79, 146 n135
Gender equality, 15(table), 43, 48 n67, 192
Giroud, Françoise, 118
Giscard d'Estaing, Valéry, 20, 34, 35, 78(table), 83, 86, 96, 101, 117, 138 n13, 140 n39, 140 n42, 187
  background of, 85, 289 n7
  cabinet and, 191, 195, 196, 197, 198, 200
  Chirac and, 83, 92, 96, 284
  defeat of, 87–88
  as deputy, 257 n61
  domestic policies of, 30
  economic planning and, 323
  European Union and, 341
  on immigrants, 102
  media and, 311
  in Parliament, 224
  party composition of government, 190(table)

as president, 27, 30, 37, 121, 168, 180–81, 195, 196, 197, 198, 199, 200, 210–11, 214 n11, 228, 233–34, 237, 251, 266, 277, 316 n61, 323, 338
as presidential candidate, 87–88
trade unions and, 149, 151
voters for, 125
women's rights and, 44
Giscardism, Giscardists, 83, 125, 138 n15, 227(table), 311
Giscardo-Centrism, 85–88, 206
Globalization, 121, 157, 331
Grandes écoles, 38, 47 n48, 261, 265. *See also individual grandes écoles*
GRECE *(Groupe de recherche et d'étude sur la civilisation européenne)*, 135
Greens, 42, 96–97, 102–3, 104, 105, 109(table), 111(table), 112, 114(table), 115, 121, 139 n27, 141 n68, 226, 253
Grenelle Agreement (1968), 323
Groupes d'action locale, 135
Groupuscules, 133
Guichard, Olivier, 83
Guigou, Elisabeth, 170, 215 n35, 304
Gulf War, 98–99, 121, 179, 258 n82, 316 n59, 352 n39

Habbash affair, 202–3, 306
Habeas corpus, 300
Heroic leadership, 6, 63, 208–13. *See also under* Gaulle, Charles de
HLMs *(habitations à loyer modéré)*, 30
Hue, Robert, 42, 78(table), 100, 104, 108, 109(table), 123(table), 140 n47, 141 n61, 146 n128, 151, 331, 345
Hunters' party. *See* CPNT

Ideology, 29, 293 n61. *See also* Political ideology; *individual political parties*
Immigration, immigrants, 15(table), 24–26, 35, 37, 65, 70 n79, 71 n82, 102, 103, 119–20, 237–38, 348
legal protection of, 305–6
Incivisme, 51
Incompatibility rule, 194, 243–45
Individualism, 53–54, 293 n61
Indochina, 8, 336, 338
Industry, 27–28, 120, 325, 327, 348

administration of nationalized, 287–88, 289 n3, 325
INSEE *(Institut national de la statistique et des études économiques)*, 321
Institut d'Etudes Politiques, 49 n72, 290 n12
Intellectuals, 339. *See also* Professors
Interest groups
access and input of, 157–59
civil service and, 162, 267
impact on laws, 267
mayors and, 133
political parties and, 159–71
See also Agriculture; Business, organized; Economic and Social Council; Education; Trade unions
Islam, 32, 35–36, 46 n34, 70 n79, 71 n82. *See also* Muslims

JAC *(Jeunesse agricole chrétienne)*, 154, 173 n22
Jacobinism, Jacobins, 5–6, 9, 36, 47 n45, 65, 98, 295 n98, 314 n30, 346
Jews, 32, 34–35, 70 n70. *See also* Anti-Semitism
Jobert, Michel, 118, 216 n39, 216 n43, 351 n35
Jospin, Lionel, 46 n28, 153, 215 n18, 215 n30, 215 n34
cabinet and, 192, 194, 195, 198, 204
defeat of, 61
economic policy of, 330–31
education reform and, 333
media and, 312
as premier, 42, 65, 108, 121, 122, 123(table), 157, 183(table), 184, 188, 189, 191(table), 206, 230, 236, 242, 243, 277, 343, 344, 346
as presidential candidate, 78(table), 103–4, 109(table), 117, 125–26, 133, 144 n113, 146 n128, 150
Judicial system, 14, 15(table), 297–300, 347, 349
constitutional provisions for, 366–68
executive and, 304–5
members of, 298, 301, 302, 312 n1
procedure in, 300
reform of, 303–4
See also Prisons

July Monarchy (1830), 4, 6, 13(table), 259
Juppé, Alain, 153, 182, 188, 215 n34
  cabinet and, 192, 197, 198, 201, 204
  economic policy, 328–30
  as premier, 42, 61, 105, 106, 149, 170, 181,
    183(table), 191(table), 234, 243, 253,
    257 n61, 257 n65, 258 n76, 270, 287,
    343
  as presidential candidate, 117, 146 n128
Juquin, Pierre, 94, 134
Justice, 300–5

Keller, Fabienne, 48 n65
Kouchner, Bernard, 118, 134

Labor. *See* Trade unions; Working class,
  workers
Labor force, 26, 31–32, 41. *See also* Working
  class, workers
Labor tribunals, 165(table), 174 n51, 298,
  299(fig.)
Laïcité (secularity), 33, 63, 156, 162
Laguiller, Arlette, 78(table), 104, 109(table),
  123(table)
Lajoinie, André, 78(table), 94
Lalonde, Brice, 96, 97, 102, 118, 140 n39,
  142 n79
Lang, Jack, 47 n45, 142 n72, 175 n71, 204,
  334, 351 n35
Larosière, Jacques, 341
LCR *(Ligue communiste révolutionnaire)*,
  109(table), 111(table), 114(table)
LDI *(La Droite indépendante)*, 77
Lecanuet, Jean, 78(table), 85, 254 n15
Left, leftists, 6, 48 n62, 55, 56, 57, 62, 63, 68
  n37, 73, 87, 115, 130, 136, 203, 208,
  342
  alliances of, 79–80, 85
  Constitutional Council and, 241
  decentralization and, 275
  ideology, 120–22
  parliamentary elections and, 74–75(table),
    97–100
  in power, 88–91, 105–6, 107–8, 206
  public educators and, 290 n27
  social class and, 29, 30
  See also Common Program of the Left;
    Communist party, Communists; FGDS;
    Socialist party, Socialists

Left Radicals. *See* MRG
Lejeune, Max, 118
Lenoir, Noëlle, 118
Léotard, François, 96, 102, 117, 142 n83,
  215 n24
Lepage, Corinne, 109(table), 346
Le Pen, Jean-Marie, 35, 42, 78(table), 92, 94,
  104, 108, 109(table), 109–10, 113, 117,
  123(table), 124, 126, 130, 141 n61,
  309, 343, 345, 348. *See also* National
  Front
Lévy, Bernard-Henri, 146 n138
Liberalism, 62(table), 63. *See also* Neoliber-
  alism
Ligue des droits de l'homme, 168
Local government. *See Arrondissements;* Com-
  munes; Departments; Mayor; Prefect;
  Regions
Localism, 3, 52, 54, 85, 121
Loi Bonnet, 305
Louis XVIII, 4
Louis-Philippe, 4. *See also* July Monarchy
Luethy, Herbert, 57
Lutte ouvrière, 104, 109(table), 111(table),
  114(table), 135
Lyons, 26(table), 285

Maastricht, Treaty of (1992), 15(table), 16,
  100, 120, 121, 132(table), 179, 198,
  216 n50, 240, 252, 255 n25, 258 n82,
  341, 343, 345
Mac-Mahon, Marshal Patrice de, 5
Madelin, Alain, 107, 109(table), 117,
  123(table), 135, 197, 346
Maghrebis, 65, 92–93
Malraux, André, 47 n47, 194
Mamère, Noël, 109(table), 123(table), 346
Marchais, Georges, 78(table), 82, 89, 94,
  100, 126, 137 n4, 149
Marseilles/Aix-en-Provence, 26(table), 285
Marxism, Marxists, 36, 80, 89
Mauroy, Pierre, 90
  cabinet and, 194, 196, 197–98, 199, 200,
    203
  as premier, 183(table), 184, 191(table),
    273, 325, 350 n6
Maurras, Charles, 46 n31
May 1968, events of, 6, 32, 39, 58–59, 64,
  68 n43, 81, 202, 307

Mayor, 54, 81, 133, 198–99, 247, 257 n622, 272–73, 274, 278, 281, 282–84, 292 n53, 294 n74, 295 n92

MEDEF *(Mouvement des entrepreneurs de France)*, 153, 166, 173 n20

Media. *See* Press; Television and radio

Mediator, 291 n41

Médicins sans frontières, 157, 340

Mégret, Bruno, 109(table), 113, 126

Mendès-France, Pierre, 118, 202, 248

Mer, Francis, 192

Mermaz, Louis, 258 n79

Messmer, Pierre, 182, 183(table), 184, 190(table), 199, 203, 256 n49, 291 n40

Middle East, 34–35, 338, 339

Millon, Charles, 113, 118–19

Minimum wage, 23. *See also* SMIC; SMIG; Wages

Ministers, ministries. *See* Cabinet

Minorities, 36, 37, 43, 246, 335
  legal protection of, 305–6

Mitterrand, François, 78(table), 101, 107, 143 n94
  burial ceremonies, 34
  cabinets and, 118, 195, 196–98, 199, 202, 203–4
  charisma and, 211–12
  Communists and, 197
  domestic policies of, 324–28
  foreign policy of, 338–39
  as leader of UDSR, 142 n81
  Parliament and, 181, 205–6, 212, 228, 251
  party composition of government, 191(table)
  party switching, 118
  as president, 16–17, 35, 61, 90, 97, 121, 122, 170, 181, 205–6, 208, 211–12, 214 n11, 228, 240, 248, 251, 255 n35, 256 n38, 266, 289 n3, 290 n22, 312, 348
  as presidential candidate, 94–95
  as president under cohabitation, 185–88
  proportional representation and, 128
  public opinion of, 144 n112
  relations with Chirac, 284–85
  relations with Rocard, 196–97, 203, 204
  as Socialist leader, 80, 88–89, 98, 99, 103, 117
  trade unions and, 149–50
  views of presidency, 20

voters and, 124, 125, 138 n19
women's rights and, 44
See also Cohabitation

MNR *(Mouvement national républicain)*, 76–77(fig.), 109(table), 111(table), 113, 114(table). *See also* Mégret, Bruno

MODEF *(Mouvement de coordination de défense des exploitants agricoles familiaux)*, 155

Moderates, 6

Mollet, Guy, 80

Monarchism, monarchy, 3, 4, 5, 6, 9, 11, 13(table), 63, 211–12

Monnerville, Gaston, 233

Monnet, Jean, 322

Monory, René, 254 n15

Montesquieu, Charles de, 9

Motiv-é-s, 122

Mouvement action égalité, 135

Mouvement des citoyens, 76–77(fig.), 98–99, 105, 108, 112, 121, 135. *See also* Chevènement, Jean-Pierre

Mouvement pour la France, 76–77(fig.), 104, 111(table), 113, 115, 121

MRG *(Mouvement des radicaux de gauche)*, 74–75(table), 76–77(fig.), 85, 88, 89, 103, 112, 227(table), 232(table). *See also* PRG

MRP *(Mouvement républicain populaire)*, 7, 32, 74–75(table), 76–77(fig.), 84, 116, 126, 148, 158, 227(table), 232(table)

Muslims, 34, 35–36, 65, 92–93, 143 n84, 192. *See also* Islam

Napoleon I, 3–4, 10(table), 12, 19, 21 n2, 208. *See also* Bonapartism

Napoleon III, 4, 10(table), 12, 19, 208

Napoleonic Code (1804), 41, 297

National Assembly, 4–5, 9, 17, 73, 223
  activities of, 230(table)
  bills in, 224, 225(fig.), 226, 231–32, 234, 249–50
  blocked vote in, 236–37, 255 n28
  censure in, 242–43
  committees in, 224, 226, 228–30, 229(table), 252, 253–54 n6
  composition of, 227(table)
  election of, 129(table)
  power of, 235

National Assembly *(continued)*
  professions of members of, 246(table)
  questions in, 241–43, 256 n42, 256 n44
  speakers of, 258 n79
  See also Deputies; Parliament
National Front, 35, 42, 65, 68 n32,
    74–75(table), 76–77(fig.), 86, 92–93,
    94, 95, 97, 100, 102–5, 109(table),
    111(table), 112, 113, 114(table),
    115–16, 118, 120, 121, 124, 127, 129,
    138–39 n23, 159, 171 n4, 308, 346
  origins and ideology, 92, 93
  in Parliament, 127, 129
  social class and, 30
National identity, 63–66, 346
Nationalization, nationalized enterprises,
    63, 287–88, 325
NATO (North Atlantic Treaty Organization),
    113, 119, 179, 336, 338, 340, 345
Naturalization, 35, 46 n32, 130
Neoliberalism, 92, 119, 167, 323, 326,
    330–31, 344, 346
New Caledonia, 15(table), 132(table), 196,
    286, 369–70
Nicoud, Gérard, 153
Notaires, 298, 313 n5
Notat, Nicole, 42, 150, 152

Ombudsman, 269–70
Ordre des médecins, 162, 174 n46
Ordres professionnels, 164
Orléanists, 5, 138 n15, 212, 259
d'Ornano, Michel, 138 n14
ORTF *(Office pour la télévision et la radiodiffu-
    sion françaises),* 311
Overseas territories, 285–86, 295 n101, 369

PACS *(Pacte civil de solidarité),* 301
Pantouflage, 152, 287
Papon, Maurice, 143 n94, 290 n20
Paris, 26(table)
  administration of, 284–85
  newspapers, 310(table)
  preeminence of, 3, 37–38
  social class and, 29
Paris Commune of 1871. *See Communards,*
    Paris Commune
Parliament, 3, 221–53
  bills in, 221–22, 224, 225(fig.), 226

cabinet and, 118, 192, 194, 198, 204
committees in, 13, 224, 226, 228–30
Constitutional Council and, 238–41
constitutional provisions for, 358–65
decree powers and, 221–23
economic planning and, 323
executive and, 12, 204–6, 217 n66,
    237–38, 250–51
Fifth Republic, 13, 222–24
Fourth Republic, 221–22, 231
incompatibility rule, 243–45
limits on decision making, 234–38
negative public view of, 248–49
position and powers of, 14, 31, 235–38,
    248–49, 347
premier and, 180, 181
questions and censure motions in, 241–43
role of deputy in, 245–53
Third Republic, 11
  See also National Assembly; Senate
Parti populaire pour la démocratie française,
    107, 141 n54, n55. *See also Perspectives et
    réalités*
Parti social-démocrate, 107
Parti socialiste autonome, 118
Pasqua, Charles, 113, 117, 254 n15, 305,
    309
Pasqua laws, 305
PCF *(Parti communiste français). See* Commu-
    nist party, Communists
PDM *(Progrès et democratie moderne),*
    76–77(fig.), 85
Penal code, 250, 297, 300, 301, 302, 308
Peretti, Achille, 258 n79
Perspectives et réalités, 91, 107, 134, 135, 138
    n16. *See also Parti populaire pour la dé-
    mocratie française*
Pétain, Marshal Philippe, 11, 14, 70 n70, 81,
    313 n11
Peyrefitte, Alain, 118
Philanthropy, 55, 67 n25
Pinay, Antoine, 269
Plebiscitarism, plebiscites, 10(table), 12, 16,
    178
Pluralism
  cultural, 37, 63–64
  of decision-making system, 160, 166–67,
    170–71, 319–20
  of Giscardists, 37

of interest groups, 160, 161, 166, 319
  media and, 312
  of party system, 98, 108, 120
Poher, Alain, 78(table), 81, 233, 239, 254
  n15
Pôle républicain, 111(table), 112. *See also*
  Chevènement, Jean-Pierre; *Mouvement
  des citoyens*
Police, 306–8
  municipal, urban, 277–78, 307, 315 n45
  national, 307
Political culture, 51–66, 331
  civic and anti-civic attitudes, 51–55
  conceptions of state, 59–63
  national identity, 63–66, 346
  verbal and practical behavior, 55–59
Political ideology, 73, 119–22, 125, 136. *See
  also* Political parties
Political justice, 300–1, 304
Political parties, 73, 115
  alliances, 76–77(fig.), 116–17
  cabinet construction and, 194–95, 200
  centrist coalitions, 84–85
  electoral system and, 126–33
  in Fifth Republic government,
    190–91(table)
  fragmentation and consolidation,
    76–77(fig.)
  functional relevance, 116–26
  irrelevance of labels, 121, 125
  local role of, 280–81
  orientations, 56, 57–58
  parliamentary, 224–25
  switching, 117–19
  women and, 42, 43, 48 n71
  See also Clubs; Elections; Political ideology;
    individual parties
Pompidou, Georges, 78(table), 81, 83, 150
  cabinet and, 196, 197, 198, 199, 200
  party composition of government,
    190(table)
  as premier, 16, 34, 182, 183(table), 184,
    190(table), 199, 202, 214 n5, 243
  as president, 180, 196, 197, 198, 199,
    200, 205, 208, 210, 214 n11, 237,
    323, 338
  as secretary-general, 216 n43
Poniatowski, Michel, 138 n14, 196, 254 n9,
  291 n40

Popular Front, 7, 21 n12, 79, 81, 320
Postmaterialism, 55, 57, 96
Poujade, Pierre, Poujadism, Poujadists, 52,
  86, 92, 153
PR *(Parti républicain)*, 87, 103
Prefect, 271–72, 273, 277, 282, 284, 295
  n92. *See also* Superprefect
Premier, prime minister, 13, 42, 177, 213
  investiture of, 16, 18(table), 204
  National Assembly and, 179, 204
  Parliament and, 204–6
  resignations, 217 n62
  role in Fifth Republic, 17, 18(table)
  selection and replacement of, 177, 179,
    180–81, 184–85
  See also individual premiers
Presidency, president
  arbitrage and, 13
  charisma and, 208–13
  Constitutional Council and, 239
  constitutional provisions for, 356–58
  deputies and, 250–51
  domestic policy responsibility of, 179–80
  election of, 3, 4, 10(table), 15(table), 16,
    129(table), 132(table), 177
  foreign-policy responsibility of, 178–79
  as interpreter of Constitution, 19
  judiciary and, 304–5
  Parliament and, 5, 20, 204–6, 215 n23,
    217 n66, 237–38, 250–51
  position and powers of, 10, 11–12,
    177–81
  premier and, 179–81, 185, 197–98
  public opinion regarding, 61
  staff of, 195, 216 n41
  strengthening of, 20
  succession in, 347–48
  term of, 11, 15(table), 18(table), 214, 214
    n11, 216 n50, 347
  in Third Republic, 5
  See also individual presidents
Press, 308–12, 317 n66
PRG *(Parti des radicaux de gauche)*,
  109(table), 111(table), 112, 142 n73
Primaires, 127
Prime minister. *See* Premier
Prisons, 303–4. *See also* Judicial system
Private members' bills, 224, 225(fig.),
  236–37, 249–50

Privatization, 67 n31, 270–71, 327–28, 329, 330, 331
Professional orders. *See Ordres professionnels*
Professors, 39, 40, 90, 192. *See also* Universities
Projets de loi. See Parliament, bills in
Proportional representation, 126, 127, 128, 129–30, 145 n119, 145 n122, 159
Propositions de loi. See Private members' bills
Protestants, Protestantism, 32, 34, 46 n28, 53, 54
PS *(Parti socialiste). See* Socialist party, Socialists
PS-MRG, 144 n106
PS-PRG, 63, 114(table)
PSU *(Parti socialiste unifié)*, 76–77(fig.), 88, 118, 144 n106
PT *(Parti des travailleurs)*, 109(table)
Public opinion polls
  on acceptable behavior, 66 n10
  on anti-Semitism, 70–71 n81
  on candidate personality, 125
  on capitalism, 69 n49
  on deputies, 249
  on Europe, 352 n52
  on Fifth Republic Constitution, 353 n53
  on free choice of schools, 67 n30
  on good citizenship, 66 n10
  on Islamic immigrants, 70 n79
  on judicial system, 313 n14
  on liberalism, 69 n49
  on Mitterrand as president, 348, 353 n56
  on national debt, 68 n32
  on Parliament, 248–49
  on political corruption, 249
  on political party identification, 68–69 n45
  on politicians, 60, 258 n71
  on politics, 60, 68 n34, 69 n63
  on presidential candidates, 144 n112
  on privatization, 67 n31
  on public institutions, 69 n61
  on reforms of institutions, 347(table)
  on responsibilities of state, 62(table)
  on security vs. liberty, 144 n107
  on socialism, 69 n49
  on societal utility of various professions, 69 n50
  on state intervention in the economy, 63(table)

Racism, 35–36, 65, 71 n82, 92, 113
Radical-Socialists, 32, 34, 73, 74–75(table), 79, 80, 83, 84, 85, 87, 88, 107, 116, 126, 155, 158, 227(table), 232(table)
Raffarin, Jean-Pierre, 43, 183(table), 184, 185, 191(table), 192, 193(table), 199, 331–32, 344
Rapporteur, 223–24, 226, 253 n6
RCV *(Radical, citoyen, vert)*, 108
Referendum, 10(table), 12, 13, 15(table), 20, 130, 216 n50
  abstentions and, 132(table)
  constitutional requirements, 14
  of 1962, 207, 216 n50
  of 1968, 233
  of 1969, 218 n77
  of 1992 (Treaty of Maastricht), 198, 216 n50
  of 2000, 216 n50
Réfondateurs, Réfondations movement, 98, 99, 118
Réformateurs, Reformers' Movement, 76–77(fig.), 85
Regions, 275–77, 279(table), 281(table)
Regional council, 129(table), 276–77
Regulations *(règlements complémentaires)*, 13, 238, 255 n29, 267–68
Religion, 1, 3, 32–35. *See also* Catholic church; Catholics, Catholicism; Islam; Jews, Muslims, Protestants, Protestantism
Republic of 1792, 13
Republicanism, 5–6, 13, 20, 116, 200
Republicans, 73, 110, 128, 190–91(table). *See also* RI; UDF
République et liberté, 118
Resistance, 64, 79, 81, 184
Revolution of 1789, 1, 3–7, 64
RI *(Républicains indépendants)*, 74–75(table), 86, 87, 138 n14. *See also* Republicans
Richelieu, Armand-Jean, Cardinal de, 3
Right, rightists, 6, 55, 56, 57, 62, 63, 68 n37, 73, 85–86, 130, 136, 208, 342
  vs. Center, 91–92

Constitutional Council and, 241
ideology of, 120–22
parliamentary elections and, 74–75(table),
    100–2, 110
public servants and, 290 n27
social class and, 30
RMI *(revenu minimum d'insertion)*, 24, 44 n4,
    327
Rocard, Michel, 46 n28, 88, 90, 102, 125,
    134, 286, 350 n6
  cabinet and, 190, 203
  as premier, 49 n74, 95, 97, 182,
    183(table), 184, 191(table), 196–97,
    215 n18, 236, 251, 287, 326
  as prospective presidential candidate, 98
  resignation of, 202
  as Socialist party leader, 98–99, 100, 103,
    216 n39
Rousseau, Jean-Jacques, 5, 9, 157
RPF *(Rassemblement du peuple français)*, 8,
    111(table), 113, 158
RPR *(Rassemblement pour la République)*,
    76–77(fig.), 83, 87, 91–95, 100–1,
    109(table), 110, 114(table), 115, 117,
    121, 127, 128, 140 n39, 145 n122, 192,
    201, 252. *See also* Gaullism, Gaullists
RPR-UDF, 63, 105, 107, 114(table), 119, 168

Saint-Josse, Jean, 109(table), 114, 345
Sarkozy, Nicolas, 192
Savary, Alain, 332
SCALP *(Section carrément anti–Le Pen)*, 157
Schengen Accords, 305, 344
Schnapper, Dominique, 255 n33
Second Empire, 4, 13(table), 284
Second Republic (1848–1852), 3, 4,
    10(table), 12, 19
Secularism. *See* Laïcité
"Security and Liberty" bill (1981), 303
Séguin, Philippe, 101, 107, 188–90, 206,
    235, 247, 252, 258 n76, 258 n79, 343
Seillière, Ernest-Antoine, 153
Senate, 5, 15(table), 27, 231–34
  bills in, 224, 225(fig.), 226, 245
  blocked vote in, 236–37, 255 n28
  committees in, 224, 228, 229
  composition of, 232(table)
  election of, 129(table)

power of, 231, 233–34, 235
questions in, 241–43, 256 n42, 256 n44
See also Parliament
SFIO *(Section française de l'Internationale ou-
    vrière)*, 76–77(fig.), 79, 117, 126, 142
    n71, 155. *See also* Socialist party, Social-
    ists
SGEN *(Syndicat général d'éducation na-
    tionale)*, 156
Shopkeepers, small business, 27, 28, 85,
    86–87, 89, 91, 153, 231
Sieyès, Abbé Emmanuel Joseph, 6
SIVOM *(syndicats intercommunaux à vocation
    multiple)*, 282
SIVU *(syndicats intercommunaux à vocation
    unique)*, 282
Small-business associations. *See* Shopkeep-
    ers, small business
SMIC *(salaire minimum interprofessionel de
    croissance)*, 23, 24, 44 n2, 331, 350 n13
SMIG *(salaire minimum industriel garanti)*,
    23, 44 n2
SNESup *(Syndicat national d'enseignement
    supérieur)*, 156, 333
SNI-PEGC *(Syndicat national des instituteurs
    et professors d'enseignement général de col-
    lège)*, 156
SNUipp *(Syndicat national unitaire des institu-
    teurs, professeurs d'école et professeurs de
    collège)*, 156
Socialist party, Socialists, 7, 12, 20, 48 n62,
    48 n71, 63, 67 n31, 68 n32, 73,
    74–75(table), 76–77(fig.), 79–80,
    88–91, 108, 109(table), 111(table), 112,
    115, 121, 125, 126–28, 134, 141 n68,
    159, 200, 226, 311
  acceptance of Fifth Republic systems by,
    346
  bourgeoisie and, 79, 90
  Catholics and, 80, 90, 138 n19
  civil service and, 264
  Communists and, 80, 82, 88–89, 90, 100,
    116
  creation of PS, 80
  defeats of, 61, 203–4
  as deputies, 245, 253 n6
  diversity within, 98, 108
  economic policy of, 325, 330

Socialist party, Socialists *(continued)*
  education and, 40
  in Fourth Republic coalition, 79
  ideology and policies of, 31, 90, 119, 136
  institutional ideas of, 181
  interest groups and, 148, 151, 158, 169
  in Left alliance, 7, 73, 79, 80, 84, 85,
    88–91, 105, 106, 115, 116, 134, 346
  media and, 309, 310, 311, 312
  in Parliament, 227(table), 232(table), 234,
    251
  parliamentary elections of 1986, 93–94
  parliamentary elections of 1988, 95
  parliamentary elections of 1993, 97–100
  parliamentary elections of 1997, 105–6
  parliamentary elections of 2002, 111–12
  in power, 88–91
  presidential elections of 1995, 103–4
  presidential elections of 2002, 109, 110
  religion and, 32, 34
  science and technology policy of, 333–34
  social class and, 29
  support base of, 28, 29, 31, 79, 89, 91, 99,
    136
  trade unions and, 148, 151, 158
  working class and, 79, 84, 89
Social partnership, 160, 166, 170
Social security, 15(table), 31(table), 165–66
  funding, 235–36
*Societé nationale d'encouragement a l'agricul-
  ture*, 155
Soisson, Jean-Pierre, 118, 134, 202
Solidarité et liberté, 134
Solidarités modernes, 134
SOS-Racisme, 135, 168, 169
Soviet Union, 339–40
State, statism, 59–63, 167–70, 175 n65
State Security Court, 37, 308
Stirn, Olivier, 118
Stoléru, Lionel, 118
Strauss-Kahn, Dominique, 202, 215 n35,
  330
Strikes. *See under* Trade unions
Students, 39–40, 58, 81, 155–57. *See also*
  Universities
Superprefect, 275, 276

Tapie, Bernard, 99, 103, 146 n138, 202, 291
  n29

Taxation, 30–31(table), 324, 326, 328, 329
  evasion of, 52–53, 66 n10
  negative income, 52
  solidarity, 329
  subnational, 278–79, 282
  value-added, 52, 273, 326
  wealth, 24
Teachers, 28, 40, 89, 90, 91, 155–57, 319
Technocracy. *See* Civil service, civil servants
Television and radio, 311–12, 317 n64
  election campaigns and, 125–26, 130, 146
    n128
  European, 342
Terrorism, 36, 121, 304, 306, 340
Thibault, Bernard, 151
Thiers, Adolphe, 5
Third Republic (1875–1940), 3, 5–7,
  10(table), 12, 13(table), 18(table), 19,
  126, 158
  civil service in, 259, 262, 263, 265, 266
  Constitution, 178
  freedom of press during, 308
  interest groups in, 158
  parties in, 73, 86, 116
  role of executive during, 10, 11, 17
  Senate in, 231
  women during, 42
  See also under Constitution
Tibéri, Jean, 215 n34, 304
Tixier-Vignancour, Jean-Louis, 78(table),
  92
Toubon, Jacques, 37, 304
Toubon law (1994), 37, 53
Touvier, Paul, 300–1, 313 n11
Trade unions, 31, 56, 147–52, 156, 158,
  163–64, 170–71, 172 n10, 266
  civil service and, 264
  Economic and Social Council and, 161,
    163(table), 292 n45
  economic planning and, 322–23, 329–30
  elections to labor relations tribunals,
    165(table)
  functional representation and, 161–62,
    163(table), 164
  political parties and, 147–48, 149–50, 151,
    172 n9
  social security boards and, 165, 166
  strikes, 58, 59, 150, 168–70, 288, 292 n45,
    307, 329

See also Interest groups; Working class, workers; *individual trade unions*
Trautmann, Catherine, 48 n65, 294 n74
Treaties, 10(table), 15(table), 178, 337, 339, 365. *See also* Maastricht, Treaty of
Tripartism, 116, 170
Trotskyists, 108, 112, 345
Truche committee, 303, 304, 314 n27
Tutelle, 154, 267, 277

UCANSS *(Union des caisses nationales de securité sociale)*, 166
UDC *(Union du centre)*, 96
UDCA *(Union pour la défense des commerçants et des artisans)*, 86, 153
UDF *(Union pour la démocratie française)*, 63, 68 n32, 73, 74–75(table), 76–77(fig.), 78(table), 83, 87, 103, 109(table), 110–11(table), 112, 114(table), 115, 118–20, 121, 127, 128, 134, 136, 141 n54, 144 n106, 145 n122, 154, 167, 226, 243, 245, 291 n41
  in cohabitation government, 201, 203, 206
  relations with RPR, 91–92, 93, 94, 95–96, 105, 107, 117, 140 n40, 252, 294 n81
  See also Giscardism, Giscardists
UDR *(Union pour la défense de la République)*, 74–75(table), 76–77(fig.), 82, 137 n6, 200
UDSR *(Union démocratique et socialiste de la Résistance)*, 76–77(fig.), 142 n81
UEM *(Union en mouvement)*, 110. *See also* UMP
UER *(Unité d'enseignement et de recherche)*, 39, 47 n49
UGDS *(Union de la gauche démocrate et socialiste)*, 74–75(table), 76–77(fig.)
UMP *(Union pour la majorité présidentielle)*, 48 n71, 73, 74–75(table), 76–77(fig.), 110, 111(table), 112, 119, 130, 136, 141 n60, 224, 226
UNAPEL *(Union nationale des parents d'élèves de l'enseignement libre)*, 156
UNEF *(Union nationale des étudiants de France)*, 155–56
UNEF–Indépendante et démocratique, 156
UNEF–Solidarité étudiante, 156
Unemployment, 24, 322, 324–25, 326, 327, 328, 329, 343, 350 n13

Union des femmes françaises, 44
Union et fraternité française, 86
Union française du travail, 172 n6
Union pour la majorité, 82
Union pour la nouvelle majorité, 88
Union pour la réforme, 110
Universities, 38, 39, 40, 59, 333. *See also* Professors; Students
UNR *(Union pour la nouvelle République)*, 76–77(fig.), 82, 127
UNSA *(Union nationale des syndicats autonomes)*, 148, 156, 173 n27
UPA *(Union professionnelle artisanale)*, 153
UPF *(Union pour la France du progrès)*, 74–75(table), 76–77(fig.), 100–1
URC *(Union du rassemblement et du centre)*, 77

Value-added tax. *See* Taxation
Vedel, Georges, 257 n63
Vedel Commission, 20, 145 n122, 258 n86, 353 n54
Védrine, Hubert, 201, 215 n26, 217 n57, 345
Veil, Simone, 42, 102, 341
Viannet, Louis, 151
Vichy regime, 7, 13(table), 14, 64, 70 n70, 86, 143 n94, 152, 174 n46, 212, 313 n11, 335
Vietnam, 8, 338
Vigipirate, 306, 315 n42
Vigouroux, Robert, 117
Villepin, Dominique de, 201
Villiers, Philippe de, 104, 112, 113, 115, 140 n46, 146 n138
Voters, voting, 122–26
  abstention, 57, 105, 110, 130, 131(table), 132(table), 145 n125, 210
  electoral system and, 126–33
  negative, 60
  proxy, 247
Voynet, Dominique, 42, 102, 104, 112, 140 n48

Waechter, Antoine, 96, 97, 102, 140 n48
Wages, 23–24, 32, 323, 325, 327, 329, 330, 331. *See also* SMIC
Welfare state, 57, 81, 85, 105, 320, 324, 331, 350 n15

Wiretapping, 228, 312, 316 n51
Withdrawals, 126–27
Women, 41–44, 47 n54, n55, n56, n57, 48
 n62, n65, n67, n71, 49 n74, n77, 174
 n51, 192, 341
Workers, white-collar *(salariat)*, 31–32, 148,
 172 n8
Working class (proletariat), workers, 3, 8,
 28, 31–32, 58, 81, 82, 122, 124,
 246(table), 262
 Communist party and, 31, 81, 119
 embourgeoisement of, 31, 119
 foreign, 24–26, 31–32

management and, 87, 149
 Socialist party and, 79, 84, 89
 unions and, 147, 148, 171 n5
 See also Labor force
WTO (World Trade Organization), 28, 101,
 327

Xenophobia, 35–36, 52, 54–55, 65, 305, 334

Youth, 54, 57, 58, 59, 60, 63(table), 68–69
 n45, 70 n70, 81

ZUPS *(zones d'urbanisation à priorité)*, 30